ספר תהלים · מהדורת קורן
The Koren Tehillim

קורן ירושלים

THE ROHR FAMILY EDITION

ספר תהלים · מהדורת קורן

THE KOREN TEHILLIM

שירו לו
זמרו לו
שיחו
בכל
נפלאותיו

WITH TRANSLATION BY

Rabbi Eli Cashdan ז״ל

WITH INTRODUCTION AND COMMENTARY BY

Rabbi Dr. Tzvi Hersh Weinreb

•

KOREN PUBLISHERS JERUSALEM

The Koren Tehillim
The Rohr Family Edition
Second Hebrew/English Edition, 2019

Koren Publishers Jerusalem Ltd.
POB 4044, Jerusalem 91040, ISRAEL
POB 8531, New Milford, CT 06776, USA

www.korenpub.com

The creation of this book was made possible through the generous support of Torah Education in Israel.

Tehillim, Hebrew/English, Standard, Hardcover, ISBN 978-965-301-206-6
Tehillim, Hebrew/English, Compact, Hardcover, ISBN 978-965-301-204-2
Tehillim, Hebrew/English, Compact, Softcover, ISBN 978-965-301-205-9
Tehillim, Hebrew/English, Compact, Decorative Hardcover by Enya Keshet, ISBN 978-965-301-207-3
Printed in PRC

TC02B

The Rohr Family Edition
of
The Koren Tehillim
pays tribute to the memory of

Mr. Sami Rohr ז״ל
ר׳ שמואל ב״ר יהושע אליהו ז״ל

who served his Maker with joy,
and whose far-reaching vision, warm open hand, love of Torah,
and love for every Jew were catalysts for the revival and growth of
vibrant Jewish life in the former Soviet Union
and in countless communities the world over,

and to the memory of his beloved wife

Mrs. Charlotte Rohr (née Kastner) ע״ה
שרה בת ר׳ יקותיאל יהודה ע״ה

who survived the fires of the Shoah to become
the elegant and gracious matriarch,
first in Colombia and later in the United States,
of three generations of a family
nurtured by her love and unstinting devotion.
She found grace in the eyes of all those whose lives she touched.

Together they merited to see all their children
build lives enriched by faithful commitment
to the spreading of Torah and *Ahavat Yisrael.*

Dedicated with love by
The Rohr Family
NEW YORK, USA

CONTENTS

Of all the books of the Tanakh, no book has brought more comfort to those in emotional pain, more joy to those celebrating, more praise and thanks to God, than *Sefer Tehillim,* the book of Psalms. It is with great pride that we present this new edition of *The Koren Tehillim.* There is something unique about a book that carries within it the words to express the gamut of human experience; our joy, gratitude, reverence, fear, sorrow, and anguish; words that seem to continually speak to us in whatever time and place we find ourselves. The age-old poetry of Tehillim has comforted our people throughout the generations, marked our celebrations, and given voice to our ongoing conversation with God.

As always, we have incorporated the textual accuracy and aesthetic design for which Koren is renowned, but there are two significant innovations to this edition.

First, the translation by Rabbi Eli Cashdan, ז״ל, is especially elegant and clear: as Rabbi Lord Jonathan Sacks writes, it is "*simple, direct, lucid and intelligible, informed not only by previous translations but also by the classic Jewish commentaries, it will allow these masterpieces of religious poetry to speak with their ageless power to a new generation.*" This is central: to seek for emotional, spiritual strength from an ancient text requires a full understanding of each. We are fortunate to have collaborated with the family of the late Rav Cashdan for the exclusive use of his work.

Secondly, we are privileged to present the commentary of Rabbi Dr. Tzvi Hersh Weinreb. A former community rabbi, leader of the Orthodox Union for over a decade, as well as a trained and practicing psychologist, Rabbi Weinreb brings together a deeply rooted knowledge of traditional texts with a compassionate understanding of the human condition, to provide an insightful commentary that explores the specific meaning of each psalm. Why do we turn to the psalms in particular situations? What can we learn from the circumstances under which a psalm was composed? Rabbi Weinreb has created a unique analysis which aims to guide the reader in his or her search for meaning and a more profound understanding of Tehillim.

We are honored by the exceptional support of the Rohr family, without whom this project would not have been possible. It is appropriate that it is dedicated to the memories of Sami Rohr, ז"ל, and Charlotte Rohr (née Kastner), ז"ל, both of whom knew the power of Tehillim and recited them daily. We extend our gratitude to their children, George and Pamela Rohr, Shmuel and Evelyn Katz, and Moshe and Lillian Tabacinic, for their generosity. On behalf of the thousands who will use this book, we thank you for advancing and deepening Jewish learning all over the world.

A project of this scope is by nature collaborative. Our small but highly professional team in Jerusalem never ceases to impress with both the quantity and quality of their work. We thank Efrat Gross for reviewing the Hebrew text; Rachel Meghnagi and Nechama Unterman for editing the English texts; and Esther Be'er and Ayelet Dagan for the typographic design.

If we have brought some comfort to the troubled, or an even greater appreciation of the beauty and depths of some of the most sublime poetry ever composed, we will be satisfied.

Matthew Miller, Publisher
Jerusalem, 5775 (2015)

It has been said that the Five Books of the Torah are meant to be studied, the Prophets are meant to heard, the Ketuvim such as Job or the Book of Esther are meant to be read. But Tehillim, Psalms, are meant to be said.

Traditionally, Tehillim are recited, unlike any of the other books of the Bible. In Yiddish, one says, "*Tehillim, menn sagt Tehillim.*"

It is for this reason that Tehillim have become so personally relevant to the religious person, Jew or gentile. People have historically turned to Tehillim in times of woe as well as in times of joy. They have discovered in the recitation of Tehillim a vehicle to express the entire range of human thoughts and emotions.

Thus, Tehillim have become the key to spirituality for all mankind. For the Jew especially, Tehillim are literally indispensable to the religious experience, to his relationship with God.

The importance of Tehillim for the inner life of the religious person necessitates that they be available to him in a manner that he can understand intellectually and integrate emotionally. Tehillim speak to both the heart and the mind.

This edition strives to make Tehillim conceptually meaningful and emotionally accessible.

Each individual psalm is preceded by a very brief meditation, written in the first person. This meditation attempts to capture the predominant mood of the psalm, the mood in which the person who turns to this psalm finds himself. The reader will be able to approach the psalm from his subjective feelings, and will be enabled to link the words of the psalm to those feelings.

These meditations are designed to evoke the array of feelings which are common to all humanity, and which are subjects of study for the existentialist philosopher and for the depth psychologist. Those feelings will include dread, hope, despair, courage, doubt, confidence, triumph, frustration, shame and pride, joie de vivre and fear of death, and more.

But psalms are not only designed to be read. They are also to be studied. And so, each psalm will be followed by a brief essay expounding upon one or two of its central teachings. Special attention will be given to those teachings which reflect the issues which the reader is likely to confront in his personal life in this day and age.

A meditation will precede, and a meaningful message will follow, each *kapitel*, Yiddish for chapter, of Tehillim. That is the design for this commentary.

But perusing the commentary will not suffice. The words must be recited; ideally, first in Hebrew, and then in the exquisite and inspiring translation of Rabbi Eli Cashdan, to whom I am personally indebted for his rich and suggestive rendition of these timeless words.

Rabbi Dr. Tzvi Hersh Weinreb
Suffern, New York, and Jerusalem, Israel
5775 (2014)

תהלים

TEHILLIM

PRAYER BEFORE READING PSALMS

Supplication to be said before reading Psalms:

יְהִי רָצוֹן May it be Your will, Lord our God, God of our ancestors, who chooses His servant David, and his descendants after him; who chooses song and praise – that You turn, in Your compassion, toward my reading of these Psalms, as if King David, peace be upon him, were reading them himself; and may the merit of the verses of the Psalms, the merit of their words and letters, their vowels and their notes, and of the names found in them, formed of the first letters and last letters of their words, all stand up for us, to bring us atonement for our rebellions and transgressions and sins; to cut down tyrants, to harvest all the thorns and thistles surrounding the heavenly lily, and to join the Bride of His youth with the Beloved, in friendship and in brotherhood and love – and from that place may plenty be drawn down to us, to soul and spirit and higher soul, to purify us of our iniquities and to forgive our sins and atone our transgressions, just as You forgave David, who first spoke these songs before You, as it is said: "And the Lord *II Sam. 12*
has passed over your sin, and you shall not die." And do not take us from this world before our time, not before our seventy years are complete; let us live such that we may be able to put right all that we have damaged. And may the merit of King David, peace be upon him, defend us, that You may withhold Your wrath until we return to You in complete repentance. Grace us with gifts undeserved from Your treasury, as it is said, "I shall be gracious *Ex. 33*
to whom I shall be gracious; I shall be merciful to whom I shall be merciful." And just as we sing songs in this world, so may we have the merit to sing before You, Lord our God, God of our ancestors, song and praise in the world to come. And through our speaking these Psalms, may the Rose of Sharon be awakened to sing with a lovely voice, rejoicing and song, for the glory of Lebanon is given to her. Glory and splendor in the house of our God, speedily *Is. 35*
in our days: Amen, Selah!

Before reading Psalms it is customary to recite these verses:

Come, let us sing joyfully to the Lord, let us acclaim the Rock of our salvation. *Ps. 95*
Let us come before His presence with thanksgiving,
and acclaim Him with songs of praise.
For the Lord is a great God, a great King above all gods.

תפילה לפני אמירת תהלים

Supplication to be said before reading Psalms:

יְהִי רָצוֹן מִלְּפָנֶיךָ, יהוה אֱלֹהֵינוּ וֵאלֹהֵי אֲבוֹתֵינוּ, הַבּוֹחֵר בְּדָוִד עַבְדּוֹ וּבְזַרְעוֹ
אַחֲרָיו, וְהַבּוֹחֵר בְּשִׁירוֹת וְתִשְׁבָּחוֹת, שֶׁתֵּפֶן בְּרַחֲמִים אֶל קְרִיאַת מִזְמוֹרֵי
תְהִלִּים שֶׁאֶקְרָא כְּאִלּוּ אֲמָרָם דָּוִד הַמֶּלֶךְ עָלָיו הַשָּׁלוֹם בְּעַצְמוֹ, זְכוּתוֹ
תָּגֵן עָלֵינוּ, וְתַעֲמָד לָנוּ זְכוּת פְּסוּקֵי תְהִלִּים וּזְכוּת תֵּבוֹתֵיהֶם וְאוֹתִיּוֹתֵיהֶם
וּנְקֻדּוֹתֵיהֶם וְטַעֲמֵיהֶם וְהַשֵּׁמוֹת הַיּוֹצְאִים מֵהֶם מֵרָאשֵׁי תֵבוֹת וּמִסּוֹפֵי
תֵבוֹת לְכַפֵּר פְּשָׁעֵינוּ וַעֲוֹנוֹתֵינוּ וְחַטֹּאתֵינוּ, וּלְזַמֵּר עָרִיצִים וּלְהַכְרִית כָּל
הַחוֹחִים וְהַקּוֹצִים הַסּוֹבְבִים אֶת הַשּׁוֹשַׁנָּה הָעֶלְיוֹנָה וּלְחַבֵּר אֵשֶׁת נְעוּרִים
עִם דּוֹדָהּ בְּאַהֲבָה וְאַחֲוָה וְרֵעוּת, וּמִשָּׁם יִמָּשֵׁךְ לָנוּ שֶׁפַע לְנֶפֶשׁ רוּחַ וּנְשָׁמָה
לְטַהֲרֵנוּ מֵעֲוֹנוֹתֵינוּ וְלִסְלֹחַ חַטֹּאתֵינוּ וּלְכַפֵּר פְּשָׁעֵינוּ, כְּמוֹ שֶׁסָּלַחְתָּ לְדָוִד
שֶׁאָמַר מִזְמוֹרִים אֵלּוּ לְפָנֶיךָ, כְּמוֹ שֶׁנֶּאֱמַר, גַּם־יהוה הֶעֱבִיר חַטָּאתְךָ לֹא שמואל ב׳ יב
תָמוּת: וְאַל תִּקָּחֵנוּ מֵהָעוֹלָם הַזֶּה קֹדֶם זְמַנֵּנוּ עַד מְלֹאת שְׁנוֹתֵינוּ בָּהֶם
שִׁבְעִים שָׁנָה, בְּאוֹפַן שֶׁנּוּכַל לְתַקֵּן אֵת אֲשֶׁר שִׁחַתְנוּ, וּזְכוּת דָּוִד הַמֶּלֶךְ
עָלָיו הַשָּׁלוֹם תָּגֵן עָלֵינוּ וּבַעֲדֵנוּ, שֶׁתַּאֲרִיךְ אַפְּךָ עַד שׁוּבֵנוּ אֵלֶיךָ בִּתְשׁוּבָה
שְׁלֵמָה לְפָנֶיךָ, וּמֵאוֹצַר מַתְּנַת חִנָּם חָנֵּנוּ, כִּדְכְתִיב, וְחַנֹּתִי אֶת־אֲשֶׁר אָחֹן שמות לג
וְרִחַמְתִּי אֶת־אֲשֶׁר אֲרַחֵם: וּכְשֵׁם שֶׁאָנוּ אוֹמְרִים לְפָנֶיךָ שִׁירָה בָּעוֹלָם
הַזֶּה, כָּךְ נִזְכֶּה לוֹמַר לְפָנֶיךָ יהוה אֱלֹהֵינוּ שִׁיר וּשְׁבָחָה לָעוֹלָם הַבָּא. וְעַל
יְדֵי אֲמִירַת תְּהִלִּים, תִּתְעוֹרֵר חֲבַצֶּלֶת הַשָּׁרוֹן וְלָשִׁיר בְּקוֹל נָעִים בְּגִילַת
וְרַנֵּן, כְּבוֹד הַלְּבָנוֹן נִתַּן־לָהּ: הוֹד וְהָדָר בְּבֵית אֱלֹהֵינוּ בִּמְהֵרָה בְיָמֵינוּ, ישעיה לה
אָמֵן סֶלָה.

Before reading Psalms it is customary to recite these verses:

לְכוּ נְרַנְּנָה לַיהוה, נָרִיעָה לְצוּר יִשְׁעֵנוּ: תהלים צה
נְקַדְּמָה פָנָיו בְּתוֹדָה, בִּזְמִרוֹת נָרִיעַ לוֹ:
כִּי אֵל גָּדוֹל יהוה, וּמֶלֶךְ גָּדוֹל עַל־כָּל־אֱלֹהִים:

PSALM 1

1. Happy is the man
who never follows the advice of the wicked,
nor lingers in the path of the sinners,
nor sits in the company of scoffers; *First day of the month* *Sunday*

2. but finds his delight in the Torah of the LORD,
and meditates in His Torah day and night.

3. He is like a tree planted beside streams of water,
that yields fruit in season, and whose leaf never withers.
He succeeds in everything he does.

4. Not so is it with the wicked.
They are like chaff which the wind blows away.

5. Therefore, when judgment comes the wicked shall not stand firm,
nor sinners in the company of the righteous.

6. For the LORD cares for the way of the righteous,
but the way of the wicked is doomed.

---

person who performs the good *never withers,* and the time eventually comes when *judgment comes for the wicked.* There is a fundamental question, however, and that is the ability to know what is Good and what is Evil. The choice between right and wrong is often a very ambiguous one. It is for this reason that this psalm speaks of the Torah and the need to *meditate in it day and night.*

There are guidelines for discriminating right from wrong, no matter how ambiguous the choice may seem. The Torah is exactly this: a set of guidelines to assist in making choices, particularly when things are fuzzy and unclear.

But the Torah's guidelines are often themselves ambiguous, and alone, one can never be certain that he has interpreted them correctly. This psalm provides two suggestions for rendering the Torah more relevant to one's choices.

One suggestion is in meditating in Torah *day and night.* Diligence and constant study is necessary. One needs to be preoccupied with Torah for it to offer its answers definitively.

Another suggestion is to *find delight* in the Torah, to cherish it. The Torah is best understood not so much by the person who studies it as if it was a book of law, but rather by the one who enjoys it and sings it as a delightful song.

מזמור א

I face a difficult choice. Good versus Evil. How can I choose? Will I not regret my choice of the former, when the latter has such obvious advantages?

א לחודש
ליום ראשון

א אַשְׁרֵי־הָאִישׁ
אֲשֶׁר ׀ לֹא הָלַךְ בַּעֲצַת רְשָׁעִים
וּבְדֶרֶךְ חַטָּאִים לֹא עָמָד
וּבְמוֹשַׁב לֵצִים לֹא יָשָׁב׃

ב כִּי אִם בְּתוֹרַת יהוה חֶפְצוֹ
וּבְתוֹרָתוֹ יֶהְגֶּה יוֹמָם וָלָיְלָה׃

ג וְהָיָה כְּעֵץ שָׁתוּל עַל־פַּלְגֵי מָיִם
אֲשֶׁר פִּרְיוֹ ׀ יִתֵּן בְּעִתּוֹ
וְעָלֵהוּ לֹא־יִבּוֹל
וְכֹל אֲשֶׁר־יַעֲשֶׂה יַצְלִיחַ׃

ד לֹא־כֵן הָרְשָׁעִים
כִּי אִם־כַּמֹּץ אֲשֶׁר־תִּדְּפֶנּוּ רוּחַ׃

ה עַל־כֵּן ׀
לֹא־יָקֻמוּ רְשָׁעִים בַּמִּשְׁפָּט
וְחַטָּאִים בַּעֲדַת צַדִּיקִים׃

ו כִּי־יוֹדֵעַ יהוה דֶּרֶךְ צַדִּיקִים
וְדֶרֶךְ רְשָׁעִים תֹּאבֵד׃

מזמור א *Psalm 1:* There is indeed Evil in the world, and it has its temptations. Its opposite, Good, is not nearly as tempting. This is especially true in the short term. Immediate gratification is what we all seek, and postponing gratification is very difficult. This is particularly true if the immediate gratification is certain, and there is no guarantee that the postponed gratification will ever be achieved.

We all need some kind of assurance that forgoing the temptations of the moment will pay off in the long run. This psalm gives that assurance. The

PSALM 2

1. Why do the nations rage,
and the peoples devise futile plots?

2. Kings of the earth stand ready,
and princes conspire together
against the LORD and against His anointed, saying,

3. "Let us break their fetters,
and cast off their bonds from us."

4. He who is enthroned in heaven laughs,
the LORD mocks at them.

5. Then He speaks to them in His anger,
and terrifies them in His wrath,

6. "I have set up My king,
on Zion, My holy mountain."

7. I will announce the decree:
The LORD said to me, "You are My son;
this day I have become your father.

The Jewish people have encountered powerful kingdoms and sadistic national forces over and over again. Often these nations had their own theology, and it was one which mocked the LORD our God. Yet, without exception, these enemies of God have all disappeared from the map of nations.

The image of God, who *enthroned in heaven, laughs and mocks at them,* is an apt and encouraging image. True, there have been circumstances in our history when the image of a "laughing and mocking God" was of insufficient comfort. The Holocaust is but a relatively recent example of such a set of circumstances. It is difficult to find consolation in the fact that the Nazis *ended in ruin.*

The Book of Psalms is not a book of theology, and does not provide easy answers to such important questions. It does provide us, however, with spiritual counsel, and near the end of this psalm, such spiritual counsel is given.

מזמור ב

I am frightened. Powerful nations abound. They threaten harm, particularly to Israel. They are serious, fanatically serious. They defy all that we hold holy. I tremble.

א לָ֭מָּה רָגְשׁ֣וּ גוֹיִ֑ם
וּ֝לְאֻמִּ֗ים יֶהְגּוּ־רִֽיק׃

ב יִ֥תְיַצְּב֨וּ ׀ מַלְכֵי־אֶ֗רֶץ
וְרוֹזְנִ֥ים נֽוֹסְדוּ־יָ֑חַד
עַל־יְ֝הוָ֗ה וְעַל־מְשִׁיחֽוֹ׃

ג נְֽ֭נַתְּקָה אֶת־מֽוֹסְרוֹתֵ֑ימוֹ
וְנַשְׁלִ֖יכָה מִמֶּ֣נּוּ עֲבֹתֵֽימוֹ׃

ד יוֹשֵׁ֣ב בַּשָּׁמַ֣יִם יִשְׂחָ֑ק
אֲ֝דֹנָ֗י יִלְעַג־לָֽמוֹ׃

ה אָ֤ז יְדַבֵּ֣ר אֵלֵ֣ימוֹ בְאַפּ֑וֹ
וּֽבַחֲרוֹנ֥וֹ יְבַהֲלֵֽמוֹ׃

ו וַ֭אֲנִי נָסַ֣כְתִּי מַלְכִּ֑י
עַל־צִ֝יּ֗וֹן הַר־קָדְשִֽׁי׃

ז אֲסַפְּרָ֗ה אֶֽ֫ל חֹ֥ק
יְֽהוָ֗ה אָמַ֘ר אֵלַ֣י בְּנִ֣י אַ֑תָּה
אֲ֝נִ֗י הַיּ֥וֹם יְלִדְתִּֽיךָ׃

מזמור ב *Psalm 2:* One of the central teachings of Judaism is that God plays a role in the international arena. He is not just a personal deity, available to the individual. Rather, He is an actor on the stage of nations.

This is one of the themes of the exodus from Egypt. Egypt was a powerful international force in its time, and God played a role in its downfall. So too has He been active throughout human history.

8. Ask of Me,
and I will give you nations as your inheritance,
the ends of the earth as your possession.

9. You will break them with a rod of iron,
and shatter them like a potter's jar."

10. So now, kings, be prudent;
be warned, you rulers of the earth.

11. Serve the LORD with reverence,
rejoice with trembling.

12. Pay homage with sincerity,
lest He be angry and you end in ruin;*
for His anger flares up in a moment.
Happy are all who find refuge in Him!

* Lit. "perish in the way."

There must be a semblance of sobriety underlying even experiences of great celebration.

But the converse is also true, and is implied in the phrase *rejoice with trembling*. In moments of trembling, times of great frustration and despair, one must somehow find a way to *rejoice*. A semblance of joy and hope must exist even in the depths of suffering. A difficult lesson to follow, but one for which the chroniclers of our tradition have many examples

ח שְׁאַל מִמֶּנִּי
וְאֶתְּנָה גוֹיִם נַחֲלָתֶךָ
וַאֲחֻזָּתְךָ אַפְסֵי־אָרֶץ׃

ט תְּרֹעֵם בְּשֵׁבֶט בַּרְזֶל
כִּכְלִי יוֹצֵר תְּנַפְּצֵם׃

י וְעַתָּה מְלָכִים הַשְׂכִּילוּ
הִוָּסְרוּ שֹׁפְטֵי אָרֶץ׃

יא עִבְדוּ אֶת־יְהוָה בְּיִרְאָה
וְגִילוּ בִּרְעָדָה׃

יב נַשְּׁקוּ־בַר
פֶּן־יֶאֱנַף ׀ וְתֹאבְדוּ דֶרֶךְ
כִּי־יִבְעַר כִּמְעַט אַפּוֹ
אַשְׁרֵי כָּל־חוֹסֵי בוֹ׃

I refer to the phrase *rejoice with trembling*. Many have found this brief phrase – just three words in English and only two in Hebrew – to contain the essential secret of Jewish spirituality.

As the Talmud (*Berakhot* 30b) has it: "In a place of great joy, there needs to be trembling." One cannot allow moments of joy to deteriorate into frivolity.

PSALM 3

1. A psalm of David,
when he fled from his son Absalom.

2. Lord, how many are my foes!
Many rise against me.

3. Many are saying of me,
"There is no help for him from God." *Selah*

4. But You, Lord, are a shield around me;
You are my glory,
You raise high my head.

5. When I call to the Lord,
He answers me from His holy mountain. *Selah*

6. I lie down to rest,
and I sleep,
I wake again for the Lord upholds me.

But we are suddenly surprised as David shifts from his overwhelming feelings of desperation to a firm expression of faith and trust:

But you, Lord, are a shield around me. So powerful is this spiritual sense of trust that he sleeps peacefully and has no fear.

Faith and trust swell within him, and enable him to assert his power and even to anticipate victory.

It is in this psalm that we first encounter the word "*Selah*." This word has been translated in many different ways over the ages, so that our translator has simply transliterated it, leaving it in the Hebrew original.

One commentator, Radak (acronym for Rabbi David Kimchi), suggests that the word has no connotative meaning at all. Rather, it derives from a Hebrew root which means to "raise high." It is a signal to those who sing this psalm, or read it aloud, to raise their voices at this point.

The word *Selah* instructs us to raise our voices at three critical points in this brief psalm, each point corresponding to a shift in King David's mood.

מזמור ג

There can be nothing worse. I must flee from my own son, my flesh and blood. Those closest to me have betrayed me. This is worse than facing enemy armies. I am overwhelmed, helpless. I am driven into hiding.

א מִזְמ֥וֹר לְדָוִ֑ד
בְּ֝בָרְח֗וֹ מִפְּנֵ֤י ׀ אַבְשָׁל֬וֹם בְּנֽוֹ׃

ב יְ֭הוָה מָֽה־רַבּ֣וּ צָרָ֑י
רַ֝בִּ֗ים קָמִ֥ים עָלָֽי׃

ג רַבִּים֮ אֹמְרִ֪ים לְנַ֫פְשִׁ֥י
אֵ֤ין יְֽשׁוּעָ֓תָה לּ֬וֹ בֵ֬אלֹהִ֬ים סֶֽלָה׃

ד וְאַתָּ֣ה יְ֭הוָה מָגֵ֣ן בַּעֲדִ֑י
כְּ֝בוֹדִ֗י וּמֵרִ֥ים רֹאשִֽׁי׃

ה ק֭וֹלִי אֶל־יְהוָ֣ה אֶקְרָ֑א
וַיַּעֲנֵ֨נִי מֵהַ֖ר קָדְשׁ֣וֹ סֶֽלָה׃

ו אֲנִ֥י שָׁכַ֗בְתִּי וָאִ֫ישָׁ֥נָה
הֱקִיצ֑וֹתִי
כִּ֖י יְהוָ֣ה יִסְמְכֵֽנִי׃

מזמור ג *Psalm 3:* King David is furious and frightened. He feels betrayed and afraid.

In the preceding psalm he remained undaunted by the raging nations.

But now that the rebellious Absalom has successfully enlisted his father's inner circle in his mutinous cause, desperate flight seems David's only resort.

Lord, how many are my foes!

Many rise against me. "Rebellion in one's own home is an even greater catastrophe than the wars of Gog and Magog," says the Talmud (*Berakhot* 7b).

7. I fear not the myriads of people
who have set themselves against me on every side.

8. Arise, LORD; save me, O my God!
Strike all my enemies on the cheek;
Smash the teeth of the wicked.

9. Victory comes from the LORD;
May Your blessing rest upon Your people. *Selah*

The second *Selah* heralds the transition from faithful trust to calm serenity.

The psalm concludes with a third *Selah,* urging us to raise our voices yet again, as if to echo David's resounding confidence in his ultimate triumph.

ז לֹֽא־אִירָא מֵרִבְב֥וֹת עָ֑ם
אֲשֶׁ֥ר סָ֝בִ֗יב שָׁ֣תוּ עָלָֽי׃

ח ק֘וּמָ֤ה יהו֨ה ׀ הוֹשִׁ֘יעֵ֤נִי אֱלֹהַ֗י
כִּֽי־הִכִּ֣יתָ אֶת־כָּל־אֹיְבַ֣י לֶ֑חִי
שִׁנֵּ֖י רְשָׁעִ֣ים שִׁבַּֽרְתָּ׃

ט לַיהו֥ה הַיְשׁוּעָ֑ה
עַֽל־עַמְּךָ֖ בִרְכָתֶ֣ךָ סֶּֽלָה׃

The first *Selah* prepares us for the abrupt change that takes place as David transcends his sense of desperation and opens himself up to feelings of trust in God.

PSALM 4

1. For the Chief Musician; with stringed instruments.
A psalm of David.

2. Answer me when I call,
O my righteous God.
When I was in distress You freed me;
now have mercy on me, and hear my prayer.

3. You men of rank,
how long will you turn my glory into shame?
How long will you love vanity,
and seek after falsehood? *Selah*

4. Know that the LORD has singled out the faithful for Himself.
The LORD hears when I call to Him.

5. Fear Him; do not sin.
Ponder on this when you rest in bed,
and be silent. *Selah*

6. Offer righteousness as your sacrifice,
and trust in the LORD.

He advises them to remember that his position is divinely sanctioned, and that it is sinful for them to persist in denying him the throne. He asks them to contemplate the righteousness of his cause dispassionately.

Almost immediately, another *Selah* instructs the reader to lift his voice in further amazement as David delineates a course of atonement for his enemies, recommending the practices of sacrifice and faith.

David assures them that he not only bears no grudge against them, but that he rejoices in their well-being and success.

He alerts opponents that he is ready to forgive them, that he longs to be at one with them. He concludes by stating that he relies upon God Himself to restore peace and harmony.

מזמור ד

I am eager to dialogue with those who have betrayed me, because I am confident that the Lord will hear my prayers. I don't want to fight with them. I wish they were sufficiently open-minded to hear my side of the story. My God is their God. Why can they not understand that? Why not forgive each other? We would accomplish so much if we could just work together.

א לַמְנַצֵּ֥חַ בִּנְגִינ֗וֹת מִזְמ֥וֹר לְדָוִֽד׃

ב בְּקָרְאִ֡י עֲנֵ֤נִי ׀ אֱלֹ֘הֵ֤י צִדְקִ֗י בַּ֭צָּר הִרְחַ֣בְתָּ לִּ֑י
חָ֝נֵּ֗נִי וּשְׁמַ֥ע תְּפִלָּתִֽי׃

ג בְּנֵי־אִ֡ישׁ עַד־מֶ֬ה כְבוֹדִ֣י לִ֭כְלִמָּה
תֶּאֱהָב֣וּן רִ֑יק
תְּבַקְשׁ֖וּ כָזָ֣ב סֶֽלָה׃

ד וּדְע֗וּ כִּֽי־הִפְלָ֣ה יהוה חָסִ֣יד ל֑וֹ
יהוה יִ֝שְׁמַ֗ע בְּקָרְאִ֥י אֵלָֽיו׃

ה רִגְז֗וּ וְֽאַל־תֶּ֫חֱטָ֥אוּ
אִמְר֣וּ בִ֭לְבַבְכֶם עַל־מִשְׁכַּבְכֶ֗ם
וְדֹ֣מּוּ סֶֽלָה׃

ו זִבְח֥וּ זִבְחֵי־צֶ֑דֶק
וּ֝בִטְח֗וּ אֶל־יְהוָֽה׃

מזמור ד *Psalm 4:* King David continues his response to Absalom's mutiny, but with a fundamental difference. He no longer confines himself to his own reaction, but rather begins to directly address the "other."

His perspective changes only after he first turns to God: *Answer me when I call... hear my prayer*. Then, sure that God heard his prayer, he abandons the monologue of Psalm 3, and begins the dialogue of Psalm 4: *You men of rank, how long will you turn my glory into shame?Selah* punctuates the psalm at this point, instructing us to raise our voices as David cuts short his rebuke of his enemies and, astoundingly, begins to counsel them.

7. There are many who say,
"If only we might see better times!"
Let the light of Your face shine upon us, LORD!

8. You have put in my heart greater joy
than others have when their corn and wine abound.

9. In peace I lie down and sleep,
for You alone,
LORD, keep me in safety.

---

planted by a readiness to engage in mutual conversation, empathic dialogue, and ultimately forgiveness.

Taken together, these two psalms teach a lesson in the dynamic nature of spirituality, as David models a style of response to dire threat that is not rigid and static, but is open to reconsideration, modification, and profound religious growth.

ז רַבִּ֥ים אֹמְרִים֮
מִֽי־יַרְאֵ֪נ֫וּ ט֥וֹב
נְֽסָה־עָ֭לֵינוּ א֨וֹר פָּנֶ֬יךָ יְהוָֽה׃

ח נָתַ֣תָּה שִׂמְחָ֣ה בְלִבִּ֑י
מֵעֵ֬ת דְּגָנָ֖ם וְתִירוֹשָׁ֣ם רָֽבּוּ׃

ט בְּשָׁל֣וֹם יַחְדָּו֮ אֶשְׁכְּבָ֪ה וְאִ֫ישָׁ֥ן
כִּֽי־אַתָּ֣ה יְהוָ֣ה לְבָדָ֑ד
לָ֝בֶ֗טַח תּוֹשִׁיבֵֽנִי׃

By interpreting Psalms 3 and 4 as being linked in this manner, we are enabled to view the progression of David's emotional reactions to the treachery perpetrated upon him. We follow the transformation of feelings of fear and anger into empathy and forgiveness. Strategies of flight and fight become sup-

PSALM 5

1. For the Chief Musician; on the *neḥilot.*
A psalm of David.

2. Give ear to my words, LORD;
pay heed to my utterance.

3. Listen to my cry for help,
my King and my God,
for to You I pray.

4. Morning after morning, LORD,
You hear my voice,
morning after morning
I set out my plea before You and wait.

5. For You are not a God who delights in wickedness;
no evil man can be a guest of Yours.

6. The boastful cannot stand in Your presence;
You hate all evildoers.

7. You destroy all who speak lies;
bloodthirsty and deceitful men the LORD detests.

Morning is precisely the right time of day for God to hear such utterances. As we awake, we have a dim and fast-fading awareness of our dreams, which revealed our innermost feelings but soon concealed them in a mysterious language of symbols and images.

With the arrival of the morning our conscious self emerges. The dream images slip beyond our reach, hidden from our conscious self. Our thoughts are no longer mysterious; their language becomes ordinary and familiar.

Will our prayers also be ordinary and familiar?

We implore God, for whom those lost utterances of the soul are ever present, to assure us that they are not lost, but remain heard, infusing our prayers with the passion and depth which our conscious minds have suppressed.

מזמור ה

Words cannot express my thoughts and emotions. My thoughts are numerous and chaotic. My emotions are frightening and overwhelming. Thus, I pray that God not only hears my words, but reads my mind.

א לַמְנַצֵּחַ אֶל־הַנְּחִילוֹת מִזְמוֹר לְדָוִד׃

ב אֲמָרַי הַאֲזִינָה ׀ יְהוָה
בִּינָה הֲגִיגִי׃

ג הַקְשִׁיבָה ׀ לְקוֹל שַׁוְעִי
מַלְכִּי וֵאלֹהָי
כִּי־אֵלֶיךָ אֶתְפַּלָּל׃

ד יְהוָה
בֹּקֶר תִּשְׁמַע קוֹלִי
בֹּקֶר אֶעֱרָךְ־לְךָ וַאֲצַפֶּה׃

ה כִּי ׀ לֹא אֵל־חָפֵץ רֶשַׁע ׀ אָתָּה
לֹא יְגֻרְךָ רָע׃

ו לֹא־יִתְיַצְּבוּ הוֹלְלִים לְנֶגֶד עֵינֶיךָ
שָׂנֵאתָ כָּל־פֹּעֲלֵי אָוֶן׃

ז תְּאַבֵּד דֹּבְרֵי כָזָב
אִישׁ־דָּמִים וּמִרְמָה יְתָעֵב ׀ יְהוָה׃

מזמור ה *Psalm 5:* Rashi puts it so well: "*Give ear to my words* when I have the ability to use words to ask You for my needs, but when I am powerless to pray, when my anxieties are enclosed within my heart, *pay heed to my utterance.*"

The root of the word translated here as utterance is *h-g-h,* which implies an "inner" utterance, one that is thought but not spoken.

Thus it is only *to You that I pray*. Only You can hear the unarticulated utterances of my soul.

8. But I, through Your great loving-kindness,
may come into Your house,
I bow down toward Your Holy Temple in awe of You.

9. Lead me, LORD, in Your righteousness, because of my foes;
make Your way straight before me.

10. For there is no truth in their talk;*
their mind is bent on destruction.
Their throat is an open grave;
they speak so smoothly with their tongue.

11. Condemn them, God,
let them fall by their own devices;
cast them out for their many crimes,
for they have rebelled against You.

12. But let all who take refuge in You rejoice,
let them ever sing for joy;
spread Your shelter over them,
so that those who love Your name exult in You.

13. For you, LORD, will bless the righteous man;
You will surround him with favor as with a shield.

* Lit. "mouth."

We must attempt to eliminate those traits from own behavioral repertoires, turning to God to help us in this process.

Our relationship with Him cannot just be spiritually edifying, but must be ethically instructive as well.

When we *come into Your house and bow down to Your Holy Temple* it is not just to worship. Rather, it is to learn right from wrong and to implore Him to help us put the lessons we learn into practice.

In His house and Holy Temple we hope to achieve both spiritual experience *and* ethical guidance.

Hence our prayer in His house: *Lead me, LORD, in Your righteousness, because of my foes; make Your way straight before me.*

ח וַאֲנִי בְּרֹב חַסְדְּךָ אָבוֹא בֵיתֶךָ
אֶשְׁתַּחֲוֶה אֶל־הֵיכַל־קָדְשְׁךָ בְּיִרְאָתֶךָ׃

ט יְהוָה ׀ נְחֵנִי בְצִדְקָתֶךָ לְמַעַן שׁוֹרְרָי
הושר לְפָנַי דַּרְכֶּךָ׃ הַיְשַׁר

י כִּי אֵין בְּפִיהוּ נְכוֹנָה
קִרְבָּם הַוּוֹת
קֶבֶר־פָּתוּחַ גְּרוֹנָם
לְשׁוֹנָם יַחֲלִיקוּן׃

יא הַאֲשִׁימֵם ׀ אֱלֹהִים
יִפְּלוּ מִמֹּעֲצוֹתֵיהֶם
בְּרֹב פִּשְׁעֵיהֶם הַדִּיחֵמוֹ
כִּי מָרוּ בָךְ׃

יב וְיִשְׂמְחוּ כָל־חוֹסֵי בָךְ
לְעוֹלָם יְרַנֵּנוּ וְתָסֵךְ עָלֵימוֹ
וְיַעְלְצוּ בְךָ אֹהֲבֵי שְׁמֶךָ׃

יג כִּי־אַתָּה תְּבָרֵךְ צַדִּיק
יְהוָה
כַּצִּנָּה רָצוֹן תַּעְטְרֶנּוּ׃

With the arrival of morning we leave the dream world and its images, and face the real world and its threats.

The threats we face are the traits which God most despises: *wickedness, boastfulness, lies, and deceit.*

Our enemies possess those traits. They are *bent on my destruction.*

Can we be confident of God's protection since He despises the very traits which our enemies have?

Yes, but only if we ourselves are devoid of those traits; only if we can rid ourselves of our own wickedness.

PSALM 6

1. For the Chief Musician;
with instrumental music on the *sheminit*.
A psalm of David.

2. LORD, do not rebuke me in Your anger;
do not punish me in Your wrath.

3. Have pity on me, LORD,
for I am weak;
heal me, LORD,
for my bones shake with terror.

4. My whole being is greatly shaken up;
but You, LORD – how long before You act?

5. Turn, LORD,
and deliver me;
save me, because of Your loving-kindness.

6. For there is no remembrance of You among the dead;
in Sheol who praises You?

---

of his own illness, to be used as a text for all who pray." David provided the words for all who are gravely ill; for all of us who struggle desperately to give vent to our emotions.

We feel rebuked and punished, and can accept that, for who among us does not experience guilt for one or another of our many sins? But we beg Him not to mete out that rebuke in an angry manner, not to punish us wrathfully. We urge Him to diminish His anger and be gentle with us. We implore Him to temper that wrath, so that we can at least tolerate the pain and somehow cope with it.

Heretofore death was a stranger; suddenly, it is a real threat.

We are obsessed with images of the grave, and protest: "What about our life's mission? Surely, that cannot be accomplished in the grave!"

The sleepless nights are the worst. We ache with loneliness. We dampen our pillow with our tears.

מזמור ו

I am sick. I mean sick! I have never felt this bad in my entire life. It hurts. It really hurts. I cannot stand the pain. I am scared out of my wits. Really scared. Can no one help me? I never felt this close to death. I do not want to die.

א לַמְנַצֵּחַ בִּנְגִינוֹת עַל־הַשְּׁמִינִית מִזְמוֹר לְדָוִד׃

ב יהוה אַל־בְּאַפְּךָ תוֹכִיחֵנִי
וְאַל־בַּחֲמָתְךָ תְיַסְּרֵנִי׃

ג חָנֵּנִי יהוה
כִּי אֻמְלַל אָנִי
רְפָאֵנִי יהוה
כִּי נִבְהֲלוּ עֲצָמָי׃

ד וְנַפְשִׁי נִבְהֲלָה מְאֹד
וְאַתְּ יהוה עַד־מָתָי׃

ה שׁוּבָה יהוה
חַלְּצָה נַפְשִׁי
הוֹשִׁיעֵנִי לְמַעַן חַסְדֶּךָ׃

ו כִּי אֵין בַּמָּוֶת זִכְרֶךָ
בִּשְׁאוֹל מִי יוֹדֶה־לָּךְ׃

מזמור ו *Psalm 6:* For most of us, suffering a serious illness is a new experience, for which we are unprepared. We have seen others in great pain, and we have performed our share of visits to the ill.

But this time it is us. It is hardly believable, but we are the ones now in unbearable pain, pitifully helpless; feeling overwhelmed and frightened, abandoned and alone.

In this psalm, David gives voice to his experience of such illness, and it is here that Radak chooses to impart the encouraging lesson, applicable to the entire Book of Psalms: "They were composed by King David in the throes

7. I am wearied with my groaning;
every night I drench my bed with weeping,
I melt my couch with tears.

8. My eyes are dimmed with sorrow,
they are worn out because of all my foes.

9. Away from me, all you evildoers,
for the LORD has heard my weeping.

10. Yes, the LORD has heard my entreaty;
He has listened to my prayer.

11. All my enemies will be ashamed and dismayed;
they will turn back in sudden confusion.

---

survive and live to see their antagonists *ashamed and dismayed* by their foiled evil schemes.

They report that they wished these would-be usurpers no terrible punishment, just that they would *turn back in sudden confusion* and experience shame.

These feelings, secretly harbored by the recovered patient, are consistent with a most insightful midrash, to be found in the collection *Yalkut Shimoni* on our psalm:

> The Holy One, blessed be He, curses the wicked in only one way: that they feel shame. He curses them doubly, as it is written (in our psalm, verse 11), "*they turn back* and are embarrassed again..."
>
> Similarly, He blesses the righteous in only one way: that they never experience shame or embarrassment, as it is written (Is. 54:4), "*they shall neither be shamed nor confounded.*"

ז יָגַעְתִּי ׀ בְּאַנְחָתִי
אַשְׂחֶה בְכׇל־לַיְלָה מִטָּתִי
בְּדִמְעָתִי עַרְשִׂי אַמְסֶה׃

ח עָשְׁשָׁה מִכַּעַס עֵינִי
עָתְקָה בְּכׇל־צוֹרְרָי׃

ט סוּרוּ מִמֶּנִּי כׇּל־פֹּעֲלֵי אָוֶן
כִּי־שָׁמַע יהוה קוֹל בִּכְיִי׃

י שָׁמַע יהוה תְּחִנָּתִי
יהוה תְּפִלָּתִי יִקָּח׃

יא יֵבֹשׁוּ ׀ וְיִבָּהֲלוּ מְאֹד כׇּל־אֹיְבָי
יָשֻׁבוּ יֵבֹשׁוּ רָגַע׃

Our eyes become our most prominent organ. They become clouded. Our vision fades, becoming effete and worn with age. We are panicked lest our eyes decay and decompose, failing us completely.

For David, his illness carries an additional anxiety. His enemies stand just outside the door to his sickroom, and eagerly wait for him to succumb to his illness.

We wonder whether we too have such perfidious enemies, standing by and wishing we were out of their way.

Those who have experienced and survived serious illness tell us that they definitely did have recurring thoughts of such enemies. Sometimes these were paranoid thoughts of imagined enemies, but sometimes they were very real people who hoped to replace the sick person, usurping his or her role in the family, in the workplace, or in the community.

Like David, they found themselves preoccupied not just with those nasty "friends" who wished them ill, but with hopeful thoughts that they would

PSALM 7

1. A *shiggayon* of David,
which he sang to the LORD,
concerning Cush, a Benjaminite.

2. LORD, my God, in You I seek refuge;
rescue me from all my pursuers and save me,

3. lest, like a lion, they tear me apart,
and rip me to pieces, with none to rescue.

4. LORD, my God,
if I had done these things,
if there is any guilt on my hands,

5. if I have done evil to him who was at peace with me, –
I who delivered him who without cause was my enemy

6. then let an enemy pursue and overtake me,
let him trample my life to the ground,
and lay my honor in the dust. *Selah*

David understood Saul, but to survive he had to flee from Saul and those he sent to pursue him, *lest, like a lion, they tear me apart, and rip me to pieces.*

Saul was stripped of his throne, and the monarchy was awarded to David by Samuel, in the name of God Himself. David knew that his cause was just. But he could not help having empathy for Saul.

He *delivered him who without cause was my enemy.*

It is impossible to fight an enemy effectively when you have mixed feelings for him.

What made matters worse for David was that Saul had many supporters. But so did David have his supporters.

How could he distinguish his own allies from those of Saul? How could he be sure who was with him and who was against him?

For that he had to rely upon God, the *searcher of the mind and heart,* the

מזמור ז

It is would be much easier if I knew exactly who my enemies were. But it is so hard to tell. What's worse, some of my enemies are not all bad; they have good sides to them. It is hard to fight someone when you feel sorry for him.

א שִׁגָּיוֹן לְדָוִד
אֲשֶׁר־שָׁר לַיהוָה
עַל־דִּבְרֵי־כוּשׁ בֶּן־יְמִינִי׃

ב יְהוָה אֱלֹהַי בְּךָ חָסִיתִי
הוֹשִׁיעֵנִי מִכָּל־רֹדְפַי וְהַצִּילֵנִי׃

ג פֶּן־יִטְרֹף כְּאַרְיֵה נַפְשִׁי
פֹּרֵק וְאֵין מַצִּיל׃

ד יְהוָה אֱלֹהַי
אִם־עָשִׂיתִי זֹאת
אִם־יֶשׁ־עָוֶל בְּכַפָּי׃

ה אִם־גָּמַלְתִּי שׁוֹלְמִי רָע
וָאֲחַלְּצָה צוֹרְרִי רֵיקָם׃

ו יִרַדֹּף אוֹיֵב ׀ נַפְשִׁי וְיַשֵּׂג
וְיִרְמֹס לָאָרֶץ חַיָּי
וּכְבוֹדִי ׀ לֶעָפָר יַשְׁכֵּן סֶלָה׃

מזמור ז *Psalm 7:* We all know something about "love/hate" relationships. They are complicated, to say the least.

David's relationship with Saul was even more complicated than most such relationships. There was a time when Saul loved David, and needed him, both as a warrior and as a soothing musician. Saul chose David as his son-in-law.

But Saul came to hate David, whom he feared as a rival for his throne. He became murderously jealous of him.

7. Arise, LORD, in Your anger,
rouse Yourself in fury against my foes;
bestir Yourself on my behalf; pronounce judgment.

8. Let the peoples assemble around You,
and for them take Your seat on high.

9. The LORD judges the peoples.
Judge me, LORD, according to my righteousness,
and according to my integrity.

10. Let the evil of the wicked come to an end,
but establish the righteous,
You searcher of the mind and heart,

11. You righteous God.
I rely on God who is my shield;
He saves the upright in heart.

12. God is a just judge;
every day He is indignant [with the wicked].

13. If a man does not repent,
God will sharpen His sword,
He will bend His bow and take aim.

14. He has prepared for him His deadly weapons,
He has made ready His arrows
for the pursuers [of the righteous].

15. See, how the wicked conceives evil, is pregnant with mischief,
and gives birth to lies.

---

this lesson, which many of us wish we had learned early in life: "Many people pretend that they are good, but are not."

David, however, is supremely confident in God's ironic justice. David knows that the wicked person *digs a pit and digs it deep, but he himself will fall into the hole he has made.*

ז קוּמָה יהוה ׀ בְּאַפֶּךָ
הִנָּשֵׂא בְּעַבְרוֹת צוֹרְרָי
וְעוּרָה אֵלַי מִשְׁפָּט צִוִּיתָ׃

ח וַעֲדַת לְאֻמִּים תְּסוֹבְבֶךָּ
וְעָלֶיהָ לַמָּרוֹם שׁוּבָה׃

ט יהוה יָדִין עַמִּים
שָׁפְטֵנִי יהוה כְּצִדְקִי וּכְתֻמִּי עָלָי׃

י יִגְמָר־נָא רַע ׀ רְשָׁעִים וּתְכוֹנֵן צַדִּיק
וּבֹחֵן לִבּוֹת וּכְלָיוֹת אֱלֹהִים צַדִּיק׃

יא מָגִנִּי עַל־אֱלֹהִים
מוֹשִׁיעַ יִשְׁרֵי־לֵב׃

יב אֱלֹהִים שׁוֹפֵט צַדִּיק
וְאֵל זֹעֵם בְּכָל־יוֹם׃

יג אִם־לֹא יָשׁוּב חַרְבּוֹ יִלְטוֹשׁ
קַשְׁתּוֹ דָרַךְ וַיְכוֹנְנֶהָ׃

יד וְלוֹ הֵכִין כְּלֵי־מָוֶת
חִצָּיו לְדֹלְקִים יִפְעָל׃

טו הִנֵּה יְחַבֶּל־אָוֶן
וְהָרָה עָמָל וְיָלַד שָׁקֶר׃

One who could help him discriminate between those whom he could trust, and those wicked ones *who conceive evil, are pregnant with mischief, and give birth to lies.*

David's bitter foes could not readily be identified. Radak pithily expresses

16. He digs a pit and digs it deep,
but he himself will fall into the hole he has made.

17. His mischief will recoil upon his own head,
his violence will come down upon his own skull.

18. I will praise the LORD for His righteousness,
and sing psalms to the name of the LORD Most High.

David intuitively knows that the evil man's *mischief will recoil upon his own head; his violence will come down upon his own skull.*

David is so certain of this ultimate outcome that he already proclaims exultantly: *I will praise the LORD for His righteousness, and sing psalms to the name of the LORD Most High.*

טז בּ֣וֹר כָּ֭רָֽה וַֽיַּחְפְּרֵ֑הוּ
וַ֝יִּפֹּ֗ל בְּשַׁ֣חַת יִפְעָֽל׃

יז יָשׁ֣וּב עֲמָל֣וֹ בְרֹאשׁ֑וֹ
וְעַ֥ל קָ֝דְקֳד֗וֹ חֲמָס֥וֹ יֵרֵֽד׃

יח אוֹדֶ֣ה יְהוָ֣ה כְּצִדְק֑וֹ
וַ֝אֲזַמְּרָ֗ה שֵׁם־יְהוָ֥ה עֶלְיֽוֹן׃

He is already aware of what subsequent history teaches us about tyrants; namely, that they are their own worst enemies, and, blinded by their madness, eventually subvert their own schemes.

PSALM 8

1. For the Chief Musician; on the *gittit*.
A psalm of David.

2. LORD, our Sovereign,
how glorious is Your name in all the earth!
Your splendor is praised as high as the heavens!

3. Out of the mouths of infants and babes
You have given proof of Your power,
because of Your foes,
to silence the enemy and the avenger.

4. When I look up at Your heavens, the work of Your fingers,
at the moon and the stars that You set in place,

5. what is man that You should be mindful of him,
a mere human, that You should take notice of him?

6. Yet You made him little less than divine,
and crowned him with glory and honor.

Your splendor is praised as high as the heavens! Out of the mouths of infants and babes You have given proof of Your power... to silence the enemy. The enemy is us. It is our stubborn refusal to open our eyes to the wondrous sights around us that renders us His enemy.

We are told that our relationship with God must be a paradoxical one: we are to love Him, but we are also to stand in awe of Him.

We feel love for Him when we *look up to Your heavens, the work of Your fingers.*

Humbly, we stand in awe of Him when we contrast ourselves with Him, and wonder *what is man that You should be mindful of him, a mere human?*

We feel puny, insignificant. But we transcend those feelings when we realize that He has made us *little less than divine... master over all Your handiwork.*

He has given us dominion over all of His creation, even over *the birds of the heaven, the fish in the sea.*

But with that power, He challenges us with a great responsibility.

מזמור ח

What a wonderful world. I look up at the heavens on a cloudless night. I gaze at the moon and stars. Amazing! Here on earth, I observe the baby nursing at its mother's breast. Astounding! At moments like these I am in awe of God. I feel like a mere speck in His infinite universe.

א לַמְנַצֵּחַ עַל־הַגִּתִּית מִזְמוֹר לְדָוִד׃

ב יְהוָה אֲדֹנֵינוּ
מָה־אַדִּיר שִׁמְךָ בְּכָל־הָאָרֶץ
אֲשֶׁר־תְּנָה הוֹדְךָ עַל־הַשָּׁמָיִם׃

ג מִפִּי עוֹלְלִים ׀ וְיֹנְקִים יִסַּדְתָּ עֹז
לְמַעַן צוֹרְרֶיךָ
לְהַשְׁבִּית אוֹיֵב וּמִתְנַקֵּם׃

ד כִּי־אֶרְאֶה שָׁמֶיךָ מַעֲשֵׂה אֶצְבְּעֹתֶיךָ
יָרֵחַ וְכוֹכָבִים אֲשֶׁר כּוֹנָנְתָּה׃

ה מָה־אֱנוֹשׁ כִּי־תִזְכְּרֶנּוּ
וּבֶן־אָדָם כִּי תִפְקְדֶנּוּ׃

ו וַתְּחַסְּרֵהוּ מְּעַט מֵאֱלֹהִים
וְכָבוֹד וְהָדָר תְּעַטְּרֵהוּ׃

מזמור ח *Psalm 8:* We often ignore the grandeur of the world around us. We hardly notice nature's marvelous beauty. We have lost the capacity to wonder.

We have thus alienated ourselves from God the Creator, from Him who perpetually reveals Himself to us through His world.

When our blindness to nature's wonders is occasionally pierced by the sudden perception of an especially impressive phenomenon, we catch a glimpse of the Almighty in action. We then draw closer to Him.

When we persist in that blindness, we distance ourselves from Him, denying ourselves the possibility of a relationship with Him.

In a sense, we become His enemy, his foe.

7. You made him master over all Your handiwork,
and put everything under his feet:

8. sheep and oxen, all of them,
and also the wild beasts;

9. the birds of the heaven, the fish in the sea,
all that swim along the ocean paths.

10. Lord, our Sovereign,
how glorious is Your name in all the earth!

Moses responds:

What is written in Your Torah? Do not worship idols, be honest in your business affairs, honor your father and mother.

Are these angels tempted to worship idols? Do they have business dealings? Do they have a father and a mother? No! Not at all!

Clearly then, the Torah cannot be kept in the heavens. It is precisely on earth that the Torah belongs, and only mortals can be expected to adhere to its demands.

God accedes to Moses' persuasive argument. The Torah is delivered into the hand of humans.

The psalm ends by repeating that opening verse, but only its first half.

Note that the second half of the verse, containing the angels' plea that the Torah be safeguarded in the heavens, is not repeated.

Lord, our Sovereign, how glorious is Your name in all the earth. Period.

The Torah belongs here on earth, with the *mere humans* of whom God *takes notice* and of whom He *is mindful.*

ז תַּמְשִׁילֵהוּ בְּמַעֲשֵׂי יָדֶיךָ
כֹּל שַׁתָּה תַֽחַת־רַגְלָיו׃

ח צֹנֶה וַאֲלָפִים כֻּלָּם
וְגַם בַּהֲמוֹת שָׂדָי׃

ט צִפּוֹר שָׁמַיִם וּדְגֵי הַיָּם
עֹבֵר אָרְחוֹת יַמִּים׃

י יְהוָה אֲדֹנֵינוּ
מָה־אַדִּיר שִׁמְךָ בְּכָל־הָאָרֶץ׃

Are we equal to that challenge?

The Talmud (*Shabbat* 88b) tells us that God thought that we were indeed equipped to handle that challenge, and that is why He planned to give us His Torah.

But the angels objected to God's plan. They felt that the Torah, God's Law, was too sacred to be entrusted to mere mortals.

The Talmud puts the opening words of our psalm in the mouths of those angels:

"*Lord, our Sovereign, how glorious is Your name in all the earth! Your splendor,* meaning Your Torah, *is praised as high as the heavens!*"

Leave it in the heavens! Do not allow earthly mortals to sully it! God hears the angels' argument, and turns to Moses to refute them.

PSALM 9

1. For the Chief Musician; on *mut labben.*
A psalm of David.

2. I will praise You, LORD, with all my heart;
I will recount all Your wonderful deeds.

3. I will rejoice and exult in You,
I will sing praise to Your name, O Most High,

4. because my enemies turn back,
they stumble and perish before You.

5. For You uphold my right and my cause,
You sit on Your throne as a righteous judge.

6. You have rebuked the nations,
You have destroyed the wicked,

7. You have blotted out their name forever.
The enemy is finished,
in ruins forever.
You uprooted their cities;
all memory of them is gone.

8. But the LORD abides forever;
He has established His throne for judgment.

---

story. But if we reread it as it appears in I Samuel chapter 17 we soon note two elements of the story that will prove vital for us to understand this psalm.

For one thing, not only does a young inexperienced lad, armed with just a slingshot, slay a giant warrior clad in armor, but he achieves a national victory for his people. After David defeats the giant and beheads him, *the men of Israel and Judah rose up with a war cry and pursued the Philistines all the way to Gai.* More importantly, before he engages Goliath in combat, David debates him verbally, and casts the debate in theological terms. You come *against me with sword and spear and javelin; but I come against you in the name of the LORD of*

מזמור ט

I am just one person, an insignificant part of the crowd. I am a single isolated member of a large community. I praise God for the triumphs of my people. I celebrate the achievements of my community. But I ask God, "What about me? Where are my triumphs?" I feel neglected, lost in the larger picture. I am a failure, and the victories of my community do nothing for me. Yes, God helps the mighty and the many. But will He help poor little me?

א לַמְנַצֵּחַ עַל־מוּת לַבֵּן מִזְמוֹר לְדָוִד׃

ב אוֹדֶה יְהוָה בְּכָל־לִבִּי
אֲסַפְּרָה כָּל־נִפְלְאוֹתֶיךָ׃

ג אֶשְׂמְחָה וְאֶעֶלְצָה בָךְ
אֲזַמְּרָה שִׁמְךָ עֶלְיוֹן׃

ד בְּשׁוּב־אוֹיְבַי אָחוֹר
יִכָּשְׁלוּ וְיֹאבְדוּ מִפָּנֶיךָ׃

ה כִּי־עָשִׂיתָ מִשְׁפָּטִי וְדִינִי
יָשַׁבְתָּ לְכִסֵּא שׁוֹפֵט צֶדֶק׃

ו גָּעַרְתָּ גוֹיִם אִבַּדְתָּ רָשָׁע
שְׁמָם מָחִיתָ לְעוֹלָם וָעֶד׃

ז הָאוֹיֵב ׀ תַּמּוּ חֳרָבוֹת לָנֶצַח
וְעָרִים נָתַשְׁתָּ
אָבַד זִכְרָם הֵמָּה׃

ח וַיהוָה לְעוֹלָם יֵשֵׁב
כּוֹנֵן לַמִּשְׁפָּט כִּסְאוֹ׃

מזמור ט *Psalm 9:* It is apparent that in this psalm, David is celebrating a very special triumph over a particularly vicious enemy. Some commentators suggest that it is the victory over Goliath that he celebrates here.

Most of us are familiar with the basic plot of the David versus Goliath

9. He will judge the world with justice;
He will rule the people with fairness.

10. The LORD is a tower of strength for the oppressed,
a tower of strength in times of trouble.

11. Let those who acknowledge Your name put their trust in You,
for You, LORD, do not abandon those who seek You.

12. Sing praises to the LORD who dwells in Zion;
declare His deeds among the peoples.

13. For the avenger of blood remembers,
He does not ignore the cry of the afflicted.

14. Have pity on me, LORD;
see how I am afflicted by my foes.
Raise me from the gates of death,

15. so that I may tell all Your praise;
in the gates of the daughter of Zion,
I will exult in Your deliverance.

---

humble) back home cannot echo that exultation. His personal misfortunes are not at all alleviated by the nation's military victory.

What cause does he have to praise God with all his heart or to recount all of His wonderful deeds?

In empathy for this individual, David begins to shift his focus from the nation to the individual. *The LORD abides forever,* not just in moments of a great war. *He will rule the people with fairness,* all people.

He is *a tower of strength in times of trouble* to all who acknowledge His name, and He does not abandon anyone who seeks Him.

He *dwells in Zion* and not just on the battlefield, so that His praise can be sung *in the gates of the daughter of Zion,* and not only by its warriors.

David delivers this ultimate reassurance to the humble and destitute: *The needy will not always be forgotten; nor will the hope of the poor be lost forever.*

ט וְהוּא יִשְׁפֹּט־תֵּבֵל בְּצֶדֶק
יָדִין לְאֻמִּים בְּמֵישָׁרִים׃

י וִיהִי יהוה מִשְׂגָּב לַדָּךְ
מִשְׂגָּב לְעִתּוֹת בַּצָּרָה׃

יא וְיִבְטְחוּ בְךָ יוֹדְעֵי שְׁמֶךָ
כִּי לֹא־עָזַבְתָּ דֹרְשֶׁיךָ יהוה׃

יב זַמְּרוּ לַיהוה יֹשֵׁב צִיּוֹן
הַגִּידוּ בָעַמִּים עֲלִילוֹתָיו׃

יג כִּי־דֹרֵשׁ דָּמִים אוֹתָם זָכָר
לֹא־שָׁכַח צַעֲקַת עניים׃ עֲנָוִים

יד חָנְנֵנִי יהוה
רְאֵה עָנְיִי מִשֹּׂנְאָי
מְרוֹמְמִי מִשַּׁעֲרֵי־מָוֶת׃

טו לְמַעַן אֲסַפְּרָה כָּל־תְּהִלָּתֶיךָ
בְּשַׁעֲרֵי בַת־צִיּוֹן
אָגִילָה בִּישׁוּעָתֶךָ׃

Hosts… whom you have blasphemed. Both the national nature of the victory and the blasphemy of the enemy are important elements in our psalm.

Because the victory is for the entire nation, David can praise God with ***all** my heart* and can *recount **all** Your wonderful deeds.* He can conceive of God as sitting on His throne, symbolic of complete dominion. He can assert: *The enemy is finished, in ruins forever. You uprooted their cities; all memory of them is gone.*

But while David can exult in the nation's complete victory, the humble and destitute citizen (Radak notes with irony that the destitute person is typically

16. The nations are sunk in the pit they made,
their foot has been caught in the net they hid.

17. The LORD makes Himself known by the justice He does;
the wicked man is trapped by his own devices. *Higgayon. Selah*

18. The wicked shall go to Sheol,
all the nations who forget God.

19. But the needy will not always be forgotten,
nor the hope of the poor be lost forever.

20. Arise, LORD, let no man prevail;
let the nations be judged in Your presence.

21. Strike them with terror, LORD;
let the nations know that they are but men.

---

they think of themselves as divine, and thus dare to blaspheme the Almighty God: *let the nations know that they are but men.*

טז טָבְע֣וּ ג֭וֹיִם בְּשַׁ֣חַת עָשׂ֑וּ
בְּרֶֽשֶׁת־ז֥וּ טָ֝מָ֗נוּ נִלְכְּדָ֥ה רַגְלָֽם׃

יז נוֹדַ֤ע ׀ יְהוָה֮ מִשְׁפָּ֪ט עָ֫שָׂ֥ה
בְּפֹ֣עַל כַּ֭פָּיו נוֹקֵ֣שׁ רָשָׁ֑ע הִגָּי֥וֹן סֶֽלָה׃

יח יָשׁ֣וּבוּ רְשָׁעִ֣ים לִשְׁא֑וֹלָה
כָּל־גּ֝וֹיִ֗ם שְׁכֵחֵ֥י אֱלֹהִֽים׃

יט כִּ֤י לֹ֣א לָ֭נֶצַח יִשָּׁכַ֣ח אֶבְי֑וֹן
תִּקְוַ֥ת ע֝נוים תֹּאבַ֥ד לָעַֽד׃ עֲנִיִּ֗ים

כ ק֣וּמָה יְ֭הוָה אַל־יָעֹ֣ז אֱנ֑וֹשׁ
יִשָּׁפְט֥וּ ג֝וֹיִ֗ם עַל־פָּנֶֽיךָ׃

כא שִׁ֘יתָ֤ה יְהוָ֨ה ׀ מוֹרָ֗ה לָ֫הֶ֥ם
יֵדְע֥וּ ג֝וֹיִ֗ם אֱנ֣וֹשׁ הֵ֣מָּה סֶּֽלָה׃

Finally, David concludes this psalm with a prayer against future would-be Goliaths; men who like Goliath are so deluded by their military prowess that

PSALM 10

1. Why, LORD, do You stand far off, *Second day of the month*
hiding Yourself in times of trouble?

2. The wicked in their arrogance hunt down the poor;
may they themselves be caught in the schemes they devise!

3. The wicked man boasts of his heart's desires;
greedy for gain, he curses and reviles the LORD.

4. The wicked man in his pride does not seek God;
there is no room for God in all his schemes.

5. His ways prosper at all times;
Your judgments are above and beyond his grasp;
he snaps his fingers at all who oppose him.

6. He thinks in his heart: I shall not be shaken;
never shall I find myself in trouble.

7. His mouth is full of curses, deceit and violence;
mischief and evil are under his tongue.

Rashi effectively uses the language of the Midrash to describe the inevitable reaction to such a foe: "There is no justice. There is no Judge."

Once again the psalmist is describing a human enemy. After all, David had many and varied enemies: opponents of Israel, rivals for his throne, a jealous father-in-law, formerly trusted friends, a rebellious son.

The Jewish people too have faced many and varied enemies throughout their history. Indeed, it is a challenge to identify a period in our history when we did not face a murderous foe.

Hence, this psalm, and others like it, have become eternally relevant.

But surely we also face other problems. What about poverty, disease, and natural disasters? How can the person who confronts such circumstances use the words of this psalm in his or her prayers?

One can do so by using the human foe of this psalm as a metaphor for the particular difficulty with which one is struggling.

מזמור י

I feel alienated, frustrated, abandoned by God. My enemy comes at me out of nowhere. He is arrogant, deceitful, and vicious. Worse, he does not seem to be accountable to God. Is there no justice?

א לָמָה יְהוָה תַּעֲמֹד בְּרָחוֹק ב לחודש
תַּעְלִים לְעִתּוֹת בַּצָּרָה׃

ב בְּגַאֲוַת רָשָׁע יִדְלַק עָנִי
יִתָּפְשׂוּ ׀ בִּמְזִמּוֹת זוּ חָשָׁבוּ׃

ג כִּי־הִלֵּל רָשָׁע עַל־תַּאֲוַת נַפְשׁוֹ
וּבֹצֵעַ בֵּרֵךְ נִאֵץ ׀ יְהוָה׃

ד רָשָׁע כְּגֹבַהּ אַפּוֹ בַּל־יִדְרֹשׁ
אֵין אֱלֹהִים כָּל־מְזִמּוֹתָיו׃

ה יָחִילוּ דְרָכָו ׀ בְּכָל־עֵת
מָרוֹם מִשְׁפָּטֶיךָ מִנֶּגְדּוֹ
כָּל־צוֹרְרָיו יָפִיחַ בָּהֶם׃

ו אָמַר בְּלִבּוֹ בַּל־אֶמּוֹט
לְדֹר וָדֹר אֲשֶׁר לֹא־בְרָע׃

ז אָלָה ׀ פִּיהוּ מָלֵא וּמִרְמוֹת וָתֹךְ
תַּחַת לְשׁוֹנוֹ עָמָל וָאָוֶן׃

מזמור י *Psalm 10:* The enemy in this psalm is treacherous in many ways.

He attacks unexpectedly, by surprise, so that the victim is not prepared to defend himself. *He lurks in hiding like a lion in its lair.*

He always achieves his objectives. He seems to never lose. *His ways prosper at all times.* He is supremely self-confident, even arrogant. *He thinks in his heart: I shall not be shaken.* He is blithely unconcerned with God, and certainly is not afraid of divine justice. *He says to himself, "God has forgotten, He has hidden His face, He never looks."*

8. He waits in ambush in the villages,
he murders the innocent by stealth;
his eyes are on the lookout for the hapless victims.

9. He lurks in hiding like a lion in its lair,
he lies in wait to seize the poor;
he seizes him and drags him away in his net.

10. He crouches, he stoops,
and the hapless fall into his strong grip.

11. He says to himself, "God has forgotten,
He has hidden His face, He never looks."

12. Arise, LORD; lift up Your hand for action, O God;
do not forget the lowly.

13. Why should the wicked man revile You, God,
and think in his heart that You will not call to account?

14. But You see it all;
You note mischief and grief;
You will take the matter in hand.
The hapless victim commits himself to You;
You have always been the helper of the fatherless.

Do not patients report that their illness appears to defy God's benevolence, and acts with impunity, as if immune from God's justice?

Does not Rashi's phrase, "There is no justice. There is no Judge," aptly describe the feelings of so many suffering patients, who silently protest God's "unfairness"?

People struggling with circumstances very different from the battlefield can easily resort to the words of this psalm to express their inner emotions, using the human enemy as a symbol for whatever other enemy they are facing.

Furthermore, they can use this psalm to give voice to feelings of alienation from God, something which many people of faith find so difficult to do. *Why, LORD, do you stand far off, hiding Yourself in times of trouble?*

They can then proceed, as does the psalmist, to appeal to God to emerge from His distant abode, from His place of hiding. *Arise, LORD; lift up Your*

ח יֵשֵׁב ׀ בְּמַאְרַב חֲצֵרִים
בַּמִּסְתָּרִים יַהֲרֹג נָקִי
עֵינָיו לְחֵלְכָה יִצְפֹּנוּ׃

ט יֶאֱרֹב בַּמִּסְתָּר ׀ כְּאַרְיֵה בְסֻכֹּה
יֶאֱרֹב לַחֲטוֹף עָנִי
יַחְטֹף עָנִי בְּמָשְׁכוֹ בְרִשְׁתּוֹ׃

י ודכה יָשֹׁחַ יִדְכֶּה
וְנָפַל בַּעֲצוּמָיו חלכאים׃ חֵל כָּאִים

יא אָמַר בְּלִבּוֹ
שָׁכַח אֵל
הִסְתִּיר פָּנָיו בַּל־רָאָה לָנֶצַח׃

יב קוּמָה יהוה
אֵל נְשָׂא יָדֶךָ
אַל־תִּשְׁכַּח עניים׃ עֲנָוִים

יג עַל־מֶה ׀ נִאֵץ רָשָׁע ׀ אֱלֹהִים
אָמַר בְּלִבּוֹ לֹא תִדְרֹשׁ׃

יד רָאִתָה
כִּי־אַתָּה ׀ עָמָל וָכַעַס ׀ תַּבִּיט
לָתֵת בְּיָדֶךָ
עָלֶיךָ יַעֲזֹב חֵלֶכָה
יָתוֹם אַתָּה ׀ הָיִיתָ עוֹזֵר׃

Take disease for example. Do not many diseases seem to come "out of nowhere," unexpectedly, like a lion lurking in its lair?

Does a sick person not sometimes imagine his illness like an arrogant, absolutely self-confident enemy that never loses a battle?

15. Break the power of the wicked and evil man;
search out his wickedness until You find no more.

16. The LORD is King forever and ever;
the nations will perish from His land.

17. You hear, LORD, the yearning of the humble;
strengthen their hearts, and pay heed to them;

18. do justice to the fatherless and the downtrodden,
so that mortal man may never again inspire terror.

---

evil man is based upon the assumption that when evil succeeds, even more evil is perpetuated. This is because others draw the conclusion that evil "pays," that it can be performed with impunity.

But if God breaks the power of evil, others will no longer draw that conclusion. Instead, they will learn that evil "does not pay." As a result, God will *search out wickedness* and *find no more.*

A world in which justice is meted out effectively is a world without evil.
A world in which disease is healed is a world of greater spiritual faith.

טו שְׁבֹר זְרוֹעַ רָשָׁע
וָרָע תִּדְרוֹשׁ־רִשְׁעוֹ בַל־תִּמְצָא׃

טז יְהוָה מֶלֶךְ עוֹלָם וָעֶד
אָבְדוּ גוֹיִם מֵאַרְצוֹ׃

יז תַּאֲוַת עֲנָוִים שָׁמַעְתָּ יְהוָה
תָּכִין לִבָּם תַּקְשִׁיב אָזְנֶךָ׃

יח לִשְׁפֹּט יָתוֹם וָדָךְ
בַּל־יוֹסִיף עוֹד לַעֲרֹץ אֱנוֹשׁ מִן־הָאָרֶץ׃

---

hand for action.... Why should the wicked man... think in his heart that You will not call him to account?

Finally, they can console themselves with the assurance that *You hear, Lord, the yearning of the humble; strengthen their hearts, and pay heed to them.* There is a most noteworthy interpretation given by Rashi to verse 15, which is an argument that victims of enemies, human or otherwise, can use as they prayerfully attempt to persuade God to eradicate the wicked or the wickedness.

Rashi asserts that the request that God *break the power of the wicked and*

PSALM 11

1. For the Chief Musician. Of David.
In the LORD I take refuge.
How then can you say to me:
"Flee like a bird to your mountain.

2. For look, the wicked are bending the bow,
they are fitting their arrows to the string,
to shoot from the darkness at the upright."

3. When the foundations are undermined,
what can the righteous man do?

4. The LORD is in His Holy Temple,
the LORD has His throne in heaven.
Yet His eyes look down [on the world],
His gaze* examines the sons of man.

* Lit. "his eyelids."

---

asserts that it is his, and evokes our protest: "How can you tell us to leave *your* mountain?!"

The third translation is that of Rabbi Yechiel Hillel of Yabrov, whose succinct commentary *Metzudat David* renders the complaint thus: "How dare you tell me that the refuge I thought to be as secure as a mountain is in reality no more than a bird in flight?"

Rabbi Samson Raphael Hirsch essentially follows *Metzudat David*, but puts it this way: "How can you say to me, 'Flee! Your mountain is but a bird!,' as if to say that I must abandon my sense of security and trust, because that which I and my like-minded brothers rely upon as a firm mountain, is no more than a feeble bird?"

All three approaches make good sense to us. We sometimes feel pursued, but at least have a destination somewhere that promises to provide us with safety. We thus expend our energies, struggling to reach that destination.

But sometimes we lack even the prospect of such a destination, and instead

מזמור יא

I once felt secure. But now I feel like a little bird, driven from place to place, never allowed to rest. My problems are vicious, unrelenting. The earth is shaking; its firm foundations withdraw from underneath me. God promised me His protection. I cling desperately to His assurance.

א לַמְנַצֵּחַ לְדָוִד
בַּיהוה ׀ חָסִיתִי
אֵיךְ תֹּאמְרוּ לְנַפְשִׁי
נודו הַרְכֶם צִפּוֹר׃
נוּדִי

ב כִּי הִנֵּה הָרְשָׁעִים יִדְרְכוּן קֶשֶׁת
כּוֹנְנוּ חִצָּם עַל־יֶתֶר
לִירוֹת בְּמוֹ־אֹפֶל לְיִשְׁרֵי־לֵב׃

ג כִּי הַשָּׁתוֹת יֵהָרֵסוּן
צַדִּיק מַה־פָּעָל׃

ד יהוה ׀ בְּהֵיכַל קָדְשׁוֹ
יהוה בַּשָּׁמַיִם כִּסְאוֹ
עֵינָיו יֶחֱזוּ
עַפְעַפָּיו יִבְחֲנוּ בְּנֵי אָדָם׃

מזמור יא *Psalm 11:* Commentators have translated the first verse of our psalm in three different ways, each powerful and each troubling:

How then can you say to me: "Flee like a bird to your mountain?"

How then can you tell me to flee like a bird from your mountain?

How dare you tell me that I must flee, because my mountain is but a bird?

The first translation, Rabbi Cashdan's, follows Rashi. The enemy expels us from our rightful place, and demands that we fly like a bird to some distant mountain.

The second translation is Radak's. The enemy expels us from the mountain,

5. The LORD examines the righteous;
but despises the wicked and the lover of violence.

6. He will rain down upon the wicked
flaming coals and brimstone;
a scorching wind will be their allotted portion.

7. For the LORD is righteous;
He loves righteous deeds;
the upright shall see His face.

To cope with such overwhelming feelings, we take consolation in our belief that *the LORD is in His Holy Temple,* that *His gaze examines the sons of man,* and that He will decisively eliminate our woes so that *a scorching wind will be their allotted portion.*

We commit ourselves to remain upright and to perform righteous deeds, for we fervently believe that He who *loves righteous deeds* will allow that *the upright shall see His face.*

ה יְהוָה֮ צַדִּ֪יק יִ֫בְחָ֥ן
וְ֭רָשָׁע וְאֹהֵ֣ב חָמָ֑ס שָֽׂנְאָ֥ה נַפְשֽׁוֹ׃

ו יַמְטֵ֥ר עַל־רְשָׁעִ֗ים פַּ֫חִ֥ים
אֵ֣שׁ וְ֭גָפְרִית וְר֥וּחַ זִלְעָפ֗וֹת מְנָ֣ת כּוֹסָֽם׃

ז כִּֽי־צַדִּ֣יק יְ֭הוָה צְדָק֣וֹת אָהֵ֑ב
יָ֝שָׁ֗ר יֶחֱז֥וּ פָנֵֽימוֹ׃

---

feel desperate. We have been uprooted and displaced. We are homeless. We have no place to go.

Worst of all is the situation portrayed by the third translation. Our hopes have been dashed. We had an illusion of security and safety. We thought we had the protection of an invincible mountain. That illusion has vanished, and we are now as vulnerable as a little bird. We feel betrayed, and wonder whether one can ever recover from disillusionment.

PSALM 12

1. For the Chief Musician; on the *sheminit*. A psalm of David.

2. Help, LORD, for the devout are no more;
the faithful have vanished from among men.

3. Men speak lies to one another,
they talk with flattering lips and double minds.

4. May the LORD cut off all flattering lips,
every boastful tongue!

5. They say, "With our tongue we shall prevail,
our lips are our own; who is LORD over us?"

6. "Because of the oppression of the poor
and the groans of the needy,
I will now arise," says the LORD;
"I will give help," He assures him.

---

century, wondered what the Angel of Truth has been doing ever since his ignominious fate. He conjectured that the Angel of Truth has been wandering the earth all these millennia, taking the form of each generation's rare truthful man.

This psalm opens by declaring that even that rare truthful man is now nowhere to be found. *The faithful have vanished from among men.* Now we live in a world in which all *men speak lies to one another* and *talk with flattering lips and double minds*

The world suffers because of all this dishonesty. *The groans of the needy* are so vociferous that the LORD Himself cannot but hear them and so promises, *"I will now arise… I will give help."*

God's help takes the form of His own words, the word of His teachings, of His Torah. Those words are pure truth, *like silver… purified seven times over.*

Those who are exposed to God's truth are at risk, however. The attractions of falsehood are many and mighty. Special protection is necessary to assure that those who are taught truth remain faithful to its teachings.

מזמור יב

It is a world of lies. Deceit and hypocrisy prevail. Falseness is used as a weapon to manipulate the naïve and the gullible. I would love to encounter pure truth. But would I recognize pure truth even if I saw it?

א לַמְנַצֵּחַ עַל־הַשְּׁמִינִית מִזְמוֹר לְדָוִד׃

ב הוֹשִׁיעָה יְהוָה כִּי־גָמַר חָסִיד
כִּי־פַסּוּ אֱמוּנִים מִבְּנֵי אָדָם׃

ג שָׁוְא ׀ יְדַבְּרוּ אִישׁ אֶת־רֵעֵהוּ
שְׂפַת חֲלָקוֹת בְּלֵב וָלֵב יְדַבֵּרוּ׃

ד יַכְרֵת יְהוָה כָּל־שִׂפְתֵי חֲלָקוֹת
לָשׁוֹן מְדַבֶּרֶת גְּדֹלוֹת׃

ה אֲשֶׁר אָמְרוּ ׀ לִלְשֹׁנֵנוּ נַגְבִּיר שְׂפָתֵינוּ אִתָּנוּ
מִי אָדוֹן לָנוּ׃

ו מִשֹּׁד עֲנִיִּים מֵאַנְקַת אֶבְיוֹנִים
עַתָּה אָקוּם יֹאמַר יְהוָה
אָשִׁית בְּיֵשַׁע יָפִיחַ לוֹ׃

מזמור יב *Psalm 12:* There is a midrash which records the debate which occurred among the angels when God consulted them about whether or not to create man. The Angel of Justice said, "Create him, for he can be just." To which the Angel of Truth countered, "Don't create him, because he is full of lies."

God then turned to the Angel of Compassion who argued that man was capable of mercy, and so deserved to be created. But the Angel of Peace protested: "He is full of petty squabbles, incapable of peace. Do not create him."

God resolved the stalemate. He hurled the Angel of Truth to the ground, eliminating him from the dispute. With the vote now two to one in favor of creating man, man was created.

Rabbi Mendel of Kotzk, that incisive hasidic leader of the late eighteenth

7. The words of the Lord are pure words,
like silver refined in an earthen crucible,
purified seven times over.

8. You, Lord, will guard them.
You will protect each one from such people forever.

9. On every side the wicked strut freely
when vileness is rated high among men.

The Talmud has its own translation of this otherwise obscure verse. It suggests that the phrase refers to those things which "stand at the highest possible sphere, and are yet treated disgracefully by the sons of man." The Talmud goes on to specify that it is prayer that "stands at the highest sphere" (*Berakhot* 4b).

Prayer is the pinnacle of human spiritual experience; yet it is often disgraced and treated with vileness. Since this verse occurs at the end of our psalm, whose very theme is falseness and the need for truth, we can easily extrapolate a vital lesson: Truth is a prerequisite for prayer. The person who is insincere in his prayers defiles those prayers. Truth is a necessity in man's relationship with his fellow man. It is all the more necessary in his relationship with his God.

ז אִמֲר֣וֹת יְהֹוָה֮ אֲמָר֪וֹת טְהֹ֫ר֥וֹת
כֶּ֣סֶף צָ֭רוּף בַּעֲלִ֣יל לָאָ֑רֶץ מְ֝זֻקָּ֗ק שִׁבְעָתָֽיִם׃

ח אַתָּֽה־יְהֹוָ֥ה תִּשְׁמְרֵ֑ם
תִּצְּרֶ֓נּוּ ׀ מִן־הַדּ֖וֹר ז֣וּ לְעוֹלָֽם׃

ט סָבִ֗יב רְשָׁעִ֥ים יִתְהַלָּכ֑וּן
כְּרֻ֥ם ז֝֗לֻּת לִבְנֵ֥י אָדָֽם׃

Rashi quotes a midrash which tells the story of the schoolchildren in the time of King David, who were so thoroughly indoctrinated in the Torah that they could expound its truths *seven times over;* that is, seven times seven, or forty-nine different ways.

Yet, David felt compelled to pray to God that He protect even such perfectly educated youth from the world's corrupt influences. *You, Lord, will guard them. You will protect each one from such people forever.*

The very last words of this psalm are exceedingly difficult to translate, so that we find ourselves with a confusing abundance of translations. This is Rabbi Cashdan's version: *when vileness is rated high among men.*

PSALM 13

1. For the Chief Musician.
A psalm of David.

2. How long, Lord? Will You forget me forever?
How long will You hide Your face from me?

3. How long must I bear anxieties in my mind,
grief in my heart day after day?
How long shall my enemy exalt himself over me?

4. Look now, and answer me, Lord my God!
Give light to my eyes,
lest I sleep the sleep of death;

5. lest my enemy say: "I have overcome him";
lest my foes rejoice when I fall.

Whereas Rabbi Cashdan translates the first half of verse 3 as *How long must I bear anxieties in my mind… ?*, the Hebrew lends itself to alternative translations, such as *How long will I think thoughts in my soul?* or *How long shall I seek counsel in my soul?*

Such translations suggest that the sufferer is undergoing a thorough course of introspection. He seeks to determine God's role in his plight. He also strives to identify the spiritual options which are available to him, to help him grow as he copes with the agony of suffering and wrestles with its mysteries.

The suffering believer discovers two kinds of options.

First of all, he does not dare to request of God that He, God, remember him, or even that He unveil His hidden face. Rather, he asks God for but one glance, one ray of light. *Look now…. Give light to my eyes.* Secondly, he discovers the array of inner inspirational sources that are available to him. He succinctly lists them in the last verse of this psalm.

It is befitting that this verse was selected by those who compiled the synagogue prayer book, the Siddur, to culminate the *Hodu* prayer, with which the *Pesukei DeZimra* (verses of song) daily liturgical service is introduced.

מזמור יג

Why am I suffering? How long will I suffer? Will it get worse? It can't possibly get worse! It is hard to believe in God when there is no hope.

א לַמְנַצֵּ֗חַ מִזְמ֥וֹר לְדָוִֽד׃

ב עַד־אָ֣נָה יְ֭הוָה תִּשְׁכָּחֵ֣נִי נֶ֑צַח
עַד־אָ֓נָה ׀ תַּסְתִּ֖יר אֶת־פָּנֶ֣יךָ מִמֶּֽנִּי׃

ג עַד־אָ֨נָה אָשִׁ֪ית עֵצ֡וֹת בְּנַפְשִׁ֗י
יָג֣וֹן בִּלְבָבִ֣י יוֹמָ֑ם
עַד־אָ֓נָה ׀ יָר֖וּם אֹיְבִ֣י עָלָֽי׃

ד הַבִּ֣יטָֽה עֲ֭נֵנִי יְהוָ֣ה אֱלֹהָ֑י
הָאִ֥ירָה עֵ֝ינַ֗י פֶּן־אִישַׁ֥ן הַמָּֽוֶת׃

ה פֶּן־יֹאמַ֣ר אֹיְבִ֣י יְכָלְתִּ֑יו
צָרַ֥י יָ֝גִ֗ילוּ כִּ֣י אֶמּֽוֹט׃

מזמור יג *Psalm 13:* There are two dimensions to the suffering of a believer. There is the pain itself – the wound, the loss, the fear. But then there is also the felt absence of God – the sense of abandonment, of having been forgotten by Him.

This second dimension has come to be termed *hester panim,* the hidden face of God. *How long will You hide Your face from me?*

Rav Hirsch points out that the phrase *How long?,* which appears four times over in the opening verses of our psalm, can also be translated *How far?* That is, where is all this suffering heading? What is its objective? Will it get worse? Or, more important, for what purpose am I suffering?

These questions are part of the inner dialogue which the true believer carries on within himself all the while he is suffering. He strives to discern what God expects of him, why He inflicted this pain upon him. He assumes that his suffering has some meaning, but he is frustrated by his inability to ascertain that meaning.

6. But I trust in Your loving-kindness,
my heart rejoices in Your deliverance.
I will sing to the LORD
for He has been good to me.

This brief psalm, with only six verses, so successfully depicts the internal struggle of the man of faith as he confronts his suffering.

ו וַאֲנִ֤י ׀ בְּחַסְדְּךָ֣ בָטַחְתִּי֮
יָ֤גֵ֥ל לִבִּ֗י בִּֽישׁ֫וּעָתֶ֥ךָ
אָשִׁ֥ירָה לַֽיהוָ֑ה כִּ֖י גָמַ֣ל עָלָֽי׃

These are the resources that he identifies within his soul:

Trust, *But I trust in your loving-kindness.* Joy, *my heart rejoices in your deliverance.* Song, *I will sing to the* Lord. Gratitude, *for He has been good to me.*

PSALM 14

1. For the Chief Musician. Of David.
The senseless man says in his heart,
"There is no God."
All are corrupt, they do abominable acts;
there is no one who does good.

2. The LORD looks down from heaven on mankind
to see if there are any who act wisely,
any who seek God.

3. But they all have gone astray,
they are all equally rotten;
there is no one who does good,
not even one.

4. Will all these evildoers never learn,
who devour My people as men eat bread,
and never call upon the LORD?

Rabbi Meir Leibush (Malbim) elucidates the close resemblance between our psalm and Psalm 53 differently.

He asserts that our psalm was written by King David in reaction to the enemies he faced. Hence, our psalm opens: *For the Chief Musician. Of David.*

But Psalm 53 begins: *For the Chief Musician; on* maḥalat. *A maskil of David.* That psalm was not written by King David, but at a much later time by others who were impressed by the close resemblance of their circumstances to those of David. See our comments on that psalm, Psalm 53.

David judges his enemies to be irredeemably evil, all bad. They are not only corrupt ethically; they are theologically brazen. They *say in their heart, "There is no God."*

We acknowledge that the rare good man occasionally exists even in a thoroughly corrupt society. However, this was not the case with David's foes. Among them, even those who seemed to be good men on the surface were found wanting when subjected to divine scrutiny. Thus, when *The LORD looks*

מזמור יד

Our entire society is corrupt. There is not a single good person out there. Spirituality? Forget about it! Everyone derides and mocks whatever smacks of religion. This must change. It can't go on this way.

א לַמְנַצֵּ֗חַ לְדָ֫וִ֥ד
אָ֘מַ֤ר נָבָ֣ל בְּ֭לִבּוֹ אֵ֣ין אֱלֹהִ֑ים
הִֽשְׁחִ֗יתוּ הִֽתְעִ֥יבוּ עֲלִ֥ילָה
אֵ֣ין עֹֽשֵׂה־טֽוֹב׃

ב יְהוָ֗ה מִשָּׁמַ֡יִם הִשְׁקִ֬יף עַֽל־בְּנֵֽי־אָ֫דָ֥ם
לִ֭רְאוֹת הֲיֵ֣שׁ מַשְׂכִּ֑יל
דֹּ֝רֵ֗שׁ אֶת־אֱלֹהִֽים׃

ג הַכֹּ֥ל סָר֮ יַחְדָּ֪ו נֶ֫אֱלָ֥חוּ
אֵ֣ין עֹֽשֵׂה־ט֑וֹב
אֵ֝֗ין גַּם־אֶחָֽד׃

ד הֲלֹ֥א יָדְעוּ֮ כָּל־פֹּ֪עֲלֵ֫י אָ֥וֶן
אֹכְלֵ֣י עַ֭מִּי אָ֣כְלוּ לֶ֑חֶם
יְ֝הוָ֗ה לֹ֣א קָרָֽאוּ׃

מזמור יד *Psalm 14:* This psalm may very well be the most pessimistic of them all. It flatly states: *There is no one who does good, not even one.*

Moreover, a later psalm, Psalm 53, pronounces a startlingly similar judgment upon another society in almost identical words.

Rashi addresses the issue of this repetition. He assigns our psalm to an earlier historical era, that of the Babylonian King Nebuchadnezzar, who destroyed the First Temple. Of him and his cohorts it could surely be said: *All are corrupt… all equally rotten; there is no one who does good, not even one.*

Psalm 53, suggests Rashi, belongs to a later era. It uses the very same language to condemn the Roman tyrant Titus, whose legions destroyed the Second Temple.

5. There they are, in terror and in dread;
for God is with the righteous generation.

6. You would confound the plans of the poor,
but the LORD is his refuge.

7. O that the deliverance of Israel might come from Zion!
When the LORD restores the fortunes of His people,
Jacob will rejoice; Israel will be glad.

---

links this term with *kol,* which means "sound" or "voice." Hence, *gil* refers to a loud expression of joy, a boisterous but short-lived emotion.

The Hebrew for "being glad," on the other hand, is *yismaḥ,* whose root is *s-m-ḥ,* related to *tz-m-ḥ,* which means "to blossom," suggesting a quiescent process of well-rooted growth. This emotion is barely expressed but it is felt deeply, and is long-lasting.

Rav Hirsch notes that *gil* precedes *simḥa* in our verse, indicating that the spontaneous joyous outburst is a transient emotion which is best eventually transformed into a more reflective, and more permanent, emotion.

He further notes that this sequence, *gil* first and then *simḥa,* is typical throughout Psalms. Thus, Psalm 31, verse 8, reads: *I will exult ("agila") and rejoice ("ve'esmeḥa") in Your constant loving-kindness.* First, active demonstrative exultation, and only later the inner joy, which is much more secure.

This is a lesson to remember as we advance in our own study of Psalms and its language.

ה שָׁ֤ם ׀ פָּ֣חֲדוּ פָ֑חַד
כִּֽי־אֱ֝לֹהִ֗ים בְּד֣וֹר צַדִּֽיק׃

ו עֲצַת־עָנִ֥י תָבִ֑ישׁוּ
כִּ֖י יְהוָ֣ה מַחְסֵֽהוּ׃

ז מִ֥י יִתֵּ֣ן מִצִּיּוֹן֮ יְשׁ֢וּעַ֫ת יִשְׂרָ֥אֵל
בְּשׁ֣וּב יְ֭הוָה שְׁב֣וּת עַמּ֑וֹ
יָגֵ֥ל יַ֝עֲקֹ֗ב יִשְׂמַ֥ח יִשְׂרָאֵֽל׃

---

down from heaven on mankind He discovers that *they have all gone astray… there is no one who does good, not even one.*

"God knows the hidden recesses of the heart," writes Malbim. "He detects the abominable behaviors that outwardly good men perform in secret."

* * *

Our final verse reads: *Jacob will rejoice; Israel will be glad.*

Is there any difference between "rejoicing" and "being glad"?

Nineteenth-century commentators such as Malbim and Rav Hirsch pay particularly close attention to such subtle differences.

Hirsch's analysis of our verse is a rewarding example of this interpretative technique.

The Hebrew original for "rejoice" is *yagel,* whose root is *gil.* Rav Hirsch

PSALM 15

1. A psalm of David.
LORD, who may dwell in Your tent?
Who may live on Your holy mountain?

2. One whose life is blameless,
who does what is right,
and speaks the truth from his heart;

3. who does not slander with his tongue,
who never wrongs his fellow,
and casts no slur on his neighbor;

4. who has nothing but contempt for a vile man,
but honors those who fear the LORD;
who holds to his oath even to his own hurt;

He whose scruples in matters of religious piety are matched by his scruples in his dealings with people is to be emulated.

Such a person is not ridden by internal conflict. His thoughts, his words, and his actions are in harmony with each other. *He speaks the truth from his heart, does not slander with his tongue,* and *never wrongs his fellow.*

No hypocrite he. He says what he thinks, and does what he says.

Despite his significant moral achievements, he does not consider himself superior to anyone else. He is free of sanctimony, and he appreciates the spiritual accomplishments of others. He *honors those who fear the LORD.*

Furthermore, in verse 5 we read that he *does not lend money at interest.* Radak asks, "Was it not already stated in verse 3 that he *never wrongs his fellow*?" Is it not repetitive to assert that he does not charge interest when we have already been told that he never wrongs his fellow?

To which Radak answers that frequently the borrower needs the money so badly that he is perfectly willing to pay interest. The borrower does not at all feel wronged by paying interest in order to get the money he needs. But even then, the hero of our psalm will not charge interest, because it is intrinsically wrong to do so.

Our good man is so upright that he will not violate ethical proscriptions

מזמור טו

He gets no attention. He receives no public acclaim, and shuns worldly recognition. Nobody notices this decent but quiet fellow who lives down the street. But he's my idea of a holy man.

א מִזְמ֗וֹר לְדָ֫וִ֥ד
יְֽהוָ֗ה מִי־יָג֥וּר בְּאָהֳלֶ֑ךָ
מִֽי־יִ֝שְׁכֹּ֗ן בְּהַ֣ר קָדְשֶֽׁךָ׃

ב הוֹלֵ֣ךְ תָּ֭מִים וּפֹעֵ֣ל צֶ֑דֶק
וְדֹבֵ֥ר אֱ֝מֶ֗ת בִּלְבָבֽוֹ׃

ג לֹֽא־רָגַ֨ל ׀ עַל־לְשֹׁנ֗וֹ
לֹא־עָשָׂ֣ה לְרֵעֵ֣הוּ רָעָ֑ה
וְ֝חֶרְפָּ֗ה לֹא־נָשָׂ֥א עַל־קְרֹבֽוֹ׃

ד נִבְזֶ֤ה ׀ בְּֽעֵינָ֘יו נִמְאָ֗ס
וְאֶת־יִרְאֵ֣י יְהוָ֣ה יְכַבֵּ֑ד
נִשְׁבַּ֥ע לְ֝הָרַ֗ע וְלֹ֣א יָמִֽר׃

מזמור טו *Psalm 15:* Our psalm speaks of no enemy, and utters no prayer. It is straightforward and descriptive. It defines the good man, unambiguously, succinctly, and inspiringly. Five verses express the lessons that philosophers throughout the ages have attempted to teach in countless volumes, with much less success.

Who deserves to *dwell in Your tent? Who may live on Your holy mountain?* Whom are we to revere and respect?

Not necessarily those who are honored in the public square, who make the headlines, receive the awards and garner the glory! God's *tent* and our high regard are reserved for the person who meets the standards of the "checklist" outlined in our psalm.

He *whose life is blameless* morally, and who *does what is right* ethically, is to be admired.

5. who does not lend his money at interest,
and accepts no bribe against the innocent.
The man who does this will never be shaken.

It is only such an upstanding fellow who can dwell in God's tent and live on His holy mountain. Only he can be assured that his residence in such sacred precincts *will never be shaken.*

ה כַּסְפּ֤וֹ ׀ לֹא־נָתַ֬ן בְּנֶ֗שֶׁךְ
וְשֹׁ֥חַד עַל־נָקִ֗י לֹ֥א לָ֫קָ֥ח
עֹֽשֵׂה־אֵ֑לֶּה לֹ֖א יִמּ֣וֹט לְעוֹלָֽם׃

---

even when doing so might arguably result in some greater good. He does not wish to be tempted by exceptions to the rule. For him a rule is a rule, to be applied in all situations, without regard for potentially misleading distinctions between one situation and another.

PSALM 16

1. A *mikhtam* of David.
Guard me, God, for I seek refuge in You.

2. I say to the LORD, "You are my Master."
You are not bound to promote my welfare;

3. but [You do so] on account of the holy ones
who were in the land,
and the noble men, in whom was all my delight.

4. Many shall be the sorrows of those who woo another god.
Never will I offer libations of blood to such gods;
never will I take their names upon my lips.

5. The LORD alone is my portion, my share, my cup of destiny;
You hold my lot secure.

6. A measured portion has fallen for me in delightful places;
excellent indeed is my heritage.

Rabbi Moses Isserles, known by the initials of his name as Rema, selects this phrase to open his notations to the *Shulḥan Arukh*, the Code of Jewish Law.

For him the key word is *always*. "The person who contemplates well that the Holy One blessed be He is always present, that He stands above us and observes our every deed, cannot help but be overwhelmed by awe, humility, dread and shame, for He is *always* present."

It is by striving to experience God at every moment and in every circumstance that one can achieve the idyllic relationship with God that is depicted in our psalm.

Rav Hirsch finds a very similar lesson in the same phrase, but not in the same word. Rather than focus upon *always*, Rav Hirsch would have us consider the Hebrew words with which our verse begins: *Shiviti Hashem*.

The standard translation of these two words is *I set the LORD*, as Rabbi Cashdan has it. But Rav Hirsch creatively introduces an alternate translation. Noting that the Hebrew root for *shiviti* is *sh-v-h*, which means "equal," he

מזמור טז

I am on a spiritual "high." I feel God close to me. I glimpse the possibility of getting even closer to Him. There are so many blessings in my life. I appreciate them. But I want more.

א מִכְתָּ֥ם לְדָוִ֑ד
שָֽׁמְרֵ֥נִי אֵ֝֗ל כִּֽי־חָסִ֥יתִי בָֽךְ׃

ב אָמַ֣רְתְּ לַ֭יהוה
אֲדֹנָ֣י אָ֑תָּה
ט֝וֹבָתִ֗י בַּל־עָלֶֽיךָ׃

ג לִ֭קְדוֹשִׁים אֲשֶׁר־בָּאָ֣רֶץ הֵ֑מָּה
וְ֝אַדִּירֵ֗י כָּל־חֶפְצִי־בָֽם׃

ד יִרְבּ֥וּ עַצְּבוֹתָם֮
אַחֵ֪ר מָ֫הָ֥רוּ
בַּל־אַסִּ֣יךְ נִסְכֵּיהֶ֣ם מִדָּ֑ם
וּבַל־אֶשָּׂ֥א אֶת־שְׁ֝מוֹתָ֗ם עַל־שְׂפָתָֽי׃

ה יהוה מְנָת־חֶלְקִ֥י וְכוֹסִ֑י
אַ֝תָּ֗ה תּוֹמִ֥יךְ גּוֹרָלִֽי׃

ו חֲבָלִ֣ים נָֽפְלוּ־לִ֭י בַּנְּעִמִ֑ים
אַף־נַ֝חֲלָ֗ת שָֽׁפְרָ֥ה עָלָֽי׃

מזמור טז *Psalm 16:* Struggle and conflict are absent from this psalm. Instead, its themes are gratitude, confidence, and hope.

You are not bound to promote my welfare, but You do. *You hold my lot secure… excellent indeed is my heritage… my whole body is secure and at rest.*

How does one achieve such a splendid existence? What is the secret path to *bliss for evermore*?

There is one phrase in this psalm which helps us find this path.

It is to be found in verse 8: *I set the Lord before me always.*

7. I will bless the LORD who gives me counsel;
at night my thoughts instruct me.

8. I set the LORD before me always;
with Him at my right hand I shall not falter.

9. Therefore my heart is glad, my soul rejoices,
my whole body is secure and at rest.

10. For You will not abandon my soul to the grave,
nor suffer Your faithful servant to see the pit.

11. You will make known to me the path of life;
in Your presence is fullness of joy,
at Your right hand bliss forevermore.

Him as somehow "equal" to me, close enough so that He can empathize with me, so that I can exclaim: *Guard me, God, for I seek refuge in You.*

Refuge can only be found with someone who is nearby, with someone whose circumstances are "equal" to mine.

To use philosophical terminology, the God of our psalm is an immanent God, and not a transcendent one. He is with us on earth, and not aloft in the heavens.

The realization that God is *equal,* that he is *always* nearby, inspires the expressions of utter confidence which permeate our psalm:

With Him at my right hand I shall not falter.... For You will not abandon my soul to the grave.... You will make known to me the path of life!

ז אֲבָרֵךְ אֶת־יהוה אֲשֶׁר יְעָצָנִי
אַף־לֵילוֹת יִסְּרוּנִי כִלְיוֹתָי׃

ח שִׁוִּיתִי יְהוָה לְנֶגְדִּי תָמִיד
כִּי מִימִינִי בַּל־אֶמּוֹט׃

ט לָכֵן ׀ שָׂמַח לִבִּי וַיָּגֶל כְּבוֹדִי
אַף־בְּשָׂרִי יִשְׁכֹּן לָבֶטַח׃

י כִּי ׀ לֹא־תַעֲזֹב נַפְשִׁי לִשְׁאוֹל
לֹא־תִתֵּן חסידיך לִרְאוֹת שָׁחַת׃ חֲסִידְךָ

יא תּוֹדִיעֵנִי אֹרַח חַיִּים
שֹׂבַע שְׂמָחוֹת אֶת־פָּנֶיךָ
נְעִמוֹת בִּימִינְךָ נֶצַח׃

suggests that we must not seek Him in some lofty and sublime place, aloof and unconcerned with all that is mundane.

Quite the contrary, he insists, we must imagine Him to be our equal. That is, the presence of God is to be found in the midst of earthly life, with all of its triviality, and even with its ugliness.

"Nothing is too small or too base to escape His gaze and His care."

The close affinity to God which is the theme of our psalm requires the awareness, which many will find heretical, that God is not high above us in some far removed celestial abode.

He is not in His sacred heaven. He is in down here with us on the same "playing field." As strange as it sounds to pious ears, *shiviti,* I must conceive of

PSALM 17

1. A prayer of David.
Hear, Lord, my righteous cause, listen to my cry.
Give ear to my prayers from lips without deceit.

2. Let my judgment come forth from You;
let Your eyes discern what is right.

3. Were You to test my heart, and watch me all night long.
Were You to try me [as in a furnace],
You would not find me innocent.
I wish that my mouth had not transgressed.

4. With regard to man's activities –
being mindful of the command of Your lips,
I have protected others from the ways of the lawless.

5. My steps have held firmly to Your paths,
my feet have never faltered.

6. I call on You, for You will answer me, God.
Turn Your ear to me; listen to my words.

7. Favor me with Your compassion,
You who rescues those who seek refuge
from Your opponents with Your right hand.

Why should God listen to his prayers? He is convinced that his faults prevent him from obtaining God's favor.

This psalm provides a solution to his dilemma with but one word.

It is a word which appears twice in this psalm, once in the very first verse and again in the last.

The word is *tzedek,* righteousness.

Hear, Lord, my righteous cause… then I, in righteousness, will behold Your face. The sages of the Talmud defined "righteousness" in very concrete and achievable terms.

Noting the similarity between the word *tzedek* and the word *tzedaka,* they defined it quite simply: "charity"!

One must first give charity. Then his prayers will be heard.

מזמור יז

I pray, but will He hear my prayers? After all, I am sure that I am far from perfect in His eyes. I have such ferocious problems. I need His mercy. What can I possibly do to earn His mercy?

א תְּפִלָּה לְדָוִד
שִׁמְעָה יְהוָה ׀ צֶדֶק
הַקְשִׁיבָה רִנָּתִי הַאֲזִינָה תְפִלָּתִי
בְּלֹא שִׂפְתֵי מִרְמָה׃

ב מִלְּפָנֶיךָ מִשְׁפָּטִי יֵצֵא
עֵינֶיךָ תֶּחֱזֶינָה מֵישָׁרִים׃

ג בָּחַנְתָּ לִבִּי ׀ פָּקַדְתָּ לַּיְלָה
צְרַפְתַּנִי בַל־תִּמְצָא
זַמֹּתִי בַּל־יַעֲבָר־פִּי׃

ד לִפְעֻלּוֹת אָדָם בִּדְבַר שְׂפָתֶיךָ
אֲנִי שָׁמַרְתִּי אָרְחוֹת פָּרִיץ׃

ה תָּמֹךְ אֲשֻׁרַי בְּמַעְגְּלוֹתֶיךָ
בַּל־נָמוֹטּוּ פְעָמָי׃

ו אֲנִי־קְרָאתִיךָ כִי־תַעֲנֵנִי אֵל
הַט־אָזְנְךָ לִי שְׁמַע אִמְרָתִי׃

ז הַפְלֵה חֲסָדֶיךָ מוֹשִׁיעַ חוֹסִים
מִמִּתְקוֹמְמִים בִּימִינֶךָ׃

מזמור יז *Psalm 17:* This psalm formulates the dilemma confronted by every sincere person of faith as he begins to pray.

He feels desperate. His problems are insoluble. He needs God to hear his prayers.

But he is hampered by his awareness of his sinfulness. He refuses to believe that he is worthy of God's attention.

8. Guard me like the apple of Your eye;
hide me in the shadow of Your wings

9. from the wicked who do me violence,
from my deadly enemies who encircle me.

10. Their fat has enclosed their hearts,
their mouths speak nothing but arrogance.

11. [They track] our steps; now they surround us;
they set their eyes to throw us to the ground.

12. They are like a lion hungry for prey,
like a young lion crouching in ambush.

13. Arise, LORD, confront them, bring them down;
save my life from the wicked who act as Your sword.

14. I prefer to die at Your hand, LORD,
among those who die of old age;
whose portion is life,
and whose bellies You will fill with Your hidden treasures.
May their sons have plenty,
and have something to leave for their offspring.

15. Then I, in righteousness, will behold Your face;
when I awake, I shall be content with the vision of You.

This practice is incorporated into the Code of Jewish Law, the *Shulḥan Arukh* (*Yoreh De'ah* 249:14). A small donation into the synagogue's charity box must precede one's daily prayer.

Self-recrimination and guilt can be alleviated with a single act of charity.

He who suffers from a sense of spiritual inadequacy can cure that suffering. He can reverse course and embark upon the path of righteousness. He can begin to do so with one almost effortless act of compassion.

Our psalm encourages the remorseful and self-doubting man of faith. It tells him: You may be riddled with despair and discontent, but with just a "penny in the *pushka*" you can dispel those feelings. You can *awake and become content with the vision* of an attentive and responsive God.

ח שָׁמְרֵנִי כְּאִישׁוֹן בַּת־עָיִן
בְּצֵל כְּנָפֶיךָ תַּסְתִּירֵנִי׃

ט מִפְּנֵי רְשָׁעִים זוּ שַׁדּוּנִי
אֹיְבַי בְּנֶפֶשׁ יַקִּיפוּ עָלָי׃

י חֶלְבָּמוֹ סָּגְרוּ
פִּימוֹ דִּבְּרוּ בְגֵאוּת׃

יא אַשֻּׁרֵינוּ עַתָּה סבבוני סְבָבוּנוּ
עֵינֵיהֶם יָשִׁיתוּ לִנְטוֹת בָּאָרֶץ׃

יב דִּמְיֹנוֹ
כְּאַרְיֵה יִכְסוֹף לִטְרוֹף
וְכִכְפִיר יֹשֵׁב בְּמִסְתָּרִים׃

יג קוּמָה יְהוָה קַדְּמָה פָנָיו הַכְרִיעֵהוּ
פַּלְּטָה נַפְשִׁי מֵרָשָׁע חַרְבֶּךָ׃

יד מִמְתִים יָדְךָ ׀ יְהוָה מִמְתִים מֵחֶלֶד
חֶלְקָם בַּחַיִּים וצפינך תְּמַלֵּא בִטְנָם וּצְפוּנְךָ
יִשְׂבְּעוּ בָנִים
וְהִנִּיחוּ יִתְרָם לְעוֹלְלֵיהֶם׃

טו אֲנִי בְּצֶדֶק אֶחֱזֶה פָנֶיךָ
אֶשְׂבְּעָה בְהָקִיץ תְּמוּנָתֶךָ׃

"R. Elazar gave a penny to a poor man, and then prayed" (*Bava Batra* 10b).

R. Elazar based his practice upon our psalm.

It opens with the phrase *my righteous cause.* A simple act of charity renders one's cause righteous.

It ends with the phrase *I, in righteousness,* having given a penny to a poor man, *will behold Your face* so that my prayers will be heard.

PSALM 18

Third day of the month

1. For the Chief Musician. Of David the servant of the Lord,
who recited to the Lord the words of this song
when the Lord had saved him from the hands
of all his enemies and from the hand of Saul.

2. He said:
I love You, Lord, my strength.

3. The Lord is my rock, my fortress, my deliverer,
my God, my stronghold in whom I take refuge,
my shield, the power of my salvation, my strong tower.

4. I call on the Lord to whom all praise is due,
and I am saved from my enemies.

5. The bonds of death entangled me,
torrents of destruction overwhelmed me;

6. the bonds of Sheol encircled me,
the snares of death confronted me.

7. In my distress I called to the Lord,
I cried to my God for help.
From His Temple He heard my voice;
my cry to Him reached His ears.

The emotions of thanksgiving, vindication, triumph, and the felt certainty of continued divine providence comprise our psalm.

Such a range of emotions can only be expressed by someone who, like this psalmist, is truly a *servant of the Lord,* one who, in the words of Radak, has "invested his physical energies and spiritual powers in all aspects of his existence in the Blessed God." Only such a devoted worshipper will experience God as *my rock, my fortress, my deliverer... my shield, the power of my salvation, my strong tower.*

A less devoted person would never attribute his life's successes to God.

מזמור יח

It has been such a long time, with so many different kinds of problems. I can hardly believe that they are all behind me. My enemies are gone, my difficulties are resolved, and my pain is relieved. How thankful I am to the One Above. He was always my only hope, and He came through.

ג לחודש

א לַמְנַצֵּחַ לְעֶבֶד יְהוָה לְדָוִד
אֲשֶׁר דִּבֶּר ׀ לַיהוָה אֶת־דִּבְרֵי הַשִּׁירָה הַזֹּאת
בְּיוֹם ׀ הִצִּיל־יְהוָה אוֹתוֹ מִכַּף כָּל־אֹיְבָיו וּמִיַּד שָׁאוּל׃

ב וַיֹּאמַר אֶרְחָמְךָ יְהוָה חִזְקִי׃

ג יְהוָה ׀ סַלְעִי וּמְצוּדָתִי וּמְפַלְטִי
אֵלִי צוּרִי אֶחֱסֶה־בּוֹ
מָגִנִּי וְקֶרֶן־יִשְׁעִי מִשְׂגַּבִּי׃

ד מְהֻלָּל אֶקְרָא יְהוָה
וּמִן־אֹיְבַי אִוָּשֵׁעַ׃

ה אֲפָפוּנִי חֶבְלֵי־מָוֶת
וְנַחֲלֵי בְלִיַּעַל יְבַעֲתוּנִי׃

ו חֶבְלֵי שְׁאוֹל סְבָבוּנִי
קִדְּמוּנִי מוֹקְשֵׁי מָוֶת׃

ז בַּצַּר־לִי ׀ אֶקְרָא יְהוָה
וְאֶל־אֱלֹהַי אֲשַׁוֵּעַ
יִשְׁמַע מֵהֵיכָלוֹ קוֹלִי
וְשַׁוְעָתִי לְפָנָיו ׀ תָּבוֹא בְאָזְנָיו׃

מזמור יח *Psalm 18:* There are many psalms which express the prayers of persons in desperate straits. Our psalm expresses the emotions of one who has been delivered from such straits.

8. The earth reeled and rocked,
the foundations of the mountains shook;
they reeled, because He was angry.

9. Smoke rose from His nostrils,
a devouring fire from His mouth,
that kindled coals into flame.

10. He bent the sky and came down,
a dark cloud lay under His feet.

11. He mounted a cherub and flew,
He soared on the wings of the wind.

12. He made darkness His screen;
the dark rain clouds of the sky
were His canopy around Him.

13. The radiance of His presence
pierced the clouds,
flashing fiery hail like blazing coals.

14. The LORD thundered from heaven,
the Most High raised His voice,
amidst a storm of hailstones and fiery coals.

15. He shot His arrows and scattered [His foes];
He hurled lightning bolts and routed them.

16. The ocean bed was revealed,
the foundations of the world were laid bare,
at Your rebuke, LORD,
at the blast of the breath of Your nostrils.

---

ous enemies, and ideological opponents. He has suffered from each of these terrible troubles for years; indeed for most of his life.

But now that these troubles are gone, he refuses to believe that his victories were in any way due to his own valiant efforts. No! It is God *who trains my hands for battle* and who has *made my enemies turn their backs in flight.*

In the midst of his struggles, when his tribulations were far from over,

ח וַתִּגְעַשׁ וַתִּרְעַשׁ ׀ הָאָרֶץ
וּמוֹסְדֵי הָרִים יִרְגָּזוּ
וַיִּתְגָּעֲשׁוּ כִּי־חָרָה לוֹ׃

ט עָלָה עָשָׁן ׀ בְּאַפּוֹ וְאֵשׁ־מִפִּיו תֹּאכֵל
גֶּחָלִים בָּעֲרוּ מִמֶּנּוּ׃

י וַיֵּט שָׁמַיִם וַיֵּרַד
וַעֲרָפֶל תַּחַת רַגְלָיו׃

יא וַיִּרְכַּב עַל־כְּרוּב וַיָּעֹף
וַיֵּדֶא עַל־כַּנְפֵי־רוּחַ׃

יב יָשֶׁת חֹשֶׁךְ ׀ סִתְרוֹ סְבִיבוֹתָיו סֻכָּתוֹ
חֶשְׁכַת־מַיִם עָבֵי שְׁחָקִים׃

יג מִנֹּגַהּ נֶגְדּוֹ
עָבָיו עָבְרוּ בָּרָד וְגַחֲלֵי־אֵשׁ׃

יד וַיַּרְעֵם בַּשָּׁמַיִם ׀ יְהוָה
וְעֶלְיוֹן יִתֵּן קֹלוֹ
בָּרָד וְגַחֲלֵי־אֵשׁ׃

טו וַיִּשְׁלַח חִצָּיו וַיְפִיצֵם
וּבְרָקִים רָב וַיְהֻמֵּם׃

טז וַיֵּרָאוּ ׀ אֲפִיקֵי מַיִם
וַיִּגָּלוּ מוֹסְדוֹת תֵּבֵל
מִגַּעֲרָתְךָ יְהוָה
מִנִּשְׁמַת רוּחַ אַפֶּךָ׃

Quite the contrary, he would credit those successes to his own skills and talents, or perhaps to arbitrary good fortune.

Not so the author of this psalm. He has known natural disasters, murder-

17. From on high He reached down and took me;
He drew me out of the mighty waters.

18. He rescued me from my powerful enemy,
from my foes who were too strong for me.

19. They confronted me in the day of my calamity,
but the LORD was my support.

20. He brought me out into freedom;
He saved me because He was pleased with me.

21. The LORD rewarded me according to my merit,
He requited me because my hands were clean.

22. For I kept the ways of the LORD,
and was not disloyal to my God.

23. All His laws are ever before me;
I have not disregarded His precepts.

24. I have always been blameless before Him,
and have kept myself from sin.

25. The LORD requited me according to my merit,
because my hands were clean
in His sight.

26. To the loyal You show Yourself loyal,
and to the blameless You show Yourself blameless.

Our psalmist knew three varieties of challenge. He knew how destructive nature could be: *The earth reeled and rocked, the foundations of the mountains shook.* He saw God's wrath take the form of *dark rain clouds* and *fiery hail like blazing coals.* He was terrified by how *the ocean bed was revealed, the foundations of the world laid bare.*

But God rescued him from those catastrophes: *He drew me out of the mighty waters.*

He also knew the ferocity of battle. Here too he is convinced that his

יז יִשְׁלַח מִמָּרוֹם יִקָּחֵנִי
יַמְשֵׁנִי מִמַּיִם רַבִּים׃

יח יַצִּילֵנִי מֵאֹיְבִי עָז
וּמִשֹּׂנְאַי
כִּי־אָמְצוּ מִמֶּנִּי׃

יט יְקַדְּמוּנִי בְיוֹם־אֵידִי
וַיְהִי־יְהוָה לְמִשְׁעָן לִי׃

כ וַיּוֹצִיאֵנִי לַמֶּרְחָב
יְחַלְּצֵנִי כִּי חָפֵץ בִּי׃

כא יִגְמְלֵנִי יְהוָה כְּצִדְקִי
כְּבֹר יָדַי יָשִׁיב לִי׃

כב כִּי־שָׁמַרְתִּי דַּרְכֵי יְהוָה
וְלֹא־רָשַׁעְתִּי מֵאֱלֹהָי׃

כג כִּי כָל־מִשְׁפָּטָיו לְנֶגְדִּי
וְחֻקֹּתָיו לֹא־אָסִיר מֶנִּי׃

כד וָאֱהִי תָמִים עִמּוֹ
וָאֶשְׁתַּמֵּר מֵעֲוֹנִי׃

כה וַיָּשֶׁב־יְהוָה לִי כְצִדְקִי
כְּבֹר יָדַי לְנֶגֶד עֵינָיו׃

כו עִם־חָסִיד תִּתְחַסָּד
עִם־גְּבַר תָּמִים תִּתַּמָּם׃

---

and the threat of failure seemed imminent, our psalmist remained a stalwart believer: *I have always been blameless before Him,* never questioning His ways, and never doubting His protection.

27. To the sincere You show Yourself sincere,
but to the perverse You show Yourself shrewd.

28. For You save the lowly people,
but humble haughty eyes.

29. For You keep my lamp alight;
the LORD, my God,
lightens my darkness.

30. With Your help I can advance against a troop;
with my God's aid I can scale a wall.

31. The way of God is perfect!
The LORD's word is flawless.
He is a shield to all who seek refuge in Him.

32. What god is there except the LORD?
What rock but our God?

33. He is the God who girds me with strength,
and makes my way straight.

34. He makes my feet swift as a deer,
and sets me secure on the heights.

35. He trains my hands for battle,
so that my arms can bend a bow of bronze.

Finally, he also knew ideological enemies, those who would judge him in their own tribunals, by their own standards of justice. But here too he triumphs: *You delivered me from the attacks of the people.*

The Hebrew original for "attack" in this verse is *riv,* which is more accurately translated as "dispute," suggesting a debate of ideas rather than military combat.

This interpretation is supported by the next verse, which reads, in Rabbi Cashdan's translation, *As soon as they hear of me, they obey me; foreigners cringe before me.*

כז עִם־נָבָר תִּתְבָּרָר
וְעִם־עִקֵּשׁ תִּתְפַּתָּל׃

כח כִּי־אַתָּה עַם־עָנִי תוֹשִׁיעַ
וְעֵינַיִם רָמוֹת תַּשְׁפִּיל׃

כט כִּי־אַתָּה תָּאִיר נֵרִי
יְהוָה אֱלֹהַי יַגִּיהַּ חָשְׁכִּי׃

ל כִּי־בְךָ אָרֻץ גְּדוּד
וּבֵאלֹהַי אֲדַלֶּג־שׁוּר׃

לא הָאֵל תָּמִים דַּרְכּוֹ
אִמְרַת־יְהוָה צְרוּפָה
מָגֵן הוּא לְכֹל ׀ הַחוֹסִים בּוֹ׃

לב כִּי מִי אֱלוֹהַּ מִבַּלְעֲדֵי יְהוָה
וּמִי צוּר זוּלָתִי אֱלֹהֵינוּ׃

לג הָאֵל הַמְאַזְּרֵנִי חָיִל
וַיִּתֵּן תָּמִים דַּרְכִּי׃

לד מְשַׁוֶּה רַגְלַי כָּאַיָּלוֹת
וְעַל בָּמֹתַי יַעֲמִידֵנִי׃

לה מְלַמֵּד יָדַי לַמִּלְחָמָה
וְנִחֲתָה קֶשֶׁת־נְחוּשָׁה זְרוֹעֹתָי׃

---

courage is abetted by his Divine Protector: *With Your help I can advance against a troop, with my God's aid I can scale a wall.*

Not only does he come to know victory, but he is able to repel his enemies: *You made my enemies turn their backs in flight.*

36. You have given me Your shield of protection;
Your right hand sustains me;
for it is Your purpose to make me great.

37. You made room for my steps;
my feet have not slipped.

38. I pursue my enemies and overtake them;
I do not turn back until I have made an end of them.

39. I strike them down and they can rise no more;
they lie fallen at my feet.

40. You have girded me with strength for battle;
You subdued my assailants before me.

41. You made my enemies turn their backs in flight;
those who hated me I destroyed.

42. They cried out, but there was no one to save them;
they cried to the LORD, but He did not answer them.

43. I crushed them fine as dust before the wind;
I poured them out like mud in the streets.

44. You delivered me from the attacks of the people;
You have set me at the head of nations;
peoples I know not serve me.

This view is supported in a previous verse, in which the psalmist's enemies despair of having their prayers answered by their own gods, and instead direct their pleas to the LORD Almighty: *They cried out, but there was no one to save them; they cried to the LORD, but He did not answer them.* When they finally do turn to the LORD, it is with insufficient sincerity, and so He rejects their prayers.

Our psalm conveys the words of an experienced man, a wise veteran of the vicissitudes of life. He has known thunderous storms, vicious violence, and blasphemous foes. He has overcome them all.

לו וַתִּתֶּן־לִי֮ מָגֵ֪ן יִ֫שְׁעֶ֥ךָ
וִֽימִינְךָ֥ תִסְעָדֵ֑נִי
וְֽעַנְוַתְךָ֥ תַרְבֵּֽנִי׃

לז תַּרְחִ֣יב צַעֲדִ֣י תַחְתָּ֑י
וְלֹ֥א מָ֝עֲד֗וּ קַרְסֻלָּֽי׃

לח אֶרְדּ֣וֹף א֭וֹיְבַי וְאַשִּׂיגֵ֑ם
וְלֹֽא־אָ֝שׁ֗וּב עַד־כַּלּוֹתָֽם׃

לט אֶ֭מְחָצֵם וְלֹא־יֻ֣כְלוּ ק֑וּם
יִ֝פְּל֗וּ תַּ֣חַת רַגְלָֽי׃

מ וַתְּאַזְּרֵ֣נִי חַ֭יִל לַמִּלְחָמָ֑ה
תַּכְרִ֖יעַ קָמַ֣י תַּחְתָּֽי׃

מא וְֽאֹיְבַ֗י נָתַ֣תָּה לִּ֣י עֹ֑רֶף
וּ֝מְשַׂנְאַ֗י אַצְמִיתֵֽם׃

מב יְשַׁוְּע֥וּ וְאֵין־מוֹשִׁ֑יעַ
עַל־יְ֝הוָ֗ה וְלֹ֣א עָנָֽם׃

מג וְ֭אֶשְׁחָקֵם כְּעָפָ֣ר עַל־פְּנֵי־ר֑וּחַ
כְּטִ֖יט חוּצ֣וֹת אֲרִיקֵֽם׃

מד תְּפַלְּטֵנִי֮ מֵרִ֪יבֵ֫י עָ֥ם
תְּ֭שִׂימֵנִי לְרֹ֣אשׁ גּוֹיִ֑ם
עַ֖ם לֹא־יָדַ֣עְתִּי יַעַבְדֽוּנִי׃

Radak has it differently: *As soon as they hear of me, they assemble; foreigners concede to me.* They come to listen to my teachings, and are so convinced by them that they reject their own beliefs, and adopt my views.

45. As soon as they hear of me, they obey me;
foreigners cringe before me.

46. Foreign people are disheartened,
they come trembling out of their strongholds.

47. The Lord lives! Blessed is my rock!
Exalted be God, my deliverer!

48. He is the God who vindicates me,
who subdues nations under me;

49. who rescues me from my enemies.
You raise me above my foes,
and deliver me from violent men.

50. Therefore, Lord, I will praise You among the nations,
and sing psalms to Your name.

51. He gives great victories to His king,
He shows loving-kindness to His anointed,
to David and his descendants forever.

And finally, words of prayer for his descendants:
He shows loving-kindness to… David and his descendants forever.

מה לְשֵׁ֣מַע אֹ֭זֶן יִשָּׁ֣מְעוּ לִ֑י
בְּנֵי־נֵ֝כָ֗ר יְכַחֲשׁוּ־לִֽי׃

מו בְּנֵי־נֵכָ֥ר יִבֹּ֑לוּ
וְ֝יַחְרְג֗וּ מִֽמִּסְגְּרֽוֹתֵיהֶֽם׃

מז חַי־יְ֭הוָה וּבָר֣וּךְ צוּרִ֑י
וְ֝יָר֗וּם אֱלוֹהֵ֥י יִשְׁעִֽי׃

מח הָאֵ֗ל הַנּוֹתֵ֣ן נְקָמ֣וֹת לִ֑י
וַיַּדְבֵּ֖ר עַמִּ֣ים תַּחְתָּֽי׃

מט מְפַלְּטִ֗י מֵאֹ֫יְבָ֥י
אַ֣ף מִן־קָ֭מַי תְּרוֹמְמֵ֑נִי
מֵאִ֥ישׁ חָ֝מָ֗ס תַּצִּילֵֽנִי׃

נ עַל־כֵּ֤ן ׀ אוֹדְךָ֖ בַגּוֹיִ֥ם ׀ יְהוָ֑ה
וּלְשִׁמְךָ֥ אֲזַמֵּֽרָה׃

נא מַגְדִּל֮ יְשׁוּע֪וֹת מַ֫לְכּ֥וֹ
וְעֹ֘שֶׂ֤ה חֶ֨סֶד ׀ לִמְשִׁיח֗וֹ
לְדָוִ֥ד וּלְזַרְע֗וֹ עַד־עוֹלָֽם׃

He feels compelled to conclude with two culminating statements, without which his message is incomplete:

First, words of thanksgiving for his past:

Therefore, Lord, I will praise You… and sing psalms to Your name.

PSALM 19

1. For the Chief Musician. A psalm of David.

2. The heavens declare the glory of God,
the sky proclaims the work of His hand.

3. Day after day they* tell their tale,
night after night they proclaim this fact.

4. No word, no utterance, no sound is heard,

5. yet their message goes out through all the earth,
and what they tell reaches to the end of the world.
In them He has set up a tent for the sun.

6. It comes out like a bridegroom from his chamber,
rejoicing like a champion to run its course.

7. It rises at one end of the heaven,
and makes its circuit to the other end;
and nothing is hidden from its heat.

* I.e., the heavens.

Nature is one source of spiritual experience.

A second source is that which we call Torah: God's instructions to man, His revealed law. Unlike nature, Torah provides more than a spiritual experience for those who study it. It changes them. It transforms them. It *refreshes their souls... makes wise the simple... gives joy to the heart,* and *brings light to the eyes.*

Skeptics often question the need to resort to divine revelation in order to attain spiritual insight. They ask, "Can one not rely upon human intelligence as a means of ascertaining spiritual truth?"

Rabbi Abraham Isaac Kook takes this question very seriously, and finds an answer in verse 8 of our psalm.

He points out that human intellect is limited. Any attempt to focus on any one subject, however important, or concentrate upon any one objective, however lofty, necessitates ignoring other subjects and other objectives. Mortals can only deal with one subject at a time. Their intense interest in the subject at hand restricts them from seeing the whole picture.

They may see the trees very well, but in the process they lose sight of the forest. What's worse is that they are left with a vague feeling of incompleteness.

מזמור יט

Days like today make it all worthwhile. Everything fits. The wonders of nature thrill me. I am blown away by God's wisdom. I am on a spiritual "high," and wish it would last forever. Why can't every day be like today?

א לַמְנַצֵּחַ מִזְמוֹר לְדָוִד׃

ב הַשָּׁמַיִם מְסַפְּרִים כְּבוֹד־אֵל
וּמַעֲשֵׂה יָדָיו מַגִּיד הָרָקִיעַ׃

ג יוֹם לְיוֹם יַבִּיעַ אֹמֶר
וְלַיְלָה לְּלַיְלָה יְחַוֶּה־דָּעַת׃

ד אֵין־אֹמֶר וְאֵין דְּבָרִים
בְּלִי נִשְׁמָע קוֹלָם׃

ה בְּכָל־הָאָרֶץ ׀ יָצָא קַוָּם
וּבִקְצֵה תֵבֵל מִלֵּיהֶם
לַשֶּׁמֶשׁ שָׂם־אֹהֶל בָּהֶם׃

ו וְהוּא כְּחָתָן יֹצֵא מֵחֻפָּתוֹ
יָשִׂישׂ כְּגִבּוֹר לָרוּץ אֹרַח׃

ז מִקְצֵה הַשָּׁמַיִם ׀ מוֹצָאוֹ
וּתְקוּפָתוֹ עַל־קְצוֹתָם
וְאֵין נִסְתָּר מֵחַמָּתוֹ׃

מזמור יט *Psalm 19:* Our world is full of people in search of meaningful spiritual experiences. Our psalm proclaims that such experiences are easily found. But we must be attuned to the world around us in order to find them.

The heavens declare the glory of God… their message goes out through all the earth, and what they tell reaches to the end of the world.

We take daily miracles for granted. The rising sun is but one of the phenomena that *tell their tale day after day.* If one takes notice of regularly recurring events, if one "listens" to the heavens, one hears wordless testimony to the existence of God and to His glory.

8. The law of the LORD is perfect, refreshing the soul; the decrees
of the LORD are trustworthy, making wise the simple.

9. The precepts of the LORD are right, giving joy to the heart;
the commandment of the LORD is clear,
bringing light to the eyes.

10. The fear of the LORD is pure, enduring forever;
the judgments of the LORD are true, righteous altogether.

11. They are more desirable than gold, than much fine gold;
they are sweeter than honey, than the drippings from the comb.

12. By them Your servant is enlightened;
in keeping them there is great reward.

13. But who can be aware of errors?
Cleanse me of hidden faults.

14. Above all, restrain Your servant from willful sins;
let them not rule over me,
then shall I be blameless, innocent of great transgression.

15. May the words of my mouth, and the thoughts of my mind,
be pleasing to You, Lord, my rock and my redeemer!

None of us is infallible. Left to our own limited intelligence, we will sooner or later make mistakes, which will doom our entire search to failure. We assume that there is no safeguard against human error.

Our psalm recognizes that there is indeed a safeguard against error. That safeguard is prayer and repentance.

In the world of mortals, errors are seldom reversible. From the divine perspective, however, errors can be forgiven.

Who can be aware of errors?

Cleanse me of hidden faults.

Above all, restrain Your servant from willful sins. The explorer in search of a new continent cannot undo the tragic consequence of steering his ship in the wrong direction.

But the explorer in search of God can reach his destination no matter how drastically he errs. He can be confident that his innocent mistakes, and even his intentional sins, can be rectified through God's forgiveness.

ח תּוֹרַת יְהוָה תְּמִימָה מְשִׁיבַת נָפֶשׁ
עֵדוּת יְהוָה נֶאֱמָנָה מַחְכִּימַת פֶּתִי:

ט פִּקּוּדֵי יְהוָה יְשָׁרִים מְשַׂמְּחֵי־לֵב
מִצְוַת יְהוָה בָּרָה מְאִירַת עֵינָיִם:

י יִרְאַת יְהוָה ׀ טְהוֹרָה עוֹמֶדֶת לָעַד
מִשְׁפְּטֵי־יְהוָה אֱמֶת צָדְקוּ יַחְדָּו:

יא הַנֶּחֱמָדִים מִזָּהָב וּמִפַּז רָב
וּמְתוּקִים מִדְּבַשׁ וְנֹפֶת צוּפִים:

יב גַּם־עַבְדְּךָ נִזְהָר בָּהֶם
בְּשָׁמְרָם עֵקֶב רָב:

יג שְׁגִיאוֹת מִי־יָבִין
מִנִּסְתָּרוֹת נַקֵּנִי:

יד גַּם מִזֵּדִים ׀ חֲשֹׂךְ עַבְדֶּךָ
אַל־יִמְשְׁלוּ־בִי אָז אֵיתָם
וְנִקֵּיתִי מִפֶּשַׁע רָב:

טו יִהְיוּ לְרָצוֹן ׀ אִמְרֵי־פִי וְהֶגְיוֹן לִבִּי לְפָנֶיךָ
יְהוָה צוּרִי וְגֹאֲלִי:

They know that they are missing something, although they know not what. They remain unsettled; they are left feeling restless, anxious.

The merit of God's Torah is that *the law of the LORD is perfect, "temima,"* a word which carries the connotation of whole, comprehensive, total. Torah allows the trees to be studied in exquisite detail, but never loses sight of the forest. The Torah's ability to be simultaneously comprehensive and intensive prevents the fatigue that the student using other methods of study often experiences. Instead, it *refreshes the soul.*

In verse 13 we find yet another way in which Torah is unlike other methods of searching for spiritual truth.

PSALM 20

1. For the Chief Musician. A psalm of David.

2. May the LORD answer you in a time of distress;
may the name of Jacob's God be a tower of strength to you.

3. May He send you help from the sanctuary,
and give you support from Zion.

4. May He remember all your offerings,
and graciously accept your burnt-offerings. *Selah*

5. May He grant you your heart's desire,
and fulfill your every plan.

6. May we shout for joy over your victory,
and in the name of our God unfurl our banners.
May the LORD grant your every request.

7. Now I know that the LORD will give victory to His anointed;
He will answer him from His holy heaven
with the saving strength of His right hand.

---

behind. He pours out his heart praying for them. This psalm is an eloquent expression of his empathy.

From the security of his royal palace, he shares his troops' anxiety. From afar, he celebrates their victory with them.

May the LORD answer you in a time of distress.
May He... give you support from Zion.
May we shout for joy over your victory.
May the LORD grant your every request.
They collapse and fall, but we rise up and stand firm.

In verse 2, David summons *Jacob's God,* prompting us to wonder, as the Talmud (*Berakhot* 64a) does, why he addresses Jacob's God and not the God of Abraham and Isaac.

The Talmud points out that it is Jacob, the patriarch who raised the first all-Jewish family, who bears a special responsibility for the Jewish people

מזמור כ

I am safe, but my buddy is in trouble – deep trouble. I feel helpless. I wish there was something I could do for him. There is something I can do for him. I can pray.

א לַמְנַצֵּחַ מִזְמוֹר לְדָוִד׃

ב יַעַנְךָ יהוה בְּיוֹם צָרָה
יְשַׂגֶּבְךָ שֵׁם ׀ אֱלֹהֵי יַעֲקֹב׃

ג יִשְׁלַח־עֶזְרְךָ מִקֹּדֶשׁ
וּמִצִּיּוֹן יִסְעָדֶךָּ׃

ד יִזְכֹּר כָּל־מִנְחוֹתֶךָ
וְעוֹלָתְךָ יְדַשְּׁנֶה סֶלָה׃

ה יִתֶּן־לְךָ כִלְבָבֶךָ
וְכָל־עֲצָתְךָ יְמַלֵּא׃

ו נְרַנְּנָה ׀ בִּישׁוּעָתֶךָ
וּבְשֵׁם־אֱלֹהֵינוּ נִדְגֹּל
יְמַלֵּא יהוה כָּל־מִשְׁאֲלוֹתֶיךָ׃

ז עַתָּה יָדַעְתִּי כִּי הוֹשִׁיעַ ׀ יהוה מְשִׁיחוֹ
יַעֲנֵהוּ מִשְּׁמֵי קָדְשׁוֹ בִּגְבוּרוֹת יֵשַׁע יְמִינוֹ׃

מזמור כ *Psalm 20:* The theme of this psalm is empathy.

When someone we care for is in danger, while we ourselves are at a safe distance from that danger, we feel empathy. We tremble at the other's fears, and experience his terror in our bones.

Rashi tells us that this psalm is part of a larger story, narrated in II Samuel, chapter 18.

David sends his troops to war. He prepares to join them on the battlefield, but his men dissuade him, saying: "*… you are worth ten thousand of us. Therefore, it is better for you to support us from the city.*" David consents, and remains

8. Some boast of chariots, some of horses,
but we boast in the name of the LORD our God.

9. They collapse and fall,
but we rise up and stand firm.

10. LORD, grant victory;
may the King answer us when we call.

---

answered me when I was in distress and who has been with me wherever I have gone" (Gen. 35:3).

God Himself is the ultimate exemplar of empathy. No wonder then that the last verse of our psalm, in which we plead for God's empathy, is evoked so very frequently in the Siddur: *LORD, grant victory; may the King answer us when we call.*

אֵלֶּה בָרֶכֶב וְאֵלֶּה בַסּוּסִים ח
וַאֲנַחְנוּ ׀ בְּשֵׁם־יהוָה אֱלֹהֵינוּ נַזְכִּיר׃

הֵמָּה כָּרְעוּ וְנָפָלוּ ט
וַאֲנַחְנוּ קַּמְנוּ וַנִּתְעוֹדָד׃

יהוָה הוֹשִׁיעָה י
הַמֶּלֶךְ יַעֲנֵנוּ בְיוֹם־קָרְאֵנוּ׃

---

throughout the ages. It is Jacob who can show the empathy which is the theme *of* this psalm. Hence it is his God that David calls upon.

Furthermore, our psalm speaks of those who find themselves in a *time of distress*. Who can empathize with them then better than Jacob, whose life was one of recurring distress? It is Jacob who builds an altar to "*the* God who

PSALM 21

1. For the Chief Musician. A psalm of David.
2. LORD, the king rejoices in Your might.
How great is his joy in Your saving power!
3. For You have given him his heart's desire,
and have not denied him the request of his lips. *Selah*
4. You welcomed him with rich blessings,
and placed a crown of fine gold on his head.
5. He asked You for life and You gave it to him,
length of days, forever and ever.
6. Great is his glory through Your victory;
You bestowed on him majesty and honor.
7. You have given him blessings forever,
You make him glad with the joy of Your presence.

We know two things about success: It takes hard work, skill, and courage; and it is tenuous, ephemeral, and easily lost.

Our psalm teaches us that success is lost when it is taken for granted. If the successful person is convinced that his achievements are the product of his own efforts, he risks losing them. If he uses his position for his own egotistical purposes, his very success will prove to be his downfall.

He must learn humility. He must see his success as a tool with which he is to perform God's mission. He can be confident of retaining his authority only if he learns to use it as an opportunity to achieve selfless goals and divine purposes.

LORD, the king rejoices in Your might. How great is his joy in Your saving power.

The first eight verses of our psalm eloquently describe the feelings of the successful man. *You have given him his heart's desire.... He asked You for life and You gave it to him.... You gave him blessings forever.*

But they conclude with a condition: Only if *the king trusts in the LORD... will he not be shaken.*

There is a difficulty with which the successful leader is confronted. God

מזמור כא

I always knew he could do it. He fought so many enemies. He overcame so many obstacles. Now he has achieved it all. But so many others are jealous of him. Success is never secure.

א לַמְנַצֵּחַ מִזְמוֹר לְדָוִד׃

ב יְהוָה בְּעָזְּךָ יִשְׂמַח־מֶלֶךְ
וּבִישׁוּעָתְךָ מַה־יָּגֶיל מְאֹד׃

יִגֶּל

ג תַּאֲוַת לִבּוֹ נָתַתָּה לּוֹ
וַאֲרֶשֶׁת שְׂפָתָיו בַּל־מָנַעְתָּ סֶּלָה׃

ד כִּי־תְקַדְּמֶנּוּ בִּרְכוֹת טוֹב
תָּשִׁית לְרֹאשׁוֹ עֲטֶרֶת פָּז׃

ה חַיִּים ׀ שָׁאַל מִמְּךָ נָתַתָּה לּוֹ
אֹרֶךְ יָמִים עוֹלָם וָעֶד׃

ו גָּדוֹל כְּבוֹדוֹ בִּישׁוּעָתֶךָ
הוֹד וְהָדָר תְּשַׁוֶּה עָלָיו׃

ז כִּי־תְשִׁיתֵהוּ בְרָכוֹת לָעַד
תְּחַדֵּהוּ בְשִׂמְחָה אֶת־פָּנֶיךָ׃

מזמור כא *Psalm 21.* Our psalm is about success. More specifically, it is about the spiritual significance of success.

Many understand our psalm as a song of victory for King David as he successfully ascends to the throne. Others interpret it as a prophetic description of the coronation of the ultimate "anointed king," the Messiah.

One thing is certain: our psalm is about a king.

From the Talmud's perspective we are all kings, or at least the children of kings.

From this perspective, our psalm is a song of praise to Everyman; a celebration of the blessing of every and any successful individual.

8. For the king trusts in the Lord,
and through the constant loving-kindness of the Most High
he will not be shaken.

9. Your hand will reach all Your enemies,
Your right hand will reach all who hate You.

10. You will burn them up as in a fiery furnace
in the time of Your anger.
The Lord will destroy them in His anger,
fire shall consume them.

11. You will wipe out their offspring from the earth,
and their posterity from among men.

12. For they planned evil against You,
and devised wicked schemes,
but could not succeed.

13. For You will make them turn their backs in flight
when You aim at their faces with Your bows.

14. Be exalted, Lord, in Your might;
we will sing and praise Your power.

Moshe ben Naḥman, Ramban) discovers in our psalm. In his description of the truly happy man, to be found in his commentary on the verse in Genesis 25:8 which reads: "*And Abraham breathed his last, dying at a good ripe age, old and contented,*" he writes:

> He desired nothing more. The future had nothing more in store for him… this is the commendable quality of the righteous – they do not long for excessive pleasures. As it is written, *You have given him his heart's desire* (our psalm, verse 3), unlike other people, of whom it is written, *A lover of money never has his fill of money* (Eccl. 5:9). The successful leader finds satisfaction in his achievements, and does not greedily seek more and more. He knows well the distinction between ambition and avarice.

ח כִּֽי־הַ֭מֶּלֶךְ בֹּטֵ֣חַ בַּיהוָ֑ה
וּבְחֶ֥סֶד עֶ֝לְי֗וֹן בַּל־יִמּֽוֹט׃

ט תִּמְצָ֣א יָ֭דְךָ לְכָל־אֹיְבֶ֑יךָ
יְ֝מִֽינְךָ֗ תִּמְצָ֥א שֹׂנְאֶֽיךָ׃

י תְּשִׁיתֵ֨מוֹ ׀ כְּתַנּ֥וּר אֵשׁ֮ לְעֵ֪ת פָּ֫נֶ֥יךָ
יְ֭הוָה בְּאַפּ֣וֹ יְבַלְּעֵ֑ם
וְֽתֹאכְלֵ֥ם אֵֽשׁ׃

יא פִּ֭רְיָמוֹ מֵאֶ֣רֶץ תְּאַבֵּ֑ד
וְ֝זַרְעָ֗ם מִבְּנֵ֥י אָדָֽם׃

יב כִּֽי־נָט֣וּ עָלֶ֣יךָ רָעָ֑ה
חָשְׁב֥וּ מְ֝זִמָּ֗ה
בַּל־יוּכָֽלוּ׃

יג כִּ֭י תְּשִׁיתֵ֣מוֹ שֶׁ֑כֶם
בְּ֝מֵיתָרֶ֗יךָ תְּכוֹנֵ֥ן עַל־פְּנֵיהֶֽם׃

יד ר֣וּמָה יְהוָ֣ה בְעֻזֶּ֑ךָ
נָשִׁ֥ירָה וּ֝נְזַמְּרָ֗ה גְּבוּרָתֶֽךָ׃

---

is a Hidden God, and His ways are typically far from apparent. How is the "king" to discern God's hand in his success?

This is the challenge of the successful person. He must use the spiritual means at his disposal to pierce God's veil. It is a struggle to attribute one's hard-earned victories to a Source outside oneself.

This is why our psalm ends with a prayer: *Be exalted, Lord, in Your might.* Be exalted, not concealed. Reveal Yourself so that I come to know that it is indeed *Your might,* and not my own, that has brought me these achievements.

There is yet another lesson about success which Nahmanides (Rabbi

PSALM 22

1. For the Chief Musician; on the strength of a new dawn.
A psalm of David.

2. My God, my God, why have You forsaken me?
Far from my salvation are the words that I roar.

3. My God, I cry by day,
but You do not answer;
and by night I am not silent.*

4. Yet You are enthroned as the Holy One,
receiving the praises of Israel.

5. In You our fathers put their trust;
they trusted, and You delivered them.

6. They cried to You and were saved;
they trusted in You, and were not disappointed.

7. But I am a worm, not a man,
scorned by men, despised by the people.

8. All who see me jeer at me,
they curl their lips and wag their heads.

* Or: "I have no respite."

---

illustrated this point with a parable: There was a king whose son the prince rebelled against him. The king exiled him to a deep forest in a remote corner of the kingdom. There the prince remained for many long years. He apprenticed himself to a woodsman, and earned his keep by chopping wood. Eventually the king decided to inquire after his son's well-being. He dispatched a messenger to him, with the instructions to tell the exiled prince that any request he made would be granted. The son was thrilled by the prospect of having his wish fulfilled, but after all those years of chopping wood, all he wished for was a new and sharper hatchet. The messenger reported the request back to the king, who was dismayed. "How tragic," he exclaimed. "He has forgotten

מזמור כב

I am worthless. Prayers work for others; for me they are futile. The odds are against me. I am helpless. I must become more hopeful, more optimistic. I will change the way I think of myself. I've got great potential.

א לַמְנַצֵּחַ עַל־אַיֶּלֶת הַשַּׁחַר מִזְמוֹר לְדָוִד׃

ב אֵלִי אֵלִי לָמָה עֲזַבְתָּנִי
רָחוֹק מִישׁוּעָתִי דִּבְרֵי שַׁאֲגָתִי׃

ג אֱלֹהַי אֶקְרָא יוֹמָם וְלֹא תַעֲנֶה
וְלַיְלָה וְלֹא־דוּמִיָּה לִי׃

ד וְאַתָּה קָדוֹשׁ
יוֹשֵׁב תְּהִלּוֹת יִשְׂרָאֵל׃

ה בְּךָ בָּטְחוּ אֲבֹתֵינוּ
בָּטְחוּ וַתְּפַלְּטֵמוֹ׃

ו אֵלֶיךָ זָעֲקוּ וְנִמְלָטוּ
בְּךָ בָטְחוּ וְלֹא־בוֹשׁוּ׃

ז וְאָנֹכִי תוֹלַעַת וְלֹא־אִישׁ
חֶרְפַּת אָדָם וּבְזוּי עָם׃

ח כָּל־רֹאַי יַלְעִגוּ לִי
יַפְטִירוּ בְשָׂפָה יָנִיעוּ רֹאשׁ׃

מזמור כב *Psalm 22:* We typically think so little of ourselves that we pray for what is trivial, and fail to pray for what is really important. *Far from my salvation are the words that I roar.* We "roar" for worldly gain, and thereby miss the opportunity to pray for the ultimate, for salvation.

The nineteenth-century hasidic sage Rabbi Yechezkel of Kuzmir (d. 1856)

9. But if one commits himself to the LORD,
He will save him. He will rescue him
because He delights in him.

10. For it was You who drew me from my mother's womb,
You who made me secure at my mother's breast.

11. From birth I was thrust upon You,
from my mother's womb You have been my God.

12. Keep not far from me,
for trouble is near, and there is no one to help.

13. Many bulls surround me,
strong bulls of Bashan encircle me.

14. They open wide their jaws against me
like ravenous, roaring lions.

15. I am poured out like water,
all my bones are out of joint;
my heart is like wax,
it melts within me.

16. My strength is dried up like a potsherd,
my tongue sticks to my palate;
You lay me in the dust of death.

17. For dogs surround me,
a mob of evildoers encircles me,
like a lion [they mangle] my hands and feet.

Our self-concepts are inadequate; hence, our prayers fall short of their mark.

We forget that we are nobility; hence, our prayers are so laughably limited.

We are princes, but our wishes are the wishes of woodchoppers.

We "roar" for petty gifts, and thereby forfeit the gifts of salvation.

ט גֹּ֣ל אֶל־יְהֹוָ֣ה יְפַלְּטֵ֑הוּ
יַ֝צִּילֵ֗הוּ כִּ֘י חָ֥פֵֽץ בּֽוֹ׃

י כִּֽי־אַתָּ֣ה גֹחִ֣י מִבָּ֑טֶן
מַ֝בְטִיחִ֗י עַל־שְׁדֵ֥י אִמִּֽי׃

יא עָ֭לֶיךָ הָשְׁלַ֣כְתִּי מֵרָ֑חֶם
מִבֶּ֥טֶן אִ֝מִּ֗י אֵ֣לִי אָֽתָּה׃

יב אַל־תִּרְחַ֣ק מִ֭מֶּנִּי כִּי־צָרָ֣ה קְרוֹבָ֑ה
כִּי־אֵ֥ין עוֹזֵֽר׃

יג סְ֭בָבוּנִי פָּרִ֣ים רַבִּ֑ים
אַבִּירֵ֖י בָשָׁ֣ן כִּתְּרֽוּנִי׃

יד פָּצ֣וּ עָלַ֣י פִּיהֶ֑ם
אַ֝רְיֵ֗ה טֹרֵ֥ף וְשֹׁאֵֽג׃

טו כַּמַּ֥יִם נִשְׁפַּכְתִּי֮ וְהִתְפָּֽרְד֡וּ כָּֽל־עַצְמ֫וֹתָ֥י
הָיָ֣ה לִ֭בִּי כַּדּוֹנָ֑ג נָ֝מֵ֗ס בְּת֣וֹךְ מֵעָֽי׃

טז יָ֘בֵ֤שׁ כַּחֶ֨רֶשׂ ׀ כֹּחִ֗י
וּ֭לְשׁוֹנִי מֻדְבָּ֣ק מַלְקוֹחָ֑י
וְֽלַעֲפַר־מָ֥וֶת תִּשְׁפְּתֵֽנִי׃

יז כִּ֤י סְבָב֗וּנִי כְּלָ֫בִ֥ים
עֲדַ֣ת מְ֭רֵעִים הִקִּיפ֑וּנִי
כָּ֝אֲרִ֗י יָדַ֥י וְרַגְלָֽי׃

---

that he is a prince. He asked for a mere hatchet, when he could have asked to return home to the palace to regain his royal position."

Far from my salvation are the words of my roaring.

18. I can count all my bones;
people stare and gloat over me.

19. They divide my clothing among them,
and cast lots for my garments.

20. But You, LORD, be not far off;
my strength, come quickly to my aid.

21. Save my life from the sword,
my precious soul from those dogs.

22. Rescue me from the lion's jaws,
deliver me from the horns of the wild ox.

23. Then I will declare Your fame to my brethren;
I will praise You in the midst of the assembly.

24. Praise Him, you who fear the LORD!
Honor Him, all you descendants of Jacob!
Stand in awe of Him, all you descendants of Israel!

25. For He has not spurned or disdained
the misery of the afflicted.
He has not hidden His face from him,
but has listened to him when he cried for help.

26. You are the theme of my praise in the great assembly;
I will pay my vows in the presence of those who revere Him.

First, he is *a worm, not a man.*

Then he remembers that he is indeed a man, drawn from *my mother's womb* and *made secure at my mother's breast.*

Despite the *bulls that surround me* and the *mob of evildoers who encircle me,* he can confidently call upon God to *not be far off.*

He becomes aware that he is not just an individual, but part of a collective: *I will declare Your fame to my brethren, I will praise You in the midst of the assembly.*

יח אֲסַפֵּר כָּל־עַצְמוֹתָי
הֵמָּה יַבִּיטוּ יִרְאוּ־בִי׃

יט יְחַלְּקוּ בְגָדַי לָהֶם
וְעַל־לְבוּשִׁי יַפִּילוּ גוֹרָל׃

כ וְאַתָּה יהוה אַל־תִּרְחָק
אֱיָלוּתִי לְעֶזְרָתִי חוּשָׁה׃

כא הַצִּילָה מֵחֶרֶב נַפְשִׁי
מִיַּד־כֶּלֶב יְחִידָתִי׃

כב הוֹשִׁיעֵנִי מִפִּי אַרְיֵה
וּמִקַּרְנֵי רֵמִים עֲנִיתָנִי׃

כג אֲסַפְּרָה שִׁמְךָ לְאֶחָי
בְּתוֹךְ קָהָל אֲהַלְלֶךָּ׃

כד יִרְאֵי יהוה ׀ הַלְלוּהוּ
כָּל־זֶרַע יַעֲקֹב כַּבְּדוּהוּ
וְגוּרוּ מִמֶּנּוּ כָּל־זֶרַע יִשְׂרָאֵל׃

כה כִּי לֹא־בָזָה וְלֹא שִׁקַּץ עֱנוּת עָנִי
וְלֹא־הִסְתִּיר פָּנָיו מִמֶּנּוּ
וּבְשַׁוְּעוֹ אֵלָיו שָׁמֵעַ׃

כו מֵאִתְּךָ תְּהִלָּתִי
בְּקָהָל רָב נְדָרַי אֲשַׁלֵּם נֶגֶד יְרֵאָיו׃

How fortunate we are that we can redefine our understanding of who we are, and in the process we can learn to pray for what is truly significant.

Such a transition takes place in our psalm, as the psalmist gradually expands his self-definition.

27. The poor shall eat and be satisfied,
those who seek the LORD shall praise Him;
may you be of good heart forever!

28. Let all the ends of the earth remember and turn to the LORD;
let all the families of the nations bow down before You;

29. for dominion belongs to the LORD
and He rules over the nations.

30. All the prosperous ones in the land shall feast and worship Him,
all who are mortal* shall kneel before Him,
even he that cannot keep his soul alive.

31. Posterity shall serve Him,
the coming generation shall be told about the LORD;

32. and they in turn shall proclaim His righteousness
to a people yet unborn,
that He has acted.

* Lit. "all who go down to the dust."

Our prayers grow in their meaningfulness as we grow in the image we have of ourselves.

Paupers pray as paupers, but we are princes and princesses, and must learn to pray accordingly.

כו יֹאכְל֬וּ עֲנָוִ֨ים ׀ וְיִשְׂבָּ֗עוּ יְהַֽלְל֣וּ יְ֭הוָה דֹּרְשָׁ֑יו
יְחִ֖י לְבַבְכֶ֣ם לָעַֽד׃

כז יִזְכְּר֤וּ ׀ וְיָשֻׁ֣בוּ אֶל־יְ֭הוָה כָּל־אַפְסֵי־אָ֑רֶץ
וְיִשְׁתַּחֲו֥וּ לְ֝פָנֶ֗יךָ כָּֽל־מִשְׁפְּח֥וֹת גּוֹיִֽם׃

כח כִּ֣י לַ֭יהוָה הַמְּלוּכָ֑ה
וּ֝מֹשֵׁ֗ל בַּגּוֹיִֽם׃

כט אָ֘כְל֤וּ וַיִּֽשְׁתַּחֲוּ֨וּ ׀ כָּֽל־דִּשְׁנֵי־אֶ֡רֶץ
לְפָנָ֣יו יִ֭כְרְעוּ כָּל־יוֹרְדֵ֣י עָפָ֑ר
וְ֝נַפְשׁ֗וֹ לֹ֣א חִיָּֽה׃

ל זֶ֥רַע יַֽעַבְדֶ֑נּוּ
יְסֻפַּ֖ר לַֽאדֹנָ֣י לַדּֽוֹר׃

לא יָ֭בֹאוּ וְיַגִּ֣ידוּ צִדְקָת֑וֹ
לְעַ֥ם נ֝וֹלָ֗ד כִּ֣י עָשָֽׂה׃

He imagines a future: *Posterity shall serve Him.*

He recognizes that there is much potential to him, that he is likened unto *a people yet unborn.*

PSALM 23

1. A psalm of David.
The Lord is my shepherd; I shall not want. *Fourth day of the month*

2. He makes me lie down in green pastures;
He leads me beside still waters.

3. He revives my soul;
He guides me in the right paths for His name's sake.

4. Though I walk through the valley of the shadow of death
I fear no evil, for You are with me;
Your rod and Your staff, they comfort me.

What he could not tolerate was his real sense that God was imprisoned along with him. He was tormented by the conviction that just as he was suffering, so was God suffering.

There is a concept in our theology of *Shekhinta beGaluta,* of the Divine Presence in Exile. The Bible abounds with passages which suggest that God is with us in our times of travail and in our times of joy. He went down to Egypt with us, and He departed Egypt with us. He traveled with us into the bondage of Babylon, and He accompanied us as we were dragged in chains through the streets of ancient Rome.

One of the very few survivors of the Treblinka death camp reports that, at one point in time, the Nazi guards suspended a synagogue curtain above the gates of the camp. The curtain was embroidered with the words of Psalm 118:20: *This is the Lord's gate; the righteous shall enter through it.*

This survivor reported that, oddly, he found comfort in those words. Although they were meant to be taunting, he found them encouraging. To him they announced that God was present, even there in the hell of Treblinka.

This was the Rabbi Israel's experience in the Czarist prison. He felt certain that God was with him, and was deeply saddened by God's suffering. He found words in our psalm which give voice to this feeling. These words, as he interprets them, convey nothing less than sympathy for God, a notion that may sound shockingly sacrilegious to our ears.

The words are the famous words of verse 4: *Though I walk through the valley*

מזמור כג

A strange calm has come over me. It is not that my troubles are gone. They are still around, believe me. But I have given them over to a "Higher Power." That relieves me from a lot of pressure. I have more freedom to solve my problems by myself.

א מִזְמ֥וֹר לְדָוִ֑ד
ד לחודש
יְהוָ֥ה רֹ֝עִ֗י לֹ֣א אֶחְסָֽר׃

ב בִּנְא֣וֹת דֶּ֭שֶׁא יַרְבִּיצֵ֑נִי
עַל־מֵ֖י מְנֻח֣וֹת יְנַהֲלֵֽנִי׃

ג נַפְשִׁ֥י יְשׁוֹבֵ֑ב
יַֽנְחֵ֥נִי בְמַעְגְּלֵי־צֶ֝֗דֶק לְמַ֣עַן שְׁמֽוֹ׃

ד גַּ֤ם כִּֽי־אֵלֵ֨ךְ בְּגֵ֪יא צַלְמָ֡וֶת לֹא־אִ֘ירָ֤א רָ֗ע
כִּי־אַתָּ֥ה עִמָּדִ֑י
שִׁבְטְךָ֥ וּ֝מִשְׁעַנְתֶּ֗ךָ הֵ֣מָּה יְנַחֲמֻֽנִי׃

מזמור כג *Psalm 23:* Our psalm is certainly the most well-known psalm of all. Its words are calming and reassuring. Its message is one of trust and hope.

There is a sub-theme to our psalm which was noticed by the nineteenth-century hasidic sage Rabbi Israel Friedman of Ruzhyn (1796–1850). The Ruzhyner, as he was known, personally experienced imprisonment in Czarist Russia. He was maliciously slandered and accused of traitorous conduct. He knew what it meant to be cast into a dungeon.

As a man of profound faith, he found our psalm particularly comforting during his prison confinement. It helped him cope with the deprivation of prison life. He could fortify himself with the words: *The Lord is my shepherd; I shall not want.*

He felt immune to the tortures inflicted upon him; tortures which are aptly described as *the valley of the shadow of death.*

He felt shielded from the threats and blows of his cruel jailors, because *You spread a table for me in the sight of my enemies.*

He tolerated the pain and the dread, the hunger and the sleeplessness, and even the horrible loneliness.

5. You spread a table for me in the sight of my enemies;
You anoint my head with oil,
my cup overflows.

6. Surely goodness and kindness will follow me
all the days of my life;
and I shall dwell in the house of the LORD
for many years to come.

"I can manage all the evil that engulfs me. What troubles me, what I find evil, is that You are with me."

Few are capable of feeling empathy for the Divine. But Rabbi Israel was.

He achieved this exquisite spiritual insight through his ordeal in the Czar's prison. Through his insight, those of us of lesser faith gained access to the teaching that not only does God accompany us to the places of our suffering, but He suffers along with us. He feels our pain. Amazingly, we can also feel His.

ה תַּעֲרֹךְ לְפָנַי ׀ שֻׁלְחָן נֶגֶד צֹרְרָי
דִּשַּׁנְתָּ בַשֶּׁמֶן רֹאשִׁי כּוֹסִי רְוָיָה׃

ו אַךְ ׀ טוֹב וָחֶסֶד יִרְדְּפוּנִי כָּל־יְמֵי חַיָּי
וְשַׁבְתִּי בְּבֵית־יהוה לְאֹרֶךְ יָמִים׃

---

of the shadow of death I fear no evil for You are with me. The Ruzhyner interprets these words differently with this unique and creative alternate punctuation: *Though I walk through the valley of the shadow of death I fear not. What is evil is that You are with me.*

This is truly an example of rare and sublime spiritual sensitivity.

PSALM 24

1. Of David. A psalm.
The earth is the LORD's, and all that is in it;
the world and all who live in it.

2. For He founded it upon the seas,
and set it firm upon the ocean currents.

3. Who may ascend the mountain of the LORD?
Who may stand in His holy place?

4. He who has clean hands and a pure heart,
who has not taken My name in vain,
and has not sworn deceitfully.

5. He shall receive a blessing from the LORD,
and generous reward from God his savior.

6. Such is the generation of those who search for Him;
they are the sons of Jacob who seek Your presence. *Selah*

7. Lift up your heads, you gates,
lift yourselves up, you everlasting doors,
that the King of Glory may come in.

Our psalm also asserts that not every man can ascend that mountain. There is only one path up that mountain, and that is the path of upright ethical behavior: *Who may ascend?... He who has clean hands and a pure heart... and has not sworn deceitfully.*

Closeness to God is reserved for those whose thoughts, words, and actions, are all meritorious. A deficiency in any of these three realms of human activity precludes access to the LORD's mountaintop.

Many have embarked upon a search for communion with the Divine. Our psalm insists that such a quest is futile unless it begins with perfect ethical behavior. Otherwise, it will go nowhere. Clean hands and a pure heart – only

מזמור כד

I definitely believe in God. I think He is awesome. Why should my silly little games matter to Him? Maybe He cares about some big shot's good deeds. But mine? No way

א לְדָוִד מִזְמוֹר
לַיהוה הָאָרֶץ וּמְלוֹאָהּ תֵּבֵל וְיֹשְׁבֵי בָהּ:

ב כִּי־הוּא עַל־יַמִּים יְסָדָהּ
וְעַל־נְהָרוֹת יְכוֹנְנֶהָ:

ג מִי־יַעֲלֶה בְהַר־יהוה
וּמִי־יָקוּם בִּמְקוֹם קָדְשׁוֹ:

ד נְקִי כַפַּיִם וּבַר־לֵבָב
אֲשֶׁר לֹא־נָשָׂא לַשָּׁוְא נפשו נַפְשִׁי
וְלֹא נִשְׁבַּע לְמִרְמָה:

ה יִשָּׂא בְרָכָה מֵאֵת יהוה
וּצְדָקָה מֵאֱלֹהֵי יִשְׁעוֹ:

ו זֶה דּוֹר דֹּרְשָׁו
מְבַקְשֵׁי פָנֶיךָ יַעֲקֹב סֶלָה:

ז שְׂאוּ שְׁעָרִים ׀ רָאשֵׁיכֶם וְהִנָּשְׂאוּ פִּתְחֵי עוֹלָם
וְיָבוֹא מֶלֶךְ הַכָּבוֹד:

מזמור כד *Psalm 24:* Our psalm asserts that God is a transcendent Being, standing outside the universe that He created. *The earth is the* L*ORD's and all that is in it.* As such, He is unreachable by man.

Can a creature address its Creator? Can a mortal relate to the Eternal? Our psalm answers those questions with a resounding "Yes." Man can *ascend the mountain of the* L*ORD.*

8. Who is the King of Glory?
The LORD, strong and mighty,
the LORD, mighty in battle.

9. Lift up your heads, you gates,
lift them up, you everlasting doors,
that the King of Glory may come in.

10. Who is He, this King of Glory?
The LORD of Hosts, He is the King of Glory. *Selah*

---

which is named the King of Glory must expand the horizons of his soul to encompass both the ethical and the spiritual. Ethical purity is necessary, but not sufficient; holiness is also required.

Ethical conduct alone will not open the gates. *Lift up your heads, you gates.* There is more to be done.

Our tradition distinguishes between the realm of "between man and his fellow," the ethical, and the realm of "between man and God," the spiritual. Both are necessary, and our psalm teaches us the proper sequence.

The journey must begin with *clean hands and a pure heart.* But it cannot end there if the King of Glory is to *come in.* For that the "gates must first lift their heads" in a supreme spiritual effort.

The precise nature of that effort is left undefined. It remains a mystery for each of us to solve on our own.

ח מִי זֶה מֶלֶךְ הַכָּבוֹד
יהוה עִזּוּז וְגִבּוֹר
יהוה גִּבּוֹר מִלְחָמָה׃

ט שְׂאוּ שְׁעָרִים ׀ רָאשֵׁיכֶם וּשְׂאוּ פִּתְחֵי עוֹלָם
וְיָבֹא מֶלֶךְ הַכָּבוֹד׃

י מִי הוּא זֶה מֶלֶךְ הַכָּבוֹד
יהוה צְבָאוֹת הוּא מֶלֶךְ הַכָּבוֹד סֶלָה׃

---

such is the generation of those who search for Him. That is the message of the first six verses of our psalm. At the end of the sixth verse the word *Selah* appears, signaling that we are about to progress to a new level, one which will require a raised voice and more intense concentration.

The person whose thought, speech, and action are without blemish is entitled to *stand in His holy place.* He earns a *generous reward from God his savior.* But he cannot yet encounter *the King of Glory.*

Such an encounter requires even more than ethical perfection. It requires holiness.

The person who strives for a glimpse of that higher aspect of the Divine

PSALM 25

1. Of David.
To You, LORD, I lift up my soul.

2. My God, in You I trust;
do not let me be put to shame,
do not let my enemies triumph over me.

3. Let no one whose hope is in You ever be put to shame;
only those are put to shame
who wantonly break faith.

4. Show me Your ways, LORD;
teach me Your paths.

5. Guide me in Your truth and teach me,
for You are the God who will save me,
and my hope is in You all day long.

6. Remember, LORD, Your tender mercy
and Your loving-kindness,
for they are from of old.

7. Do not remember the sins of my youth and my faults,
but remember me according to Your loving-kindness,
in keeping with Your goodness, LORD.

Our psalm differs from the preceding ones in yet another way. It is the first of several psalms in which the verses are arranged alphabetically. Wherever such is the case, we will discover that the theme of the psalm is of special importance.

The brevity and directness of our psalm's beginning, and the fact that its verses follow the alphabetical sequence, suggest that David is here expressing thoughts and feelings which are particularly personal, and unique to the historic role he plays.

He is a leader; indeed, he is the leader. None is above him. As such, he bears the ultimate responsibility for the people he leads.

David carries the burden of leadership alone. David incorporates his

מזמור כה

I never asked for all of these responsibilities. I am stuck with them. I am in way over my head. Who can help me handle it all? Can God be my guide? There is no one else for me to rely on.

א לְדָוִד
אֵלֶיךָ יְהוָה נַפְשִׁי אֶשָּׂא׃

ב אֱלֹהַי
בְּךָ בָטַחְתִּי אַל־אֵבוֹשָׁה
אַל־יַעַלְצוּ אוֹיְבַי לִי׃

ג גַּם כָּל־קוֶֹיךָ לֹא יֵבֹשׁוּ
יֵבֹשׁוּ הַבּוֹגְדִים רֵיקָם׃

ד דְּרָכֶיךָ יְהוָה הוֹדִיעֵנִי
אֹרְחוֹתֶיךָ לַמְּדֵנִי׃

ה הַדְרִיכֵנִי בַאֲמִתֶּךָ ׀ וְלַמְּדֵנִי
כִּי־אַתָּה אֱלֹהֵי יִשְׁעִי
אוֹתְךָ קִוִּיתִי כָּל־הַיּוֹם׃

ו זְכֹר־רַחֲמֶיךָ יְהוָה וַחֲסָדֶיךָ
כִּי מֵעוֹלָם הֵמָּה׃

ז חַטֹּאות נְעוּרַי ׀ וּפְשָׁעַי אַל־תִּזְכֹּר
כְּחַסְדְּךָ זְכָר־לִי־אַתָּה
לְמַעַן טוּבְךָ יְהוָה׃

מזמור כה *Psalm 25:* Our psalm begins simply – *Of David.* Unlike any of the preceding psalms, there are no other words in its title. It is not *Of David. A psalm,* and not *A psalm of David,* and certainly not *For the Chief Musician. A psalm of David.*

8. Good and upright is the Lord,
therefore He instructs sinners the way they should go.

9. He guides the humble in the right path,
and teaches the humble His way.

10. All the ways of the Lord are kindness and truth
to those who keep His covenant and His rules.

11. For the sake of Your name, Lord,
forgive my iniquity, though it is great.

12. Who, then, is the man who fears the Lord?
He will guide him along the path he will choose.

13. Such a man shall live in prosperity,
and his children shall inherit the land.

14. The Lord confides in those who fear Him;
to them He makes known His covenant.

15. My eyes are ever on the Lord,
for only He can free my feet from the net.

16. Turn to me and show me favor,
for I am alone and in pain.

As the Midrash has it: "I am praying for me and for Your people Israel. The eyes of all of Israel are looking up at me, and my eyes are looking up at You. If You hear my prayer, You will be hearing their prayers as well."

David knows yet another advantage of leadership. The leader can call upon special guidance from the Almighty, and depend with great confidence that he will obtain that guidance. He dares to ask: *Show me Your ways, Lord; teach me Your paths.* He believes that God *instructs sinners in the way they should go,* and trusts Him to *guide him along the path he will choose*

The lesson here, a common one in the Bible, is that when God chooses a leader, He does not abandon him. He stands by him, inspires him with special wisdom, and blesses him with His guidance. *The Lord confides in those who fear Him.*

Because he is not blind to his own shortcomings, David also prays: *Do*

ח טוֹב־וְיָשָׁר יְהוָה
עַל־כֵּן יוֹרֶה חַטָּאִים בַּדָּרֶךְ׃

ט יַדְרֵךְ עֲנָוִים בַּמִּשְׁפָּט
וִילַמֵּד עֲנָוִים דַּרְכּוֹ׃

י כָּל־אָרְחוֹת יְהוָה חֶסֶד וֶאֱמֶת
לְנֹצְרֵי בְרִיתוֹ וְעֵדֹתָיו׃

יא לְמַעַן־שִׁמְךָ יְהוָה
וְסָלַחְתָּ לַעֲוֺנִי כִּי רַב־הוּא׃

יב מִי־זֶה הָאִישׁ יְרֵא יְהוָה
יוֹרֶנּוּ בְּדֶרֶךְ יִבְחָר׃

יג נַפְשׁוֹ בְּטוֹב תָּלִין
וְזַרְעוֹ יִירַשׁ אָרֶץ׃

יד סוֹד יְהוָה לִירֵאָיו
וּבְרִיתוֹ לְהוֹדִיעָם׃

טו עֵינַי תָּמִיד אֶל־יְהוָה
כִּי הוּא־יוֹצִיא מֵרֶשֶׁת רַגְלָי׃

טז פְּנֵה־אֵלַי וְחָנֵּנִי
כִּי־יָחִיד וְעָנִי אָנִי׃

---

aloneness into his prayer, and attempts to use it to persuade God to grant him special favor. *Turn to me and show me favor, for I am alone and in pain.* The very fact that he is alone is sufficient for him to feel assured that God will hear his prayer.

As leader, David is not just praying for himself. He is praying for an entire people, all of whom trust in God. This gives him further cause for confidence in God's succor. *Let no one whose hope is in You ever be put to shame.*

17. The troubles of my heart have increased;
lead me out of my distress.

18. Consider my pain and my toil,
and tolerate all my sins.

19. See how numerous are my enemies,
how they hate me for naught.

20. Guard me and deliver me;
let me not be put to shame,
for I seek refuge in You.

21. May integrity and uprightness protect me,
for in You, Lord, is my hope.

22. O God, redeem Israel
from all its troubles.

---

mighty kings like David. The lessons of this psalm are lessons for us all: none of us is alone; we all bear responsibility for others; we all can beseech God to grant us His benevolent guidance; and we all must seek His forgiveness if we are to overcome our faults and succeed in our life's mission.

We may not all be kings, but however modest our circumstances, we are all leaders.

יז צָר֣וֹת לְבָבִ֣י הִרְחִ֑יבוּ
מִ֝מְּצֽוּקוֹתַ֗י הוֹצִיאֵֽנִי׃

יח רְאֵ֣ה עָ֭נְיִי וַעֲמָלִ֑י
וְ֝שָׂ֗א לְכָל־חַטֹּאותָֽי׃

יט רְאֵֽה־אוֹיְבַ֥י כִּי־רָ֑בּוּ
וְשִׂנְאַ֖ת חָמָ֣ס שְׂנֵאֽוּנִי׃

כ שָׁמְרָ֣ה נַ֭פְשִׁי וְהַצִּילֵ֑נִי
אַל־אֵ֝ב֗וֹשׁ כִּֽי־חָסִ֥יתִי בָֽךְ׃

כא תֹּם־וָיֹ֥שֶׁר יִצְּר֑וּנִי
כִּ֝֗י קִוִּיתִֽיךָ׃

כב פְּדֵ֣ה אֱ֭לֹהִים אֶת־יִשְׂרָאֵ֑ל
מִ֝כֹּ֗ל צָֽרוֹתָיו׃

---

not remember the sins of my youth and my faults, but remember me according to Your loving-kindness.

He faces his weaknesses. He has forgotten neither the misdeeds of his past nor his present imperfections. He most certainly does not want his people to suffer because of his faults.

The reader of our psalm misses an opportunity if he limits its lessons to

PSALM 26

1. Of David.
Judge me, LORD, for I have led a blameless life;
I have trusted in the LORD;
I have not wavered.

2. Test me, LORD, and try me,
probe my heart and mind.

3. For Your loving-kindness is ever before my eyes;
I walk continually in Your truth.

4. I do not sit in the company of false men,
or associate with hypocrites.

5. I detest the company of evildoers,
and refuse to sit with the wicked.

6. I wash my hands in innocence,
and join the procession round Your altar,

7. singing songs of thanksgiving,
and telling all Your wondrous deeds.

---

the *Kabbalat Shabbat* service every Friday evening, contains this phrase: *Let the heavens rejoice and the earth be glad…for He is coming to judge the earth.*

The Midrash addresses this problem, albeit indirectly, by seeking to reconcile the verse in our psalm: "*Judge me, LORD, for I have led a blameless life*" with the second verse in Psalm 143, which reads: "*Do not enter into judgment with Your servant, for no man living is righteous before You.*"

In our psalm David asks for God's judgment. In the later psalm, he beseeches God not to judge him. How are we to comprehend this inconsistency?

The Midrash ingeniously resolves the contradiction as follows: "Said David before the Holy One blessed be He: 'During those times when You judge the wicked, *Judge me, LORD*. But when You are busy judging the righteous, *Do not enter into judgment with Your servant!*'"

מזמור כו

I can't tolerate phonies. I may not be perfect, but at least I am sincere. I don't preach one thing and then do another. I dislike hypocrites. I avoid them when I can.

א לְדָוִד ׀ שָׁפְטֵנִי יְהוָה כִּי־אֲנִי בְּתֻמִּי הָלַכְתִּי
וּבַיהוָה בָּטַחְתִּי לֹא אֶמְעָד׃

ב בְּחָנֵנִי יְהוָה וְנַסֵּנִי
צרופה כִלְיוֹתַי וְלִבִּי׃ צָרְפָה

ג כִּי־חַסְדְּךָ לְנֶגֶד עֵינָי
וְהִתְהַלַּכְתִּי בַּאֲמִתֶּךָ׃

ד לֹא־יָשַׁבְתִּי עִם־מְתֵי־שָׁוְא
וְעִם נַעֲלָמִים לֹא אָבוֹא׃

ה שָׂנֵאתִי קְהַל מְרֵעִים
וְעִם־רְשָׁעִים לֹא אֵשֵׁב׃

ו אֶרְחַץ בְּנִקָּיוֹן כַּפָּי
וַאֲסֹבְבָה אֶת־מִזְבַּחֲךָ יְהוָה׃

ז לַשְׁמִעַ בְּקוֹל תּוֹדָה
וּלְסַפֵּר כָּל־נִפְלְאוֹתֶיךָ׃

מזמור כו *Psalm 26:* The great Christian writer C. S. Lewis found psalms such as ours very difficult from his religious perspective. He writes that "it was with great surprise that I first noticed how the psalmists talk about the judgments of God." He explains that, for a Christian, God's judgment is something to be feared, not something to be desired. He wonders how David can begin our psalm by asking God to judge him.

Lewis' surprise was magnified when he discovered that, in some psalms, God's judgment is not only longed for, but is an occasion for rejoicing. For example, Psalm 96, with which Jews are familiar because it is recited during

8. Lord, I love the house where You dwell,
the place where Your glory resides.

9. Do not sweep my soul away with sinners,
nor my life with bloodthirsty men,

10. in whose hands are evil schemes,
and whose right hand is full of bribes.

11. As for me, I lead a blameless life;
redeem me, and be merciful to me.

12. My foot stands on level ground;
in the assemblies I will bless the Lord.

"It is only with regard to his actions and deeds," continues Radak, "that David says *Do not enter into judgment with Your servant.*" He does not fear being judged for his thoughts.

C. S. Lewis shares with us his Christian surprise at David's willingness to be judged. But the Jewish attitude is that there are indeed many circumstances in which the quest to be judged is warranted and perfectly understandable. The Midrash and Radak provide us with two such circumstances. The reader who takes the trouble to study other Jewish commentaries will discover many more.

One other such circumstance is the appreciation of God's loving-kindness. He who is convinced, as David was, that *Your loving-kindness is ever before my eyes,* will not be reluctant to confront God's judgment. Indeed, he will be eager to do so.

ח יְהוָה אָהַבְתִּי מְעוֹן בֵּיתֶךָ
וּמְקוֹם מִשְׁכַּן כְּבוֹדֶךָ׃

ט אַל־תֶּאֱסֹף עִם־חַטָּאִים נַפְשִׁי
וְעִם־אַנְשֵׁי דָמִים חַיָּי׃

י אֲשֶׁר־בִּידֵיהֶם זִמָּה
וִימִינָם מָלְאָה שֹּׁחַד׃

יא וַאֲנִי בְּתֻמִּי אֵלֵךְ
פְּדֵנִי וְחָנֵּנִי׃

יב רַגְלִי עָמְדָה בְמִישׁוֹר
בְּמַקְהֵלִים אֲבָרֵךְ יְהוָה׃

The Midrash knows well that the degree of one's guilt or innocence is a relative matter. Compared to the truly wicked, David could be confident in his righteousness, and did not need to fear God's judgment. However, in comparison with the truly righteous, he felt that he stood no chance, and thus prayed that he not be judged.

Radak suggests another approach to resolving the contradiction. He draws our attention to the phrase in verse 2 which reads *probe my heart and mind*. David is willing to be judged for what he is feeling and thinking. It is his actual behavior for which he wishes to escape judgment.

Radak paraphrases David's words: "*Judge me* according to my intentions, for even though my actions are occasionally improper, my heart is upright at all times."

PSALM 27

1. Of David.
The LORD is my light and my salvation;
whom shall I fear?
The LORD is the stronghold of my life;
of whom shall I be afraid?

2. When evildoers close in on me to devour my flesh –
it is they, my adversaries and my foes, who stumble and fall.

3. If an army should encamp against me,
my heart would not fear;
if war should break out against me,
I would still be confident.

4. One thing I ask of the LORD, this only I seek:
to live in the house of the LORD all the days of my life,
to gaze upon the beauty of the LORD,
and to worship in His Temple.

5. For He will shelter me in His pavilion
on the day of trouble,
He will hide me under cover of His tent,
He will set me high upon a rock.

This same pair of words appears repetitively in the Book of Esther. There the King asks Esther: *What is your wish (ma she'elatekh)? And what is your request (ma bakashatekh)?* Esther replies with the same couplet: *My wish… my request (she'elati uvakashati)* (Est. 5:6–7).

Rabbi Yonatan Eybeschutz, a prolific eighteenth-century rabbinic scholar, elucidates the subtle difference between these two closely related words. "A request for something which is transient is termed *she'ela*. But for a request for something which is enduring, and certainly for something which is eternal, the term *bakasha* is used."

Rabbi Eybeschutz' application of his distinction to the Esther narrative

מזמור כז

My outer life is full. But my inner life is empty. A voice inside of me is calling. I strain to hear it. What is it saying?

א לְדָוִד ׀ יְהוָה ׀ אוֹרִי וְיִשְׁעִי מִמִּי אִירָא
יְהוָה מָעוֹז־חַיַּי מִמִּי אֶפְחָד׃

ב בִּקְרֹב עָלַי ׀ מְרֵעִים לֶאֱכֹל אֶת־בְּשָׂרִי
צָרַי וְאֹיְבַי לִי
הֵמָּה כָשְׁלוּ וְנָפָלוּ׃

ג אִם־תַּחֲנֶה עָלַי ׀ מַחֲנֶה לֹא־יִירָא לִבִּי
אִם־תָּקוּם עָלַי מִלְחָמָה בְּזֹאת אֲנִי בוֹטֵחַ׃

ד אַחַת ׀ שָׁאַלְתִּי מֵאֵת־יְהוָה אוֹתָהּ אֲבַקֵּשׁ
שִׁבְתִּי בְּבֵית־יְהוָה כָּל־יְמֵי חַיַּי
לַחֲזוֹת בְּנֹעַם־יְהוָה וּלְבַקֵּר בְּהֵיכָלוֹ׃

ה כִּי יִצְפְּנֵנִי ׀ בְּסֻכֹּה בְּיוֹם רָעָה
יַסְתִּרֵנִי בְּסֵתֶר אָהֳלוֹ
בְּצוּר יְרוֹמְמֵנִי׃

מזמור כז *Psalm 27:* In our psalm David expresses his trust in God. In spite of his many enemies he asks, *of whom shall I be afraid?* He is sure that his adversaries will *stumble and fall.* He is ready to do battle, and feels certain of victory.

But he wants more than worldly achievements, victories for his body. His soul calls out to him: *On Your behalf my heart says, "Seek My face!"*

He searches for meaning and purpose. He wants opportunities for prayer and meditation. *One thing I ask of the Lord, this only I seek: to live in the house of the Lord all the days of my life, to gaze upon the beauty of the Lord.*

He "asks" (Hebrew: *sha'alti*) and he "seeks" (Hebrew: *avakesh*). Are these words perfectly synonymous, or do they have slightly different shades of meaning?

6. Now my head is raised high above my enemies around me;
I will sacrifice in His tent with shouts of joy,
I will sing and chant praises to the LORD.

7. LORD, hear my voice when I call;
be gracious to me, and answer me.

8. On Your behalf my heart says,
"Seek My face!"
Therefore I will seek Your face, LORD.

9. Do not hide Your face from me;
do not turn Your servant away in anger.
You have always been my help.
Do not reject me nor forsake me, God, my savior.

10. Though my father and mother forsake me,
the LORD will take me in.

11. Teach me Your way, LORD,
and lead me on a level path,
because of my foes who threaten me.

12. Do not hand me over to the will of my adversaries;
for false witnesses have risen up against me,
breathing out violence.

---

his fleeting this-worldly life in the house of God, engaged in prayer and contemplation."

But as a consequence of the fulfillment of his *she'ela,* his "temporary" residence in God's earthly abode, he anticipated that his *bakasha,* his eternal request *to gaze upon the beauty of the LORD,* would be granted to him as well.

Rabbi Eybeschutz imparts a basic Jewish teaching here. The mundane world and the eternal world are not identical to each other. But they are somehow parallel to each other, so that when we achieve our earthly spiritual objectives, we already partake of celestial spiritual rewards.

ו וְעַתָּה יָרוּם רֹאשִׁי עַל אֹיְבַי סְבִיבוֹתַי
וְאֶזְבְּחָה בְאָהֳלוֹ זִבְחֵי תְרוּעָה
אָשִׁירָה וַאֲזַמְּרָה לַיהוָה׃

ז שְׁמַע־יְהוָה קוֹלִי אֶקְרָא וְחָנֵּנִי וַעֲנֵנִי׃

ח לְךָ ׀ אָמַר לִבִּי בַּקְּשׁוּ פָנָי
אֶת־פָּנֶיךָ יְהוָה אֲבַקֵּשׁ׃

ט אַל־תַּסְתֵּר פָּנֶיךָ ׀ מִמֶּנִּי אַל תַּט־בְּאַף עַבְדֶּךָ
עֶזְרָתִי הָיִיתָ
אַל־תִּטְּשֵׁנִי וְאַל־תַּעַזְבֵנִי אֱלֹהֵי יִשְׁעִי׃

י כִּי־אָבִי וְאִמִּי עֲזָבוּנִי
וַיהוָה יַאַסְפֵנִי׃

יא הוֹרֵנִי יְהוָה דַּרְכֶּךָ
וּנְחֵנִי בְּאֹרַח מִישׁוֹר לְמַעַן שׁוֹרְרָי׃

יב אַל־תִּתְּנֵנִי בְּנֶפֶשׁ צָרָי
כִּי קָמוּ־בִי עֵדֵי־שֶׁקֶר וִיפֵחַ חָמָס׃

---

need not concern us here. The interested reader can find it in his collection of sermons, *Yaarot Devash*, Part I, Sermon 17.

But let us see how Rabbi Eybeschutz uses his nuanced distinction to interpret our text.

One thing I ask of the Lord (aḥat sha'alti). David asks that he spend *all the days of my life* in God's house. Rabbi Eybeschutz surprises us by insisting that "all of one's life" is a short-term request. "This is because," he writes, "few in number are a man's days on this earth."

"Thus," he continues, "David's *she'ela,* or short-term wish, was to spend

13. Had I not believed that I would see the LORD's goodness
in the land of the living....*

14. Place your hope in the LORD, be courageous and He will
strengthen your heart;
and place your hope in the LORD!

* The verse is left unfinished for effect, the concluding thought being "I would have despaired."

---

a foretaste of the World to Come, here and now. Live in God's house on earth, and you are already *gazing upon the beauty of the LORD.*

יג לׅׄוּלֵׅׄ֗אׅׄ הֶ֭אֱמַנְתִּי לִרְא֥וֹת בְּֽטוּב־יְהוָ֗ה
בְּאֶ֣רֶץ חַיִּֽים׃

יד קַוֵּ֗ה אֶל־יְה֫וָ֥ה
חֲ֭זַק וְיַאֲמֵ֣ץ לִבֶּ֑ךָ
וְ֝קַוֵּ֗ה אֶל־יְהוָֽה׃

David's two requests, his *she'ela* and his *bakasha,* are thus in some sense one and the same: If one sojourns in this world's "house of God," one experiences

PSALM 28

1. Of David.
To You, LORD, I call;
O my rock, be not deaf to my cry.
For if You remain silent,
I shall be like those who go down to the grave.

2. Hear my cry when I call to You for help,
when I lift my hands toward Your holy sanctuary.

3. Do not drag me away with the wicked,
with evildoers, who speak peace with their neighbors
while malice is in their hearts.

4. Repay them for their deeds and their malicious acts;
repay them for what their hands have done;
give them their deserts.

5. For they give no thought to the works of the LORD,
and what His hands have done;
may He tear them down and never build them up!

---

be qualified for the tasks that he assigned them, and he could never know for sure that they would be faithful to him.

Characteristically, when David feels that a situation is impossible, he turns to God. He teaches us in our psalm, and in so many others, that one must humbly recognize and courageously acknowledge one's helplessness, and then call upon the Almighty.

David teaches us to turn to God when we feel that there is no other resort. *For if You remain silent, I shall be like those who go down to the grave.*

David knows that he must choose colleagues and allies. He cannot govern alone. But men are so hard to read. He can never be sure of his own choices. He prays: *do not drag me away with the wicked.*

When he is confident that he has successfully found the right inner circle to help him lead effectively he enthusiastically thanks God. He does not take

מזמור כח

I couldn't survive without friends. But some of them have let me down in a big way. How can I learn to choose the right friends? I can pray to God to help me. I can celebrate when He steers me in the right direction.

א לְדָוִד אֵלֶיךָ יהוה ׀ אֶקְרָא
צוּרִי אַל־תֶּחֱרַשׁ מִמֶּנִּי
פֶּן־תֶּחֱשֶׁה מִמֶּנִּי
וְנִמְשַׁלְתִּי עִם־יוֹרְדֵי בוֹר׃

ב שְׁמַע קוֹל תַּחֲנוּנַי בְּשַׁוְּעִי אֵלֶיךָ
בְּנָשְׂאִי יָדַי אֶל־דְּבִיר קָדְשֶׁךָ׃

ג אַל־תִּמְשְׁכֵנִי עִם־רְשָׁעִים וְעִם־פֹּעֲלֵי אָוֶן
דֹּבְרֵי שָׁלוֹם עִם־רֵעֵיהֶם
וְרָעָה בִּלְבָבָם׃

ד תֶּן־לָהֶם כְּפָעֳלָם וּכְרֹעַ מַעַלְלֵיהֶם
כְּמַעֲשֵׂה יְדֵיהֶם תֵּן לָהֶם
הָשֵׁב גְּמוּלָם לָהֶם׃

ה כִּי לֹא יָבִינוּ אֶל־פְּעֻלֹּת יהוה וְאֶל־מַעֲשֵׂה יָדָיו
יֶהֶרְסֵם וְלֹא יִבְנֵם׃

מזמור כח *Psalm 28:* No man is an island. We need others for companionship, for advice, and for assistance in times of need.

Leaders especially cannot go it alone. Many are tempted to do so. Others surround themselves with advisors, only to be disappointed by their incompetence, or betrayed by their untrustworthiness.

David knew well that he could not lead the People of Israel without the help of capable assistants and advisors. But he also knew from bitter experience that he could never be assured that the men he chose as associates would

6. Blessed be the LORD
for He has heard my cry for mercy.

7. The LORD is my strength and my shield;
in Him my heart trusts, and I am helped.
Now my heart exults,
and I praise Him with my song.

8. The LORD is the strength of those* [loyal to Him],
a safe refuge for His anointed.

9. O save Your people, bless Your heritage;
feed them and sustain them forever!

* Or: "His people."

Here too he turns to God: *O save Your people, bless Your heritage; feed them and sustain them forever.*

No wonder then that we find the following description of David as he first began his leadership career, even before he was crowned king: "*David was successful in all his undertakings, for the LORD was with him*" (1 Sam. 18:14).

ו בָּר֥וּךְ יְהוָ֑ה כִּֽי־שָׁ֝מַע ק֣וֹל תַּחֲנוּנָֽי׃

ז יְהוָ֤ה ׀ עֻזִּ֥י וּמָגִנִּ֗י
בּ֤וֹ בָטַ֥ח לִבִּ֗י וְֽנֶעֱזָ֫רְתִּי
וַיַּעֲלֹ֥ז לִבִּ֑י וּֽמִשִּׁירִ֥י אֲהוֹדֶֽנּוּ׃

ח יְהוָ֥ה עֹֽז־לָ֑מוֹ
וּמָ֘ע֤וֹז יְשׁוּע֖וֹת מְשִׁיח֣וֹ הֽוּא׃

ט הוֹשִׁ֤יעָה ׀ אֶת־עַמֶּ֗ךָ וּבָרֵ֥ךְ אֶת־נַחֲלָתֶ֑ךָ
וּֽרְעֵ֥ם וְ֝נַשְּׂאֵ֗ם עַד־הָעוֹלָֽם׃

---

credit personally for his wise choices of personnel. *The Lord is my strength and my shield; in Him my heart trusts, and I am helped.*

But a skilled and devoted leadership team is not enough. He must creatively and effectively engage his followers, who are quite likely to be unable or unwilling to follow his lead.

PSALM 29

1. A psalm of David. *Fifth day of the month*
Ascribe to the LORD, you divine beings,
ascribe to the LORD glory and strength.

2. Ascribe to the LORD the glory due to His name,
worship Him in the splendor of holiness.

3. The voice of the LORD echoes over the waters;
the God of glory, the LORD, thunders over the mighty waters.

4. The voice of the LORD is full of power;
the voice of the LORD is full of majesty.

5. The voice of the LORD breaks cedars,
the LORD shatters the cedars of Lebanon.

6. He makes Lebanon skip like a calf,
Sirion like a young wild ox.

---

several psalms which comprise the *Kabbalat Shabbat* service, ushering in the Sabbath every Friday evening.

But there is a deeper connection which he perceives in the Talmudic passage which discusses the structure of the *Amida,* or central set of prayers, on the Sabbath. Unlike the weekday *Amida,* which originally had eighteen blessings, the Sabbath *Amida* has but seven.

The Talmud asks (*Berakhot* 29a):

"Corresponding to what were these seven blessings of the Sabbath *Amida* instituted?"

It answers:

"R. Ḥalafta b. Shaul said: 'Corresponding to the seven "voices" which David mentioned on the waters.'" In other words, the very structure of the Sabbath *Amida* is based upon the seven times that the phrase "voice of God" is mentioned in our psalm.

What hidden relationship exists between our psalm and the Sabbath?

This is Rav Kook's answer, freely translated from his commentary on the Prayer Book, *Olat Re'iya*:

מזמור כט

Have you ever really felt God?
I never did until that camping trip.
We were outdoors in a hurricane, for three days and three nights.
Trees were falling, streams were overflowing, thunder was roaring.
That's when I first felt God.

ה לחודש

א מִזְמ֗וֹר לְדָ֫וִ֥ד
הָב֣וּ לַֽ֭יהוה בְּנֵ֣י אֵלִ֑ים
הָב֥וּ לַ֝יהוה כָּב֥וֹד וָעֹֽז׃

ב הָב֣וּ לַֽ֭יהוה כְּב֣וֹד שְׁמ֑וֹ
הִשְׁתַּחֲו֥וּ לַ֝יהוה בְּהַדְרַת־קֹֽדֶשׁ׃

ג ק֥וֹל יהוה עַל־הַ֫מָּ֥יִם
אֵֽל־הַכָּב֥וֹד הִרְעִ֑ים
יהוה עַל־מַ֥יִם רַבִּֽים׃

ד קוֹל־יהוה בַּכֹּ֑חַ
ק֥וֹל יהוה בֶּהָדָֽר׃

ה ק֣וֹל יהוה שֹׁבֵ֣ר אֲרָזִ֑ים
וַיְשַׁבֵּ֥ר יהוה אֶת־אַרְזֵ֥י הַלְּבָנֽוֹן׃

ו וַיַּרְקִידֵ֥ם כְּמוֹ־עֵ֑גֶל
לְ֝בָנ֥וֹן וְשִׂרְיֹ֗ן כְּמ֣וֹ בֶן־רְאֵמִֽים׃

מזמור כט *Psalm 29:* How are we to understand our psalm? Does it describe God's power in the context of nature? Or is it a metaphor, as some commentators would have it, for some event of great grandeur? Might it depict the Revelation on Mount Sinai, for example; or perhaps the apocalyptic wars of Gog and Magog?

Rav Kook finds in our psalm a profound mystical teaching. He notes the connection between our psalm and the Sabbath. For one thing, it is one of

7. The voice of the LORD flashes flames of fire.

8. The voice of the LORD makes the desert quake;
the LORD makes the wilderness of Kadesh tremble.

9. The voice of the LORD makes hinds calve,
and strips the forests bare;
while in His Temple all cry: "Glory!"

10. The LORD was enthroned at the flood;
the LORD sits enthroned as King forever.

11. The LORD will give strength to His people;
the LORD will bless His people with peace.

"So it is," concludes Rav Kook, "with Man's glory. At first glance, we observe Man's greatness only in his physical accomplishments, in his works of art and his technological achievements. We dismiss his day of rest as an episode of sloth, decay, boredom, and nothingness.

"But in truth it is that Sabbath day which is his crown of perfection. It is the seventh day which brings meaning and purpose to the other six."

The seven voices of our psalm correspond to the seven days of the week. Our psalm drives home the point that just as God's ultimate glory is to be found precisely where it is not apparent, so too man's ultimate creative spirit will not be found in farm, factory, and urban hubbub. It will be found around the Sabbath table, in the light of its modest candles, and in the music of its melodies.

ז קוֹל־יְהוָה חֹצֵב לַהֲבוֹת אֵשׁ׃

ח קוֹל יְהוָה יָחִיל מִדְבָּר
יָחִיל יְהוָה מִדְבַּר קָדֵשׁ׃

ט קוֹל יְהוָה ׀ יְחוֹלֵל אַיָּלוֹת וַיֶּחֱשֹׂף יְעָרוֹת
וּבְהֵיכָלוֹ כֻּלּוֹ אֹמֵר כָּבוֹד׃

י יְהוָה לַמַּבּוּל יָשָׁב
וַיֵּשֶׁב יְהוָה מֶלֶךְ לְעוֹלָם׃

יא יְהוָה עֹז לְעַמּוֹ יִתֵּן
יְהוָה ׀ יְבָרֵךְ אֶת־עַמּוֹ בַשָּׁלוֹם׃

We see perfection in the universe when we behold intact, unspoiled, and flourishing nature. We do not see perfection in ruins, destruction, and desolation. But when we contemplate the latter more carefully, subjecting them to scientific analysis, we detect signs of divine wisdom in what we thought were nature's wastelands.

This is the significance of David "seven voices" on the water. *The voice of the LORD breaks cedars;* it *shatters the cedars of Lebanon.* His voice *flashes flames of fire,* it *makes the desert quake.* It *strips the forest bare.* Yet in that abyss of destruction can be found God's glory. That desolation is where He *sits enthroned as King forever.*

PSALM 30

1. A psalm. A song for the dedication of the Temple. Of David. *Monday*

2. I will extol You, Lord,
for You have lifted me up,
and have not let my enemies rejoice over me.

3. Lord, my God, I cried out to You,
and You healed me.

4. Lord, You brought up my soul from Sheol,
You saved my life from going down to the pit.

5. Sing to the Lord, O you His faithful ones,
and praise His holy name.

6. For His anger lasts but a moment,
His favor a lifetime;
weeping may linger at nightfall,
but joy comes in the morning.

7. When I was carefree, I thought,
"I shall never be shaken."

---

to the pit. Sheol and *the pit* are both synonyms for the grave. The two halves of this verse are generally understood as saying the same thing in different words for poetic effect.

One commentator, however, suggests that the two terms, while similar, are not synonymous, and the two halves of the verse are not mere mirror images of each other.

That commentator is Rav Kook. His interpretation is found in *Olat Re'iya*, his commentary on the Siddur, or Daily Prayer Book. Our psalm is the first psalm recited in our daily prayers.

Rav Kook explains that a person's vitality can be so diminished by "panic, fear, anxiety, and anguish of the soul" that almost all traces of humanity vanish. All that is left is the desire to survive. All the means of achieving that desire are lacking, but the will to live remains. Such a person has descended

מזמור ל

I was complacent. I thought I had it made. Everything changed in the blink of an eye. Joyous dance turned into heartbreak. Another blink of an eye, and again everything changed. I danced once more.

א מִזְמוֹר שִׁיר־חֲנֻכַּת הַבַּיִת לְדָוִד׃ ליום שני

ב אֲרוֹמִמְךָ יהוה כִּי דִלִּיתָנִי
וְלֹא־שִׂמַּחְתָּ אֹיְבַי לִי׃

ג יְהוָה אֱלֹהָי
שִׁוַּעְתִּי אֵלֶיךָ וַתִּרְפָּאֵנִי׃

ד יְהוָה הֶעֱלִיתָ מִן־שְׁאוֹל נַפְשִׁי
חִיִּיתַנִי מיורדי־בוֹר׃ מִיָּרְדִי־

ה זַמְּרוּ לַיהוָה חֲסִידָיו
וְהוֹדוּ לְזֵכֶר קָדְשׁוֹ׃

ו כִּי רֶגַע ׀ בְּאַפּוֹ חַיִּים בִּרְצוֹנוֹ
בָּעֶרֶב יָלִין בֶּכִי וְלַבֹּקֶר רִנָּה׃

ז וַאֲנִי אָמַרְתִּי בְשַׁלְוִי
בַּל־אֶמּוֹט לְעוֹלָם׃

מזמור ל *Psalm 30:* Our psalm is an eloquent expression of what we all know, but choose to forget. Life is tenuous.

One day we are arrogantly confident that we *shall never be shaken,* but the next day dawns, *God hides His face,* and we find ourselves cowering in terror.

Luckily, that terror too can be astonishingly short-lived. *Weeping may linger at nightfall, but joy comes in the morning.* Nothing is permanent, everything is ephemeral.

Depictions of the transience of life are somber enough. But there is another verse in our psalm which is yet gloomier, evoking images of the nether world: *Lord, You brought up my soul from Sheol, You saved my life from going down*

8. Lord, when I enjoyed Your favor,
You made me stand firm as a mighty mountain;
when You hid Your face,
I was terrified.

9. To You, Lord, I called;
to the Lord I pleaded:

10. "What profit is there in my death,*
in my going down into the pit?
Can the dust acknowledge You?
Can it proclaim Your truth?"

11. Hear, Lord, and be gracious to me;
Lord, be my helper.

12. You turned my lament into dancing;
You removed my sackcloth and girded me with joy,

13. that my soul may sing Your praises and never cease.
I will acknowledge You forever, Lord my God.

*Lit. "blood."

---

vival. They had descended drastically, but not quite to *the pit.* They fell only as far as *Sheol.* But others, known in the *lager* as *Muselmänner,* were not that resilient. They led a vacuous existence, wandering about the camps in a daze, like robots bereft of every trace of humanity. These men had fallen into *the pit.* They were doomed.

God brings up our souls from *Sheol,* from that state of emotional depletion in which only the rudimentary will to live remains. *Lord, You brought up my soul from Sheol.* More than that, concludes Rav Kook, "heavenly loving-kindness penetrates to the depths, and revives even those so mired in despair that they are oblivious of life itself." God's loving-kindness can even resuscitate the *Muselmänner* of the *lager. You saved my life from going down to the pit.*

ח יְֽהֹוָ֗ה בִּרְצוֹנְךָ֮ הֶעֱמַ֪דְתָּה לְֽהַרְרִ֫י עֹ֥ז
הִסְתַּ֥רְתָּ פָנֶ֗יךָ הָיִ֥יתִי נִבְהָֽל׃

ט אֵלֶ֣יךָ יְהֹוָ֣ה אֶקְרָ֑א
וְאֶל־אֲ֝דֹנָ֗י אֶתְחַנָּֽן׃

י מַה־בֶּ֥צַע בְּדָמִי֮ בְּרִדְתִּ֪י אֶ֫ל שָׁ֥חַת
הֲיוֹדְךָ֥ עָפָ֑ר הֲיַגִּ֥יד אֲמִתֶּֽךָ׃

יא שְׁמַע־יְהֹוָ֥ה וְחָנֵּ֑נִי
יְ֝הֹוָ֗ה הֱֽיֵה־עֹזֵ֥ר לִֽי׃

יב הָפַ֥כְתָּ מִסְפְּדִי֮ לְמָח֪וֹל לִ֥֫י
פִּתַּ֥חְתָּ שַׂקִּ֑י וַתְּאַזְּרֵ֥נִי שִׂמְחָֽה׃

יג לְמַ֤עַן ׀ יְזַמֶּרְךָ֣ כָ֭בוֹד וְלֹ֣א יִדֹּ֑ם
יְהֹוָ֥ה אֱ֝לֹהַ֗י לְעוֹלָ֥ם אוֹדֶֽךָּ׃

---

to *Sheol.* Rav Kook seems to relate the word *Sheol* to the Hebrew word *sho'el,* to request or to desire.

But there is an even more pitiful state into which man can fall. That is *the pit.* Such a person has no wish to survive. "The channel of ambition which leads out of the innermost will is blocked." The Hebrew word for *the pit* is *bor*: barren, empty, void.

Although Rav Kook departed this world several years before the Holocaust, accounts written about the *lager,* the Nazi concentration camp, corroborate his distinction. Some of the inmates of those camps were in the first category. They fought to survive by any means available. They stood a chance at sur-

PSALM 31

1. For the Chief Musician. A psalm of David.

2. In You, LORD, I take refuge,
may I never be put to shame;
in Your righteousness rescue me.

3. Incline Your ear to me;
speedily deliver me.
Be a rock of refuge for me,
a stronghold to save me.

4. For You are my rock and my fortress;
for the honor of Your name lead me and guide me.

5. Free me from the net they have hidden for me,
for You are my refuge.

6. Into Your hand I commit my spirit;
redeem me, LORD, You God of truth.

7. I detest those who look to worthless vanities;
for my part I put my trust in the LORD.

8. I will exult and rejoice in Your constant loving-kindness,
for You have seen my affliction.
You know the distress of my soul,

9. and You have not handed me over to the enemy,
but have set my feet at large.

At some level we all know that one day we will die. But for most of our lives we delude ourselves and imagine that we are immortal. We do not think of our day of death. We certainly do not prepare for it.

We find that our sages did indeed imagine their dying day, and spiritually prepared themselves for it. They caution us to repent on the day before we die, and since none of us knows for sure when that day will occur, we must repent every day, for we might die tomorrow.

Furthermore, they inform us that there are several ways to resolve internal moral conflict. One is Torah study. Another is reciting the *Shema* prayer. If

מזמור לא

I struggle in two ways. I struggle to escape a sly and determined enemy. I struggle to trust God. It came to me in a flash. There is but one struggle.

א לַמְנַצֵּחַ מִזְמוֹר לְדָוִד׃

ב בְּךָ־יְהוָה חָסִיתִי אַל־אֵבוֹשָׁה לְעוֹלָם
בְּצִדְקָתְךָ פַלְּטֵנִי׃

ג הַטֵּה אֵלַי ׀ אָזְנְךָ מְהֵרָה הַצִּילֵנִי
הֱיֵה לִי ׀ לְצוּר־מָעוֹז לְבֵית מְצוּדוֹת לְהוֹשִׁיעֵנִי׃

ד כִּי־סַלְעִי וּמְצוּדָתִי אָתָּה
וּלְמַעַן שִׁמְךָ תַּנְחֵנִי וּתְנַהֲלֵנִי׃

ה תּוֹצִיאֵנִי מֵרֶשֶׁת זוּ טָמְנוּ לִי
כִּי־אַתָּה מָעוּזִּי׃

ו בְּיָדְךָ אַפְקִיד רוּחִי
פָּדִיתָה אוֹתִי יְהוָה אֵל אֱמֶת׃

ז שָׂנֵאתִי הַשֹּׁמְרִים הַבְלֵי־שָׁוְא
וַאֲנִי אֶל־יְהוָה בָּטָחְתִּי׃

ח אָגִילָה וְאֶשְׂמְחָה בְּחַסְדֶּךָ
אֲשֶׁר רָאִיתָ אֶת־עָנְיִי
יָדַעְתָּ בְּצָרוֹת נַפְשִׁי׃

ט וְלֹא הִסְגַּרְתַּנִי בְּיַד־אוֹיֵב
הֶעֱמַדְתָּ בַמֶּרְחָב רַגְלָי׃

מזמור לא *Psalm 31:* After attending his best friend's funeral, an old and ailing man once quipped, in Yiddish: "I always thought that there was a *ḥevra shtarbers*, an exclusive club to which only those who will die belong. I never thought that my good friend belonged to that club. Now I see that he did. But not me. I surely don't belong to that *ḥevra*!"

10. Have mercy on me, LORD,
for I am in distress;
my eye wastes away with sorrow,
my body and soul too.

11. My life is spent with grief,
and my years with groaning;
my strength fails because of my iniquity,
and my bones waste away.

12. Because of all my foes I have become an object of scorn,
especially so to my neighbors;
I am a horror to my friends;
those who see me in the street flee from me.

13. I have passed out of mind like the dead,
I have become like a discarded vessel.

14. For I hear the whispering of many;
there is terror on every side,
as they conspire against me
and plot to take my life.

15. But I trust in You, LORD;
I say, "You are my God."

16. My fate* lies in Your hand;
rescue me from my enemies and my pursuers.

17. Let Your face shine upon Your servant;
save me in Your constant loving-kindness.

18. LORD, let me not be put to shame when I call You;
let the wicked be ashamed and reduced to silence in Sheol.

*Lit. "my times."

"old man," whose proper name was Rabbi Simcha Zissel Ziv, lay upon his deathbed. Much to the chagrin of his disciples, he was notified by his doctor that he had but one day to live.

The disciples protested: "How can you tell the poor man such news?"

י חָנֵּנִי יהוה כִּי צַר לִי
עָשְׁשָׁה בְכַעַס עֵינִי נַפְשִׁי וּבִטְנִי:

יא כִּי כָלוּ בְיָגוֹן חַיַּי וּשְׁנוֹתַי בַּאֲנָחָה
כָּשַׁל בַּעֲוֺנִי כֹחִי וַעֲצָמַי עָשֵׁשׁוּ:

יב מִכׇּל־צֹרְרַי הָיִיתִי חֶרְפָּה וְלִשְׁכֵנַי ׀ מְאֹד
וּפַחַד לִמְיֻדָּעָי
רֹאַי בַּחוּץ נָדְדוּ מִמֶּנִּי:

יג נִשְׁכַּחְתִּי כְּמֵת מִלֵּב
הָיִיתִי כִּכְלִי אֹבֵד:

יד כִּי שָׁמַעְתִּי ׀ דִּבַּת רַבִּים מָגוֹר מִסָּבִיב
בְּהִוָּסְדָם יַחַד עָלַי
לָקַחַת נַפְשִׁי זָמָמוּ:

טו וַאֲנִי ׀ עָלֶיךָ בָטַחְתִּי יהוה
אָמַרְתִּי אֱלֹהַי אָתָּה:

טז בְּיָדְךָ עִתֹּתָי
הַצִּילֵנִי מִיַּד־אוֹיְבַי וּמֵרֹדְפָי:

יז הָאִירָה פָנֶיךָ עַל־עַבְדֶּךָ
הוֹשִׁיעֵנִי בְחַסְדֶּךָ:

יח יהוה אַל־אֵבוֹשָׁה כִּי קְרָאתִיךָ
יֵבֹשׁוּ רְשָׁעִים יִדְּמוּ לִשְׁאוֹל:

---

these don't work, there is a third method, a last resort: "He should remind himself of the day of death" (*Berakhot* 5a).

Nowadays, doctors do not hesitate to inform terminally ill patients that their days are numbered.

Back in the days of the revered "old man" of Kelm, a hundred years ago or more, doctors did not share such information with their dying patients. The

19. Let lying lips be struck dumb
that speak haughtily against the righteous
with arrogance and contempt.

20. How great is the goodness
that You have stored up for those who fear You,
that You have bestowed on those who take refuge in You
in the sight of men.

21. You hide them in the shelter of Your presence
from the intrigues of men;
You shield them in Your tent
from quarrelsome tongues.

22. Blessed be the LORD,
for He has shown to me His wonderful kindness
in a besieged city.

23. In my alarm, I said,
"I am thrust out from Your sight";
yet You heard my cry for mercy
when I called to You for help.

24. Love the LORD, all you loyal to Him!
The LORD protects the faithful,
but repays in full him who acts with pride.

25. Be strong, and let your heart take courage,
all you who wait for the LORD.

---

he was even more afraid, as he felt inadequately prepared to face God's final judgment.

However, he knew how to cope with that dreadful fear. He committed his spirit to God, trusting His mercy and understanding. He felt absolutely certain that by accepting his imminent death he was but yielding his soul to the hands of His Blessed Name, whose benevolence and kindness know no bounds.

יט תֵּאָלַמְנָה שִׂפְתֵי שָׁקֶר
הַדֹּבְרוֹת עַל־צַדִּיק עָתָק בְּגַאֲוָה וָבוּז:

כ מָה רַב טוּבְךָ אֲשֶׁר־צָפַנְתָּ לִּירֵאֶיךָ
פָּעַלְתָּ לַחֹסִים בָּךְ נֶגֶד בְּנֵי אָדָם:

כא תַּסְתִּירֵם ׀ בְּסֵתֶר פָּנֶיךָ מֵרֻכְסֵי אִישׁ
תִּצְפְּנֵם בְּסֻכָּה מֵרִיב לְשֹׁנוֹת:

כב בָּרוּךְ יְהוָה
כִּי הִפְלִיא חַסְדּוֹ לִי בְּעִיר מָצוֹר:

כג וַאֲנִי ׀ אָמַרְתִּי בְחָפְזִי נִגְרַזְתִּי מִנֶּגֶד עֵינֶיךָ
אָכֵן שָׁמַעְתָּ קוֹל תַּחֲנוּנַי בְּשַׁוְּעִי אֵלֶיךָ:

כד אֶהֱבוּ אֶת־יְהוָה כָּל־חֲסִידָיו
אֱמוּנִים נֹצֵר יְהוָה
וּמְשַׁלֵּם עַל־יֶתֶר עֹשֵׂה גַאֲוָה:

כה חִזְקוּ וְיַאֲמֵץ לְבַבְכֶם
כָּל־הַמְיַחֲלִים לַיהוָה:

To which the doctor answered: "I knew this old Jew. He was always fully aware that one day he would die. I simply told him when that day was."

One astute disciple rephrased the doctor's message in words his peers could understand. "Our Rebbe," he explained, "prepared to die every day. That is why he read aloud one particular biblical phrase as part of his evening routine."

That biblical phrase is to be found in our psalm, verse 6. It defines the central theme of our entire psalm: *Into Your hand I commit my spirit.*

The "old man" of Kelm was as afraid of death as everyone else. Arguably,

PSALM 32

1. Of David. A *maskil.*
Happy is he whose transgression is forgiven,
whose sin is covered up.

2. Happy is the man to whom the LORD imputes no guilt,
and in whose spirit there is no deceit.

3. All the time I suffered in silence, my body wasted away
through my groaning all day long.

4. For day and night Your hand lay heavy upon me;
the sap in me dried up as by the summer's heat. *Selah*

5. Then I acknowledged my sin to You,
I did not cover up my guilt.
I said, "I will confess my transgressions to the LORD";
and You forgave the guilt of my sin. *Selah*

6. Therefore let every faithful man pray to You
at the time when You may be found;
so that when a great flood of water comes rushing in
it will not reach him.

7. You are my shelter,
You will shield me from distress;
You will surround me with songs of deliverance. *Selah*

---

for them the way to rise from the pit of their misdeeds and escape the trap of their offenses.... In His great goodness He has taught them to turn to Him... He has not closed the doors of repentance to them."

The sinner experiences guilt, but also has the opportunity to attain God's forgiveness. One component of the process of gaining His forgiveness is the attitude of trust in God, *bitaḥon.* Our psalm culminates with the verse *and the man who trusts in the LORD is surrounded by loving-kindness.*

But that is only the second half of that verse. The first half reads *Many are the sorrows of the wicked man.* Is the *wicked man* being contrasted here with

מזמור לב

People talk about Jewish guilt as if it is a bad thing. To some extent, they are correct. I know. I've been there. I've sinned and been shamed. I've suffered the pain of remorse. I discovered that God forgives. He even brought me close to Him.

א לְדָוִד מַשְׂכִּיל
אַשְׁרֵי נְשׂוּי־פֶּשַׁע כְּסוּי חֲטָאָה׃

ב אַשְׁרֵי־אָדָם לֹא יַחְשֹׁב יְהוָה לוֹ עָוֹן
וְאֵין בְּרוּחוֹ רְמִיָּה׃

ג כִּי־הֶחֱרַשְׁתִּי בָּלוּ עֲצָמָי
בְּשַׁאֲגָתִי כׇּל־הַיּוֹם׃

ד כִּי ׀ יוֹמָם וָלַיְלָה תִּכְבַּד עָלַי יָדֶךָ
נֶהְפַּךְ לְשַׁדִּי בְּחַרְבֹנֵי קַיִץ סֶלָה׃

ה חַטָּאתִי אוֹדִיעֲךָ
וַעֲוֺנִי לֹא־כִסִּיתִי
אָמַרְתִּי אוֹדֶה עֲלֵי פְשָׁעַי לַיהוָה
וְאַתָּה נָשָׂאתָ עֲוֺן חַטָּאתִי סֶלָה׃

ו עַל־זֹאת יִתְפַּלֵּל כׇּל־חָסִיד ׀ אֵלֶיךָ לְעֵת מְצֹא
רַק לְשֵׁטֶף מַיִם רַבִּים
אֵלָיו לֹא יַגִּיעוּ׃

ז אַתָּה ׀ סֵתֶר לִי מִצַּר תִּצְּרֵנִי
רָנֵּי פַלֵּט תְּסוֹבְבֵנִי סֶלָה׃

מזמור לב *Psalm 32:* The theme of our psalm is summed up in the opening sentences of the medieval treatise *The Gates of Repentance,* written by Rabbeinu Yona of Gerona:

"Among the Blessed One's kindnesses to his creations is having prepared

8. I will instruct you and show you
the way you should go;
I will counsel you, and keep My eye on you.

9. Do not be like the horse or the mule, senseless creatures,
whose spirit must be curbed by bit and bridle,
so that they do not come near to you.

10. Many are the sorrows of the wicked man,
and the man who trusts in the LORD is surrounded by loving-kindness;

11. Rejoice in the LORD and be glad, you righteous;
sing aloud, all you upright of heart.

---

other merits. Even the *wicked man*, stained with sin and full of faults, can obtain God's favor merely by trusting in Him.

This is basic Jewish theology. God's love and mercy are not just for the righteous. The wicked too can enjoy His favor.

Psalm 103, verses 10–11, eloquently confirms this teaching:

He has not dealt with us as our sins deserve.... For as the heavens are high above the earth, So great is His loving-kindness.

ח אַשְׂכִּֽילְךָ֨ ׀ וְֽאוֹרְךָ֗ בְּדֶֽרֶךְ־ז֥וּ תֵלֵ֑ךְ
אִֽיעֲצָ֖ה עָלֶ֣יךָ עֵינִֽי׃

ט אַל־תִּהְי֤וּ ׀ כְּס֥וּס כְּפֶרֶד֮ אֵ֤ין הָ֫בִ֥ין
בְּמֶתֶג־וָרֶ֣סֶן עֶדְי֣וֹ לִבְל֑וֹם בַּ֝֗ל קְרֹ֣ב אֵלֶֽיךָ׃

י רַבִּ֥ים מַכְאוֹבִ֗ים לָרָ֫שָׁ֥ע
וְהַבּוֹטֵ֥חַ בַּיהוָ֑ה חֶ֝֗סֶד יְסוֹבְבֶֽנּוּ׃

יא שִׂמְח֬וּ בַיהוָ֣ה וְ֭גִילוּ צַדִּיקִ֑ים
וְ֝הַרְנִ֗ינוּ כָּל־יִשְׁרֵי־לֵֽב׃

---

the man who trusts in the Lord? Most readers, scholars and laymen alike, certainly interpret it that way.

The Midrash, however, offers a startling alternative interpretation:

"Said R. Elazar in the name of R. Abba: 'Even the wicked man, if he but trusts in God, will be surrounded by loving-kindness.'"

Bitaḥon, trust in the Lord, is sufficient to earn God's mercy even without

PSALM 33

1. Sing joyfully to the LORD, you righteous;
it is fitting for the upright to praise Him.

2. Praise the LORD with the harp;
sing to Him with the ten-stringed lute.

3. Sing to Him a new song;
play skillfully amid shouts of joy.

4. For the word of the LORD is right;
His every deed is trustworthy.

5. He loves righteousness and justice;
the earth is full of the goodness of the LORD.

6. By the word of the LORD the heavens were made,
and all their host by the breath of His mouth.

7. He gathers the waters of the sea as in a heap;
He puts the deep in storehouses.

8. Let all the earth fear the LORD;
let all the inhabitants of the world stand in awe of Him.

Music inspires. It motivates us to achieve ever loftier objectives.

Music assists. It raises us up from the depths of depression, and illuminates the darkest despair.

What is there to sing about? What themes does our psalm suggest to writers of songs and composers of music?

Our psalm offers a series of answers to those questions.

The first theme is the contrast of justice and mercy. *He loves righteousness and justice*. But do they always prevail? Does not His mercy often override His insistence upon obedience to the law? The earth contains its share of injustice and lawlessness, true. But *the earth is full of the goodness of the LORD.* What a theme for an epic poem or a dramatic opera!

Another theme is the majesty and grandeur of God's creation. *By the word*

מזמור לג

They deride me behind my back. They spread lies about me. They scheme to rid the world of me. I toil in vain to win them over. For what can I possibly apologize? I have harmed no one who hasn't harmed me. I have come to the aid of those who hate me. I must trust God to frustrate their plans. I have no other recourse.

א רַנְּנ֣וּ צַ֭דִּיקִים בַּיהֹוָ֑ה
לַ֝יְשָׁרִ֗ים נָאוָ֥ה תְהִלָּֽה׃

ב הוֹד֣וּ לַיהֹוָ֣ה בְּכִנּ֑וֹר
בְּנֵ֥בֶל עָ֝שׂ֗וֹר זַמְּרוּ־לֽוֹ׃

ג שִֽׁירוּ־ל֭וֹ שִׁ֣יר חָדָ֑שׁ
הֵיטִ֥יבוּ נַ֝גֵּ֗ן בִּתְרוּעָֽה׃

ד כִּֽי־יָשָׁ֥ר דְּבַר־יְהֹוָ֑ה
וְכָל־מַ֝עֲשֵׂ֗הוּ בֶּאֱמוּנָֽה׃

ה אֹ֭הֵב צְדָקָ֣ה וּמִשְׁפָּ֑ט
חֶ֥סֶד יְ֝הֹוָ֗ה מָלְאָ֥ה הָאָֽרֶץ׃

ו בִּדְבַ֣ר יְ֭הֹוָה שָׁמַ֣יִם נַעֲשׂ֑וּ
וּבְר֥וּחַ פִּ֝֗יו כָּל־צְבָאָֽם׃

ז כֹּנֵ֣ס כַּ֭נֵּד מֵ֣י הַיָּ֑ם
נֹתֵ֖ן בְּאֹצָר֣וֹת תְּהוֹמֽוֹת׃

ח יִֽירְא֣וּ מֵ֭יְהֹוָה כָּל־הָאָ֑רֶץ
מִ֝מֶּ֗נּוּ יָ֝ג֗וּרוּ כָּל־יֹשְׁבֵ֥י תֵבֵֽל׃

מזמור לג *Psalm 33:* Our psalm asks that we sing with our voices. It recognizes the power of song.

Our psalm asks that we use our hands to play musical instruments. It understands the effect that melody has upon the soul.

As Radak puts it, "musical instruments inspire the wise soul, and assist it."

9. For He spoke, and it was;
He commanded, and there it stood.

10. The LORD frustrates the plans of nations;
He thwarts the designs of peoples.

11. But the LORD's own plan stands forever,
the designs of His heart endure for all generations.

12. Happy is the nation whose God is the LORD;
the people He has chosen for His own heritage.

13. The LORD looks down from heaven,
He sees all mankind.

14. From His dwelling-place He surveys
all the inhabitants of the earth.

15. It is He who fashions the hearts of them all,
He notes all their doings.

16. No king is saved by the size of his army;
no warrior is delivered by his great strength.

17. The horse is a vain hope for deliverance;
despite its great strength, it provides no escape.

The theme of war is a favorite choice of writers and composers. But the role of God in the ultimate outcome of wars has been a far less frequent theme. Our psalm confronts us with the fact that the plans of those who initiate wars are seldom realized. It asks: "Is it not the LORD who *frustrates the plans of nations*? Do His plans not indeed *endure for all generations*?"

Our psalm provides other suggestions for the poet's and musician's consideration: God *surveys all the inhabitants of the earth ... no warrior is delivered by his great strength ... the eye of the LORD is on those who fear Him ... to deliver them from death.*

Rav Kook was one of the few traditional rabbis to recognize and acknowledge the role of fine literature in human cultural development. But he bemoaned the

ט כִּ֤י ה֣וּא אָמַ֣ר וַיֶּ֑הִי
הֽוּא־צִ֝וָּ֗ה וַֽיַּעֲמֹֽד׃

י יְֽהוָ֗ה הֵפִ֥יר עֲצַת־גּוֹיִ֑ם
הֵ֝נִ֗יא מַחְשְׁב֥וֹת עַמִּֽים׃

יא עֲצַ֣ת יְ֭הוָה לְעוֹלָ֣ם תַּעֲמֹ֑ד
מַחְשְׁב֥וֹת לִ֝בּ֗וֹ לְדֹ֣ר וָדֹֽר׃

יב אַשְׁרֵ֣י הַ֭גּוֹי אֲשֶׁר־יְהוָ֣ה אֱלֹהָ֑יו
הָעָ֓ם ׀ בָּחַ֖ר לְנַחֲלָ֣ה לֽוֹ׃

יג מִ֭שָּׁמַיִם הִבִּ֣יט יְהוָ֑ה
רָ֝אָ֗ה אֶֽת־כׇּל־בְּנֵ֥י הָאָדָֽם׃

יד מִמְּכוֹן־שִׁבְתּ֥וֹ הִשְׁגִּ֑יחַ
אֶ֝֗ל כׇּל־יֹשְׁבֵ֥י הָאָֽרֶץ׃

טו הַיֹּצֵ֣ר יַ֣חַד לִבָּ֑ם
הַ֝מֵּבִ֗ין אֶל־כׇּל־מַעֲשֵׂיהֶֽם׃

טז אֵֽין־הַ֭מֶּלֶךְ נוֹשָׁ֣ע בְּרׇב־חָ֑יִל
גִּ֝בּ֗וֹר לֹֽא־יִנָּצֵ֥ל בְּרׇב־כֹּֽחַ׃

יז שֶׁ֣קֶר הַ֭סּוּס לִתְשׁוּעָ֑ה
וּבְרֹ֥ב חֵ֝יל֗וֹ לֹ֣א יְמַלֵּֽט׃

---

of the Lord the heavens were made. Nature and God's role in it have been perennial themes of the poet and musician.

Fear of God is another potential theme. *Let all the inhabitants of the world stand in awe of Him.* Granted, it may take being in a "foxhole," under a threat to one's life, to evoke it, but fear of God is a prevalent, if often denied, human emotion.

18. But the eye of the Lord is on those who fear Him,
who wait for His loving care,

19. to deliver them from death,
and to keep them alive in famine.

20. Our soul waits for the Lord; He is our help and our shield.

21. In Him our hearts rejoice, for we trust in His holy name.

22. Let Your loving care, Lord, rest upon us,
as we put our hope in You.

---

to ponder them, and, more than that, to transform them into melodies and poems, symphonies and songs.

Our psalm issues a simple plea to each of us: Make music!

יח הִנֵּ֤ה עֵ֣ין יְ֭הֹוָה אֶל־יְרֵאָ֑יו
לַֽמְיַחֲלִ֥ים לְחַסְדּֽוֹ׃

יט לְהַצִּ֣יל מִמָּ֣וֶת נַפְשָׁ֑ם
וּ֝לְחַיּוֹתָ֗ם בָּרָעָֽב׃

כ נַ֭פְשֵׁנוּ חִכְּתָ֣ה לַיהֹוָ֑ה
עֶזְרֵ֖נוּ וּמָגִנֵּ֣נוּ הֽוּא׃

כא כִּי־ב֭וֹ יִשְׂמַ֣ח לִבֵּ֑נוּ
כִּ֤י בְשֵׁ֖ם קָדְשׁ֣וֹ בָטָֽחְנוּ׃

כב יְהִי־חַסְדְּךָ֣ יְהֹוָ֣ה עָלֵ֑ינוּ
כַּ֝אֲשֶׁ֗ר יִחַ֥לְנוּ לָֽךְ׃

failure of much of that literature to address the kinds of existential issues which are contained in our psalm.

Few of us are gifted poets and creative musicians. But, as humans we all grapple with life's major themes. Our psalm attempts to motivate all of us

PSALM 34

1. Of David,
when he feigned madness before Abimelech
and was driven away, and he departed.*

2. I will bless the LORD at all times;
His praise is ever in my mouth.

3. My soul glories in the LORD;
let the humble hear it and rejoice.

4. Glorify the LORD with me;
together let us exalt His name.

5. I sought the LORD and He answered me;
He delivered me from all my terrors.

6. Men look to Him and are radiant;
their faces never blush with shame.

7. This poor man cried out,
and the LORD heard him;
He saved him from all his troubles.

8. The angel of the LORD
camps round those who fear Him
and rescues them.

* See 1 Sam. 21:12–16.

Some argue that God wants us to demonstrate our obedience to Him. He therefore issued a long list of decrees to test whether or not we will obey Him. In this view, there are no intrinsic benefits to obeying the mitzvot.

Others insist that God issued a particular set of mitzvot because they are intrinsically beneficial. He issued these decrees because they are good for us. Indeed, mitzvot are not decrees at all. They are guidelines for a life of happiness, health, peace, and contentment.

מזמור לד

My tongue is inside me. It symbolizes my inner self: Thoughts of a spiritual life. I keep my tongue from evil. I desire that life. My lips are visible externally. They symbolize my outer self: Everyday concerns. I keep my lips from uttering deceit. I long for many days to enjoy prosperity.

א לְדָוִד
בְּשַׁנּוֹתוֹ אֶת־טַעְמוֹ לִפְנֵי אֲבִימֶלֶךְ
וַיְגָרְשֵׁהוּ וַיֵּלַךְ׃

ב אֲבָרְכָה אֶת־יְהוָה בְּכָל־עֵת
תָּמִיד תְּהִלָּתוֹ בְּפִי׃

ג בַּיהוָה תִּתְהַלֵּל נַפְשִׁי
יִשְׁמְעוּ עֲנָוִים וְיִשְׂמָחוּ׃

ד גַּדְּלוּ לַיהוָה אִתִּי
וּנְרוֹמְמָה שְׁמוֹ יַחְדָּו׃

ה דָּרַשְׁתִּי אֶת־יְהוָה וְעָנָנִי
וּמִכָּל־מְגוּרוֹתַי הִצִּילָנִי׃

ו הִבִּיטוּ אֵלָיו וְנָהָרוּ
וּפְנֵיהֶם אַל־יֶחְפָּרוּ׃

ז זֶה עָנִי קָרָא וַיהוָה שָׁמֵעַ
וּמִכָּל־צָרוֹתָיו הוֹשִׁיעוֹ׃

ח חֹנֶה מַלְאַךְ־יְהוָה סָבִיב לִירֵאָיו
וַיְחַלְּצֵם׃

מזמור לד *Psalm 34:* Our psalm resolves an ancient theological debate. What is the nature of God's mitzvot? For what reason did He give us His commandments, prescribing hundreds of actions and prohibiting even more?

9. Taste and see how good the LORD is;
happy the man who finds refuge in Him.

10. Fear the LORD, you His holy people;
for those who fear Him lack nothing.

11. Young lions may suffer want and go hungry,
but those who seek the LORD lack no good thing.

12. Come, children, listen to me;
I will teach you the fear of the LORD.

13. Who is the man who desires life,
and longs for many days to enjoy prosperity?

14. Then keep your tongue from evil,
and your lips from uttering deceit.

15. Shun evil and do good;
seek peace and pursue it.

16. The eyes of the LORD are on the righteous;
His ears are open to their cry.

17. The LORD's face is set against evildoers,
to cut off all memory of them from the earth.

18. When they [the righteous] cry for help the LORD hears,
and delivers them from all their troubles.

---

from evil, and your lips from uttering deceit. Honesty and discretion will ensure the good life, the life and prosperity that you seek.

And if you pursue the path of evil, be prepared for the consequences. Not in Hell, or Purgatory, but in this mundane world, where *evil brings death to the wicked* and *those who hate the righteous will suffer.* David learned the lesson that obeying God's will brings about tangible rewards when he concocted a bizarre stratagem to escape a dire predicament.

The story is told in the Book of Samuel (1 Sam. 21:11–16). David was entrapped in the land of Akhish, king of Gat. The king's servants begged him to execute David, who was, after all, their enemy's hero.

Realizing the danger he was in, David *changed his behavior before them,*

ט טַעֲמוּ וּרְאוּ כִּי־טוֹב יְהֹוָה
אַשְׁרֵי הַגֶּבֶר יֶחֱסֶה־בּוֹ׃

י יְראוּ אֶת־יְהֹוָה קְדֹשָׁיו
כִּי־אֵין מַחְסוֹר לִירֵאָיו׃

יא כְּפִירִים רָשׁוּ וְרָעֵבוּ
וְדֹרְשֵׁי יהוה לֹא־יַחְסְרוּ כׇל־טוֹב׃

יב לְכוּ־בָנִים שִׁמְעוּ־לִי
יִרְאַת יהוה אֲלַמֶּדְכֶם׃

יג מִי־הָאִישׁ הֶחָפֵץ חַיִּים
אֹהֵב יָמִים לִרְאוֹת טוֹב׃

יד נְצֹר לְשׁוֹנְךָ מֵרָע
וּשְׂפָתֶיךָ מִדַּבֵּר מִרְמָה׃

טו סוּר מֵרָע וַעֲשֵׂה־טוֹב
בַּקֵּשׁ שָׁלוֹם וְרׇדְפֵהוּ׃

טז עֵינֵי יהוה אֶל־צַדִּיקִים
וְאׇזְנָיו אֶל־שַׁוְעָתָם׃

יז פְּנֵי יהוה בְּעֹשֵׂי רָע
לְהַכְרִית מֵאֶרֶץ זִכְרָם׃

יח צָעֲקוּ וַיהֹוָה שָׁמֵעַ
וּמִכׇּל־צָרוֹתָם הִצִּילָם׃

Our psalm sides with this latter view. *Taste and see how good the Lord is.* Not "obey the Lord for He is powerful," but "taste and see how good He is." *Those who seek the Lord lack no good thing.*

Do you *desire life*? Do you wish *to enjoy prosperity*? *Then keep your tongue*

19. The LORD is close to the broken-hearted;
He saves those who are crushed in spirit.

20. Many evils may confront the righteous man,
but the LORD delivers him from them all.

21. He guards every bone of his body,
not one of them is broken.

22. Evil brings death to the wicked;
those who hate the righteous will suffer.

23. The LORD redeems the lives of His servants;
none will regret having taken refuge in Him.

He learned the lesson that God answers a man's prayers in unimaginably practical ways; in this case, by inspiring him with a strange and unpredictable exit strategy from a seemingly impossible dilemma.

David memorialized his experience in our psalm: *I sought the LORD and… He delivered me from all my terrors.*

יט קָר֣וֹב יְ֭הוָה לְנִשְׁבְּרֵי־לֵ֑ב
וְֽאֶת־דַּכְּאֵי־ר֥וּחַ יוֹשִֽׁיעַ׃

כ רַ֭בּוֹת רָע֣וֹת צַדִּ֑יק
וּ֝מִכֻּלָּ֗ם יַצִּילֶ֥נּוּ יְהוָֽה׃

כא שֹׁמֵ֥ר כָּל־עַצְמוֹתָ֑יו
אַחַ֥ת מֵ֝הֵ֗נָּה לֹ֣א נִשְׁבָּֽרָה׃

כב תְּמוֹתֵ֣ת רָשָׁ֣ע רָעָ֑ה
וְשֹׂנְאֵ֖י צַדִּ֣יק יֶאְשָֽׁמוּ׃

כג פּוֹדֶ֣ה יְ֭הוָה נֶ֣פֶשׁ עֲבָדָ֑יו
וְלֹ֥א יֶ֝אְשְׁמ֗וּ כָּל־הַחֹסִ֥ים בּֽוֹ׃

---

and feigned himself mad in their hands, and scratched on the doors of the gate, and let his spittle run down upon his beard. To which Akhish famously responded: *"Do I lack mad men that you have brought this fellow to play the mad man in my presence?"* Freed, David then hastened to find refuge in a different venue.

David thus learned that madness too has its purpose in God's world.

PSALM 35

Sixth day of the month

1. Of David.
Strive, LORD, with those who strive against me,
fight those who fight against me.

2. Take up shield and buckler,
and come to my defense.

3. Uncover the spear,
and bar the way in the face of my pursuers;
say to me: "I am your salvation."

4. May those who seek my life be disgraced and shamed;
may those who plot my ruin be turned back in disgrace.

5. May they be like chaff before the wind,
with the angel of the LORD driving them on.

6. May their path be dark and slippery,
with the angel of the LORD pursuing them.

7. For without cause they have laid their net for me;
without cause they have dug a pit for me.

8. But destruction will overtake them unawares,
and the net they laid will catch them;
they will fall into it to their destruction.

But in our psalm David transcends that theme and discloses a behavior which is astounding, and which is an expression of his rare spiritual stature. He tells us that he prays for his enemies.

Yet when they were sick I put on sackcloth... I went about as though grieving for a friend or brother. Malbim interprets verses 13 through 16 in a manner which provides a glimpse of each detail of David's interaction with his foes. Here is a rewording of his comments:

> He describes how he sought their well-being. He was so pained by their suffering that he himself was bedridden.

מזמור לה

When I pray, I do not stand still. I sway. My entire body prays. I fell ill. Every limb was vulnerable. I did battle. Each muscle was endangered. I recovered from my disease. I vanquished my foe. Every limb now prays, and every muscle sways. Lord, You are incomparable!

א לְדָוִד ׀ ולחודש
רִיבָה יהוה אֶת־יְרִיבַי
לְחַם אֶת־לֹחֲמָי׃

ב הַחֲזֵק מָגֵן וְצִנָּה
וְקוּמָה בְּעֶזְרָתִי׃

ג וְהָרֵק חֲנִית וּסְגֹר לִקְרַאת רֹדְפָי
אֱמֹר לְנַפְשִׁי יְשֻׁעָתֵךְ אָנִי׃

ד יֵבֹשׁוּ וְיִכָּלְמוּ מְבַקְשֵׁי נַפְשִׁי
יִסֹּגוּ אָחוֹר וְיַחְפְּרוּ חֹשְׁבֵי רָעָתִי׃

ה יִהְיוּ כְּמֹץ לִפְנֵי־רוּחַ
וּמַלְאַךְ יהוה דּוֹחֶה׃

ו יְהִי־דַרְכָּם חֹשֶׁךְ וַחֲלַקְלַקֹּת
וּמַלְאַךְ יהוה רֹדְפָם׃

ז כִּי־חִנָּם טָמְנוּ־לִי שַׁחַת רִשְׁתָּם
חִנָּם חָפְרוּ לְנַפְשִׁי׃

ח תְּבוֹאֵהוּ שׁוֹאָה לֹא־יֵדָע
וְרִשְׁתּוֹ אֲשֶׁר־טָמַן תִּלְכְּדוֹ
בְּשׁוֹאָה יִפָּל־בָּהּ׃

מזמור לה *Psalm 35:* In our psalm David prays that he be delivered from his enemies. Beseeching God for victory in battle is a frequent theme in David's prayers.

9. Then my soul will rejoice in the LORD,
and delight in His deliverance.

10. All my bones will say,
"LORD, who is like You?
You save the poor from one stronger than he,
the poor and the needy from his despoiler."

11. Malicious witnesses come forward,
they question me on things of which I know nothing.

12. They repay me evil for good;
[they seek] my undoing.

13. Yet when they were sick I put on sackcloth,
I afflicted myself with fasting.
May it come to me what I prayed for them!

14. I went about as [though grieving] for a friend or a brother,
bowed in gloom as though mourning for a mother.

15. But when I stumble they gather round with glee;
even cripples gather against me;
and those I do not know tear me to pieces without ceasing.

16. With profane mocking gestures
they gnash their teeth at me.

---

sackcloth. I even *afflicted myself with fasting.* I prayed intensely, but privately, so that others would not witness my intercession on their behalf.

Not just once did I pray, but again and again. *I went about,* that is, I visited them in their private rooms, *as though for a friend or brother.* I mourned for them so that I was so *bowed in gloom* that I became infirm myself.

They reacted with glee when they gathered by themselves, but when they visited me they pretended to be crippled in pain.

I did not know their true feelings. They tore their clothing as if they

ט וְנַפְשִׁי תָּגִיל בַּיהוָה
תָּשִׂישׂ בִּישׁוּעָתוֹ׃

י כׇּל עַצְמוֹתַי ׀ תֹּאמַרְנָה
יְהוָה מִי כָמוֹךָ
מַצִּיל עָנִי מֵחָזָק מִמֶּנּוּ
וְעָנִי וְאֶבְיוֹן מִגֹּזְלוֹ׃

יא יְקוּמוּן עֵדֵי חָמָס
אֲשֶׁר לֹא־יָדַעְתִּי יִשְׁאָלוּנִי׃

יב יְשַׁלְּמוּנִי רָעָה תַּחַת טוֹבָה
שְׁכוֹל לְנַפְשִׁי׃

יג וַאֲנִי ׀ בַּחֲלוֹתָם לְבוּשִׁי שָׂק
עִנֵּיתִי בַצּוֹם נַפְשִׁי
וּתְפִלָּתִי עַל־חֵיקִי תָשׁוּב׃

יד כְּרֵעַ־כְּאָח לִי הִתְהַלָּכְתִּי
כַּאֲבֶל־אֵם קֹדֵר שַׁחוֹתִי׃

טו וּבְצַלְעִי שָׂמְחוּ וְנֶאֱסָפוּ
נֶאֶסְפוּ עָלַי נֵכִים וְלֹא יָדַעְתִּי
קָרְעוּ וְלֹא־דָמּוּ׃

טז בְּחַנְפֵי לַעֲגֵי מָעוֹג
חָרֹק עָלַי שִׁנֵּימוֹ׃

But they ungratefully rejoiced that he was confined to his bed. They eagerly anticipated his death.

When they were sick I immediately did everything possible. *I put on*

17. How long, Lord, will You look on?
Rescue my life from their onslaughts,
my precious soul from the lions.

18. Then I will praise You in the great assembly,
extol You before a mighty throng.

19. Let not my treacherous enemies rejoice over me;
let not those who hate me without cause wink maliciously.

20. For they do not speak of peace,
but devise deceitful schemes against the oppressed in the land.

21. They open wide their mouths against me,
crying: "Hurrah! Hurrah! Our eye has seen it."

22. You have seen it all, Lord; be not silent.
Do not be far from me, Lord.

23. Awake, and rise to my defense,
to plead my cause, my God and Lord.

24. Do me justice as You are just Yourself,
Lord my God;
do not let them gloat over me.

25. Do not let them say to themselves,
"Hurrah!, that's what we wished!"
Let them not say,
"We have swallowed him up."

These poignant details are evidence of David's exquisite humanity; nay, of his nobility. David is more than a warrior and the sweet singer of Israel. He is a moral hero.

His *menschlichkeit*, his heroic empathy, his ability to "feel the pain" of even his foes, are the reasons why David endures as the most majestic figure in our tradition.

אֲדֹנָי֮ כַּמָּ֪ה תִּ֫רְאֶ֥ה יז
הָשִׁ֣יבָה נַ֭פְשִׁי מִשֹּׁאֵיהֶ֑ם
מִ֝כְּפִירִ֗ים יְחִידָתִֽי׃

א֭וֹדְךָ בְּקָהָ֣ל רָ֑ב יח
בְּעַ֖ם עָצ֣וּם אֲהַלְלֶֽךָּ׃

אַֽל־יִשְׂמְחוּ־לִ֣י אֹיְבַ֣י שֶׁ֑קֶר יט
שֹׂנְאַ֥י חִ֝נָּ֗ם יִקְרְצוּ־עָֽיִן׃

כִּ֤י לֹ֪א שָׁ֫ל֥וֹם יְדַ֫בֵּ֥רוּ כ
וְעַ֥ל רִגְעֵי־אֶ֑רֶץ דִּבְרֵ֥י מִ֝רְמ֗וֹת יַחֲשֹׁבֽוּן׃

וַיַּרְחִ֣יבוּ עָלַי֮ פִּ֫יהֶ֥ם כא
אָ֭מְרוּ הֶאָ֣ח ׀ הֶאָ֑ח רָאֲתָ֥ה עֵינֵֽנוּ׃

רָאִ֣יתָה יְ֭הוָה אַֽל־תֶּחֱרַ֑שׁ כב
אֲ֝דֹנָ֗י אַל־תִּרְחַ֥ק מִמֶּֽנִּי׃

הָעִ֣ירָה וְ֭הָקִיצָה לְמִשְׁפָּטִ֑י כג
אֱלֹהַ֖י וַאדֹנָ֣י לְרִיבִֽי׃

שָׁפְטֵ֣נִי כְ֭צִדְקְךָ יְהוָ֣ה אֱלֹהָ֑י כד
וְאַל־יִשְׂמְחוּ־לִֽי׃

אַל־יֹאמְר֣וּ בְ֭לִבָּם הֶאָ֣ח נַפְשֵׁ֑נוּ כה
אַל־יֹ֝אמְר֗וּ בִּלַּעֲנֽוּהוּ׃

---

were mourning for me, but they were insincere. When they left my bedside they resumed their *profane mocking gestures; they gnashed their teeth at me.*

26. May those who gloat over my misfortune
be shamed and disgraced;
may those who exalt themselves over me
be covered with shame and confusion.

27. But may those who would see me vindicated
shout for joy and gladness;
may they always say,
"Magnified be the LORD,
who delights in the success of His servant!"

28. Then shall my tongue speak of Your justice,
and all day long of Your praise.

כו יֵבֹשׁוּ וְיַחְפְּרוּ ׀ יַחְדָּו שְׂמֵחֵי רָעָתִי
יִלְבְּשׁוּ־בֹשֶׁת וּכְלִמָּה
הַמַּגְדִּילִים עָלָי:

כז יָרֹנּוּ וְיִשְׂמְחוּ חֲפֵצֵי צִדְקִי
וְיֹאמְרוּ תָמִיד יִגְדַּל יְהוָה
הֶחָפֵץ שְׁלוֹם עַבְדּוֹ:

כח וּלְשׁוֹנִי תֶּהְגֶּה צִדְקֶךָ
כָּל־הַיּוֹם תְּהִלָּתֶךָ:

PSALM 36

1. For the Chief Musician. Of David, the servant of the LORD.

2. I do believe* that sin inspires the wicked man.
There is no fear of God before his eyes.

3. For he flatters himself in his own mind,
thinking, none can find out or hate his sin.**

4. The words of his mouth are mischievous and deceitful;
he has given up acting sensibly or doing good.

5. In bed he plots mischief;
he sets himself on a wicked course,
he does not reject evil.

6. LORD, Your loving-kindness reaches to heaven,
Your faithfulness to the skies.

7. Your righteousness is like the high mountains,
Your judgments like the great deep.
LORD, You give protection to man and beast.

* Lit. "It is in my heart"; i.e., "It is my belief."

** I.e., "The wicked man deceives himself that God will neither find out nor punish his sin."

Few of us qualify as "righteous." Since the rest of us are either wicked, or, at best, average, it behooves us to become better acquainted with our evil inclinations.

Our psalm allows us to do precisely that. Very near its beginning, it declares: *there is no fear of God before his eyes.*

Fyodor Dostoevsky, the great Russian novelist, phrased it so succinctly: "If there is no God, then everything is permitted."

This is the fundamental attitude of the wicked inclination. There is no God. There is certainly no reason to fear Him. So, *none can find out or hate his sin.* Morality is a consequence of faith in God. Absent God, moral behavior lacks a motive. Conversely, immoral behavior is certain evidence of lack of

מזמור לו

I had a free day; free from work, and free, I thought, from God. I went down to the sea. I saw a bird swoop down from the sky and scoop up a fish. I exclaimed: Your judgments are like the great deep. I had a free day; free to play, and free, I thought, from God. I strolled in the woods, and saw an anthill, protruding but an inch from the ground. I exclaimed: Your righteousness is like the high mountains.

א לַמְנַצֵּ֬חַ ׀ לְעֶֽבֶד־יְהֹוָ֬ה לְדָוִֽד׃

ב נְאֻֽם־פֶּ֣שַׁע לָ֭רָשָׁע בְּקֶ֣רֶב לִבִּ֑י
אֵֽין־פַּ֥חַד אֱ֝לֹהִ֗ים לְנֶ֣גֶד עֵינָֽיו׃

ג כִּֽי־הֶחֱלִ֣יק אֵלָ֣יו בְּעֵינָ֑יו
לִמְצֹ֖א עֲוֺנ֣וֹ לִשְׂנֹֽא׃

ד דִּבְרֵי־פִ֭יו אָ֣וֶן וּמִרְמָ֑ה
חָדַ֖ל לְהַשְׂכִּ֣יל לְהֵיטִֽיב׃

ה אָ֤וֶן ׀ יַחְשֹׁ֗ב עַֽל־מִשְׁכָּ֫ב֥וֹ
יִ֭תְיַצֵּב עַל־דֶּ֣רֶךְ לֹא־ט֑וֹב
רָ֝֗ע לֹ֣א יִמְאָֽס׃

ו יְ֭הֹוָה בְּהַשָּׁמַ֣יִם חַסְדֶּ֑ךָ
אֱ֝מ֥וּנָתְךָ֗ עַד־שְׁחָקִֽים׃

ז צִדְקָתְךָ֤ ׀ כְּֽהַרְרֵי־אֵ֗ל
מִ֭שְׁפָּטֶךָ תְּה֣וֹם רַבָּ֑ה
אָ֤דָֽם וּבְהֵמָ֖ה תוֹשִׁ֣יעַ ׀ יְהֹוָֽה׃

מזמור לו *Psalm 36:* Our psalm is all about evil, the evil that lurks within us all.

Our tradition teaches us of a *yetzer hara*, an evil inclination that is born when we are born. There is also inclination toward good. It joins us as we mature.

"R. Yose HaGelili says: 'The good inclination rules the righteous. The evil inclination rules the wicked. The average person is ruled by both'" (*Berakhot* 61b).

8. How precious is Your loving-kindness, God!
Men find refuge in the shadow of Your wings.

9. They feast on the rich abundance of Your house;
You give them to drink of the stream of Your delights.

10. For with You is the fountain of life;
by Your light do we see light.

11. Continue Your loving-kindness to those who know You,
and Your kindness to the upright in heart.

12. Let not the proud foot approach me,
let not the wicked hand drive me away.

13. There the evildoers lie fallen,
thrust down, unable to rise.

---

to do what is good. That too is linked to faith. *By Your light do we see light.* The darkness of evil is dispelled by the light of faith in Him.

Indeed, if there is no God, then all is permissible. But if there is a God, and if *we find refuge in the shadow of His wings*, then it becomes clear that all is not permissible. Not only is there a right and a wrong, but, *in His light,* we have the capacity to discern one from the other.

ח מַה־יָּקָר חַסְדְּךָ אֱלֹהִים
וּבְנֵי אָדָם בְּצֵל כְּנָפֶיךָ יֶחֱסָיוּן׃

ט יִרְוְיֻן מִדֶּשֶׁן בֵּיתֶךָ
וְנַחַל עֲדָנֶיךָ תַשְׁקֵם׃

י כִּי־עִמְּךָ מְקוֹר חַיִּים
בְּאוֹרְךָ נִרְאֶה־אוֹר׃

יא מְשֹׁךְ חַסְדְּךָ לְיֹדְעֶיךָ
וְצִדְקָתְךָ לְיִשְׁרֵי־לֵב׃

יב אַל־תְּבוֹאֵנִי רֶגֶל גַּאֲוָה
וְיַד־רְשָׁעִים אַל־תְּנִדֵנִי׃

יג שָׁם נָפְלוּ פֹּעֲלֵי אָוֶן
דֹּחוּ וְלֹא־יָכְלוּ קוּם׃

---

faith in God. That there is a linkage between our belief in God and our moral practice is a fundamental teaching of our Bible and Talmud, and one which is especially prevalent in Psalms.

Our psalm is equally attentive to the other force within us, the inclination

PSALM 37

1. Of David.
Do not fret because of evildoers,
nor envy wrongdoers;

2. for like grass they soon wither,
and like the green herbs they fade away;

3. Trust in the LORD and do good,
wherever you dwell, shepherd others faithfully.*

4. Take delight in the LORD,
and He will grant you your heart's desire.

5. Commit your way to the LORD;
trust in Him and He will act.

6. He will make your righteousness shine like the light,
and the justice of your cause like the brightness of noon.

7. Be patient and wait for the LORD;
do not fret over the man who prospers in his dealings,
when he carries out his evil schemes.

8. Desist from anger and forsake wrath;
do not fret; it can only bring harm.

9. For evil men will be cut off,
while they who hope in the LORD will inherit the land.

* Lit. "feed on."

מזמור לז *Psalm 37:* Choosing a vocation is a challenge. The person of faith wants a vocation consistent with his faith. He hopes that his vocation will enhance his personal faith, and will advance the cause he professes.

The vocation that best fits these objectives is the profession of teaching. Teaching need not be done in the formal context of a classroom. The coach

מזמור לז

Envy poisons the soul. Yet I am envious. Competition exhausts the body. But if I don't compete I will lose. Anger is harmful. But I cannot resist expressing my wrath. I must learn to be satisfied with what I have. Then my soul will be whole. And my body revived. And my temper calmed. Those are the benefits of trusting in God.

א לְדָוִ֨ד ׀
אַל־תִּתְחַ֥ר בַּמְּרֵעִ֑ים
אַל־תְּ֝קַנֵּ֗א בְּעֹשֵׂ֥י עַוְלָֽה׃

ב כִּ֣י כֶ֭חָצִיר מְהֵרָ֣ה יִמָּ֑לוּ
וּכְיֶ֥רֶק דֶּ֝֗שֶׁא יִבּוֹלֽוּן׃

ג בְּטַ֣ח בַּ֭יהוָה וַעֲשֵׂה־ט֑וֹב
שְׁכָן־אֶ֝֗רֶץ וּרְעֵ֥ה אֱמוּנָֽה׃

ד וְהִתְעַנַּ֥ג עַל־יְהוָ֑ה
וְיִֽתֶּן־לְ֝ךָ֗ מִשְׁאֲלֹ֥ת לִבֶּֽךָ׃

ה גּ֣וֹל עַל־יְהוָ֣ה דַּרְכֶּ֑ךָ
וּבְטַ֥ח עָ֝לָ֗יו וְה֣וּא יַעֲשֶֽׂה׃

ו וְהוֹצִ֣יא כָא֣וֹר צִדְקֶ֑ךָ
וּ֝מִשְׁפָּטֶ֗ךָ כַּֽצָּהֳרָֽיִם׃

ז דּ֤וֹם ׀ לַיהוָה֮ וְהִתְח֪וֹלֵֽל ל֫וֹ
אַל־תִּ֭תְחַר בְּמַצְלִ֣יחַ דַּרְכּ֑וֹ
בְּ֝אִ֗ישׁ עֹשֶׂ֥ה מְזִמּֽוֹת׃

ח הֶ֣רֶף מֵ֭אַף וַעֲזֹ֣ב חֵמָ֑ה
אַל־תִּ֝תְחַ֗ר אַךְ־לְהָרֵֽעַ׃

ט כִּֽי־מְ֭רֵעִים יִכָּרֵת֑וּן
וְקֹוֵ֥י יְ֝הוָ֗ה הֵ֣מָּה יִֽירְשׁוּ־אָֽרֶץ׃

10. A little longer, and the wicked will be no more;
search his place well, and he will not be there.

11. But the humble shall inherit the land;
and enjoy abundant prosperity.

12. The wicked man plots against the righteous
and gnashes his teeth at him;

13. but the LORD laughs at him,
for He knows that his day will come.

14. The wicked draw their swords and bend their bows
to lay low the poor and the needy,
to slaughter those who walk the straight path.

15. Their swords shall pierce their own hearts,
and their bows shall be broken.

16. Better is the little which the righteous man has
than the great wealth of the wicked;

17. for the power of the wicked shall be broken,
but the LORD supports the righteous.

18. The LORD cares for the lives** of the blameless,
and their inheritance will last forever.

19. They will not suffer shame in bad times;
in days of famine they shall have plenty.

20. But the wicked will perish;
the enemies of the LORD will vanish
like the beauty of the meadows;
they shall vanish like smoke.

** Lit. "days."

---

on the football field, the rabbi in his pulpit, the poet at her writing desk, and the Jewish communal worker – all are teachers.

A biblical metaphor for the teacher is the shepherd. Radak finds this

י וְע֣וֹד מְ֭עַט וְאֵ֣ין רָשָׁ֑ע
וְהִתְבּוֹנַ֖נְתָּ עַל־מְקוֹמ֣וֹ וְאֵינֶֽנּוּ׃

יא וַעֲנָוִ֥ים יִֽירְשׁוּ־אָ֑רֶץ
וְ֝הִתְעַנְּג֗וּ עַל־רֹ֥ב שָׁלֽוֹם׃

יב זֹמֵ֣ם רָ֭שָׁע לַצַּדִּ֑יק
וְחֹרֵ֖ק עָלָ֣יו שִׁנָּֽיו׃

יג אֲדֹנָ֥י יִשְׂחַק־ל֑וֹ
כִּֽי־רָ֝אָ֗ה כִּֽי־יָבֹ֥א יוֹמֽוֹ׃

יד חֶ֤רֶב ׀ פָּתְח֣וּ רְשָׁעִים֮ וְדָרְכ֪וּ קַ֫שְׁתָּ֥ם
לְ֭הַפִּיל עָנִ֣י וְאֶבְי֑וֹן
לִ֝טְב֗וֹחַ יִשְׁרֵי־דָֽרֶךְ׃

טו חַ֭רְבָּם תָּב֣וֹא בְלִבָּ֑ם
וְ֝קַשְּׁתוֹתָ֗ם תִּשָּׁבַֽרְנָה׃

טז טֽוֹב־מְ֭עַט לַצַּדִּ֑יק
מֵ֝הֲמ֗וֹן רְשָׁעִ֥ים רַבִּֽים׃

יז כִּ֤י זְרוֹע֣וֹת רְ֭שָׁעִים תִּשָּׁבַ֑רְנָה
וְסוֹמֵ֖ךְ צַדִּיקִ֣ים יְהוָֽה׃

יח יוֹדֵ֣עַ יְ֭הוָה יְמֵ֣י תְמִימִ֑ם
וְ֝נַחֲלָתָ֗ם לְעוֹלָ֥ם תִּהְיֶֽה׃

יט לֹֽא־יֵ֭בֹשׁוּ בְּעֵ֣ת רָעָ֑ה
וּבִימֵ֖י רְעָב֣וֹן יִשְׂבָּֽעוּ׃

כ כִּ֤י רְשָׁעִ֨ים ׀ יֹאבֵ֗דוּ
וְאֹיְבֵ֣י יְ֭הוָה כִּיקַ֣ר כָּרִ֑ים
כָּל֖וּ בֶעָשָׁ֣ן כָּֽלוּ׃

21. The wicked man borrows and does not repay;
the righteous is generous and gives again.

22. Those blessed by Him will inherit the land,
but those cursed by Him will be cut off.

23. The steps of a man are made steady by the LORD,
when He delights in the path that he takes.

24. Though he stumbles, he will not fall headlong,
for the LORD holds him by the hand.

25. I have been young and now am grown old,
yet I have never seen the righteous man forsaken,
or his children begging bread.

26. At all times he is generous and lends freely,
and his children become a blessing.

27. Shun evil and do good,
and you shall always live at peace.

28. For the LORD loves justice,
and does not forsake His faithful.
They are safeguarded forever;
but the children of the wicked will be cut off.

The teacher "shepherds" others. *"And I will give you shepherds after my own heart, who will pasture you with knowledge and skill"* (Jer. 3:15).

Teaching others, in whatever form, is challenging. Its material rewards are few. Glory and prestige are seldom forthcoming. Many smugly utter that insidious witticism: Those who can, do; those who can't, teach.

Insufficiently rewarded, unappreciated, insulted – how is a teacher to cope?

Our psalm offers encouragement: *Do not fret.... Desist from anger... the humble shall inherit the land.... Better is the little which the righteous man has*

כא לֹוֶה רָשָׁע וְלֹא יְשַׁלֵּם
וְצַדִּיק חוֹנֵן וְנוֹתֵן׃

כב כִּי מְבֹרָכָיו יִירְשׁוּ אָרֶץ
וּמְקֻלָּלָיו יִכָּרֵתוּ׃

כג מֵיְהוָה מִצְעֲדֵי־גֶבֶר כּוֹנָנוּ
וְדַרְכּוֹ יֶחְפָּץ׃

כד כִּי־יִפֹּל לֹא־יוּטָל
כִּי־יְהוָה סוֹמֵךְ יָדוֹ׃

כה נַעַר ׀ הָיִיתִי גַּם־זָקַנְתִּי
וְלֹא־רָאִיתִי צַדִּיק נֶעֱזָב
וְזַרְעוֹ מְבַקֶּשׁ־לָחֶם׃

כו כָּל־הַיּוֹם חוֹנֵן וּמַלְוֶה
וְזַרְעוֹ לִבְרָכָה׃

כז סוּר מֵרָע וַעֲשֵׂה־טוֹב
וּשְׁכֹן לְעוֹלָם׃

כח כִּי יְהוָה ׀ אֹהֵב מִשְׁפָּט
וְלֹא־יַעֲזֹב אֶת־חֲסִידָיו
לְעוֹלָם נִשְׁמָרוּ
וְזֶרַע רְשָׁעִים נִכְרָת׃

---

metaphor in the third verse of our psalm: *Wherever you dwell, shepherd others faithfully*. In whatever circumstances you find yourself, there is an opportunity to teach.

29. The righteous will inherit the land,
and dwell in it forever.

30. The mouth of the righteous man utters wisdom,
and his tongue speaks what is right.

31. The law of his God is in his heart;
his footsteps will never falter.

32. The wicked watches out for the righteous,
seeking to bring about his death;

33. but the Lord will not leave him in his power,
nor let him be condemned when he is on trial.

34. Wait for the Lord and keep His way,
and He will raise you to possess the land.
When the wicked are cut off, you will see it.

35. I have seen a wicked and ruthless man,
well-rooted like a luxurious tree in its native soil;

36. but he soon passed away and was no more;
I sought him, but he was not to be found.

37. Watch the blameless, observe the upright,
for there is a future for the peace-loving man.

38. But transgressors shall be utterly destroyed;
the future of the wicked shall be cut off.

---

worldly success and honor." One sage, a teacher in his own right, found the opposite lesson in verse 23 of our psalm. His name was Rabbi Yaakov Loberbaum, rabbi of the community of Lyssa in early nineteenth-century Poland. Among his numerous works is a precious commentary on the Pentateuch, *Naḥalat Yaakov*.

There he writes:

> A person must make every effort to succeed in life. He must not passively rely upon omens or miracles. This is the meaning of the verse: *The steps of*

כט צַדִּיקִים יִירְשׁוּ־אָרֶץ
וְיִשְׁכְּנוּ לָעַד עָלֶיהָ׃

ל פִּי־צַדִּיק יֶהְגֶּה חָכְמָה
וּלְשׁוֹנוֹ תְּדַבֵּר מִשְׁפָּט׃

לא תּוֹרַת אֱלֹהָיו בְּלִבּוֹ
לֹא תִמְעַד אֲשֻׁרָיו׃

לב צוֹפֶה רָשָׁע לַצַּדִּיק
וּמְבַקֵּשׁ לַהֲמִיתוֹ׃

לג יְהוָה לֹא־יַעַזְבֶנּוּ בְיָדוֹ
וְלֹא יַרְשִׁיעֶנּוּ בְּהִשָּׁפְטוֹ׃

לד קַוֵּה אֶל־יְהוָה ׀ וּשְׁמֹר דַּרְכּוֹ
וִירוֹמִמְךָ לָרֶשֶׁת אָרֶץ
בְּהִכָּרֵת רְשָׁעִים תִּרְאֶה׃

לה רָאִיתִי רָשָׁע עָרִיץ
וּמִתְעָרֶה כְּאֶזְרָח רַעֲנָן׃

לו וַיַּעֲבֹר וְהִנֵּה אֵינֶנּוּ
וָאֲבַקְשֵׁהוּ וְלֹא נִמְצָא׃

לז שְׁמָר־תָּם וּרְאֵה יָשָׁר
כִּי־אַחֲרִית לְאִישׁ שָׁלוֹם׃

לח וּפֹשְׁעִים נִשְׁמְדוּ יַחְדָּו
אַחֲרִית רְשָׁעִים נִכְרָתָה׃

---

than the great wealth of the wicked. Some "teachers" adopt an attitude of resignation and passivity. "Such is the lot of the teacher or rabbi or communal worker," they say. "My rewards are of an eternal nature. I am willing to forgo

39. The deliverance of the righteous comes from the LORD;
He is their stronghold in time of trouble.

40. The LORD helps them and delivers them;
He delivers them from the wicked and saves them,
because they seek refuge in Him.

---

of Lyssa asserts the contrary: devout trust in God is perfectly consistent with insistence upon deserved rewards, due recognition, and maintenance of self-respect.

The spiritual benefits of public service must not come at the expense of appropriate material rewards.

לט וּתְשׁוּעַת צַדִּיקִים מֵיְהוָה
מָעוּזָּם בְּעֵת צָרָה׃

מ וַיַּעְזְרֵם יהוה וַיְפַלְּטֵם
יְפַלְּטֵם מֵרְשָׁעִים וְיוֹשִׁיעֵם
כִּי־חָסוּ בוֹ׃

---

a man are made steady by the LORD, when He delights in the path that he takes. Although God directs the fate of every person, thus making his steps steady, He nevertheless desires that a person exert every means at his disposal to succeed. Then He will grant him providential abundance.

An image prevails of the communal worker as a servile individual who is fundamentally naïve, long-suffering, and willing to tolerate abuse. Rav Yaakov

PSALM 38

1. A psalm of David; *lehazkir,* to remember.

2. LORD, do not rebuke me in Your anger,
or chastise me in Your wrath.

3. For Your arrows have sunk deep into me,
and Your hand has come down upon me.

4. There is no soundness in my body
because of Your indignation;
there is no health in my limbs
because of my sin.

5. For my iniquities overwhelm me,
like a heavy load they are too heavy for me to bear.

6. My wounds stink and fester
because of my folly.

7. I am bent double, I am utterly bowed down;
all day long I go about in deep gloom.

8. For my loins are full of fever;
there is no soundness in my body.

9. I am benumbed and badly crushed;
I groan in anguish of heart.

Fear: *My heart is throbbing.*
Depression: *All day long I go about in deep gloom.*
Despair: *My strength fails me.*
Loneliness: *My friends and my companions stand back.*
Danger: *Those who seek my life lay snares.*
Betrayal: *They plot treachery.*
Helplessness: *I am like a dumb man who cannot speak up.*

Radak informs us that David composed our psalm "for every person crushed by illness, every tormented soul, to use in his prayers. It was written to encourage every broken spirit to pray."

מזמור לח

I wish I could forget the pain, and the shame, and the unspeakable horror. Lehazkir: To remind myself. I suffered in silence. I never talk about it. Lehazkir: To record for eternity. I was desperate, hopeless, alone and abandoned. Lehazkir: To have Him remember me.

א מִזְמ֖וֹר לְדָוִ֣ד לְהַזְכִּֽיר׃

ב יְֽהוָ֗ה אַל־בְּקֶצְפְּךָ֥ תוֹכִיחֵ֑נִי
וּֽבַחֲמָתְךָ֥ תְיַסְּרֵֽנִי׃

ג כִּֽי־חִ֭צֶּיךָ נִ֣חֲתוּ בִ֑י
וַתִּנְחַ֖ת עָלַ֣י יָדֶֽךָ׃

ד אֵין־מְתֹ֣ם בִּ֭בְשָׂרִי מִפְּנֵ֣י זַעְמֶ֑ךָ
אֵין־שָׁל֥וֹם בַּ֝עֲצָמַ֗י מִפְּנֵ֥י חַטָּאתִֽי׃

ה כִּ֣י עֲ֭וֺנֹתַי עָבְר֣וּ רֹאשִׁ֑י
כְּמַשָּׂ֥א כָ֝בֵ֗ד יִכְבְּד֥וּ מִמֶּֽנִּי׃

ו הִבְאִ֣ישׁוּ נָ֭מַקּוּ חַבּוּרֹתָ֑י
מִ֝פְּנֵ֗י אִוַּלְתִּֽי׃

ז נַעֲוֵ֣יתִי שַׁחֹ֣תִי עַד־מְאֹ֑ד
כָּל־הַ֝יּ֗וֹם קֹדֵ֥ר הִלָּֽכְתִּי׃

ח כִּֽי־כְ֭סָלַי מָלְא֣וּ נִקְלֶ֑ה
וְאֵ֥ין מְ֝תֹ֗ם בִּבְשָׂרִֽי׃

ט נְפוּג֣וֹתִי וְנִדְכֵּ֣יתִי עַד־מְאֹ֑ד
שָׁ֝אַ֗גְתִּי מִנַּהֲמַ֥ת לִבִּֽי׃

מזמור לח *Psalm 38:* Our psalm is an unparalleled expression of misery, a most eloquent catalog of human suffering.

Disease: *There is no health in my limbs.*

Guilt: *My iniquities are too heavy for me to bear.*

10. Lord, all my longing lies open before You;
my groaning is not hidden from You.

11. My heart is throbbing, my strength fails me;
even the light has gone from my eyes.

12. My friends and my companions stand back from my affliction;
my kinsmen stand far away.

13. Those who seek my life lay snares,
those who mean to harm me talk of my ruin;
they plot treachery all day long.

14. But I am like a deaf man who cannot hear,
like a dumb man who cannot speak up.

15. I behave like one who does not hear,
whose mouth offers no retort.

16. But I wait for You, Lord;
You will answer, Lord my God.

17. For I said,
"Let them not rejoice over me;
let them not gloat over me when my foot slips."

18. For I am on the verge of disaster;*
my pain is always with me.

*Lit. "for I am ready to fall."

In the final two verses the sufferer turns to God with words of prayer, at long last. There is a spiritual message in these verses: with each phrase of the prayer comes more and more hope.

First, *Lord, do not forsake me.* Total abandonment would be the worst possible consequence.

Having uttered that phrase, the sufferer feels assured of at least this much: he will not be forsaken.

י אֲדֹנָי נֶגְדְּךָ כָל־תַּאֲוָתִי
וְאַנְחָתִי מִמְּךָ לֹא־נִסְתָּרָה׃

יא לִבִּי סְחַרְחַר עֲזָבַנִי כֹחִי
וְאוֹר־עֵינַי גַּם־הֵם אֵין אִתִּי׃

יב אֹהֲבַי ׀ וְרֵעַי מִנֶּגֶד נִגְעִי יַעֲמֹדוּ
וּקְרוֹבַי מֵרָחֹק עָמָדוּ׃

יג וַיְנַקְשׁוּ ׀ מְבַקְשֵׁי נַפְשִׁי
וְדֹרְשֵׁי רָעָתִי דִּבְּרוּ הַוּוֹת
וּמִרְמוֹת כָּל־הַיּוֹם יֶהְגּוּ׃

יד וַאֲנִי כְחֵרֵשׁ לֹא אֶשְׁמָע
וּכְאִלֵּם לֹא יִפְתַּח־פִּיו׃

טו וָאֱהִי כְּאִישׁ אֲשֶׁר לֹא־שֹׁמֵעַ
וְאֵין בְּפִיו תּוֹכָחוֹת׃

טז כִּי־לְךָ יְהוָה הוֹחָלְתִּי
אַתָּה תַעֲנֶה אֲדֹנָי אֱלֹהָי׃

יז כִּי־אָמַרְתִּי פֶּן־יִשְׂמְחוּ־לִי
בְּמוֹט רַגְלִי עָלַי הִגְדִּילוּ׃

יח כִּי־אֲנִי לְצֶלַע נָכוֹן
וּמַכְאוֹבִי נֶגְדִּי תָמִיד׃

Our psalm captures every emotional nuance of the anguished person at length and in poignant detail.

All but the concluding verses give voice exclusively to extreme pain. There is hardly a hint of hope in them.

19. For I confess my iniquity;
I am troubled because of my sin.

20. My enemies are vigorous and strong;
numerous are those who hate me without reason.

21. Those who repay good with evil,
oppose me for pursuing good.

22. LORD, do not forsake me;
my God, be not far from me.

23. Hasten to my aid, LORD, my deliverer.

---

close to him. He is then emboldened to request even more: *Hasten to my aid, LORD, my deliverer.* He will not be forsaken. God will remain close to him. But he wants more than that. He wants deliverance from his suffering. Still more, he dares demand that it come quickly.

With each phrase of prayer comes ever increasing hope.

יט כִּי־עֲוֺנִי אַגִּיד
אֶדְאַג מֵחַטָּאתִי׃

כ וְאֹיְבַי חַיִּים עָצֵמוּ
וְרַבּוּ שֹׂנְאַי שָׁקֶר׃

כא וּמְשַׁלְּמֵי רָעָה תַּחַת טוֹבָה
יִשְׂטְנוּנִי תַּחַת רדופי־טוֹב׃ רָדְפִי־

כב אַל־תַּעַזְבֵנִי יְהוָה
אֱלֹהַי אַל־תִּרְחַק מִמֶּנִּי׃

כג חוּשָׁה לְעֶזְרָתִי
אֲדֹנָי תְּשׁוּעָתִי׃

So he proceeds to ask for a bit more: *My God, be not far from me*. The sufferer wants more than to merely not be forsaken. He desires God's closeness. After this second phrase he becomes confident that God will indeed be

PSALM 39

1. For the Chief Musician; for Yedutun. A psalm of David. *Seventh day of the month*

2. I said, I will watch my ways,
lest I sin with my tongue;
I will put a curb on my mouth,
while the wicked man stands before me.

3. I kept utterly silent;
not a word did I say, not even anything good;
but my pain only grew worse.

4. My heart burned within me;
the more I thought of it, the fire flared up;
then I spoke out without restraint:

5. "LORD, let me know my end
and what is the number of my days;
tell me how short my life is to be."

6. Look, You have made my life but a few handbreadths;
my life-span is as nothing before You.
Alas, every man, however firm he stands,
is but a mere breath. *Selah*

---

it no longer. At least tell me how much longer this exile will last. If I knew when it would end I could somehow cope. But it seems endless.

I accept that it is because of my sins that I suffer. But I am a mere mortal. Surely you can find it in Your heart to forgive me, and free me from unbearable persecution.

There is a concept in our tradition of *tzidduk haDin,* acceptance of God's judgment. For Rashi, our psalm is an eloquent *tzidduk haDin,* followed by the desperate question, "When will it all end?"

When one reads this psalm aloud, which is the way all psalms need to be read, he experiences an irrepressible urge to identify with the speaker's voice. He is tempted to exclaim, "It is not the nation of Israel that is speaking. It is me! The psalmist is expressing my own inner anguish, the anguish of my soul."

מזמור לט

How does one get close to God? Some seek Him in nature's wonders. Some find Him in His words. Some embrace Him, grateful for His blessings. I come closest to Him. I need Him.

ז לחודש

לִידוּתוּן

א לַמְנַצֵּחַ לִידִיתוּן מִזְמוֹר לְדָוִד׃

ב אָמַרְתִּי
אֶשְׁמְרָה דְרָכַי מֵחֲטוֹא בִלְשׁוֹנִי
אֶשְׁמְרָה־לְפִי מַחְסוֹם
בְּעֹד רָשָׁע לְנֶגְדִּי׃

ג נֶאֱלַמְתִּי דוּמִיָּה הֶחֱשֵׁיתִי מִטּוֹב
וּכְאֵבִי נֶעְכָּר׃

ד חַם־לִבִּי ׀ בְּקִרְבִּי
בַּהֲגִיגִי תִבְעַר־אֵשׁ
דִּבַּרְתִּי בִּלְשׁוֹנִי׃

ה הוֹדִיעֵנִי יהוה ׀ קִצִּי
וּמִדַּת יָמַי מַה־הִיא
אֵדְעָה מֶה־חָדֵל אָנִי׃

ו הִנֵּה טְפָחוֹת ׀ נָתַתָּה יָמַי
וְחֶלְדִּי כְאַיִן נֶגְדֶּךָ
אַךְ כָּל־הֶבֶל כָּל־אָדָם נִצָּב סֶלָה׃

מזמור לט *Psalm 39:* Rashi interprets our psalm as an expression of the reaction of the Jewish people to their centuries of exile. Although our psalm is written in the first person singular, *I said… I kept… My heart…,* Rashi affirms that it is not an individual who is speaking. It is the nation as a whole.

The nation is saying:

I have suffered in silence, careful not to complain aloud. I will not voice sacrilegious protest. I have resisted questioning Your ways. I can tolerate

7. Alas, every man walks about as a shadow;
alas, in vain is his restless bustle;
he piles up wealth, not knowing who will get it.

8. And now, what can I expect, LORD?
My hope lies only in You.

9. Deliver me from all my transgressions;
do not make me the scorn of fools.

10. I am dumb; I shall not open my mouth;
for this is all Your doing.

11. Remove Your scourge from me;
I waste away from Your blows.

12. When with rebukes You punish a man for his sin,
You make all that he treasures melt away like a moth.
Alas, man is no more than a breath. *Selah*

13. Hear my prayer, LORD; listen to my cry;
do not disregard my tears.
For I am a wayfarer before you,
a sojourner, as all my fathers were.

14. Look away from me that I may have some respite,
before I pass away and am no more.

---

way it is coming from You. You are angry with me, but I dare not protest lest You become even angrier.

I know I deserve what I got. I know I have sinned, and sinned terribly and repeatedly. I am scared to death. Will I die? When? So soon?

If I die, what have I lived for? It has all been worthless.

I turn to You. Only You can help me. Forgive me. Heal me. *Hear my prayer, LORD; listen to my cry; do not disregard my tears... before I pass away and am no more.*

Too often, when one prays this fervently, this sincerely, it is too late. Death is already imminent. Our psalm provides the words for each of us to contemplate, and to utter, while there is still time, while there is still life.

ז אַךְ־בְּצֶלֶם ׀ יִתְהַלֶּךְ־אִישׁ
אַךְ־הֶבֶל יֶהֱמָיוּן
יִצְבֹּר
וְלֹא־יֵדַע מִי־אֹסְפָם׃

ח וְעַתָּה מַה־קִּוִּיתִי אֲדֹנָי
תּוֹחַלְתִּי לְךָ הִיא׃

ט מִכׇּל־פְּשָׁעַי הַצִּילֵנִי
חֶרְפַּת נָבָל אַל־תְּשִׂימֵנִי׃

י נֶאֱלַמְתִּי לֹא אֶפְתַּח־פִּי
כִּי אַתָּה עָשִׂיתָ׃

יא הָסֵר מֵעָלַי נִגְעֶךָ
מִתִּגְרַת יָדְךָ אֲנִי כָלִיתִי׃

יב בְּתוֹכָחוֹת עַל־עָוֺן ׀ יִסַּרְתָּ אִישׁ
וַתֶּמֶס כָּעָשׁ חֲמוּדוֹ
אַךְ הֶבֶל כׇּל־אָדָם סֶלָה׃

יג שִׁמְעָה תְפִלָּתִי ׀ יהוה וְשַׁוְעָתִי ׀ הַאֲזִינָה
אֶל־דִּמְעָתִי אַל־תֶּחֱרַשׁ
כִּי גֵר אָנֹכִי עִמָּךְ
תּוֹשָׁב כְּכׇל־אֲבוֹתָי׃

יד הָשַׁע מִמֶּנִּי וְאַבְלִיגָה
בְּטֶרֶם אֵלֵךְ וְאֵינֶנִּי׃

Read as an articulation of one's own deepest feelings, this is what the psalm is saying:

I am ill. I sense that my illness is an affliction. In some incomprehensible

PSALM 40

1. For the Chief Musician. Of David. A psalm.

2. I waited patiently for the Lord;
He bent down to me, and heard my cry.

3. He lifted me out of the horrible pit,
out of the miry mud;
He set my feet upon a rock,
and steadied my footsteps.

4. He put a new song into my mouth,
a song of praise to our God.
Many will look and stand in awe,
and put their trust in the Lord.

5. Happy is the man who makes the Lord his trust,
and does not turn to the proud
or to followers of falsehood.

6. My Lord God, You have done great things;
Your wonders and Your plans are for us;
none can compare with You.
Were I to speak and tell of them,
they would be too many to declare.

7. You do not desire sacrifice or meal-offering;
You do not ask for burnt-offering or sin-offering,
but You have given me receptive ears [to obey You].

Specifically, when one feels gratitude for his freedom or health or rescue, is it preferable that he donate a thanksgiving sacrifice out of a sense of fidelity to the Torah's commandment, or because of one's autonomous motivation to do so?

Malbim clearly advocates for the superiority of personal motivation over conformity to divine law. He sustains his view by a creative but careful re-reading of our psalm. Here is how he does it:

מזמור מ

Is it blasphemous to say to God, "Keep up the good work"? Usually, I pray to God when I am really hurting. But this time, things are going well. I am singing a new song. Sing along with me. I am praying a new prayer. Join me. Together we can make the good times last.

א לַמְנַצֵּ֬חַ לְדָוִ֬ד מִזְמֽוֹר׃

ב קַוֹּ֣ה קִוִּ֣יתִי יְהוָ֑ה
וַיֵּ֥ט אֵ֝לַ֗י וַיִּשְׁמַ֥ע שַׁוְעָתִֽי׃

ג וַיַּעֲלֵ֤נִי ׀ מִבּ֥וֹר שָׁאוֹן֮ מִטִּ֪יט הַיָּ֫וֵ֥ן
וַיָּ֖קֶם עַל־סֶ֥לַע רַגְלַ֗י כּוֹנֵ֥ן אֲשֻׁרָֽי׃

ד וַיִּתֵּ֬ן בְּפִ֨י ׀ שִׁ֥יר חָדָשׁ֮ תְּהִלָּ֪ה לֵֽאלֹ֫הֵ֥ינוּ
יִרְא֣וּ רַבִּ֣ים וְיִירָ֑אוּ
וְ֝יִבְטְח֗וּ בַּיהוָֽה׃

ה אַ֥שְֽׁרֵי־הַגֶּ֗בֶר אֲשֶׁר־שָׂ֣ם יְ֭הוָה מִבְטַח֑וֹ
וְלֹא־פָנָ֥ה אֶל־רְ֝הָבִ֗ים וְשָׂטֵ֥י כָזָֽב׃

ו רַבּ֤וֹת עָשִׂ֨יתָ ׀ אַתָּ֤ה ׀ יְהוָ֣ה אֱלֹהַי֮
נִֽפְלְאֹתֶ֥יךָ וּמַחְשְׁבֹתֶ֗יךָ אֵ֫לֵ֥ינוּ
אֵ֤ין ׀ עֲרֹ֬ךְ אֵלֶ֗יךָ אַגִּ֥ידָה וַאֲדַבֵּ֑רָה
עָ֝צְמ֗וּ מִסַּפֵּֽר׃

ז זֶ֤בַח וּמִנְחָ֨ה ׀ לֹֽא־חָפַ֗צְתָּ
אָ֭זְנַיִם כָּרִ֣יתָ לִּ֑י
עוֹלָ֥ה וַ֝חֲטָאָ֗ה לֹ֣א שָׁאָֽלְתָּ׃

מזמור מ *Psalm 40:* Malbim finds in our psalm the answer to an old and troublesome theological dilemma. Should one act religiously out of a sense of obedience to God's will? Or, is it better to act spontaneously, because one is personally inspired to do so?

8. Then I said, "Look;
I come with the scroll written for me."

9. My God, my whole desire is to do Your will;
Your teaching is in my inmost parts.

10. I have proclaimed [Your] righteousness in the great assembly;
I did not seal my lips, as You know, Lord.

11. I have not kept Your kindness hidden in my heart;
I have always spoken of Your faithfulness and saving power;
I have never concealed Your loving-kindness and Your truth
from the great assembly.

12. You, Lord, will not withhold Your compassion from me;
Your kindness and true loving-kindness will always protect me.

13. For troubles without number beset me;
my iniquities have caught up with me;
I can no longer see.
They are more than the hairs of my head;
my courage fails me.

14. Be pleased, Lord, to save me;
Lord, hasten to my aid.

He begins with verse 6, inserting his own words between each phrase, thus elaborating upon that phrase's literal meaning. *My Lord God, You have done great things.* This refers to the wonders of His creation of the universe. *Your wonders and Your plans are for us.* These are the miraculous events that occur in each generation. *Were I to speak of them ... they would be too many to declare.* This refers to both types of divine actions. They are both inexpressible.

He proceeds to verses 7 and 8: Because these divine actions are so wondrous that words cannot describe them, it follows that even if *You did not desire sacrifice or meal-offering,* which, of course, You actually did prescribe in Your Torah, and *gave me receptive ears to obey You,* and even if You had not *asked for burnt-offering or sin-offering,* I would have brought these offerings on

אָז אָמַרְתִּי הִנֵּה־בָאתִי ח
בִּמְגִלַּת־סֵפֶר כָּתוּב עָלָי׃

לַעֲשׂוֹת־רְצוֹנְךָ אֱלֹהַי חָפָצְתִּי ט
וְתוֹרָתְךָ בְּתוֹךְ מֵעָי׃

בִּשַּׂרְתִּי צֶדֶק ׀ בְּקָהָל רָב י
הִנֵּה שְׂפָתַי לֹא אֶכְלָא
יהוה אַתָּה יָדָעְתָּ׃

צִדְקָתְךָ לֹא־כִסִּיתִי ׀ בְּתוֹךְ לִבִּי יא
אֱמוּנָתְךָ וּתְשׁוּעָתְךָ אָמָרְתִּי
לֹא־כִחַדְתִּי חַסְדְּךָ וַאֲמִתְּךָ לְקָהָל רָב׃

אַתָּה יהוה לֹא־תִכְלָא רַחֲמֶיךָ מִמֶּנִּי יב
חַסְדְּךָ וַאֲמִתְּךָ תָּמִיד יִצְּרוּנִי׃

כִּי אָפְפוּ־עָלַי ׀ רָעוֹת עַד־אֵין מִסְפָּר יג
הִשִּׂיגוּנִי עֲוֺנֹתַי
וְלֹא־יָכֹלְתִּי לִרְאוֹת
עָצְמוּ מִשַּׂעֲרוֹת רֹאשִׁי
וְלִבִּי עֲזָבָנִי׃

רְצֵה יהוה לְהַצִּילֵנִי יד
יהוה לְעֶזְרָתִי חוּשָׁה׃

He begins by asserting that all of the Torah's commandments have their root in our own psyche and natural intellect. Bringing a sacrificial offering to the Holy Temple when one has occasion to be grateful is a mitzva, granted. But gratitude is also an attitude which is built into the emotional composition of every human being. As Malbim puts it, it is written in God's book, but it is also written upon the heart of man.

15. Let those who seek to take my life
be put to shame and confusion;
let those who desire my ruin
be turned back and disgraced.

16. Let those who cry "Hurrah! Hurrah!" at me
be appalled over their shame.

17. But let all who seek You be glad and rejoice in You;
let those who love Your saving help always say,
"Exalted be the LORD!"

18. But I am poor and needy,
may the LORD think of me;
You are my help and my rescuer;
my God, do not delay.

---

subsequent verses: It is only because *Your teaching is in my inmost parts* that *I have proclaimed Your righteousness in the great assembly* and *have not kept Your kindness hidden in my heart.* The psalms are a manual for those who seek the spiritual life. With this psalm, and Malbim's interpretation, such seekers now have the encouragement to rely upon their own intuitive wellsprings in order to express their spirituality. They can transcend conformity to religious regulations and let their spirits fly.

טו יֵבֹשׁוּ וְיַחְפְּרוּ ׀ יַחַד
מְבַקְשֵׁי נַפְשִׁי לִסְפּוֹתָהּ
יִסֹּגוּ אָחוֹר וְיִכָּלְמוּ
חֲפֵצֵי רָעָתִי׃

טז יָשֹׁמּוּ עַל־עֵקֶב בָּשְׁתָּם
הָאֹמְרִים לִי הֶאָח ׀ הֶאָח׃

יז יָשִׂישׂוּ וְיִשְׂמְחוּ ׀ בְּךָ כָּל־מְבַקְשֶׁיךָ
יֹאמְרוּ תָמִיד יִגְדַּל יְהוָה
אֹהֲבֵי תְּשׁוּעָתֶךָ׃

יח וַאֲנִי ׀ עָנִי וְאֶבְיוֹן
אֲדֹנָי יַחֲשָׁב לִי
עֶזְרָתִי וּמְפַלְטִי אַתָּה
אֱלֹהַי אַל־תְּאַחַר׃

---

my own accord, because of *the scroll written for* me. I would have discovered that commandment inscribed upon the scroll of my own heart!

Compliance with a God-given written commandment would not have generated the outbursts of song and praise. Only the felt "peak experience" can motivate the public expression of gratitude that is articulated in the

PSALM 41

1. For the Chief Musician. A psalm of David.

2. Happy is he who is thoughtful for the helpless!
The LORD will deliver him on the day of trouble.

3. The LORD will protect him, and keep him alive,
and he will be counted happy in the land.
You will not give him up to the will of his enemies.

4. The LORD will sustain him on his sickbed;
You transformed his entire bed in his illness.

5. I pray, "LORD, have mercy on me,
heal me, for I have sinned against You."

6. My enemies say cruel things about me:
"When will he die and his name perish?"

7. If one comes to visit me, he speaks falsehood;
in his heart he stores up malice;
when he leaves, he spreads it abroad.

8. All who hate me whisper together about me,
imagining the worst for me.

---

he who supports the helpless," or "gives to the helpless," or "who helps the helpless." Thoughtfulness is crucial.

Based on this verse the Talmudic sage R. Yona teaches that one must perform all good deeds with forethought and consideration, assuring that the assistance be delivered in a manner which will not offend the sensibilities of the recipient (Y. *Shekalim* 15a).

The proper procedures for visiting the sick are spelled out in detail in the Talmud and Codes. The common denominator of these regulations is the requirement of concern for the patient's psyche, as well as for his body. After the visit, the patient should feel moved to thank the visitor, saying of him *May the LORD protect him, and keep him alive… and sustain him on his sickbed* should he ever fall ill.

מזמור מא

It is good to visit a sick person. That's sympathy. It is admirable to understand what he is feeling. That's empathy. It is wonderful when he knows that you understand. That's compassion. That's "Love your neighbor as you love yourself."

א לַמְנַצֵּחַ מִזְמוֹר לְדָוִד׃

ב אַשְׁרֵי מַשְׂכִּיל אֶל־דָּל
בְּיוֹם רָעָה יְמַלְּטֵהוּ יְהוָה׃

ג יְהוָה ׀ יִשְׁמְרֵהוּ וִיחַיֵּהוּ יאשר בָּאָרֶץ וְאֻשַּׁר
וְאַל־תִּתְּנֵהוּ בְּנֶפֶשׁ אֹיְבָיו׃

ד יְהוָה יִסְעָדֶנּוּ עַל־עֶרֶשׂ דְּוָי
כָּל־מִשְׁכָּבוֹ הָפַכְתָּ בְחָלְיוֹ׃

ה אֲנִי־אָמַרְתִּי יְהוָה חָנֵּנִי
רְפָאָה נַפְשִׁי כִּי־חָטָאתִי לָךְ׃

ו אוֹיְבַי יֹאמְרוּ רַע לִי
מָתַי יָמוּת וְאָבַד שְׁמוֹ׃

ז וְאִם־בָּא לִרְאוֹת ׀ שָׁוְא יְדַבֵּר
לִבּוֹ יִקְבָּץ־אָוֶן לוֹ
יֵצֵא לַחוּץ יְדַבֵּר׃

ח יַחַד עָלַי יִתְלַחֲשׁוּ כָּל־שֹׂנְאָי
עָלַי ׀ יַחְשְׁבוּ רָעָה לִי׃

מזמור מא *Psalm 41:* Our psalm is an insightful study of the phenomenology of illness. Its helps us understand the subjective experience of the sick person, and to comprehend his attitude toward those who surround him.

Our psalm begins *Happy is he who is thoughtful for the helpless.* The key word is *maskil,* "thoughtful." Our sages note that the text does not read "Happy is

9. "A vile disease courses through his body;
now that he is bedridden, he will never rise again."

10. Even my best friend whom I trusted,
who ate bread with me,
lifted his heel against me.*

11. But You, LORD, have mercy on me,
restore me, that I may repay them.

12. Then I shall know that You delight in me,
and that my enemy will not triumph over me.

13. You have always upheld me because of my integrity,
and kept me in Your presence forever.

14. Blessed be the LORD, the God of Israel,
from eternity to eternity.
Amen and Amen!

*Or: "lies in wait for me" (Rashi).

From the patient's point of view, as Radak points out, everyone is his enemy, and when we are ill, especially if we are feverishly ill, we begin to confuse our friends for enemies, thinking that those *whom I trusted, who ate bread with me* have now betrayed me.

The psalms are divided into five sections, or books. Our psalm is the last of the first section. Hence it ends with verse 14, which contains, not the words of the poor sick man, but the words of the poet, or psalmist, himself. He celebrates the conclusion of his book, thanking God for the inspiration and skill which has brought him to this point. He blesses God *from eternity to eternity,* from the time he began his work until now, when he is about to begin the next section.

Amen and Amen. Amen for Your blessing inspiring me throughout this work thus far, and Amen for blessing me with the persistence to continue and to complete it.

ט דְּבַר־בְּלִיַּעַל יָצוּק בּוֹ
וַאֲשֶׁר שָׁכַב לֹא־יוֹסִיף לָקוּם׃

י גַּם־אִישׁ שְׁלוֹמִי ׀ אֲשֶׁר־בָּטַחְתִּי בוֹ
אוֹכֵל לַחְמִי
הִגְדִּיל עָלַי עָקֵב׃

יא וְאַתָּה יהוה חָנֵּנִי וַהֲקִימֵנִי
וַאֲשַׁלְּמָה לָהֶם׃

יב בְּזֹאת יָדַעְתִּי כִּי־חָפַצְתָּ בִּי
כִּי לֹא־יָרִיעַ אֹיְבִי עָלָי׃

יג וַאֲנִי בְּתֻמִּי תָּמַכְתָּ בִּי
וַתַּצִּיבֵנִי לְפָנֶיךָ לְעוֹלָם׃

יד בָּרוּךְ יהוה ׀ אֱלֹהֵי יִשְׂרָאֵל
מֵהָעוֹלָם וְעַד־הָעוֹלָם אָמֵן ׀ וְאָמֵן׃

The Talmud provides a poignant example of the mysterious phrase, *You transformed*, in verse 4. What transformation occurs to the patient's *entire bed*? The Talmud (*Nedarim* 41a), relates the tragic story of R. Yosef, who suffered a traumatic injury, after which forgot much of his learning. His favorite disciple, Abaye, would frequently interrupt his master's post-traumatic lectures with the gentle reminder, "Rabbi, you yourself once taught us differently."

R. Yosef's *entire bed*, nay, his entire being, was *transformed*.

The bed-ridden person feels abandoned, certainly by his foes, but even by his former friends. *My enemies say cruel things about me.... Even my best friend... lifted his heel against me*. We all know how we ourselves begin to ignore our sick friends, if only because we feel inadequate and uncomfortable when we visit their bedside.

PSALM 42

1. For the Chief Musician. A *maskil* of the sons of Korah.

2. As a deer yearns for running streams,
so does my soul yearn for You, God.

3. My soul thirsts for God, the living God.
O when will I go and appear before God!

4. My tears have been my food day and night,
while men say to me all day long, "Where is your God?"

5. These things I remember as I pour out my soul:
how I used to move with the throng,
leading them in procession to the house of God,
amid shouts of joy and thanksgiving,
a truly festive throng.

6. Why are you downcast, my soul?
Why so disturbed within me?
Hope in God; for I will yet praise Him
for the salvation of His presence.

7. My God, my soul is downcast within me,
therefore I shall remember You from the land of Jordan,
from the Hermon range and Mount Mizar,

---

important to us. Criticize an athlete for his scholarly ignorance, or the scholar for his lack of athletic prowess, and your words have had little effect. Criticize an athlete for his failures in the sports arena, or the scholar for his intellectual deficiencies, and you have caused great psychic pain.

Our psalm describes a person who is God-intoxicated. He has felt God's presence, and longs for Him when he feels His absence. At such moments his *soul is downcast,* he asks God *why have You forgotten me?* He *goes about in mourning.*

To say that God is precious to such a person is a gross understatement. What is the worst pain that can be inflicted upon this lover of the Almighty?

מזמור מב

I obey God's will. I'm religious. I pray to God and sing to Him. I'm spiritual. I thirst for God. I yearn for Him. I miss Him. I am a mystic.

א לַמְנַצֵּחַ מַשְׂכִּיל לִבְנֵי־קֹרַח׃

ב כְּאַיָּל תַּעֲרֹג עַל־אֲפִיקֵי־מָיִם
כֵּן נַפְשִׁי תַעֲרֹג אֵלֶיךָ אֱלֹהִים׃

ג צָמְאָה נַפְשִׁי ׀ לֵאלֹהִים לְאֵל חָי
מָתַי אָבוֹא וְאֵרָאֶה פְּנֵי אֱלֹהִים׃

ד הָיְתָה־לִּי דִמְעָתִי לֶחֶם יוֹמָם וָלָיְלָה
בֶּאֱמֹר אֵלַי כָּל־הַיּוֹם אַיֵּה אֱלֹהֶיךָ׃

ה אֵלֶּה אֶזְכְּרָה ׀ וְאֶשְׁפְּכָה עָלַי ׀ נַפְשִׁי
כִּי אֶעֱבֹר ׀ בַּסָּךְ אֶדַּדֵּם עַד־בֵּית אֱלֹהִים
בְּקוֹל־רִנָּה וְתוֹדָה הָמוֹן חוֹגֵג׃

ו מַה־תִּשְׁתּוֹחֲחִי ׀ נַפְשִׁי וַתֶּהֱמִי עָלָי
הוֹחִלִי לֵאלֹהִים כִּי־עוֹד אוֹדֶנּוּ יְשׁוּעוֹת פָּנָיו׃

ז אֱלֹהַי עָלַי נַפְשִׁי תִשְׁתּוֹחָח
עַל־כֵּן אֶזְכָּרְךָ מֵאֶרֶץ יַרְדֵּן וְחֶרְמוֹנִים מֵהַר מִצְעָר׃

מזמור מב *Psalm 42:* There is a nursery school rhyme that many of us remember from childhood. "Sticks and stones may break my bones, but names will never harm me." It was a useful lesson, because it enabled us to endure the insults and teasing of the schoolyard bullies.

But there is fallacy in that old chant. Names can indeed harm us. Verbal insults can sometimes hurt us more than sticks and stones. Verbal abuse can cause injuries far worse than physical abuse, and it can leave deeper and longer-lasting wounds.

Words hurt most of all when they attack the attitudes or ideas which are

8. where deep calls to deep in the roar of Your cataracts,
where all Your waves and breakers have swept over me.

9. By day the Lord bestows His loving-kindness,
and at night a song to Him is on my lips,
a prayer to the God of my life.

10. I will say to God my rock,
"Why have You forgotten me?
Why must I go about mourning,
oppressed by the enemy?"

11. Like murder in my bones
are the taunts of my foes,
when all day long they say to me,
"Where is your God?"

12. Why are you downcast, O my soul?
Why so disturbed within me?
Hope in God, for I will yet praise Him,
my salvation and my God.

---

describes incidents in which extreme physical torture was made even more unbearable by precisely this taunt, "Where is your God?"

Among those stories is one related by a survivor of the Warsaw Ghetto, Yosef Friedensohn. He tells of a brave hasidic Jew whom he witnessed being whipped by a Gestapo officer. At one point the Nazi paused and said to his victim, "God has abandoned you, hasn't He?" Mr. Friedensohn, standing at some distance from the scene, felt those words piercing his flesh like daggers.

But the brave victim proudly stood his ground, and proclaimed in Yiddish, "*Yah! Aber nisht auf eibik und nisht total!*" "Yes, He has abandoned us, but not forever, and not totally."

How very similar is the response to the taunt in the last verse of our psalm: *Hope in God, for I will yet praise Him, my salvation and my God.*

ח תְּהוֹם־אֶל־תְּהוֹם קוֹרֵא לְקוֹל צִנּוֹרֶיךָ
כׇּל־מִשְׁבָּרֶיךָ וְגַלֶּיךָ עָלַי עָבָרוּ׃

ט יוֹמָם ׀ יְצַוֶּה יהוה ׀ חַסְדּוֹ
וּבַלַּיְלָה שִׁירֹה עִמִּי
תְּפִלָּה לְאֵל חַיָּי׃

י אוֹמְרָה ׀ לְאֵל סַלְעִי
לָמָה שְׁכַחְתָּנִי
לָמָּה־קֹדֵר אֵלֵךְ בְּלַחַץ אוֹיֵב׃

יא בְּרֶצַח ׀ בְּעַצְמוֹתַי חֵרְפוּנִי צוֹרְרָי
בְּאׇמְרָם אֵלַי כׇּל־הַיּוֹם אַיֵּה אֱלֹהֶיךָ׃

יב מַה־תִּשְׁתּוֹחֲחִי ׀ נַפְשִׁי וּמַה־תֶּהֱמִי עָלָי
הוֹחִילִי לֵאלֹהִים כִּי־עוֹד אוֹדֶנּוּ
יְשׁוּעֹת פָּנַי וֵאלֹהָי׃

Insulting God will be painful for him, surely. But taunting him about God is pouring salt on an open wound.

Asking him, in the throes of his troubles and woes, *"Where is your God?"* is nothing short of murder. *Like murder in my bones are the taunts of my foes, when all day long they say to me, "Where is your God?"*

The many persecutions that the Jewish people suffered over the centuries were often exacerbated by such mocking statements. Many a Holocaust story

PSALM 43

1. Grant me justice, God, plead my cause,
against a nation which is not righteous;
deliver me from men who are deceitful and unjust.

2. For You are my God, my stronghold;
why have You rejected me?
Why must I go about mourning,
oppressed by the enemy?

3. Send forth Your light and Your truth,
to guide me;
let them bring me to Your holy mountain,
to the place where You dwell.

---

refer to You as "*my stronghold*" – that's how much I trust You! So, *why have You rejected me?*

The Midrash continues: "*Why must I go about mourning, oppressed by the enemy?*"

There are many Hebrew words for oppression, but the word used in our psalm is *laḥatz,* the same word which the Almighty used to describe the oppression He witnessed in Egypt: "I have seen the *laḥatz,* the oppression, by which Egypt oppressed them" (Ex. 3:9).

The petitioner thus has a two-pronged argument for his redemption: "I showed greater trust in You than did the slaves in Egypt, and my suffering is not one whit less than theirs. Why, then, do You not redeem me?"

The Midrash has the petitioner continue:

> You sent the Jewish people two saviors to redeem from Egypt, Moses and Aaron. I too demand two saviors: *Send forth Your light and Your truth to guide me.* Furthermore, just as the words of the Song of the Sea contain the assurance: "You will bring them and plant them in Your own mountain… the sanctuary, O Lord, which Your hands established," so too do I pray that You *bring me to Your holy mountain, to the place where You dwell.*

מזמור מג

I firmly believe that my cause is just. My opponent believes, just as firmly, that his cause is just. There are those who say that we are both right. We just have different "narratives." Sometimes I think that they may have a point. Why can't we just negotiate a compromise? We could if he was trustworthy, honest, and fair. But he is fraudulent, deceitful, and unjust. I hope that God will grant me justice, that He will plead my cause.

א שָׁפְטֵנִי אֱלֹהִים ׀
וְרִיבָה רִיבִי מִגּוֹי לֹא־חָסִיד
מֵאִישׁ־מִרְמָה וְעַוְלָה תְפַלְּטֵנִי׃

ב כִּי־אַתָּה ׀ אֱלֹהֵי מָעוּזִּי
לָמָה זְנַחְתָּנִי
לָמָּה־קֹדֵר אֶתְהַלֵּךְ בְּלַחַץ אוֹיֵב׃

ג שְׁלַח־אוֹרְךָ וַאֲמִתְּךָ
הֵמָּה יַנְחוּנִי
יְבִיאוּנִי אֶל־הַר־קָדְשְׁךָ
וְאֶל־מִשְׁכְּנוֹתֶיךָ׃

מזמור מג *Psalm 43:* The Midrash (in the collection known as *Yalkut Shimoni*) views our psalm as a plea for redemption which could have been uttered by any Jewish exile, at any time during the seemingly endless centuries of Jewish persecution. The exile in our psalm compares his plight to that of the Jewish exiles during their period of enslavement in Egypt, and begs the Almighty to reenact the redemption that we experienced then.

As the Midrash interprets it, our psalm's petitioner begins his argument for the LORD's intercession from a position of superiority:

> LORD, before You redeemed the Jewish people from Egypt, not one of them referred to You as "*my stronghold.*" Only after You redeemed them, at the Song of the Sea, did they finally say, "The LORD is my strength and my might" (Ex. 15:2). As for me, You haven't redeemed me yet, but I already

4. And I will come to the altar of God,
God who is my joy and my delight;
and I will praise You with the lyre,
God, my God.

5. Why are you downcast, my soul?
Why so disturbed within me?
Hope in God; for I will yet praise Him,
my salvation and my God.

As we say in the Passover Haggada: "In every generation one must look upon himself as if he had personally left Egypt.... For not only did God save our fathers from Egypt, but He also saved us with them."

ד וְאָב֤וֹאָה ׀ אֶל־מִזְבַּ֬ח אֱלֹהִ֗ים
אֶל־אֵל֮ שִׂמְחַ֪ת גִּ֫ילִ֥י
וְאוֹדְךָ֥ בְכִנּ֗וֹר אֱלֹהִ֥ים אֱלֹהָֽי׃

ה מַה־תִּשְׁתּ֬וֹחֲחִ֨י ׀ נַפְשִׁי֮
וּמַה־תֶּהֱמִ֪י עָ֫לָ֥י
הוֹחִ֣ילִי לֵ֭אלֹהִים כִּי־ע֣וֹד אוֹדֶ֑נּוּ
יְשׁוּעֹ֥ת פָּ֝נַ֗י וֵאלֹהָֽי׃

By finding so many parallels between our psalm's prayer for deliverance and the redemption from Egypt, the Midrash is making an important statement: The period of slavery in Egypt is a paradigm for all Jewish suffering throughout history, and the Exodus from Egypt is the archetypal redemption, one which we pray for fervently, and ultimately anticipate.

PSALM 44

1. For the Chief Musician. A *maskil* of the sons of Korah. *Eighth day of the month*

2. God, we ourselves have heard,
our fathers have told us,
of the deeds You performed in their days,
in days long ago.

3. With Your hand You displaced nations,
and planted our fathers in their place;
You punished the peoples and drove them out.

4. It was not by their sword that they won the land,
nor did their arm bring them victory;
but it was Your right hand and Your arm,
and the light of Your presence,
because You favored them.

5. God, You are my King;
command victory for Jacob.

6. Through You we gore our foes;
by Your name we trample our aggressors.

7. For I do not trust in my bow;
it is not my sword that brings me victory;

8. but You give us victory over our foes;
You put to shame those who hate us.

In defeat, the believer retains his belief. He affirms: *All this has befallen us, yet we have not forgotten You.*

Our psalm emphasizes the role of our ancestors in our victories: *Our* fathers *have told us of the deeds You performed.* Similarly, their role is emphasized in the opening phrase in our daily *Amida* prayer: "Blessed are You, our God and the God of our forefathers."

Ramban interprets verse 4 of our psalm in an unusual manner, which enables

מזמור מד

When we see the hand of God, we praise Him. Then, our enemy is speechless. At times God's hand cannot be seen. Then, our enemy taunts us. He asks, "Where is your God?" Then, we are speechless. But we have not forgotten Him.

א לַמְנַצֵּחַ לִבְנֵי־קֹרַח מַשְׂכִּיל׃ ח לחודש

ב אֱלֹהִים ׀ בְּאָזְנֵינוּ שָׁמַעְנוּ
אֲבוֹתֵינוּ סִפְּרוּ־לָנוּ
פֹּעַל־פָּעַלְתָּ בִימֵיהֶם בִּימֵי קֶדֶם׃

ג אַתָּה ׀ יָדְךָ גּוֹיִם הוֹרַשְׁתָּ וַתִּטָּעֵם
תָּרַע לְאֻמִּים וַתְּשַׁלְּחֵם׃

ד כִּי לֹא בְחַרְבָּם יָרְשׁוּ אָרֶץ
וּזְרוֹעָם לֹא־הוֹשִׁיעָה לָּמוֹ
כִּי־יְמִינְךָ וּזְרוֹעֲךָ וְאוֹר פָּנֶיךָ כִּי רְצִיתָם׃

ה אַתָּה־הוּא מַלְכִּי אֱלֹהִים
צַוֵּה יְשׁוּעוֹת יַעֲקֹב׃

ו בְּךָ צָרֵינוּ נְנַגֵּחַ
בְּשִׁמְךָ נָבוּס קָמֵינוּ׃

ז כִּי לֹא בְקַשְׁתִּי אֶבְטָח
וְחַרְבִּי לֹא תוֹשִׁיעֵנִי׃

ח כִּי הוֹשַׁעְתָּנוּ מִצָּרֵינוּ
וּמְשַׂנְאֵינוּ הֱבִישׁוֹתָ׃

מזמור מד *Psalm 44:* For the person of perfect faith, God is present in victory and in defeat.

In victory, the believer does not credit his own skill. He acknowledges the hand of God.

9. In God we glory all day long,
and praise Your name forever. *Selah*

10. But now You have rejected and humiliated us;
You no longer go out with our armies.

11. You have made us retreat before the foe;
those who hate us plunder us at will.

12. You have given us up to be devoured like sheep,
and scattered us among the nations.

13. You sold Your people for next to nothing,
and made no profit from their sale.

14. You have made us the scorn of our neighbors,
the mockery and contempt of those around us.

15. You have made us a byword among the nations;
the people shake their heads [at us].

16. My disgrace confronts me all day long;
shame covers my face,

17. at the shout of those who taunt and revile me,
because of the enemy who is bent on revenge.

18. All this has befallen us, yet we have not forgotten You,
nor have we been false to Your covenant.

---

people because of *zekhut avot*, the merit of the patriarchs. In his comment on Genesis 48:22, dealing particularly with the patriarch Jacob, he writes:

> It was his merit which waged war for them and fought on their behalf, not they themselves, even as the verse states it: *It was not by their sword that they won the land... but it was Your right hand and Your arm and the light of Your presence.* This is a reference to the merit of the patriarchs, for by the way of truth, *Your right hand* is a reference to the merit of Abraham, *Your arm* to that of Isaac, and *the light of Your presence* to that of Jacob.

ט בֵּאלֹהִים הִלַּלְנוּ כָּל־הַיּוֹם
וְשִׁמְךָ ׀ לְעוֹלָם נוֹדֶה סֶלָה׃

י אַף־זָנַחְתָּ וַתַּכְלִימֵנוּ
וְלֹא־תֵצֵא בְּצִבְאוֹתֵינוּ׃

יא תְּשִׁיבֵנוּ אָחוֹר מִנִּי־צָר
וּמְשַׂנְאֵינוּ שָׁסוּ לָמוֹ׃

יב תִּתְּנֵנוּ כְּצֹאן מַאֲכָל
וּבַגּוֹיִם זֵרִיתָנוּ׃

יג תִּמְכֹּר־עַמְּךָ בְלֹא־הוֹן
וְלֹא־רִבִּיתָ בִּמְחִירֵיהֶם׃

יד תְּשִׂימֵנוּ חֶרְפָּה לִשְׁכֵנֵינוּ
לַעַג וָקֶלֶס לִסְבִיבוֹתֵינוּ׃

טו תְּשִׂימֵנוּ מָשָׁל בַּגּוֹיִם
מְנוֹד־רֹאשׁ בַּלְאֻמִּים׃

טז כָּל־הַיּוֹם כְּלִמָּתִי נֶגְדִּי
וּבֹשֶׁת פָּנַי כִּסָּתְנִי׃

יז מִקּוֹל מְחָרֵף וּמְגַדֵּף
מִפְּנֵי אוֹיֵב וּמִתְנַקֵּם׃

יח כָּל־זֹאת בָּאַתְנוּ וְלֹא שְׁכַחֲנוּךָ
וְלֹא־שִׁקַּרְנוּ בִּבְרִיתֶךָ׃

---

him to assert that God intervenes on behalf of our people solely because of his love for our ancestors.

Ramban argues that God's will is, so to speak, swayed to assist the Jewish

19. Our heart has not turned back,
nor have our feet strayed from Your path.

20. Yet You have crushed us [and cast us] into the haunt of jackals,
and covered us with deep darkness.

21. Had we forgotten the name of our God,
and spread out our hands to a foreign god,

22. would not God have discovered it,
since He knows the secrets of the heart?

23. For Your sake we face death all day long,
we are considered as sheep for slaughter.

24. Awake! Why do You sleep, LORD?
Rouse Yourself, do not reject us forever.

25. Why do You hide Your face,
and forget our misery and oppression?

26. We are brought down to the dust,
our bodies cling to the ground.

27. Arise and help us;
for the sake of your loving-kindness redeem us.

For those of us who may be "mystically challenged," Ramban's teaching can be simplified as follows:

If a human factor was in some small way involved in our victories, we ourselves were not that factor. Rather, it was the result of the deeds of our patriarchs, and the merit that those deeds earned them in the eyes of God, that contributed to His granting us the favor of His divine providence.

It is not my sword that brings me victory; but You give us victory over our foes.

יט לֹא־נָס֣וֹג אָח֣וֹר לִבֵּ֑נוּ
וַתֵּ֥ט אֲ֝שֻׁרֵ֗ינוּ מִנִּ֥י אָרְחֶֽךָ׃

כ כִּ֣י דִ֭כִּיתָנוּ בִּמְק֣וֹם תַּנִּ֑ים
וַתְּכַ֖ס עָלֵ֣ינוּ בְצַלְמָֽוֶת׃

כא אִם־שָׁ֭כַחְנוּ שֵׁ֣ם אֱלֹהֵ֑ינוּ
וַנִּפְרֹ֥שׂ כַּ֝פֵּ֗ינוּ לְאֵ֣ל זָֽר׃

כב הֲלֹ֣א אֱ֭לֹהִים יַֽחֲקָר־זֹ֑את
כִּי־ה֥וּא יֹ֝דֵ֗עַ תַּעֲלֻמ֥וֹת לֵֽב׃

כג כִּֽי־עָ֭לֶיךָ הֹרַ֣גְנוּ כָל־הַיּ֑וֹם
נֶ֝חְשַׁ֗בְנוּ כְּצֹ֣אן טִבְחָֽה׃

כד ע֤וּרָה ׀ לָ֖מָּה תִישַׁ֥ן ׀ אֲדֹנָ֑י
הָ֝קִ֗יצָה אַל־תִּזְנַ֥ח לָנֶֽצַח׃

כה לָֽמָּה־פָנֶ֥יךָ תַסְתִּ֑יר
תִּשְׁכַּ֖ח עָנְיֵ֣נוּ וְֽלַחֲצֵֽנוּ׃

כו כִּ֤י שָׁ֣חָה לֶעָפָ֣ר נַפְשֵׁ֑נוּ
דָּבְקָ֖ה לָאָ֣רֶץ בִּטְנֵֽנוּ׃

כז ק֭וּמָה עֶזְרָ֣תָה לָּ֑נוּ
וּ֝פְדֵ֗נוּ לְמַ֣עַן חַסְדֶּֽךָ׃

Those familiar with Ramban's commentary know that when he offers an interpretation "by the way of truth," he is telling us that this teaching has its roots in the Kabbala, in Jewish mysticism. Only such a source would dare substitute the names of the patriarchs for phrases that are clear references to God.

PSALM 45

1. For the Chief Musician of the sons of Korah; set to *shoshanim*.
A *maskil*. A love song.

2. My heart is stirred by a noble theme,
I dedicate my poem to the king.
My tongue runs like the pen of a skillful scribe.

3. You are fairer than all mortals,
charm flows from your lips,
for God has blessed you forever.

4. Gird your sword upon your thigh, O mighty hero,
in glory and majesty.

5. And in your majesty ride on triumphant
for the cause of truth, humility and justice;
and may your right hand lead you to awesome deeds.

6. Your arrows are sharp,
they pierce the hearts of your enemies;
nations fall at your feet.

We must begin by reflecting upon the special heroism of the sons of Korah. Their father led a revolt against Moses. He was shrewd, charismatic, a master of persuasion, a demagogue. He rallied a large group of followers to his cause. His sons were able to resist both the charisma of their father and the pressure of the crowd. Thus, they are memorialized in Psalms as spiritual heroes.

Shoshanim, roses, are universal symbols of beauty, because of their lovely color and delicate fragrance. But they grow surrounded by thorns. "*Like a rose among thorns, so is my beloved among the maidens*" (Song. 2:2). The sons of Korah too were surrounded by thorns. Their ability to transcend their natural environment enhanced their beauty. The rose is a metaphor which fits them well.

This psalm is a *maskil*, an instructive poem, for it teaches a powerful and practical lesson. One can rise above one's social background. One need not submit to the temptations of demagoguery; one need not be swayed by the frenzy of the crowd.

מזמור מה

In our tradition, study is a form of worship. It is the highest form of worship. Others study in silence and solitude. We study together, and we study aloud. We do battle with each other. Our words are swords, our arguments arrows. "War" is a harsh metaphor for study. But it is an apt metaphor for Torah study.

א לַמְנַצֵּ֥חַ עַל־שֹׁשַׁנִּ֗ים לִבְנֵי־קֹ֑רַח
מַ֝שְׂכִּ֗יל שִׁ֣יר יְדִידֹֽת׃

ב רָ֘חַ֤שׁ לִבִּ֨י ׀ דָּ֘בָ֤ר ט֗וֹב
אֹמֵ֣ר אָ֭נִי מַעֲשַׂ֣י לְמֶ֑לֶךְ
לְ֝שׁוֹנִ֗י עֵ֤ט ׀ סוֹפֵ֬ר מָהִֽיר׃

ג יָפְיָפִ֡יתָ מִבְּנֵ֬י אָדָ֗ם
ה֣וּצַק חֵ֭ן בְּשְׂפְתוֹתֶ֑יךָ
עַל־כֵּ֤ן בֵּרַכְךָ֖ אֱלֹהִ֣ים לְעוֹלָֽם׃

ד חֲגוֹר־חַרְבְּךָ֣ עַל־יָרֵ֣ךְ גִּבּ֑וֹר
ה֝וֹדְךָ֗ וַהֲדָרֶֽךָ׃

ה וַהֲדָרְךָ֬ ׀ צְלַ֬ח רְכַ֗ב
עַֽל־דְּבַר־אֱ֭מֶת וְעַנְוָה־צֶ֑דֶק
וְתוֹרְךָ֖ נוֹרָא֣וֹת יְמִינֶֽךָ׃

ו חִצֶּ֗יךָ שְׁנוּנִ֥ים
עַ֭מִּים תַּחְתֶּ֣יךָ יִפְּל֑וּ
בְּ֝לֵ֗ב אוֹיְבֵ֥י הַמֶּֽלֶךְ׃

מזמור מה *Psalm 45:* The first verse of our psalm, the title verse, consists of several phrases which resemble pieces of a jigsaw puzzle. It is dedicated to *the sons of Korah.* It is set to *shoshanim,* which many understand to be some kind of musical instrument, but which literally translates as roses or lilies. It is labeled a *maskil,* an "instructive" poem. And it is *a love song.* How do these disparate terms fit together?

7. Your divine throne is eternal,
Your royal scepter is a scepter of justice.

8. You love right and hate wrong;
therefore God, your God, has anointed you
with oil of gladness above your fellows.

9. Your robes are all fragrant with myrrh and aloes and cassia;
stringed music from ivory palaces delights you.

10. Princesses are among your noble ladies;
at your right stands the queen in gold of Ophir.

11. Listen, daughter, and consider; hear my words:
forget your own people and your father's house;

12. let the king desire your beauty;
for he is your LORD, bow to him.

13. The people of Tyre, the richest of all peoples,
will court your favor with gifts.

14. All glorious is the princess within the palace;
her gown is inwrought with gold.

15. In embroidered apparel she is led to the king;
the maidens in her train,
her bridesmaids, are brought to you.

For the Chief Musician of the sons of Korah; set to shoshanim. This is what is meant by the verse *"My beloved has gone down to his garden... to browse in the gardens and to pick shoshanim"* (Song. 6:2). The *shoshanim* (roses) were initially not discernible. Whoever saw them said that they were thorns, because they were surrounded by thorns. But the sons of Korah were *shoshanim* (roses), and were plucked from among the thorns.

This is to be compared to a king who visits one of his provinces. The

ז כִּסְאֲךָ אֱלֹהִים עוֹלָם וָעֶד
שֵׁבֶט מִישֹׁר שֵׁבֶט מַלְכוּתֶךָ׃

ח אָהַבְתָּ צֶּדֶק וַתִּשְׂנָא רֶשַׁע
עַל־כֵּן ׀ מְשָׁחֲךָ אֱלֹהִים אֱלֹהֶיךָ
שֶׁמֶן שָׂשׂוֹן מֵחֲבֵרֶךָ׃

ט מֹר־וַאֲהָלוֹת קְצִיעוֹת כׇּל־בִּגְדֹתֶיךָ
מִן־הֵיכְלֵי שֵׁן מִנִּי שִׂמְּחוּךָ׃

י בְּנוֹת מְלָכִים בְּיִקְּרוֹתֶיךָ
נִצְּבָה שֵׁגַל לִימִינְךָ בְּכֶתֶם אוֹפִיר׃

יא שִׁמְעִי־בַת וּרְאִי וְהַטִּי אׇזְנֵךְ
וְשִׁכְחִי עַמֵּךְ וּבֵית אָבִיךְ׃

יב וְיִתְאָו הַמֶּלֶךְ יׇפְיֵךְ
כִּי־הוּא אֲדֹנַיִךְ וְהִשְׁתַּחֲוִי־לוֹ׃

יג וּבַת־צֹר ׀ בְּמִנְחָה פָּנַיִךְ יְחַלּוּ עֲשִׁירֵי עָם׃

יד כׇּל־כְּבוּדָּה בַת־מֶלֶךְ פְּנִימָה
מִמִּשְׁבְּצוֹת זָהָב לְבוּשָׁהּ׃

טו לִרְקָמוֹת תּוּבַל לַמֶּלֶךְ
בְּתוּלוֹת אַחֲרֶיהָ רֵעוֹתֶיהָ מוּבָאוֹת לָךְ׃

This psalm is indeed a love song, arguably the ultimate love song. The lover is the Almighty, and the beloved are the sons of Korah. But the sons of Korah are not the only ones who are beloved. Beloved too are all who retain their faith despite the tests and trials of life.

How exquisitely are the themes of this psalm captured in this passage from the Midrash on Psalms:

16. They are led in with gladness and joy;
they enter the palace of the king.

17. Your sons will succeed your fathers;
you will make them princes throughout the land.

18. I will perpetuate your name throughout all generations;
therefore peoples shall praise you forever and ever.

It is the same with the King of kings. "*Silver is Mine and gold is Mine – says the* L*ORD of Hosts*" (Hag. 2:8). Material gifts are meaningless to Him. A wreath of roses is all He desires. A wreath of love for Him, demonstrated by the human heroism of people like the sons of Korah, is His most precious gift.

טז תּוּבַלְנָה בִּשְׂמָחוֹת וָגִיל
תְּבֹאֶינָה בְּהֵיכַל מֶלֶךְ׃

יז תַּחַת אֲבֹתֶיךָ יִהְיוּ בָנֶיךָ
תְּשִׁיתֵמוֹ לְשָׂרִים בְּכָל־הָאָרֶץ׃

יח אַזְכִּירָה שִׁמְךָ בְּכָל־דֹּר וָדֹר
עַל־כֵּן עַמִּים יְהוֹדוּךָ לְעוֹלָם וָעֶד׃

---

citizens greet him to crown him with a crown of gold, inlaid with precious stones and diamonds. The king's retinue objects:"The king has no need for gold and silver. What he desires is a crown of roses." Immediately all the people rejoiced.

PSALM 46

1. For the Chief Musician. A song of the sons of Korah.
On *alamot.*

2. God is our refuge and strength,
ever ready to help in time of trouble.

3. Therefore we are not afraid when the earth is shaken,
when mountains tumble into the heart of the sea;

4. when its waters roar and foam
and the mountains quake at its surging. *Selah*

5. There is a river whose streams bring joy to the City of God,
the holy dwelling place of the Most High.

6. God is within her, she will never fall;
God will help her at the break of day.

7. Nations rage, kingdoms topple;
the earth melts when He lifts His voice.

8. The LORD of Hosts is with us,
the God of Jacob is our fortress. *Selah*

There is no beseeching in our psalm, no complaint of illness or suffering, no expression of fear, no plea for the enemy's defeat.

The source of this firm confidence in divine protection is made clear in that very same phrase: *A song of the sons of Korah.* Korah's sons were spared from the devastation which surrounded them. The earth swallowed up their father and his band, but they enjoyed God's special providence. Their message to all generations is the message of our psalm: *We are not afraid when the earth is shaken.*

Note well the use of the word *Selah* at the end of each of our psalm's three stanzas. Remember Radak's contention that *Selah* is a signal to those who sing this psalm to raise their voices with mounting enthusiasm.

מזמור מו

Trouble is brewing. But I feel protected. My faith gives me hope. I feel secure. Am I hopelessly naïve? Am I foolishly optimistic? No. I am a realist. I believe in miracles.

א לַמְנַצֵּחַ לִבְנֵי־קֹרַח עַל־עֲלָמוֹת שִׁיר׃

ב אֱלֹהִים לָנוּ מַחֲסֶה וָעֹז
עֶזְרָה בְצָרוֹת נִמְצָא מְאֹד׃

ג עַל־כֵּן לֹא־נִירָא בְּהָמִיר אָרֶץ
וּבְמוֹט הָרִים בְּלֵב יַמִּים׃

ד יֶהֱמוּ יֶחְמְרוּ מֵימָיו
יִרְעֲשׁוּ־הָרִים בְּגַאֲוָתוֹ סֶלָה׃

ה נָהָר פְּלָגָיו יְשַׂמְּחוּ עִיר־אֱלֹהִים
קְדֹשׁ מִשְׁכְּנֵי עֶלְיוֹן׃

ו אֱלֹהִים בְּקִרְבָּהּ בַּל־תִּמּוֹט
יַעְזְרֶהָ אֱלֹהִים לִפְנוֹת בֹּקֶר׃

ז הָמוּ גוֹיִם מָטוּ מַמְלָכוֹת
נָתַן בְּקוֹלוֹ תָּמוּג אָרֶץ׃

ח יְהוָה צְבָאוֹת עִמָּנוּ
מִשְׂגָּב לָנוּ אֱלֹהֵי יַעֲקֹב סֶלָה׃

מזמור מו *Psalm 46:* Although the word "song," in one form or another, has appeared several times in preceding psalms, our psalm is the first to entirely be designated as a song. *A song of the sons of Korah.*

It is a song of pure confidence: *God is our refuge and strength*; pure hope: *God will help her at the break of day*; and pure joy: *There is a river whose streams bring joy.*

9. Come and see the works of the LORD,
the astounding things He has wrought on earth.

10. He puts an end to wars throughout the earth,
He breaks the bow, He snaps the spear;
the shield He burns with fire.

11. Be still and know that I am God,
exalted among the nations, exalted over the earth.

12. The LORD of Hosts is with us,
The God of Jacob is our fortress. *Selah*

And finally, the climactic third stanza, which avows: *He puts an end to wars throughout the earth.* This is the occasion for the most jubilant *Selah* of all, the *Selah* which celebrates the *broken bow* and the *snapped spear.*

Our psalm thus culminates with the ultimate cause for song, the end of war. Its message will be echoed in a future generation by the prophet Isaiah: "*They shall beat their swords into plowshares and their spears into pruning hooks. Nation shall not take up sword against nation; they shall never again know war*" (Is. 2:4).

ט לְכוּ־חֲזוּ מִפְעֲלוֹת יְהוָה
אֲשֶׁר־שָׂם שַׁמּוֹת בָּאָרֶץ׃

י מַשְׁבִּית מִלְחָמוֹת עַד־קְצֵה הָאָרֶץ
קֶשֶׁת יְשַׁבֵּר וְקִצֵּץ חֲנִית
עֲגָלוֹת יִשְׂרֹף בָּאֵשׁ׃

יא הַרְפּוּ וּדְעוּ כִּי־אָנֹכִי אֱלֹהִים
אָרוּם בַּגּוֹיִם אָרוּם בָּאָרֶץ׃

יב יְהוָה צְבָאוֹת עִמָּנוּ
מִשְׂגָּב לָנוּ אֱלֹהֵי יַעֲקֹב סֶלָה׃

Our first stanza portrays natural disasters, and promises a safe haven for those who take refuge in God. That is sufficient cause for the first exuberant *Selah*.

The second stanza assures the faithful that they will be immune from catastrophes caused by mankind. Although *nations rage* and *kingdoms topple,* the *City of God… will never fail.* At this point, another *Selah* is in order, more exultant than the first.

PSALM 47

1. For the Chief Musician. A psalm of the sons of Korah.

2. Clap your hands, all you peoples,
acclaim God with shouts of joy.

3. For the Lord, the Most High, is to be revered;
He is the Great King over all the earth.

4. He subdues peoples under us,
He puts nations at our feet.

5. He chose for us our heritage;
the pride of Jacob, whom He loved. *Selah*

6. God ascends His throne amid shouts of joy,
the Lord, amid blasts of the horn.

7. Sing to the Lord, sing!
Sing to our King, sing!

8. For God is king over all the earth;
sing with keen understanding.

---

of hands and shouts of joy. We can all clap our hands and we can all shout. Neither action calls for any special talent.

But in verses 7 and 8 our psalm progresses from mere hand clapping and shouting to something much higher – song. *Sing… sing with keen understanding.*

Radak calls our attention to the unusual usage of the word *maskil,* which we have translated as a person with keen understanding. "The ordinary person can applaud and can shout," writes Radak, "but he is incapable of creating poetry; he cannot compose songs. Those skills require the keen understanding of the *maskil.*"

Radak, whose commentary is indispensable for the proper understanding of Psalms, often shares with us his father's incisive interpretations of Scripture.

Here is the senior Kimchi's alternative understanding of this verse and of

מזמור מז

There are two types of applause: I applaud your performance. You did a fine job. We all applaud together. We celebrate as one. On that great day, the nations will applaud us. Better still, they will join us as we applaud Him.

א לַֽמְנַצֵּ֬חַ לִבְנֵי־קֹ֬רַח מִזְמֽוֹר׃

ב כָּֽל־הָ֭עַמִּים תִּקְעוּ־כָ֑ף
הָרִ֥יעוּ לֵ֝אלֹהִ֗ים בְּק֣וֹל רִנָּֽה׃

ג כִּֽי־יהוה עֶלְי֣וֹן נוֹרָ֑א
מֶ֥לֶךְ גָּ֝ד֗וֹל עַל־כָּל־הָאָֽרֶץ׃

ד יַדְבֵּ֣ר עַמִּ֣ים תַּחְתֵּ֑ינוּ
וּ֝לְאֻמִּ֗ים תַּ֣חַת רַגְלֵֽינוּ׃

ה יִבְחַר־לָ֥נוּ אֶת־נַחֲלָתֵ֑נוּ
אֶ֬ת גְּא֨וֹן יַעֲקֹ֖ב אֲשֶׁר־אָהֵ֣ב סֶֽלָה׃

ו עָלָ֣ה אֱ֭לֹהִים בִּתְרוּעָ֑ה
יהוה֗ בְּק֣וֹל שׁוֹפָֽר׃

ז זַמְּר֣וּ אֱלֹהִ֣ים זַמֵּ֑רוּ
זַמְּר֖וּ לְמַלְכֵּ֣נוּ זַמֵּֽרוּ׃

ח כִּ֤י מֶ֖לֶךְ כָּל־הָאָ֥רֶץ אֱלֹהִ֗ים
זַמְּר֥וּ מַשְׂכִּֽיל׃

מזמור מז *Psalm 47:* The sons of Korah had the gift of prophecy. They could envision a time when all mankind will acknowledge God's dominion. All of humanity will acclaim God's majesty, and rejoice along with the People of Israel. He who was formerly just *our King,* is now *King over all the earth.*

Expressions of elation vary in degree. Our psalm begins with clapping

9. God reigns over the nations,
God is seated on His holy throne.

10. O princes of the people, gather together,
you people, who are faithful to the God of Abraham;
for the guardians* of the earth belong to God,
and He is exalted above them all.

* Lit. "the shields."

Both the elder and younger Kimchi agree that the song we will sing in the ultimate future will be much more than mere words accompanied by pretty music. Rather, that song's lyrics will articulate the deepest motifs of mankind's soul, and its melody will strike chords in the hearts of all humanity.

ט מָלַ֣ךְ אֱ֭לֹהִים עַל־גּוֹיִ֑ם
אֱלֹהִ֗ים יָשַׁ֤ב ׀ עַל־כִּסֵּ֬א קָדְשֽׁוֹ׃

י נְדִ֘יבֵ֤י עַמִּ֨ים ׀ נֶאֱסָ֗פוּ עַם֮ אֱלֹהֵ֪י אַבְרָ֫הָ֥ם
כִּ֣י לֵ֭אלֹהִים מָֽגִנֵּי־אֶ֗רֶץ
מְאֹ֣ד נַעֲלָֽה׃

---

the phrase *maskil*: "The psalmist asks us to sing a song so inspiring that it will bring keen understanding to all mankind, so that all will be wise enough to acknowledge that God alone *is King over all the earth.*"

PSALM 48

1. A song. A psalm of the sons of Korah.

2. Great is the LORD, and most worthy of praise,
in the city of our God, on His holy mountain.

3. Beautiful in elevation,
the joy of the whole earth is Mount Zion;
in the recesses of the north is the city of the great King.

4. In her palaces God is known
as a tower of strength.

5. See, the kings join forces,
advancing together.

6. They saw, and they were astounded;
they panicked; they fled in fear.

7. Trembling seized them there,
like the pains of a woman in labor;

8. like the ships of Tarshish
when an east wind wrecks them.

---

we are overcome with self-criticism and remorse. Such feelings do not make for happiness.

Jerusalem had a cure for such feelings. That cure was forgiveness. Forgiveness, in times of the Holy Temple, was achieved through sacrificial offerings, which could only be brought in Jerusalem. According to our sages the phrase *in the recesses of the north* is an allusion to the northern flank of the altar, where the first of the sacrificial procedures were performed.

In the words of the Midrash: "R. Naḥman said, 'When a man sins he becomes distraught. His heart is humbled and sad. He ascends to Jerusalem, brings his sacrifice and is forgiven. He leaves the city as a happy man. Hence Jerusalem is called *the joy of the whole earth*.'"

Another cause of sadness is worry. Everyday circumstances inevitably cause us to worry. The Midrash Raba, at the very end of the Book of Exodus,

מזמור מח

What makes Jerusalem beautiful? The mountains which surround her? The ramparts and towers which can be seen from afar? Eyes don't see what makes her beautiful. Hearts feel her beauty. Hearts know loving-kindness. Hearts rejoice. Hearts find solace in His guidance, even unto death.

א שִׁיר מִזְמוֹר לִבְנֵי־קֹרַח׃

ב גָּדוֹל יְהוָה וּמְהֻלָּל מְאֹד
בְּעִיר אֱלֹהֵינוּ הַר־קׇדְשׁוֹ׃

ג יְפֵה נוֹף מְשׂוֹשׂ כׇּל־הָאָרֶץ
הַר־צִיּוֹן יַרְכְּתֵי צָפוֹן
קִרְיַת מֶלֶךְ רָב׃

ד אֱלֹהִים בְּאַרְמְנוֹתֶיהָ
נוֹדַע לְמִשְׂגָּב׃

ה כִּי־הִנֵּה הַמְּלָכִים נוֹעֲדוּ
עָבְרוּ יַחְדָּו׃

ו הֵמָּה רָאוּ כֵּן תָּמָהוּ
נִבְהֲלוּ נֶחְפָּזוּ׃

ז רְעָדָה אֲחָזָתַם שָׁם
חִיל כַּיּוֹלֵדָה׃

ח בְּרוּחַ קָדִים
תְּשַׁבֵּר אֳנִיּוֹת תַּרְשִׁישׁ׃

מזמור מח *Psalm 48:* What is it about Jerusalem that makes it *the joy of the whole earth*? What is it about the Holy City that makes *mount Zion rejoice* and *the cities of Judah be glad*?

There are several answers to these questions.

One of the causes of sadness is guilt. When we are aware of our wrongdoings

9. What we have heard, we have now seen,
in the city of the LORD of Hosts,
in the city of our God.
May God establish her forever! *Selah*

10. In Your Temple, God,
we reflect on Your loving-kindness.

11. Your praise, God, like Your name,
reaches to the ends of the earth.
Your right hand is filled with righteousness.

12. Let Mount Zion rejoice;
let the cities* of Judah be glad,
because of Your judgments.

13. Walk about Zion, go all round her;
count her towers.

14. Take note of her ramparts, view her citadels,
that you may tell it to the next generation;

15. that this God is our God forever;
He will guide us even unto death.

* Lit. "daughters."

---

and abandonment. *In her palaces God is known.* Magically, mysteriously, God feels close to us when we are in His Holy City.

Even today, when there are no longer sacrificial offerings with which to gain forgiveness, and the platform for worries is long gone, the closeness to God that we feel there dispels the dark clouds of sadness and despair. Jerusalem provides the hopefulness and inspiration that allows her to retain the title *joy of the whole earth.*

So powerful is this mystical mood that fills the streets of Jerusalem that even our natural fear of death is alleviated there. For it is in Jerusalem, more than anywhere else on earth, that one is moved to recite aloud the closing verse of our psalm: *God is our God forever; He will guide us even unto death.*

ט כַּאֲשֶׁר שָׁמַעְנוּ ׀ כֵּן רָאִינוּ
בְּעִיר־יְהוָה צְבָאוֹת בְּעִיר אֱלֹהֵינוּ
אֱלֹהִים יְכוֹנְנֶהָ עַד־עוֹלָם סֶלָה׃

י דִּמִּינוּ אֱלֹהִים חַסְדֶּךָ
בְּקֶרֶב הֵיכָלֶךָ׃

יא כְּשִׁמְךָ ׀ אֱלֹהִים
כֵּן תְּהִלָּתְךָ עַל־קַצְוֵי־אֶרֶץ
צֶדֶק מָלְאָה יְמִינֶךָ׃

יב יִשְׂמַח ׀ הַר־צִיּוֹן תָּגֵלְנָה בְּנוֹת יְהוּדָה
לְמַעַן מִשְׁפָּטֶיךָ׃

יג סֹבּוּ צִיּוֹן וְהַקִּיפוּהָ
סִפְרוּ מִגְדָּלֶיהָ׃

יד שִׁיתוּ לִבְּכֶם ׀ לְחֵילָה פַּסְּגוּ אַרְמְנוֹתֶיהָ
לְמַעַן תְּסַפְּרוּ לְדוֹר אַחֲרוֹן׃

טו כִּי זֶה ׀ אֱלֹהִים אֱלֹהֵינוּ עוֹלָם וָעֶד
הוּא יְנַהֲגֵנוּ עַל־מוּת׃

---

tells us that there was a rock platform in Jerusalem where people would come to ponder their business accounts. The anxiety that usually accompanies monetary reckonings was inconsistent with the mood of the city. So a special place, presumably just outside the city limits, was designated as the site for worries and anxieties to be aired. The city proper was a respite from worry, reserved for undisturbed happiness.

Another source of sadness is the sense of alienation and abandonment which is common to those for whom God feels absent. In Jerusalem one cannot escape God's presence. Jerusalem is an antidote for feelings of alienation

PSALM 49

1. For the Chief Musician. A psalm of the sons of Korah. *Ninth day of the month*

2. Hear this, all you peoples;
listen, all you inhabitants of the world,

3. both high and low,
rich and poor alike.

4. My mouth shall speak words of wisdom;
the utterance of my heart shall give you understanding.

5. I will turn my ear to a parable,
I will expound my riddle to the music of the harp.

6. Why should I fear in bad times
when the sins I trod upon surround me?

7. As for them who trust in their riches
and boast of their great wealth?

8. Alas! In no way can a man redeem his brother,
or pay God the price of his release –

9. for the ransom of a life is too costly;
he must abandon the idea forever.

It is a message which we do not wish to hear; a message about our inevitable fate, our mortality.

There are other messages here, no doubt: the ultimate equality of rich and poor, mighty and helpless; the futility of material pursuits; and the meaninglessness of the life that most men lead.

Traditionally, Jews hold daily prayer services in the house of the mourner during the first week of the mourning period. Our psalm is read at the conclusion of those services. Scripture has no equal to our psalm in capturing the despondent mood of the mourner: *To think that one can live on forever and never see the grave.... But man, despite his splendor, does not endure.... He will never again see the light.*

מזמור מט

We strolled along the old cemetery's path every sunny Sunday. We passed unmarked graves and modest headstones; We stared at monuments; We studied wordy tributes on mausoleum doors. The newest grave was dug long before I was born. All the dead there were forgotten, unnoticed; except on sunny Sundays.

א לַמְנַצֵּחַ לִבְנֵי־קֹרַח מִזְמוֹר׃ ט לחודש

ב שִׁמְעוּ־זֹאת כָּל־הָעַמִּים
הַאֲזִינוּ כָּל־יֹשְׁבֵי חָלֶד׃

ג גַּם־בְּנֵי אָדָם גַּם־בְּנֵי־אִישׁ
יַחַד עָשִׁיר וְאֶבְיוֹן׃

ד פִּי יְדַבֵּר חָכְמוֹת
וְהָגוּת לִבִּי תְבוּנוֹת׃

ה אַטֶּה לְמָשָׁל אָזְנִי
אֶפְתַּח בְּכִנּוֹר חִידָתִי׃

ו לָמָּה אִירָא בִּימֵי רָע
עֲוֺן עֲקֵבַי יְסוּבֵּנִי׃

ז הַבֹּטְחִים עַל־חֵילָם
וּבְרֹב עָשְׁרָם יִתְהַלָּלוּ׃

ח אָח לֹא־פָדֹה יִפְדֶּה אִישׁ
לֹא־יִתֵּן לֵאלֹהִים כָּפְרוֹ׃

ט וְיֵקַר פִּדְיוֹן נַפְשָׁם
וְחָדַל לְעוֹלָם׃

מזמור מט *Psalm 49:* Our psalm concludes a series of five psalms composed by, or dedicated to, the sons of Korah. The previous four had lessons specifically addressed to the Jewish people. Our psalm has a universal message, a message for all mankind.

10. To think that one can live on forever
and never see the grave!

11. Surely he sees that wise men die,
that the foolish and the senseless both perish,
leaving their wealth to others.

12. They inwardly think that their houses will continue forever,
their dwellings for all generations;
they even name lands after themselves.

13. But man, despite his splendor, does not endure;
he is like the beasts that perish.

14. Such is the fate of foolish men,
and of their followers who approve their words. *Selah*

15. Like sheep they are destined for the grave;
death is their shepherd.
While the upright shall have overcome them in the morning,
and their spirit is destined to endure beyond the grave.
It shall not remain their dwelling-place.

16. But God will redeem my soul from the grasp of the grave,
by taking me to Himself. *Selah*

17. Fear not when a man grows rich,
when the wealth of his house increases;

18. for he can take nothing with him when he dies,
his wealth will not follow after him.

---

ments of the mourning process early on, in verse 5. There he speaks of expounding his message in *a parable* – somber contemplation. But he surprises by giving notice that he will also use *the music of the harp* – soothing consolation.

That music is finally heard in verses 15 and 16. There we learn that there is a class of men who can spiritually transcend the limits of mortality, who can escape the inevitable destiny of the grave.

י וִיחִי־ע֥וֹד לָנֶ֑צַח
לֹ֖א יִרְאֶ֣ה הַשָּֽׁחַת׃

יא כִּ֤י יִרְאֶ֨ה ׀ חֲכָמִ֣ים יָמ֗וּתוּ
יַ֤חַד כְּסִ֣יל וָבַ֣עַר יֹאבֵ֑דוּ
וְעָזְב֖וּ לַאֲחֵרִ֣ים חֵילָֽם׃

יב קִרְבָּ֤ם בָּתֵּ֨ימוֹ ׀ לְֽעוֹלָ֗ם מִ֭שְׁכְּנֹתָם לְדֹ֣ר וָדֹ֑ר
קָֽרְא֥וּ בִ֝שְׁמוֹתָ֗ם עֲלֵ֣י אֲדָמֽוֹת׃

יג וְאָדָ֣ם בִּ֭יקָר בַּל־יָלִ֑ין
נִמְשַׁ֖ל כַּבְּהֵמ֣וֹת נִדְמֽוּ׃

יד זֶ֣ה דַ֭רְכָּם כֵּ֣סֶל לָ֑מוֹ
וְאַחֲרֵיהֶ֓ם ׀ בְּפִיהֶ֖ם יִרְצ֣וּ סֶֽלָה׃

טו כַּצֹּ֤אן ׀ לִֽשְׁא֣וֹל שַׁתּוּ֮ מָ֤וֶת יִרְעֵ֗ם
וַיִּרְדּ֨וּ בָ֤ם יְשָׁרִ֨ים ׀ לַבֹּ֗קֶר
וצירם לְבַלּ֥וֹת שְׁ֝א֗וֹל מִזְּבֻ֥ל לֽוֹ׃ וְצוּרָם

טז אַךְ־אֱלֹהִ֗ים יִפְדֶּ֣ה נַ֭פְשִׁי מִיַּ֣ד שְׁא֑וֹל
כִּ֖י יִקָּחֵ֣נִי סֶֽלָה׃

יז אַל־תִּ֭ירָא כִּֽי־יַעֲשִׁ֣ר אִ֑ישׁ
כִּֽי־יִ֝רְבֶּה כְּב֣וֹד בֵּיתֽוֹ׃

יח כִּ֤י לֹ֣א בְ֭מוֹתוֹ יִקַּ֣ח הַכֹּ֑ל
לֹא־יֵרֵ֖ד אַחֲרָ֣יו כְּבוֹדֽוֹ׃

There are, however, two elements in the process of mourning. One is the stark contemplation of the loss that has been suffered. The other element is consolation. Where are the words of consolation in our psalm?

Note that the psalmist proclaims his intention of facilitating both ele-

19. Though in his lifetime he counted himself happy –
men always praise you when you do well for yourself –

20. he must join the company of his ancestors,
who will never again see the light.

21. A man who has riches, but no understanding,
is like the beasts that perish.

---

demise merely marks the dawn of a new day. They are destined to live beyond the grave, so that it shall not be a permanent dwelling-place for them."

Here at last is *the music of the harp,* comforting words which ameliorate the otherwise disquieting themes of our psalm.

יט כִּֽי־נַ֭פְשׁוֹ בְּחַיָּ֣יו יְבָרֵ֑ךְ
וְ֝יוֹדֻ֗ךָ כִּי־תֵיטִ֥יב לָֽךְ׃

כ תָּ֭בוֹא עַד־דּ֣וֹר אֲבוֹתָ֑יו
עַד־נֵ֝֗צַח לֹ֣א יִרְאוּ־אֽוֹר׃

כא אָדָ֣ם בִּ֭יקָר וְלֹ֣א יָבִ֑ין
נִמְשַׁ֖ל כַּבְּהֵמ֣וֹת נִדְמֽוּ׃

Our translation follows Rabbi Samson Raphael Hirsh, who puts it this way: "*The upright shall overcome them* – not overcome the wicked, but overcome death and the grave. The upright, who have lived without deviating from the path of duty, shall have overcome both death and the grave. Their physical

PSALM 50

1. A psalm of Asaph.
God, the LORD God, speaks;
He summons the whole world from east to west.

2. From Zion, the city perfect in beauty,
God shines forth.

3. Our God is coming, and will not be silent;
before Him is a devouring fire,
around Him a raging storm.

4. He summons the heavens above, and the earth,
for the trial of His people.

5. "Gather to Me My devout people,
those who made a covenant with Me by sacrifice."

6. The heavens proclaim His justice,
for God Himself is the judge. *Selah*

7. Listen, My people, and I will speak;
Israel, I will testify against you:
I am God, your God.

8. I do not rebuke you for your sacrifices,
nor for your burnt-offerings which are ever before Me.

---

to publicize their philosophies. Still others use fame, often achieved with their superficial charismatic appeal, to model lifestyles for us to emulate.

We are seduced into adopting the beliefs and practices of these gurus, who seldom have substantive qualifications for their influential roles. Some of us follow them quite consciously. Others remain unaware that they have been subliminally indoctrinated into an alien weltanschauung, to which they would never intentionally adhere.

The Bible speaks frequently and explicitly of false prophets, and warns us to diligently avoid being misled by them. But the Jewish people have fallen prey to such false prophets repeatedly over the course of our history.

מזמור נ

"Thank you" is a confession. It is an admission that I need You; that I couldn't have done it myself. Who wants to feel inadequate? It is hard to say "thank you." Yet, all You want from me is my gratitude. You have everything else.

א מִזְמוֹר לְאָסָף
אֵל ׀ אֱלֹהִים יהוה דִּבֶּר וַיִּקְרָא־אָרֶץ
מִמִּזְרַח־שֶׁמֶשׁ עַד־מְבֹאוֹ׃

ב מִצִּיּוֹן מִכְלַל־יֹפִי אֱלֹהִים הוֹפִיעַ׃

ג יָבֹא אֱלֹהֵינוּ וְאַל־יֶחֱרַשׁ
אֵשׁ־לְפָנָיו תֹּאכֵל וּסְבִיבָיו נִשְׂעֲרָה מְאֹד׃

ד יִקְרָא אֶל־הַשָּׁמַיִם מֵעָל
וְאֶל־הָאָרֶץ לָדִין עַמּוֹ׃

ה אִסְפוּ־לִי חֲסִידָי
כֹּרְתֵי בְרִיתִי עֲלֵי־זָבַח׃

ו וַיַּגִּידוּ שָׁמַיִם צִדְקוֹ
כִּי־אֱלֹהִים ׀ שֹׁפֵט הוּא סֶלָה׃

ז שִׁמְעָה עַמִּי ׀ וַאֲדַבֵּרָה
יִשְׂרָאֵל וְאָעִידָה בָּךְ
אֱלֹהִים אֱלֹהֶיךָ אָנֹכִי׃

ח לֹא עַל־זְבָחֶיךָ אוֹכִיחֶךָ
וְעוֹלֹתֶיךָ לְנֶגְדִּי תָמִיד׃

מזמור נ *Psalm 50:* The world is full of preachers and teachers who claim to know the answers to the grand questions of life. "How can I find happiness?" "How can I determine what is right and what is wrong?" "What is the secret of spirituality?"

Some answer these questions in novels or essays. Others use mass media

9. I have no need to take bulls from your farmstead,
or he-goats from your folds;

10. for Mine is every beast of the forest
and the cattle on thousands of hills.

11. I know every bird on the mountains;
everything that moves in the field belongs to Me.

12. If I were hungry, I would not tell you,
for the world is Mine and all that it holds.

13. Do I eat the flesh of bulls,
or drink the blood of he-goats?

14. Offer to God a sacrifice of thanksgiving,
and pay your vows to the Most High.

15. Then call upon Me in time of trouble,
I will rescue you, and you will honor Me.

16. But to the wicked man God says:
"What right have you to recite My laws,
and mouth the words of My covenant,

17. seeing that you hate correction,
and cast My words behind you?

18. When you see a thief you associate with him;
you throw in your lot with adulterers.

---

than the Rabbi's preaching. They asserted that they could ignore the religious content of the sermon, and assimilate only its universal ethical message.

The Rabbi protested this practice with eloquence and passion, first with a parable and then with the words of our psalm.

The parable tells of a peasant who came to the royal castle seeking an audience with the king. The guards at the gate denied him entry, demanding his credentials.

When they asked him if they could announce him to the king as a visiting peasant, he insisted, "I am much more than that." They asked if he was a general or military hero, to which he again replied, "I am much higher than that." They asked him if he himself was a king, or perhaps even the emperor,

ט לֹא־אֶקַּח מִבֵּיתְךָ פָר
מִמִּכְלְאֹתֶיךָ עַתּוּדִים׃

י כִּי־לִי כָל־חַיְתוֹ־יָעַר
בְּהֵמוֹת בְּהַרְרֵי־אָלֶף׃

יא יָדַעְתִּי כָּל־עוֹף הָרִים
וְזִיז שָׂדַי עִמָּדִי׃

יב אִם־אֶרְעַב לֹא־אֹמַר לָךְ
כִּי־לִי תֵבֵל וּמְלֹאָהּ׃

יג הַאוֹכַל בְּשַׂר אַבִּירִים
וְדַם עַתּוּדִים אֶשְׁתֶּה׃

יד זְבַח לֵאלֹהִים תּוֹדָה
וְשַׁלֵּם לְעֶלְיוֹן נְדָרֶיךָ׃

טו וּקְרָאֵנִי בְּיוֹם צָרָה
אֲחַלֶּצְךָ וּתְכַבְּדֵנִי׃

טז וְלָרָשָׁע ׀ אָמַר אֱלֹהִים
מַה־לְּךָ לְסַפֵּר חֻקָּי
וַתִּשָּׂא בְרִיתִי עֲלֵי־פִיךָ׃

יז וְאַתָּה שָׂנֵאתָ מוּסָר
וַתַּשְׁלֵךְ דְּבָרַי אַחֲרֶיךָ׃

יח אִם־רָאִיתָ גַנָּב וַתִּרֶץ עִמּוֹ
וְעִם מְנָאֲפִים חֶלְקֶךָ׃

In the sermons of Rabbi Yaakov of Lyssa, a nineteenth-century rabbinic scholar, we learn of a problem he faced in his community. Many members of his flock would attend the sermons of local Christian clergy. They found them inspiring, and claimed that they were more relevant to their daily lives

19. You give free rein to your mouth for evil,
and harness your tongue to deceit.

20. You sit and malign your brother,
and slander your own mother's son.

21. All this you have done, and I said nothing,
you thought that I was like you.
But now I will rebuke you, and indict you to your face.

22. Consider this, you who forget God,
lest I tear you apart and there be no one to save you.

23. He who offers a sacrifice of thanksgiving honors Me,
and to him who sets himself on My way
I will show the salvation of God."

---

faults. How dare you pretend to know the will of God? You are grossly unqualified to gain entry into the King's palace, let alone to speak on His behalf!"

Our psalm teaches us a very useful lesson. As we seek spiritual counsel or religious guidance, we are well advised to search for a mentor who is himself spiritually authentic and religiously scrupulous. We must avoid charlatans and hypocrites, and struggle to see behind their deceptive facades.

To him who sets himself on My way I will show the salvation of God. We must attempt to set ourselves on His way, aware of the obstacles which are strewn along that way. With prayer, wisdom, and dogged commitment to discovering truth, we can avoid those obstacles and achieve His salvation.

יט פִּיךָ שָׁלַחְתָּ בְרָעָה
וּלְשׁוֹנְךָ תַּצְמִיד מִרְמָה׃

כ תֵּשֵׁב בְּאָחִיךָ תְדַבֵּר
בְּבֶן־אִמְּךָ תִּתֶּן־דֹּפִי׃

כא אֵלֶּה עָשִׂיתָ ׀ וְהֶחֱרַשְׁתִּי
דִּמִּיתָ הֱיוֹת־אֶהְיֶה כָמוֹךָ
אוֹכִיחֲךָ וְאֶעֶרְכָה לְעֵינֶיךָ׃

כב בִּינוּ־נָא זֹאת שֹׁכְחֵי אֱלוֹהַּ
פֶּן־אֶטְרֹף וְאֵין מַצִּיל׃

כג זֹבֵחַ תּוֹדָה יְכַבְּדָנְנִי
וְשָׂם דֶּרֶךְ
אַרְאֶנּוּ בְּיֵשַׁע אֱלֹהִים׃

---

to which he responded, "No. I am much higher than that." Exasperated, they asked him if he was God, and again he replied, "No. I am even higher than that." Finally they asked him to please reveal exactly who he was and what did. He said, "I am a sculptor and I sculpt gods for all who would believe in them. I am thus even higher than God, for I make gods."

The Rabbi of Lyssa then linked this parable to the words of our psalm. *What right have you to recite My laws...? When you see a thief you associate with him.... You give free rein to your mouth for evil.... You sit and malign your brother.* The Rabbi paraphrased the psalm, driving home the point of the parable: "You are a mere mortal. You yourself are ridden with moral flaws and ethical

PSALM 51

1. For the Chief Musician. A psalm of David, *Tuesday*

2. when Nathan the prophet came to him
after he had taken Bathsheba.*

3. God, be merciful to me in Your loving-kindness;
in Your great compassion blot out my transgressions.

4. Wash me thoroughly of my iniquity,
and cleanse me from my sin.

5. For I know my transgressions,
I am always aware of my sin.

6. Against You, You only, have I sinned,
and done what is evil in Your sight;
so You are right when You pass sentence,
and fair in Your judgment.

7. Truly, I have been a sinner from birth,
sinful from the time my mother conceived me.

8. Surely, You desire truth in our inward selves,
so teach me wisdom about hidden things.

* See II Sam. 12.

David said to Nathan, "I stand guilty before the LORD!" And Nathan replied to David, "The LORD has remitted your sin; you shall not die."

One might wonder then why David is prays in our psalm. He has already confessed. He has already been forgiven.

Rabbeinu Yona of Gerona wrote a masterwork entitled *The Gates of Repentance.* In it he teaches us that, even after he has been granted forgiveness, the penitent must continue to pray for three things.

He must continue to pray for forgiveness, for he cannot ever be certain of the permanence of that forgiveness.

He must pray for divine assistance in the never-ending arduous process of repentance.

מזמור נא

I will not deny my guilt. I am guilty. I am obsessed. Visions of my sinful act haunt me. I was born in sin. Sin is a part of me. I would make any sacrifice to be able to shed my sin. God does not want sacrifice. He wants my broken heart. He has it.

א לַמְנַצֵּחַ מִזְמוֹר לְדָוִד׃ ליום שלישי

ב בְּבוֹא־אֵלָיו נָתָן הַנָּבִיא
כַּאֲשֶׁר־בָּא אֶל־בַּת־שָׁבַע׃

ג חָנֵּנִי אֱלֹהִים כְּחַסְדֶּךָ
כְּרֹב רַחֲמֶיךָ מְחֵה פְשָׁעָי׃

ד הרבה כַּבְּסֵנִי מֵעֲוֺנִי הֶרֶב
וּמֵחַטָּאתִי טַהֲרֵנִי׃

ה כִּי־פְשָׁעַי אֲנִי אֵדָע
וְחַטָּאתִי נֶגְדִּי תָמִיד׃

ו לְךָ לְבַדְּךָ ׀ חָטָאתִי
וְהָרַע בְּעֵינֶיךָ עָשִׂיתִי
לְמַעַן תִּצְדַּק בְּדָבְרֶךָ
תִּזְכֶּה בְשָׁפְטֶךָ׃

ז הֵן־בְּעָווֹן חוֹלָלְתִּי
וּבְחֵטְא יֶחֱמַתְנִי אִמִּי׃

ח הֵן־אֱמֶת חָפַצְתָּ בַטֻּחוֹת
וּבְסָתֻם חָכְמָה תוֹדִיעֵנִי׃

מזמור נא *Psalm 51:* Our psalm is the prayer of a confessed and forgiven sinner.

David committed adultery with Bathsheba and plotted to have her husband Uriah killed on the battlefield. In the twelfth chapter of II Samuel we read David's response to the prophet Nathan's accusation:

9. Purge me with hyssop and I shall be pure;
wash me and I shall be whiter than snow.

10. Let me hear the sound of joy and gladness;
let the bones You have crushed rejoice.

11. Hide Your face from my sins
and blot out all my iniquities.

12. Create in me a pure heart, God,
and put a new steadfast spirit within me.

13. Do not cast me away from Your presence,
or take Your holy spirit away from me.

14. Grant me once again the joy of Your saving power;
let Your noble spirit sustain me.

15. Then I will teach transgressors Your ways,
and sinners will return to You.

16. Deliver me from bloodshed, O God, God my deliverer,
and my tongue will sing of Your righteousness.

17. LORD, open my lips,
and my mouth will declare Your praise.

---

hoping that God's miracles and redemptive power will remain with him as before. Rabbi Yitzḥak Hutner, a twentieth-century Yeshiva dean, analyzes this three-fold prayer in his collection of essays entitled *Paḥad Yitzḥak*. He finds yet a fourth component of this post-penitential prayer in a later passage of Rabbeinu Yona's masterwork.

When discussing the solemn meal which Jews customarily eat on the eve of the fast of Yom Kippur, Rabbeinu Yona writes, "By partaking in the festive meal the penitent expresses his joy and gladness in the moment of his imminent atonement."

Rav Hutner comments, "This is another aspect of the penitent's prayer: voicing joy in conjunction with God's forgiveness."

This additional prayer component has its basis in our psalm. Besides verse

ט תְּחַטְּאֵנִי בְאֵזוֹב וְאֶטְהָר
תְּכַבְּסֵנִי וּמִשֶּׁלֶג אַלְבִּין׃

י תַּשְׁמִיעֵנִי שָׂשׂוֹן וְשִׂמְחָה
תָּגֵלְנָה עֲצָמוֹת דִּכִּיתָ׃

יא הַסְתֵּר פָּנֶיךָ מֵחֲטָאָי
וְכָל־עֲוֺנֹתַי מְחֵה׃

יב לֵב טָהוֹר בְּרָא־לִי אֱלֹהִים
וְרוּחַ נָכוֹן חַדֵּשׁ בְּקִרְבִּי׃

יג אַל־תַּשְׁלִיכֵנִי מִלְּפָנֶיךָ
וְרוּחַ קָדְשְׁךָ אַל־תִּקַּח מִמֶּנִּי׃

יד הָשִׁיבָה לִּי שְׂשׂוֹן יִשְׁעֶךָ
וְרוּחַ נְדִיבָה תִסְמְכֵנִי׃

טו אֲלַמְּדָה פֹשְׁעִים דְּרָכֶיךָ
וְחַטָּאִים אֵלֶיךָ יָשׁוּבוּ׃

טז הַצִּילֵנִי מִדָּמִים ׀ אֱלֹהִים
אֱלֹהֵי תְּשׁוּעָתִי
תְּרַנֵּן לְשׁוֹנִי צִדְקָתֶךָ׃

יז אֲדֹנָי שְׂפָתַי תִּפְתָּח
וּפִי יַגִּיד תְּהִלָּתֶךָ׃

And he must pray that he be restored to God's favor. He must aspire to regain the "light of God's countenance." David asks, *Wash me thoroughly of my iniquity, and cleanse me from my sin*. He goes on to seek to experience God's favor as he had before sinning. Thus he pleads *Do not take Your holy spirit away from me*. He begs God to *Grant me once again the joy of Your saving power,*

18. You take no delight in sacrifice,
or I would bring it;
You do not desire burnt-offerings.

19. The sacrifice acceptable to God is a broken spirit;
a wounded and contrite heart,
You, God, will not despise.

20. May it be Your pleasure to make Zion prosper;
rebuild the walls of Jerusalem.

21. Then You will delight in sincere offerings,
in burnt-offerings and whole offerings;
then bullocks will be offered on Your altar.

David, that search was part of a dialogue with God that endured long after Nathan had accepted his confession and proclaimed his forgiveness.

Our psalm teaches us that repentance must persist long after initial forgiveness has been granted. There is much more to pray for: permanent forgiveness, assistance in the process of repentance, regaining God's favor, and, very simply, the capacity to be happy again.

יח כִּי ׀ לֹא־תַחְפֹּץ זֶבַח וְאֶתֵּנָה
עוֹלָה לֹא תִרְצֶה׃

יט זִבְחֵי אֱלֹהִים רוּחַ נִשְׁבָּרָה
לֵב־נִשְׁבָּר וְנִדְכֶּה
אֱלֹהִים לֹא תִבְזֶה׃

כ הֵיטִיבָה בִרְצוֹנְךָ אֶת־צִיּוֹן
תִּבְנֶה חוֹמוֹת יְרוּשָׁלָםִ׃

כא אָז תַּחְפֹּץ זִבְחֵי־צֶדֶק עוֹלָה וְכָלִיל
אָז יַעֲלוּ עַל־מִזְבַּחֲךָ פָרִים׃

14, *Grant me once again the joy of Your saving power,* which is a plea to regain God's favor, in an earlier verse (10), *Let me hear the sound of joy and gladness,* David searches to retrieve the happiness he knew before he sinned.

For all Jews, that search is linked to the pre-Yom Kippur festive meal. For

PSALM 52

1. For the Chief Musician. A *maskil*. Of David,

2. when Doeg the Edomite came and told Saul
that David had gone to Achimelech's house.*

3. Why do you boast of your wickedness, you brave man?
God's loving-kindness is all day long.

4. You plot ruin,
your tongue is sharp as a razor, you mischief-maker.

5. You love evil rather than good,
falsehood rather than speaking the truth. *Selah*

6. You love the destructive word,
the deceitful tongue.

7. Surely God will utterly destroy you,
He will snatch you up and pluck you from your tent,
and uproot you out of the land of the living. *Selah*

8. The righteous will look on, awestruck;

* See 1 Sam. 22:9 ff.

Somehow, word of this horrible massacre reached David in his hiding place. Our psalm is his response.

In it, his feelings of horror and anger are expressed, but its central message is not an emotional one. On the contrary, the opening verse defines our psalm as a *maskil*, a Hebrew word which suggests wisdom, not passion.

That is because there is a lesson to the wise which David wishes to impart in our psalm. It is a lesson to individuals who are blessed with skills and talents and intelligence. David advises such people that they too can be blinded by their malice. He counsels them that they are as prone to error as are those who are devoid of such blessings.

Although brief, our psalm consists of three distinct sections, which are delineated by the word *Selah*. We know that this word signals the reader to pause, and to begin the next passage in a slightly louder voice.

מזמור נב

I am stunned, shocked, disillusioned. I thought you were a pious man, an honest man, and a friend. I was vulnerable. You were in a position to help me. But you betrayed me. No punishment is sufficient for your murderous treachery.

א לַמְנַצֵּ֗חַ מַשְׂכִּ֥יל לְדָוִֽד׃

ב בְּב֤וֹא ׀ דּוֹאֵ֣ג הָאֲדֹמִי֮ וַיַּגֵּ֪ד לְשָׁ֫א֥וּל
וַיֹּ֣אמֶר ל֑וֹ
בָּ֥א דָ֝וִ֗ד אֶל־בֵּ֥ית אֲחִימֶֽלֶךְ׃

ג מַה־תִּתְהַלֵּ֣ל בְּ֭רָעָה הַגִּבּ֑וֹר
חֶ֥סֶד אֵ֝֗ל כָּל־הַיּֽוֹם׃

ד הַוּ֭וֹת תַּחְשֹׁ֣ב לְשׁוֹנֶ֑ךָ
כְּתַ֥עַר מְ֝לֻטָּ֗שׁ עֹשֵׂ֥ה רְמִיָּֽה׃

ה אָהַ֣בְתָּ רָּ֣ע מִטּ֑וֹב
שֶׁ֓קֶר ׀ מִדַּבֵּ֖ר צֶ֣דֶק סֶֽלָה׃

ו אָהַ֥בְתָּ כָל־דִּבְרֵי־בָ֑לַע
לְשׁ֥וֹן מִרְמָֽה׃

ז גַּם־אֵל֮ יִתָּצְךָ֪ לָ֫נֶ֥צַח
יַחְתְּךָ֣ וְיִסָּחֲךָ֣ מֵאֹ֑הֶל
וְשֵׁרֶשְׁךָ֨ מֵאֶ֖רֶץ חַיִּ֣ים סֶֽלָה׃

מזמור נב *Psalm 52:* There is a story here that must be told. It is the story of Doeg, King Saul's "chief herdsman" and one of his most powerful courtiers. The sages portray him as a master of Torah, but one whose scholarship was too superficial to have an effect upon his moral character.

David had to flee King Saul's wrath. He took refuge in Nob, a community of priests, over which Achimelech presided. Achimelech gave David shelter, food, and the sword of Goliath. Doeg secretly witnessed this. He treacherously reported the entire episode to the king, who ordered the execution of the entire community. Doeg himself was the executioner.

8. they will gloat over him and say,

9. "So this is the man who would not make God his refuge,
9. but trusted in his great wealth,
and grew powerful by his mischief."

10. But I am like a flourishing olive tree in God's house;
I trust in the goodness of God forever and ever.

11. I will praise You forever for what You have done;
I will proclaim that Your name is good
in the presence of Your loyal ones.

---

who considers himself righteous must come to fear Doeg's fate, for he too is not immune from moral error and may easily succumb to Doeg's temptations. He too may *trust in his great wealth, and grow powerful by his mischief.*

This is the lesson of our psalm. This is the reason why it is termed a *maskil,* a word to the wise, and not a *mizmor,* a song.

No matter how pious we think we are, and no matter how learned or prestigious we may be, we must be ever vigilant in moral matters. We must contemplate our choices well, and struggle to distinguish right from wrong. We must not follow Doeg's example.

ח וְיִרְאוּ צַדִּיקִים וְיִירָאוּ
וְעָלָיו יִשְׂחָקוּ:

ט הִנֵּה הַגֶּבֶר לֹא יָשִׂים אֱלֹהִים מָעוּזּוֹ
וַיִּבְטַח בְּרֹב עָשְׁרוֹ
יָעֹז בְּהַוָּתוֹ:

י וַאֲנִי ׀ כְּזַיִת רַעֲנָן בְּבֵית אֱלֹהִים
בָּטַחְתִּי בְחֶסֶד־אֱלֹהִים עוֹלָם וָעֶד:

יא אוֹדְךָ לְעוֹלָם כִּי עָשִׂיתָ
וַאֲקַוֶּה שִׁמְךָ כִי־טוֹב נֶגֶד חֲסִידֶיךָ:

In the first section, David tells Doeg what he thinks of him. *Why do you boast of your wickedness? You plot ruin. You love… falsehood rather than speaking the truth. Selah.* That *Selah* instructs us to lift our voices, for we have concluded our confrontation with Doeg. Now, with a slightly raised voice, we inform him of the consequences of his treachery: *Surely God will utterly destroy you… and uproot you out of the land of the living. Selah.*

We take our cue from this second *Selah* and proceed with an even louder voice to proclaim the reaction of the righteous to the actions of Doeg and to his just punishment: *The righteous will look on, awe-struck.* The righteous person will be awe-struck because he is fearful lest he too, upright and well-intentioned as he may be, may fall into the same trap as Doeg did. The person

PSALM 53

1. *For the Chief Musician; on *maḥalat*. A *maskil* of David.

2. The fool says in his heart,
"There is no God."
All are corrupt, they do abominable deeds;
no one does good.

3. God looks down from heaven on mankind
to see if there are any who act wisely,
any who seek God.

4. But they are all dross,
all rotten to the core;
there is no one who does good,
not even one.

* This psalm is a revised form of Psalm 14. Here the divine name is exclusively "God," whereas in Psalm 14 "the LORD" is used.

This fact can help us further explicate the need for both psalms, teaches Rav Hirsch.

The dual forms of the divine name exemplify two different modes of God's interaction with the world. The name "God," spelled *YHWH*, represents His mercy, His way of guiding history according to His own plan, independent of the actions of men. "The LORD," *Elohim*, on the other hand, represents God as Judge, the mode by which He guides the world according to the merits of mankind.

Psalm 14 employs the name of God, *YHWH*, who deals with the evil enemy when He chooses to do so, whatever the merits of mankind.

Our psalm refers exclusively to *Elohim*, the Judge. In this mode, the LORD redeems because redemption has been earned by a righteous people, whose actions have been judged meritorious.

This helps us comprehend another difference between the two psalms, one so subtle that it cannot be detected in Rabbi Cashdan's translation.

מזמור נג

Once again, look what I'm up against. My enemy is thoroughly evil; blasphemous, cynical, derisive. I so wish that my salvation would be as complete as is the hostility I face. I wish I could be happy again.

א לַמְנַצֵּחַ עַל־מָחֲלַת מַשְׂכִּיל לְדָוִד׃

ב אָמַר נָבָל בְּלִבּוֹ אֵין אֱלֹהִים
הִשְׁחִיתוּ וְהִתְעִיבוּ עָוֶל
אֵין עֹשֵׂה־טוֹב׃

ג אֱלֹהִים מִשָּׁמַיִם הִשְׁקִיף עַל־בְּנֵי־אָדָם
לִרְאוֹת הֲיֵשׁ מַשְׂכִּיל
דֹּרֵשׁ אֶת־אֱלֹהִים׃

ד כֻּלּוֹ סָג יַחְדָּו נֶאֱלָחוּ
אֵין עֹשֵׂה־טוֹב אֵין גַּם־אֶחָד׃

מזמור נג *Psalm 53:* In our comments on Psalm 14 we noted the similarity between it and our psalm, Psalm 53. We mentioned that this repetition could be explained by assigning each version to a different period in Jewish history.

Malbim asserts that, whereas Psalm 14 was composed by David, our psalm was composed in the time of King Hezekiah, whose arch enemy was Sennacherib, king of Assyria. The people of that time were so struck by the resemblance between their enemy and David that they echoed, with but a few variations, the psalm composed by David so many centuries earlier.

Malbim notes that the opening verse in our psalm does not directly attribute its composition to David. Instead, it instructs the Chief Musician to use a very specific instrument, *maḥalat,* and it uses the term *maskil,* "intelligent one," in recognition of David's prophetic insight, which enabled him to foresee that his circumstances would be mirrored by the experiences of a later generation.

Rabbi Cashdan, in a footnote to his translation, alerts us to another difference between the two psalms. "Here the divine name is exclusively 'God,' whereas in Psalm 14 'the Lord' is used."

5. Will the evildoers never learn,
who devour My people as men eat bread,
and never call upon God?

6. There they are, in dire terror;
never was there such terror.
For God has scattered the bones of your attackers.
You have put them to shame,
for God has rejected them.

7. O that the deliverance of Israel might come from Zion!
When God restores the fortunes of His people,
Jacob will rejoice, Israel will be glad.

In Psalm 14 *the deliverance* is a favor, an unearned gift. It is therefore in the singular, signifying that it limited, insufficient.

In our psalm, however, the Divine Judge rewards the people with what they have earned and merited, *deliverances* in the plural. This signifies an abundant and comprehensive redemption.

O that the deliverances of Israel might come from Zion… Jacob will rejoice, Israel will be glad.

ה הֲלֹא יָדְעוּ פֹּעֲלֵי אָוֶן
אֹכְלֵי עַמִּי אָכְלוּ לֶחֶם
אֱלֹהִים לֹא קָרָאוּ׃

ו שָׁם ׀ פָּחֲדוּ־פַחַד לֹא־הָיָה פָחַד
כִּי־אֱלֹהִים פִּזַּר עַצְמוֹת חֹנָךְ
הֱבִישֹׁתָה כִּי־אֱלֹהִים מְאָסָם׃

ז מִי יִתֵּן מִצִּיּוֹן יְשֻׁעוֹת יִשְׂרָאֵל
בְּשׁוּב אֱלֹהִים שְׁבוּת עַמּוֹ
יָגֵל יַעֲקֹב יִשְׂמַח יִשְׂרָאֵל׃

Rabbi Cashdan translates the culmination of both psalms, verse 7: *O that the deliverance of Israel might come from Zion.*

But the sensitive reader of the Hebrew original will note that in Psalm 14 the word is indeed "*yeshuat,*" singular, *the deliverance of.*

However, in our psalm, the Hebrew is "*yeshuot,*" plural, *the deliverances of.* This may be a minor difference, but it is not a trivial one.

PSALM 54

1. For the Chief Musician; with stringed instruments.
A *maskil* of David,

2. when the Ziphites came and told Saul:
"We are sure David is in hiding among us."*

3. Save me, God, by Your name;
vindicate me, by Your might.

4. God, hear my prayer;
give ear to the words of my mouth.

5. For strangers have risen up against me,
ruthless men seek my life,
men who have no regard for God. *Selah*

6. But God is my helper;
the LORD is with them who sustain my soul.

* See 1 Sam. 23:19.

Ziphites he does not call for their destruction. Certainly not with the same ferocity as he foretells Doeg's fate: *God will utterly destroy you… and uproot you from the land of the living.*

Doeg, as we have seen, is a person of great distinction, who should have known better. The Ziphites are a tribe of desert wanderers; malicious to be sure, but hardly as culpable for their crime as Doeg was for his.

David refers to them as *those who seek out my faults.* Lacking motives for opposing David, the Ziphites scrutinize him, and search urgently for a rationale for their hostility.

With this background, we can understand why the opening verse of our psalm identifies it as a *maskil.* We have already noted in Psalm 52 that this term implies that there is wisdom to be gained by carefully contemplating our psalm.

The lesson here is one that the Ziphites tragically did not learn. They failed to recognize how important it is, when one encounters two adversaries in the

מזמור נד

They are strangers, coming out of nowhere. Yet they betray me, joining my enemies. Whom can I trust? I can only trust the Almighty.

א לַמְנַצֵּחַ בִּנְגִינֹת מַשְׂכִּיל לְדָוִד׃

ב בְּבוֹא הַזִּיפִים וַיֹּאמְרוּ לְשָׁאוּל
הֲלֹא דָוִד מִסְתַּתֵּר עִמָּנוּ׃

ג אֱלֹהִים בְּשִׁמְךָ הוֹשִׁיעֵנִי
וּבִגְבוּרָתְךָ תְדִינֵנִי׃

ד אֱלֹהִים שְׁמַע תְּפִלָּתִי
הַאֲזִינָה לְאִמְרֵי־פִי׃

ה כִּי זָרִים | קָמוּ עָלַי
וְעָרִיצִים בִּקְשׁוּ נַפְשִׁי
לֹא שָׂמוּ אֱלֹהִים לְנֶגְדָּם סֶלָה׃

ו הִנֵּה אֱלֹהִים עֹזֵר לִי
אֲדֹנָי בְּסֹמְכֵי נַפְשִׁי׃

מזמור נד *Psalm 54:* This is the third consecutive psalm in which David confronts a treacherous enemy. The enemies described in the two immediately preceding psalms are substantial, if evil, men. In Psalm 52 the foe is Doeg the Edomite, a ranking member of the royal court. In Psalm 53 it is the thoroughly wicked fool, who is *rotten to the core.*

In our psalm there is no one villain. It is an anonymous band of nonentities, the Ziphites, who attempt to deliver David to King Saul.

David is not so much angry as he surprised by their enmity. *For strangers have risen up against me!* These are people with whom neither David nor King Saul had any significant previous relationship. They have neither justification to hunt down David, nor prior political allegiance with King Saul.

Although David is confident that God *will repay the evil* perpetrated by the

7. He will repay the evil of those who seek out my faults;
by Your faithfulness You will destroy them.

8. Then I will willingly offer sacrifice to You;
I will praise Your name, LORD, for it is good.

9. For He has delivered me from all trouble,
and my eyes have seen the downfall of my enemies.

---

for God. They plunged into the fray impetuously, with no regard for the God who requires contemplation and forethought before rushing to judgment.

David believes that he has learned that lesson well, and that he can therefore be confident that *God is my helper; the LORD is with them who sustain my soul.*

ז יָשׁוּב הָרַע לְשֹׁרְרָי — יָשִׁיב
בַּאֲמִתְּךָ הַצְמִיתֵם׃

ח בִּנְדָבָה אֶזְבְּחָה־לָּךְ
אוֹדֶה שִּׁמְךָ יְהוָה כִּי־טוֹב׃

ט כִּי מִכָּל־צָרָה הִצִּילָנִי
וּבְאֹיְבַי רָאֲתָה עֵינִי׃

---

midst of a conflict, to be judicious and circumspect before choosing sides. They did not consider the option, for example, of remaining neutral and playing a pacifying role in the conflict they witnessed.

Perhaps that is why David describes the Ziphites as *men who have no regard*

PSALM 55

1. For the Chief Musician; with stringed instruments. *Tenth day of the month*
A *maskil* of David.

2. Give ear, God, to my prayer;
do not hide Yourself from my plea.

3. Listen to me and answer me;
I am restless in my grief, and am distraught

4. at the clamor of the enemy,
because of the oppression of the wicked;
for they bring down misery upon me,
and fiercely assail me.

5. My heart is in anguish within me,
the terrors of death bear down on me.

6. Fear and trembling have beset me,
horror overwhelms me.

7. I said, "O that I had the wings of a dove!
I would fly away and be at rest;

8. I would flee far away,
I would lodge in the wilderness. *Selah*

They stand together under the marriage canopy. They dream of a life together.

They begin to achieve that dream. They find a place to live. She conceives, and gives birth to a child.

One day he turns on her cruelly; mocks her, and teases her mercilessly.

Then he assaults her, viciously. Lover and beloved become perpetrator and victim.

The dream becomes a nightmare.

This scenario, sadly not uncommon, is just one variation on the theme of betrayal, and the disillusionment that follows in its wake.

מזמור נה

You taught me all I know. You were my confidant. We dreamed dreams together. We were so close. I cannot believe that you betrayed me, slyly and viciously. I will fight back, and I will win.

א לַמְנַצֵּחַ בִּנְגִינֹת מַשְׂכִּיל לְדָוִד׃ י לחודש

ב הַאֲזִינָה אֱלֹהִים תְּפִלָּתִי
וְאַל־תִּתְעַלַּם מִתְּחִנָּתִי׃

ג הַקְשִׁיבָה לִּי וַעֲנֵנִי
אָרִיד בְּשִׂיחִי וְאָהִימָה׃

ד מִקּוֹל אוֹיֵב מִפְּנֵי עָקַת רָשָׁע
כִּי־יָמִיטוּ עָלַי אָוֶן וּבְאַף יִשְׂטְמוּנִי׃

ה לִבִּי יָחִיל בְּקִרְבִּי
וְאֵימוֹת מָוֶת נָפְלוּ עָלָי׃

ו יִרְאָה וָרַעַד יָבֹא בִי
וַתְּכַסֵּנִי פַּלָּצוּת׃

ז וָאֹמַר
מִי־יִתֶּן־לִּי אֵבֶר כַּיּוֹנָה
אָעוּפָה וְאֶשְׁכֹּנָה׃

ח הִנֵּה אַרְחִיק נְדֹד
אָלִין בַּמִּדְבָּר סֶלָה׃

מזמור נה *Psalm 55:* Imagine a man and a woman in love. He courts her, and promises her the world.

They share intimate secrets, and confide their fondest hopes to each other. He whispers words to her that make her blush and glow.

9. I would quickly find a shelter for myself
from the raging wind and the tempest."

10. LORD, confuse and break up their schemes!*
For I see violence and strife in the city;

11. day and night they go around its walls;
trouble and mischief are in its midst.

12. There is destruction everywhere;
fraud and deceit never depart from its streets.

13. Yet, it is not an enemy who reviles me – that I could bear;
nor is it a foe of mine who treats me with scorn – for then I could hide from him.

14. But it is you, a man like myself,
my mentor, my intimate friend;

15. we used to take sweet counsel together,
as we walked with the throng** to the house of God.

16. May He incite death against them;
may they go down alive into Sheol,
for evil is in their dwellings, in their very midst.

17. But I call to God,
and the LORD will save me.

* Lit. "their tongue."

** Or: "with ecstasy."

My mentor, my intimate friend; we used to take sweet counsel together, as we walked with the throng to the house of God.

One day, without warning, Achitophel joined the ranks of those who rebelled against David's reign.

David felt betrayal, and expresses it: *It is not an enemy who reviles me – that I could bear... it is you!*

But David has more pressing needs than expressing his emotions. He is in

ט אָחִ֣ישָׁה מִפְלָ֣ט לִ֑י
מֵר֖וּחַ סֹעָ֣ה מִסָּֽעַר׃

י בַּלַּ֣ע אֲ֭דֹנָי פַּלַּ֣ג לְשׁוֹנָ֑ם
כִּֽי־רָאִ֨יתִי חָמָ֖ס וְרִ֣יב בָּעִֽיר׃

יא יוֹמָ֤ם וָלַ֗יְלָה יְסוֹבְבֻ֥הָ עַל־חוֹמֹתֶ֑יהָ
וְאָ֖וֶן וְעָמָ֣ל בְּקִרְבָּֽהּ׃

יב הַוּ֥וֹת בְּקִרְבָּ֑הּ
וְלֹא־יָמִ֥ישׁ מֵ֝רְחֹבָ֗הּ תֹּ֣ךְ וּמִרְמָֽה׃

יג כִּ֤י לֹא־אוֹיֵ֣ב יְחָרְפֵ֣נִי וְאֶ֫שָּׂ֥א
לֹֽא־מְ֭שַׂנְאִי עָלַ֣י הִגְדִּ֑יל וְאֶסָּתֵ֥ר מִמֶּֽנּוּ׃

יד וְאַתָּ֣ה אֱנ֣וֹשׁ כְּעֶרְכִּ֑י
אַ֝לּוּפִ֗י וּמְיֻדָּעִֽי׃

טו אֲשֶׁ֣ר יַ֭חְדָּו נַמְתִּ֣יק ס֑וֹד
בְּבֵ֥ית אֱ֝לֹהִ֗ים נְהַלֵּ֥ךְ בְּרָֽגֶשׁ׃

טז יְשִׁ֤ימָ֨וֶת ׀ עָלֵ֗ימוֹ יַשִּׁ֤יא מָ֨וֶת
יֵרְד֣וּ שְׁא֣וֹל חַיִּ֑ים
כִּֽי־רָע֖וֹת בִּמְגוּרָ֣ם בְּקִרְבָּֽם׃

יז אֲ֭נִי אֶל־אֱלֹהִ֣ים אֶקְרָ֑א
וַ֝יהוָ֗ה יוֹשִׁיעֵֽנִי׃

Our psalm is a heart-rending description of such a betrayal. Its tale is not a domestic tale of a marriage gone awry.

It is rather, our sages tell us, the tale of King David and the most treacherous of his enemies, Achitophel.

Achitophel and David studied together, worshipped together, and planned together.

18. Evening, morning and noon
I complain and moan,
and He hears my voice.

19. He rescues me unharmed from the battle
that is waged against me;
for many are hostile to me.

20. God, who is enthroned from of old,
will hear and humble them. *Selah*
For these people never change,
and have no fear of God.

21. That man* attacked those who were at peace with him,
he violated his covenant of friendship.

22. His speech was smoother than butter,
yet war was in his heart;
his words were more soothing than oil,
yet they were swords, drawn.

23. Cast your cares upon the LORD and He will sustain you;
He will never let the righteous man fall.

24. For You, God, will bring them down into the deepest pit;
bloodthirsty and deceitful men
shall not live out half their days;
but I, for my part, will put my trust in You.

* I.e., the "friend" of v. 14.

David's concluding words serve as advice to our betrayed wife, and to all overwhelmed by traitorous enemies:

Cast your cares upon the LORD and He will sustain you;
He will never let the righteous man fall.

יח עֶ֤רֶב וָבֹ֣קֶר וְ֭צׇהֳרַיִם אָשִׂ֣יחָה וְאֶהֱמֶ֑ה
וַיִּשְׁמַ֥ע קוֹלִֽי׃

יט פָּ֘דָ֤ה בְשָׁל֣וֹם נַ֭פְשִׁי מִקְּרׇב־לִ֑י
כִּֽי־בְ֝רַבִּ֗ים הָי֥וּ עִמָּדִֽי׃

כ יִשְׁמַ֤ע ׀ אֵ֨ל ׀ וְיַעֲנֵ֗ם וְיֹ֘שֵׁ֤ב קֶ֗דֶם סֶ֥לָה
אֲשֶׁ֤ר אֵ֣ין חֲלִיפ֣וֹת לָ֑מוֹ
וְלֹ֖א יָרְא֣וּ אֱלֹהִֽים׃

כא שָׁלַ֣ח יָ֭דָיו בִּשְׁלֹמָ֗יו
חִלֵּ֥ל בְּרִיתֽוֹ׃

כב חָלְק֤וּ ׀ מַחְמָאֹ֡ת פִּ֗יו וּֽקְרׇב־לִ֫בּ֥וֹ
רַכּ֣וּ דְבָרָ֣יו מִשֶּׁ֑מֶן
וְהֵ֥מָּה פְתִחֽוֹת׃

כג הַשְׁלֵ֤ךְ עַל־יהוה ׀ יְהָבְךָ֮ וְה֪וּא יְכַ֫לְכְּלֶ֥ךָ
לֹא־יִתֵּ֖ן לְעוֹלָ֥ם מ֝֗וֹט לַצַּדִּֽיק׃

כד וְאַתָּ֤ה אֱלֹהִ֨ים ׀ תּוֹרִדֵ֡ם לִבְאֵ֬ר שַׁ֗חַת
אַנְשֵׁ֤י דָמִ֣ים וּ֭מִרְמָה לֹא־יֶחֱצ֣וּ יְמֵיהֶ֑ם
וַ֝אֲנִ֗י אֶבְטַח־בָּֽךְ׃

---

grave danger and wishes he could flee to some secluded somewhere. But he cannot. He must defend himself.

The unfortunate woman who suffered her husband's treachery can take David as a model as she struggles to defend herself.

David exemplifies the spiritual response to suffering. His first line of defense is turning to God. He is a man of action and he will take action. But first he turns his eyes heavenward.

PSALM 56

1. For the Chief Musician; on *yonat elem reḥokim*. Of David.
A *mikhtam*, when the Philistines seized him in Gath.

2. Have mercy on me, God, for men trample me underfoot;
all day long assailants harass me.

3. My foes trample on me all day long;
for many are those who assail me, O Most High.

4. On the day of my great fear, I put my trust in You.

5. In God, whose word I praise,
in God I trust, I shall not fear;
what can mortal man do to me?

6. All day long they distort my words,*
all their thought is to harm me.

7. They band together, they lie in wait,
they watch my steps, eager to take my life.

8. For such crimes are they to go unpunished?**
God, in Your anger cast down such people.

* Or: "they vex me for my words."

** Lit. "is deliverance for them."

But there are a number of spiritual stratagems at his disposal. He uses them all, and in the process provides guidance for all eternity to those who feel hopelessly trapped by their circumstances.

First of all, he is not in denial. He readily admits to himself that he is afraid, and for good reason. Although he trusts in God, he is not blind to the danger he faces. *On the day of my great fear, I put my trust in You.*

Rabbi Naḥman of Breslov (*Likkutei Moharan* II, 13–14) finds a second spiritual lesson in the latter half of verse 3: *for many are those who assail me, O Most High.* He creatively suggests an alternate translation, which also fits the Hebrew: *for many are those who assail me from on high.*

מזמור נו

This time things are really bad. There is no exit. I am scared to death. But God feels near. I can pray to Him. I can even thank Him. Things will work out.

א לַמְנַצֵּחַ ׀ עַל־יוֹנַת אֵלֶם רְחֹקִים לְדָוִד מִכְתָּם
בֶּאֱחֹז אֹתוֹ פְלִשְׁתִּים בְּגַת׃

ב חָנֵּנִי אֱלֹהִים כִּי־שְׁאָפַנִי אֱנוֹשׁ
כָּל־הַיּוֹם לֹחֵם יִלְחָצֵנִי׃

ג שָׁאֲפוּ שׁוֹרְרַי כָּל־הַיּוֹם
כִּי־רַבִּים לֹחֲמִים לִי מָרוֹם׃

ד יוֹם אִירָא
אֲנִי אֵלֶיךָ אֶבְטָח׃

ה בֵּאלֹהִים אֲהַלֵּל דְּבָרוֹ
בֵּאלֹהִים בָּטַחְתִּי לֹא אִירָא
מַה־יַּעֲשֶׂה בָשָׂר לִי׃

ו כָּל־הַיּוֹם דְּבָרַי יְעַצֵּבוּ
עָלַי כָּל־מַחְשְׁבֹתָם לָרָע׃

ז יָגוּרוּ ׀ יצפינו הֵמָּה עֲקֵבַי יִשְׁמֹרוּ יְצְפּוֹנוּ
כַּאֲשֶׁר קִוּוּ נַפְשִׁי׃

ח עַל־אָוֶן פַּלֶּט־לָמוֹ
בְּאַף עַמִּים ׀ הוֹרֵד אֱלֹהִים׃

מזמור נו *Psalm 56:* In the preceding four psalms we find David beset by a variety of enemies: First Doeg, then the unnamed knave, followed by the Ziphites and Achitophel.

In our psalm he is in the grips of the worst enemy of all: the Philistines. David slew their hero Goliath. He finds himself a captive in their territory. Escaping their vengeance seems impossible.

9. Do keep count of my wanderings;
store my tears in Your flask.
Surely they are recorded in Your book.

10. Then my enemies will turn back
when I call for help;
for this I know, that God is on my side.

11. In God, whose word I praise,
in the LORD, whose word I praise,

12. in God I trust, I shall not fear;
what can man do to me?

13. I must pay the vows I made to You, God;
I will render thank-offerings to You.

14. For You have rescued my soul from death,
my feet from stumbling,
that I may walk before God in the light of life.

---

does more than convey the value of genuine tears. It assures us that God preserves tears shed on past occasions, however long ago.

In the heat of battle, in the throes of crisis, it is impossible to properly pray. At such moments we can still be confident that God recalls our prayers; prayers that we ourselves have long forgotten. Our tears of earlier times are stored and recorded forever.

ט נֹדִי סָפַרְתָּה אָתָּה
שִׂימָה דִמְעָתִי בְנֹאדֶךָ
הֲלֹא בְּסִפְרָתֶךָ׃

י אָז ׀ יָשׁוּבוּ אוֹיְבַי אָחוֹר בְּיוֹם אֶקְרָא
זֶה־יָדַעְתִּי כִּי־אֱלֹהִים לִי׃

יא בֵּאלֹהִים אֲהַלֵּל דָּבָר
בַּיהוה אֲהַלֵּל דָּבָר׃

יב בֵּאלֹהִים בָּטַחְתִּי לֹא אִירָא
מַה־יַּעֲשֶׂה אָדָם לִי׃

יג עָלַי אֱלֹהִים נְדָרֶיךָ
אֲשַׁלֵּם תּוֹדֹת לָךְ׃

יד כִּי הִצַּלְתָּ נַפְשִׁי מִמָּוֶת
הֲלֹא רַגְלַי מִדֶּחִי
לְהִתְהַלֵּךְ לִפְנֵי אֱלֹהִים בְּאוֹר הַחַיִּים׃

This translation is consistent with the Talmud's teaching (*Sanhedrin* 44b): "There are enemies below; there are also enemies above." One must first reconcile with the enemies above, with *those who assail me from on high,* before one can address his earthly antagonists.

If a person's suffering drives him closer to God, he is then enabled to call upon God for His help in alleviating that suffering.

Yet another spiritual lesson pertains to the provocative image in verse 9: *store my tears in Your flask. Surely they are recorded in Your book.* This phrase

PSALM 57

1. For the Chief Musician; *al tashḥet.* Of David. A *mikhtam,*
when he fled from Saul into a cave.

2. God, have mercy on me, have mercy,
for in You does my soul take refuge.
In the shadow of Your wings I take refuge
until the storms of destruction have passed.

3. I call to God Most High,
to God who will make all end well for me.

4. He will send from heaven and save me
from the reproach of him who would trample me down. *Selah*
God will send His loving-kindness and His faithfulness.

5. I am among lions;
I lie down among hotheads,
men whose teeth are spears and arrows,
whose tongue is a sharp sword.

6. Be exalted, God, above the heavens;
let Your glory be over all the earth.

7. They have spread a net for my feet,
my spirit is low;
they have dug a pit in my path,
but have themselves fallen into it. *Selah*

---

important ways. For one thing, in it David is so confident in his ultimate deliverance that he is already planning to take up his harp and lyre and sing God's praises.

There is another new element that is introduced in our psalm, one with great theological significance. It centers about verse 3: *I call to God Most High, to God who will make all end well for me.* The latter half of this verse can be paraphrased as *to God who will finish what I have started.*

מזמור נז

I am trapped in a cave. I am surrounded by lions, hotheads, spears and arrows and swords. I don't know why, but I am confident that I will escape to safety. Bring me my harp now! Strange as it may seem, I am ready to sing.

א לַמְנַצֵּחַ אַל־תַּשְׁחֵת לְדָוִד מִכְתָּם
בְּבָרְחוֹ מִפְּנֵי־שָׁאוּל בַּמְּעָרָה׃

ב חָנֵּנִי אֱלֹהִים ׀ חָנֵּנִי
כִּי בְךָ חָסָיָה נַפְשִׁי
וּבְצֵל־כְּנָפֶיךָ אֶחְסֶה עַד יַעֲבֹר הַוּוֹת׃

ג אֶקְרָא לֵאלֹהִים עֶלְיוֹן
לָאֵל גֹּמֵר עָלָי׃

ד יִשְׁלַח מִשָּׁמַיִם ׀ וְיוֹשִׁיעֵנִי חֵרֵף שֹׁאֲפִי סֶלָה
יִשְׁלַח אֱלֹהִים חַסְדּוֹ וַאֲמִתּוֹ׃

ה נַפְשִׁי ׀ בְּתוֹךְ לְבָאִם אֶשְׁכְּבָה לֹהֲטִים
בְּנֵי־אָדָם שִׁנֵּיהֶם חֲנִית וְחִצִּים
וּלְשׁוֹנָם חֶרֶב חַדָּה׃

ו רוּמָה עַל־הַשָּׁמַיִם אֱלֹהִים
עַל כָּל־הָאָרֶץ כְּבוֹדֶךָ׃

ז רֶשֶׁת ׀ הֵכִינוּ לִפְעָמַי כָּפַף נַפְשִׁי
כָּרוּ לְפָנַי שִׁיחָה
נָפְלוּ בְתוֹכָהּ סֶלָה׃

מזמור נז *Psalm 57:* Our psalm is the sixth in a succession of psalms in which David prays desperately to be delivered from his enemies. This time it is Saul from whom he is fleeing, and it is from a cave that he beseeches God for mercy.

But our psalm differs from the preceding ones in this series in several

8. My heart is steadfast, God,
my heart is steadfast;
I will sing and chant praises.

9. Awake, O my soul!
Awake, harp and lyre!
I will awaken the dawn.

10. I will praise You, LORD, among the nations;
I will sing praises to You among the peoples.

11. For Your loving-kindness is as high as the heavens;
Your faithfulness reaches to the sky.

12. Be exalted, God, above the heavens;
let Your glory be over all the earth.

> To which the king responded reassuringly, "You just dabble with your paints, and I will gladly yield some of my glory."

In simple terms the king was saying: "You just do your best. I'll meet you more than halfway."

When Man attempts to serve God he need not feel paralyzed by the frustration expressed by Solomon. Yes, he realizes that his acts of worship are not just inadequate, but must appear ludicrous from God's perspective. But he can feel reassured by the words of our psalm: *God will make all end well for me.*

In the metaphor of the Midrash's parable, God equates our playful dabbling in paints with an exquisite work of art. In the metaphor of our psalm, He empowers the music of the mere harp and lyre with the ability to *awaken the dawn.*

Did not the sage R. Tarfon express this very notion when he taught: "It is not for you to complete the task, but neither are you free to stand aside from it" (*Pirkei Avot* 2:21)?

We can use the words of our psalm when we feel overwhelmed by the religious duties with which we are constantly confronted: *I call to God Most High, to God who will finish what I have started.*

ח נָכ֣וֹן לִבִּ֣י אֱ֭לֹהִים נָכ֣וֹן לִבִּ֑י
אָ֝שִׁ֗ירָה וַאֲזַמֵּֽרָה׃

ט ע֤וּרָה כְבוֹדִ֗י ע֭וּרָֽה הַנֵּ֥בֶל וְכִנּ֗וֹר
אָעִ֥ירָה שָּֽׁחַר׃

י אוֹדְךָ֖ בָעַמִּ֥ים ׀ אֲדֹנָ֑י
אֲ֝זַמֶּרְךָ֗ בַּלְאֻמִּֽים׃

יא כִּֽי־גָדֹ֣ל עַד־שָׁמַ֣יִם חַסְדֶּ֑ךָ
וְעַד־שְׁחָקִ֣ים אֲמִתֶּֽךָ׃

יב ר֣וּמָה עַל־שָׁמַ֣יִם אֱלֹהִ֑ים
עַ֖ל כָּל־הָאָ֣רֶץ כְּבוֹדֶֽךָ׃

Man is limited; God is infinite. Our spiritual leaders from Moses on down have struggled with the question of how puny humans, of negligible significance from a cosmic perspective, can possibly presume to worship the eternal and omnipotent God.

Solomon put it perhaps best. As he set out to build the Holy Temple in Jerusalem he hesitated. The task was daunting, and the very notion of building an abode for God seemed audacious.

He asked, *But will God really dwell on earth? Even the heavens to their utmost reaches cannot contain You, how much less this house, which I have built?* (1 Kings 8:27)

The Midrash (*Shemot Raba* 35:60) offers a fascinating parable to express this very dilemma.

> There was once a king who had a most handsome face. He asked his servant to paint his portrait. The servant protested: "My royal master, how can I paint a picture to even remotely resemble your wondrous countenance?"

PSALM 58

1. For the Chief Musician; *al tashḥet.* Of David.
A *mikhtam.*

2. Do you really assemble to dispense justice?
Do you judge people with fairness?

3. In your heart you work injustice;
with your hands you justify violence in the land.

4. The wicked are estranged from birth,
those liars go astray as soon as they are born!

5. Their venom is like the venom of serpents;
they are like the deaf asp which stops its ears

6. so as not to listen to the sound of the charmer,
or to the expert caster of spells.

7. God, break the teeth in their mouths;
Lord, shatter the fangs of these young lions.

8. May they melt and vanish like water.
May He aim His arrows till they are cut to pieces.

---

justice? You *are like the deaf asp which stops its ears so as not to listen* to the conclusive evidence of my innocence.

One dramatic example is David's ire against Saul's trusted general, Abner, for failing to take note of that palpable evidence, as described in I Samuel, chapter 26. There we read:

> David went… to the place where Saul had encamped, and David saw the spot where Saul and his army commander, Abner son of Ner, lay asleep…. David and Abishai approached the troops by night, and found Saul fast asleep inside the barricade. And Abishai said to David, "…let me pin him to the ground with a single thrust of the spear…" But David said to Abishai, "Don't do him violence! …God forbid that I should lay a hand upon the Lord's anointed"… So David took away the spear and the water jar at Saul's head.

מזמור נח

They know that I am right. They see the injustice which has been perpetrated against me. Yet they remain silent. Are they malicious? Are they corrupt? Are they cowardly? Do I not matter to them? I know. They are indifferent. That's the worst sin of all.

א לַמְנַצֵּחַ אַל־תַּשְׁחֵת לְדָוִד מִכְתָּם׃

ב הַאֻמְנָם אֵלֶם צֶדֶק תְּדַבֵּרוּן
מֵישָׁרִים תִּשְׁפְּטוּ בְּנֵי אָדָם׃

ג אַף־בְּלֵב עוֹלֹת תִּפְעָלוּן
בָּאָרֶץ חֲמַס יְדֵיכֶם תְּפַלֵּסוּן׃

ד זֹרוּ רְשָׁעִים מֵרָחֶם
תָּעוּ מִבֶּטֶן דֹּבְרֵי כָזָב׃

ה חֲמַת־לָמוֹ כִּדְמוּת חֲמַת־נָחָשׁ
כְּמוֹ־פֶתֶן חֵרֵשׁ יַאְטֵם אָזְנוֹ׃

ו אֲשֶׁר לֹא־יִשְׁמַע לְקוֹל מְלַחֲשִׁים
חוֹבֵר חֲבָרִים מְחֻכָּם׃

ז אֱלֹהִים הֲרָס־שִׁנֵּימוֹ בְּפִימוֹ
מַלְתְּעוֹת כְּפִירִים נְתֹץ ׀ יְהוָה׃

ח יִמָּאֲסוּ כְמוֹ־מַיִם יִתְהַלְּכוּ־לָמוֹ
יִדְרֹךְ חִצָּו כְּמוֹ יִתְמֹלָלוּ׃

מזמור נח *Psalm 58:* Our psalm continues the sequence, begun in Psalm 51, in which we are privy to David's inner emotional reactions to the wave of predicaments which were his lot in life. Not the least of these predicaments was the enmity of his father-in-law, King Saul.

What frustrated David most of all was the collusion of Saul's advisors in his attempts to murder David. It is to these advisors that David addresses the complaints that are recorded in our psalm: *Do you really assemble to dispense*

9. May they be like the snail which dissolves as it slithers away,
like a stillborn child, like a mole, which never see the sun!

10. Before your pots can feel [the heat of] the thorns,
He will whirl them away by His might and in His fury.

11. The righteous man shall rejoice when he sees vengeance done;
he will bathe his feet in the blood of the wicked.

12. Then men will say:
There is, after all, reward for the righteous;
there is, indeed, a God who does justice on earth.

---

with him and his baseless suspicions of my murderous and rebellious intentions? How dare you be so unjust? *Your hands justify violence! Your venom is like the venom of serpents!*"

In anger and frustration, David understandably invokes the LORD's retribution against Abner and his fellows in Saul's entourage: *LORD, shatter the fangs of these young lions!*

How justified is his hope to witness the time when *the righteous man shall rejoice when he sees vengeance done*! How appropriate is our sympathy with his impatient anticipation of the time when *men will say ... there is, indeed, a God who does justice on earth*!

ט כְּמוֹ שַׁבְּלוּל תֶּמֶס יַהֲלֹךְ
נֵפֶל אֵשֶׁת בַּל־חָזוּ שָׁמֶשׁ׃

י בְּטֶרֶם יָבִינוּ סִּירֹתֵיכֶם אָטָד
כְּמוֹ־חַי כְּמוֹ־חָרוֹן יִשְׂעָרֶנּוּ׃

יא יִשְׂמַח צַדִּיק כִּי־חָזָה נָקָם
פְּעָמָיו יִרְחַץ בְּדַם הָרָשָׁע׃

יב וְיֹאמַר אָדָם
אַךְ־פְּרִי לַצַּדִּיק
אַךְ יֵשׁ־אֱלֹהִים שֹׁפְטִים בָּאָרֶץ׃

The narrative continues with a description of David's subsequent confrontation with Abner, in which he accuses him of negligence in his duty to safeguard the king, and allowing David and Abishai to penetrate the perimeter of Saul's barricade undetected, and carry away the spear and water jar, rather than killing him, as they easily could have done.

At that point, we can imagine for ourselves that David would have confronted Abner with the words of our psalm. "How can you now deny my innocence? I could easily have assassinated Saul, but you persist in colluding

PSALM 59

1. For the Chief Musician; *al tashḥet.*
Of David. A *mikhtam,*
when Saul sent men to watch on David's house to kill him.*

2. Rescue me from my enemies, O my God;
be my strong tower against my assailants.

3. Rescue me from evildoers;
save me from bloodthirsty men.

4. See, they lie in wait for my life;
fierce men band together against me
for no offense or sin of mine, LORD.

5. For no guilt of mine they rush and are ready [to attack].
Rouse Yourself on my behalf; see my plight.

6. For You, LORD God of Hosts, are the God of Israel;
bestir Yourself, and punish all the nations;
show no mercy to wicked traitors. *Selah*

7. They come out at nightfall, snarling like dogs,
and prowl about the city.

8. See, they emit a stream of abuse from their mouths,
words like swords are on their lips;
[They say,] "Who can hear us?"

* See 1 Sam. 19:11.

Our psalm reports David's understandably harsh reaction to this entrapment, and to Saul's men who surround him, in vivid detail. *Rescue me… they lie in wait for my life…. Destroy them in Your anger.*

But there is another fact in the story which David does not disclose in our psalm. Indeed, the very name of the heroine of the story, David's wife Michal, is omitted. Had David mentioned her name and shared with us the details of his rescue at her hands, our psalm would have a very different message, a message of hope and courage. After all, Michal was not just David's wife. She was Saul's daughter.

מזמור נט

I don't want my enemies punished. Rather, may they reform themselves. I don't want them to disappear. Rather, may they change their ways. I certainly don't want to see them perish. Rather, have them learn the lessons of their misdeeds. Then I'll sing a song, But I won't sing it alone. They'll all join me.

א לַמְנַצֵּ֣חַ אַל־תַּשְׁחֵת֮ לְדָוִ֪ד מִ֫כְתָּ֥ם
בִּשְׁלֹ֥חַ שָׁא֑וּל וַֽיִּשְׁמְר֥וּ אֶת־הַ֝בַּ֗יִת לַהֲמִיתֽוֹ׃

ב הַצִּילֵ֣נִי מֵאֹיְבַ֣י ׀ אֱלֹהָ֑י
מִּמִּתְקוֹמְמַ֥י תְּשַׂגְּבֵֽנִי׃

ג הַ֭צִּילֵנִי מִפֹּ֣עֲלֵי אָ֑וֶן
וּֽמֵאַנְשֵׁ֥י דָ֝מִ֗ים הוֹשִׁיעֵֽנִי׃

ד כִּ֤י הִנֵּ֪ה אָֽרְב֡וּ לְנַפְשִׁ֗י יָג֣וּרוּ עָלַ֣י עַזִּ֑ים
לֹֽא־פִשְׁעִ֖י וְלֹֽא־חַטָּאתִ֣י יְהוָֽה׃

ה בְּֽלִי־עָ֭וֺן יְרֻצ֣וּן וְיִכּוֹנָ֑נוּ
ע֖וּרָה לִקְרָאתִ֣י וּרְאֵֽה׃

ו וְאַתָּ֤ה יְהוָֽה־אֱלֹהִ֥ים ׀ צְבָא֡וֹת אֱלֹ֘הֵ֤י יִשְׂרָאֵ֗ל
הָקִ֗יצָה לִפְקֹ֥ד כָּל־הַגּוֹיִ֑ם
אַל־תָּ֝חֹ֗ן כָּל־בֹּ֥גְדֵי אָ֣וֶן סֶֽלָה׃

ז יָשׁ֣וּבוּ לָ֭עֶרֶב יֶהֱמ֥וּ כַכָּ֗לֶב
וִ֣יס֣וֹבְבוּ עִֽיר׃

ח הִנֵּ֤ה ׀ יַבִּ֘יע֤וּן בְּפִיהֶ֗ם חֲ֭רָבוֹת בְּשִׂפְתוֹתֵיהֶ֑ם
כִּי־מִ֥י שֹׁמֵֽעַ׃

מזמור נט *Psalm 59:* Our psalm continues the series which began with Psalm 51, which documents David's reactions to his many harrowing trials. It conveys David's reaction to yet another of King Saul's attempts to do him in.

This attempt is described in 1 Samuel 19:11: *"That night Saul sent messengers to David's home to keep watch on him and to kill him in the morning."*

9. But You, Lord, laugh at them;
You mock all the nations.

10. O Mighty One!* I wait for You,
for God is my strong tower.

11. God who shows me loving-kindness will go before me;
God will let me gloat over my foes.

12. But do not kill them, lest my people forget;
scatter them by Your might.
Bring them to ruin, Lord, our shield,

13. for the sins they have uttered,
for the words of their lips.
Let them be taken in their pride,
for the curses and the lies which they utter.

14. Destroy them in Your anger,
destroy them till they are no more,
then it will be known to the ends of the earth,
that God is ruler in Jacob. *Selah*

15. They come out at nightfall, snarling like dogs,
as they prowl about the city.

* Taking the Hebrew word *uzzo* (or *uzzu*) as the archaic form of the noun *oz*, meaning strength or might. The psalmist appeals to God for help, addressing Him as the Mighty One. After receiving help from God in v. 18, he addresses God as "my Mighty One."

"Two are better than one... For should they fall, one can raise the other, but woe betide him who is alone and falls with no companion to raise him!" (Eccl. 4:9–10). This verse refers to Michal and Jonathan, both Saul's progeny, and both of whom loved David. Michal rescued him from within the house, and Jonathan from without. Indeed, *two are better than one.*

David's failure to acknowledge Michal's role in this episode was compensated

ט וְאַתָּ֣ה יְ֭הוָה תִּשְׂחַק־לָ֑מוֹ
תִּ֝לְעַ֗ג לְכָל־גּוֹיִֽם׃

י עֻ֭זּוֹ אֵלֶ֣יךָ אֶשְׁמֹ֑רָה
כִּֽי־אֱ֝לֹהִ֗ים מִשְׂגַּבִּֽי׃

יא אֱלֹהֵ֣י חסדו יְקַדְּמֵ֑נִי חַסְדִּ֥י
אֱ֝לֹהִ֗ים יַרְאֵ֥נִי בְשֹׁרְרָֽי׃

יב אַל־תַּהַרְגֵ֤ם ׀ פֶּֽן־יִשְׁכְּח֬וּ עַמִּ֗י
הֲנִיעֵ֣מוֹ בְ֭חֵילְךָ וְהוֹרִידֵ֑מוֹ
מָֽגִנֵּ֣נוּ אֲדֹנָֽי׃

יג חַטַּאת־פִּ֗ימוֹ דְּֽבַר־שְׂפָ֫תֵ֥ימוֹ
וְיִלָּכְד֥וּ בִגְאוֹנָ֑ם
וּמֵאָלָ֖ה וּמִכַּ֣חַשׁ יְסַפֵּֽרוּ׃

יד כַּלֵּ֥ה בְחֵמָה֮ כַּלֵּ֪ה וְֽאֵ֫ינֵ֥מוֹ
וְֽיֵדְע֗וּ כִּֽי־אֱ֭לֹהִים מֹשֵׁ֣ל בְּיַעֲקֹ֑ב
לְאַפְסֵ֖י הָאָ֣רֶץ סֶֽלָה׃

טו וְיָשֻׁ֣בוּ לָ֭עֶרֶב יֶהֱמ֥וּ כַכָּ֗לֶב
וִיס֥וֹבְבוּ עִֽיר׃

For this is the rest of the story: *But David's wife Michal told him, "Unless you run for your life tonight, you will be killed tomorrow."* Michal let David down from the window and he escaped and fled. Michal defied her own father and stood by her beloved husband David.

For reasons about which we can only conjecture, David chose to focus our psalm on his enemies, and not on the loving and courageous actions of Michal. But whereas our psalm disappointingly neglects Michal, the midrash on our psalm highlights her heroism and her love.

Here are selected passages from that midrash, freely translated:

16. They wander about in search of food,
and howl if they are not satisfied.

17. But I will sing of Your strength,
every morning I will extol Your loving-kindness;
for You have been to me a tower of strength,
a refuge in times of trouble.

18. O my Mighty One, I will sing praise to You;
for God is my strong tower,
the God who shows me loving-kindness.

The careful student of both the Book of Psalms and the Book of Proverbs will discover that the latter often fills in gaps left by the former, the son complementing his father's work.

The faithful student of Torah will similarly often find how the Oral Torah, in this case the Midrash, will recover seeming omissions in the scriptural text.

The person who recites psalms will be well advised not to forget valiant Michal's role in the "rest of the story."

טז הֵ֭מָּה ינועון לֶאֱכֹ֑ל יְנִיע֣וּן
אִם־לֹ֥א יִ֝שְׂבְּע֗וּ וַיָּלִֽינוּ׃

יז וַאֲנִ֤י ׀ אָשִׁ֬יר עֻזֶּ֗ךָ וַאֲרַנֵּ֣ן לַבֹּקֶר֮ חַֽסְדֶּ֥ךָ
כִּֽי־הָיִ֣יתָ מִשְׂגָּ֣ב לִ֑י
וּ֝מָנ֗וֹס בְּי֣וֹם צַר־לִֽי׃

יח עֻ֭זִּי אֵלֶ֣יךָ אֲזַמֵּ֑רָה
כִּֽי־אֱלֹהִ֥ים מִ֝שְׂגַּבִּ֗י אֱלֹהֵ֥י חַסְדִּֽי׃

---

for by his son Solomon, who wrote, in his wisdom: *He who finds a wife has found good fortune* (Prov. 18:22). Upon which the Midrash comments: "This verse refers to Michal the daughter of Saul, who loved her husband David more than she loved her father, and who saved his life from her father. When? *When Saul sent men to watch on David's house to kill him*. Thus it is written (as our psalm begins): *For the Chief Musician;* al tashḥet. *A psalm of David.*"

PSALM 60

1. For the Chief Musician; on *shushan edut.* *Eleventh day of the month*
A *mikhtam* of David, for instruction:

2. *when he fought against Aram-Naharaim and Aram-Zobah,
while Joab returned and killed twelve thousand Edomites in
the Valley of Salt.

3. God, You have rejected us and shattered us;
You have been angry; restore us!

4. You have shaken the land and torn it open;
repair its ruins, for it is falling apart.

5. You have made Your people suffer hardship;
You have given us wine that makes us stagger.

6. But You have raised a banner for those who fear You
round which they may rally for the sake of truth. *Selah*

7. **That those dear to You may be delivered,
save with Your right hand and answer me.

* See II Sam. 8, and I Chr. 18.

** An alphabetical psalm; the "*nun*" verse is missing.

In our psalm, David conducts a war, but whether or not the war is a just war is open to debate. Hence, the outcome is neither resounding victory, nor ignominious defeat.

The Midrash questions the very legitimacy of David's waging war with Aram. It tells of the opposition which Joab confronted when he first faced the enemy. They asked him:

> Are you not a descendant of Jacob? Did not Laban the Aramean, Jacob's father-in-law, enact an eternal peace treaty between himself and Jacob? Did not Laban say: "*Come, then, let us make a pact, you and I... ?*" And did not Jacob himself gather the stones to erect a mound and a pillar which were to serve as a *witness that I am not to cross to you past this mound, and you are not to cross to me past this mound and this pillar, with hostile intent*? And did Laban and Jacob not swear, each to his own deity, to abide by this treaty? (See Gen. 31:4–54)

מזמור ס

Life is never perfect. Even when we win, we lose. In war there are casualties. Successful surgery leaves scars. Effective medicines have side effects. We praise God for helping us achieve victory. Yet we think He has abandoned us.

א לַמְנַצֵּחַ עַל־שׁוּשַׁן עֵדוּת יא לחודש
מִכְתָּם לְדָוִד לְלַמֵּד׃

ב בְּהַצּוֹתוֹ ׀ אֶת אֲרַם נַהֲרַיִם וְאֶת־אֲרַם צוֹבָה
וַיָּשָׁב יוֹאָב וַיַּךְ אֶת־אֱדוֹם בְּגֵיא־מֶלַח
שְׁנֵים עָשָׂר אָלֶף׃

ג אֱלֹהִים זְנַחְתָּנוּ פְרַצְתָּנוּ
אָנַפְתָּ תְּשׁוֹבֵב לָנוּ׃

ד הִרְעַשְׁתָּה אֶרֶץ פְּצַמְתָּהּ
רְפָה שְׁבָרֶיהָ כִי־מָטָה׃

ה הִרְאִיתָ עַמְּךָ קָשָׁה
הִשְׁקִיתָנוּ יַיִן תַּרְעֵלָה׃

ו נָתַתָּה לִּירֵאֶיךָ נֵּס לְהִתְנוֹסֵס
מִפְּנֵי קֹשֶׁט סֶלָה׃

ז לְמַעַן יֵחָלְצוּן יְדִידֶיךָ
הוֹשִׁיעָה יְמִינְךָ ועננו׃ וַעֲנֵנִי

מזמור ס *Psalm 60:* The reader of our psalm is confronted by its internal contradictions. On the one hand, David's general Joab *killed twelve thousand Edomites in the Valley of Salt*. Nevertheless, David feels that God has *rejected us and shattered us*. David feels assured of God's support: *God declared in His sanctuary that I would triumph,* and yet he asks, *have You not rejected us, God?*

How is the reader to resolve these contradictions? The answer lies in the fact that only seldom do the dilemmas of life have answers which are unequivocally right or definitely wrong, and rarely do our efforts result in outcomes which are unambiguously good or clearly bad.

8. God declared in His sanctuary that I would triumph;
I would divide Shechem,
and measure off the Valley of Sukkoth.

9. Gilead would be mine, Manasseh mine;
Ephraim my chief stronghold, Judah my scepter.

10. Moab would be my wash-basin,
over Edom I would fling my shoe;
Philistia, come and join me.

11. But who will conduct me to the fortified city?
Who will lead me to Edom?

12. Have You not rejected us, God?
No longer, God, do You come out with our armies.

13. Grant us aid against the foe,
for worthless is the help of man.

14. Through God we shall do valiantly,
for He will trample our foes.

---

orphaned. Soldiers were maimed, remaining cripples for life. Such is the cost of all wars, and it is no wonder that David felt God's *aid against the foe* at the same time that he saw God make His *people suffer hardship.*

The lesson of our psalm is apparent, and it applies not just to military situations, but to all of life's struggles. Rarely does one taste the sweetness of pure victory, or of total cure, or of absolute resolution of thorny interpersonal conflicts. Much more commonly, the results of our prayers appear to us to be mixtures of great blessings and painful disappointments. No wonder we are torn between praising God, and imploring Him not to reject us.

This is the nature of religious experience. It is seldom crystal clear. It is more typically laden with persistent doubt and ongoing conflict. That is the lesson of our psalm. *You have given us wine that makes us stagger. But You have raised a banner for those who fear You.*

Rarely do our struggles in this world conclude with the pronouncement: "And they lived happily ever after."

ח אֱלֹהִים ׀ דִּבֶּר בְּקׇדְשׁוֹ אֶעְלֹזָה
אֲחַלְּקָה שְׁכֶם וְעֵמֶק סֻכּוֹת אֲמַדֵּד׃

ט לִי גִלְעָד ׀ וְלִי מְנַשֶּׁה וְאֶפְרַיִם מָעוֹז רֹאשִׁי
יְהוּדָה מְחֹקְקִי׃

י מוֹאָב ׀ סִיר רַחְצִי
עַל־אֱדוֹם אַשְׁלִיךְ נַעֲלִי
עָלַי פְּלֶשֶׁת הִתְרוֹעָעִי׃

יא מִי יֹבִלֵנִי עִיר מָצוֹר
מִי נָחַנִי עַד־אֱדוֹם׃

יב הֲלֹא־אַתָּה אֱלֹהִים זְנַחְתָּנוּ
וְלֹא־תֵצֵא אֱלֹהִים בְּצִבְאוֹתֵינוּ׃

יג הָבָה־לָּנוּ עֶזְרָת מִצָּר
וְשָׁוְא תְּשׁוּעַת אָדָם׃

יד בֵּאלֹהִים נַעֲשֶׂה־חָיִל
וְהוּא יָבוּס צָרֵינוּ׃

How then was David permitted to order Joab to attack Aram?

The Midrash justifies the attack by demonstrating that Aram broke the treaty first, once when it sent Balaam to lay a curse upon Israel (See Num. 23:7: "*From Aram has Balak brought me*") and then again during the time that the Israelites were oppressed by the king of Aram (See Judges 3:8: "*The Lord became incensed at Israel and surrendered them to King Cushan-rishathaim of Aram-Naharaim; and the Israelites were subject to Cushan-rishathaim for eight years*").

Was the fact that Aram broke the treaty first sufficient justification for the Israelites to break it as well? This remains an open question.

Just as the original justification of the war was questionable, so was its outcome ambiguous. Yes, the Israelites were victorious. But they suffered casualties; thousands of Jewish women were widowed and their children

PSALM 61

1. For the Chief Musician; with a stringed instrument.
Of David.

2. God, hear my cry,
listen to my prayer.

3. From the end of the earth I call to You
when my heart grows faint;
lead me to a rock that is high above me.

4. For You have been my refuge,
a tower of strength against the foe.

5. O that I may dwell in Your tent forever,
and take refuge in the shelter of Your wings. *Selah*

6. For You, God, have heard my vows;
You have restored the heritage to those who fear Your name.

We Jews, who have survived centuries of exile, can easily imagine that we are the ones who are calling to God in our psalm. We are quite literally at *the end of the earth*; indeed, we are scattered to the four corners of the earth. It is no wonder that our *heart grows faint.*

The root of the Hebrew word which we translated as "*grows faint*" is *a-t-f*, "*atifa*," and Radak tells us that the word refers to a condition which results from "excessive prayer in a time of trouble." This word is often used in Psalms, and refers to a condition which is all too familiar to those who have known true suffering.

If we adopt this latter approach, and identify the speaker in our psalm as the exiled Jewish people, then we must assume that the king we are praying for is the Messiah, the ultimate King.

We pray for his reign to *extend over many generations* once he finally does arrive. But we also pray that God *add days to the life of the king*; that God hasten the Messiah's arrival so that he will come before the preordained time, and hence have days added not only to the end, but also to the beginning, of his tenure.

מזמור סא

I am here today. I do not want to be gone tomorrow. You can say that I am selfish. I want both worlds. I want my words heard, here and now. I want my lips to murmur forever, even in the grave.

א לַמְנַצֵּ֬חַ ׀ עַֽל־נְגִינַ֬ת לְדָוִֽד׃

ב שִׁמְעָ֣ה אֱ֭לֹהִים רִנָּתִ֑י
הַ֝קְשִׁ֗יבָה תְּפִלָּתִֽי׃

ג מִקְצֵ֤ה הָאָ֨רֶץ ׀ אֵלֶ֣יךָ אֶ֭קְרָא בַּעֲטֹ֣ף לִבִּ֑י
בְּצוּר־יָר֖וּם מִמֶּ֣נִּי תַנְחֵֽנִי׃

ד כִּֽי־הָיִ֣יתָ מַחְסֶ֣ה לִ֑י
מִגְדַּל־עֹ֝֗ז מִפְּנֵ֥י אוֹיֵֽב׃

ה אָג֣וּרָה בְ֭אָהָלְךָ עוֹלָמִ֑ים
אֶֽחֱסֶ֨ה בְסֵ֖תֶר כְּנָפֶ֣יךָ סֶּֽלָה׃

ו כִּֽי־אַתָּ֣ה אֱ֭לֹהִים שָׁמַ֣עְתָּ לִנְדָרָ֑י
נָתַ֥תָּ יְ֝רֻשַּׁ֗ת יִרְאֵ֥י שְׁמֶֽךָ׃

מזמור סא *Psalm 61:* Who is speaking in our psalm? Who is calling *from the end of the earth*?

It might be David, praying from his safe refuge, far from the soldiers he has sent into battle. This is Rashi's approach. David's *heart grows faint* as he empathizes with the plight of the warriors whom he has ordered into harm's way.

Or it could be the prayer of David on the run, a common experience for him. He calls to God because he has been forced to flee from his pursuers, and is cut off from his home and people. He feels as if he is calling God *from the end of the earth.*

If either of these approaches is true, we have no trouble understanding verses 7 and 8. They are David's prayers for himself. It is for himself as the anointed king that he wishes additional days and extended years. He prays that he himself will *sit enthroned in God's presence forever.*

7. Add days to the life of the king!
May his years extend over many generations!

8. May he sit enthroned in God's presence forever;
appoint Your constant loving-kindness to protect him!

9. So I will ever sing praises to Your name,
as I fulfill my vows day after day.

We can understand that, in our great gratitude, we will not only offer vows, but commit to fulfill them *day after day*, through daily prayer, daily Torah study, and daily deeds of kindness and compassion.

ז יָמִים עַל־יְמֵי־מֶלֶךְ תּוֹסִיף
שְׁנוֹתָיו כְּמוֹ־דֹר וָדֹר:

ח יֵשֵׁב עוֹלָם לִפְנֵי אֱלֹהִים
חֶסֶד וֶאֱמֶת מַן יִנְצְרֻהוּ:

ט כֵּן אֲזַמְּרָה שִׁמְךָ לָעַד
לְשַׁלְּמִי נְדָרַי יוֹם ׀ יוֹם:

If it is the Messiah whom we wish to see *enthroned in God's presence forever*, then we can readily understand our urge, expressed in the very last verse, to *sing praises to Your name.*

PSALM 62

1. For the Chief Musician; on Yedutun. A psalm of David.

2. For God alone my soul waits patiently,
my deliverance comes only from Him.

3. He alone is my rock and my deliverance;
He is my fortress; I shall never be shaken.

4. How long will all of you assault a man
and batter him down,
as if he were a leaning wall,
a tottering fence?

5. They plan only to topple him from his height;
they delight in lies.
With their mouths they bless,
but in their hearts they curse. *Selah*

6. For God alone wait patiently, O my soul;
for my hope comes only from Him.

7. He alone is my rock and my deliverance;
He is my fortress; I shall not be shaken.

---

to us and informed us of His will by imparting the Torah to us through Moses. Moses had a role to play in transmitting the Torah, but he did not write it and he did not add to it. He merely taught it.

Another principle reads: "I believe with perfect faith that the Creator, blessed be His name, rewards those who keep His commandments, and punishes those who transgress them."

Both of these principles are addressed in our psalm. Verse 11 admonishes those who gained their wealth though illegitimate means: *Put not your trust in extortion … though your riches increase, set not your heart on it.* The Creator punishes those who violate His prohibitions.

Verse 12 tells us that God has spoken, and that we heard Him speak. But it presents us with a puzzle: *One thing God has spoken, two things have I learnt.* How can we learn two things from one utterance?

מזמור סב

We all want security. Some find it in status and power. Others find it in wealth. Those things don't last. I trust God. I have learned to wait for Him with great patience. He has never let me down.

א לַמְנַצֵּחַ עַל־יְדוּתוּן מִזְמוֹר לְדָוִד׃

ב אַךְ אֶל־אֱלֹהִים דּוּמִיָּה נַפְשִׁי
מִמֶּנּוּ יְשׁוּעָתִי׃

ג אַךְ־הוּא צוּרִי וִישׁוּעָתִי
מִשְׂגַּבִּי לֹא־אֶמּוֹט רַבָּה׃

ד עַד־אָנָה תְּהוֹתְתוּ עַל־אִישׁ
תְּרָצְּחוּ כֻלְּכֶם
כְּקִיר נָטוּי גָּדֵר הַדְּחוּיָה׃

ה אַךְ מִשְּׂאֵתוֹ יָעֲצוּ לְהַדִּיחַ יִרְצוּ כָזָב
בְּפִיו יְבָרֵכוּ
וּבְקִרְבָּם יְקַלְלוּ־סֶלָה׃

ו אַךְ לֵאלֹהִים דּוֹמִּי נַפְשִׁי
כִּי־מִמֶּנּוּ תִּקְוָתִי׃

ז אַךְ־הוּא צוּרִי וִישׁוּעָתִי
מִשְׂגַּבִּי לֹא אֶמּוֹט׃

מזמור סב *Psalm 62:* Many have tried to list the major principles of Jewish belief. Most famous is the list compiled by Maimonides containing thirteen major principles. Our psalm offers us the occasion to reflect upon two of them.

The eighth of Maimonides' principles, as expressed in the *Yigdal* poem, reads: "I believe with perfect faith that the entire Torah now in our hands is the same one that was given to Moses our teacher."

Implicit in this statement is the belief that Almighty God revealed Himself

8. Upon God depend my deliverance and honor;
He is the rock of my strength.
In God is my refuge.

9. Trust in Him at all times, O people;
pour out your hearts before Him,
for God is our refuge. *Selah*

10. Men of low degree are a mere breath,
men of high degree are but an illusion;
placed on the scales all together,
they are lighter than a breath.

11. Put not your trust in extortion,
nor place vain hope in robbery;
though your riches increase,
set not your heart on it.

12. One thing God has spoken,
two things indeed have I learnt:

13. that power belongs to God,
and that with You, LORD, is loving-kindness.
And You will reward each man according to his deeds.

But Rashi then points out that a careful reading of the Hebrew suggests otherwise. It does not read "*ish maasehu*," in which case our translation would be correct. Rather it reads "*ish kemaasehu*," which is better translated as *You will reward each man approximately in accordance with his deeds.* This injects a large measure of love into God's justice. There is room for forgiveness, for the consideration of mitigating circumstances, and for taking into account the sinner's state of mind, in order to minimize the degree of his guilt.

Maimonides' list of principles mentions only reward and punishment. There is no mention of love. Our psalm objects to such stringency, and insists that even when exercising His power, God does not lose sight of His merciful forgiveness.

ח עַל־אֱלֹהִים יִשְׁעִי וּכְבוֹדִי
צוּר־עֻזִּי מַחְסִי בֵּאלֹהִים׃

ט בִּטְחוּ בוֹ בְכָל־עֵת ׀ עָם
שִׁפְכוּ־לְפָנָיו לְבַבְכֶם
אֱלֹהִים מַחֲסֶה־לָּנוּ סֶלָה׃

י אַךְ ׀ הֶבֶל בְּנֵי־אָדָם כָּזָב בְּנֵי אִישׁ
בְּמֹאזְנַיִם לַעֲלוֹת
הֵמָּה מֵהֶבֶל יָחַד׃

יא אַל־תִּבְטְחוּ בְעֹשֶׁק וּבְגָזֵל אַל־תֶּהְבָּלוּ
חַיִל ׀ כִּי־יָנוּב אַל־תָּשִׁיתוּ לֵב׃

יב אַחַת ׀ דִּבֶּר אֱלֹהִים שְׁתַּיִם־זוּ שָׁמָעְתִּי
כִּי עֹז לֵאלֹהִים׃

יג וּלְךָ־אֲדֹנָי חָסֶד
כִּי־אַתָּה תְשַׁלֵּם לְאִישׁ כְּמַעֲשֵׂהוּ׃

One approach to this problem is to be found in the Targum's rendition of our verse: "God spoke the words of Torah once, but I heard it twice from Moses." From God's perspective the Torah was given but once, but the people heard it more than once from their teacher.

What were the two lessons that the psalmist learned from the one Torah?

First of all, he learned *that power belongs to God*. He metes out justice powerfully, punishing the wicked as they deserve to be punished.

The second lesson he learned contravenes the first: *and that with You, Lord, is loving-kindness.* Yes, God punishes without mercy. But His love leaves open a path for the wicked to change their ways, and then they too will experience His love.

Rashi examines the very last words of our psalm: *And You will reward each man according to his deeds.* We are each held accountable for our deeds, and there is no escaping God's retribution for our misdeeds.

PSALM 63

1. A psalm of David, when he was in the wilderness of Judah.

2. God, You are my God; eagerly I seek You.
My soul thirsts for You,
my body longs for You,
like a parched and weary land that has no water.

3. So do I long to see You in the sanctuary,
and to behold Your power and glory!

4. For Your loving-kindness is better than life itself;
therefore my lips will sing Your praises.

5. Thus I will bless You all my life;
in Your name I lift up my hands [in prayer].

6. My soul is satisfied as with the richest of foods;*
my mouth shall praise You with joyous lips.

7. When I lie in bed I remember You;
through the watches of the night I think of You;

*Lit. "marrow and fat."

---

with God: *When I lie in bed I remember You; through the watches of the night I think of You.*

Would we, if we were threatened with danger, react similarly? Would we, at such moments, give voice to such sublime concerns?

How can we make our psalm relevant to our own lesser levels of spirituality? The Talmud (*Berakhot* 16b) responds by connecting one of the verses in our psalm to the liturgy which we recite daily:

> R. Elazar said:
> *Thus I will bless You all my life* refers to the recitation of the *Shema*.
> *In Your name I lift up my hands* refers to prayer (that is, to the *Amida* prayer, or the *Shemoneh Esrei*).
> If he does so (that is, if he recites *Shema* and prays the *Amida* properly), to him the verse applies: *My soul is satisfied as with the richest of foods.*

מזמור סג

I am not a mystic. But sometimes I feel that God is with me, at my side. I feel such a glow, such warmth, so connected. It is like sitting in my grandfather's lap when I was little. While it lasts, it feels better than life itself. It doesn't last long. When it is over I feel dry and empty. He left me. Suddenly, out of nowhere, the feeling returns. He is back. He decides when to be near me and when to be far away. I wish He would let me decide.

א מִזְמ֥וֹר לְדָוִ֑ד בִּ֝הְיוֹת֗וֹ בְּמִדְבַּ֥ר יְהוּדָֽה׃

ב אֱלֹהִ֤ים ׀ אֵלִ֣י אַתָּה֮ אֲֽשַׁחֲ֫רֶ֥ךָּ
צָמְאָ֬ה לְךָ֨ ׀ נַפְשִׁ֗י כָּמַ֣הּ לְךָ֣ בְשָׂרִ֑י
בְּאֶֽרֶץ־צִיָּ֖ה וְעָיֵ֣ף בְּלִי־מָֽיִם׃

ג כֵּ֭ן בַּקֹּ֣דֶשׁ חֲזִיתִ֑יךָ
לִרְא֥וֹת עֻ֝זְּךָ֗ וּכְבוֹדֶֽךָ׃

ד כִּי־ט֣וֹב חַ֭סְדְּךָ מֵֽחַיִּ֗ים
שְׂפָתַ֥י יְשַׁבְּחֽוּנְךָ׃

ה כֵּ֣ן אֲבָרֶכְךָ֣ בְחַיָּ֑י
בְּ֝שִׁמְךָ֗ אֶשָּׂ֥א כַפָּֽי׃

ו כְּמ֤וֹ חֵ֣לֶב וָ֭דֶשֶׁן תִּשְׂבַּ֣ע נַפְשִׁ֑י
וְשִׂפְתֵ֥י רְ֝נָנ֗וֹת יְהַלֶּל־פִּֽי׃

ז אִם־זְכַרְתִּ֥יךָ עַל־יְצוּעָ֑י
בְּ֝אַשְׁמֻר֗וֹת אֶהְגֶּה־בָּֽךְ׃

מזמור סג *Psalm 63:* Our psalm was composed by David *when he was in the wilderness of Judah,* pursued by Saul. It thus does not surprise us that he prays that *those who seek to destroy my life sink into the depths of the earth.* We too would utter those very words if we were pursued by enemies.

What does surprise us is that, despite his precarious circumstances, David's expresses yearning for God: *My soul thirsts for You, my body longs for You.* He is not obsessed with his fear of those who pursue him. Instead, he is obsessed

8. for You have always been my help;
in the shadow of Your wings I sing for joy.

9. My soul clings to You;
Your right hand supports me.

10. May those who seek to destroy my life
sink into the depths of the earth.

11. May they be given over to the sword,
and become the prey of foxes.

12. But the king shall rejoice in God;
all who swear by Him shall glory,
while the mouths of liars will be stopped.

The recitation of *Shema* represents that first level; namely, the utilization of natural gifts for a higher purpose. The verse *I will bless You all my life* refers to that level, blessing God with one's "life," with one's inborn talents and skills.

When one proceeds to the *Amida*, moving from recitation to prayer, one ascends to a higher level, and develops greater powers than those with which he was naturally endowed.

When one masters both levels, he experiences unique spiritual pleasure. One's *soul is satisfied as with the richest of foods.*

Such a person inherits two worlds: This world because of the exemplary use he has made of his this-worldly powers; and the World to Come, which he has earned with his newly attained other-worldly powers.

Our psalm demonstrates that we have the capacity to elevate ourselves to ever higher levels of spirituality. David did it in the wilderness, by moving beyond his daunting concerns to yearn and search for God. We are no less capable, whatever our challenges, of attaining a spiritual sense of certainty that we are *in the shadow of Your wings*, where we *sing for joy*.

ח כִּי־הָיִיתָ עֶזְרָתָה לִּי
וּבְצֵל כְּנָפֶיךָ אֲרַנֵּן:

ט דָּבְקָה נַפְשִׁי אַחֲרֶיךָ
בִּי תָּמְכָה יְמִינֶךָ:

י וְהֵמָּה לְשׁוֹאָה יְבַקְשׁוּ נַפְשִׁי
יָבֹאוּ בְּתַחְתִּיּוֹת הָאָרֶץ:

יא יַגִּירֻהוּ עַל־יְדֵי־חָרֶב
מְנָת שֻׁעָלִים יִהְיוּ:

יב וְהַמֶּלֶךְ יִשְׂמַח בֵּאלֹהִים
יִתְהַלֵּל כָּל־הַנִּשְׁבָּע בּוֹ
כִּי יִסָּכֵר פִּי דוֹבְרֵי־שָׁקֶר:

Not only that, but he inherits two worlds; this world and the World to Come. As it is written: *My mouth shall praise You with joyous lips* ("lips" in the plural, two worlds).

Rav Kook, in his commentary on the Daily Prayer Book, *Olat Re'iya*, insightfully analyzes this passage.

He points out that we all have natural abilities. We generally use them for mundane purposes. We use our powers of speech to communicate, and our senses of vision and hearing to see and hear matters of practical concern.

If we attain a rudimentary level of spirituality, we learn to use these talents and skills for higher purposes; for prayer, Torah study, or performing mitzvot, good deeds. We devote our natural gifts to a sacred objective.

There is, however, writes Rav Kook, a higher spiritual level. "When one fully recognizes the lofty value of divine purpose, then one develops inner strength, stamina, and courage, which allow him to transcend the natural gifts of life with which he was born." He can now devote "supernatural" gifts to a sacred objective.

PSALM 64

1. For the Chief Musician. A psalm of David.

2. Hear my voice, God, when I plead;
guard my life from the terror of the enemy.

3. Hide me from the council of wicked men,
from the riotous mob of evildoers,

4. who sharpen their tongues like swords,
and aim venomous words like arrows,

5. to shoot from ambush at the innocent,
shooting at him suddenly, without fear.

6. They encourage each other in their evil scheme;
they talk about laying hidden snares.
They say, "Who can see them?"

7. They thoroughly test their plots;
they conceal a well-devised scheme –
deep indeed is the heart and mind of man.

8. But God shoots an arrow at them,
suddenly they are stricken.

He wishes to be hidden *from the council of wicked men*, who plot and scheme behind closed doors. Even the *riotous mob of evildoers* does not fight with weapons of war. Instead, these evildoers resort to *venomous words*, which *they shoot from ambush … suddenly, without fear.*

If they were out in the open, the psalmist would not feel the desperate need for prayer. He exerts his own power in his own defense. But they lay *hidden snares*, they are confident that they cannot be seen, and they choose *the heart and mind of man* as their battlefield.

Our psalmist's foe is very familiar to modern man. His weapons are propaganda, slander, and rumor. His greatest weapon is his anonymity. Who can fight an unknown foe?

מזמור סד

I am in trouble. I am under attack. I am terrified. I'm able to fight power and might. But the terror I feel cripples me. If only I were not so frightened. Lord, save me from the fear of my enemies.

א לַמְנַצֵּחַ מִזְמוֹר לְדָוִד׃

ב שְׁמַע־אֱלֹהִים קוֹלִי בְשִׂיחִי
מִפַּחַד אוֹיֵב תִּצֹּר חַיָּי׃

ג תַּסְתִּירֵנִי מִסּוֹד מְרֵעִים
מֵרִגְשַׁת פֹּעֲלֵי אָוֶן׃

ד אֲשֶׁר שָׁנְנוּ כַחֶרֶב לְשׁוֹנָם
דָּרְכוּ חִצָּם דָּבָר מָר׃

ה לִירוֹת בַּמִּסְתָּרִים תָּם
פִּתְאֹם יֹרֻהוּ וְלֹא יִירָאוּ׃

ו יְחַזְּקוּ־לָמוֹ ׀ דָּבָר רָע
יְסַפְּרוּ לִטְמוֹן מוֹקְשִׁים
אָמְרוּ מִי יִרְאֶה־לָּמוֹ׃

ז יַחְפְּשׂוּ־עוֹלֹת תַּמְנוּ חֵפֶשׂ מְחֻפָּשׂ
וְקֶרֶב אִישׁ וְלֵב עָמֹק׃

ח וַיֹּרֵם אֱלֹהִים
חֵץ פִּתְאוֹם
הָיוּ מַכּוֹתָם׃

מזמור סד *Psalm 64:* In our psalm the psalmist speaks of a different kind of enemy. He is no longer afraid of physical danger. Rather, he fears his opponent's treachery and secretiveness.

It is as if he is saying, "Come out and fight like a man!"

9. Their own tongue shall trip them up,
all who see them shall flee in horror.

10. Then all men shall stand in awe;
they will declare the work of God
and understand what He has done.

11. The righteous will rejoice in the LORD,
and take refuge in Him;
all the upright in heart will exult.

---

knew what it was, we could combat it with the cures available to modern medicine. But it is a mystery, and we know not where to turn. When the enemy is defeated, when the disease inexplicably goes into remission, we know that it was not achieved by the hands of man. We are forced to see the hand of God.

When we witness such a mysterious triumph, whether over a human enemy or over a disease, we *stand in awe*. We echo the words of the climax of our psalm and we *declare the work of God and understand what He has done.*

ט וַיַּכְשִׁילֻהוּ עָלֵימוֹ לְשׁוֹנָם
יִתְנֹדְדוּ כָּל־רֹאֵה בָם׃

י וַיִּירְאוּ כָּל־אָדָם
וַיַּגִּידוּ פֹּעַל אֱלֹהִים וּמַעֲשֵׂהוּ הִשְׂכִּילוּ׃

יא יִשְׂמַח צַדִּיק בַּיהוה וְחָסָה בוֹ
וְיִתְהַלְלוּ כָּל־יִשְׁרֵי־לֵב׃

Our psalmist recognizes man's impotence in the face of such a foe. He turns to God because he accepts the fact that without God he is helpless.

He celebrates the fact that his enemy is defeated not because of his own efforts, but because the enemy's *own tongue shall trip them up.* He recognizes the hand of God in the fact that the enemy's weapons backfire; the tactics at which he excels are the very tactics that do him in.

This enemy resembles a malicious illness, an undiagnosed disease. If we

PSALM 65

1. For the Chief Musician. A psalm of David. A song.

2. To You, God in Zion, silence is praise;
to You vows are paid.

3. Hearer of prayer,
to You all men shall come.

4. When sinfulness overwhelms me;
only You can forgive our transgressions.

5. Happy is he whom You choose and bring near
to dwell in Your courts!
May we be filled with the bounty of Your house,
of Your Holy Temple!

6. By Your righteousness answer us with wondrous deeds,
God, our deliverer,
in whom all the ends of the earth and the distant seas
put their trust.

7. It is He who by His might made the mountains firm;
so girded with power is He.

8. He stills the raging of the seas,
the roaring of their waves,
and the tumult of the peoples.

Others suggest that it means "appropriate" or befitting": *To You alone is praise appropriate.*

The straightforward, literal translation which we have adopted, following Rashi, *To You… silence is praise,* is based upon a profound insight. Silence can communicate. Enter a house of worship where all in attendance are silent, and a sense of utter devotion is instantly communicated to you.

The story is told of the famed "*tzaddik*" of Jerusalem, Rav Aryeh Levin. He was a confidant of the great Chief Rabbi Avraham Yitzḥak Kook. One day, he needed to consult Rav Kook about an urgent dilemma, but Rav Kook was

מזמור סה

For some, He is to be found in the tempest. Thunder and lightning are His signs. Others find Him in His Law. Mercy and Forgiveness are His signs. I find Him when I walk along a country road. His signs are His wheat fields, swaying in His wind; His pastures well-watered; grape leaves in His vineyards glistening in His sun. They make no sound, but they sing a joyous song.

א לַמְנַצֵּחַ מִזְמוֹר לְדָוִד שִׁיר׃

ב לְךָ דֻמִיָּה תְהִלָּה אֱלֹהִים בְּצִיּוֹן
וּלְךָ יְשֻׁלַּם־נֶדֶר׃

ג שֹׁמֵעַ תְּפִלָּה
עָדֶיךָ כָּל־בָּשָׂר יָבֹאוּ׃

ד דִּבְרֵי עֲוֺנֹת גָּבְרוּ מֶנִּי
פְּשָׁעֵינוּ אַתָּה תְכַפְּרֵם׃

ה אַשְׁרֵי ׀ תִּבְחַר וּתְקָרֵב יִשְׁכֹּן חֲצֵרֶיךָ
נִשְׂבְּעָה בְּטוּב בֵּיתֶךָ קְדֹשׁ הֵיכָלֶךָ׃

ו נוֹרָאוֹת ׀ בְּצֶדֶק תַּעֲנֵנוּ אֱלֹהֵי יִשְׁעֵנוּ
מִבְטָח כָּל־קַצְוֵי־אֶרֶץ וְיָם רְחֹקִים׃

ז מֵכִין הָרִים בְּכֹחוֹ
נֶאְזָר בִּגְבוּרָה׃

ח מַשְׁבִּיחַ ׀ שְׁאוֹן יַמִּים שְׁאוֹן גַּלֵּיהֶם
וַהֲמוֹן לְאֻמִּים׃

מזמור סה *Psalm 65:* The opening phrase of our psalm is a puzzling one: *To You… silence is praise.* How can silence be praise? Praise requires words. Praise is a means of communication. Can one communicate silently?

The Hebrew word which we have translated as *silence* is *"dumiya."* To avoid the perplexity involved with the word "silence" in this context, others have suggested alternative translations. Some render it "hope": *Hope is your praise.*

9. Those who live at the ends of the earth
are overawed by Your signs.
You make the lands of sunrise and sunset sing with joyous song.

10. You care for the land and water it;
You enrich it greatly
with God's stream that is full of water;
and so You provide grain [for man].
In this manner You prepare the earth:

11. You water its furrows,
You level its ridges,
You soften it with showers,
You bless its growth.

12. You crown the year with Your goodness;
Your tracks drip with abundance.

13. The desert pastures drip with moisture,
the hills are girded with joy.

14. The meadows are clothed with sheep,
the valleys are decked with grain;
they shout for joy, they break into song.

---

his dilemma occurred to him without a word having passed between him and the Nazir.

Later, when Rav Kook returned, Rav Aryeh jokingly teased him: "Your disciple is a better counselor than you are. You require words. He advised me wonderfully, but in silence."

Rav Kook responded: "Silence is the highest form of communication!"

Indeed, it is. And that is the message of this psalm. There is no louder or clearer praise of God than the silent message of the wonders of nature, which are described so delicately in our psalm:

The meadows are clothed with sheep,
The valleys are decked with grain;
they shout for joy, they break into song.

ט וַיִּירְא֨וּ ׀ יֹשְׁבֵ֣י קְ֭צָוֺת מֵאוֹתֹתֶ֑יךָ
מ֤וֹצָֽאֵי־בֹ֖קֶר וָעֶ֣רֶב תַּרְנִֽין׃

י פָּקַ֥דְתָּ הָאָ֨רֶץ ׀ וַתְּשֹׁ֬קְקֶ֗הָ
רַבַּ֬ת תַּעְשְׁרֶ֗נָּה
פֶּ֣לֶג אֱ֭לֹהִים מָ֣לֵא מָ֑יִם
תָּכִ֥ין דְּ֝גָנָ֗ם כִּי־כֵ֥ן תְּכִינֶֽהָ׃

יא תְּלָמֶ֣יהָ רַ֭וֵּה נַחֵ֣ת גְּדוּדֶ֑הָ
בִּרְבִיבִ֥ים תְּ֝מֹגְגֶ֗נָּה
צִמְחָ֥הּ תְּבָרֵֽךְ׃

יב עִ֭טַּרְתָּ שְׁנַ֣ת טוֹבָתֶ֑ךָ
וּ֝מַעְגָּלֶ֗יךָ יִרְעֲפ֥וּן דָּֽשֶׁן׃

יג יִ֭רְעֲפוּ נְא֣וֹת מִדְבָּ֑ר
וְ֝גִ֗יל גְּבָע֥וֹת תַּחְגֹּֽרְנָה׃

יד לָבְשׁ֬וּ כָרִ֨ים ׀ הַצֹּ֗אן
וַעֲמָקִ֥ים יַֽעַטְפוּ־בָ֑ר
יִ֝תְרוֹעֲע֗וּ אַף־יָשִֽׁירוּ׃

---

away. The only person present in Rav Kook's study hall was his disciple, the saintly Rav David HaKohen. Because he abstained from fruits of the vine, and from other earthly pleasures, he was known as the Nazir.

Occasionally, and that particular day was one such occasion, the Nazir would vow to abstain entirely from all conversation. Rav Aryeh sat down next to him, hoping to get his counsel in the absence of Rav Kook. But he received the "silent treatment," and quickly understood that he would get no verbal response from the Nazir that day.

Rav Aryeh sat down next to the Nazir, silently and meditatively. After just a few moments, he was struck by a flash of insight, and a perfect solution to

PSALM 66

Twelfth day of the month

1. For the Chief Musician. A song. A psalm.
Shout with joy to God, all you on earth.

2. Sing to the glory of His name;
make glorious His praise.

3. Say to God, "How awesome are Your deeds!"
Because of Your mighty power
Your enemies feign homage to You.

4. All the earth bows to You
and sings praises to You;
they sing praises in honor of Your name. *Selah*

5. Come and see the works of God;
awesome are His deeds among men.

6. He turned the sea into dry land,
that men may pass through the river on foot;
therefore let us rejoice in Him.

7. He rules forever by His power,
His eyes keep watch on the nations;
let not the rebellious exalt themselves. *Selah*

8. Bless our God, O nations;
let the sound of His praise be heard,

---

gratitude when they will visit the rebuilt Holy Temple. It is a psalm for a nation to sing, and it calls upon all nations to accompany them in that song.

In the last several verses there is a dramatic shift. The voice of the psalmist becomes intensely personal. He no longer speaks to others; not to his people, and certainly not to all mankind. Rather he resorts to the first person, and, by doing so, reveals some of the secrets of the process of prayer.

These verses read: *Had I evil thoughts in my mind, the LORD would not have listened. But God did listen; He gave heed to my prayer. Blessed be God who has not turned away my prayer nor His loving-kindness from me.*

מזמור סו

Some ponder, some wonder. I ponder the suffering of our long exile. I wonder at our survival. When I ponder, I pray. When I wonder, I sing. When will we all ponder and wonder? Then we will all pray. Then we will all sing.

יב לחודש

א לַמְנַצֵּחַ שִׁיר מִזְמוֹר
הָרִיעוּ לֵאלֹהִים כָּל־הָאָרֶץ׃

ב זַמְּרוּ כְבוֹד־שְׁמוֹ
שִׂימוּ כָבוֹד תְּהִלָּתוֹ׃

ג אִמְרוּ לֵאלֹהִים מַה־נּוֹרָא מַעֲשֶׂיךָ
בְּרֹב עֻזְּךָ יְכַחֲשׁוּ לְךָ אֹיְבֶיךָ׃

ד כָּל־הָאָרֶץ ׀ יִשְׁתַּחֲווּ לְךָ וִיזַמְּרוּ־לָךְ
יְזַמְּרוּ שִׁמְךָ סֶלָה׃

ה לְכוּ וּרְאוּ מִפְעֲלוֹת אֱלֹהִים
נוֹרָא עֲלִילָה עַל־בְּנֵי אָדָם׃

ו הָפַךְ יָם ׀ לְיַבָּשָׁה
בַּנָּהָר יַעַבְרוּ בְרָגֶל
שָׁם נִשְׂמְחָה־בּוֹ׃

ז מֹשֵׁל בִּגְבוּרָתוֹ ׀ עוֹלָם
עֵינָיו בַּגּוֹיִם תִּצְפֶּינָה
הַסּוֹרְרִים ׀ אַל־יָרִימוּ לָמוֹ סֶלָה׃ יָרוּמוּ

ח בָּרְכוּ עַמִּים ׀ אֱלֹהֵינוּ
וְהַשְׁמִיעוּ קוֹל תְּהִלָּתוֹ׃

מזמור סו *Psalm 66:* Most of our psalm describes the powers of the Almighty as He sustained the Jewish people throughout their long exile. It culminates with the promise of those who experienced His deliverance to express their

9. for He has kept us among the living,
and has not let our feet slip.

10. For You, God, have put us to the test,
and refined us as one refines silver;

11. You have led us into a snare,
and placed shackles around our loins;

12. You have let men ride over our heads;
we went through fire and water,
but You led us forth to overflowing ease.

13. I enter Your house with burnt-offerings,
and pay my vows to You –

14. vows which my lips pronounced,
and my mouth uttered when I was in distress.

15. I will offer up to You fat beasts as burnt-offerings,
and the soothing odor of burning rams;
I will make ready bulls and he-goats. *Selah*

16. Come and hear, all you God-fearing men,
and I will tell you what He did for me.

17. With my mouth I called to Him,
high praise was on my tongue.

---

that the psalmist's thoughts must have been pure. Ibn Ezra's premise is that impure thoughts do indeed render a prayer invalid.

Rashi, however, understands these verses differently. For him, the psalmist's thoughts were in fact evil, and might very well have undermined the spoken prayer. However, God in His mercy chose to overlook the mere thoughts, and attended only to the spoken words. The psalmist thus exclaims: *He gave heed to my prayer*, not as a sign that he was found innocent of evil thoughts, as Ibn Ezra would have it, but as an expression of God's mercy. In His mercy, God ignored the evil thoughts in the mind of the psalmist.

ט הַשָּׂם נַפְשֵׁנוּ בַּחַיִּים
וְלֹא־נָתַן לַמּוֹט רַגְלֵנוּ׃

י כִּי־בְחַנְתָּנוּ אֱלֹהִים
צְרַפְתָּנוּ כִּצְרׇף־כָּסֶף׃

יא הֲבֵאתָנוּ בַמְּצוּדָה
שַׂמְתָּ מוּעָקָה בְמׇתְנֵינוּ׃

יב הִרְכַּבְתָּ אֱנוֹשׁ לְרֹאשֵׁנוּ
בָּאנוּ־בָאֵשׁ וּבַמַּיִם וַתּוֹצִיאֵנוּ לָרְוָיָה׃

יג אָבוֹא בֵיתְךָ בְעוֹלוֹת
אֲשַׁלֵּם לְךָ נְדָרָי׃

יד אֲשֶׁר־פָּצוּ שְׂפָתָי
וְדִבֶּר־פִּי בַּצַּר־לִי׃

טו עֹלוֹת מֵחִים אַעֲלֶה־לָּךְ עִם־קְטֹרֶת אֵילִים
אֶעֱשֶׂה בָקָר עִם־עַתּוּדִים סֶלָה׃

טז לְכוּ־שִׁמְעוּ וַאֲסַפְּרָה כׇּל־יִרְאֵי אֱלֹהִים
אֲשֶׁר עָשָׂה לְנַפְשִׁי׃

יז אֵלָיו פִּי־קָרָאתִי
וְרוֹמַם תַּחַת לְשׁוֹנִי׃

There are two radically different ways to understand the meaning of these verses.

Avraham ibn Ezra understands the psalmist to be saying that if his thoughts had indeed been evil, no matter what his actual spoken words would have been, God would not have listened to his prayers. God reads one's mind, and had He descried impure thoughts, He would have rejected the prayer. Since God did not reject the prayer, but *did listen* and did *give heed,* this is a sign

18. Had I evil thoughts in my mind,
the LORD would not have listened.

19. But God did listen;He gave heed to my prayer.

20. Blessed be God who has not turned away my prayer
nor His loving-kindness from me.

Rashi, on the other hand, recognizes that God will often ignore the malicious thoughts of the person who prays. After all, they are only thoughts, and our merciful God chooses to pay them no heed. He takes only the overt spoken words into account, and not the intent.

God will answer even imperfect prayers. *Blessed be God who has not turned away my prayer,* despite my insincerity. *Blessed be God who has not turned away... His loving-kindness from me,* despite the fact that I was unworthy.

יח אָ֭וֶן אִם־רָאִ֣יתִי בְלִבִּ֑י
לֹ֖א יִשְׁמַ֥ע ׀ אֲדֹנָֽי׃

יט אָ֭כֵן שָׁמַ֣ע אֱלֹהִ֑ים
הִ֝קְשִׁ֗יב בְּק֣וֹל תְּפִלָּתִֽי׃

כ בָּר֥וּךְ אֱלֹהִ֑ים
אֲשֶׁ֤ר לֹֽא־הֵסִ֘יר תְּפִלָּתִ֥י וְ֝חַסְדּ֗וֹ מֵאִתִּֽי׃

This difference in exegetical approach between these two master commentators reflects a profound difference of opinion between them about the nature of prayer.

For Ibn Ezra, prayerful words without sincere thoughts are not valid and will be rejected by God. If one's prayers are heard, that is evidence that the intentions behind those prayers were clean and pure.

PSALM 67

1. For the Chief Musician; with stringed instruments.
A psalm. A song.

2. May God be gracious to us and bless us;
may He cause His face to shine upon us, *Selah*

3. that Your way may be known on earth,
Your salvation, among all nations.

4. May the peoples praise You, God;
may all the peoples praise You!

5. The nations will rejoice and break into song;
for You judge the peoples with equity
and guide the nations of the earth. *Selah*

But they are still primitive. They are not yet able to move beyond mere verbal praise to more communicative modalities of expression. They cannot effectively convey the religious message to others.

Only in verse 5, writes Malbim, does the psalmist describe "*leumim*," civilizations which possess a distinct and highly developed culture, one which enables them to *rejoice and break into song.* Only the more intellectually advanced "*leumim*" can appreciate that *You judge the peoples with equity and guide the nations of the earth.* Only they can communicate their religious discoveries to the rest of the world.

Malbim keeps us aware of the difference between different national groups, and the degree to which they differ from each other. Some are better able than others to integrate their religious experiences into their cultural consciousness.

He forces us to confront ourselves with the difficult question: How verbally prepared are we to express our religious experiences? Are we at the first level, barely able to sense something numinous, but not even able to put our experience into words?

Or can we at least find words of praise by which to thank God for His blessings, but are we incapable of being the "light unto the nations" which is our mission?

מזמור סז

Have you ever gone to court? I think I'm totally right, and you think you are. The judge decides. We're both disappointed. It won't be long now before all the nations face His court. He, the Judge, will decide. Amazing! They'll all be so happy. They'll all sing and dance.

א לַמְנַצֵּחַ בִּנְגִינֹת מִזְמוֹר שִׁיר׃

ב אֱלֹהִים יְחָנֵּנוּ וִיבָרְכֵנוּ
יָאֵר פָּנָיו אִתָּנוּ סֶלָה׃

ג לָדַעַת בָּאָרֶץ דַּרְכֶּךָ
בְּכָל־גּוֹיִם יְשׁוּעָתֶךָ׃

ד יוֹדוּךָ עַמִּים ׀ אֱלֹהִים
יוֹדוּךָ עַמִּים כֻּלָּם׃

ה יִשְׂמְחוּ וִירַנְּנוּ לְאֻמִּים
כִּי־תִשְׁפֹּט עַמִּים מִישֹׁר
וּלְאֻמִּים ׀ בָּאָרֶץ תַּנְחֵם סֶלָה׃

מזמור סז *Psalm 67:* There are many Hebrew words for "nation." Our psalm uses three of them. In verse 3 it refers to "*goyim,*" in verse 4, twice, to "*amim,*" and in verse 5, again twice, to "*leumim.*"

English translations typically ignore the subtle distinctions that exist between these three terms, and translate all three as "nations" or "peoples." Many commentators insist that these terms are not at all synonymous.

Malbim, for example, maintains that the term "*goyim*" refers to loosely organized groups of people. They are capable, as verse 3 has it, of experiencing and knowing God's salvation, but are not sufficiently cohesive to respond in unison to that salvation. They are deficient in the language of praise. They feel God's salvation but cannot articulate their response.

For Malbim, the term "*amim*" of verse 4 refers to a group of people who are better organized. They are led by a common ruler, a sovereign king. They can articulate their experience of salvation. They know the language of praise.

6. May the peoples praise You, God;
may all the peoples praise You!

7. The earth has yielded its produce;
may God, our God, bless us.

8. May God bless us,
and may all the ends of the earth be in awe of Him!

---

excellence that testifies that we, the people of the psalms, have progressed beyond the stages of "*goyim*" and "*amim*." We have attained the stage of "*leumim*." We are indeed a civilization capable of bringing the message of the Almighty to all humanity. *May God bless us, and may all the ends of the earth be in awe of Him.*

ו יוֹדוּךָ עַמִּים ׀ אֱלֹהִים
יוֹדוּךָ עַמִּים כֻּלָּם׃

ז אֶרֶץ נָתְנָה יְבוּלָהּ
יְבָרְכֵנוּ אֱלֹהִים אֱלֹהֵינוּ׃

ח יְבָרְכֵנוּ אֱלֹהִים
וְיִירְאוּ אוֹתוֹ כָּל־אַפְסֵי־אָרֶץ׃

Or ideally, is our language up to the task where we can fully express the religious message, in our emotions, in our songs, and in our way of life, so that others will look up to us and become inspired to follow our example?

The best proofs that we have advanced to the latter level are the psalms themselves. Without fail, each and every psalm advances to a level of literary

PSALM 68

1. For the Chief Musician. A psalm. A song of David.

2. May God arise, may His enemies be scattered;
may those who hate Him flee before Him!

3. As smoke is dispersed [by the wind],
so disperse them;
as wax melts before fire, so shall the wicked perish before God.

4. But the righteous shall rejoice and exult before God;
they shall be happy and joyful.

5. Sing to God; sing praises to His name;
extol Him who rides on the clouds.
The LORD is His name; exult before Him.

6. The father of the fatherless,
the defender of the widow,
is God in His holy dwelling.

7. God gives the lonely a home,
He leads out the imprisoned to prosperity;
but the rebellious shall live in a parched land.

8. God, when You went forth before Your people,
when You marched through the wasteland, *Selah*

---

convinced that it must refer to the defeat of the armies of Sennacherib, who all abandoned their siege of Jerusalem and ran for their lives.

Another theme is the experience of Sinai, God's revelation which took place on that holy but humble mountain. And still another theme is God's concern for the lowliest of humans, the poor and desolate, along with the recognition that *the LORD bears our burdens day by day.*

If we had to identify one underlying unifying theme for this entire complex psalm, it might very well be that our psalm prescribes the antidote for the old adage, attributed to Lord Acton, which exclaims: "Power corrupts, and absolute power corrupts absolutely."

Lord Acton was onto something very true, and the subsequent popularity

מזמור סח

There are all the mighty, and there is the Mightiest of All. All the mighty are indifferent to the little guy. Why should they care about him? They have other concerns, bigger things to worry about. The Mightiest of All is not that way. He cares, especially for the little guy. He rides on the clouds. But He fathers the fatherless and defends the widow. He gives the lonely a home. There's a message here for all the mighty. Come down from the clouds.

א לַמְנַצֵּחַ לְדָוִד מִזְמוֹר שִׁיר׃

ב יָקוּם אֱלֹהִים יָפוּצוּ אוֹיְבָיו
וְיָנוּסוּ מְשַׂנְאָיו מִפָּנָיו׃

ג כְּהִנְדֹּף עָשָׁן תִּנְדֹּף
כְּהִמֵּס דּוֹנַג מִפְּנֵי־אֵשׁ
יֹאבְדוּ רְשָׁעִים מִפְּנֵי אֱלֹהִים׃

ד וְצַדִּיקִים יִשְׂמְחוּ יַעַלְצוּ לִפְנֵי אֱלֹהִים
וְיָשִׂישׂוּ בְשִׂמְחָה׃

ה שִׁירוּ ׀ לֵאלֹהִים זַמְּרוּ שְׁמוֹ
סֹלּוּ לָרֹכֵב בָּעֲרָבוֹת בְּיָהּ שְׁמוֹ
וְעִלְזוּ לְפָנָיו׃

ו אֲבִי יְתוֹמִים וְדַיַּן אַלְמָנוֹת
אֱלֹהִים בִּמְעוֹן קָדְשׁוֹ׃

ז אֱלֹהִים ׀ מוֹשִׁיב יְחִידִים ׀ בַּיְתָה
מוֹצִיא אֲסִירִים בַּכּוֹשָׁרוֹת
אַךְ סוֹרְרִים שָׁכְנוּ צְחִיחָה׃

ח אֱלֹהִים בְּצֵאתְךָ לִפְנֵי עַמֶּךָ
בְּצַעְדְּךָ בִישִׁימוֹן סֶלָה׃

מזמור סח *Psalm 68:* Our psalm is a long one, and seems to contain many different themes. One is the utter defeat of one of Israel's enemies. Our psalm describes the defeat as being so comprehensive, that many commentators are

9. the earth trembled, the heavens poured down rain,
at the sight of God;
Sinai too [quaked], at the sight of God, the God of Israel.

10. You, God, poured down a generous rain,
and refreshed Your weary heritage.

11. Then Your own people settled there;
in Your goodness, God, You provided for the needy.

12. The LORD spoke the tidings [of victory],
a great host of women spread the news:

13. "Kings with their armies are in flight, in flight,
while the women at home divide the spoil."

14. Even for those of you who lie idly among the sheepfolds,
there were wings of a dove sheathed in silver,
its pinions in glittering gold.*

15. When the Almighty scattered the kings,
it was like snow falling on Mount Zalmon.

16. Mount Bashan is a lofty mountain,
Mount Bashan with its many peaks.

17. Why gaze in envy, you many-peaked mount,
at the mountain God desired for His dwelling?
The LORD will abide there forever.

18. The chariots of God are many myriads,
thousands upon thousands;
the LORD was among them.
So it was at Sinai, so, too, as He entered the sanctuary.

* These were the trophies taken from the enemy.

---

of his witty remark serves to corroborate that truth. There is something about power that corrupts the person who possesses it. It makes him preoccupied with himself, and removes the natural concerns that human beings have for each other. It distorts his judgment, and renders him not just indifferent to the suffering of others, but cruelly callous to all whom he deems lower than himself.

ט אֶ֤רֶץ רָעָ֨שָׁה ׀ אַף־שָׁמַ֣יִם נָטְפוּ֮
מִפְּנֵ֪י אֱלֹ֫הִ֥ים
זֶ֥ה סִינַ֑י
מִפְּנֵ֥י אֱ֝לֹהִ֗ים אֱלֹהֵ֥י יִשְׂרָאֵֽל׃

י גֶּ֣שֶׁם נְ֭דָבוֹת תָּנִ֣יף אֱלֹהִ֑ים
נַחֲלָתְךָ֥ וְ֝נִלְאָ֗ה אַתָּ֥ה כוֹנַנְתָּֽהּ׃

יא חַיָּתְךָ֥ יָֽשְׁבוּ־בָ֑הּ
תָּ֤כִין בְּטוֹבָתְךָ֖ לֶעָנִ֣י אֱלֹהִֽים׃

יב אֲדֹנָ֥י יִתֶּן־אֹ֑מֶר
הַ֝מְבַשְּׂר֗וֹת צָבָ֥א רָֽב׃

יג מַלְכֵ֣י צְ֭בָאוֹת יִדֹּד֣וּן יִדֹּד֑וּן
וּנְוַת־בַּ֝֗יִת תְּחַלֵּ֥ק שָׁלָֽל׃

יד אִם־תִּשְׁכְּבוּן֮ בֵּ֪ין שְׁפַ֫תָּ֥יִם
כַּנְפֵ֣י י֭וֹנָה נֶחְפָּ֣ה בַכֶּ֑סֶף
וְ֝אֶבְרוֹתֶ֗יהָ בִּירַקְרַ֥ק חָרֽוּץ׃

טו בְּפָרֵ֣שׂ שַׁ֭דַּי מְלָכִ֥ים בָּ֗הּ
תַּשְׁלֵ֥ג בְּצַלְמֽוֹן׃

טז הַר־אֱלֹהִ֥ים הַר־בָּשָׁ֑ן
הַ֥ר גַּ֝בְנֻנִּ֗ים הַר־בָּשָֽׁן׃

יז לָ֤מָּה ׀ תְּֽרַצְּדוּן֮ הָרִ֪ים גַּבְנֻ֫נִּ֥ים
הָהָ֗ר חָמַ֣ד אֱלֹהִ֣ים לְשִׁבְתּ֑וֹ
אַף־יְ֝הוָ֗ה יִשְׁכֹּ֥ן לָנֶֽצַח׃

יח רֶ֤כֶב אֱלֹהִ֗ים
רִבֹּתַ֣יִם אַלְפֵ֣י שִׁנְאָ֑ן
אֲדֹנָ֥י בָ֝ם סִינַ֗י בַּקֹּֽדֶשׁ׃

19. You, God, ascended the heights, You carried off captives,
You received tributes from men, even from rebels,
that the LORD God might dwell there.

20. Blessed be the LORD who bears our burdens day by day;
God is our salvation. *Selah*

21. Our God is a God who saves;
the LORD God can provide escape from death.

22. But God will crush the heads of His enemies,
the hairy scalp of him who persists in his guilt.

23. The LORD said, "I will bring them back from Bashan,
I will bring them back from the depths of the sea,

24. that your feet may wade through blood,
and the tongues of your dogs
may have their share of the enemy."

25. The people saw Your processions, God,
the processions of my God, my King, into the sanctuary;

26. the singers in the lead, the minstrels following,
among them maidens beating timbrels.

27. In full assemblies bless God;
[bless] the LORD, you who are from the fountain of Israel.

28. There was the little tribe of Benjamin leading them,
there the princes of Judah in their brocaded robes,
there too the princes of Zebulun and the princes of Naphtali.

Our psalm counters this tendency by teaching a lesson which is derived from Him who is the most powerful of all. Thus, R. Yoḥanan makes use of the fifth and sixth verses of our psalm in his famous remark, quoted in the Talmud (*Megilla* 31a):

> R. Yoḥanan said: Wherever you find the greatness of the Holy One, blessed be He, there you find His humility. This is written in the Torah, repeated

יט עָלִיתָ לַמָּרוֹם ׀ שָׁבִיתָ שֶּׁבִי
לָקַחְתָּ מַתָּנוֹת בָּאָדָם
וְאַף סוֹרְרִים לִשְׁכֹּן ׀ יָהּ אֱלֹהִים׃

כ בָּרוּךְ אֲדֹנָי יוֹם ׀ יוֹם
יַעֲמָס־לָנוּ הָאֵל יְשׁוּעָתֵנוּ סֶלָה׃

כא הָאֵל ׀ לָנוּ אֵל לְמוֹשָׁעוֹת
וְלֵיהוִה אֲדֹנָי לַמָּוֶת תּוֹצָאוֹת׃

כב אַךְ־אֱלֹהִים יִמְחַץ רֹאשׁ אֹיְבָיו
קָדְקֹד שֵׂעָר מִתְהַלֵּךְ בַּאֲשָׁמָיו׃

כג אָמַר אֲדֹנָי
מִבָּשָׁן אָשִׁיב
אָשִׁיב מִמְּצֻלוֹת יָם׃

כד לְמַעַן ׀ תִּמְחַץ רַגְלְךָ בְּדָם
לְשׁוֹן כְּלָבֶיךָ מֵאֹיְבִים מִנֵּהוּ׃

כה רָאוּ הֲלִיכוֹתֶיךָ אֱלֹהִים
הֲלִיכוֹת אֵלִי מַלְכִּי בַקֹּדֶשׁ׃

כו קִדְּמוּ שָׁרִים אַחַר נֹגְנִים
בְּתוֹךְ עֲלָמוֹת תּוֹפֵפוֹת׃

כז בְּמַקְהֵלוֹת בָּרְכוּ אֱלֹהִים
אֲדֹנָי מִמְּקוֹר יִשְׂרָאֵל׃

כח שָׁם בִּנְיָמִן ׀ צָעִיר רֹדֵם
שָׂרֵי יְהוּדָה רִגְמָתָם
שָׂרֵי זְבֻלוּן שָׂרֵי נַפְתָּלִי׃

29. Your God endowed you with strength [in the past];
display again, God, that strength which You wrought for us.

30. For the honor of Your Temple at Jerusalem
kings will bring You gifts.

31. Rebuke the wild beast of the reeds,
the herd of bulls with the calves of the nations,
until, humbled, they each come with pieces of silver.
Scatter the peoples who delight in wars.

32. Envoys will come from Egypt,
Ethiopia will stretch out her hands to God.

33. Sing to God, O kingdoms of the earth;
Sing praises to the LORD, *Selah*

34. to Him who rides on the heavens, the ancient heavens.
Listen! His voice thunders with mighty power.

35. Ascribe power to God,
whose majesty is over Israel,
whose might is in the skies.

36. You are awesome, God, in Your holy places!
It is the God of Israel who gives might
and strength to the people.
May God be blessed!

> Him." Immediately afterward it is written: "The father of the fatherless, the defender of the widow, is God in His holy dwelling."

Rabbi Lord Jonathan Sacks, in his translation of the prayer books, puts it so eloquently: "This magnificent passage from the Talmud is telling us to learn from God that greatness is humility, and humility greatness. The Creator of all cares for all; the Power of powers cares for the powerless. The deeper our compassion the higher we stand."

כט צִוָּה אֱלֹהֶיךָ עֻזֶּךָ
עוּזָּה אֱלֹהִים
זוּ פָּעַלְתָּ לָּנוּ׃

ל מֵהֵיכָלֶךָ עַל־יְרוּשָׁלָ‍ִם
לְךָ יוֹבִילוּ מְלָכִים שָׁי׃

לא גְּעַר חַיַּת קָנֶה
עֲדַת אַבִּירִים ׀ בְּעֶגְלֵי עַמִּים
מִתְרַפֵּס בְּרַצֵּי־כָסֶף
בִּזַּר עַמִּים קְרָבוֹת יֶחְפָּצוּ׃

לב יֶאֱתָיוּ חַשְׁמַנִּים מִנִּי מִצְרָיִם
כּוּשׁ תָּרִיץ יָדָיו לֵאלֹהִים׃

לג מַמְלְכוֹת הָאָרֶץ שִׁירוּ לֵאלֹהִים
זַמְּרוּ אֲדֹנָי סֶלָה׃

לד לָרֹכֵב בִּשְׁמֵי שְׁמֵי־קֶדֶם
הֵן יִתֵּן בְּקוֹלוֹ קוֹל עֹז׃

לה תְּנוּ עֹז לֵאלֹהִים
עַל־יִשְׂרָאֵל גַּאֲוָתוֹ וְעֻזּוֹ בַּשְּׁחָקִים׃

לו נוֹרָא אֱלֹהִים ׀ מִמִּקְדָּשֶׁיךָ
אֵל יִשְׂרָאֵל
הוּא נֹתֵן ׀ עֹז וְתַעֲצֻמוֹת לָעָם
בָּרוּךְ אֱלֹהִים׃

---

in the Prophets, and stated a third time in the Writings.... It is stated a third time in the Writings: "Sing to God, sing praises to His name, and extol Him who rides on the clouds. The Lord is His name; exult before

PSALM 69

Thirteenth day of the month

1. For the Chief Musician; on *shoshanim*. Of David.

2. Save me, God, for the waters have come up to my neck.

3. I have sunk into the miry depths, where there is no foothold;
I have come into deep waters,
and the flood carries me away.

4. I am weary with crying, my throat is parched;
my eyes are exhausted, waiting for my God.

5. More numerous than the hairs of my head
are those who hate me without cause;
many are those who would destroy me,
who are wrongfully my enemies.
How can I restore what I have not stolen?

6. God, You know how foolish I have been;
my guilty deeds are not hidden from You.

7. LORD God of Hosts, let not those who hope in You
be put to shame because of me.
Let not those who seek You be dismayed
because of me, O God of Israel.

8. It is for Your sake that I suffer reproach,
that shame covers my face.

9. I have become a stranger to my brothers,
an alien to the sons of my own mother.

מזמור סט *Psalm 69:* There is an emotional state that public figures know well, especially if they are in leadership positions. David describes this state exquisitely in our psalm.

On the one hand, the leader feels privileged to have been chosen for this position. A religious leader, convinced that his position has been divinely ordained, feels especially privileged. But, on the other hand, the pressures of his office are often overwhelming. He experiences reproach from his critics,

מזמור סט

I am drowning. It is futile to hope for rescue. It is senseless to even try to pray. Desperately, I say to Him: "Don't let me down." Daringly, I say much more: "Don't let down those who rely upon me." "Don't disappoint those who look up to me." "Don't deny the dreams of those who count on me." I don't deserve that You hear my prayers. But they do deserve that You hear theirs.

א לַמְנַצֵּחַ עַל־שׁוֹשַׁנִּים לְדָוִד׃ יג לחודש

ב הוֹשִׁיעֵנִי אֱלֹהִים
כִּי בָאוּ מַיִם עַד־נָפֶשׁ׃

ג טָבַעְתִּי ׀ בִּיוֵן מְצוּלָה
וְאֵין מָעֳמָד
בָּאתִי בְמַעֲמַקֵּי־מַיִם
וְשִׁבֹּלֶת שְׁטָפָתְנִי׃

ד יָגַעְתִּי בְקָרְאִי נִחַר גְּרוֹנִי
כָּלוּ עֵינַי מְיַחֵל לֵאלֹהָי׃

ה רַבּוּ ׀ מִשַּׂעֲרוֹת רֹאשִׁי שֹׂנְאַי חִנָּם
עָצְמוּ מַצְמִיתַי אֹיְבַי שֶׁקֶר
אֲשֶׁר לֹא־גָזַלְתִּי אָז אָשִׁיב׃

ו אֱלֹהִים אַתָּה יָדַעְתָּ לְאִוַּלְתִּי
וְאַשְׁמוֹתַי מִמְּךָ לֹא־נִכְחָדוּ׃

ז אַל־יֵבֹשׁוּ בִי ׀ קֹוֶיךָ אֲדֹנָי יֱהוִה צְבָאוֹת
אַל־יִכָּלְמוּ בִי מְבַקְשֶׁיךָ אֱלֹהֵי יִשְׂרָאֵל׃

ח כִּי־עָלֶיךָ נָשָׂאתִי חֶרְפָּה
כִּסְּתָה כְלִמָּה פָנָי׃

ט מוּזָר הָיִיתִי לְאֶחָי
וְנָכְרִי לִבְנֵי אִמִּי׃

10. Zeal for Your house has consumed me;
the insults of those who revile You have fallen upon me.

11. When I wept and fasted,
I was taunted for it.

12. When I put on sackcloth,
I became a byword among them.

13. Those who sit by the town gate talk about me;
I am the song of drunkards.

14. But I, LORD, I pray to You – may it be at a favorable moment!
God, in Your abundant loving-kindness answer me with Your true deliverance.

15. Rescue me from the mire; let me not sink;
let me be rescued from my enemies,
and from the deep waters.

16. Let not the flood waters carry me away;
do not let the deep swallow me up,
and let not the Pit close its mouth over me.

17. Answer me, LORD, according to Your loving-kindness;
in Your great compassion turn to me.

18. Do not hide Your face from Your servant;
answer me quickly for I am in great trouble.

19. Come near to me and redeem me;
free me from my foes.

20. You know my reproach, my shame and my disgrace;
all who harass me are well known to You.

---

and that stings him to his very core. He is painfully embarrassed by the taunts which are mercilessly hurled at him, undermining the self-assurance he requires if he is to lead successfully.

At such moments he cannot suppress the resentment which threatens to poison his soul. He is moved to exclaim to God, as did David: *It is for Your sake that I suffer reproach, that shame covers my face.*

י כִּֽי־קִנְאַ֣ת בֵּיתְךָ֣ אֲכָלָ֑תְנִי
וְחֶרְפּ֥וֹת ח֝וֹרְפֶ֗יךָ נָפְל֥וּ עָלָֽי׃

יא וָאֶבְכֶּ֣ה בַצּ֣וֹם נַפְשִׁ֑י
וַתְּהִ֖י לַחֲרָפ֣וֹת לִֽי׃

יב וָאֶתְּנָ֣ה לְבוּשִׁ֣י שָׂ֑ק
וָאֱהִ֥י לָ֝הֶ֗ם לְמָשָֽׁל׃

יג יָשִׂ֣יחוּ בִ֭י יֹ֣שְׁבֵי שָׁ֑עַר
וּ֝נְגִינ֗וֹת שׁוֹתֵ֥י שֵׁכָֽר׃

יד וַאֲנִ֤י תְפִלָּֽתִי־לְךָ֨ ׀ יְהוָ֡ה עֵ֤ת רָצ֗וֹן
אֱלֹהִ֥ים בְּרָב־חַסְדֶּ֑ךָ
עֲ֝נֵ֗נִי בֶּאֱמֶ֥ת יִשְׁעֶֽךָ׃

טו הַצִּילֵ֣נִי מִ֭טִּיט וְאַל־אֶטְבָּ֑עָה
אִנָּצְלָ֥ה מִ֝שֹּׂנְאַ֗י וּמִמַּֽעֲמַקֵּי־מָֽיִם׃

טז אַל־תִּשְׁטְפֵ֤נִי ׀ שִׁבֹּ֬לֶת מַ֗יִם
וְאַל־תִּבְלָעֵ֥נִי מְצוּלָ֑ה
וְאַל־תֶּאְטַר־עָלַ֖י בְּאֵ֣ר פִּֽיהָ׃

יז עֲנֵ֣נִי יְ֭הוָה כִּי־ט֣וֹב חַסְדֶּ֑ךָ
כְּרֹ֥ב רַ֝חֲמֶ֗יךָ פְּנֵ֣ה אֵלָֽי׃

יח וְאַל־תַּסְתֵּ֣ר פָּ֭נֶיךָ מֵעַבְדֶּ֑ךָ
כִּי־צַר־לִ֝֗י מַהֵ֥ר עֲנֵֽנִי׃

יט קָרְבָ֣ה אֶל־נַפְשִׁ֣י גְאָלָ֑הּ
לְמַ֖עַן אֹיְבַ֣י פְּדֵֽנִי׃

כ אַתָּ֤ה יָדַ֗עְתָּ חֶרְפָּתִ֣י וּ֭בָשְׁתִּי וּכְלִמָּתִ֑י
נֶ֝גְדְּךָ֗ כָּל־צוֹרְרָֽי׃

21. Their insults have broken my heart,
and I am desperately sick;
I look for sympathy, but there is none,
for comforters, but find none.

22. They put poison in my food;
for my thirst they gave me vinegar to drink.

23. May their table be a snare to them,
and a trap to them in their security.

24. May their eyes be darkened so that they cannot see;
make their loins shake continually.

25. Pour out Your wrath upon them;
and let Your fierce anger overtake them.

26. May their settlements be deserted,
let there be no one to live in their tents.

27. For they persecute him whom You have struck down,
and gossip about the pain of those whom You have wounded.

28. Charge them with crime upon crime,
and let them not enjoy Your favor.

29. Let them be blotted out from the book of life,
and not be inscribed among the righteous.

More unbearable than the burdens of office and the hostile challenges to his authority is the loneliness which inevitably comes with positions of leadership. *I have become a stranger to my brothers, an alien to the sons of my own mother.* Not only does the leader feel the distance between him and his constituency, but he can no longer be comforted by those who were once closest to him.

No man is a prophet in his own home town. David's brothers "knew him when." They cannot bring themselves to see him as he is now: a charismatic leader, a hero, a king. They still see him as a youngster motivated by naïve curiosity and preoccupied with childish daydreams. They cannot take him seriously, and he knows it. His adult self will forever be estranged from them.

כא חֶרְפָּה ׀ שָׁבְרָה לִבִּי וָאָנוּשָׁה
וָאֲקַוֶּה לָנוּד וָאַיִן
וְלַמְנַחֲמִים וְלֹא מָצָאתִי׃

כב וַיִּתְּנוּ בְּבָרוּתִי רֹאשׁ
וְלִצְמָאִי יַשְׁקוּנִי חֹמֶץ׃

כג יְהִי־שֻׁלְחָנָם לִפְנֵיהֶם לְפָח
וְלִשְׁלוֹמִים לְמוֹקֵשׁ׃

כד תֶּחְשַׁכְנָה עֵינֵיהֶם מֵרְאוֹת
וּמָתְנֵיהֶם תָּמִיד הַמְעַד׃

כה שְׁפָךְ־עֲלֵיהֶם זַעְמֶךָ
וַחֲרוֹן אַפְּךָ יַשִּׂיגֵם׃

כו תְּהִי־טִירָתָם נְשַׁמָּה
בְּאָהֳלֵיהֶם אַל־יְהִי יֹשֵׁב׃

רז כִּי־אַתָּה אֲשֶׁר־הִכִּיתָ רָדָפוּ
וְאֶל־מַכְאוֹב חֲלָלֶיךָ יְסַפֵּרוּ׃

כח תְּנָה־עָוֺן עַל־עֲוֺנָם
וְאַל־יָבֹאוּ בְּצִדְקָתֶךָ׃

כט יִמָּחוּ מִסֵּפֶר חַיִּים
וְעִם צַדִּיקִים אַל־יִכָּתֵבוּ׃

One can easily imagine David saying to himself, "Who needed all this? I could have remained a humble shepherd, the kid brother in a close-knit family. Had I stayed back on the homestead, I would never have provoked all of these envious schemes. I wouldn't have incurred all this enmity. The weight of endless royal responsibilities would not be on my shoulders, and I would have avoided all this palace intrigue."

30. But I am afflicted and in pain;
let Your help, God, raise me on high.

31. Then will I praise God's name with a song,
and exalt Him with thanksgiving.

32. This will please the LORD more than any bull,
or bullock with horns and cloven hoof.

33. The humble will see this and rejoice;
take heart, you seekers after God.

34. For the LORD listens to the needy,
and does not despise His captive people.

35. Let heaven and earth praise Him,
the seas and all that moves in them.

36. For God will save Zion,
and rebuild the cities of Judah;
they shall live there and inherit it.

37. The descendants of His servants shall possess it,
and those who love His name shall dwell there.

Such loneliness can ruin a man. It can easily lead him to forfeit his office, by either abusing his privilege of office or relinquishing it altogether. David finds a different alternative. He turns to God. The tragic misfortunes which are his lot are the very factors which make him, not only the most glorious of kings, but the biblical spiritual exemplar par excellence. He turns all of his trials into opportunities to draw close to the Almighty who ordained him for leadership in the first place.

Hence, he exclaims, in a verse which is incorporated more than once in Jewish liturgy: *But I, LORD, I pray to You – may it be at a favorable moment! God, in Your abundant loving-kindness answer me with Your true deliverance.*

The Talmudic sages wonder: What is *a favorable moment* for prayer? They respond that such favorable moments exist when the community prays in unison, and not necessarily when one prays alone. David feels the pain of loneliness and turns to God in search of His companionship. He asks God for a *favorable moment.* How ironic it is that that favorable moment can readily be found, but only in the fellowship of others.

ל וַאֲנִי עָנִי וְכוֹאֵב
יְשׁוּעָתְךָ אֱלֹהִים תְּשַׂגְּבֵנִי׃

לא אֲהַלְלָה שֵׁם־אֱלֹהִים בְּשִׁיר
וַאֲגַדְּלֶנּוּ בְתוֹדָה׃

לב וְתִיטַב לַיהוָה מִשּׁוֹר פָּר
מַקְרִן מַפְרִיס׃

לג רָאוּ עֲנָוִים יִשְׂמָחוּ
דֹּרְשֵׁי אֱלֹהִים וִיחִי לְבַבְכֶם׃

לד כִּי־שֹׁמֵעַ אֶל־אֶבְיוֹנִים יְהוָה
וְאֶת־אֲסִירָיו לֹא בָזָה׃

לה יְהַלְלוּהוּ שָׁמַיִם וָאָרֶץ
יַמִּים וְכָל־רֹמֵשׂ בָּם׃

לו כִּי אֱלֹהִים ׀ יוֹשִׁיעַ צִיּוֹן
וְיִבְנֶה עָרֵי יְהוּדָה
וְיָשְׁבוּ שָׁם וִירֵשׁוּהָ׃

לז וְזֶרַע עֲבָדָיו יִנְחָלוּהָ
וְאֹהֲבֵי שְׁמוֹ יִשְׁכְּנוּ־בָהּ׃

David is a deeply spiritual person, "the sweet singer of Israel." He is sincerely devoted to God, and hopes to find succor, if not with his friends of yore, then perhaps with those who share his profound religious experiences. But here too he is disappointed. *When I wept and fasted, I was taunted for it.* They doubt the sincerity of my religious activities. They consider me a hypocrite.

He is tempted to turn to others in leadership roles to allay his desperate loneliness. Surely, he reasons, those *who sit by the town gate,* those who occupy judicial positions, will empathize with him and at least allow him their compassionate company. But, alas, they too *talk about me* derisively and sing *the song of drunkards.*

PSALM 70

1. For the Chief Musician. Of David;
lehazkir, to remember.

2. Make haste, God, to save me;
come quickly to my aid!

3. Ashamed and confounded be those who seek my life!
Routed and disgraced be those who desire my ruin!

4. May they withdraw in their shame
who jeer, crying, Hurrah! Hurrah!

---

the flock of sheep, found them and gathered them back to him. He rebuilt the barn for them to again take shelter there. But he did not remember the shepherd, and abandoned him, forlorn and forgotten.

The shepherd protested: "The sheep have been returned, the barn restored, and I have been forgotten?!"So too, at the end of the previous psalm we read: *for God will save Zion, and rebuild the cities of Judah.* There! The barn is rebuilt!

The descendants of His servants shall possess it, and those who love His name shall dwell there. There! The sheep are returned!

But I, the shepherd, am not mentioned! Am I not to be remembered?!

Thus, our psalm begins, *A psalm of David; lehazkir, to remember.*

David begins our psalm with a prayer that he be remembered. He foresaw the restoration of Zion and the rebuilt cities of Judah. He envisioned the return thereto of the Jewish people. But he was pained because he was glaringly absent from this prophetic picture. Was he not to receive the credit he was due for his role in this dramatic achievement?

Many a leader has experienced similar ignominy. This is indeed a common tale but true. History is replete with tragic stories of how these leaders struggled with this great frustration, typically in futility.

David dealt with it in the way he knew best. He turned to the God he knew as a just God, and pleaded for justice. He asked to be remembered, not to be cast into oblivion. He begged that a place of honor be reserved for him at the ultimate victory celebration.

But I am poor and needy... You are my help and my deliverer... do not tarry!

מזמור ע

People tell me, "You're a man of faith." "Hang in there." "Be patient." But men of faith can't wait. Faith makes us impatient. God's salvation comes in the blink of an eye. Make haste... come quickly... Now! Now! Now!

א לַמְנַצֵּחַ לְדָוִד לְהַזְכִּיר׃

ב אֱלֹהִים לְהַצִּילֵנִי
יְהוָה לְעֶזְרָתִי חוּשָׁה׃

ג יֵבֹשׁוּ וְיַחְפְּרוּ מְבַקְשֵׁי נַפְשִׁי
יִסֹּגוּ אָחוֹר וְיִכָּלְמוּ חֲפֵצֵי רָעָתִי׃

ד יָשׁוּבוּ עַל־עֵקֶב בָּשְׁתָּם
הָאֹמְרִים הֶאָח ׀ הֶאָח׃

מזמור ע *Psalm 70:* Our psalm takes us one step further, and much deeper, into the psyche of the leader. In the previous psalm we learned of the difficulties he experiences. As if physical danger was not enough, he suffers unbearable loneliness, constant criticism, and assaults upon his self-esteem. No wonder that he often resents the burdens of his high office, and comes to regret the choices he made which led him to his position.

Our psalm asks us to contemplate the plight of the leader after he has been victorious, after he has accomplished his leadership mission. One would think that at that point he could put the burdens of office behind him. We assume that surely, having achieved his objectives, he would no longer be subject to opposition and embarrassment.

However, the leader is often forgotten. He comes to be seen as a figure who may have had historical importance, once upon a time, but who is no longer relevant. Accustomed to center stage, he must now accommodate to oblivion.

This insight is conveyed by Rashi in his remarks on the mysterious phrase in the very first verse of our psalm: *A psalm of David; lehazkir, to remember*:

> In the Midrash on Psalms I came across this parable: A king was once angry at his flock of sheep. In his wrath, he drove the sheep into the wild, dismantled the barn in which they took shelter, and dismissed the shepherd who tended to them. After a while, he calmed down. He sought after

5. But may all who seek You be glad and jubilant in You;
may those who love Your saving power
forever say, "God is great!"

6. But I am poor and needy,
God, come quickly to me.
You are my help and my deliverer,
LORD, do not tarry!

ה יָשִׂ֥ישׂוּ וְיִשְׂמְח֨וּ ׀ בְּךָ֮ כָּֽל־מְבַקְשֶׁ֥יךָ
וְיֹאמְר֣וּ תָ֭מִיד יִגְדַּ֣ל אֱלֹהִ֑ים אֹ֝הֲבֵ֗י יְשׁוּעָתֶֽךָ׃

ו וַאֲנִ֤י ׀ עָנִ֣י וְאֶבְי֮וֹן
אֱלֹהִ֪ים ח֫וּשָׁה לִּ֥י
עֶזְרִ֣י וּמְפַלְטִ֣י אַ֑תָּה
יְ֝הוָ֗ה אַל־תְּאַחַֽר׃

PSALM 71

1. In You, Lord, I take refuge;
may I never be put to shame.

2. In Your righteousness deliver me and rescue me;
turn Your ear to me and save me.

3. Be my stronghold, my shelter,
to which I may come at all times;
order my deliverance,
for You are my rock and my fortress.

4. Rescue me, O my God, from the power of the wicked,
from the grasp of evil and violent men.

5. For You are my hope, Lord God,
my trust since my childhood.

6. In the womb I was dependent on You:
it was You who brought me forth from my mother's womb.
I will praise You at all times.

7. I have become a source of wonder to many;
but You are my strong refuge.

8. My mouth is full of praise to You,
singing Your glory all day long.

---

emotional skills which each life stage presents have also been studied and described.

But the developmental tasks which relate to the spiritual aspects of life have been largely ignored by social scientists. Men and women of faith know a great deal about the obstacles to spirituality which each life passage entails. They know well, for example, that one can never rely upon the spiritual skills learned in youth to meet the challenges of adulthood.

They know even better that new difficulties emerge in old age which threaten to annihilate spiritual attainments altogether. But they also sense that old age brings with it opportunities for previously unimaginable spiritual growth.

Our psalm gives voice to those who have known the struggle to master the

מזמור עא

"What is life all about?" He answered his own question: "It's all about struggle." He's wrong. It's also about song. That's the lesson of the psalms: Deliver me and rescue me… revive me once more! Struggle. Lyre… harp… lips… tongue! Song. Sing along!

א בְּךָֽ־יְהֹוָ֥ה חָסִ֑יתִי
אַל־אֵב֥וֹשָׁה לְעוֹלָֽם׃

ב בְּצִדְקָתְךָ֗ תַּצִּילֵ֥נִי וּֽתְפַלְּטֵ֑נִי
הַטֵּֽה־אֵלַ֥י אׇ֝זְנְךָ֗ וְהוֹשִׁיעֵֽנִי׃

ג הֱיֵ֤ה לִ֨י ׀ לְצ֬וּר מָע֗וֹן
לָב֗וֹא תָּ֫מִ֥יד צִוִּ֥יתָ לְהוֹשִׁיעֵ֑נִי
כִּֽי־סַלְעִ֖י וּמְצוּדָתִ֣י אָֽתָּה׃

ד אֱֽלֹהַ֗י פַּ֭לְּטֵנִי מִיַּ֣ד רָשָׁ֑ע
מִכַּ֖ף מְעַוֵּ֣ל וְחוֹמֵֽץ׃

ה כִּֽי־אַתָּ֥ה תִקְוָתִ֑י
אֲדֹנָ֥י יֱ֝הֹוִ֗ה מִבְטַחִ֥י מִנְּעוּרָֽי׃

ו עָלֶ֤יךָ ׀ נִסְמַ֬כְתִּי מִבֶּ֗טֶן
מִמְּעֵ֣י אִ֭מִּי אַתָּ֣ה גוֹזִ֑י
בְּךָ֖ תְהִלָּתִ֣י תָמִֽיד׃

ז כְּ֭מוֹפֵת הָיִ֣יתִי לְרַבִּ֑ים
וְ֝אַתָּ֗ה מַחֲסִי־עֹֽז׃

ח יִמָּ֣לֵא פִ֭י תְּהִלָּתֶ֑ךָ
כׇּל־הַ֝יּ֗וֹם תִּפְאַרְתֶּֽךָ׃

מזמור עא *Psalm 71:* Life has its stages, and at each stage there are new challenges to master, new skills to learn. Psychologists call these "developmental tasks." Much has been written about the sensory-motor, verbal, and intellectual tasks which must be mastered. The social challenges and

9. Do not cast me off in old age,
do not forsake me when my strength fails.

10. For my enemies talk against me,
those who watch for my life take counsel together,

11. saying, "God has forsaken him;
pursue him, catch him; for there is no one to save him."

12. God, be not far from me;
my God, hasten to my help.

13. May my accusers be shamed and ruined;
may those who seek my hurt be covered with scorn and disgrace!

14. But as for me, I will always hope,
and praise You ever more and more.

15. My mouth will tell of Your righteousness,
all day long of Your saving acts,
though I know not how to tell it all.

16. I come [to praise You] for Your mighty acts, LORD God;
and I will proclaim Your righteousness, Yours alone.

17. God, You have been my teacher from my youth,
and to this day I tell of Your marvelous deeds.

---

during his earliest life stages will vanish with the approach of old age: *Do not cast me off in old age, do not forsake me when my strength fails.*

The person of faith is thoroughly familiar with the sense of closeness to God which is among the great benefits of belief. But he also knows how ephemeral that sense of closeness can be. As he experiences the conclusion of one stage, he fears that that sense of closeness will disappear as he enters the next stage. No wonder that such a developmental crisis moves him to exclaim: *God, be not far from me... hasten to my help.*

He not only pleads that God remain close; he begs that God help him cope with the difficulties of the transition from one stage of life to another.

For the person of faith, God's closeness is but one benefit of spirituality.

ט אַל־תַּשְׁלִיכֵנִי לְעֵת זִקְנָה
כִּכְלוֹת כֹּחִי אַל־תַּעַזְבֵנִי׃

י כִּי־אָמְרוּ אוֹיְבַי לִי
וְשֹׁמְרֵי נַפְשִׁי נוֹעֲצוּ יַחְדָּו׃

יא לֵאמֹר אֱלֹהִים עֲזָבוֹ
רִדְפוּ וְתִפְשׂוּהוּ כִּי־אֵין מַצִּיל׃

יב אֱלֹהִים אַל־תִּרְחַק מִמֶּנִּי
אֱלֹהַי לְעֶזְרָתִי חִישה׃ (חוּשָׁה)

יג יֵבֹשׁוּ יִכְלוּ שֹׂטְנֵי נַפְשִׁי
יַעֲטוּ חֶרְפָּה וּכְלִמָּה מְבַקְשֵׁי רָעָתִי׃

יד וַאֲנִי תָּמִיד אֲיַחֵל
וְהוֹסַפְתִּי עַל־כָּל־תְּהִלָּתֶךָ׃

טו פִּי ׀ יְסַפֵּר צִדְקָתֶךָ כָּל־הַיּוֹם תְּשׁוּעָתֶךָ
כִּי לֹא יָדַעְתִּי סְפֹרוֹת׃

טז אָבוֹא בִּגְבֻרוֹת אֲדֹנָי יֱהֹוִה
אַזְכִּיר צִדְקָתְךָ לְבַדֶּךָ׃

יז אֱלֹהִים לִמַּדְתַּנִי מִנְּעוּרָי
וְעַד־הֵנָּה אַגִּיד נִפְלְאוֹתֶיךָ׃

---

developmental tasks of spirituality over the course of a lifetime. And it does so with profound empathy and understated eloquence.

The psalmist recollects the hope and trust he had in God since his childhood. He knows full well that this relationship preceded his very capacity to remember: *In the womb I was dependent on You.*

His greatest fear is that the strong spiritual bond which he experienced

18. So now that I am old and gray-headed,
do not forsake me, God,
until I proclaim Your power to the next generation,
and Your might, to all who are to come.

19. Your righteousness, God, reaches to highest heaven,
for great are the things You have done.
Who is there like You, God?

20. Though You have made me undergo many bitter troubles,
yet You will revive me once more,
and raise me once more from the depths of the earth.

21. You will increase my honor,
and comfort me again.

22. Then I will praise You with the lyre
for Your faithfulness, O my God.
I will sing praises to You with the harp, O Holy One of Israel.

23. My lips shall greatly rejoice as I sing praises to You;
my whole being, too, which You have redeemed.

24. All day long my tongue shall tell of Your righteousness,
how those who sought my hurt were shamed and disgraced.

---

person feels a unique urgency to perpetuate his religious beliefs and spiritual discoveries to those to whom the future belongs. Not only does such a person not wish to be forsaken, but he begs to be privileged to endure *until I proclaim Your power to the next generation, and Your might, to all who are to come.*

Finally, the psalmist knows what has eluded even students of human development, a secret of which even astute gerontologists are largely ignorant. As we progress through the passages of life our songs change. The songs of nursery school differ from the songs of adolescence. The love songs of early adulthood do not calm the turmoil of mid-life. And old age reserves for itself a special repertoire of songs, nourished by nostalgia to be sure, but also addressing the existential concerns of those facing finitude.

Hence our psalm concludes: *I will praise You with the lyre... with the harp.... My lips shall greatly rejoice as I sing... my whole being, too, which You have redeemed.*

יח וְגַם עַד־זִקְנָה ׀ וְשֵׂיבָה
אֱלֹהִים אַל־תַּעַזְבֵנִי
עַד־אַגִּיד זְרוֹעֲךָ לְדוֹר
לְכָל־יָבוֹא גְּבוּרָתֶךָ׃

יט וְצִדְקָתְךָ אֱלֹהִים עַד־מָרוֹם
אֲשֶׁר־עָשִׂיתָ גְדֹלוֹת
אֱלֹהִים מִי כָמוֹךָ׃

כ אֲשֶׁר הראיתנו ׀ צָרוֹת רַבּוֹת וְרָעוֹת הִרְאִיתַנִי
תָּשׁוּב תחיינו תְּחַיֵּנִי
וּמִתְּהֹמוֹת הָאָרֶץ תָּשׁוּב תעלנו׃ תַּעֲלֵנִי

כא תֶּרֶב ׀ גְּדֻלָּתִי
וְתִסֹּב תְּנַחֲמֵנִי׃

כב גַּם־אֲנִי ׀ אוֹדְךָ בִכְלִי־נֶבֶל אֲמִתְּךָ אֱלֹהָי
אֲזַמְּרָה לְךָ בְכִנּוֹר קְדוֹשׁ יִשְׂרָאֵל׃

כג תְּרַנֵּנָּה שְׂפָתַי כִּי אֲזַמְּרָה־לָּךְ
וְנַפְשִׁי אֲשֶׁר פָּדִיתָ׃

כד גַּם־לְשׁוֹנִי כָּל־הַיּוֹם תֶּהְגֶּה צִדְקָתֶךָ
כִּי־בֹשׁוּ כִי־חָפְרוּ מְבַקְשֵׁי רָעָתִי׃

Another benefit is the sense that God guides him, advises him, and teaches him. As we progress to later stages of life we need new and different guidance, advice relevant to our changed circumstances, and life lessons more appropriate for this suddenly unfamiliar experience.

How apt at such a time is our psalmist's prayer: *God, You have been my teacher from my youth… so now that I am old and gray-headed, do not forsake me!* Continue to guide me and teach me.

With age there is a new developmental task, one which younger individuals hardly anticipate. That is the need for a sense of immortality, best achieved by passing on one's experiences and values to a later generation. The devout

PSALM 72

Fourteenth day of the month

1. Of Solomon.
God, endow the king with Your justice,
the royal son with Your righteousness,

2. that he may judge Your people with righteousness,
and Your poor with equity.

3. May the mountains bring forth prosperity for the people,
the hills too, because of [his] justice.

4. May he defend the poor among the people;
may he save the children of the needy,
and crush the oppressor.

5. Then all will revere You as long as the sun endures,
and as long as the moon lasts, throughout the ages.

6. May he come down
like rain falling on a mown field,
like showers watering the earth!

7. In his days may the righteous flourish,
and peace abound till the moon be no more.

Solomon his successor. It affords us a glimpse into David's psyche, and additionally sheds light on the thought processes of all loving fathers. To some extent, our psalm contains a universal theme.

Like every good father, David wants only the best for his son. But he goes further than most fathers would, and volunteers to himself suffer all the pain that might be destined for his son. Thus, he prays: *God, endow the king with Your justice, the royal son with Your righteousness.* As Rashi interprets this verse, David is referring to himself as "the king" and using the phrase "the royal son" to refer to Solomon. He is telling God to endow him, David, with the painful consequences of harsh justice, and to spare Solomon from those consequences. Instead, Solomon, "the royal son," should never know harsh "justice," but only experience compassionate "righteousness." What are

מזמור עב

God does His work in the tunnels. We live on the surface. We don't see what He is doing. We don't have a clue. Blessed be the Lord… who alone does wondrous things! Better – who does wondrous things alone! As the Talmud puts it, "The beneficiary of the miracle is unaware of his own miracle." What He did for you in the tunnel saved your life. But you'll never know.

א לִשְׁלֹמֹה ׀ יד לחודש
אֱלֹהִים מִשְׁפָּטֶיךָ לְמֶלֶךְ תֵּן
וְצִדְקָתְךָ לְבֶן־מֶלֶךְ׃

ב יָדִין עַמְּךָ בְצֶדֶק
וַעֲנִיֶּיךָ בְמִשְׁפָּט׃

ג יִשְׂאוּ הָרִים שָׁלוֹם לָעָם
וּגְבָעוֹת בִּצְדָקָה׃

ד יִשְׁפֹּט ׀ עֲנִיֵּי־עָם יוֹשִׁיעַ לִבְנֵי אֶבְיוֹן
וִידַכֵּא עוֹשֵׁק׃

ה יִירָאוּךָ עִם־שָׁמֶשׁ
וְלִפְנֵי יָרֵחַ דּוֹר דּוֹרִים׃

ו יֵרֵד כְּמָטָר עַל־גֵּז
כִּרְבִיבִים זַרְזִיף אָרֶץ׃

ז יִפְרַח־בְּיָמָיו צַדִּיק
וְרֹב שָׁלוֹם עַד־בְּלִי יָרֵחַ׃

מזמור עב *Psalm 72:* David was a warrior, a king, and a poet. But some of the most poignant biblical narratives about him describe him as a loving father. He prayed desperately for the sick child born to him and Bathsheba. He bitterly mourned even Absalom, the son who rebelled against him.

Our psalm gives us insight into his hopes and prayers for yet another son,

8. May he rule from sea to sea,
from the River to the ends of the earth.

9. Desert dwellers shall kneel before him;
his enemies shall lick the dust.

10. The kings of Tarshish and of the isles shall pay him tribute,
the kings of Sheba and Seba shall offer gifts;

11. all kings shall bow to him,
all nations shall serve him.

12. For he saves the needy who call for help,
and the poor who have no protector.

13. He has pity on the poor and the needy,
and saves the lives of the helpless.

14. He redeems their lives from oppression and violence,
for their blood is precious in his eyes.

15. Long may he live with them, sharing the gold he received from
Sheba, So that they will pray for him constantly, and bless him
each day.

---

complish other objectives as well. As Ibn Ezra, noting that the phrase "*crush the oppressor*" is followed immediately by the phrase "*then all will revere You as long as the sun endures,*" comments: "Your success in crushing the oppressors of the world will bring about universal reverence of the LORD."

Similarly, the nations of the world will yield power to Solomon not because of his might or wealth, but because they will recognize in him a person who sympathizes with the needy of all nations. *All nations shall serve him…for he saves the needy who call for help, and the poor who have no protector.*

We have followed Radak's translation of verse 15, for it insightfully connects that verse with the earlier verse 10. In the earlier verse Solomon receives tribute from a foreign power. In the latter verse we see how he dispenses those gifts. He shares them with the helpless from whom he never distances himself, but among whom he insists upon dwelling.

With our psalm the second book of Psalms comes to an end. Hence the concluding verse: *Here end the prayers of David, son of Jesse.*

ח וְיֵרְדְּ מִיָּם עַד־יָם
וּמִנָּהָר עַד־אַפְסֵי־אָרֶץ׃

ט לְפָנָיו יִכְרְעוּ צִיִּים
וְאֹיְבָיו עָפָר יְלַחֵכוּ׃

י מַלְכֵי תַרְשִׁישׁ וְאִיִּים מִנְחָה יָשִׁיבוּ
מַלְכֵי שְׁבָא וּסְבָא אֶשְׁכָּר יַקְרִיבוּ׃

יא וְיִשְׁתַּחֲווּ־לוֹ כָל־מְלָכִים
כָּל־גּוֹיִם יַעַבְדוּהוּ׃

יב כִּי־יַצִּיל אֶבְיוֹן מְשַׁוֵּעַ
וְעָנִי וְאֵין־עֹזֵר לוֹ׃

יג יָחֹס עַל־דַּל וְאֶבְיוֹן
וְנַפְשׁוֹת אֶבְיוֹנִים יוֹשִׁיעַ׃

יד מִתּוֹךְ וּמֵחָמָס יִגְאַל נַפְשָׁם
וְיֵיקַר דָּמָם בְּעֵינָיו׃

טו וִיחִי וְיִתֶּן־לוֹ מִזְּהַב שְׁבָא
וְיִתְפַּלֵּל בַּעֲדוֹ תָמִיד
כָּל־הַיּוֹם יְבָרְכֶנְהוּ׃

David's ambitions for his son? Some have understood our psalm as an expression of David's dream that Solomon surpass him and achieve the power and dominion that he never did. But a careful reading of our psalm demonstrates quite clearly that David's prayer was not that Solomon rule the world. Rather, his prayer was that Solomon would bring justice into the world, especially justice for the poor and needy.

May he defend the poor… may he save the children… may he crush the oppressor.

David believed that in his pursuit of justice Solomon would inevitably ac-

16. May there be an abundance of corn in the land,
even on the mountain tops;
may its crops rustle like Lebanon;
and men shall thrive in the cities like grass in the fields!

17. May his name endure forever;
as long as the sun lasts may his name continue;
men shall wish to be blessed as he was;
all nations shall call him happy!

18. Blessed be the Lord, the God of Israel,
who alone does wondrous things!

19. Blessed be His glorious name forever;
let the whole earth be filled with His glory!
Amen and Amen!

20. Here end the prayers of David, son of Jesse.

---

reads, "Here end David's prayers." Once the nations of the world are at peace, and David's scion, the Messiah, reigns over them, there is no longer a need for forgiveness or rescue or prosperity. All that has been achieved.

The need for prayers is finally over. We can now proceed to songs of praise and thanksgiving.

טז יְהִ֤י פִסַּת־בַּ֨ר ׀ בָּאָרֶץ֮ בְּרֹ֪אשׁ הָ֫רִ֥ים
יִרְעַ֣שׁ כַּלְּבָנ֣וֹן פִּרְי֑וֹ
וְיָצִ֥יצוּ מֵ֝עִ֗יר כְּעֵ֣שֶׂב הָאָֽרֶץ׃

יז יְהִ֤י שְׁמ֨וֹ ׀ לְֽעוֹלָ֗ם לִפְנֵי־שֶׁ֮מֶשׁ֮ ינין שְׁ֫מ֥וֹ יִנּ֥וֹן
וְיִתְבָּ֥רְכוּ ב֑וֹ כָּל־גּ֝וֹיִ֗ם יְאַשְּׁרֽוּהוּ׃

יח בָּר֤וּךְ ׀ יְהוָ֣ה אֱ֭לֹהִים אֱלֹהֵ֣י יִשְׂרָאֵ֑ל
עֹשֵׂ֖ה נִפְלָא֣וֹת לְבַדּֽוֹ׃

יט וּבָר֤וּךְ ׀ שֵׁ֥ם כְּבוֹד֗וֹ לְע֫וֹלָ֥ם
וְיִמָּלֵ֣א כְ֭בוֹדוֹ אֶת־כֹּ֥ל־הָאָ֗רֶץ
אָ֘מֵ֤ן ׀ וְאָמֵֽן׃

כ כָּלּ֥וּ תְפִלּ֑וֹת דָּ֝וִ֗ד בֶּן־יִשָֽׁי׃

The commentators are puzzled by the placement of this verse; after all, more than half of the psalms still remain. David is hardly done.

Radak, Rabbi David Kimchi, quotes, as he often does, his own father's succinct resolution of this problem. The elder Kimchi notes that the verse does not say, "Here end David's songs of praise or thanksgiving." Rather it

PSALM 73

1. A psalm of Asaph. *Wednesday*
Truly, God is good to Israel,
to those who are pure in heart.

2. But as for me, my feet had almost slipped,
my foothold had nearly given way.

3. For I envied the revelers,
when I saw the prosperity of the wicked.

4. They have no pangs at death;
their body is sound.

5. They are free from the sorrows common to man;
they are not afflicted like other people.

6. Therefore they wear pride as a necklace;
they clothe themselves with a mantle of violence.

7. Their eyes peep through folds of fat;
they succeed far beyond their expectations.

8. They scoff, they speak with malice;
from their high position they plan oppression.

---

suffering, stands in the company of other biblical figures: Job, Jeremiah, Jonah, and even Moses.

The reader of his psalm, who has also asked these questions, and who has experienced similar feelings, is astounded by the uncanny accuracy of Asaph's words: *They are free from the sorrows common to man; they are not afflicted like other people... when all day long I am afflicted with pain, every morning I suffer further punishment.*

Nowhere does the Bible give facile answers to these haunting questions. Asaph finds some solace when he attains to *God's sanctuary,* and there gains a glimpse of the contrast between the current triumphs of the wicked and their ultimate destiny. Some find comfort in taking this long view, the perspective of the course of history. Ultimately the perpetrators of evil will receive their just deserts, and the faithful will achieve the rewards which are their due.

מזמור עג

Sh...sh...sh... We don't dare ask these questions aloud. But we all have our doubts. We wonder, "Why be good? The righteous suffer so, And good things happen to bad people!" Asaph struggled with his doubts. He found his answer. Find yours.

א מִזְמוֹר לְאָסָף ליום רביעי
אַךְ טוֹב לְיִשְׂרָאֵל אֱלֹהִים לְבָרֵי לֵבָב׃

ב וַאֲנִי כִּמְעַט נטוי רַגְלָי נָטָיוּ
כְּאַיִן שפכה אֲשֻׁרָי׃ שֻׁפְּכוּ

ג כִּי־קִנֵּאתִי בַּהוֹלְלִים
שְׁלוֹם רְשָׁעִים אֶרְאֶה׃

ד כִּי אֵין חַרְצֻבּוֹת לְמוֹתָם
וּבָרִיא אוּלָם׃

ה בַּעֲמַל אֱנוֹשׁ אֵינֵמוֹ
וְעִם־אָדָם לֹא יְנֻגָּעוּ׃

ו לָכֵן עֲנָקַתְמוֹ גַאֲוָה
יַעֲטָף־שִׁית חָמָס לָמוֹ׃

ז יָצָא מֵחֵלֶב עֵינֵמוֹ
עָבְרוּ מַשְׂכִּיּוֹת לֵבָב׃

ח יָמִיקוּ ׀ וִידַבְּרוּ בְרָע עֹשֶׁק
מִמָּרוֹם יְדַבֵּרוּ׃

מזמור עג *Psalm 73:* Our psalm elaborates upon one of the most troublesome dilemmas confronted by people of faith. The twin questions "why do bad things happen to good people?" and "why do good things happen to bad people?" gnaw at the sensitivities of all who believe in a benevolent and just God.

Asaph, who witnessed the grandiose and undeserved success of the wicked, while personally experiencing confounding frustration and unbearable

9. They set their mouths against heaven,
their tongue roams over the earth.

10. Therefore His own people turn to [follow] them,
and drain to the dregs their abundant waters.*

11. They say, "How could God know?
Does the Most High have knowledge?

12. Look at these wicked men,
always at ease, piling up wealth.

13. Surely, in vain have I kept my heart pure,
and washed my hands in innocence,

14. when all day long I am afflicted with pain,
every morning I suffer further punishment."

15. Had I decided to speak out in this fashion
I would be betraying the generation of Your children.

16. So I tried to understand it all,
but it was too much for me,

17. until I entered God's sanctuary;
then I perceived what their destiny would be.

18. You set them on a slippery road,
and hurl them to destruction.

* Swallowing thirstily the philosophy of the ungodly.

---

ignorant. He is guided by God's own counsel, and states, in words that border on blasphemy, that he "has God": *And having You, I desire nothing else on earth.*

It is not the assurance of events in a far-off history that finally allays Asaph's doubts. Rather it is a felt spiritual phenomenon that not only reassures him, but inspires in him a sense of holy mission and divine purpose, and motivates him to tell others of the tasks with which God has charged him.

Rabbi Shneur Zalman of Liadi, the "Alter Rebbe" of the Chabad Hasidim, puts Asaph's spiritual enlightenment into these words in chapter 46 of his acclaimed work, the Tanya:

This is the meaning of what Asaph said ... on behalf of the whole community

ט שַׁתּוּ בַשָּׁמַיִם פִּיהֶם
וּלְשׁוֹנָם תִּהֲלַךְ בָּאָרֶץ׃

י לָכֵן ׀ יָשִׁיב עַמּוֹ הֲלֹם   יָשׁוּב
וּמֵי מָלֵא יִמָּצוּ לָמוֹ׃

יא וְאָמְרוּ אֵיכָה יָדַע־אֵל
וְיֵשׁ דֵּעָה בְעֶלְיוֹן׃

יב הִנֵּה־אֵלֶּה רְשָׁעִים
וְשַׁלְוֵי עוֹלָם הִשְׂגּוּ־חָיִל׃

יג אַךְ־רִיק זִכִּיתִי לְבָבִי
וָאֶרְחַץ בְּנִקָּיוֹן כַּפָּי׃

יד וָאֱהִי נָגוּעַ כָּל־הַיּוֹם
וְתוֹכַחְתִּי לַבְּקָרִים׃

טו אִם־אָמַרְתִּי אֲסַפְּרָה כְמוֹ
הִנֵּה דוֹר בָּנֶיךָ בָגָדְתִּי׃

טז וָאֲחַשְּׁבָה לָדַעַת זֹאת
עָמָל הִיא בְעֵינָי׃   הוּא

יז עַד־אָבוֹא אֶל־מִקְדְּשֵׁי־אֵל
אָבִינָה לְאַחֲרִיתָם׃

יח אַךְ בַּחֲלָקוֹת תָּשִׁית לָמוֹ
הִפַּלְתָּם לְמַשּׁוּאוֹת׃

But the last several verses of our psalm suggest that it is not the promise of a far-off future that comforts Asaph. Rather, his comfort takes a spiritual form. He experiences God's closeness, in the midst of his suffering, despite *these wicked men, always at ease, piling up wealth.* Once he experiences God's closeness, he becomes aware that his previous questions and doubts were *stupid and*

19. How suddenly they are ruined,
wiped out, destroyed by terrors!

20. As a dream vanishes when one awakes,
so You, LORD, will lay waste to their icons in the royal city.

21. Long was my mind in ferment
and my feelings in turmoil;*

22. I was stupid and ignorant,
I was like a beast in Your sight.

23. Yet I am always with You,
You hold my right hand.

24. You guide me with Your counsel;
and in the end You will receive me with glory.

25. Whom else have I in heaven?
And having You, I desire nothing else on earth.

26. Though my body and mind fail,
yet God is the rock of my heart
and my portion forever.

27. For those who are far from You are lost;
You destroy all who are unfaithful to You.

28. But as for me, my chief good is to be near to God;
so I have made the LORD God my refuge,
that I may tell of all the ways You inspire me.

* Lit. "were pierced."

---

not prevent the union of the soul with the light of the blessed *Ein Sof* (the Infinite One), who fills all worlds, and as is written: "*Yea, the darkness hides not from You*" (Ps. 139:12).

This profound sense of union of one's soul with the Infinite, albeit mystical, is what allows a person of faith to cope with the injustices which seem to pervade our daily reality.

Though my body and mind fail... my chief good is to be near to God... that I may tell of all the ways You inspire me.

יט אֵיךְ הָיוּ לְשַׁמָּה כְרָגַע
סָפוּ תַמּוּ מִן־בַּלָּהוֹת׃

כ כַּחֲלוֹם מֵהָקִיץ
אֲדֹנָי בָּעִיר ׀ צַלְמָם תִּבְזֶה׃

כא כִּי יִתְחַמֵּץ לְבָבִי
וְכִלְיוֹתַי אֶשְׁתּוֹנָן׃

כב וַאֲנִי־בַעַר וְלֹא אֵדָע
בְּהֵמוֹת הָיִיתִי עִמָּךְ׃

כג וַאֲנִי תָמִיד עִמָּךְ
אָחַזְתָּ בְּיַד־יְמִינִי׃

כד בַּעֲצָתְךָ תַנְחֵנִי
וְאַחַר כָּבוֹד תִּקָּחֵנִי׃

כה מִי־לִי בַשָּׁמָיִם
וְעִמְּךָ לֹא־חָפַצְתִּי בָאָרֶץ׃

כו כָּלָה שְׁאֵרִי וּלְבָבִי
צוּר־לְבָבִי וְחֶלְקִי אֱלֹהִים לְעוֹלָם׃

כז כִּי־הִנֵּה רְחֵקֶיךָ יֹאבֵדוּ
הִצְמַתָּה כָּל־זוֹנֶה מִמֶּךָּ׃

כח וַאֲנִי ׀ קִרֲבַת אֱלֹהִים לִי טוֹב
שַׁתִּי ׀ בַּאדֹנָי יֱהֹוִה מַחְסִי
לְסַפֵּר כָּל־מַלְאֲכוֹתֶיךָ׃

---

of Israel: “I was stupid and ignorant, I was like a beast in Your sight. Yet I am always with You.” This means that even though I am as a “beast” when I am with You, being unaware of and insensitive to this union (of man and Divine), yet “I am always with You,” for the corporeality of the body does

PSALM 74

1. A *maskil* of Asaph.
God, why have You cast us off forever?
Why does Your anger continue to smolder
against the sheep of Your pasture?

2. Remember the community You made Yours long ago,
the tribe You redeemed as Your inheritance,
Mount Zion, which You made as Your abode.

3. Direct Your steps toward the terrible desolations;
[see] all the havoc the enemy has wrought in the sanctuary.

4. Your foes roar in Your meeting place,
they have set up their standards as signs [of victory].

5. It looked as though they had been wielding axes
upon the intricate woodwork,

6. and then hacking away at its carved work
with pick and hatchet.

7. They set fire to Your sanctuary;
they profanely razed to the ground
the dwelling-place sacred to Your name.

What is noteworthy about our psalm is that the psalmist, while disappointed that God seems to have gone over to the side of the enemy, does not express anger. He pleads with God, and praises Him, but does not even vent his displeasure. Instead, he presents his case to God, listing reasons why He should restore the relationship, turn against the enemy and punish him.

Malbim analyzes the concluding verses of our psalms, from verse 16 onward. He uncovers a tightly organized list of persuasive arguments:

1. God, begins the psalmist, You control nature. The entire world knows that and acknowledges that. The day is Yours and the night is Yours.... Summer and winter, You created them both. The enemy sees nature; he observes the wonders of the natural world. But he sees no sign that You control nature.

מזמור עד

Dare I ask You whose side You are on? The enemy's every tactic works for him. Nothing works for me. It was once very different. I could do no wrong. You were on my side then. Come back! Please, come back.

א מַשְׂכִּיל לְאָסָף
לָמָה אֱלֹהִים זָנַחְתָּ לָנֶצַח
יֶעְשַׁן אַפְּךָ בְּצֹאן מַרְעִיתֶךָ:

ב זְכֹר עֲדָתְךָ ׀ קָנִיתָ קֶּדֶם
גָּאַלְתָּ שֵׁבֶט נַחֲלָתֶךָ
הַר־צִיּוֹן זֶה ׀ שָׁכַנְתָּ בּוֹ:

ג הָרִימָה פְעָמֶיךָ לְמַשֻּׁאוֹת נֶצַח
כָּל־הֵרַע אוֹיֵב בַּקֹּדֶשׁ:

ד שָׁאֲגוּ צֹרְרֶיךָ בְּקֶרֶב מוֹעֲדֶךָ
שָׂמוּ אוֹתֹתָם אֹתוֹת:

ה יִוָּדַע כְּמֵבִיא לְמָעְלָה
בִּסֲבָךְ־עֵץ קַרְדֻּמּוֹת:

ו וְעַתָּ פִּתּוּחֶיהָ יָּחַד
בְּכַשִּׁיל וְכֵילַפֹּת יַהֲלֹמוּן:

ז שִׁלְחוּ בָאֵשׁ מִקְדָּשֶׁךָ
לָאָרֶץ חִלְּלוּ מִשְׁכַּן־שְׁמֶךָ:

מזמור עד *Psalm 74:* Our psalm eloquently expresses the devastation felt by a people who have witnessed total defeat. The defeat is made all the more difficult to bear because the people have known victory in the past. Coming to terms with abandonment is much more difficult when the "good old days" of attachment can still be remembered.

8. They said to themselves, "We will utterly crush them";
and they burnt all God's meeting places in the land.

9. No sign has come to us;
no prophets are left;
no one among us knows how long this will last.

10. How much longer, God, will the foe blaspheme?
Will the enemy insult Your name forever?

11. Why do You hold back Your hand, Your right hand?
[Draw it] out of Your bosom, and destroy them.

12. Yet God is my King from of old,
who brings deliverance throughout the land.

13. It was You who split the sea by Your power,
and shattered the heads of the monsters in the sea.

14. It was You who crushed the heads of Leviathan,
and gave them as food to seafaring men.

15. It was You who opened springs and streams [in the desert];
and dried up ever-flowing rivers.

16. The day is Yours and the night is Yours;
it was You who set in place the moon and the sun;

---

2. The psalmist proceeds with another, more subtle, argument. Granted, Your people are like a turtle dove, tame and passive, defenseless against the beasts of the wild. But they are infused with "life," with a breath of the divine, which compensates for their physical vulnerability with a spiritual power. Therefore, Do not deliver Your turtle dove to the wild beasts; do not forget the lives (the spiritual lives which connect them to the divine source of life) of your afflicted people.

3. Look to the covenant! You promised that there will be a time when the land will be forsaken and desolate, but at that very time You will remember Your covenant with us: "*Then I will remember My covenant with Jacob… and I will remember the land…for the land shall be forsaken… I will remember in*

ח אָמְרוּ בְלִבָּם נִינָם יָחַד
שָׂרְפוּ כָל־מוֹעֲדֵי־אֵל בָּאָרֶץ׃

ט אוֹתֹתֵינוּ לֹא־רָאִינוּ
אֵין־עוֹד נָבִיא וְלֹא־אִתָּנוּ יֹדֵעַ עַד־מָה׃

י עַד־מָתַי אֱלֹהִים יְחָרֶף צָר
יְנָאֵץ אוֹיֵב שִׁמְךָ לָנֶצַח׃

יא לָמָּה תָשִׁיב יָדְךָ וִימִינֶךָ
מִקֶּרֶב חוקך כַלֵּה׃ חֵיקְךָ

יב וֵאלֹהִים מַלְכִּי מִקֶּדֶם
פֹּעֵל יְשׁוּעוֹת בְּקֶרֶב הָאָרֶץ׃

יג אַתָּה פוֹרַרְתָּ בְעָזְּךָ יָם
שִׁבַּרְתָּ רָאשֵׁי תַנִּינִים עַל־הַמָּיִם׃

יד אַתָּה רִצַּצְתָּ רָאשֵׁי לִוְיָתָן
תִּתְּנֶנּוּ מַאֲכָל לְעָם לְצִיִּים׃

טו אַתָּה בָקַעְתָּ מַעְיָן וָנָחַל
אַתָּה הוֹבַשְׁתָּ נַהֲרוֹת אֵיתָן׃

טז לְךָ יוֹם אַף־לְךָ לָיְלָה
אַתָּה הֲכִינוֹתָ מָאוֹר וָשָׁמֶשׁ׃

You allow the world to proceed without protesting evil, without protecting the innocent. The enemy concludes that Nature is neutral on matters of right or wrong. "There is neither justice, nor judge," no benevolent God, just blind natural forces. Hence, remember this, Lord; how the enemy blasphemes You! The psalmist turns this into his first argument to persuade God to intervene and demonstrate that He, the Lord of Justice and Mercy, is also the Lord of Nature.

17. it was You who fixed the boundaries of the earth;
summer and winter, You created them both.

18. Remember this, LORD; how the enemy blasphemes You!
How vile people insult Your name!

19. Do not deliver Your turtle dove to the wild beasts;
do not forget the lives of Your afflicted people forever.

20. Look to the covenant;
for all the dark places in the land are haunts of violence.

21. Let not the downtrodden turn away in shame;
let the poor and the needy praise Your name.

22. Arise, LORD! Defend Your cause!
Remember how vile men taunt You all day long.

23. Do not forget the clamor of Your foes,
the ever-rising uproar of Your adversaries.

---

very notion that You will not forget us. It is they who laughingly imitate us and with an ever-rising uproar mockingly declare our prayer: *Do not forget the clamor of Your foes.*

Malbim, alone among the commentators, puts these words, not in the mouth of the psalmist, but in the mouth of the enemy.

Our psalm concludes not with a prayer, but with a series of persuasive arguments designed to convince God to act justly toward us. How consistent is this creative interpretation with the experience of the faithful person, who often suspends prayer and entreaty, and adopts the strategy of arguing with God, attempting to persuade Him to do what is right!

יז אַתָּה הִצַּבְתָּ כׇּל־גְּבוּלוֹת אָרֶץ
קַיִץ וָחֹרֶף אַתָּה יְצַרְתָּם׃

יח זְכׇר־זֹאת אוֹיֵב חֵרֵף ׀ יְהֹוָה
וְעַם־נָבָל נִאֲצוּ שְׁמֶךָ׃

יט אַל־תִּתֵּן לְחַיַּת נֶפֶשׁ תּוֹרֶךָ
חַיַּת עֲנִיֶּיךָ אַל־תִּשְׁכַּח לָנֶצַח׃

כ הַבֵּט לַבְּרִית
כִּי־מָלְאוּ מַחֲשַׁכֵּי־אֶרֶץ נְאוֹת חָמָס׃

כא אַל־יָשֹׁב דַּךְ נִכְלָם
עָנִי וְאֶבְיוֹן יְהַלְלוּ שְׁמֶךָ׃

כב קוּמָה אֱלֹהִים רִיבָה רִיבֶךָ
זְכֹר חֶרְפָּתְךָ מִנִּי־נָבָל כׇּל־הַיּוֹם׃

כג אַל־תִּשְׁכַּח קוֹל צֹרְרֶיךָ
שְׁאוֹן קָמֶיךָ עֹלֶה תָמִיד׃

their favor the covenant" (Lev. 26:42–45). That time has come. The land is forsaken and desolate: ... the dark places in the land are haunts of violence! Now is the time to look to the covenant.

4. God, Your special attribute is the mercy You show to the helpless. We call upon that attribute now, for we are totally helpless, as never before: Let not the downtrodden turn away in shame, nor the poor and needy.

5. You must help us for Your sake. It is You who is being mocked, Your prestige which is being derided. *Defend Your cause*! Look at the source of this derision: *vile men taunt You*. Look at the duration of this mockery: *all day long*! And finally, do not forget how they sarcastically poke fun at the

PSALM 75

1. For the Chief Musician; *al tashḥet.*
A psalm of Asaph. A song.

2. We praise You, God, we praise You,
for Your name is near to us;
men have told us of Your wonderful deeds.

3. When I set the appointed time
I will judge with absolute fairness.

4. Though the earth and all its inhabitants melt away,
I still hold its pillars firm. *Selah*

5. To the boastful I say, "Do not boast,"
and to the wicked, "Do not flaunt your strength."*

6. Do not flaunt your strength against heaven;
or speak with insolent arrogance.

7. No influence from the east or from the west
or from the wilderness can exalt man,

* Lit. "Do not lift up your horn."

According to one version R. Yose responded that He occupies Himself with matchmaking, finding suitable spouses for each human being.

In another version, the "matron" asks the same question, but R. Yose answers very differently. He says: "The Holy One blessed be He sits and builds ladders." Astonished, the "matron" responds: "Ladders! What sort of an occupation is that for God?" To which R. Yose replies: "He lowers one person and raises up another. He causes one to go down, and He promotes another."

R. Yose then quotes the biblical basis for his statement, from the eighth verse of our psalm: *It is God who gives judgment: one man He brings down, another He lifts up.*

There is a great lesson in R. Yose's retort, and in the verses in our psalm which he quotes. This lesson is especially relevant nowadays, when the search for material success is so prevalent.

We tend to search for success in many ways. Some work long hours, others

מזמור עה

The world is not as solid as we think. The earth and all its inhabitants melt away. There are times when God considers destroying it. One such time was in the days of Noah. Another such time was at Mount Sinai. No one wanted the Torah; it was just too cumbersome. God was ready to return the world to its primeval chaos. The Jewish people accepted the Torah, willingly and eagerly. I still hold its pillars firm. And so the world still stands.

א לַמְנַצֵּ֥חַ אַל־תַּשְׁחֵ֑ת
מִזְמ֖וֹר לְאָסָ֣ף שִֽׁיר׃

ב ה֘וֹדִ֤ינוּ לְּךָ֨ ׀ אֱֽלֹהִ֗ים
ה֭וֹדִינוּ וְקָר֣וֹב שְׁמֶ֑ךָ
סִ֝פְּר֗וּ נִפְלְאוֹתֶֽיךָ׃

ג כִּ֭י אֶקַּ֣ח מוֹעֵ֑ד
אֲ֝נִ֗י מֵישָׁרִ֥ים אֶשְׁפֹּֽט׃

ד נְֽמוֹגִ֣ים אֶ֭רֶץ וְכָל־יֹשְׁבֶ֑יהָ
אָֽנֹכִ֨י תִכַּ֖נְתִּי עַמּוּדֶ֣יהָ סֶּֽלָה׃

ה אָמַ֣רְתִּי לַ֭הוֹלְלִים אַל־תָּהֹ֑לּוּ
וְ֝לָרְשָׁעִ֗ים אַל־תָּרִ֥ימוּ קָֽרֶן׃

ו אַל־תָּרִ֣ימוּ לַמָּר֣וֹם קַרְנְכֶ֑ם
תְּדַבְּר֖וּ בְצַוָּ֣אר עָתָֽק׃

ז כִּ֤י לֹ֣א מִ֭מּוֹצָא וּמִֽמַּעֲרָ֑ב
וְ֝לֹ֗א מִמִּדְבַּ֥ר הָרִֽים׃

מזמור עה *Psalm 75:* One theme of our psalm is well explicated in a passage in the Midrash which records two versions of a fascinating discussion between a "certain matron" and R. Yose bar Ḥalafta. The "matron," presumably a member of the Roman royal entourage, asked him how long it took for the Almighty to create the world. When he responded that it took Him only six days she asked, "Well, what then does He do from then until now? How does He keep Himself busy?"

8. but it is God who gives judgment:
one man He brings down, another He lifts up.

9. For in the hand of the Lord there is a cup,
full of foaming wine, mixed with spices;
from this He pours,
and all the wicked of the earth must drink
and drain it to the very dregs.

10. As for me, I will declare [His glory] forever;
I will sing praises to the God of Jacob.

11. I will cut down the power* of evil men,
but the power* of the righteous shall be raised high.

* *Lit. "the horns."*

---

of the Talmud phrase it, "success is like a revolving wheel." *One man He brings down, another He lifts up.*

The lesson of our psalm is not a fatalistic one. It does not forbid legitimate efforts to pursue success. But it does call upon each of to realize that ultimately success is not ours to secure. It is God's to grant, and His to withdraw.

Such an attitude toward life, cultivated properly, is a great blessing. It helps a person arrange his priorities properly and achieve proper balance in his life. It helps him deal with frustration and failure. And it inculcates in him a sense of humility, so that he does not allow success to go to his head and become arrogantly indifferent to the plight of others.

ח כִּֽי־אֱלֹהִ֥ים שֹׁפֵ֑ט
זֶ֥ה יַ֝שְׁפִּ֗יל וְזֶ֣ה יָרִֽים׃

ט כִּ֤י כ֪וֹס בְּֽיַד־יְהֹוָ֡ה
וְיַ֤יִן חָמַ֨ר ׀ מָ֥לֵא מֶסֶךְ֮
וַיַּגֵּ֪ר מִ֫זֶּ֥ה
אַךְ־שְׁ֭מָרֶיהָ יִמְצ֣וּ יִשְׁתּ֑וּ
כֹּ֝֗ל רִשְׁעֵי־אָֽרֶץ׃

י וַ֭אֲנִי אַגִּ֣יד לְעֹלָ֑ם
אֲ֝זַמְּרָ֗ה לֵאלֹהֵ֥י יַעֲקֹֽב׃

יא וְֽכׇל־קַרְנֵ֣י רְשָׁעִ֣ים אֲגַדֵּ֑עַ
תְּ֝רוֹמַ֗מְנָה קַרְנ֥וֹת צַדִּֽיק׃

---

lie and cheat; some travel to the ends of the earth in search of treasure, and others devise creative schemes.

Our psalm admonishes all who seek success so desperately: *No influence from the east or from the west or from the wilderness can exalt man.* Man's position in life is not advanced by frantic effort. Neither diligence nor skill nor power nor sycophancy will guarantee success.

Indeed, even success itself does not assure continued success. As the sages

PSALM 76

1. For the Chief Musician; with many melodies.
A psalm of Asaph. A song.

2. God is renowned in Judah,
His name is great in Israel.

3. His tent is in Salem,
His dwelling-place in Zion.

4. There He broke the fiery arrows of the bow,
the shield, the sword and the weapons of war. *Selah*

5. You, LORD, were resplendent and majestic
on the mountains of prey.

6. Stout-hearted men were despoiled;
they slept their last sleep;
the valiant could not lift a hand.

7. At Your rebuke, O God of Jacob,
horse and chariot lay still.

8. You, You alone are terrifying!
Who can stand before You
once Your anger is roused?

Others, like Radak, understand our psalm as a prophecy of the war of Gog and Magog at the end of days. Then the People of Israel will achieve the complete victory which our psalm describes.

Yet another approach is suggested by passages in the Talmud which find allusions in our psalm to God's revelation at Mount Sinai, when the Torah was offered to the People of Israel.

One such passage, (*Shabbat* 88a), questions verse 9 of our psalm: *From heaven You pronounced the Law, the earth feared and was still.* The Talmud asks, "If it feared, why was it still? If it was still, why did it fear? Apparently, it first feared and subsequently became still."

The Talmud proceeds to explain that the earth first feared that the Jewish

מזמור עו

"We attain spiritual victory through the art of music." So wrote Rav Hirsch. "Music soothes the savage breast." So wrote William Congreve. What propels man to compose music? Victory motivates him. It matters not whether he triumphs over an enemy from without, Or vanquishes the enemy within. Either way, melody ensues.

א לַמְנַצֵּחַ בִּנְגִינֹת מִזְמוֹר לְאָסָף שִׁיר׃

ב נוֹדָע בִּיהוּדָה אֱלֹהִים
בְּיִשְׂרָאֵל גָּדוֹל שְׁמוֹ׃

ג וַיְהִי בְשָׁלֵם סֻכּוֹ
וּמְעוֹנָתוֹ בְצִיּוֹן׃

ד שָׁמָּה שִׁבַּר רִשְׁפֵי־קָשֶׁת
מָגֵן וְחֶרֶב וּמִלְחָמָה סֶלָה׃

ה נָאוֹר אַתָּה אַדִּיר מֵהַרְרֵי־טָרֶף׃

ו אֶשְׁתּוֹלְלוּ ׀ אַבִּירֵי לֵב נָמוּ שְׁנָתָם
וְלֹא־מָצְאוּ כָל־אַנְשֵׁי־חַיִל יְדֵיהֶם׃

ז מִגַּעֲרָתְךָ אֱלֹהֵי יַעֲקֹב
נִרְדָּם וְרֶכֶב וָסוּס׃

ח אַתָּה ׀ נוֹרָא אַתָּה
וּמִי־יַעֲמֹד לְפָנֶיךָ מֵאָז אַפֶּךָ׃

מזמור עו *Psalm 76:* Our psalm is one of the few that contains no prayer, but only praise. The psalmist expresses no fear and tells of no danger. He describes no suffering, except for that of the enemy.

The commentators struggle to find a time in our history when there was such perfect success, such a total victory.

Some, like Rashi, affirm that our psalm refers to the story of Sennacherib, who besieged Jerusalem in the time of King Hezekiah, but whose troops fled in utter panic with no harm befalling its inhabitants.

9. From heaven You pronounced the Law;
the earth feared and was still,

10. as God arose to judge,
to save all the humble of the earth. *Selah*

11. When the fury of man will [turn to] praise You,
You will, on Your part, hold back all that remains
of Your fierce anger.

12. Make vows to the LORD your God and fulfill them;
let all who are around Him bring tribute
to His dread majesty.

13. For He curbs the spirit of princes;
He is the terror of the kings on earth.

---

world exists only as a context for proper human conduct. Thus, the earth *feared.*

The people did not fail the test. They joyfully and sincerely committed to follow the Torah's dictates. The world was now assured that it would not be reduced to chaos. It then *became still.*

Our psalm continues with a description of the further effects of society's commitment to God's Torah. That society will *save all the humble of the earth.* Even the untamed *fury of man will turn to praise You.... All who are around Him* will *bring tribute to His dread majesty.*

For the Talmud, the victory described in our psalm is not a victory over a brutal army. It is a triumph over moral chaos, a victory for humanity.

Such a victory indeed deserves that *the Chief Musician, with many melodies,* compose a song.

ט מִ֭שָּׁמַיִם הִשְׁמַ֣עְתָּ דִּ֑ין
אֶ֖רֶץ יָֽרְאָ֣ה וְשָׁקָֽטָה׃

י בְּקוּם־לַמִּשְׁפָּ֣ט אֱלֹהִ֑ים
לְהוֹשִׁ֖יעַ כָּל־עַנְוֵי־אֶ֣רֶץ סֶֽלָה׃

יא כִּֽי־חֲמַ֣ת אָדָ֣ם תּוֹדֶ֑ךָּ
שְׁאֵרִ֖ית חֵמֹ֣ת תַּחְגֹּֽר׃

יב נִֽדֲר֣וּ וְשַׁלְּמוּ֮ לַיהוָ֪ה אֱלֹהֵ֫יכֶ֥ם
כָּל־סְבִיבָ֑יו יֹבִ֥ילוּ שַׁ֝֗י לַמּוֹרָֽא׃

יג יִ֭בְצֹר ר֣וּחַ נְגִידִ֑ים
נ֝וֹרָ֗א לְמַלְכֵי־אָֽרֶץ׃

---

people would reject the Torah, and that God, whose purpose for creating the world was so that the Torah would be accepted by Man, would return the world to primeval chaos.

Whereas the first two approaches understand the battle in our psalm as one between two rival nations, the Talmud understands the battle in terms of a spiritual conflict. Will human beings adopt the divine code of ethic and morality, or will they spurn it?

The earth, the cosmos, waited with bated breath. Its fate hung in the balance. Bereft of Torah, the cosmos would evaporate into nothingness. The

PSALM 77

1. For the Chief Musician; on Yedutun. A psalm of Asaph.

Fifteenth day of the month

2. I cry aloud to God,
I cry aloud to God that He may hear me.

3. In the day of my distress I seek the LORD;
at night my hand is stretched out unceasingly [in prayer];
my soul refuses to be comforted.

4. I think of God, and groan,
I complain, and my spirit faints. *Selah*

5. You have kept my eyes from closing;I am distraught,
I cannot speak.

6. I thought of the days of old,
of the years long past.

7. I remember my songs of praise at night;
now I ponder in my heart,
and my spirit searches for an answer:

8. "Will the LORD reject forever,
and never again show favor?

But the psalmist does not remain mired in despair. He transforms the despair into hope. He employs several different tactics in order to achieve this transformation.

One tactic is the use of memory. By recollecting the past the psalmist averts fixation upon the present. He convinces himself that if God once redeemed His people from impossible pressures, He can do so again.

Memory does not merely console him; it empowers him.

Not only does he recall God's protection. He remembers his own past activities, especially the songs he once sang. *I remember my songs of praise at night.* Others, entrapped by dire circumstances, will sing songs of suffering and sorrow. He refuses to do so, and insists on reviving the songs of praise that he once sang. Old songs of praise become new songs of hope.

He also dares to look inward, to determine whether he is to blame for his

מזמור עז

Despair is crippling. It paralyzes us. It feels total, "no exit." We have options. We must be strong enough to remember them. But we are too feeble to hope. We no longer know who we are. And we have forgotten how to pray.

טו לחודש

א לַמְנַצֵּחַ עַל־יְדִיתוּן לְאָסָף מִזְמוֹר׃ (יְדוּתוּן)

ב קוֹלִי אֶל־אֱלֹהִים וְאֶצְעָקָה
קוֹלִי אֶל־אֱלֹהִים וְהַאֲזִין אֵלָי׃

ג בְּיוֹם צָרָתִי אֲדֹנָי דָּרָשְׁתִּי
יָדִי ׀ לַיְלָה נִגְּרָה וְלֹא תָפוּג
מֵאֲנָה הִנָּחֵם נַפְשִׁי׃

ד אֶזְכְּרָה אֱלֹהִים וְאֶהֱמָיָה
אָשִׂיחָה ׀ וְתִתְעַטֵּף רוּחִי סֶלָה׃

ה אָחַזְתָּ שְׁמֻרוֹת עֵינָי
נִפְעַמְתִּי וְלֹא אֲדַבֵּר׃

ו חִשַּׁבְתִּי יָמִים מִקֶּדֶם
שְׁנוֹת עוֹלָמִים׃

ז אֶזְכְּרָה נְגִינָתִי בַּלָּיְלָה
עִם־לְבָבִי אָשִׂיחָה
וַיְחַפֵּשׂ רוּחִי׃

ח הַלְעוֹלָמִים יִזְנַח ׀ אֲדֹנָי
וְלֹא־יֹסִיף לִרְצוֹת עוֹד׃

מזמור עז *Psalm 77:* Our psalm deals with the problem that has confronted our people for millennia. How does one cope with utter despair? How can we persist when there seems to be no hope whatsoever?

The extent of this despair is articulated with unique force in our psalm: *"Will the* L*ORD reject forever?... Has His promise failed forevermore?*

9. Has His loving-kindness vanished forever?
Has His promise failed forevermore?

10. Has God forgotten to show pity?
Has He in anger withheld His compassion?" *Selah*

11. I concluded, "It was because of my debility,
that the right hand of the Most High has changed."

12. I recall the deeds of the Lord,
I recall Your wonderful acts of old.

13. I meditate on all Your works
and ponder on Your acts.

14. God, Your way is holy;
what god is as great as our God?

15. You are the God who works wonders;
You have shown Your power among the nations.

16. With Your arm You redeemed Your people,
the children of Jacob and Joseph. *Selah*

17. The waters saw You, God,
the waters saw You and writhed;
the very depths were convulsed.

The Almighty did not arbitrarily change His relationship with His people. Their sinful conduct instigated that change.

The psalmist has not only restored hope. He has also learned to accept responsibility. Motivated by hope, and armed with a sense of personal responsibility, he is now equipped to effect change in his dark circumstances.

One phrase is easily ignored by a superficial reading of our psalm, but it did not escape the notice of the sages of the Talmud. It is the phrase in verse 16: *With Your arm You redeemed Your people, the children of Jacob and Joseph.*

The mention of Joseph troubles R. Elazar in a passage in *Sanhedrin* 19a. "Our people are all children of Jacob, but by no means are we all children of

ט הֶאָפֵס לָנֶצַח חַסְדּוֹ
גָּמַר אֹמֶר לְדֹר וָדֹר׃

י הֲשָׁכַח חַנּוֹת אֵל
אִם־קָפַץ בְּאַף רַחֲמָיו סֶלָה׃

יא וָאֹמַר חַלּוֹתִי הִיא
שְׁנוֹת יְמִין עֶלְיוֹן׃

יב אזכיר מַעַלְלֵי־יָהּ אֶזְכּוֹר
כִּי־אֶזְכְּרָה מִקֶּדֶם פִּלְאֶךָ׃

יג וְהָגִיתִי בְכָל־פָּעֳלֶךָ
וּבַעֲלִילוֹתֶיךָ אָשִׂיחָה׃

יד אֱלֹהִים בַּקֹּדֶשׁ דַּרְכֶּךָ
מִי־אֵל גָּדוֹל כֵּאלֹהִים׃

טו אַתָּה הָאֵל עֹשֵׂה פֶלֶא
הוֹדַעְתָּ בָעַמִּים עֻזֶּךָ׃

טז גָּאַלְתָּ בִּזְרוֹעַ עַמֶּךָ
בְּנֵי־יַעֲקֹב וְיוֹסֵף סֶלָה׃

יז רָאוּךָ מַּיִם ׀ אֱלֹהִים
רָאוּךָ מַּיִם יָחִילוּ
אַף יִרְגְּזוּ תְהֹמוֹת׃

---

ruptured relationship with God. This introspection allows him to conclude that his own moral and spiritual debility was a factor in that ruined relationship: *It is because of my debility that the right hand of the Most High has changed.*

18. The clouds poured down water,
the skies thundered,
Your arrows sped on every side.

19. The noise of Your thunder was like the rattling of wheels;
lightning lit up the world;
the earth trembled and quaked.

20. You made Your way through the sea
and Your path through the mighty waters,
though Your footprints could not be seen.

21. You led Your people like a flock
by the hand of Moses and Aaron.

Joseph coped with despair with the same tactics that our psalmist extols. He remembered his origins, he retained hope, and his sense of responsibility made him successful.

As a "father" of all the children of Israel, Joseph epitomizes the lesson that our psalmist wishes to teach. Memory, hope, and personal responsibility can vanquish pessimism and despair.

יח זֹ֤רְמוּ מַ֨יִם ׀ עָב֗וֹת
ק֭וֹל נָתְנ֣וּ שְׁחָקִ֑ים
אַף־חֲ֝צָצֶ֗יךָ יִתְהַלָּֽכוּ׃

יט ק֤וֹל רַֽעַמְךָ֨ ׀ בַּגַּלְגַּ֗ל
הֵאִ֣ירוּ בְרָקִ֣ים תֵּבֵ֑ל
רָגְזָ֖ה וַתִּרְעַ֣שׁ הָאָֽרֶץ׃

כ בַּיָּ֤ם דַּרְכֶּ֗ךָ
וּ֯שביליך בְּמַ֣יִם רַבִּ֑ים וּשְׁבִילְךָ
וְ֝עִקְּבוֹתֶ֗יךָ לֹ֣א נֹדָֽעוּ׃

כא נָחִ֣יתָ כַצֹּ֣אן עַמֶּ֑ךָ
בְּֽיַד־מֹשֶׁ֥ה וְאַהֲרֹֽן׃

Joseph," he protests. He explains that Joseph supported all of the children of Israel when they came down to Egypt. Just as a person who raises an orphaned child as his own is adjudged to be that child's parent, so did Joseph merit having all of his brothers reckoned as his children.

Our psalmist incorporates the image of Joseph in our psalm because he exemplified the capacity to dispel despair.

PSALM 78

1. A *maskil* of Asaph.
Listen, my people, to my teaching,
incline your ear to the words of my mouth.

2. I will begin my discourse with a parable,
I will expound hidden lessons of the past.

3. What we have heard and know,
and what our fathers have declared to us,

4. we will not hide from their children,
but will tell to the next generation:
the praises of the LORD and His might,
and the wonderful acts He performed.

5. He decreed precepts for Jacob,
and established the Torah in Israel,
bidding our forefathers
to make it known to their sons,

6. so that the next generation might know it,
the children yet unborn,
and they in turn would tell it to their sons:

7. charging them to put their trust in God,
and not forget the works of God,
but keep His commandments;

מזמור עח *Psalm 78:* Our psalm is a "historical psalm." It recounts the history of the Jewish people, from the days of slavery in Egypt, through their ordeals in the wilderness. It culminates with God's selection of David as their king.

It is a tale of spiritual ups and downs. The people constantly "test" God. They rebel, complain, and seem to never be satisfied with God's favors. Whatever He gives them is insufficient. They want more.

מזמור עח

Is He the riddle, or are we? Which of us is the greater mystery? He is inscrutable, granted. But we're even harder to figure out. What does it take to get us to learn our lesson? Can we never be satisfied? Will He forever put up with our persistent backsliding? Our stubborn ingratitude is our mystery. Forgiveness is His.

א מַשְׂכִּ֗יל לְאָ֫סָ֥ף
הַאֲזִ֣ינָה עַ֭מִּי תּוֹרָתִ֑י
הַטּ֥וּ אָ֝זְנְכֶ֗ם לְאִמְרֵי־פִֽי׃

ב אֶפְתְּחָ֣ה בְמָשָׁ֣ל פִּ֑י
אַבִּ֥יעָה חִ֝יד֗וֹת מִנִּי־קֶֽדֶם׃

ג אֲשֶׁ֣ר שָׁ֭מַעְנוּ וַנֵּדָעֵ֑ם
וַ֝אֲבוֹתֵ֗ינוּ סִפְּרוּ־לָֽנוּ׃

ד לֹ֤א נְכַחֵ֨ד ׀ מִבְּנֵיהֶ֗ם
לְד֣וֹר אַ֭חֲרוֹן מְסַפְּרִ֣ים תְּהִלּ֣וֹת יְהוָ֑ה
וֶעֱזוּז֥וֹ וְ֝נִפְלְאוֹתָ֗יו אֲשֶׁ֣ר עָשָֽׂה׃

ה וַיָּ֤קֶם עֵד֨וּת ׀ בְּֽיַעֲקֹ֗ב
וְתוֹרָה֮ שָׂ֤ם בְּיִשְׂרָ֫אֵ֥ל
אֲשֶׁ֣ר צִ֭וָּה אֶת־אֲבוֹתֵ֑ינוּ
לְ֝הוֹדִיעָ֗ם לִבְנֵיהֶֽם׃

ו לְמַ֤עַן יֵדְע֨וּ ׀ דּ֤וֹר אַחֲר֗וֹן
בָּנִ֥ים יִוָּלֵ֑דוּ
יָ֝קֻ֗מוּ וִיסַפְּר֥וּ לִבְנֵיהֶֽם׃

ז וְיָשִׂ֥ימוּ בֵֽאלֹהִ֗ים כִּ֫סְלָ֥ם
וְלֹ֣א יִ֭שְׁכְּחוּ מַֽעַלְלֵי־אֵ֑ל
וּמִצְוֺתָ֥יו יִנְצֹֽרוּ׃

8. and not be like their fathers
a stubborn and defiant generation,
a generation whose heart was not steadfast,
and whose spirit was not faithful to God.

9. [So it was with] the men of Ephraim,*
who, though well equipped and armed with bows,
turned and fled in the day of battle.

10. For they did not keep God's covenant,
and refused to live according to His law;

11. they forgot what He had done
and the wonderful acts He had shown them.

12. He performed wonders in the sight of their fathers,
in the land of Egypt, in the fields of Zoan.

13. He divided the sea and led them through it;
He made the waters stand firm like a wall.

14. He led them with a cloud by day,
and all night long by the light of fire.

15. He split rocks in the wilderness,
and gave them water to drink
as if drawn from the great deep.

16. He brought out flowing streams from a rock
and made the water run down like torrents.

17. But they continued to sin against Him,
defying the Most High in the desert.

18. They willfully put God to the test
by demanding food for themselves.

* The early commentators, Rashi and Ibn Ezra, refer to an ancient tradition, based on the verse in 1 Chr. 7:21, that the Ephraimites, impatient with their long servitude in Egypt, left that land prematurely, and set out on their own for the Promised Land. On the way they were confronted by the Philistines in Gath and suffered a heavy defeat.

ח וְלֹ֤א יִהְי֨וּ ׀ כַּאֲבוֹתָ֗ם
דּוֹר֮ סוֹרֵ֪ר וּמֹ֫רֶ֥ה
דּ֭וֹר לֹא־הֵכִ֣ין לִבּ֑וֹ
וְלֹא־נֶאֶמְנָ֖ה אֶת־אֵ֣ל רוּחֽוֹ׃

ט בְּֽנֵי־אֶ֭פְרַיִם נוֹשְׁקֵ֣י רוֹמֵי־קָ֑שֶׁת
הָ֝פְכ֗וּ בְּי֣וֹם קְרָֽב׃

י לֹ֣א שָׁ֭מְרוּ בְּרִ֣ית אֱלֹהִ֑ים
וּ֝בְתוֹרָת֗וֹ מֵאֲנ֥וּ לָלֶֽכֶת׃

יא וַיִּשְׁכְּח֥וּ עֲלִילוֹתָ֑יו
וְ֝נִפְלְאוֹתָ֗יו אֲשֶׁ֣ר הֶרְאָֽם׃

יב נֶ֣גֶד אֲ֭בוֹתָם עָ֣שָׂה פֶ֑לֶא
בְּאֶ֖רֶץ מִצְרַ֣יִם שְׂדֵה־צֹֽעַן׃

יג בָּ֣קַע יָ֭ם וַיַּעֲבִירֵ֑ם
וַיַּצֶּב־מַ֥יִם כְּמוֹ־נֵֽד׃

יד וַיַּנְחֵ֣ם בֶּעָנָ֣ן יוֹמָ֑ם
וְכָל־הַ֝לַּ֗יְלָה בְּא֣וֹר אֵֽשׁ׃

טו יְבַקַּ֣ע צֻ֭רִים בַּמִּדְבָּ֑ר
וַ֝יַּ֗שְׁקְ כִּתְהֹמ֥וֹת רַבָּֽה׃

טז וַיּוֹצִ֣א נוֹזְלִ֣ים מִסָּ֑לַע
וַיּ֖וֹרֶד כַּנְּהָר֣וֹת מָֽיִם׃

יז וַיּוֹסִ֣יפוּ ע֭וֹד לַחֲטֹא־ל֑וֹ
לַֽמְר֥וֹת עֶ֝לְי֗וֹן בַּצִּיָּֽה׃

יח וַיְנַסּוּ־אֵ֥ל בִּלְבָבָ֑ם
לִֽשְׁאָל־אֹ֥כֶל לְנַפְשָֽׁם׃

19. They spoke against God and said,
"Can God spread a table in the wilderness?

20. True, He struck a rock and waters flowed,
and streams gushed forth.
But can He also give bread,
or provide meat for His people?"

21. When the LORD heard this He was enraged;
fire broke out against Jacob,
wrath blazed against Israel,

22. because they put no faith in God,
no confidence in His power to save.

23. Nevertheless He commanded the clouds above,
and opened the doors of heaven.

24. He rained down manna for them to eat,
and gave them the grain of heaven.

25. Men ate the bread of angels;
He sent them provision in plenty.

26. He stirred up the east wind in heaven,
and drove the south wind by His might.

27. He rained meat on them like dust,
winged birds like the sand on the seashore.

28. He made them fall in the midst of their camp,
all around their dwellings.

29. So they ate and had their fill;
He gave them what they craved for.

They provoke His wrath time and again. They repent, but their repentance is facile and superficial. Yet He continues to forgive them.

This pattern of human waywardness and spiritual fragility, alternating with divine grace and forbearance, is not just the story of one people at one time in history. It is the story of all mankind. It is a description of the human condition, of the back-and-forth nature of the relationship between man and God.

יט וַיְדַבְּר֗וּ בֵּֽאלֹ֫הִ֥ים
אָ֭מְרוּ הֲי֣וּכַל אֵ֑ל
לַעֲרֹ֥ךְ שֻׁ֝לְחָ֗ן בַּמִּדְבָּֽר׃

כ הֵ֤ן הִכָּה־צ֨וּר ׀ וַיָּז֣וּבוּ מַיִם֮ וּנְחָלִ֪ים יִ֫שְׁטֹ֥פוּ
הֲגַם־לֶ֭חֶם י֣וּכַל תֵּ֑ת
אִם־יָכִ֖ין שְׁאֵ֣ר לְעַמּֽוֹ׃

כא לָכֵ֤ן ׀ שָׁמַ֥ע יהוה וַֽיִּתְעַבָּ֥ר
וְ֭אֵשׁ נִשְּׂקָ֣ה בְיַעֲקֹ֑ב
וְגַם־אַ֝֗ף עָלָ֥ה בְיִשְׂרָאֵֽל׃

כב כִּ֤י לֹ֣א הֶ֭אֱמִינוּ בֵּאלֹהִ֑ים
וְלֹ֥א בָ֝טְח֗וּ בִּישׁוּעָתֽוֹ׃

כג וַיְצַ֣ו שְׁחָקִ֣ים מִמָּ֑עַל
וְדַלְתֵ֖י שָׁמַ֣יִם פָּתָֽח׃

כד וַיַּמְטֵ֬ר עֲלֵיהֶ֣ם מָ֣ן לֶאֱכֹ֑ל
וּדְגַן־שָׁ֝מַ֗יִם נָ֣תַן לָֽמוֹ׃

כה לֶ֣חֶם אַ֭בִּירִים אָ֣כַל אִ֑ישׁ
צֵידָ֬ה שָׁלַ֖ח לָהֶ֣ם לָשֹֽׂבַע׃

כו יַסַּ֣ע קָ֭דִים בַּשָּׁמָ֑יִם
וַיְנַהֵ֖ג בְּעֻזּ֣וֹ תֵימָֽן׃

כז וַיַּמְטֵ֬ר עֲלֵיהֶ֣ם כֶּעָפָ֣ר שְׁאֵ֑ר
וּֽכְח֥וֹל יַ֝מִּ֗ים ע֣וֹף כָּנָֽף׃

כח וַ֭יַּפֵּל בְּקֶ֣רֶב מַחֲנֵ֑הוּ
סָ֝בִ֗יב לְמִשְׁכְּנֹתָֽיו׃

כט וַיֹּאכְל֣וּ וַיִּשְׂבְּע֣וּ מְאֹ֑ד
וְ֝תַאֲוָתָ֗ם יָבִ֥א לָהֶֽם׃

30. They were not yet done with their craving,
the food was still in their mouths,

31. when God's anger flared up against them.
He slew the sturdiest among them,
and laid low their choicest young men.

32. Despite all this they went on sinning,
and had no faith in His wonders.

33. So He ended their days like a breath,
and their years in sudden terror.

34. When He brought death among them, they began to seek Him,
they would repent and seek Him in earnest.

35. They remembered that God was their rock,
God the Most High, their redeemer.

36. But they beguiled Him with their mouth,
they lied to Him with their tongue.

37. For in their heart they were not true to Him,
they were not faithful to His covenant.

38. But He is merciful;
He forgives iniquity and does not destroy –
He suppresses His anger repeatedly,
and never rouses His full wrath.

39. He remembered that they were but flesh,
a breath that passes and does not return.

40. How often did they defy Him in the wilderness
and grieve Him in the desert!

Man enjoys God's grace. He is ungrateful. He sins. God punishes. Man repents. God forgives. And the cycle repeats itself, perennially.

The focal verse in our lengthy psalm is verse 38: *But He is merciful; He forgives iniquity and does not destroy. He suppresses His anger repeatedly, and never rouses His full wrath.*

ל לֹא־זָרוּ מִתַּאֲוָתָם
עוֹד אָכְלָם בְּפִיהֶם׃

לא וְאַף אֱלֹהִים ׀ עָלָה בָהֶם
וַיַּהֲרֹג בְּמִשְׁמַנֵּיהֶם
וּבַחוּרֵי יִשְׂרָאֵל הִכְרִיעַ׃

לב בְּכָל־זֹאת חָטְאוּ־עוֹד
וְלֹא הֶאֱמִינוּ בְּנִפְלְאוֹתָיו׃

לג וַיְכַל־בַּהֶבֶל יְמֵיהֶם
וּשְׁנוֹתָם בַּבֶּהָלָה׃

לד אִם־הֲרָגָם וּדְרָשׁוּהוּ
וְשָׁבוּ וְשִׁחֲרוּ־אֵל׃

לה וַיִּזְכְּרוּ כִּי־אֱלֹהִים צוּרָם
וְאֵל עֶלְיוֹן גֹּאֲלָם׃

לו וַיְפַתּוּהוּ בְּפִיהֶם
וּבִלְשׁוֹנָם יְכַזְּבוּ־לוֹ׃

לז וְלִבָּם לֹא־נָכוֹן עִמּוֹ
וְלֹא נֶאֶמְנוּ בִּבְרִיתוֹ׃

לח וְהוּא רַחוּם ׀ יְכַפֵּר עָוֺן וְלֹא־יַשְׁחִית
וְהִרְבָּה לְהָשִׁיב אַפּוֹ
וְלֹא־יָעִיר כָּל־חֲמָתוֹ׃

לט וַיִּזְכֹּר כִּי־בָשָׂר הֵמָּה
רוּחַ הוֹלֵךְ וְלֹא יָשׁוּב׃

מ כַּמָּה יַמְרוּהוּ בַמִּדְבָּר
יַעֲצִיבוּהוּ בִּישִׁימוֹן׃

41. Again and again they put God to the test,
and set a limit to the Holy One of Israel.

42. They did not remember His power,
nor the day He redeemed them from the foe;

43. how He displayed His signs in Egypt,
His wonders in the land of Zoan.

44. He turned their rivers into blood;
they could not drink from their streams.

45. He sent against them swarms of wild beasts
which devoured them,
and frogs which destroyed them.

46. He gave their crops over to the grubs,
their produce to the locusts.

47. He destroyed their vines with hail,
their sycamore trees with frost.

48. He abandoned their cattle to the hail,
their livestock to lightning bolts.

49. He let loose upon them His fierce anger,
fury, rage and misery,
a band of destroying angels.

50. He blazed a path for His anger.
He did not spare them from death,
but gave them over to the plague.

51. He struck down every first-born in Egypt,
the first fruits of their manhood in the tents of Ham.

Rav Kook, in his commentary upon the Prayer Book, *Olat Re'iya*, expounds upon this verse from his unique kabbalistic perspective. Freely translated, his comment reads:

> God's mercy is here referred to in the third person: *He is merciful*, and not *You are merciful*. This is because the psalmist is here alluding to the most

מא וַיָּשׁוּבוּ וַיְנַסּוּ אֵל
וּקְדוֹשׁ יִשְׂרָאֵל הִתְווּ׃

מב לֹא־זָכְרוּ אֶת־יָדוֹ
יוֹם אֲשֶׁר־פָּדָם מִנִּי־צָר׃

מג אֲשֶׁר־שָׂם בְּמִצְרַיִם אֹתוֹתָיו
וּמוֹפְתָיו בִּשְׂדֵה־צֹעַן׃

מד וַיַּהֲפֹךְ לְדָם יְאֹרֵיהֶם
וְנֹזְלֵיהֶם בַּל־יִשְׁתָּיוּן׃

מה יְשַׁלַּח בָּהֶם עָרֹב וַיֹּאכְלֵם
וּצְפַרְדֵּעַ וַתַּשְׁחִיתֵם׃

מו וַיִּתֵּן לֶחָסִיל יְבוּלָם
וִיגִיעָם לָאַרְבֶּה׃

מז יַהֲרֹג בַּבָּרָד גַּפְנָם
וְשִׁקְמוֹתָם בַּחֲנָמַל׃

מח וַיַּסְגֵּר לַבָּרָד בְּעִירָם
וּמִקְנֵיהֶם לָרְשָׁפִים׃

מט יְשַׁלַּח־בָּם ׀ חֲרוֹן אַפּוֹ
עֶבְרָה וָזַעַם וְצָרָה
מִשְׁלַחַת מַלְאֲכֵי רָעִים׃

נ יְפַלֵּס נָתִיב לְאַפּוֹ
לֹא־חָשַׂךְ מִמָּוֶת נַפְשָׁם
וְחַיָּתָם לַדֶּבֶר הִסְגִּיר׃

נא וַיַּךְ כָּל־בְּכוֹר בְּמִצְרָיִם
רֵאשִׁית אוֹנִים בְּאָהֳלֵי־חָם׃

52. Then He led forth His own people like sheep;
like a flock He guided them in the wilderness.

53. He led them in safety; they feared nothing;
while the sea closed over their enemies.

54. And so He brought them to His holy territory,
to the mountain which His right hand had won.

55. He drove out the nations before them,
allotting to each [tribe] his portion by the line,
and settled the tribes of Israel
in the homes [of the dispossessed].

56. They still tested and defied God Most High,
and did not keep His decrees.

57. They turned away, and were disloyal like their fathers,
they were unreliable like a slack bow.

58. They provoked Him with their high places,
they aroused His jealousy with their carved images.

59. God heard and was enraged;
He utterly rejected Israel.

60. He abandoned the tabernacle of Shiloh,
the tent in which He dwelt among men.

61. He let the symbol of His might go into captivity,
His glorious [ark] into enemy hands.

62. He gave up His people to the sword;
so enraged was He with His heritage.

---

profound and hidden aspect of God's attribute of mercy. Whereas the earth is founded upon His principles of justice and righteousness, this hidden attribute of mercy is always mysteriously present, providing forgiveness even for sins of commission which are otherwise unforgivable.

נב וַיַּסַּע כַּצֹּאן עַמּוֹ
וַיְנַהֲגֵם כָּעֵדֶר בַּמִּדְבָּר׃

נג וַיַּנְחֵם לָבֶטַח וְלֹא פָחָדוּ
וְאֶת־אוֹיְבֵיהֶם כִּסָּה הַיָּם׃

נד וַיְבִיאֵם אֶל־גְּבוּל קָדְשׁוֹ
הַר־זֶה קָנְתָה יְמִינוֹ׃

נה וַיְגָרֶשׁ מִפְּנֵיהֶם ׀ גּוֹיִם
וַיַּפִּילֵם בְּחֶבֶל נַחֲלָה
וַיַּשְׁכֵּן בְּאָהֳלֵיהֶם שִׁבְטֵי יִשְׂרָאֵל׃

נו וַיְנַסּוּ וַיַּמְרוּ אֶת־אֱלֹהִים עֶלְיוֹן
וְעֵדוֹתָיו לֹא שָׁמָרוּ׃

נז וַיִּסֹּגוּ וַיִּבְגְּדוּ כַּאֲבוֹתָם
נֶהְפְּכוּ כְּקֶשֶׁת רְמִיָּה׃

נח וַיַּכְעִיסוּהוּ בְּבָמוֹתָם
וּבִפְסִילֵיהֶם יַקְנִיאוּהוּ׃

נט שָׁמַע אֱלֹהִים וַיִּתְעַבָּר
וַיִּמְאַס מְאֹד בְּיִשְׂרָאֵל׃

ס וַיִּטֹּשׁ מִשְׁכַּן שִׁלוֹ
אֹהֶל שִׁכֵּן בָּאָדָם׃

סא וַיִּתֵּן לַשְּׁבִי עֻזּוֹ
וְתִפְאַרְתּוֹ בְיַד־צָר׃

סב וַיַּסְגֵּר לַחֶרֶב עַמּוֹ
וּבְנַחֲלָתוֹ הִתְעַבָּר׃

63. Fire devoured their young men,
their maidens had no wedding songs.

64. Their priests fell by the sword,
and their widows sang no dirges.

65. Then the LORD awoke as from sleep,
like a warrior recovering from wine.

66. He beat back His enemies, putting them to lasting shame.

67. He rejected the tent of Joseph;
He did not choose the tribe of Ephraim,

68. but chose the tribe of Judah,
Mount Zion, which He loved.

69. He built His sanctuary [high] like the high heavens,
and firm like the earth which He established forever.

70. He chose David, His servant,
and took him from the sheepfolds;

71. He brought him from tending the ewes
to be the shepherd of His people Jacob,
of Israel His own possession.

72. He tended them with blameless heart;
with skillful hands he led them.

This is the power of *teshuva*. It resides in the innermost chambers of the celestial treasure house, and so overrides the realities of human existence. Sin is real, and has its consequences, but the power of *teshuva* transcends forgiveness. This "hidden" mercy expunges sin, rendering it as if it never occurred.

He forgives… He suppresses… He never rouses His full wrath.

This understanding of God's forgiveness is the message of hope which sustains mankind. Despite our tendencies to continually regress, we can trust in the forgiveness which is built into our relationship with the Divine, a relationship which is ever renewed.

סג בַּחוּרָיו אָכְלָה־אֵשׁ
וּבְתוּלֹתָיו לֹא הוּלָּלוּ׃

סד כֹּהֲנָיו בַּחֶרֶב נָפָלוּ
וְאַלְמְנֹתָיו לֹא תִבְכֶּינָה׃

סה וַיִּקַץ כְּיָשֵׁן ׀ אֲדֹנָי
כְּגִבּוֹר מִתְרוֹנֵן מִיָּיִן׃

סו וַיַּךְ־צָרָיו אָחוֹר
חֶרְפַּת עוֹלָם נָתַן לָמוֹ׃

סז וַיִּמְאַס בְּאֹהֶל יוֹסֵף
וּבְשֵׁבֶט אֶפְרַיִם לֹא בָחָר׃

סח וַיִּבְחַר אֶת־שֵׁבֶט יְהוּדָה
אֶת־הַר צִיּוֹן אֲשֶׁר אָהֵב׃

סט וַיִּבֶן כְּמוֹ־רָמִים מִקְדָּשׁוֹ
כְּאֶרֶץ יְסָדָהּ לְעוֹלָם׃

ע וַיִּבְחַר בְּדָוִד עַבְדּוֹ
וַיִּקָּחֵהוּ מִמִּכְלְאֹת צֹאן׃

עא מֵאַחַר עָלוֹת הֱבִיאוֹ
לִרְעוֹת בְּיַעֲקֹב עַמּוֹ וּבְיִשְׂרָאֵל נַחֲלָתוֹ׃

עב וַיִּרְעֵם כְּתֹם לְבָבוֹ
וּבִתְבוּנוֹת כַּפָּיו יַנְחֵם׃

This hidden attribute is so powerful that it delivers total forgiveness, with no punitive trace. It leaves no destruction in its wake. It is immediate and it is total. It is operative from the very moment of the sin, so that the sin never leaves its imprint. It is negated at its inception.

PSALM 79

1. A psalm of Asaph. *Sixteenth day of the month*
O God, the nations have invaded Your inheritance,
they have defiled Your Holy Temple.
They have made Jerusalem a heap of ruins.

2. They have left the dead bodies of Your servants
as food for the birds of heaven,
and the flesh of Your faithful for the wild beasts.

3. Their blood was shed like water around Jerusalem,
with none to bury them.

4. We have become the scorn of our neighbors,
the mockery and derision of those around us.

5. How long, Lord?
Will You be angry forever?
Will Your indignation blaze like fire?

---

emphatic cries for vengeance in the Book of Psalms, it is certainly not the only instance in which the psalmist calls upon God to take revenge against His enemies.

Some faiths find such calls for revenge inconsistent with the concept of a merciful and forgiving God. They preach radical forgiveness, calling upon their adherents to forgive even the most heinous of crimes.

Judaism, based very much upon biblical passages such as ours, believes that there are crimes which cannot be forgiven, and for which revenge is justified.

Yet Judaism certainly believes in a forgiving God, and in forgiveness as an essential human virtue. "*Bless the Lord… He forgives all your sins; He heals all your ills*" (Ps. 103:3).

Our psalm contains an important lesson about forgiveness. The commentators are troubled by two phrases in the verse which are quoted at the beginning of our discussion: *Dead bodies of Your servants*? *Flesh of Your faithful*?

מזמור עט

I met them both on the streets of Brooklyn, when I was still in my teens. One, a refusenik, knew the dungeons of the Communist "utopia." Now, his spirit freed, he gaily led the circle of dancing Torahs. Let the prisoner's sighs come before You. The other was a ghost of a man. He was a kazetnik, resurrected from the hell of Auschwitz. He sang soothing melodies to ease the Sabbath's departure. With Your strong arm unchain those who stand at the brink of death.

טז לחודש

א מִזְמוֹר לְאָסָף
אֱלֹהִים בָּאוּ גוֹיִם ׀ בְּנַחֲלָתֶךָ
טִמְּאוּ אֶת־הֵיכַל קָדְשֶׁךָ
שָׂמוּ אֶת־יְרוּשָׁלִַם לְעִיִּים׃

ב נָתְנוּ אֶת־נִבְלַת עֲבָדֶיךָ
מַאֲכָל לְעוֹף הַשָּׁמָיִם
בְּשַׂר חֲסִידֶיךָ לְחַיְתוֹ־אָרֶץ׃

ג שָׁפְכוּ דָמָם ׀ כַּמַּיִם סְבִיבוֹת יְרוּשָׁלִָם
וְאֵין קוֹבֵר׃

ד הָיִינוּ חֶרְפָּה לִשְׁכֵנֵינוּ
לַעַג וָקֶלֶס לִסְבִיבוֹתֵינוּ׃

ה עַד־מָה יְהוָה תֶּאֱנַף לָנֶצַח
תִּבְעַר כְּמוֹ־אֵשׁ קִנְאָתֶךָ׃

מזמור עט *Psalm 79:* Our psalm paints a painfully brutal picture of what Jerusalem's enemies wrought. *They have made Jerusalem a heap of ruins. They have left the dead bodies of Your servants as food for the birds of heaven, and the flesh of Your faithful for the wild beasts.*

It is no wonder that the psalmist responds to such savagery with a plea for revenge. *Pour out Your wrath on the nations.... Let it be known... that You avenge the blood of Your servants.* Although this may be one of the most

6. Pour out Your wrath on the nations that do not know You,
and on the kingdoms that do not call on You by name;

7. for they have devoured Jacob,
and laid waste his homeland.

8. Do not hold against us the sins of past generations.
Let Your mercy hasten to our aid,
for we have sunk very low.

9. Help us, God our deliverer,
for the glory of Your name;
rescue us and forgive our sins
for the sake of Your name.

10. Why should the nations say, "Where is their God?"
Before our eyes let it be known among the nations
that You avenge the blood of Your servants that was shed.

11. Let the prisoner's sighs come before You;
with Your strong arm unchain those who stand
at the brink of death.

---

been administered. Their suffering eradicates their sins. Those who fell victim during the siege of Jerusalem are now again termed God's "servants."

There is room for forgiveness. But it is achieved only after justice has been done. Our psalm calls for revenge because justice against the enemy has not yet been achieved. Forgiveness is premature. The call for revenge is a call for justice to be done, for wrongs to be righted.

This tension between the quest for justice and the virtue of forgiveness is the crux of one of the central conflicts of modern times, raised in Simon Wiesenthal's book *The Sunflower*. Wiesenthal describes his summons to the deathbed of a dying Nazi soldier, whom he knew to be guilty of cruelly murdering dozens of innocents. Wiesenthal refused to express forgiveness to this soldier, but subsequently questioned his decision and presented his story to a long list of Jewish and non-Jewish thinkers.

These thinkers came to differing conclusions as they struggled with the dilemma which is the focus of our psalm: when to forgive and when to seek revenge.

ו שְׁפֹ֤ךְ חֲמָתְךָ֨ ׀ אֶֽל־הַגּוֹיִ֮ אֲשֶׁ֪ר לֹֽא־יְדָ֫ע֥וּךָ
וְעַ֥ל מַמְלָכ֑וֹת אֲשֶׁ֥ר בְּ֝שִׁמְךָ֗ לֹ֣א קָרָֽאוּ׃

ז כִּ֭י אָכַ֣ל אֶֽת־יַעֲקֹ֑ב
וְֽאֶת־נָוֵ֥הוּ הֵשַֽׁמּוּ׃

ח אַֽל־תִּזְכָּר־לָנוּ֮ עֲוֺנֹ֪ת רִאשֹׁ֫נִ֥ים
מַ֭הֵר יְקַדְּמ֣וּנוּ רַחֲמֶ֑יךָ
כִּ֖י דַלּ֣וֹנוּ מְאֹֽד׃

ט עָזְרֵ֤נוּ ׀ אֱלֹהֵ֣י יִ֭שְׁעֵנוּ עַל־דְּבַ֣ר כְּבֽוֹד־שְׁמֶ֑ךָ
וְהַצִּילֵ֥נוּ וְכַפֵּ֥ר עַל־חַ֝טֹּאתֵ֗ינוּ לְמַ֣עַן שְׁמֶֽךָ׃

י לָ֤מָּה ׀ יֹאמְר֣וּ הַגּוֹיִם֮ אַיֵּ֪ה אֱלֹהֵ֫יהֶ֥ם
יִוָּדַ֣ע בגיים לְעֵינֵ֑ינוּ בַּגּוֹיִ֣ם
נִ֝קְמַ֗ת דַּם־עֲבָדֶ֥יךָ הַשָּׁפֽוּךְ׃

יא תָּב֤וֹא לְפָנֶ֗יךָ אֶנְקַ֫ת אָ֥סִ֑יר
כְּגֹ֥דֶל זְרוֹעֲךָ֑ ה֝וֹתֵ֗ר בְּנֵ֣י תְמוּתָֽה׃

"Would a just God permit His 'servants' and His 'faithful' to suffer such gruesome ignominy?" these commentators ask. Surely those whose corpses were strewn, unburied, upon the streets of Jerusalem could not have been "faithful servants" of the Lord.

There are various approaches to this difficulty. Some concede that there were pious individuals who did fall victim to the enemy's sword, and the justice of their fate is known only to God Himself.

Others point out that although those abandoned corpses deserved their horrible punishment, they are nevertheless "servants" and "faithful" when compared to the evil enemy.

Still others prefer the Talmud's approach to this problem. The Talmud (*Sanhedrin* 47a) explains that even those who have committed sins which deserve punishment are forgiven their trespasses once that punishment has

12. Pay back into the laps of our neighbors sevenfold
for the insults which they hurled against You, Lord.

13. Then we, Your people, the sheep of Your pasture,
will praise You forever;
from generation to generation we will recount Your praise.

יב וְהָשֵׁ֬ב לִשְׁכֵנֵ֣ינוּ שִׁ֭בְעָתַיִם אֶל־חֵיקָ֑ם
חֶרְפָּתָ֥ם אֲשֶׁ֣ר חֵרְפ֣וּךָ אֲדֹנָֽי׃

יג וַאֲנַ֤חְנוּ עַמְּךָ֨ ׀ וְצֹ֘אן מַרְעִיתֶ֗ךָ
נ֤וֹדֶה לְּךָ֗ לְע֫וֹלָ֥ם
לְד֥וֹר וָדֹ֑ר נְ֝סַפֵּ֗ר תְּהִלָּתֶֽךָ׃

PSALM 80

1. For the Chief Musician; on *shoshanim*, a testimony.
Of Asaph. A psalm.

2. Give ear, O Shepherd of Israel,
who leads Joseph like a flock!
You who sit enthroned on the cherubim reveal Yourself

3. at the head of Ephraim, Benjamin and Manasseh.
Rouse Your might and come to our help.

4. Restore us, O God;
make Your face shine upon us, that we may be saved.

5. Lord, God of Hosts,
how much longer will You fume at the prayers of Your people?

6. You fed them with tears for their bread,
You have made them drink tears by the bowlful.

7. You have made us a source of strife to our neighbors;
our enemies mock us to their heart's content.

---

the Babylonian exile to the Holy Land. These stages are strikingly similar to the challenges faced by the State of Israel in modern times.

The first stage is one of struggle and battle. The nation must struggle against those forces which seek to restrain it from returning to the Holy Land.

Once the nation has a foothold in the land, however tiny and however tenuous, it must consolidate its victory and build upon it. It must secure its boundaries so that its people can live in peace, and it must provide for its people's material needs.

Finally, it must build a society worthy of God's favor. It must rebuild the Holy Temple, and until that proves feasible, it must construct a society consistent with God's mission for His people.

God has roles to play in each of these three stages, and those roles are named in the three phrases which comprise verse 2. He *leads Joseph like a*

מזמור פ

Where does God sit? Some consider such a question naïve, Others find it blasphemous. Our psalm knows where He sits. He sits enthroned upon the cherubim. The cherubim face each other in friendship and love. Where does God sit? He sits where He can best bless lovers and friends.

א לַמְנַצֵּחַ אֶל־שֹׁשַׁנִּים
עֵדוּת לְאָסָף מִזְמוֹר:

ב רֹעֵה יִשְׂרָאֵל ׀ הַאֲזִינָה
נֹהֵג כַּצֹּאן יוֹסֵף
יֹשֵׁב הַכְּרוּבִים הוֹפִיעָה:

ג לִפְנֵי אֶפְרַיִם ׀ וּבִנְיָמִן וּמְנַשֶּׁה
עוֹרְרָה אֶת־גְּבוּרָתֶךָ
וּלְכָה לִישֻׁעָתָה לָּנוּ:

ד אֱלֹהִים הֲשִׁיבֵנוּ
וְהָאֵר פָּנֶיךָ וְנִוָּשֵׁעָה:

ה יְהוָה אֱלֹהִים צְבָאוֹת
עַד־מָתַי עָשַׁנְתָּ בִּתְפִלַּת עַמֶּךָ:

ו הֶאֱכַלְתָּם לֶחֶם דִּמְעָה
וַתַּשְׁקֵמוֹ בִּדְמָעוֹת שָׁלִישׁ:

ז תְּשִׂימֵנוּ מָדוֹן לִשְׁכֵנֵינוּ
וְאֹיְבֵינוּ יִלְעֲגוּ־לָמוֹ:

מזמור פ *Psalm 80:* Our psalm is unique. It has a refrain. Verses 4, 8, and 20 are almost identical, and each heralds the conclusion of the preceding section.

Malbim views the three sections of our psalm as reflecting three distinct stages of challenge that the Jewish people faced when they first returned from

8. Restore us, O God of Hosts;
make Your face shine upon us, that we may be saved.

9. You brought a vine out of Egypt,
You drove out the nations and planted it.

10. You cleared the ground for it;
it took root and filled the land.

11. The mountains were covered with its shade,
the mighty cedars with its boughs.

12. It extended its branches to the Sea,
its shoots as far as the River.

13. Why have You broken down its walls,
so that every passer-by can pluck its fruit?

14. The wild boar of the forest gnaws it,
and the creatures of the field feed on it.

15. O God of Hosts, relent!
Look down from heaven and see;
take care of this vine,

16. the stock which Your right hand planted,
the bough which You raised up for Yourself.

God to rouse His might and come to the aid of His warriors Ephraim, Benjamin, and Manasseh. That phase concludes with the refrain: *Restore us, O God; make Your face shine upon us.*

Verses 5–7 give voice to the trials of the second stage, the establishment of firm political and economic foundations. Prayer is central to success, and we beg God to accept our prayers. It is now urgent to move beyond tears of failure. No longer can we tolerate the mockery of our neighbors. They must recognize us as a legitimate and sovereign nation. The verses of this stage again conclude: *Restore us, O God of Hosts; make Your face shine upon us.*

Verses 9–19 spell out the objectives of the third stage. The psalmist prays for the restoration of the full glory of the Jewish people – the Kingdom of David and the rebuilding of the Holy Temple. Mere survival is not enough. Return is

ח אֱלֹהִ֣ים צְבָא֣וֹת הֲשִׁיבֵ֑נוּ
וְהָאֵ֥ר פָּ֝נֶ֗יךָ וְנִוָּשֵֽׁעָה׃

ט גֶּ֭פֶן מִמִּצְרַ֣יִם תַּסִּ֑יעַ
תְּגָ֥רֶשׁ גּ֝וֹיִ֗ם וַֽתִּטָּעֶֽהָ׃

י פִּנִּ֥יתָ לְפָנֶ֑יהָ
וַתַּשְׁרֵ֥שׁ שָׁ֝רָשֶׁ֗יהָ וַתְּמַלֵּא־אָֽרֶץ׃

יא כָּסּ֣וּ הָרִ֣ים צִלָּ֑הּ
וַ֝עֲנָפֶ֗יהָ אַֽרְזֵי־אֵֽל׃

יב תְּשַׁלַּ֣ח קְצִירֶ֣הָ עַד־יָ֑ם
וְאֶל־נָ֝הָ֗ר יוֹנְקוֹתֶֽיהָ׃

יג לָ֣מָּה פָּ֭רַצְתָּ גְדֵרֶ֑יהָ
וְ֝אָר֗וּהָ כָּל־עֹ֥בְרֵי דָֽרֶךְ׃

יד יְכַרְסְמֶ֣נָּה חֲזִ֣יר מִיָּ֑עַר
וְזִ֖יז שָׂדַ֣י יִרְעֶֽנָּה׃

טו אֱלֹהִ֣ים צְבָאוֹת֮ שֽׁ֫וּב נָ֥א
הַבֵּ֣ט מִשָּׁמַ֣יִם וּרְאֵ֑ה
וּ֝פְקֹ֗ד גֶּ֣פֶן זֹֽאת׃

טז וְ֭כַנָּה אֲשֶׁר־נָטְעָ֣ה יְמִינֶ֑ךָ
וְעַל־בֵּ֝֗ן אִמַּ֥צְתָּה לָּֽךְ׃

---

flock. He defends His sheep against the many wolves that would devour it as it struggles to return to the Land. He is the *Shepherd of Israel,* sustaining them and enabling them to prosper. Finally, He *sits enthroned on the cherubim,* entrenched in the very epicenter of the rebuilt Holy Temple.

Our psalm then goes on to provide more detail about each of the stages.

Verse 3, describing the initial stage of war and physical struggle, calls upon

17. It has been burnt by fire and cut down [by our enemies].
May they perish by Your fierce rebuke!

18. Let Your hand rest on the man at Your right hand,
on the son of man whom You raised up for Yourself.

19. Then we will no more turn away from You;
Grant us new life, and we will call upon Your name.

20. Restore us, Lord God of Hosts;
make Your face shine upon us, that we may be saved.

This third stage, the apex of our prophetic vision, ends with the same refrain, but this time God's very name is uttered, as befits the Holy Temple: *Restore us, Lord (YHWH) God of Hosts; make Your face shine upon us.*

יז שְׂרֻפָ֣ה בָאֵ֣שׁ כְּסוּחָ֑ה
מִגַּעֲרַ֖ת פָּנֶ֣יךָ יֹאבֵֽדוּ׃

יח תְּֽהִי־יָ֭דְךָ עַל־אִ֣ישׁ יְמִינֶ֑ךָ
עַל־בֶּן־אָ֝דָ֗ם אִמַּ֥צְתָּ לָּֽךְ׃

יט וְֽלֹא־נָס֥וֹג מִמֶּ֑ךָּ
תְּ֝חַיֵּ֗נוּ וּבְשִׁמְךָ֥ נִקְרָֽא׃

כ יְהוָ֬ה אֱלֹהִ֣ים צְבָא֣וֹת הֲשִׁיבֵ֑נוּ
הָאֵ֥ר פָּ֝נֶ֗יךָ וְנִוָּשֵֽׁעָה׃

---

just the beginning. Political and economic viability is not the ultimate objective. He calls for no less than the restoration of the vine, that powerful symbol of all that is sacred and exalted in the history of our people. *Take care of this vine, the stock which Your right hand planted…. Grant us new life!*

PSALM 81

1. For the Chief Musician; on the *gittit*. A psalm of Asaph.

2. Sing joyfully to God our strength;
shout for joy to the God of Jacob.

3. Raise a song, beat the drum,
play the sweet harp and the lyre.

4. Blow the ram's horn in that month
on the day when the moon is covered up for our feast day;*

5. for this is a statute for Israel,
an ordinance of the God of Jacob.

6. He ordained it as a decree upon Joseph,
when He went forth from the land of Egypt.
It was then that I heard words unfamiliar to me:

7. "I removed his shoulder from the burden,
his hands were freed from the builder's basket.

8. In distress you called and I rescued you;
I answered you from the cover of the thundercloud;
I tested you at the waters of Meribah. *Selah*

* I.e., on Rosh HaShana, which is always on the first day of the month, when the moon is not seen.

The careful reader of our psalm will note that it reverses the sequence of the two verses from the order in which they appear in the Ten Commandments. Rabbi Israel Meir HaKohen, the revered early twentieth-century author of the book *Ḥafetz Ḥayim,* helps us understand this reversal by drawing our attention to this passage in the Talmud (*Shabbat* 105b):

> A person who expresses his anger by tearing his garments, or smashing his dishes, or tossing his money about haphazardly, should be considered an idolatrous person. For that is the strategy of the evil urge: Today he'll convince you to commit some trivial sin; tomorrow, he'll goad you to do something a little bit worse. Eventually, he'll even have you worshipping idols. R. Avin noted that there is scriptural source for this teaching: *There*

מזמור פא

I quiver with pangs of guilt, fearful of judgment. I pluck the strings of the harp and the lyre with joyous abandon. I shudder at the shofar's demand that I repent. Yet it relieves me of my sins. Am I hopelessly confused? No. It is Rosh HaShana, a day of paradox. It spite of God's sure knowledge that I will sin again, He forgives me, and assures me "I'll feed you honey from the rock."

א לַמְנַצֵּחַ ׀ עַל־הַגִּתִּית לְאָסָף׃

ב הַרְנִינוּ לֵאלֹהִים עוּזֵּנוּ
הָרִיעוּ לֵאלֹהֵי יַעֲקֹב׃

ג שְׂאוּ־זִמְרָה וּתְנוּ־תֹף
כִּנּוֹר נָעִים עִם־נָבֶל׃

ד תִּקְעוּ בַחֹדֶשׁ שׁוֹפָר
בַּכֵּסֶה לְיוֹם חַגֵּנוּ׃

ה כִּי חֹק לְיִשְׂרָאֵל הוּא
מִשְׁפָּט לֵאלֹהֵי יַעֲקֹב׃

ו עֵדוּת ׀ בִּיהוֹסֵף שָׂמוֹ
בְּצֵאתוֹ עַל־אֶרֶץ מִצְרָיִם
שְׂפַת לֹא־יָדַעְתִּי אֶשְׁמָע׃

ז הֲסִירוֹתִי מִסֵּבֶל שִׁכְמוֹ
כַּפָּיו מִדּוּד תַּעֲבֹרְנָה׃

ח בַּצָּרָה קָרָאתָ וָאֲחַלְּצֶךָּ
אֶעֶנְךָ בְּסֵתֶר רַעַם
אֶבְחָנְךָ עַל־מֵי מְרִיבָה סֶלָה׃

מזמור פא *Psalm 81:* Verses 10 and 11 in our psalm remind us of the opening verses of the Ten Commandments. Our verses read: *There shall be no strange god in you.... I am the Lord your God, who brought you up from the land of Egypt.*

The Ten Commandments begin *I am the Lord your God who has taken you out of the land of Egypt... You shall have no other gods before Me.*

9. Hear, My people, and I will admonish you;
Israel, if only you would listen to Me!

10. There shall be no strange god in you;
and you shall not bow down to an alien god.

11. I am the LORD your God,
who brought you up from the land of Egypt;
open your mouth wide and I will fill it."

12. But My people would not listen to Me;
Israel would have none of Me.

13. So I let them go after their stubborn hearts,
to follow their own devices.

14. If only My people would listen to Me,
if Israel would walk in My ways!

15. I would soon subdue their enemies,
and turn My hand against their foes.

16. Those who hate the LORD would come cringing to Him,
and their punishment would last forever.

17. But Israel* He would feed with the finest wheat;
"I would satisfy you with honey from the rock."

* Lit. "him."

---

is thus a consequence of His proclamation of His role in delivering us from slavery. That explains the sequence of verses in the Ten Commandments.

However, there is a prerequisite to deliverance from Egypt and the lifestyle prescribed by the Torah. One must first purge himself of the "internal idols," the passions which rage within. Before we can start on the road out of Egypt and toward Sinai we must develop self-control. Absent that self-control, the prohibitions against idolatry are futile.

Our psalm is thus teaching us the necessity of self-examination and the cultivation of positive character traits. Only when those steps are taken will God set into motion the process of redemption, epitomized by the exodus from Egypt.

Then, if we *open our mouths wide*, revealing our inner purity to all, we can be assured that He will satiate us with all that is symbolized by His *honey from the rock.*

ט שְׁמַע עַמִּי וְאָעִידָה בָּךְ
יִשְׂרָאֵל אִם־תִּשְׁמַע־לִי׃

י לֹא־יִהְיֶה בְךָ אֵל זָר
וְלֹא תִשְׁתַּחֲוֶה לְאֵל נֵכָר׃

יא אָנֹכִי ׀ יהוה אֱלֹהֶיךָ הַמַּעַלְךָ מֵאֶרֶץ מִצְרָיִם
הַרְחֶב־פִּיךָ וַאֲמַלְאֵהוּ׃

יב וְלֹא־שָׁמַע עַמִּי לְקוֹלִי
וְיִשְׂרָאֵל לֹא־אָבָה לִי׃

יג וָאֲשַׁלְּחֵהוּ בִּשְׁרִירוּת לִבָּם
יֵלְכוּ בְּמוֹעֲצוֹתֵיהֶם׃

יד לוּ עַמִּי שֹׁמֵעַ לִי
יִשְׂרָאֵל בִּדְרָכַי יְהַלֵּכוּ׃

טו כִּמְעַט אוֹיְבֵיהֶם אַכְנִיעַ
וְעַל־צָרֵיהֶם אָשִׁיב יָדִי׃

טז מְשַׂנְאֵי יהוה יְכַחֲשׁוּ־לוֹ
וִיהִי עִתָּם לְעוֹלָם׃

יז וַיַּאֲכִילֵהוּ מֵחֵלֶב חִטָּה
וּמִצּוּר דְּבַשׁ אַשְׂבִּיעֶךָ׃

---

shall be no strange God in you. What kind of a god is within you, inside your body? It is the evil urge!

Bearing this powerful psychological lesson in mind, we can understand the reversal of the verses very well. The Ten Commandments begin with God's proclamation that He brought us out of Egypt. He did so in order to bring us to Sinai, and to give us there a Torah by which to live a noble and refined life. He admonished us not to worship strange gods, because such worship entailed moral depravity. The prohibition against worship of "external idols"

PSALM 82

1. A psalm of Asaph.
God stands in the divine assembly;
among the divines* He delivers judgment.

2. How long will you judge unjustly,
and show favor to the wicked? *Selah*

3. Do justice to the poor and the orphan;
vindicate the lowly and the destitute.

4. Rescue the poor and the needy,
save them from the hand of the wicked.

5. But they neither know nor understand;
they walk about in darkness,
while all the earth's foundations are tottering.

* These are the judges who are considered as God's agents.

---

gather in prayer, or wherever three men sit down together to try to promote justice. God stands in their presence.

This is very encouraging, but it is also very frightening. God can be very demanding. If He is there when we pray, we had better show proper decorum. If He is listening in on our deliberations as we attempt to mete out justice, we had better be sure that we are honest and upright. Otherwise, we can expect to hear Him confront us angrily: *How long will you judge unjustly, and show favor to the wicked?*

He has high expectations of us, knowing that we have the potential to be *godlike beings… sons of the Most High*. But He is typically disappointed in us and knows full well that we can *fall like any prince.*

The central message is that He is present, right there in our midst, in the pews of our houses of worship, and in the chambers in which we listen to the complaints of the weak and the cries of the helpless.

Moreover, not only do we discover where He is to be found, but we learn that His concerns are not limited to any particular group of men. Quite the

מזמור פב

I had high hopes. I put my trust in him. He was a rabbi, a teacher, a judge. I thought he was on God's side. But he was no better than the worst of men. He let me down. He used me. Now I trust no one, not even myself. I am disillusioned. Disillusionment is the worst form of despair.

א מִזְמ֗וֹר לְאָ֫סָ֥ף
אֱֽלֹהִ֗ים נִצָּ֥ב בַּעֲדַת־אֵ֑ל
בְּקֶ֖רֶב אֱלֹהִ֣ים יִשְׁפֹּֽט׃

ב עַד־מָתַ֥י תִּשְׁפְּטוּ־עָ֑וֶל
וּפְנֵ֥י רְ֝שָׁעִ֗ים תִּשְׂאוּ־סֶֽלָה׃

ג שִׁפְטוּ־דַ֥ל וְיָת֑וֹם
עָנִ֖י וָרָ֣שׁ הַצְדִּֽיקוּ׃

ד פַּלְּטוּ־דַ֥ל וְאֶבְי֑וֹן
מִיַּ֖ד רְשָׁעִ֣ים הַצִּֽילוּ׃

ה לֹ֤א יָֽדְע֨וּ ׀ וְלֹ֥א יָבִ֗ינוּ בַּחֲשֵׁכָ֥ה יִתְהַלָּ֑כוּ
יִ֝מּ֗וֹטוּ כָּל־מ֥וֹסְדֵי אָֽרֶץ׃

מזמור פב *Psalm 82:* We err in two very different ways when we think of God. Sometimes, we think of Him as totally transcendent. We believe He exists, but imagine that He is distant and removed from us. We relegate Him to the high heavens. We don't experience His presence right here on earth.

Sometimes, we err in the extreme opposite direction. We believe He exists, but only for our in-group. We convince ourselves that He is available to the pious but not to the irreverent. We are certain that He favors the faithful, and not the faithless. We are sure that He answers the prayers of our co-religionists, but not those of the rest of mankind.

This psalm disabuses us of both misconceptions. In it we discover that God is close. *God stands in the divine assembly.* The Talmud (*Berakhot* 6a) defines that *divine assembly* as either the synagogue, or wherever ten individuals

6. I had said, "You are godlike beings,
all of you sons of the Most High."

7. But no, you shall die as men do,
and fall like any prince.

8. Arise, God, judge the earth;
for all the nations are Your possession.

Asaph, the author of our psalm, pleads the cause of all mankind. He teaches us that the welfare of all mankind is dependent upon an equitable and fair system of justice, and its proper enforcement.

Rav Hirsch puts is so well when he writes: "There is nothing that reveals God to the straight-thinking man more clearly than the sense of justice which was ingrained into the spirit and conscience of man at the time of Creation." All men have this "ingrained conscience." Not all men use it. That is the theme of our psalm.

ו אֲֽנִי־אָ֭מַרְתִּי אֱלֹהִ֣ים אַתֶּ֑ם
וּבְנֵ֖י עֶלְי֣וֹן כֻּלְּכֶֽם׃

ז אָ֭כֵן כְּאָדָ֣ם תְּמוּת֑וּן
וּכְאַחַ֖ד הַשָּׂרִ֣ים תִּפֹּֽלוּ׃

ח ק֣וּמָה אֱ֭לֹהִים שָׁפְטָ֣ה הָאָ֑רֶץ
כִּֽי־אַתָּ֥ה תִ֝נְחַ֗ל בְּכָל־הַגּוֹיִֽם׃

---

contrary, the scope of His interests is universal. Thus our psalm concludes by calling for God Himself to compensate for our failures to achieve justice.

We ask Him to do so for the entire world, *for all the nations are Your possession.*

Radak expresses it explicitly and emphatically: "The poor and persecuted of every nation is Your portion; typically, it is they who are humble in spirit, and men of truth."

PSALM 83

Seventeenth day of the month

1. A song, a psalm of Asaph.

2. God, do not be silent;
do not be quiet,
do not be still, O God.

3. See, Your enemies raise a tumult,
Your foes lift up their heads.

4. They devise crafty schemes against Your people,
they conspire against Your treasured ones.

5. They say, "Come, let us destroy them as a nation;
let Israel's name be remembered no more."

6. With a single mind they take counsel together,
they form an alliance against You –

7. the clans of Edom, the Ishmaelites,
Moab and the Hagrites,

8. Gebal, Ammon and Amalek,
Philistia and the inhabitants of Tyre;

---

nor plunder that they seek. They seek to undo a nation, to strip a people of its sovereignty, to eradicate the name of Israel. Why? What lies behind this enmity?

Our psalm's answer is clear: *With a single mind they take counsel together, they form an alliance against You!* Their enmity is theologically motivated. Their hostility is not aimed at the People of Israel. It is directed against the God of Israel.

What unites the enemies of Israel is an ideology of rejection of ethical monotheism and the lifestyle that it entails. Thus the psalmist prays not just for a military victory. He prays that the enemy will be forced to concede that its ideologies are false. He asks that the foe become ashamed of their pagan beliefs and disgraced by their way of life.

מזמור פג

It's an old story. It has happened many times before. It is the story of seventy wolves against one sheep. What unites the seventy wolves? What do they hope to gain from one meager sheep? It is not the sheep alone that they pursue. It is the Shepherd.

א שִׁיר מִזְמוֹר לְאָסָף׃ יז לחודש

ב אֱלֹהִים אַל־דֳּמִי־לָךְ
אַל־תֶּחֱרַשׁ וְאַל־תִּשְׁקֹט אֵל׃

ג כִּי־הִנֵּה אוֹיְבֶיךָ יֶהֱמָיוּן
וּמְשַׂנְאֶיךָ נָשְׂאוּ רֹאשׁ׃

ד עַל־עַמְּךָ יַעֲרִימוּ סוֹד
וְיִתְיָעֲצוּ עַל־צְפוּנֶיךָ׃

ה אָמְרוּ לְכוּ וְנַכְחִידֵם מִגּוֹי
וְלֹא־יִזָּכֵר שֵׁם־יִשְׂרָאֵל עוֹד׃

ו כִּי נוֹעֲצוּ לֵב יַחְדָּו
עָלֶיךָ בְּרִית יִכְרֹתוּ׃

ז אָהֳלֵי אֱדוֹם וְיִשְׁמְעֵאלִים
מוֹאָב וְהַגְרִים׃

ח גְּבָל וְעַמּוֹן וַעֲמָלֵק
פְּלֶשֶׁת עִם־יֹשְׁבֵי צוֹר׃

מזמור פג *Psalm 83:* Our psalm describes a scene which is tragically familiar to observers of Jewish history. A wide array of enemies has united against a single foe: the nation of Israel. What has brought such a heterogeneous group together? What possible common interest do they have?

A careful reading of our psalm demonstrates that it is neither territory

9. Assyria, too, is in league with them,
giving aid to the descendants of Lot. *Selah*

10. *Deal with them as You did with the Midianites,
with Sisera and Jabin at the brook, Kishon,

11. who perished at Endor,
and were spread over the field like dung.

12. Treat their nobles like Oreb and Zeeb,
all their princes like Zebah and Zalmunna,

13. who said, "Let us take for ourselves
the pasture lands of God."

14. My God, make them like thistledown,
like chaff driven by the wind.

15. As fire consumes a forest,
as the flame sets the mountains ablaze,

16. so pursue them with Your tempest,
and terrify them with Your whirlwind.

* For the historical events referred to in verses 10–12 see Judges chapters 4–8.

---

the others. The psalmist thus expresses surprise that Assyria has ventured forth from so far away.

Radak also reverently quotes "my father, of blessed memory," who reminds us that a previous king of Assyria, Sennacherib, suffered an ignominious defeat when he besieged Jerusalem in the times of King Hezekiah. The psalmist is thus surprised that Assyria had not learned its lesson, but was once again enlisting in a war against Israel.

Finally, Radak shares with us the Midrash's fascinating comment upon the verse in Genesis 10:11 which reads: *From that land Assyria went forth.*

The Midrash takes that to mean that Assyria was once the courageous

ט גַּם־אַשּׁוּר נִלְוָה עִמָּם
הָיוּ זְרוֹעַ לִבְנֵי־לוֹט סֶלָה׃

י עֲשֵׂה־לָהֶם כְּמִדְיָן
כְּסִיסְרָא כְיָבִין בְּנַחַל קִישׁוֹן׃

יא נִשְׁמְדוּ בְעֵין־דֹּאר
הָיוּ דֹּמֶן לָאֲדָמָה׃

יב שִׁיתֵמוֹ נְדִיבֵמוֹ כְּעֹרֵב וְכִזְאֵב
וּכְזֶבַח וּכְצַלְמֻנָּע כָּל־נְסִיכֵמוֹ׃

יג אֲשֶׁר אָמְרוּ נִירְשָׁה לָּנוּ
אֵת נְאוֹת אֱלֹהִים׃

יד אֱלֹהַי שִׁיתֵמוֹ כַגַּלְגַּל
כְּקַשׁ לִפְנֵי־רוּחַ׃

טו כְּאֵשׁ תִּבְעַר־יָעַר
וּכְלֶהָבָה תְּלַהֵט הָרִים׃

טז כֵּן תִּרְדְּפֵם בְּסַעֲרֶךָ
וּבְסוּפָתְךָ תְבַהֲלֵם׃

Ultimately, he longs to see them *seek Your name* and *know that You are alone supreme over all the earth.*

Such an understanding of our psalm enables us to illuminate verse 9, which reads: *Assyria, too, is in league with them.* Why is Assyria singled out from the others on the lengthy list of foes? Why is the psalmist surprised that Assyria has joined the rest?

Radak offers three answers to these questions. First of all, he notes that Assyria is geographically much more distant from the Land of Israel than

17. Cover their faces with shame
until they seek Your name, Lord.

18. May they ever be dismayed and terrified;
may they be disgraced and may they perish!

19. Then they will know that You – whose name is the Lord – are
alone supreme over all the earth.

Our psalm perceives the sinister rationale behind the hatred we have historically faced. We may not always see ourselves as the People of God, but others see us that way. When they take aim at us, it is our God who is their target.

יז מַלֵּ֣א פְנֵיהֶ֣ם קָל֑וֹן
וִֽיבַקְשׁ֖וּ שִׁמְךָ֣ יְהוָֽה׃

יח יֵבֹ֖שׁוּ וְיִבָּהֲל֥וּ עֲדֵי־עַ֗ד
וְֽיַחְפְּר֥וּ וְיֹאבֵֽדוּ׃

יט וְֽיֵדְע֗וּ כִּֽי־אַתָּ֬ה שִׁמְךָ֣ יְהוָ֣ה לְבַדֶּ֑ךָ
עֶ֝לְי֗וֹן עַל־כָּל־הָאָֽרֶץ׃

---

paragon of morality, and refused to participate in the construction of the Tower of Babel. He, Assyria, *went forth,* detaching himself from that blasphemous project. The psalmist is thus surprised that the once brave and noble Assyria has now fallen in with those who *form an alliance against You.*

PSALM 84

1. For the Chief Musician; on the *gittit*.
A psalm of the sons of Korah.

2. How beloved are Your dwelling-places, LORD of Hosts!

3. My soul longs and pines for the courts of the LORD;
my heart and my body cry out for the living God.

4. Even the sparrow has found a home,
and the swallow a nest
in which she rears her young – *
[but I yearn] for Your altars,
LORD of Hosts, my King and my God.

5. Happy are they who dwell in Your house,
ever singing Your praise! *Selah*

6. Happy is the man who finds his strength in You!
When their heart is set on the highways [to Zion],

7. even as they pass through the vale of Baca**
they regard it as a place of springs,
as if the early rain has covered it with blessings.

* This division of the words in this verse follows the Masoretic notation, which places the main pause at "her young"; cf. Ibn Ezra.

** An arid and inhospitable valley through which the pilgrims passed en route to Jerusalem. The name *Baca*, meaning "weeping," is taken from a species of gum-exuding (weeping) tree, which grew along its course.

---

the LORD your God with all your heart (Deut. 6:5). It is within the Temple's precincts that God reciprocates that love.

Our psalm begins with the exclamation "*Mah yedidot mishkenotekha*," which we have translated as *How beloved are Your dwelling-places*. But Rav Hirsch prefers to translate the phrase a bit differently. His translation reads:

מזמור פד

It is a challenge to remain challenged. After an arduous climb we relish a plateau. Even Jacob yearned for serenity. He had climbed enough. But he never knew Zion in her glory. Those who knew her glory never rest again. They strive for more, always more. They go from strength to strength.

א לַמְנַצֵּחַ עַל־הַגִּתִּית לִבְנֵי־קֹרַח מִזְמוֹר׃

ב מַה־יְּדִידוֹת מִשְׁכְּנוֹתֶיךָ
יְהוָה צְבָאוֹת׃

ג נִכְסְפָה וְגַם־כָּלְתָה ׀ נַפְשִׁי לְחַצְרוֹת יְהוָה
לִבִּי וּבְשָׂרִי יְרַנְּנוּ אֶל אֵל־חָי׃

ד גַּם־צִפּוֹר ׀ מָצְאָה בַיִת
וּדְרוֹר ׀ קֵן ׀ לָהּ
אֲשֶׁר־שָׁתָה אֶפְרֹחֶיהָ
אֶת־מִזְבְּחוֹתֶיךָ יְהוָה צְבָאוֹת
מַלְכִּי וֵאלֹהָי׃

ה אַשְׁרֵי יוֹשְׁבֵי בֵיתֶךָ
עוֹד יְהַלְלוּךָ סֶּלָה׃

ו אַשְׁרֵי אָדָם עוֹז־לוֹ בָךְ
מְסִלּוֹת בִּלְבָבָם׃

ז עֹבְרֵי ׀ בְּעֵמֶק הַבָּכָא
מַעְיָן יְשִׁיתוּהוּ
גַּם־בְּרָכוֹת יַעְטֶה מוֹרֶה׃

מזמור פד *Psalm 84:* We commonly think of the Holy Temple as a place of worship. We associate it with prayer, sacrifice, awe, and devotion. Our psalm teaches us otherwise. The Temple is a context for friendship and love. It is the place to discover the meaning of the commandment *and you shall love*

8. So they go from strength to strength
till they appear before God in Zion.

9. Lord, God of Hosts, hear my prayer;
give ear, God of Jacob. *Selah*

10. God, behold our shield [the King],
and look upon the face of Your anointed.

11. Better one day in Your courts
than a thousand elsewhere,
I would rather stand on the threshold of the house of my God
than live in the dwellings of the wicked.

12. Truly, the Lord God is a sun and shield;
the Lord bestows favor and honor.
No good thing will He hold back
from those who walk with integrity.

13. Lord of Hosts,
happy is the man who trusts in You!

---

which we find Solomon, Abraham, the Temple, God, Benjamin, and Israel, all referred to as *yedid.*

The message is clear: loving friendship is essential to the very nature of the Holy Temple. Only a loving friend such as Solomon, a worthy descendant of the loving friend Abraham, could undertake its construction. It had to be situated in the territory of Benjamin, another loving friend. The Temple is a loving friend and so is Almighty God. The defining purpose of the Temple is to serve as a place to achieve forgiveness, for which loving friendship is an absolute prerequisite.

Once we understand that the courtyards of the Temple are where abundant loving friendship is located we can accept on face value the statement *Better one day in Your courts than a thousand elsewhere.* This is not hyperbole. True friendship, loving friendship, is in fact worth a thousand days spent where such friendship is absent.

No wonder then that the visitor to such a Temple *would rather stand on the threshold of the house of my God than live in the dwellings of the wicked.*

ח יֵלְכוּ מֵחַיִל אֶל־חָיִל
יֵרָאֶה אֶל־אֱלֹהִים בְּצִיּוֹן׃

ט יְהוָה אֱלֹהִים צְבָאוֹת
שִׁמְעָה תְפִלָּתִי
הַאֲזִינָה אֱלֹהֵי יַעֲקֹב סֶלָה׃

י מָגִנֵּנוּ רְאֵה אֱלֹהִים
וְהַבֵּט פְּנֵי מְשִׁיחֶךָ׃

יא כִּי טוֹב־יוֹם בַּחֲצֵרֶיךָ מֵאָלֶף
בָּחַרְתִּי הִסְתּוֹפֵף בְּבֵית אֱלֹהַי
מִדּוּר בְּאָהֳלֵי־רֶשַׁע׃

יב כִּי שֶׁמֶשׁ ׀ וּמָגֵן יְהוָה אֱלֹהִים
חֵן וְכָבוֹד יִתֵּן יְהוָה
לֹא יִמְנַע־טוֹב לַהֹלְכִים בְּתָמִים׃

יג יְהוָה צְבָאוֹת
אַשְׁרֵי אָדָם בֹּטֵחַ בָּךְ׃

What beloved friends are Your dwelling-places The word "*yedid*" conveys a love that contains the quality of friendship, a quality that is not necessarily present in all types of love.

Perhaps the best way to define "*yedid*" is as a "loving friend." Such a definition will help us appreciate the following cryptic Talmudic passage (*Menaḥot* 53a):

"Let *yedid,* son of *yedid,* build a *yedid* for the *yedid,* in the territory of *yedid,* so that the *yedidim* can achieve forgiveness there."

The Talmud proceeds to decipher this statement: "Let Solomon, descendant of Abraham, build the Holy Temple for the Holy One blessed be He, in Benjamin's territory, so that the People of Israel can achieve forgiveness there." The Talmud marshals a dazzling array of proof texts, including our psalm, in

PSALM 85

1. For the Chief Musician. Of the sons of Korah. A psalm.

2. Lord, show favor* to Your land,
restore the fortunes of Jacob.

3. Forgive the iniquity of Your people,
cover up all their sins. *Selah*

4. Withdraw all Your wrath,
turn from Your fierce anger.

5. Turn us God of our salvation,
put an end to Your displeasure against us.

6. Will You be angry with us forever?
Will You prolong Your wrath for all generations?

7. Will You not give us new life,
so that Your people may rejoice in You?

8. Lord, show us Your true loving-kindness
and grant us Your salvation.

* The verbs in verses 2–4 are in the perfect tense, which can either describe events of the past or express a fervid prayer. The latter alternative is adopted in our translation.

---

expects us to act mercifully in response to His show of mercy. And on the contrary, He reserves His harsh discipline for our harsh treatment of others.

Which of these two attributes of God is His "real self"? Is He essentially the God of love and forgiveness, or the angry God of law? The *Midrash Tanḥuma* puts this question in the mouth of Moses:

> R. Yudan the son of R. Shimon said: "It happened on the day that the Tabernacle was first erected. Moses entered. He heard a glorious voice, a beautiful and praiseworthy voice. He said: '*I wish to hear what God, the Almighty, has to say.* Is it with *din*, with strict justice, that He speaks? Or is it with *raḥamim*, with compassion, that He speaks?' The Holy One, blessed

מזמור פה

You first! No, you first! It is the old disagreement between God and Man. He says, "Return to Me. Change your ways. Then I'll return to you." We stubbornly respond, "You return to us. Then we'll change." There is a way for Him to break this ancient deadlock. He can help us turn to each other, at the same instant. Turn us, God of our salvation…

א לַמְנַצֵּ֬חַ ׀ לִבְנֵי־קֹ֬רַח מִזְמֽוֹר׃

ב רָצִ֣יתָ יְהֹוָ֣ה אַרְצֶ֑ךָ
שַׁ֝֗בְתָּ שבות יַעֲקֹֽב׃ שְׁבִ֥ית

ג נָ֭שָׂאתָ עֲוֺ֣ן עַמֶּ֑ךָ
כִּסִּ֖יתָ כׇל־חַטָּאתָ֣ם סֶֽלָה׃

ד אָסַ֥פְתָּ כׇל־עֶבְרָתֶ֑ךָ
הֱ֝שִׁיב֗וֹתָ מֵחֲר֥וֹן אַפֶּֽךָ׃

ה שׁ֭וּבֵנוּ אֱלֹהֵ֣י יִשְׁעֵ֑נוּ
וְהָפֵ֖ר כַּֽעַסְךָ֣ עִמָּֽנוּ׃

ו הַלְעוֹלָ֥ם תֶּאֱנַף־בָּ֑נוּ
תִּמְשֹׁ֥ךְ אַ֝פְּךָ֗ לְדֹ֣ר וָדֹֽר׃

ז הֲֽלֹא־אַ֭תָּה תָּשׁ֣וּב תְּחַיֵּ֑נוּ
וְ֝עַמְּךָ֗ יִשְׂמְחוּ־בָֽךְ׃

ח הַרְאֵ֣נוּ יְהֹוָ֣ה חַסְדֶּ֑ךָ
וְ֝יֶשְׁעֲךָ֗ תִּתֶּן־לָֽנוּ׃

מזמור פה *Psalm 85:* Our psalm conveys this basic teaching regarding Judaism's theology: our relationship with God is a reciprocal one. He responds to our conduct, and He expects us to respond to His.

He, so to speak, has two modes of relationship to humanity. One is *raḥamim:* mercy and compassion. The other is *din*: discipline, justice, and strict accountability. He responds with mercy to our merciful behavior, and

9. I wish to hear what God, the Almighty, has to say:
He will speak peace for His people and for His devoted ones –
but let them not return to folly.

10. Surely His help is near to those who fear Him,
and His glory will once again dwell in our land.

11. Loving-kindness and truth meet,
righteousness and peace embrace.

12. Truth will spring up from the earth,
justice will look down from heaven.

13. The LORD will bestow prosperity,
and our land will yield its fruit.

14. Righteousness will go before Him
as He sets out on His way.

The person, guided in his life by truth and truth alone, never tempering truth with loving-kindness, must expect to be judged by God with strict righteousness, unadulterated with sympathetic peace. "Righteousness" is synonymous with justice or discipline. "Peace" bespeaks forbearance and forgiveness.

Thus, the person for whom *loving-kindness and truth meet* in his daily conduct is assured that the Almighty will cause *righteousness and peace to embrace.* He will apply a bountiful measure of His compassion to His harsh discipline. His *raḥamim* will embrace His *din.*

Our psalm is not only a prayer for God's understanding and forgiveness. It is an assurance that that prayer will be granted.

ט אֶשְׁמְעָה מַה־יְדַבֵּר הָאֵל ׀ יְהוָה
כִּי ׀ יְדַבֵּר שָׁלוֹם אֶל־עַמּוֹ וְאֶל־חֲסִידָיו
וְאַל־יָשׁוּבוּ לְכִסְלָה׃

י אַךְ קָרוֹב לִירֵאָיו יִשְׁעוֹ
לִשְׁכֹּן כָּבוֹד בְּאַרְצֵנוּ׃

יא חֶסֶד־וֶאֱמֶת נִפְגָּשׁוּ
צֶדֶק וְשָׁלוֹם נָשָׁקוּ׃

יב אֱמֶת מֵאֶרֶץ תִּצְמָח
וְצֶדֶק מִשָּׁמַיִם נִשְׁקָף׃

יג גַּם־יְהוָה יִתֵּן הַטּוֹב
וְאַרְצֵנוּ תִּתֵּן יְבוּלָהּ׃

יד צֶדֶק לְפָנָיו יְהַלֵּךְ
וְיָשֵׂם לְדֶרֶךְ פְּעָמָיו׃

---

be He, responded: 'Moses, it is with *shalom,* with peace that I speak to them. I have nothing in My heart against My children, as it is written, *He will speak peace for His people and for His devoted ones.*'"

In his book *Ahavat Ḥesed,* Rabbi Israel Meir HaKohen, known by the title of his masterpiece *Ḥafetz Ḥayim,* uses this teaching to interpret verse 11 of our psalm, *Loving-kindness and truth meet, righteousness and peace embrace.*

Ḥafetz Ḥayim is puzzled by how abstract behavioral traits can meet and embrace. He explains that the first half of our verse is the precondition for the second half. A life in which loving-kindness "meets" truth will be rewarded by the Almighty with righteousness that is "embraced" by peace.

PSALM 86

1. A prayer of David.
Incline Your ear, Lord, and answer me,
for I am poor and needy.

2. Preserve my life, for I am a devoted person;
as You are my God, save Your servant
who trusts in You.

3. Have mercy on me, Lord,
for I call to You all day long.

4. Bring joy to the life of Your servant,
for to You, Lord, I lift up my soul.

5. For You, Lord, are kind and forgiving,
full of loving-kindness to all who call on You.

6. Give ear, Lord, to my prayer,
heed the cry of my supplications.

7. In the day of my distress I call on You,
for You will surely answer me.

---

it *a devoted person*, but others have used words like "loyal," "pious," "steadfast," and "righteous" as alternatives. Whatever the translation, the central question remains: How can David insist, to God no less, that he is a *ḥasid*?

Let us survey some of the approaches that have been offered to resolve this dilemma. The Midrash on our psalm first intensifies the question by noting that God Himself is referred to as a *ḥasid* (see Jer. 3:12), rendering it even more inappropriate for David to do so. The Midrash proceeds to comment: "He who hears himself castigated, and yet remains silent, although he has the capability to reciprocate, becomes a 'partner' to the Holy One blessed be He. God constantly hears Himself blasphemed, but does not respond. So too David heard himself castigated and yet remained silent. He could rightly claim to be a *ḥasid*. He could consider himself *a devoted person*, deserving God's protection."

מזמור פו

If you sin, feel guilty. Feelings of guilt prompt repentance. But feelings of guilt can be destructive. They can leave a person paralyzed, unable to move on. God's greatest gift is forgiveness. He forgives us so that we are free to progress. He teaches us to forgive others. He teaches us to forgive ourselves. Those are hard lessons to learn.

א תְּפִלָּה לְדָוִד
הַטֵּה־יהוה אׇזְנְךָ עֲנֵנִי
כִּי־עָנִי וְאֶבְיוֹן אָנִי׃

ב שׇׁמְרָה נַפְשִׁי כִּי־חָסִיד אָנִי
הוֹשַׁע עַבְדְּךָ אַתָּה אֱלֹהַי
הַבּוֹטֵחַ אֵלֶיךָ׃

ג חׇנֵּנִי אֲדֹנָי
כִּי־אֵלֶיךָ אֶקְרָא כׇּל־הַיּוֹם׃

ד שַׂמֵּחַ נֶפֶשׁ עַבְדֶּךָ
כִּי־אֵלֶיךָ אֲדֹנָי נַפְשִׁי אֶשָּׂא׃

ה כִּי־אַתָּה אֲדֹנָי טוֹב וְסַלָּח
וְרַב־חֶסֶד לְכׇל־קֹרְאֶיךָ׃

ו הַאֲזִינָה יהוה תְּפִלָּתִי
וְהַקְשִׁיבָה בְּקוֹל תַּחֲנוּנוֹתָי׃

ז בְּיוֹם צָרָתִי אֶקְרָאֶךָּ
כִּי תַעֲנֵנִי׃

מזמור פו *Psalm 86:* In our psalm David makes a statement which raises the reader's eyebrows in astonishment. *Preserve my life, for I am a devoted person!* I am a *ḥasid*! Is this not the height of arrogance? Declaring himself a *ḥasid*? Where is his humility?

Commentaries struggle with this question. Much of their discussion revolves around the preferred translation of the word *ḥasid*. We have translated

8. There is none like You among the gods, LORD;
there are no deeds like Yours.

9. All the nations You have made
will come to bow down before You, LORD,
and honor Your name.

10. For You are great and do marvelous deeds;
You alone are God.

11. Teach me, LORD, Your way
that I may walk in Your truth;
let my heart be undivided in reverence for Your name.

12. I will praise You, LORD my God, with all my heart,
and honor Your name forever.

13. For great is Your loving-kindness toward me;
You have delivered my soul from the depths of Sheol.

14. O God, proud men have risen against me,
a mob of ruthless men seek my life –
they have no regard for You.

15. But You, LORD, are a God, compassionate and merciful,
slow to anger, and abounding in loving-kindness and truth.

> and West who gather in luxurious assemblies, while I dirty my hands in my efforts to purify ritual uncleanliness. And furthermore, I consult my teacher and mentor Mephiboshet for all that I do.

The point is clear. David is not arrogantly claiming to meet all the criteria for the title *ḥasid*. He is saying that in comparison with other royalty, who spend their days in leisure and luxury and tyranny, he is *a devoted person*, devoted to God, to the needs of his people, and to those he considers wiser than himself.

Ibn Ezra presents the unique interpretation of a Rabbi Yehuda ben Balaam, who suggests that the psalm must be translated not *Preserve my life because I am a* ḥasid, but rather, *Preserve my life so that I can one day become a* ḥasid. Ibn Ezra himself dismisses this unusual translation.

ח אֵין־כָּמוֹךָ בָאֱלֹהִים | אֲדֹנָי
וְאֵין כְּמַעֲשֶׂיךָ׃

ט כָּל־גּוֹיִם | אֲשֶׁר עָשִׂיתָ
יָבוֹאוּ | וְיִשְׁתַּחֲווּ לְפָנֶיךָ אֲדֹנָי
וִיכַבְּדוּ לִשְׁמֶךָ׃

י כִּי־גָדוֹל אַתָּה וְעֹשֵׂה נִפְלָאוֹת
אַתָּה אֱלֹהִים לְבַדֶּךָ׃

יא הוֹרֵנִי יהוה | דַּרְכֶּךָ אֲהַלֵּךְ בַּאֲמִתֶּךָ
יַחֵד לְבָבִי לְיִרְאָה שְׁמֶךָ׃

יב אוֹדְךָ | אֲדֹנָי אֱלֹהַי בְּכָל־לְבָבִי
וַאֲכַבְּדָה שִׁמְךָ לְעוֹלָם׃

יג כִּי־חַסְדְּךָ גָּדוֹל עָלָי
וְהִצַּלְתָּ נַפְשִׁי מִשְּׁאוֹל תַּחְתִּיָּה׃

יד אֱלֹהִים | זֵדִים קָמוּ־עָלַי
וַעֲדַת עָרִיצִים בִּקְשׁוּ נַפְשִׁי
וְלֹא שָׂמוּךָ לְנֶגְדָּם׃

טו וְאַתָּה אֲדֹנָי אֵל־רַחוּם וְחַנּוּן
אֶרֶךְ אַפַּיִם וְרַב־חֶסֶד וֶאֱמֶת׃

The Talmud (*Berakhot* 4a) raises the same question. To answer it, it puts these words in David's mouth:

Master of the universe, am I not *a devoted person*? Compare me to all the kings of East and West! They sleep until three hours past dawn, whereas I awake at midnight to sing Your praises. Compare me to the kings of East

16. Turn to me and show me favor;
grant Your strength to Your servant,
and save the son of Your handmaid.

17. Show me a sign of Your favor,
so that those who hate me will be shamed.
For You, Lord, helped me and comforted me.

---

intentioned, he regrets his wrongdoings, and doesn't gloat over the shortcomings of others. He wishes no one harm, even his enemies.

Radak does not consider it presumptuous for David to consider himself a devoted person. David does not claim to be a saint, he accepts his imperfections. He feels assured that God forgives him. More importantly, he forgives himself.

טז פְּנֵ֥ה אֵלַ֗י וְחָ֫נֵּ֥נִי
תְּנָֽה־עֻזְּךָ֥ לְעַבְדֶּ֑ךָ
וְ֝הוֹשִׁ֗יעָה לְבֶן־אֲמָתֶֽךָ׃

יז עֲשֵֽׂה־עִמִּ֥י א֗וֹת לְט֫וֹבָ֥ה
וְיִרְא֣וּ שֹׂנְאַ֣י וְיֵבֹ֑שׁוּ
כִּֽי־אַתָּ֥ה יְ֝הוָ֗ה עֲזַרְתַּ֥נִי וְנִחַמְתָּֽנִי׃

Radak is far less troubled by the question of David's expropriation of the title *ḥasid*. He writes:

> Others are astonished by how David can consider himself a *ḥasid*.... But I am not similarly concerned. For me, a *ḥasid* is someone who tries to do what is right by God and by man, but who occasionally errs. He is well

PSALM 87

1. A psalm. A song of the sons of Korah.
On the holy hills stands the city which He founded.

2. The LORD loves the gates of Zion
more than all the dwellings of Jacob.

3. Glorious things are said of you, O eternal city of God.

4. When I mention Rahab* and Babylon to my friends,
or even Philistia, Tyre and Ethiopia,
[people say,] "This man was born there."

5. But when speaking of Zion,
[people say,] "One and all were born in her."**
The Most High Himself establishes her.

* A poetic name for Egypt. The word means haughtiness, arrogance.

** Ibn Ezra interprets verses 4 and 5 thus: Whereas the other nations occasionally produce one or two great men, Zion produces time and time again men of stature.

---

of any one vital part. An example, of course, is the human body, where the constituent parts each play a role in its maintenance. Absent any part, and the body is defective, and in many cases ceases to function.

This, says Malbim, is the difference between Zion and the other nations enumerated. *When I mention Rahab and Babylon to my friends* I mention the names of nations. I do not mention the individuals except to say that this person was born here or that person was born there. No single person is essential to defining the nation. The nation is a crowd, and as such is no more than a homogenous mass of people, undifferentiated, and subject to what has come to be called a "crowd mentality." On the other hand, when *speaking of Zion*, each and every person counts. Zion is not Zion if one of her citizens is absent. Zion is not a sum of individuals. It is an organic whole, where each and every individual is essential to the national identity. Hence, *one and all were born in her.*

Malbim takes his point further in his interpretation of verse 6, *The LORD will record in the register of peoples.* He understands the verse to mean that

מזמור פז

Ancient cities had gates. That's where the wise men sat. Justice could be found there. God loved those gates. He loved them more than Jacob's other dwellings. Today, cities have no gates. So God loves the halls where justice is studied. I know a city which has those gates. Zion.

א לִבְנֵי־קֹרַח מִזְמוֹר שִׁיר
יְסוּדָתוֹ בְּהַרְרֵי־קֹדֶשׁ׃

ב אֹהֵב יהוה שַׁעֲרֵי צִיּוֹן
מִכֹּל מִשְׁכְּנוֹת יַעֲקֹב׃

ג נִכְבָּדוֹת מְדֻבָּר בָּךְ
עִיר הָאֱלֹהִים סֶלָה׃

ד אַזְכִּיר ׀ רַהַב וּבָבֶל לְיֹדְעָי
הִנֵּה פְלֶשֶׁת וְצוֹר עִם־כּוּשׁ
זֶה יֻלַּד־שָׁם׃

ה וּלְצִיּוֹן ׀ יֵאָמַר אִישׁ וְאִישׁ יֻלַּד־בָּהּ
וְהוּא יְכוֹנְנֶהָ עֶלְיוֹן׃

מזמור פז *Psalm 87:* Our psalm has the advantage of brevity. But many commentators have found its meaning obscure. Perhaps that is why it has so many diverse interpretations, and even differing literal translations.

Malbim offers a creative approach. It is based upon the manner in which our psalm contrasts Zion with Rahab, Babylon, and the other nations listed in verse 4.

He begins by distinguishing between two types of combinations or groups. One is the group which is the sum of a large number of parts, but to which no single part is essential. As an example of this he points to a bushel of wheat. It is comprised of thousands of single kernels, but the absence of one kernel, or even several, would have no effect upon the nature of the bushel. It remains a bushel of wheat.

The other combination or group is an organic one. Each and every part plays a role, and the organism dies, or loses its identity, with the absence

6. The LORD will record in the register of peoples:
"This [follower of mine] was born in her." *Selah*

7. Then all shall declare in song and dance:
"The source of all our blessings is in you [Zion]."

---

have ideas of their own is preferable to blind conformity and mass obedience to authority.

Was Malbim expressing his personal views in his interpretation of our psalm? Some have argued that Malbim, as a late-nineteenth-century Central European, was reading prevailing ideologies of his time into a work written in the biblical era. Whether or not this is true, he certainly has helped us find a special meaning to a psalm which otherwise presents interpretative challenges.

Although many would vehemently disagree, understanding ancient sacred texts in terms of one's contemporary categories may be entirely legitimate. Arguably, Malbim thought so.

ו יְהוָה יִסְפֹּר בִּכְתוֹב עַמִּים
זֶה יֻלַּד־שָׁם סֶלָה׃

ז וְשָׁרִים כְּחֹלְלִים
כָּל־מַעְיָנַי בָּךְ׃

---

each individual member of Zion is as significant as an entire nation, and hence each person is recorded in the register of peoples, not in the register of single individuals.

Malbim sees individuality and autonomy as traits which ideally characterize Zion. Other nations, he argues, downplay the significance of the individual, and view him as subordinate to the collective. Members of Zion are all equally important, and so the needs of the collective are secondary to the needs of the individual.

Malbim would argue that the dignity and worth of each individual is a supreme principle, overriding other considerations. Insuring the individual's privilege of self-expression and self-assertion is of far greater importance than coerced unity or superficial harmony. Vigorous debate by individuals who

PSALM 88

1. A song, a psalm of the sons of Korah.
For the Chief Musician; on *maḥalat le'annot.*
A *maskil* of Heman the Ezrahite.

Eighteenth day of the month

2. O Lord, God who saves me:
By day I cry to You, and also by night;

3. let my prayer reach You;
incline Your ear to my cry.

4. For my soul is sated with troubles;
my life is on the verge of the grave.

5. I am already counted with those who go down to the pit;
I have become like a man bereft of strength.

6. I am abandoned among the dead,
like the slain who lie in the grave,
whom You no longer remember,
and who are cut off from Your care.

7. You have put me into the deepest pit,
into the darkness, into the lowest depths.

The subject of our psalm knows full well that his *life is on the verge of the grave*. But he clings to life. He prays, day and night. But those around him, family and friends, have given up hope. And this troubles him greatly.

He is haunted by a common nightmare. He is alive, but is mistaken for a dead man. Others are preparing his funeral. They are ready to bury him. He urgently wants to protest: "I am alive!" But he is too weak to utter those words. He is about to be buried alive. The coffin lies open next to his bed and he can feel himself being gently lifted into it.

A person who is mortally ill dreads just such a fate. He is alive, and still struggling to recover. But others have given up on him. They have resigned

מזמור פח

Death is not a mystery. We know a lot about death. The dead are free from pain and suffering. They are free of obligation and opportunity. They have no friends. They are forgotten. No wonder we pray for life. We want obligations and opportunity. We want friendship, and fear being forgotten. We'll tolerate the pain and suffering. Life is a mystery.

א שִׁיר מִזְמוֹר לִבְנֵי קֹרַח יח לחודש
לַמְנַצֵּחַ עַל־מָחֲלַת לְעַנּוֹת
מַשְׂכִּיל לְהֵימָן הָאֶזְרָחִי׃

ב יְהוָה אֱלֹהֵי יְשׁוּעָתִי
יוֹם־צָעַקְתִּי בַלַּיְלָה נֶגְדֶּךָ׃

ג תָּבוֹא לְפָנֶיךָ תְּפִלָּתִי
הַטֵּה אָזְנְךָ לְרִנָּתִי׃

ד כִּי־שָׂבְעָה בְרָעוֹת נַפְשִׁי
וְחַיַּי לִשְׁאוֹל הִגִּיעוּ׃

ה נֶחְשַׁבְתִּי עִם־יוֹרְדֵי בוֹר
הָיִיתִי כְּגֶבֶר אֵין־אֱיָל׃

ו בַּמֵּתִים חָפְשִׁי
כְּמוֹ חֲלָלִים ׀ שֹׁכְבֵי קֶבֶר
אֲשֶׁר לֹא זְכַרְתָּם עוֹד
וְהֵמָּה מִיָּדְךָ נִגְזָרוּ׃

ז שַׁתַּנִי בְּבוֹר תַּחְתִּיּוֹת
בְּמַחֲשַׁכִּים בִּמְצֹלוֹת׃

מזמור פח *Psalm 88:* Our psalm is a gripping description of the feelings and fears of a dying person. It provides an accurate description of the inner experience of a man upon his deathbed.

8. Your fury lies heavily upon me;
You have afflicted me with wave after wave [of trouble]. *Selah*

9. You have removed my friends far from me,
You have made me loathsome to them.
I am shut in and cannot get out.

10. My eyes ache through affliction.
I call to You, LORD, every day;
I stretch out my hands to You in prayer.

11. Will You work wonders for the dead?
Will the shades rise up to praise You? *Selah*

12. Will Your loving-kindness be spoken of in the grave,
Your faithfulness in the realm of destruction?

13. Will Your wonders be known in the place of darkness,
Your justice in the land of oblivion?

14. But I, I call to You, LORD, for help;
my prayer greets You every morning.

15. Why, LORD, do You reject me?
Why do You hide Your face from me?

---

has long ago learned of God's promise of immortality, of a future resurrection. But these beliefs elude him now. He anticipates instead death's utter finality. He discovers that the fervently held theological tenets he once held are now meaningless. He persistently questions God: *Will You work wonders for the dead? Will Your loving-kindness be spoken of in the grave?*

When our dying man is on the brink of the grave he finds small comfort in his many years of life. He looks back on all his years as one unbroken chain of suffering and affliction. *From my youth... I have borne Your terrors* and I continue to be *in constant fear of further calamities.*

Our psalm is among the starkest, perhaps the starkest, in the entire Book of Psalms. The psalmist tells us that he has prayed, but we are not privy to

ח עָ֭לַי סָמְכָ֣ה חֲמָתֶ֑ךָ
וְכָל־מִ֝שְׁבָּרֶ֗יךָ עִנִּ֥יתָ סֶּֽלָה׃

ט הִרְחַ֥קְתָּ מְיֻדָּעַ֗י מִ֫מֶּ֥נִּי
שַׁתַּ֣נִי תוֹעֵב֣וֹת לָ֑מוֹ
כָּ֝לֻ֗א וְלֹ֣א אֵצֵֽא׃

י עֵינִ֥י דָאֲבָ֗ה מִנִּ֫י
עֹ֥נִי קְרָאתִ֣יךָ יְהֹוָ֣ה בְּכָל־י֑וֹם
שִׁטַּ֖חְתִּי אֵלֶ֣יךָ כַפָּֽי׃

יא הֲלַמֵּתִ֥ים תַּעֲשֶׂה־פֶּ֑לֶא
אִם־רְ֝פָאִ֗ים יָק֤וּמוּ ׀ יוֹד֬וּךָ סֶּֽלָה׃

יב הַיְסֻפַּ֣ר בַּקֶּ֣בֶר חַסְדֶּ֑ךָ
אֱ֝מוּנָתְךָ֗ בָּאֲבַדּֽוֹן׃

יג הֲיִוָּדַ֣ע בַּחֹ֣שֶׁךְ פִּלְאֶ֑ךָ
וְ֝צִדְקָתְךָ֗ בְּאֶ֣רֶץ נְשִׁיָּֽה׃

יד וַאֲנִ֤י ׀ אֵלֶ֣יךָ יְהֹוָ֣ה שִׁוַּ֑עְתִּי
וּ֝בַבֹּ֗קֶר תְּֽפִלָּתִ֥י תְקַדְּמֶֽךָּ׃

טו לָמָ֣ה יְ֭הֹוָה תִּזְנַ֣ח נַפְשִׁ֑י
תַּסְתִּ֖יר פָּנֶ֣יךָ מִמֶּֽנִּי׃

---

themselves to the patient's demise. *I am already counted with those who go down to the pit… I am abandoned… like the slain who lie in the grave.*

The man on his deathbed experiences more than panic and horror. He is also angry, furious at those who have given up on him. His loneliness fuels his fury. No one can know what he is feeling, and no one cares enough to even try. *You have removed my friends far from me.*

Our dying man is a man of great faith. He has not despaired of prayer. He

16. From my youth I have been afflicted
and been near to death;
I have borne Your terrors,
but am in constant fear [of further calamities].

17. Your fierce wrath overwhelms me,
Your terrors are destroying me.

18. All day long they surround me like a flood,
they completely engulf me.

19. You have put lover and friend far from me,
and my close companions into darkness.

The very last word of the psalm leaves with a taste of its entire theme: *Darkness*!

Our psalm is a masterful example of empathy for a dying man. It does not try to soothe him or argue against his feelings. It respectfully leaves him as he is, and reserves assurances of life and promises of hope for other occasions, and other psalms.

טז עָ֘נִ֤י אֲנִ֣י וְגֹוֵ֣עַ מִנֹּ֑עַר
נָשָׂ֖אתִי אֵמֶ֣יךָ אָפֽוּנָה׃

יז עָ֭לַי עָבְר֣וּ חֲרוֹנֶ֑יךָ
בִּ֝עוּתֶ֗יךָ צִמְּתֻתֽוּנִי׃

יח סַבּ֣וּנִי כַ֭מַּיִם כָּל־הַיּ֑וֹם
הִקִּ֖יפוּ עָלַ֣י יָֽחַד׃

יט הִרְחַ֣קְתָּ מִ֭מֶּנִּי אֹהֵ֣ב וָרֵ֑עַ
מְֽיֻדָּעַ֥י מַחְשָֽׁךְ׃

---

those prayers. There is nary a word of prayer in this psalm, not a sliver of hope. Instead there are questions, yes, but they serve only as expressions of dread, terror, and fury.

PSALM 89

1. A *maskil* of Ethan the Ezrahite.

2. I will sing of the Lord's loving-kindness forever;
I will make known with my mouth Your faithfulness
to all generations.

3. I declare that Your loving-kindness stands firm forever;
constant as the heavens You established with Your faithfulness.

4. "I have made a covenant with My chosen one,
I have sworn to My servant David:

5. I will establish your line forever;
I will build up your throne firm for all generations." *Selah*

6. The heavens praise Your wonders, Lord,
Your faithfulness, too, [is praised]
in the assembly of the holy beings.

7. For who in the skies can compare with the Lord?
Who is like the Lord among the heavenly beings,

8. a God greatly revered in the council of the holy ones,
awesome to all who surround Him?

9. Lord, God of Hosts, who is like You?
Lord, You are mighty; Your faithfulness surrounds You.

10. You rule over the surging sea;
when its waves mount high, You still them.

מזמור פט *Psalm 89:* The theme of our psalm is paradox, especially the paradoxical nature of the Master of the Universe.

On the one hand, He is the Almighty Creator: *the heavens praise Your wonders*. On the other hand, He has *made a covenant with My chosen one*, and seems to be exclusively concerned for one mere mortal, *My servant David*. He *rules over the surging* sea, yet devotes His divine energies to human enemies: *With Your strong arm You scattered Your enemies.*

מזמור פט

God's loving-kindness is forever. But I won't live forever. The LORD knows the rest of the story. Will I live long enough to see how it all turns out? If I don't, will my life have been worth living? I've seen suffering in my time. I wonder, "Will it cease before I die?" That's why I pray for longevity. I want to be there when the curtain falls.

א מַשְׂכִּיל לְאֵיתָן הָאֶזְרָחִי׃

ב חַסְדֵי יְהוָה עוֹלָם אָשִׁירָה
לְדֹר וָדֹר ׀ אוֹדִיעַ אֱמוּנָתְךָ בְּפִי׃

ג כִּי־אָמַרְתִּי עוֹלָם חֶסֶד יִבָּנֶה
שָׁמַיִם ׀ תָּכִן אֱמוּנָתְךָ בָהֶם׃

ד כָּרַתִּי בְרִית לִבְחִירִי
נִשְׁבַּעְתִּי לְדָוִד עַבְדִּי׃

ה עַד־עוֹלָם אָכִין זַרְעֶךָ
וּבָנִיתִי לְדֹר־וָדוֹר כִּסְאֲךָ סֶלָה׃

ו וְיוֹדוּ שָׁמַיִם פִּלְאֲךָ יְהוָה
אַף־אֱמוּנָתְךָ בִּקְהַל קְדֹשִׁים׃

ז כִּי מִי בַשַּׁחַק יַעֲרֹךְ לַיהוָה
יִדְמֶה לַיהוָה בִּבְנֵי אֵלִים׃

ח אֵל נַעֲרָץ בְּסוֹד־קְדֹשִׁים רַבָּה
וְנוֹרָא עַל־כָּל־סְבִיבָיו׃

ט יְהוָה ׀ אֱלֹהֵי צְבָאוֹת
מִי־כָמוֹךָ חֲסִין ׀ יָהּ
וֶאֱמוּנָתְךָ סְבִיבוֹתֶיךָ׃

י אַתָּה מוֹשֵׁל בְּגֵאוּת הַיָּם
בְּשׂוֹא גַלָּיו אַתָּה תְשַׁבְּחֵם׃

11. You crushed the monster Rahab dead like a corpse;
with Your strong arm You scattered Your enemies.

12. The heavens are Yours, the earth also is Yours;
You founded the world and all that is in it.

13. It is You who created the north and the south;
Tabor and Hermon hail Your name with joy.

14. Yours is an arm endowed with power;
Your hand is strong, Your right hand raised high.

15. Righteousness and justice are the foundation of Your throne,
loving-kindness and truth go before You.

16. Happy the people who know how the joyful sound;
LORD! They walk in the light of Your countenance.

17. They rejoice in Your name all day long,
and are exalted through Your righteousness.

18. Indeed, You are their glory and strength;
through Your favor our horn is exalted.

19. For our shield belongs to the LORD,
our king to the Holy One of Israel.

20. Once You spoke to Your faithful in a vision,
You said, "I have given help to a great warrior,
I have exalted one chosen from the people.

21. I have found David, My servant;
with My holy oil I have anointed him.

Is He the Master of the Cosmos, or is he a tribal god?

For Him *ḥesed,* loving-kindness, is paramount. The focal phrase in verse three, *olam ḥesed yibaneh,* can mean that loving-kindness stands firm forever, or it can mean that the entire world is built upon loving-kindness. Either way loving-kindness reigns supreme.

יא אַתָּה דִכִּאתָ כֶחָלָל רָהַב
בִּזְרוֹעַ עֻזְּךָ פִּזַּרְתָּ אוֹיְבֶיךָ׃

יב לְךָ שָׁמַיִם אַף־לְךָ אָרֶץ
תֵּבֵל וּמְלֹאָהּ אַתָּה יְסַדְתָּם׃

יג צָפוֹן וְיָמִין אַתָּה בְרָאתָם
תָּבוֹר וְחֶרְמוֹן בְּשִׁמְךָ יְרַנֵּנוּ׃

יד לְךָ זְרוֹעַ עִם־גְּבוּרָה
תָּעֹז יָדְךָ תָּרוּם יְמִינֶךָ׃

טו צֶדֶק וּמִשְׁפָּט מְכוֹן כִּסְאֶךָ
חֶסֶד וֶאֱמֶת יְקַדְּמוּ פָנֶיךָ׃

טז אַשְׁרֵי הָעָם יוֹדְעֵי תְרוּעָה
יהוה בְּאוֹר־פָּנֶיךָ יְהַלֵּכוּן׃

יז בְּשִׁמְךָ יְגִילוּן כָּל־הַיּוֹם
וּבְצִדְקָתְךָ יָרוּמוּ׃

יח כִּי־תִפְאֶרֶת עֻזָּמוֹ אָתָּה
וּבִרְצוֹנְךָ תרים קַרְנֵנוּ׃ תָּרוּם

יט כִּי לַיהוה מָגִנֵּנוּ
וְלִקְדוֹשׁ יִשְׂרָאֵל מַלְכֵּנוּ׃

כ אָז דִּבַּרְתָּ בְחָזוֹן לַחֲסִידֶיךָ
וַתֹּאמֶר שִׁוִּיתִי עֵזֶר עַל־גִּבּוֹר
הֲרִימוֹתִי בָחוּר מֵעָם׃

כא מָצָאתִי דָּוִד עַבְדִּי
בְּשֶׁמֶן קָדְשִׁי מְשַׁחְתִּיו׃

22. My hand shall be ready to help him,
My arm to strengthen him.

23. No enemy will outwit him,
no wicked man oppress him.

24. I will beat down his foes before him,
and strike down those who hate him.

25. My faithfulness and loving-kindness shall be with him,
and through My name his horn shall be raised high.

26. I will set his hand upon the sea,
and his right hand upon the rivers.

27. He will say to Me, 'You are my father,
my God, the rock who saves me.'

28. And I will make him My first-born,
highest of the kings of the earth.

29. I will keep My loving-kindness for him always,
and My covenant with him shall endure.

30. I will establish his line forever,
his throne to be as lasting as the heavens.

31. If his sons forsake My law
and do not follow My orders;

32. if they violate My precepts
and do not observe My commands,

33. I will punish their transgression with the rod
and their iniquity with lashes.

Yet He punishes *transgression with the rod and iniquity with lashes.* He will *cut short the days of a man's youth* and has ordained a world in which no one *can save himself from the grasp of the grave.*

He has made an eternal covenant with David, and promises to *make him*

כב אֲשֶׁר יָדִי תִּכּוֹן עִמּוֹ
אַף־זְרוֹעִי תְאַמְּצֶנּוּ׃

כג לֹא־יַשִּׁא אוֹיֵב בּוֹ
וּבֶן־עַוְלָה לֹא יְעַנֶּנּוּ׃

כד וְכַתּוֹתִי מִפָּנָיו צָרָיו
וּמְשַׂנְאָיו אֶגּוֹף׃

כה וֶאֱמוּנָתִי וְחַסְדִּי עִמּוֹ
וּבִשְׁמִי תָּרוּם קַרְנוֹ׃

כו וְשַׂמְתִּי בַיָּם יָדוֹ
וּבַנְּהָרוֹת יְמִינוֹ׃

כז הוּא יִקְרָאֵנִי אָבִי אָתָּה
אֵלִי וְצוּר יְשׁוּעָתִי׃

כח אַף־אָנִי בְּכוֹר אֶתְּנֵהוּ
עֶלְיוֹן לְמַלְכֵי־אָרֶץ׃

כט לְעוֹלָם אשמור־לוֹ חַסְדִּי אֶשְׁמָר־
וּבְרִיתִי נֶאֱמֶנֶת לוֹ׃

ל וְשַׂמְתִּי לָעַד זַרְעוֹ
וְכִסְאוֹ כִּימֵי שָׁמָיִם׃

לא אִם־יַעַזְבוּ בָנָיו תּוֹרָתִי
וּבְמִשְׁפָּטַי לֹא יֵלֵכוּן׃

לב אִם־חֻקֹּתַי יְחַלֵּלוּ
וּמִצְוֹתַי לֹא יִשְׁמֹרוּ׃

לג וּפָקַדְתִּי בְשֵׁבֶט פִּשְׁעָם
וּבִנְגָעִים עֲוֺנָם׃

34. But I will not withdraw My loving-kindness from him,
or belie My faithfulness.

35. I will not violate My covenant,
or alter what My lips have uttered.

36. Once and for all I have sworn by My holiness;
I will not be false to David.

37. His line will continue forever,
his throne will endure before Me like the sun;

38. it will be established forever like the moon –
that faithful witness in the sky." *Selah*

39. Yet You have rejected, spurned,
and raged at Your anointed.

40. You have renounced the covenant with Your servant;
You have defiled his crown in the dust.

41. You have broken down all his walls
and reduced his fortresses to ruins.

42. All who pass by plunder him;
he has become the scorn of his neighbors.

43. You have raised the right hand of his foes,
You have made all his enemies rejoice,

44. You have also turned back the sharp edge of his sword,
and have not supported him in battle.

45. You have brought to an end his splendor,
and hurled his throne to the ground.

My first-born. Yet, woe to David or his descendants if they forsake His law or do not follow His orders. Then He will reject them, spurn them, render them victim to His rage.

R. Tanḥum, in the Midrash, finds other examples of paradox in his reflections upon verse 49 in our psalm, which so eloquently expresses the

לד וְחַסְדִּי לֹא־אָפִיר מֵעִמּוֹ
וְלֹא אֲשַׁקֵּר בֶּאֱמוּנָתִי׃

לה לֹא־אֲחַלֵּל בְּרִיתִי
וּמוֹצָא שְׂפָתַי לֹא אֲשַׁנֶּה׃

לו אַחַת נִשְׁבַּעְתִּי בְקׇדְשִׁי
אִם־לְדָוִד אֲכַזֵּב׃

לז זַרְעוֹ לְעוֹלָם יִהְיֶה
וְכִסְאוֹ כַשֶּׁמֶשׁ נֶגְדִּי׃

לח כְּיָרֵחַ יִכּוֹן עוֹלָם
וְעֵד בַּשַּׁחַק נֶאֱמָן סֶלָה׃

לט וְאַתָּה זָנַחְתָּ וַתִּמְאָס
הִתְעַבַּרְתָּ עִם־מְשִׁיחֶךָ׃

מ נֵאַרְתָּה בְּרִית עַבְדֶּךָ
חִלַּלְתָּ לָאָרֶץ נִזְרוֹ׃

מא פָּרַצְתָּ כׇל־גְּדֵרֹתָיו
שַׂמְתָּ מִבְצָרָיו מְחִתָּה׃

מב שַׁסֻּהוּ כׇּל־עֹבְרֵי דָרֶךְ
הָיָה חֶרְפָּה לִשְׁכֵנָיו׃

מג הֲרִימוֹתָ יְמִין צָרָיו
הִשְׂמַחְתָּ כׇּל־אוֹיְבָיו׃

מד אַף־תָּשִׁיב צוּר חַרְבּוֹ
וְלֹא הֲקֵמֹתוֹ בַּמִּלְחָמָה׃

מה הִשְׁבַּתָּ מִטְּהָרוֹ
וְכִסְאוֹ לָאָרֶץ מִגַּרְתָּה׃

46. You have cut short the days of his youth,
and covered him with shame. *Selah*

47. How long, LORD?
Will You hide Yourself forever?
How long will Your wrath blaze like fire?

48. O remember how short my life is.
Was it to no purpose that You created all men?

49. What man can live and not see death,
or save himself from the grasp of the grave? *Selah*

50. LORD, where are Your former deeds of loving-kindness
which in Your faithfulness You swore to David?

51. Remember, LORD, the abuse hurled at Your servant
that I have borne in my bosom from many people.

52. [Remember,] LORD, the taunts of Your enemies,
how they mocked Your anointed at every step.

53. Blessed be the LORD forever.
Amen and Amen.

Life on earth is not utopia. Loving-kindness lies at our world's foundations, but it lies there concealed, waiting to be revealed. Reward must be earned; wrongdoing does not escape punishment. God promises an ultimate better future, but we may not see that future in our lifetimes.

Although the psalmist faces these realities, including his own mortality and experiences of rejection and defeat, he does not despair. He ends our psalm with a prayer that God remember the abuse he has suffered and the taunts which have been hurled at him. And he signs off with a familiar expression of hope and faith: *Blessed be the LORD forever. Amen and Amen.*

הִ֭קְצַרְתָּ יְמֵ֣י עֲלוּמָ֑יו מו
הֶ֥עֱטִ֨יתָ עָלָ֗יו בּוּשָׁ֥ה סֶֽלָה׃

עַד־מָ֣ה יְ֭הוָה תִּסָּתֵ֣ר לָנֶ֑צַח מז
תִּבְעַ֖ר כְּמוֹ־אֵ֣שׁ חֲמָתֶֽךָ׃

זְכָר־אֲנִ֥י מֶה־חָ֑לֶד מח
עַל־מַה־שָּׁ֝֗וְא בָּרָ֥אתָ כָל־בְּנֵי־אָדָֽם׃

מִ֤י גֶ֣בֶר יִ֭חְיֶה וְלֹ֣א יִרְאֶה־מָּ֑וֶת מט
יְמַלֵּ֖ט נַפְשׁ֥וֹ מִיַּד־שְׁא֣וֹל סֶֽלָה׃

אַיֵּ֤ה ׀ חֲסָדֶ֖יךָ הָרִאשֹׁנִ֥ים ׀ אֲדֹנָ֑י נ
נִשְׁבַּ֥עְתָּ לְ֝דָוִ֗ד בֶּאֱמוּנָתֶֽךָ׃

זְכֹ֣ר אֲ֭דֹנָי חֶרְפַּ֣ת עֲבָדֶ֑יךָ נא
שְׂאֵתִ֥י בְ֝חֵיקִ֗י כָּל־רַבִּ֥ים עַמִּֽים׃

אֲשֶׁ֤ר חֵרְפ֖וּ אוֹיְבֶ֥יךָ ׀ יְהוָ֑ה נב
אֲשֶׁ֥ר חֵ֝רְפ֗וּ עִקְּב֥וֹת מְשִׁיחֶֽךָ׃

בָּר֖וּךְ יְהוָ֥ה לְ֝עוֹלָ֗ם אָ֘מֵ֥ן ׀ וְאָמֵֽן׃ נג

---

inevitability of death. Abraham survived the fiery furnace, only to *expire and die*. Isaac stretched his neck out on the altar, but survived, only to eventually declare, *behold I am old and do not know the day of my death*. Jacob wrestled an angel and vanquished him, yet *the days of his death dr*[illegible] Moses spoke to his Creator face to face, but was [illegible] *of your death are approaching*. R. Tanḥum undersc[illegible]est paradox of all: We typically delude ourselves tha[illegible]forever. But we won't.

Our psalm conclude[illegible] book of psalms on a disappointing note.

PSALM 90

Nineteenth day of the month

Thursday

1. A prayer of Moses, the man of God.
LORD, You have been our refuge in every generation.

2. Before the mountains were born,
before You brought forth the earth and the world,
from eternity to eternity You are God.

3. You turn man back to dust,
saying, "Turn from sin, you sons of man."

4. For in Your sight a thousand years
are like yesterday that has passed,
or like a watch of the night.

5. You sweep men away, and they are asleep [in death].
They are like grass which springs up in the morning;

6. yes, in the morning it sprouts and flourishes,
but by evening it droops and withers.

7. For we are consumed by Your anger,
and shattered by Your fury.

---

absolutely know that he died. He died as a deeply disappointed man. His greatest wish, to enter the Holy Land, was denied him.

It is no wonder then that our psalm contains two themes. It begins with the assertion that there is a world beyond the world we know. There is a primeval world, which precedes Creation. In that realm the soul of man originates, and there it will return to dwell eternally. This is *the refuge in every generation* which existed *before the mountains were born*. Only Moses could speak of this realm. He, alone of all men, was privileged to glimpse, and merely glimpse, God's world.

Our psalm also portrays the earthly world, the [illegible] in which we reside, the world of the body. For Moses the central theme of this world is disappointment. He is disappointed with our brief life span. He is disappointed with

מזמור צ

Life is much too short. I've accomplished but a little. My misdeeds are many. I sense that God is angry with me. I'd like to repent. Is there enough time? Our sages tell us that Moses composed eleven psalms. Our psalm is one of them. We can expect to hear unique words in our psalm, words that could not have been expressed by anyone other than Moses.

יט לחודש
ליום חמישי

א תְּפִלָּה לְמֹשֶׁה אִישׁ־הָאֱלֹהִים
אֲדֹנָי מָעוֹן אַתָּה הָיִיתָ לָּנוּ בְּדֹר וָדֹר:

ב בְּטֶרֶם ׀ הָרִים יֻלָּדוּ וַתְּחוֹלֵל אֶרֶץ וְתֵבֵל
וּמֵעוֹלָם עַד־עוֹלָם אַתָּה אֵל:

ג תָּשֵׁב אֱנוֹשׁ עַד־דַּכָּא
וַתֹּאמֶר שׁוּבוּ בְנֵי־אָדָם:

ד כִּי אֶלֶף שָׁנִים בְּעֵינֶיךָ
כְּיוֹם אֶתְמוֹל כִּי יַעֲבֹר
וְאַשְׁמוּרָה בַלָּיְלָה:

ה זְרַמְתָּם שֵׁנָה יִהְיוּ
בַּבֹּקֶר כֶּחָצִיר יַחֲלֹף:

ו בַּבֹּקֶר יָצִיץ וְחָלָף
לָעֶרֶב יְמוֹלֵל וְיָבֵשׁ:

ז כִּי־כָלִינוּ בְאַפֶּךָ
וּבַחֲמָתְךָ נִבְהָלְנוּ:

מזמור צ *Psalm 90:* The second phrase in the first verse tells us what sets Moses apart. He is *the man of God*. He is a man, and he is of God.

In some respects he is God-like. He certainly was more familiar with the celestial realm than any other human being before him or after him.

But he is also a man, a mortal. We know not where he was buried, but we

8. You have set out our iniquities before You,
our hidden sins in the light of Your presence.

9. All our days pass away under Your wrath,
we spend our years like a sigh.

10. Seventy years, then,* is the span of our life,
or, given the strength, eighty years;
at their best** they are but toil and trouble;
for soon it is over, and we fly away.

11. Who knows the power of Your anger?
Your wrath equals the reverence due to You.

12. Teach us to number our days rightly,
that we may gain a heart of wisdom.

13. Relent, LORD! How long [will You be angry]?
Have compassion on Your servants.

14. Satisfy us in the morning with Your loving-kindness,
that we may sing and rejoice all our days.

15. Grant us joy for the days You have afflicted us,
for the years we have known misery.

* In consequence of God's fury life is limited to seventy years.

** Or: "most of them."

Emerging from this psalm are questions. Why is life so short? Why are our years *but toil and trouble*? *How long will You be angry*? Why can we not see *Your glory*? What must we do to *establish the work of our hands,* so that our accomplishments endure?

These questions are addressed in the very next psalm, Psalm 91.

ח שַׁתָּ עֲוֺנֹתֵינוּ לְנֶגְדֶּךָ
עֲלֻמֵנוּ לִמְאוֹר פָּנֶיךָ׃

ט כִּי כׇל־יָמֵינוּ פָּנוּ בְעֶבְרָתֶךָ
כִּלִּינוּ שָׁנֵינוּ כְמוֹ־הֶגֶה׃

י יְמֵי־שְׁנוֹתֵינוּ בָהֶם שִׁבְעִים שָׁנָה
וְאִם בִּגְבוּרֹת ׀ שְׁמוֹנִים שָׁנָה
וְרׇהְבָּם עָמָל וָאָוֶן
כִּי־גָז חִישׁ וַנָּעֻפָה׃

יא מִי־יוֹדֵעַ עֹז אַפֶּךָ
וּכְיִרְאָתְךָ עֶבְרָתֶךָ׃

יב לִמְנוֹת יָמֵינוּ כֵּן הוֹדַע
וְנָבִא לְבַב חׇכְמָה׃

יג שׁוּבָה יהוה עַד־מָתָי
וְהִנָּחֵם עַל־עֲבָדֶיךָ׃

יד שַׂבְּעֵנוּ בַבֹּקֶר חַסְדֶּךָ
וּנְרַנְּנָה וְנִשְׂמְחָה בְּכׇל־יָמֵינוּ׃

טו שַׂמְּחֵנוּ כִּימוֹת עִנִּיתָנוּ
שְׁנוֹת רָאִינוּ רָעָה׃

---

the swift passage of time, which deprives man of lasting accomplishment. Finally, he is disappointed with God's implacable wrath. It was because of that wrath that God rejected his many fervent prayers to be forgiven and granted entrance into the Holy Land.

16. Let Your actions be seen by Your servants,
and Your glory by their children.

17. May the pleasantness of the LORD our God be upon us.
Establish for us the work of our hands.
O do establish the work of our hands!

טז יראה אל־עבדיך פעלך
והדרך על־בניהם׃

יז ויהי ׀ נעם אדני אלהינו עלינו
ומעשה ידינו כוננה עלינו
ומעשה ידינו כוננהו׃

PSALM 91

1. You who dwell in the shelter of the Most High,
and abide in the shadow of the Almighty,

2. I say [to you], on behalf of the LORD,
who is my refuge, my stronghold, my God in whom I trust,

3. that He will deliver you from the fowler's snare,
from the destructive plague.

4. He will cover you with His pinions;
under His wings you will find safety.
His faithfulness is your shield and buckler.

5. You will not fear the terrors of the night,
or the arrow that flies by day;

6. the plague that stalks in the darkness,
or the pestilence that ravages at noon.

7. A thousand may fall at your side,
ten thousand at your right hand;
but you it will not reach.

8. You have but to look around
and see the punishment of the wicked.

---

replying to Moses. The angel is telling Moses that his soul, and the souls of all men, *dwells in the shelter of the Most High.* The angel proceeds to assure Moses that so do the bodies of all men *abide in the shadow of the Almighty.*

Man is not the insignificant creature that Moses supposed him to be. God Almighty shelters all of mankind. A personal relationship with God is achievable by all men.

"The questions you asked," the angel tells Moses, "are not questions at all."

Why do the wicked prosper? Just *look around and see the punishment of the wicked.*

Why must man suffer the *terrors of the night*? Why is he exposed to *the plague that stalks in the darkness*?

מזמור צא

I am vulnerable. I am terrified of plagues and pestilence. I am deathly frightened of lions, and vipers, and snakes. I am surrounded by ten thousand enemies. God, please protect me. Be my refuge, my shelter, and my shield.

א יֹשֵׁב בְּסֵתֶר עֶלְיוֹן
בְּצֵל שַׁדַּי יִתְלוֹנָן׃

ב אֹמַר לַיהוה מַחְסִי וּמְצוּדָתִי
אֱלֹהַי אֶבְטַח־בּוֹ׃

ג כִּי הוּא יַצִּילְךָ מִפַּח יָקוּשׁ
מִדֶּבֶר הַוּוֹת׃

ד בְּאֶבְרָתוֹ ׀ יָסֶךְ לָךְ
וְתַחַת־כְּנָפָיו תֶּחְסֶה
צִנָּה וְסֹחֵרָה אֲמִתּוֹ׃

ה לֹא־תִירָא מִפַּחַד לָיְלָה
מֵחֵץ יָעוּף יוֹמָם׃

ו מִדֶּבֶר בָּאֹפֶל יַהֲלֹךְ
מִקֶּטֶב יָשׁוּד צָהֳרָיִם׃

ז יִפֹּל מִצִּדְּךָ ׀ אֶלֶף וּרְבָבָה מִימִינֶךָ
אֵלֶיךָ לֹא יִגָּשׁ׃

ח רַק בְּעֵינֶיךָ תַבִּיט
וְשִׁלֻּמַת רְשָׁעִים תִּרְאֶה׃

מזמור צא *Psalm 91:* The great nineteenth-century commentator Malbim views our psalm as a reply to the troubling questions articulated in the preceding psalm. He sees Psalm 90 as Moses' prayer, and our psalm as an answer to that prayer.

Malbim asks us to imagine that a celestial being, perhaps an angel, is here

9. Because you [have said:] "The LORD is my refuge";
because you have made the Most High your dwelling,

10. no evil shall befall you,
no plague shall come near your dwelling.

11. For He will charge His angels concerning you,
to guard you wherever you go.

12. They will carry you in their hands,
lest you strike your foot against a stone.

13. You will tread on lion and viper.
You will trample on young lion and snake.

14. "Because he desires Me, [says the LORD,]
I will deliver him.
I will set him on high, for he knows My name.

15. Let him call to Me, so that I might answer him
that I will be with him in time of trouble
and so that I might rescue him and honor him.

16. With length of days I will satisfy him;
I will show him My salvation."

Rav Kook expounds upon this verse in his *Olat Re'iya*, using his exquisite poetic gifts and resorting to his affinity for the mystical. He writes:

> Time flows by and vanishes only when life is viewed within the context of material things, which indeed are ever-changing and which cease to be. But from a higher perspective, within the context of life in its divine eternity, nothing vanishes, everything endures. Every day of one's life is preserved in fullest detail, and all that was achieved during that day remains aglow, filling the soul with brightness, vigor, and sweet satisfaction.

ט כִּֽי־אַתָּ֣ה יְהֹוָ֣ה מַחְסִ֑י
עֶ֝לְי֗וֹן שַׂ֣מְתָּ מְעוֹנֶֽךָ׃

י לֹֽא־תְאֻנֶּ֣ה אֵלֶ֣יךָ רָעָ֑ה
וְ֝נֶ֗גַע לֹא־יִקְרַ֥ב בְּאָהֳלֶֽךָ׃

יא כִּ֣י מַ֭לְאָכָיו יְצַוֶּה־לָּ֑ךְ
לִ֝שְׁמָרְךָ֗ בְּכָל־דְּרָכֶֽיךָ׃

יב עַל־כַּפַּ֥יִם יִשָּׂא֑וּנְךָ
פֶּן־תִּגֹּ֖ף בָּאֶ֣בֶן רַגְלֶֽךָ׃

יג עַל־שַׁ֣חַל וָפֶ֣תֶן תִּדְרֹ֑ךְ
תִּרְמֹ֖ס כְּפִ֣יר וְתַנִּֽין׃

יד כִּ֤י בִ֣י חָ֭שַׁק וַאֲפַלְּטֵ֑הוּ
אֲ֝שַׂגְּבֵ֗הוּ כִּֽי־יָדַ֥ע שְׁמִֽי׃

טו יִקְרָאֵ֨נִי ׀ וְֽאֶעֱנֵ֗הוּ עִמּֽוֹ־אָנֹכִ֥י בְצָרָ֑ה
אֲ֝חַלְּצֵ֗הוּ וַאֲכַבְּדֵֽהוּ׃

טז אֹ֣רֶךְ יָ֭מִים אַשְׂבִּיעֵ֑הוּ
וְ֝אַרְאֵ֗הוּ בִּישׁוּעָתִֽי׃

The angel answers, speaking for God: "I put man through these hardships because I want him to turn to Me in prayer. *Let him call to Me so that I might answer him.* I want him to understand that I *will be with him in time of trouble.* I want him to experience for himself what it means to be rescued by My hand. I want to reward him with My glory. *So that I might rescue him and honor him.*"

And finally, why is life so brutally short?

The angel answers, again speaking for God: *With length of days I will satisfy him.*

PSALM 92

1. A psalm. A song for the Sabbath day.

2. It is good to praise the LORD,
to sing psalms to Your name, Most High;

3. to proclaim Your loving-kindness in the morning,
and Your faithfulness during the nights,

4. to the music of the ten-stringed lyre,
with the melody of the harp.

5. For You have made me glad by Your deeds, LORD;
I sing for joy at Your handiwork.

6. How great are Your works, LORD!
How very profound are Your plans!

7. The brutish man cannot know it,
the fool cannot understand it.

8. Though the wicked flourish like grass,
and all evildoers thrive,
it is only that they may be destroyed forever.

---

ed in the Holy Temple on the Sabbath day because it sung of an ideal Sabbath, a Sabbath in the Messianic future, which will be a pure and timeless Sabbath.

But he insists that our psalm also refers to an earthly Sabbath, the Sabbath that we can all experience each week.

All week long we are preoccupied, distracted by mundane affairs. We can find neither the time nor the feelings nor the words to express our spirituality. But on the Sabbath day we find those resources, and discover that *it is good to praise the LORD.*

Each weekday morning, we awake to thoughts of the new day, its problems and its pressures. On Sabbath morning we awake instead to recognition of God's loving-kindness. We appreciate that the Sabbath day itself a precious example of that loving-kindness. On the Sabbath morning, instead of worries and concerns, we open our eyes to the prospect of a day of rest and pleasure.

In verse 3, Radak detects a subtle distinction between *morning,* in the

מזמור צב

My weekdays are workdays. I have no time to think. On Shabbat, I have time to think. That is just one of Shabbat's gifts to me. I think back to that primeval Shabbat. All was perfect then, but is no longer so. On Shabbat I taste perfection. Shabbat brings me another gift: belief. Belief that all will one day be perfect again.

א מִזְמוֹר שִׁיר לְיוֹם הַשַּׁבָּת׃

ב טוֹב לְהֹדוֹת לַיהוָה
וּלְזַמֵּר לְשִׁמְךָ עֶלְיוֹן׃

ג לְהַגִּיד בַּבֹּקֶר חַסְדֶּךָ
וֶאֱמוּנָתְךָ בַּלֵּילוֹת׃

ד עֲלֵי־עָשׂוֹר וַעֲלֵי־נָבֶל
עֲלֵי הִגָּיוֹן בְּכִנּוֹר׃

ה כִּי שִׂמַּחְתַּנִי יהוה בְּפָעֳלֶךָ
בְּמַעֲשֵׂי יָדֶיךָ אֲרַנֵּן׃

ו מַה־גָּדְלוּ מַעֲשֶׂיךָ יְהוָה
מְאֹד עָמְקוּ מַחְשְׁבֹתֶיךָ׃

ז אִישׁ־בַּעַר לֹא יֵדָע
וּכְסִיל לֹא־יָבִין אֶת־זֹאת׃

ח בִּפְרֹחַ רְשָׁעִים ׀ כְּמוֹ עֵשֶׂב
וַיָּצִיצוּ כָּל־פֹּעֲלֵי אָוֶן
לְהִשָּׁמְדָם עֲדֵי־עַד׃

מזמור צב *Psalm 92:* Our psalm is entitled *a song for the Sabbath day,* yet there is no overt reference to the Sabbath in it. Commentators have struggled valiantly to find in it some hint, however tenuous or esoteric, of the Sabbath theme.

Radak's approach is simple and direct. He asserts that our psalm was recit-

9. But You, LORD, are eternally supreme.

10. Behold, Your enemies, LORD,
behold, Your enemies perish;
all evildoers are scattered.

11. But You have raised my horn high like that of a wild ox;
I am anointed with rich oil.

12. My eyes see the defeat of my adversaries,
my ears hear the downfall of the wicked who attack me.

13. The righteous shall flourish like the palm tree,
and grow like a cedar in Lebanon;

14. planted in the house of the LORD,
they shall flourish in the courts of our God.

15. In old age they shall bear fruit;
still full of sap, still fresh are they,

16. proclaiming that the LORD is upright,
my rock, in whom there is no wrong.

---

contemplation and introspection. Thus, Our psalm encourages us to reflect deeply upon the eternal questions of existence, many of which are seldom, if ever, answered to our satisfaction. These questions include our curiosity about the origins of the universe, and about the often inscrutable ways of God. One such question is "why do the righteous suffer, and why do the wicked prosper?"

But our psalm does not permit us to remain troubled by such questions. The Sabbath is not a time for pessimism and despair. Instead it ends with the assurance that *the righteous shall flourish like the palm tree* and with the proclamation that *the LORD is upright* and that in Him *there is no wrong.*

ט וְאַתָּה מָרוֹם לְעֹלָם יהוה׃

י כִּי הִנֵּה אֹיְבֶיךָ יהוה
כִּי־הִנֵּה אֹיְבֶיךָ יֹאבֵדוּ
יִתְפָּרְדוּ כָּל־פֹּעֲלֵי אָוֶן׃

יא וַתָּרֶם כִּרְאֵים קַרְנִי
בַּלֹּתִי בְּשֶׁמֶן רַעֲנָן׃

יב וַתַּבֵּט עֵינִי בְּשׁוּרָי
בַּקָּמִים עָלַי מְרֵעִים תִּשְׁמַעְנָה אָזְנָי׃

יג צַדִּיק כַּתָּמָר יִפְרָח
כְּאֶרֶז בַּלְּבָנוֹן יִשְׂגֶּה׃

יד שְׁתוּלִים בְּבֵית יהוה
בְּחַצְרוֹת אֱלֹהֵינוּ יַפְרִיחוּ׃

טו עוֹד יְנוּבוּן בְּשֵׂיבָה
דְּשֵׁנִים וְרַעֲנַנִּים יִהְיוּ׃

טז לְהַגִּיד כִּי־יָשָׁר יהוה
צוּרִי וְלֹא־עלתה בּוֹ׃ — עַוְלָתָה

---

singular, and *nights*, in the plural. He explains that whereas the Sabbath provides but one anxiety-free morning each week, it provides two such nights. First, there is Friday night, which ushers in the Sabbath. Then there is a bonus: Saturday night, when the Sabbath departs, which is also a night for repose. Few of us return to work immediately when the Sabbath concludes. We wait instead for Sunday morning. And Motza'ei Shabbat, Saturday night, is an opportunity to extend the Sabbath atmosphere and to spiritually prepare for the oncoming week.

The Sabbath is not just a day of physical rest. It is a time for profound

PSALM 93

1. The LORD reigns, He is robed in majesty;
the LORD is robed, He is girded with strength.
The world is firmly established, it cannot be shaken.

2. Your throne stands firm from of old,
You are from all eternity.

3. The rivers have lifted up, LORD,
the rivers have lifted up their voices,
the rivers lift up their pounding waves.

4. But above the roar of the great and many waters,
above the mighty breakers of the sea,
the LORD on high is mightiest.

5. Your testimonies are most trustworthy;
holiness adorns Your house, LORD,
for days without end.

---

vention. Hence, *He is robed in majesty* when He manifests Himself in miracles, and *He is girded with strength* in His "ordinary" conduct.

The person of faith sees the hand of God in both modes, the ordinary and the extraordinary. Miracles are reserved for those of lesser faith, who require more dramatic evidence of His hand.

When God does perform a miracle, there is a secondary miracle which only the spiritually perceptive observe. For when He performs a miracle, for example when He splits the sea or draws water from a rock, the rest of nature proceeds in its ordinary routine. The miracle is confined to one time and place, and the rest of world "doesn't miss a beat," but continues to function flawlessly. The apple cart is not upset by the dislodging of some of the apples.

This, argues Malbim, is the meaning of the final phrase. Although *He is robed in the majesty* of miracles, the natural order is not disrupted by those miracles. Rather, *the world … cannot be shaken.*

Radak has a much simpler approach to our phrase. He understands it to mean that in that idyllic future time, when God will reveal Himself *robed in majesty,* there will no longer be war. *The world will be firmly established* because all humanity will be at peace.

That might very well be the greatest miracle of all.

מזמור צג

We all wear costumes. We disguise ourselves. What about God? He disguises Himself so well that we often cannot find Him. At times, He dons the clothes of a warrior. He frequently wears the garb of a wise old sage. He camouflages Himself to look like nature. Our psalm tells us that He is robed in majesty. In what costume has He appeared to you?

א יְהוָה מָלָךְ גֵּאוּת לָבֵשׁ
לָבֵשׁ יְהוָה עֹז הִתְאַזָּר
אַף־תִּכּוֹן תֵּבֵל בַּל־תִּמּוֹט׃

ב נָכוֹן כִּסְאֲךָ מֵאָז
מֵעוֹלָם אָתָּה׃

ג נָשְׂאוּ נְהָרוֹת ׀ יְהוָה נָשְׂאוּ נְהָרוֹת קוֹלָם
יִשְׂאוּ נְהָרוֹת דָּכְיָם׃

ד מִקֹּלוֹת ׀ מַיִם רַבִּים אַדִּירִים מִשְׁבְּרֵי־יָם
אַדִּיר בַּמָּרוֹם יְהוָה׃

ה עֵדֹתֶיךָ ׀ נֶאֶמְנוּ מְאֹד לְבֵיתְךָ נַאֲוָה־קֹדֶשׁ
יְהוָה לְאֹרֶךְ יָמִים׃

מזמור צג *Psalm 93:* Our psalm is one of the many to illustrate that brevity does not always equal simplicity. Commentators and translators have found our psalm especially challenging. Even the simple term "rivers," which appears three times in verse 3, is understood by some to represent Israel's enemies; for others it is a reference to the nations of Gog and Magog in Messianic times; and for still others it is symbolic of nature in its entirety. Of course, there are those for whom a river is a river is a river.

And what is the significance of the phrase in the very first verse which reads *the world is firmly established, it cannot be shaken*?

Malbim sees in this phrase a profound expression of the God's *modus operandi* in His role of Master of the Universe. He explains, following earlier Jewish philosophers, that God typically manifests Himself through nature, and only rarely resorts to miracles. The term *oz*, which we have translated as "strength," refers to His customary mode. The word *geut*, majesty, connotes His supernatural inter-

PSALM 94

1. God of vengeance, LORD,
God of vengeance, appear!

2. Arise, O Judge of the earth;
give the proud their deserts.

3. How long shall the wicked, O LORD,
how long shall the wicked triumph?

4. They pour out a stream of arrogant words;
all the evildoers brag about themselves.

5. They crush Your people, LORD,
and afflict Your own heritage.

6. They kill the widow and the stranger;
they murder the fatherless.

7. And they say, "The LORD does not see;
the God of Jacob pays no heed."

8. Take heed, you most stupid people;
you fools, when will you be wise?

9. Can He who implanted the ear not hear;
He who formed the eye not see?

When we are blessed to live in less tragic times, we look to God for less drastic intervention. Everyday life has its natural anxieties, and the conditions of our daily existence require "the help of Heaven." Our psalm speaks to those moments as well:

When I thought my foot was slipping, Your loving-kindness, LORD, supported me.

When anxieties increased within me, Your consolations cheered my soul.

Who has not occasionally felt that his "foot was slipping"? Who has not had his confidence shaken by some unforeseen event? Such experiences hardly qualify as tragic. They are the stuff of ordinary life. But such lesser occasions also prompt prayer, and turning to God even at such routine moments is an expression of great religious faith.

מזמור צד

I see a picture taken during the Holocaust. I cannot get it out of my mind. It is a picture of a torture chamber. There are two words written on the wall. They are written in blood, human blood. "Yidden, nekama!" "Jews, revenge!" A voice within me shrieks: "God, revenge!"

א אֵל־נְקָמוֹת יְהוָה
אֵל נְקָמוֹת הוֹפִיעַ׃

ב הִנָּשֵׂא שֹׁפֵט הָאָרֶץ
הָשֵׁב גְּמוּל עַל־גֵּאִים׃

ג עַד־מָתַי רְשָׁעִים ׀ יְהוָה
עַד־מָתַי רְשָׁעִים יַעֲלֹזוּ׃

ד יַבִּיעוּ יְדַבְּרוּ עָתָק
יִתְאַמְּרוּ כׇּל־פֹּעֲלֵי אָוֶן׃

ה עַמְּךָ יְהוָה יְדַכְּאוּ
וְנַחֲלָתְךָ יְעַנּוּ׃

ו אַלְמָנָה וְגֵר יַהֲרֹגוּ
וִיתוֹמִים יְרַצֵּחוּ׃

ז וַיֹּאמְרוּ לֹא יִרְאֶה־יָּהּ
וְלֹא־יָבִין אֱלֹהֵי יַעֲקֹב׃

ח בִּינוּ בֹּעֲרִים בָּעָם
וּכְסִילִים מָתַי תַּשְׂכִּילוּ׃

ט הֲנֹטַע אֹזֶן הֲלֹא יִשְׁמָע
אִם־יֹצֵר עַיִן הֲלֹא יַבִּיט׃

מזמור צד *Psalm 94:* Many times, too many times in our history, the persecutions we suffered warranted cries for revenge. The opening of our psalm gives voice to those cries. *Lord, God of vengeance, appear! How long shall the wicked triumph?*

10. Shall He who disciplines nations,
and teaches mankind knowledge, not punish?

11. The LORD knows the thoughts of man,
that they are but an empty breath.

12. Happy is the man whom You discipline, LORD,
and teach him out of Your law,

13. giving him peace in days of trouble,
until a pit is dug for the wicked.

14. For the LORD will not abandon His people,
nor forsake His own heritage.

15. For justice shall again accord with righteousness,
and all the upright in heart will follow it.

16. Who will rise up for me against evil men?
Who will stand up for me against wrongdoers?

17. Had not the LORD been my help,
I should soon have dwelt in the silent grave.

18. When I thought my foot was slipping,
Your loving-kindness, LORD, supported me.

19. When anxieties increased within me,
Your consolations cheered my soul.

---

which is not at all a response to present danger. Rather, it is an integral part of the human condition, related to our awareness, however dim, that we will one day die.

At moments of anxiety, whatever its source, the person of faith turns to God and finds consolation. Moreover, he feels cheered.

The verb used in the Hebrew text for "cheered" can be translated as "delighted" and even as "entertained." When one opts for an authentic relationship with God, one realizes his anxieties were without foundation, perhaps even laughably trivial. Turning to God brings cheer.

Rav Hirsch translates our verse a bit differently, exposing another dimension

י הֲיֹסֵר גּוֹיִם הֲלֹא יוֹכִיחַ
הַמְלַמֵּד אָדָם דָּעַת׃

יא יְהוָה יֹדֵעַ מַחְשְׁבוֹת אָדָם
כִּי־הֵמָּה הָבֶל׃

יב אַשְׁרֵי הַגֶּבֶר אֲשֶׁר־תְּיַסְּרֶנּוּ יָּהּ
וּמִתּוֹרָתְךָ תְלַמְּדֶנּוּ׃

יג לְהַשְׁקִיט לוֹ מִימֵי רָע
עַד יִכָּרֶה לָרָשָׁע שָׁחַת׃

יד כִּי ׀ לֹא־יִטֹּשׁ יְהוָה עַמּוֹ
וְנַחֲלָתוֹ לֹא יַעֲזֹב׃

טו כִּי־עַד־צֶדֶק יָשׁוּב מִשְׁפָּט
וְאַחֲרָיו כָּל־יִשְׁרֵי־לֵב׃

טז מִי־יָקוּם לִי עִם־מְרֵעִים
מִי־יִתְיַצֵּב לִי עִם־פֹּעֲלֵי אָוֶן׃

יז לוּלֵי יְהוָה עֶזְרָתָה לִּי
כִּמְעַט ׀ שָׁכְנָה דוּמָה נַפְשִׁי׃

יח אִם־אָמַרְתִּי מָטָה רַגְלִי
חַסְדְּךָ יְהוָה יִסְעָדֵנִי׃

יט בְּרֹב שַׂרְעַפַּי בְּקִרְבִּי
תַּנְחוּמֶיךָ יְשַׁעַשְׁעוּ נַפְשִׁי׃

We appreciate God's loving-kindness even as we heal from minor illness or recover from the setbacks which beset us as we pursue our careers.

Anxiety is a similarly common experience. Real threats to our safety exist, and imagined threats abound. Psychologists speak of existential anxiety,

20. Can a corrupt throne be Your associate,
one that brings on misery by its decrees?

21. They band together against the life of the righteous,
and condemn the innocent to death.

22. But the LORD is my strong tower,
my God is the rock where I take refuge.

23. He will repay them for their wickedness,
and destroy them for their evil deeds.
The LORD, our God, will destroy them.

---

yeshiva. As a Jewish delegate to the Polish parliament he faced the pressures of anti-Semitism. He certainly knew times when his foot was slipping and anxieties were overwhelming, and when his thoughts were at war within him.

One way he was able to cope was by composing a beautiful song, pensive yet uplifting, to the words of our two verses. This song was sung enthusiastically by his disciples, most of whom tragically perished in the Holocaust.

Is it any wonder that his song continues to be sung today, for who does not face the emotional problems of living? Rabbi Shapiro's melody and King David's words bring solace to those who experience life's common misfortunes as well as to those who face genuine catastrophe.

Rabbi Shapiro taught us a lesson we must never forget when we study or recite psalms: they were meant to be sung!

כ הַיְחָבְרְךָ כִּסֵּא הַוּוֹת
יֹצֵר עָמָל עֲלֵי־חֹק׃

כא יָגוֹדּוּ עַל־נֶפֶשׁ צַדִּיק
וְדָם נָקִי יַרְשִׁיעוּ׃

כב וַיְהִי יהוה לִי לְמִשְׂגָּב
וֵאלֹהַי לְצוּר מַחְסִי׃

כג וַיָּשֶׁב עֲלֵיהֶם ׀ אֶת־אוֹנָם
וּבְרָעָתָם יַצְמִיתֵם
יַצְמִיתֵם יהוה אֱלֹהֵינוּ׃

---

of meaning: *When my thoughts were at war within me, Your comforts soothed my soul.*

Not only are our anxieties and fears allayed, but the inner conflicts which paralyze us with indecisiveness are also resolved by the Almighty's comforts. The person of faith finds a certain clarity in turning to God. He discovers a sense of certainty which dispels the fog of ambivalence and the clouds of doubt. God helps us make decisions.

Rabbi Meir Shapiro, the orator and educator who initiated the Daf Yomi Talmud study program, died several years before the terrible Holocaust. He had a difficult life. He had no children. He traveled the length and breadth of the Jewish world to raise funds to relieve the great debt which burdened his

PSALM 95

1. Come, let us sing joyfully to the Lord,
let us acclaim the rock of our salvation.

2. Let us come before His presence with thanksgiving,
and acclaim Him with songs of praise.

3. For the Lord is a great God,
a great King above all gods.

4. In His hand are the depths of the earth;
the mountain peaks belong to Him.

5. The sea is His, for He made it;
and the dry land too, which His hands fashioned.

6. Come, let us bow down and kneel,
let us bend the knee before the Lord our Maker.

---

down and kneel... before the Lord our Maker. Their devotional experience is one of awe and wonder.

Some such individuals don't stop there, but proceed to reason from "general to particular." They conclude that such a God must also care for the particulars of the universe, and must therefore be concerned with man and his actions. But many others do not follow this deductive method of reasoning. They remain with their initial perception of God as an impersonal cosmic force, oblivious to petty human concerns.

But for many there is an entirely different approach to belief in God. It does not start with reflection upon the wonders of the natural world. Rather, it proceeds from the historical experience of God's people, beginning with the Exodus from Egypt. Such individuals reason inductively, from the specific experiences of a Chosen People to a wondrous Master of the Universe. They begin with a sense of themselves as *the people of His pasture, the flock that is under His care.*

For them God is much more than a sublime awe-inspiring Being. He is very near, and quite concerned with the affairs of Man. Moreover, He makes demands of Man, and expects His people to live up to His expectations. He asks us not to harden our hearts, and quarrels with us when we go astray.

מזמור צה

Today. God's salvation comes as quickly as the blink of an eye. But we can't just stand there and blink. We must do our part, today. Perform good deeds, today. Keep just one Shabbat, today. The Messiah says he'll come today. The Messiah doesn't lie. Listen to His voice, today. Our psalm is especially well known as the first of the introductory psalms with which we welcome Shabbat each week. It is especially significant as an introduction because it summons us to sing God's praises.

א לְכוּ נְרַנְּנָה לַיהוָה
נָרִיעָה לְצוּר יִשְׁעֵנוּ׃

ב נְקַדְּמָה פָנָיו בְּתוֹדָה
בִּזְמִרוֹת נָרִיעַ לוֹ׃

ג כִּי אֵל גָּדוֹל יְהוָה
וּמֶלֶךְ גָּדוֹל עַל־כָּל־אֱלֹהִים׃

ד אֲשֶׁר בְּיָדוֹ מֶחְקְרֵי־אָרֶץ
וְתוֹעֲפוֹת הָרִים לוֹ׃

ה אֲשֶׁר־לוֹ הַיָּם וְהוּא עָשָׂהוּ
וְיַבֶּשֶׁת יָדָיו יָצָרוּ׃

ו בֹּאוּ נִשְׁתַּחֲוֶה וְנִכְרָעָה
נִבְרְכָה לִפְנֵי־יְהוָה עֹשֵׂנוּ׃

מזמור צה *Psalm 95:* Our psalm is especially well known as the first of the introductory psalms with which we welcome Shabbat each week. It is especially significant as an introduction because it summons us to sing God's praises.

Our psalm describes two modes of worship. It speaks of the Almighty as the God of the cosmos, and also asserts His special relationship with His people.

There are two types of believers. There are those who are impressed by the natural wonders of the universe, and envision God as the creative force behind those wonders. He is, for them, the God above all gods. *In His hand are the depths of the earth…the sea is His, for He made it.* They readily *bow*

7. For He is our God, and we the people of His pasture,
the flock that is under His care.
Even today if you would but listen to His voice!

8. Do not harden your hearts as at Meribah,*
as on that day at Massah** in the wilderness;

9. when your fathers put Me to the test;
they tried Me, though they had seen My work.

10. For forty years I quarreled with that generation;
I said, "They are a people whose hearts go astray,
refusing to know My ways."

11. Therefore I swore in My anger:
"They shall never enter My resting-place."

* See Ex. 17:7.

** Ibid.

Our psalm additionally emphasizes that not only is He to be worshipped by bowing, kneeling, and obedience, but He is also, and perhaps best, worshipped through songs of joy and gratitude: *Come, let us sing joyfully to the Lord... and acclaim Him with songs of praise.*

ז כִּי הוּא אֱלֹהֵינוּ
וַאֲנַחְנוּ ׀ עַם מַרְעִיתוֹ וְצֹאן יָדוֹ
הַיּוֹם אִם־בְּקֹלוֹ תִשְׁמָעוּ׃

ח אַל־תַּקְשׁוּ לְבַבְכֶם כִּמְרִיבָה
כְּיוֹם מַסָּה בַּמִּדְבָּר׃

ט אֲשֶׁר נִסּוּנִי אֲבוֹתֵיכֶם
בְּחָנוּנִי גַּם־רָאוּ פָעֳלִי׃

י אַרְבָּעִים שָׁנָה ׀ אָקוּט בְּדוֹר
וָאֹמַר עַם תֹּעֵי לֵבָב הֵם
וְהֵם לֹא־יָדְעוּ דְרָכָי׃

יא אֲשֶׁר־נִשְׁבַּעְתִּי בְאַפִּי
אִם־יְבֹאוּן אֶל־מְנוּחָתִי׃

Our psalm was chosen to usher in Shabbat because it alludes to both of these spiritual experiences which occur on that sacred day. We acknowledge God as the Creator of the Cosmos who completed His creation on Shabbat. We also use Shabbat as the occasion to commemorate God's role in our personal lives, and especially His role as our moral and ethical guide.

PSALM 96

1. O sing to the LORD a new song,
sing to the LORD, all the earth.

2. Sing to the LORD, bless His name;
proclaim His salvation anew, day after day.

3. Declare His glory among the nations,
His marvelous deeds among all peoples.

4. For great is the LORD, and highly to be praised;
He is to be feared above all gods.

5. For all the gods of the peoples are idols;
but the LORD made the heavens.

6. Splendor and majesty are before Him;
Strength and glory are in His sanctuary.

7. Ascribe to the LORD, O families of all peoples,
ascribe to the LORD glory and strength.

8. Ascribe to the LORD the glory due to His name;
bring an offering and enter His courts.

---

metaphorically. The world will enjoy such great peace, that even the world of nature will seem to be celebrating.

Rav Kook understands this phenomenon in a more literal manner. He offers us a very profound and inspiring message. His words, loosely translated below, can be found in his commentary on the Prayer Book, *Olat Re'iya,* pages 209–210, with reference to similar phrases in 1 Chronicles, chapter 16, verses 32–33.

For Rav Kook, our psalm envisions a time in the history of humanity when mankind will have developed intellectually and culturally to sublime heights. The entire cosmos will be equally uplifted, along with mankind. Even life in the depths of the ocean, normally hidden from our human experience, will pulsate with a richer form of life, which will loudly communicate itself to the ears of men. *Let the sea and all that is in it thunder* its message to the ears of mankind.

The indifference now demonstrated by the different realms of nature to

מזמור צו

It is a wonderful vision, a hopeful vision. It is a calming vision. But it seems such a long way off. It is a vision of peace and of justice. When true justice is achieved, real peace follows in its wake. Never has the world known such peace. A song must be sung, a song for us all. A new song must be sung, one never sung before. How soon will we sing it?

א שִׁירוּ לַיהוה שִׁיר חָדָשׁ
שִׁירוּ לַיהוה כׇּל־הָאָרֶץ׃

ב שִׁירוּ לַיהוה בָּרְכוּ שְׁמוֹ
בַּשְּׂרוּ מִיּוֹם־לְיוֹם יְשׁוּעָתוֹ׃

ג סַפְּרוּ בַגּוֹיִם כְּבוֹדוֹ
בְּכׇל־הָעַמִּים נִפְלְאוֹתָיו׃

ד כִּי גָדוֹל יהוה וּמְהֻלָּל מְאֹד
נוֹרָא הוּא עַל־כׇּל־אֱלֹהִים׃

ה כִּי ׀ כׇּל־אֱלֹהֵי הָעַמִּים אֱלִילִים
וַיהוה שָׁמַיִם עָשָׂה׃

ו הוֹד־וְהָדָר לְפָנָיו
עֹז וְתִפְאֶרֶת בְּמִקְדָּשׁוֹ׃

ז הָבוּ לַיהוה מִשְׁפְּחוֹת עַמִּים
הָבוּ לַיהוה כָּבוֹד וָעֹז׃

ח הָבוּ לַיהוה כְּבוֹד שְׁמוֹ
שְׂאוּ־מִנְחָה וּבֹאוּ לְחַצְרוֹתָיו׃

מזמור צו *Psalm 96:* Our psalm speaks of a wondrous time in the future, a time when God's glory will be celebrated by all mankind. The last several verses foretell a celebration in which the world of nature will share. The heavens, the fields, the sea, and the trees will all participate.

Commentators such as Ibn Ezra and Radak understand such celebration

9. Bow down to the LORD in the splendor of holiness;
tremble before Him all the earth.

10. Say among the nations, "The LORD reigns."
The world is firmly established and cannot be moved;
He will judge the peoples with equity.

11. Let the heavens rejoice and the earth be glad,
let the sea and all that is in it thunder;

12. let the fields and all that is in them exult;
then shall all the trees of the forest shout with joy

13. at the presence of the LORD for He is coming,
for He is coming to judge the earth;
He will judge the world with righteousness,
and the peoples with His faithfulness.

"How like mourners are the trees of the forest, forced as they are to provide shelter for this wickedness and violence!"

But when the vision of our psalm is realized, and mankind, along with all of creation, develops spiritually, that violence abates. That is when the trees sing. They sense that justice and peace will now prevail, even in the forest

The law of the jungle has been abolished. The goal of creation has now been achieved. Even the world of nature is at peace, not just mankind. The trees too, and the fields and the sea, now can join in a new song, a song occasioned by an utterly different reality.

Our response to the psalmist's vision of such a different reality must have no precedent in the songbooks of human history. It must be totally new. *O, sing to the LORD a new song,* a song in which *the fields and all that is in them exult* in unison with *the families of all peoples.*

ט הִשְׁתַּחֲווּ לַיהוה בְּהַדְרַת־קֹדֶשׁ
חִילוּ מִפָּנָיו כָּל־הָאָרֶץ׃

י אִמְרוּ בַגּוֹיִם ׀ יהוה מָלָךְ
אַף־תִּכּוֹן תֵּבֵל בַּל־תִּמּוֹט
יָדִין עַמִּים בְּמֵישָׁרִים׃

יא יִשְׂמְחוּ הַשָּׁמַיִם וְתָגֵל הָאָרֶץ
יִרְעַם הַיָּם וּמְלֹאוֹ׃

יב יַעֲלֹז שָׂדַי וְכָל־אֲשֶׁר־בּוֹ
אָז יְרַנְּנוּ כָּל־עֲצֵי־יָעַר׃

יג לִפְנֵי יהוה ׀ כִּי בָא
כִּי בָא לִשְׁפֹּט הָאָרֶץ
יִשְׁפֹּט־תֵּבֵל בְּצֶדֶק
וְעַמִּים בֶּאֱמוּנָתוֹ׃

---

each other will be healed. The disconnectedness of each component of nature from all other components will be bridged. No longer will mankind suffer the pervasive alienation from nature which is one of the curses of modern times. Instead the essential unity of all existence will become so apparent that man will feel it in his innermost soul. *Then shall all the trees of the forest shout with joy*, and we will hear their shout.

Rav Kook finds further depth of meaning in this phrase. The forest is the locale in which lawlessness and cruelty have prevailed throughout the course of natural history. It is there that beasts of prey pounce upon their victims. It is there that the mighty prevail over the weak. The trees, of which the forest consists, are forced to witness this bloody scene. Moreover, they keep it hidden from sight, using their leafy branches to keep bloody tooth and murderous claw deep dark secrets.

PSALM 97

Twentieth day of the month

1. The LORD reigns, let the earth be glad;
let the many islands rejoice.

2. Clouds and thick darkness are around Him,
righteousness and justice are the foundation of His throne.

3. Fire goes before Him,
and burns up His foes all around.

4. His lightnings light up the world;
the earth sees and trembles.

5. Mountains melt like wax before the LORD,
before the LORD of all the earth.

6. The heavens proclaim His righteousness,
and all peoples see His glory.

7. All who worship images, who boast of their idols,
are put to shame;
bow down to Him, all you gods.

8. Zion heard and rejoiced, the cities* of Judah were glad,
because of Your judgments, LORD.

* Lit. "daughters."

---

righteous and who are the upright, and why is one promised joy and the other light?

Rav Kook has a fascinating approach to these questions. (It appears in his commentary *Olat Re'iya,* vol. 2, p. 17.)

He begins by noting the comment in the Talmud (*Taanit* 15a): "The righteous earn light, the upright earn joy." He proceeds to argue that when light illuminates physical space, it simultaneously stimulates spiritual joy. First light and then joy, as we find in the Book of Esther (8:16), *and the Jews had light, and joy and gladness and honor.* Joy is the objective, the purpose, the goal. Light facilitates the experience of joy. Light is but the means to that end.

To help us understand in detail the distinction between the righteous and the upright, the *tzaddik* and the *yashar,* Rav Kook quotes a passage

מזמור צז

I need this psalm. I am in deep and dark despair. There is tragedy in the world, and great evil. Where is hope? This psalm is a message of hope. It was written for people like me. It brings us joy. It assures us that we have our priorities straight. It helps us know where we stand. It lights up the darkness.

כ לחודש

א יְהֹוָה מָלָךְ תָּגֵל הָאָרֶץ
יִשְׂמְחוּ אִיִּים רַבִּים׃

ב עָנָן וַעֲרָפֶל סְבִיבָיו צֶדֶק
וּמִשְׁפָּט מְכוֹן כִּסְאוֹ׃

ג אֵשׁ לְפָנָיו תֵּלֵךְ
וּתְלַהֵט סָבִיב צָרָיו׃

ד הֵאִירוּ בְרָקָיו תֵּבֵל
רָאֲתָה וַתָּחֵל הָאָרֶץ׃

ה הָרִים כַּדּוֹנַג נָמַסּוּ מִלִּפְנֵי יְהֹוָה
מִלִּפְנֵי אֲדוֹן כָּל־הָאָרֶץ׃

ו הִגִּידוּ הַשָּׁמַיִם צִדְקוֹ
וְרָאוּ כָל־הָעַמִּים כְּבוֹדוֹ׃

ז יֵבֹשׁוּ ׀ כָּל־עֹבְדֵי פֶסֶל הַמִּתְהַלְלִים בָּאֱלִילִים
הִשְׁתַּחֲווּ־לוֹ כָּל־אֱלֹהִים׃

ח שָׁמְעָה וַתִּשְׂמַח ׀ צִיּוֹן וַתָּגֵלְנָה בְּנוֹת יְהוּדָה
לְמַעַן מִשְׁפָּטֶיךָ יְהֹוָה׃

מזמור צז *Psalm 97: Light is sown for the righteous, and joy for the upright in heart.*

This verse, although it appears toward the end of our psalm, is its focal point. It is a verse which appears in the liturgy beyond the context of our psalm, most notoriously in the service for Yom Kippur eve, where it is recited repetitively by the cantor.

What message does this verse carry that makes it so special? Who are the

9. For You, Lord, are supreme over all the earth;
You are exalted far above all gods.

10. O lovers of the Lord, hate evil!
He guards the lives of His loyal ones,
and delivers them from the hand of the wicked.

11. Light is sown* for the righteous,
and joy for the upright in heart.

12. Rejoice in the Lord, you righteous,
and praise His holy name.

* I.e., "stored up" – so Targum.

---

not yet joy. For him, light is but a seed which he has planted, which will only eventually lead to full spiritual satisfaction.

The upright *yashar*, on the other hand, experiences pure joy immediately. He does not need to go through a process of resolving his doubts and overcoming his regrets. No temptations interfere with his path toward doing God's will, and he thus requires no intermediaries between his actions and their spiritual consequences. He proceeds directly to "joy" and need not stop at the way station of "light." Few of us nowadays are "upright" in the Maimonidean sense. Would that we would all be "merely righteous"!

But now we are in a position to understand why, when we do behave righteously, we do not immediately experience heavenly bliss. We are not yet at that end game.

We have done no more than plant a seed. If we sow many more such seeds, and patiently cultivate the garden, we will one day experience the pure joy which the "upright" reached more expeditiously.

The religious path is one of struggle. Its ultimate objectives are not achieved easily or quickly. But as sure as a seed properly tended will sprout into a gorgeous plant, so will our good deeds earn us the reward of great spiritual joy.

ט כִּי־אַתָּה יהוה עֶלְיוֹן עַל־כׇּל־הָאָרֶץ
מְאֹד נַעֲלֵיתָ עַל־כׇּל־אֱלֹהִים׃

י אֹהֲבֵי יהוה שִׂנְאוּ רָע
שֹׁמֵר נַפְשׁוֹת חֲסִידָיו
מִיַּד רְשָׁעִים יַצִּילֵם׃

יא אוֹר זָרֻעַ לַצַּדִּיק
וּלְיִשְׁרֵי־לֵב שִׂמְחָה׃

יב שִׂמְחוּ צַדִּיקִים בַּיהוה
וְהוֹדוּ לְזֵכֶר קׇדְשׁוֹ׃

---

from Maimonides' early work, The Eight Chapters. There Maimonides distinguishes between two types of religious individuals. One who naturally is attracted to the good and to what is right. He suffers no inner conflict, and need not overcome any tendencies to do otherwise than God's will. He is the *yashar*, the upright person. Moral and ethical behaviors come naturally to him.

Maimonides presents a second type of person. He wants to do what is right, but resists doing so. He has temptations, has an evil urge, which he must conquer in order to remain on the straight and narrow. Every good deed comes at a cost for him. His passions stand between him and God and he must overcome those passions. He is the *tzaddik*, the righteous person, who must struggle valiantly to conform to proper ethical and moral norms.

Maimonides speculates at length as to who stands higher in the eyes of God: the pure and saintly *yashar* or the struggling *tzaddik*. Rav Kook bypasses that discussion, but instead examines our verse from the perspective of Maimonides' dichotomy.

For the righteous *tzaddik* the full joy of doing God's will is not immediately experienced. He lives with regret, having forgone the pleasures he would have enjoyed had he submitted to his temptations. He experiences light, but

PSALM 98

1. Sing to the LORD a new song,
for He has worked wonders;
His right hand and His holy arm have brought Him victory.

2. The LORD has made known His salvation;
He has displayed His righteousness in the sight of the nations.

3. He has remembered His loving-kindness and His loyalty
toward the house of Israel;
all the ends of the earth have seen the salvation of our God.

4. Shout for joy to the LORD, all the earth;
break into songs of joy, and make music.

5. Make music to the LORD on the harp,
on the harp with melodious song.

6. With trumpets and the sound of the horn
shout for joy before the King, the LORD.

Malbim draws our attention to the progression from songs sung to the harp's melody to shouts of joy which are accompanied by trumpets and the sounds of the horn. The King advances outward from the chambers of His palace, within which the soft sounds of the harp are appropriate, to the public parade grounds, where trumpets blast and horns herald His presence. Thus is royalty revealed.

The Talmud (*Rosh HaShana* 27a) tells us about the relationship between the trumpets and horn or shofar.

> In a place where the trumpets are sounded, the shofar is not. Where the shofar is sounded, the trumpets are not. They are sounded together only in the Eastern Gate of the Holy Temple. Rava said, and others attributed this to R. Yehoshua b. Levi, that the scriptural basis for this practice is the verse [in our psalm] *with trumpets and the sound of the horn shout for joy before the King, the LORD.* Only in the presence of the King, the LORD, which is in the Holy Temple, are both instruments sounded. But nowhere else.

מזמור צח

God works wonders. When Israel triumphs and celebrates, that's a wonder. When other nations celebrate too, that's a wonder of wonders. That's an occasion for a new song. Everyone will sing it, the rivers will applaud, the hills will rejoice. But wait – there is another wonder to come. God will then judge the world with righteousness. Will the singing continue? If it does, that's a wondrous wonder. God works wondrous wonders too.

א מִזְמוֹר
שִׁירוּ לַיהוָה ׀ שִׁיר חָדָשׁ
כִּי־נִפְלָאוֹת עָשָׂה
הוֹשִׁיעָה־לּוֹ יְמִינוֹ וּזְרוֹעַ קָדְשׁוֹ׃

ב הוֹדִיעַ יְהוָה יְשׁוּעָתוֹ
לְעֵינֵי הַגּוֹיִם גִּלָּה צִדְקָתוֹ׃

ג זָכַר חַסְדּוֹ ׀ וֶאֱמוּנָתוֹ לְבֵית יִשְׂרָאֵל
רָאוּ כָל־אַפְסֵי־אָרֶץ אֵת יְשׁוּעַת אֱלֹהֵינוּ׃

ד הָרִיעוּ לַיהוָה כָּל־הָאָרֶץ
פִּצְחוּ וְרַנְּנוּ וְזַמֵּרוּ׃

ה זַמְּרוּ לַיהוָה בְּכִנּוֹר
בְּכִנּוֹר וְקוֹל זִמְרָה׃

ו בַּחֲצֹצְרוֹת וְקוֹל שׁוֹפָר
הָרִיעוּ לִפְנֵי ׀ הַמֶּלֶךְ יְהוָה׃

מזמור צח *Psalm 98:* Our psalm is a jubilant one. It envisions a new song, and begs to be put to music. It has indeed come to be sung communally in the synagogue.

Our psalm describes a revelation of the Almighty that rivals His revelation at Sinai. The entire world acknowledges God, and does so in response to Israel's triumph. The world finally recognizes that Israel's triumph is beneficial to all of humanity. This seems nothing short of miraculous.

7. Let the sea and all within it thunder,
the world and all who live in it.

8. Let the rivers clap their hands,
the mountains sing together for joy,

9. before the LORD, for He comes to judge the earth.
He will judge the world with righteousness,
and the peoples with equity.

---

the somber prospect of judgment. The unbounded joy expressed by blaring trumpets is spiritually exciting, but it is ephemeral and threatens to deteriorate into a Dionysian orgy. God's revelation contains not only the trumpet's call for celebration, but also the shofar's call for self-examination and subordination to the ethical demands of the Creator.

Our final verse assures us that we need not fear that judgment. It will be based upon righteousness and equity. It will be uplifting, and ultimately its own cause for a new song of celebration.

ז יִרְעַ֣ם הַ֭יָּם וּמְלֹא֑וֹ
תֵּ֝בֵ֗ל וְיֹ֣שְׁבֵי בָֽהּ׃

ח נְהָר֥וֹת יִמְחֲאוּ־כָ֑ף
יַ֝֗חַד הָרִ֥ים יְרַנֵּֽנוּ׃

ט לִֽפְנֵ֥י־יהוה
כִּ֥י בָא֮ לִשְׁפֹּ֪ט הָ֫אָ֥רֶץ
יִשְׁפֹּֽט־תֵּבֵ֥ל בְּצֶ֑דֶק
וְ֝עַמִּ֗ים בְּמֵישָׁרִֽים׃

The culmination of God's revelation takes place in the Holy Temple. Only there are the two resounding instruments, trumpets and shofar, joined together.

Rav Hirsch shares a profound insight here. The trumpet calls man to come to the aid of others, and asks God to come to the aid of man. The shofar, on the other hand, calls man to himself, summoning him to follow God and to obey Him. The trumpets alone call forth only a vague spiritual sense. Only when coupled with the shofar are we summoned to follow God and live in accordance with His will. This is how Rav Hirsch puts it: "If we expect Him to be our Helper, then we must first accept Him as our King."

Rav Hirsch's approach helps us understand the last verse of our psalm, which otherwise surprises us by suddenly shifting from celebratory joy to

PSALM 99

1. The Lord reigns, let the peoples tremble;
He is enthroned on the cherubim,
let the earth quake.

2. The Lord is great in Zion,
He is exalted above all the peoples.

3. Let them praise Your name as great and awesome.
He is holy!

4. You are a powerful King, a lover of justice.
You Yourself have established equity,
You Yourself have wrought justice and righteousness in Jacob.

5. Exalt the Lord our God,
and bow down at His footstool;
He is holy!

---

on this aspect of the Divine. How can we draw close to Him if He is so exalted? How can we begin to know what He expects of us? How can we pray to a God who is transcendent?

Our psalm answers these questions by encouraging us to first connect to the *other* aspect of God, His immanence. Then, gradually, we can ascend spiritually and approach His transcendent aspect.

Thus, in verse 5, we are asked to *exalt the Lord*; that is, to acclaim His transcendence. We are overawed by this and, quite naturally, feel inept and helpless in relating to such exaltation. But we are immediately advised: *bow down at His footstool*; that is, relate to that much lower aspect of His presence, symbolized by His footstool. The footstool is an incomparable metaphor for a facet of majesty which is available to all.

The verse concludes by warning us that as we progress from the awe of His transcendence to the joyous familiarity with *His footstool*, we must be prepared to revert to that original awe: *He is holy*. The word *holy, kadosh,* signifies separateness and utter distance.

Verse 9, the last verse of our psalm, uses an almost identical vocabulary. It

מזמור צט

It is Friday evening and the sun is setting. I prepare for Shabbat by singing songs of David. I sing: The LORD reigns, let the earth be glad (Ps. 97:1). I sing: The LORD reigns, the world cannot be shaken (Ps. 93:1). And I sing: The LORD reigns, let the peoples tremble… let the earth quake (our psalm, verse 1). Are we glad, and cannot be shaken? Or do we tremble and quake? Is this one of the LORD's many mysteries? Or is it our choice? This week, this Shabbat, let the world neither tremble nor quake. Let the earth be glad.

א יְהוָה מָלָךְ יִרְגְּזוּ עַמִּים
יֹשֵׁב כְּרוּבִים תָּנוּט הָאָרֶץ׃

ב יְהוָה בְּצִיּוֹן גָּדוֹל
וְרָם הוּא עַל־כָּל־הָעַמִּים׃

ג יוֹדוּ שִׁמְךָ גָּדוֹל וְנוֹרָא
קָדוֹשׁ הוּא׃

ד וְעֹז מֶלֶךְ מִשְׁפָּט אָהֵב
אַתָּה כּוֹנַנְתָּ מֵישָׁרִים
מִשְׁפָּט וּצְדָקָה בְּיַעֲקֹב ׀ אַתָּה עָשִׂיתָ׃

ה רוֹמְמוּ יְהוָה אֱלֹהֵינוּ
וְהִשְׁתַּחֲווּ לַהֲדֹם רַגְלָיו
קָדוֹשׁ הוּא׃

מזמור צט *Psalm 99:* Theologians have long ago distinguished between two modes of God's relationship to the world. On the one hand he is *transcendent*. That is, He is immeasurably greater than we can imagine, and hence we experience Him as distant. On the other hand, He is *immanent* in the world; the world is infused by His presence. He is closer than close.

Kabbalists have devised two different terms to describe these two modes. They use the term "He encompasses the world" to describe His transcendence, and the term "He fills the world" as synonymous with His immanence.

Our psalm emphasizes His transcendence: *The LORD reigns… He is enthroned… He is exalted above all.* We have great difficulties when we focus

6. Among His priests were Moses and Aaron;
among those who call on His name was Samuel;
they called to the LORD, and He answered them.

7. He spoke to them in a pillar of cloud;
they kept His decrees and the law that He gave them.

8. O LORD our God, You answered them;
You were for them a forgiving God,
even though You punished their misdeeds.

9. Exalt the LORD our God,
and bow down at His holy mountain;
for the LORD our God is holy.

The mountain is a particularly apt metaphor for our struggle to relate to the divine. For while it symbolizes the path upward, it also allows for failure and regression. We ascend, but can also descend. This is the nature of our relationship with the Master of the Universe. We vacillate, as mortals must, between His wondrous and sometimes frightful transcendence and the warmth and security of His immanence.

We cherish His footstool, we struggle to climb His holy mountain and not fall backward. But we always remain aware that *the LORD our God is holy.*

ו מֹשֶׁה וְאַהֲרֹן ׀ בְּכֹהֲנָיו
וּשְׁמוּאֵל בְּקֹרְאֵי שְׁמוֹ
קֹרִאים אֶל־יהוה וְהוּא יַעֲנֵם:

ז בְּעַמּוּד עָנָן יְדַבֵּר אֲלֵיהֶם
שָׁמְרוּ עֵדֹתָיו וְחֹק נָתַן־לָמוֹ:

ח יהוה אֱלֹהֵינוּ אַתָּה עֲנִיתָם
אֵל נֹשֵׂא הָיִיתָ לָהֶם
וְנֹקֵם עַל־עֲלִילוֹתָם:

ט רוֹמְמוּ יהוה אֱלֹהֵינוּ
וְהִשְׁתַּחֲווּ לְהַר קָדְשׁוֹ
כִּי־קָדוֹשׁ יהוה אֱלֹהֵינוּ:

---

too begins by imploring us to *Exalt the Lord,* to acknowledge His transcendence. And it too proceeds with advice to *bow down*. But this time it is not to *His footstool* that we are encouraged to bow down. It is to *His holy mountain*!

We have progressed toward Him. We began at His footstool, relishing His closeness and accessibility. We are now enabled to move up *His holy mountain,* a metaphor for His immanence, but also a path upward toward His transcendence.

PSALM 100

1. A psalm of thanksgiving.
   Shout for joy to the LORD, all men on earth.

2. Serve the LORD with gladness;
   enter His presence with singing.

3. Know that the LORD is God;
   He made us and we are His,
   His people, and the flock of His pasture.

4. Enter His gates with thanksgiving,
   His courts with praise;
   give thanks to Him, and bless His name.

5. For the LORD is good,
   His loving-kindness is everlasting;
   His faithfulness lasts through all generations.

The Midrash, commenting on our psalm, expresses this dimension of gratitude in a statement which we many find theologically provocative, but which we can easily understand once we have internalized our psalm and its message.

Here is the text of this Midrash:

"All modes of prayer will be abolished in the 'future to come,' but prayers of thanksgiving will not be abolished. All sacrificial offerings will be abolished, but the thanksgiving offering will never be abolished."

Commentaries on this midrash have explained: In a world without pain and sorrow, where none experience wants or woes, prayers are not necessary. The only prayers which remain meaningful are prayers of thanksgiving for this wonderful new world and its blessings. Similarly, in this World to Come there is no sin, and thus sacrificial offerings, almost all of which are for the purpose of achieving forgiveness for sin, become obsolete. Only offerings expressing thanksgiving remain meaningful.

A perfect world certainly is a world in which gratitude prevails. Our task is to cultivate gratitude even in the imperfect world which we occupy. Our psalm inspires us, and enables us to perform this task effectively.

מזמור ק

There is something about gratitude. It can't be expressed in solitude. Sure, it is a very spiritual feeling. It makes you feel close to God. But it also makes you shout for joy. It makes you sing and dance. It makes you want to tell your story. It makes you want to throw a party.

א מִזְמ֥וֹר לְתוֹדָ֑ה
הָרִ֥יעוּ לַ֝יהֹוָ֗ה כׇּל־הָאָֽרֶץ׃

ב עִבְד֣וּ אֶת־יְהֹוָ֣ה בְּשִׂמְחָ֑ה
בֹּ֥אוּ לְ֝פָנָ֗יו בִּרְנָנָֽה׃

ג דְּע֗וּ כִּֽי־יְהֹוָה֮ ה֤וּא אֱלֹ֫הִ֥ים
ה֣וּא עָ֭שָׂנוּ ולא אֲנַ֑חְנוּ וְל֣וֹ
עַ֝מּ֗וֹ וְצֹ֣אן מַרְעִיתֽוֹ׃

ד בֹּ֤אוּ שְׁעָרָ֨יו ׀ בְּתוֹדָ֗ה
חֲצֵרֹתָ֥יו בִּתְהִלָּ֑ה
הֽוֹדוּ־ל֝֗וֹ בָּרְכ֥וּ שְׁמֽוֹ׃

ה כִּי־ט֣וֹב יְ֭הֹוָה לְעוֹלָ֣ם חַסְדּ֑וֹ
וְעַד־דֹּ֥ר וָ֝דֹ֗ר אֱמוּנָתֽוֹ׃

מזמור ק *Psalm 100:* Our brief psalm gives expression to that most sublime of emotions, thankfulness. Our psalm emphasizes the religious nature of thankfulness, the connection to God that one experiences concomitantly with gratitude: *He made us and we are His... give thanks to Him.*

There is a circular relationship between gratitude and faith. The person of faith is more likely to experience gratitude; for he realizes that he is entitled to little, so that every one of his benefits is experienced as a divine blessing.

Gratefulness also produces faith, because it is an emotion which demands expression. There is no more effective expression of that emotion than prayers of praise to God.

Our psalm also suggests that not only is thankfulness naturally shared with others, by *all men on earth*, but it resounds forever, throughout eternity: *His faithfulness lasts through all generations.*

PSALM 101

1. Of David. A psalm.
I will sing of [Your] loving-kindness and justice,
I will sing praises to You, Lord.

2. I will give heed to the perfect way – when will it come to me?*
I will walk with a blameless heart within my house.

3. I will not set before my eyes any vile thing.
I hate crooked practices.
Such shall not cling to me.

4. Men of perverse heart shall be far from me,
I will have nothing to do with evil.

5. The man who slanders his neighbor in secret
him I will destroy;
the man of proud looks and haughty heart
him I will not tolerate.

* Or: "When will You come to me?"

The way demands self-discipline and courage, and the rare ability to "just say no" to friends who are magnetically attractive. *The man of proud looks... I will not tolerate.*

The way entails simplicity, although it is in not at all simple. It requires struggling with inner conflicts, and involves pacing the floor of one's abode in a painful process of self-examination. It necessitates confronting one's inner demons, as well as enlisting the support of one's inner angels.

The way demands that we take control of our social life, and choose our friends and companions wisely and bravely. We must rigorously avoid the company of knaves, and even of fools. *Men of perverse heart shall be far from me.*

We cannot associate with the arrogant, or with those who speak ill of others. We must shun the deceitful.

Our psalm assures us that we will eventually find this task easy. We will come to despise evil in all of its many guises. It will become our second nature to hate falsehood. We will find hypocrisy and malicious gossip unbearable.

We will be surprised to learn that there are others, many more than we

מזמור קא

I have a job. Thank God, it is a good job. I earn a living helping others. I spend my work day doing charity, achieving justice. My colleagues share my goals and we work together. I love going to work each day. I sing on my way there. I sing on the way home. Thank You, God, for assigning me this job, my job.

א לְדָוִד מִזְמוֹר
חֶסֶד־וּמִשְׁפָּט אָשִׁירָה
לְךָ יְהוָה אֲזַמֵּרָה׃

ב אַשְׂכִּילָה ׀ בְּדֶרֶךְ תָּמִים
מָתַי תָּבוֹא אֵלָי
אֶתְהַלֵּךְ בְּתָם־לְבָבִי בְּקֶרֶב בֵּיתִי׃

ג לֹא־אָשִׁית ׀ לְנֶגֶד עֵינַי דְּבַר־בְּלִיָּעַל
עֲשֹׂה־סֵטִים שָׂנֵאתִי
לֹא יִדְבַּק בִּי׃

ד לֵבָב עִקֵּשׁ יָסוּר מִמֶּנִּי
רָע לֹא אֵדָע׃

ה מלושני בַסֵּתֶר ׀ רֵעֵהוּ מְלָשְׁנִי
אוֹתוֹ אַצְמִית
גְּבַהּ־עֵינַיִם וּרְחַב לֵבָב
אֹתוֹ לֹא אוּכָל׃

מזמור קא *Psalm 101:* We all search. We search to discover who we are. We search for a way of life, one that will be meaningful, purposeful, and rewarding. We search for a "*derekh*," a path.

Our psalm tells us where to begin. It shows us the way, but it warns us that the way is long and arduous. It informs us that the way begins in intimate privacy, in solitude and contemplation. It requires walking *with a blameless heart within my house.*

6. My eyes are on the honest men in the land,
to have them live with me.
He who walks in the way of integrity
shall serve me.

7. No one who practices deceit shall live in my house;
no one who speaks lies shall endure in my presence.

8. Morning after morning I will destroy
all the wicked of the land,
ridding the Lord's city of all evildoers.

The path leads to the *Lord's city* where *the wicked of the land* have no place. *Evildoers* are not tolerated there. There David says, *My eyes are on the honest men… no one who speaks lies shall endure in my presence.*

We all look for that way, search for that path, and yearn for that destination. Our psalm assures us that we can find that way. Even more, it tells us how to do so.

ו עֵינַ֤י ׀ בְּנֶאֶמְנֵי־אֶ֡רֶץ
לָשֶׁ֬בֶת עִמָּדִ֗י
הֹ֭לֵךְ בְּדֶ֣רֶךְ תָּמִ֑ים
ה֝֗וּא יְשָֽׁרְתֵֽנִי׃

ז לֹֽא־יֵשֵׁ֨ב ׀ בְּקֶ֣רֶב בֵּיתִי֮ עֹשֵׂ֪ה רְמִ֫יָּ֥ה
דֹּבֵ֥ר שְׁקָרִ֑ים
לֹֽא־יִ֝כּ֗וֹן לְנֶ֣גֶד עֵינָֽי׃

ח לַבְּקָרִ֗ים אַצְמִ֥ית כָּל־רִשְׁעֵי־אָ֑רֶץ
לְהַכְרִ֥ית מֵֽעִיר־יְ֝הוָ֗ה כָּל־פֹּ֥עֲלֵי אָֽוֶן׃

---

imagined, who share in our search for such a lofty way of life. They are the *honest men in the land* who walk *in the way of integrity.*

The path is a long one, but it has a destination. For the individual, reaching that destination may take a lifetime. For the Jewish people it has taken two millennia, and we are still not quite there.

PSALM 102

1. A prayer by a poor man who is overwhelmed,
and pours out his speech before the LORD.

2. LORD, hear my prayer;
let my cry for help come to You!

3. Do not hide Your face from me in the day of my distress;
turn Your ear to me;
answer me quickly when I call.

4. For my days vanish like smoke;
my bones are charred as in an oven.

5. My heart is blighted and withered like grass;
I neglect to eat my food.

6. Because of my loud groaning
my bones cling to my flesh.

7. I am like a pelican in the wilderness,
like an owl among ruins.

8. I lie awake;
I am like a lone bird on a rooftop.

9. All day long my enemies revile me;
those who mock me use my name as a curse.

10. I have eaten ashes for bread,
and mingled my drink with tears.

מזמור קב *Psalm 102:* Our psalm is one of just three which begin "A prayer of..." The others are Psalm 86, which begins "A prayer of David," and Psalm 90, which begins "A prayer of Moses." The Zohar points this out, and asks which of these three is most precious. The Zohar answers that our psalm is most precious, because the poor man is broken hearted, and God is therefore closest to him. "The prayers of the poor man open all the windows of heaven."

We are all poor men, although few of us allow ourselves to be aware of

מזמור קב

God, don't file away my prayer in some folder. Give it Your special attention. I know that I pester You with my prayers. You've heard them before and they are not Your priority. You've got more important prayers to listen to than mine. But for me, these prayers are urgent. I have nowhere else to turn. Hear my prayers, and may they bear fruit.

א תְּפִלָּה לְעָנִי כִי־יַעֲטֹף
וְלִפְנֵי יהוה יִשְׁפֹּךְ שִׂיחוֹ׃

ב יהוה שִׁמְעָה תְפִלָּתִי
וְשַׁוְעָתִי אֵלֶיךָ תָבוֹא׃

ג אַל־תַּסְתֵּר פָּנֶיךָ ׀ מִמֶּנִּי בְּיוֹם צַר לִי
הַטֵּה־אֵלַי אָזְנֶךָ
בְּיוֹם אֶקְרָא מַהֵר עֲנֵנִי׃

ד כִּי־כָלוּ בְעָשָׁן יָמָי
וְעַצְמוֹתַי כְּמוֹקֵד נִחָרוּ׃

ה הוּכָּה כָעֵשֶׂב וַיִּבַשׁ לִבִּי
כִּי־שָׁכַחְתִּי מֵאֲכֹל לַחְמִי׃

ו מִקּוֹל אַנְחָתִי
דָּבְקָה עַצְמִי לִבְשָׂרִי׃

ז דָּמִיתִי לִקְאַת מִדְבָּר
הָיִיתִי כְּכוֹס חֳרָבוֹת׃

ח שָׁקַדְתִּי וָאֶהְיֶה
כְּצִפּוֹר בּוֹדֵד עַל־גָּג׃

ט כָּל־הַיּוֹם חֵרְפוּנִי אוֹיְבָי
מְהוֹלָלַי בִּי נִשְׁבָּעוּ׃

י כִּי־אֵפֶר כַּלֶּחֶם אָכָלְתִּי
וְשִׁקֻּוַי בִּבְכִי מָסָכְתִּי׃

11. In Your wrath and fury
You lifted me high only to cast me down.

12. My days are like a declining shadow;
I wither away like grass.

13. But You, LORD, are enthroned forever,
Your renown endures through all ages.

14. You will arise and have compassion on Zion,
for it is time to be gracious to her;
the appointed time has come.

15. For Your servants love her very stones,
they cherish even her dust.

16. The nations will revere the name of the LORD,
and all the kings of the earth Your glory.

17. For the LORD has built Zion;
He has shown Himself in all His glory.

18. He heeds the prayer of the destitute,
and does not despise their prayer.

19. May this be written down for a coming generation,
that people yet unborn may praise the LORD.

20. For the LORD looks down from His holy height;
from heaven He surveys the earth,

21. to hear the groans of the prisoner,
to set free those condemned to death.

22. And so the fame of the LORD will be talked about in Zion,
and His praise in Jerusalem,

---

that fact. If we would admit our impoverishment to ourselves, and pray as the overwhelmed poor person does, the windows of heaven would all open.

Our opening verse uses the word *siaḥ* to describe the poor man's prayers. We have translated *siaḥ* as "speech," although "conversation," "thought," or "meditation" might be preferable renditions. This word is found in Genesis 24:63:

יא מִפְּנֵי־זַעַמְךָ וְקִצְפֶּךָ
כִּי נְשָׂאתַנִי וַתַּשְׁלִיכֵנִי:

יב יָמַי כְּצֵל נָטוּי
וַאֲנִי כָּעֵשֶׂב אִיבָשׁ:

יג וְאַתָּה יְהוָה לְעוֹלָם תֵּשֵׁב
וְזִכְרְךָ לְדֹר וָדֹר:

יד אַתָּה תָקוּם תְּרַחֵם צִיּוֹן
כִּי־עֵת לְחֶנְנָהּ כִּי־בָא מוֹעֵד:

טו כִּי־רָצוּ עֲבָדֶיךָ אֶת־אֲבָנֶיהָ
וְאֶת־עֲפָרָהּ יְחֹנֵנוּ:

טז וְיִירְאוּ גוֹיִם אֶת־שֵׁם יְהוָה
וְכָל־מַלְכֵי הָאָרֶץ אֶת־כְּבוֹדֶךָ:

יז כִּי־בָנָה יְהוָה צִיּוֹן
נִרְאָה בִּכְבוֹדוֹ:

יח פָּנָה אֶל־תְּפִלַּת הָעַרְעָר
וְלֹא־בָזָה אֶת־תְּפִלָּתָם:

יט תִּכָּתֶב זֹאת לְדוֹר אַחֲרוֹן
וְעַם נִבְרָא יְהַלֶּל־יָהּ:

כ כִּי־הִשְׁקִיף מִמְּרוֹם קָדְשׁוֹ
יְהוָה מִשָּׁמַיִם ׀ אֶל־אֶרֶץ הִבִּיט:

כא לִשְׁמֹעַ אֶנְקַת אָסִיר
לְפַתֵּחַ בְּנֵי תְמוּתָה:

כב לְסַפֵּר בְּצִיּוֹן שֵׁם יְהוָה
וּתְהִלָּתוֹ בִּירוּשָׁלִָם:

23. when the nations are gathered together,
and also the kingdoms, to serve the LORD.

24. He has weakened my strength in mid-course,
He has cut short my days.

25. I say, "O my God, do not take me away
when only half my days are done,
You, whose years go on through all generations."

26. Long ago You founded the earth,
and the heavens are the work of Your hands.

27. They will perish, but You remain;
they will all wear out like a garment;
like clothing You will change them, and they will vanish.

28. But You are always the same, and Your years never end.

29. The children of Your servants will dwell securely,
and their descendants will be established in Your presence.

---

connection to the Divinity. He demands nothing; he is *poor and overwhelmed and pours out his speech* to God.

He describes his condition: *my bones are charred... my heart is blighted... I am like a lone bird on a rooftop.* But note: he asks for nothing.

He interrupts his meditation as his thoughts wander from his pain to the contemplation of God's glory and His special devotion to Zion. *You, LORD, are enthroned forever... from heaven He surveys the earth... His fame will be talked about in Zion.*

But he abruptly interrupts this meditative interlude and returns to focus on his own pain. *He has weakened my strength... half my days are done.*

But he never makes demands. That is the nature of *the prayer of the poor man.* He ends hopefully: *the children of Your servants will dwell securely,* but he never directly asks for that security.

He thinks, he meditates, he contemplates, and he converses. But he is much too humble to demand. Such was the nature of Isaac's prayer. Such is the *prayer of the poor man.*

כג בְּהִקָּבֵץ עַמִּים יַחְדָּו
וּמַמְלָכוֹת לַעֲבֹד אֶת־יְהוָה׃

כד עִנָּה בַדֶּרֶךְ כחו — כֹּחִי
קִצַּר יָמָי׃

כה אֹמַר אֵלִי אַל־תַּעֲלֵנִי בַּחֲצִי יָמָי
בְּדוֹר דּוֹרִים שְׁנוֹתֶיךָ׃

כו לְפָנִים הָאָרֶץ יָסַדְתָּ
וּמַעֲשֵׂה יָדֶיךָ שָׁמָיִם׃

כז הֵמָּה ׀ יֹאבֵדוּ וְאַתָּה תַעֲמֹד
וְכֻלָּם כַּבֶּגֶד יִבְלוּ
כַּלְּבוּשׁ תַּחֲלִיפֵם וְיַחֲלֹפוּ׃

כח וְאַתָּה־הוּא
וּשְׁנוֹתֶיךָ לֹא יִתָּמּוּ׃

כט בְּנֵי־עֲבָדֶיךָ יִשְׁכּוֹנוּ
וְזַרְעָם לְפָנֶיךָ יִכּוֹן׃

And Isaac went out to meditate (converse with God) in the field toward evening. The word *siah* is unique to Isaac, perhaps because as the least worldly of the three patriarchs he had a special relationship with God, one that required not petitionary prayer, but rather meditation, conversation, sharing of thoughts.

Isaac simply shared with God what was going through his mind, his raw experience. He asked God for nothing, because his material needs were negligible. He simply said, "God, this is what is going on with me."

So it is with the profoundly spiritual individual. He simply says to God, "This is what is happening to me now. I don't know how I am going to handle this. I feel helpless." He may not even say, "Help me." His is a simple and direct

PSALM 103

1. Of David.
Bless the LORD, O my soul;
let all my being [bless] His holy name.

2. Bless the LORD, O my soul,
and never forget all His benefits.

3. He forgives all your sins,
He heals all your ills.

4. He redeems your life from the pit;
He crowns you with loving-kindness and compassion.

5. He satisfies the prime* of your life with good things;
your youth is renewed like the eagle's.

6. The LORD executes righteousness
and justice for all who are oppressed.

7. He made known His ways to Moses,
His deeds to the people of Israel.

8. The LORD is compassionate and gracious,
slow to anger, and abounding in loving-kindness.

* Or: your old age (Targum), your mouth (Rashi).

He forgives all your sins, He heals all your ills... He satisfies your old age with good things.

Why is God so kind to us? What is the basis of His compassion? Our psalm outlines five reasons for His tolerance for a flawed humanity.

He knows how we are formed. He has given us free will, but He knows well that we are dominated by our passions. We have the capacity to do good, but we find it difficult to activate that capacity. It is much easier for us to slip into mischief and misdeeds. He tolerates us because *He knows how we are formed.*

He remembers that we are but dust. He is constantly conscious of the fact

מזמור קג

We pass through five worlds. In each the soul sings God's praises; in each, a different song. In the womb it sings a song of anticipation. When it is born it sings exuberant songs. Songs of hope help it cope with life's twists and turns. It departs the body, and returns to God to sing in His presence. When the world is perfect, it will sing once again. In each world the soul sings a different song. But it sings, always and forever.

א לְדָוִ֨ד ׀ בָּרְכִ֣י נַ֭פְשִׁי אֶת־יְהֹוָ֑ה
וְכׇל־קְ֝רָבַ֗י אֶת־שֵׁ֥ם קׇדְשֽׁוֹ׃

ב בָּרְכִ֣י נַ֭פְשִׁי אֶת־יְהֹוָ֑ה
וְאַל־תִּ֝שְׁכְּחִ֗י כׇּל־גְּמוּלָֽיו׃

ג הַסֹּלֵ֥חַ לְכׇל־עֲוֺנֵ֑כִי
הָ֝רֹפֵ֗א לְכׇל־תַּחֲלוּאָֽיְכִי׃

ד הַגּוֹאֵ֣ל מִשַּׁ֣חַת חַיָּ֑יְכִי
הַ֝מְעַטְּרֵ֗כִי חֶ֣סֶד וְרַחֲמִֽים׃

ה הַמַּשְׂבִּ֣יעַ בַּטּ֣וֹב עֶדְיֵ֑ךְ
תִּתְחַדֵּ֥שׁ כַּ֝נֶּ֗שֶׁר נְעוּרָֽיְכִי׃

ו עֹשֵׂ֣ה צְדָק֣וֹת יְהֹוָ֑ה
וּ֝מִשְׁפָּטִ֗ים לְכׇל־עֲשׁוּקִֽים׃

ז יוֹדִ֣יעַ דְּרָכָ֣יו לְמֹשֶׁ֑ה
לִבְנֵ֥י יִ֝שְׂרָאֵ֗ל עֲלִילוֹתָֽיו׃

ח רַח֣וּם וְחַנּ֣וּן יְהֹוָ֑ה
אֶ֖רֶךְ אַפַּ֣יִם וְרַב־חָֽסֶד׃

מזמור קג *Psalm 103:* Our psalm contrasts sharply with the preceding one. There we read of charred bones and loud groaning. Here we read of forgiveness, loving-kindness, and compassion.

In our psalm we learn of some of the components of God's magnanimity:

9. He will not always rage,
or nurse His anger forever.

10. He has not dealt with us as our sins deserve,
nor requited us according to our iniquities.

11. For as the heavens are high above the earth,
so great is His loving-kindness toward those who fear Him.

12. As far as east is from west,
so far has He removed our transgressions from us.

13. As a father has compassion on his children,
so the LORD has compassion on those who fear Him.

14. For He knows how we are formed;
He remembers that we are but dust.

15. Man's days are as grass;
he blossoms like a flower of the field.

16. When the wind passes over it, it is gone,
and its place knows it no more.

17. But the LORD's loving-kindness is for all eternity
toward those who fear Him,
and His righteousness reaches out to the children's children

---

been granted longer lives we might have repented of our ways early on, and continued on to live in a more exemplary fashion. But we typically wake up too late. By the time we mature spiritually, we no longer have opportunities to implement our newly gained good intentions.

He blossoms like a flower of the field. True, we sometimes blossom gloriously, but those rare moments are tragically brief, and already contain the seeds of imminent decay. Our most noble achievements are vulnerable to sudden and disastrous reversals. God recognizes these limitations as part of our existential condition, and therefore forgives us and understands our limits.

ט לֹא־לָנֶצַח יָרִיב
וְלֹא לְעוֹלָם יִטּוֹר׃

י לֹא כַחֲטָאֵינוּ עָשָׂה לָנוּ
וְלֹא כַעֲוֺנֹתֵינוּ גָּמַל עָלֵינוּ׃

יא כִּי כִגְבֹהַּ שָׁמַיִם עַל־הָאָרֶץ
גָּבַר חַסְדּוֹ עַל־יְרֵאָיו׃

יב כִּרְחֹק מִזְרָח מִמַּעֲרָב
הִרְחִיק מִמֶּנּוּ אֶת־פְּשָׁעֵינוּ׃

יג כְּרַחֵם אָב עַל־בָּנִים
רִחַם יהוה עַל־יְרֵאָיו׃

יד כִּי־הוּא יָדַע יִצְרֵנוּ
זָכוּר כִּי־עָפָר אֲנָחְנוּ׃

טו אֱנוֹשׁ כֶּחָצִיר יָמָיו
כְּצִיץ הַשָּׂדֶה כֵּן יָצִיץ׃

טז כִּי רוּחַ עָבְרָה־בּוֹ וְאֵינֶנּוּ
וְלֹא־יַכִּירֶנּוּ עוֹד מְקוֹמוֹ׃

יז וְחֶסֶד יהוה ׀ מֵעוֹלָם וְעַד־עוֹלָם עַל־יְרֵאָיו
וְצִדְקָתוֹ לִבְנֵי בָנִים׃

---

that He breathed His spirit into us, but it was into an earthly body that He breathed it. We have spiritual potential, but we resist it because we are but dust. We can rise above our earthly bodies, but He sympathizes with the fact that we seldom do so.

Man's days are as grass. Our days on earth are numbered, limited. Had we

18. of those who keep His covenant,
and remember to observe His precepts.

19. The LORD has established His throne in heaven,
and His kingdom rules over all.

20. Bless the LORD, you His angels,
mighty in power, who do His bidding,
and obey His spoken word.

21. Bless the LORD, all His Hosts,
you His servants who do His will.

22. Bless the LORD, all His works,
everywhere in His domain.
Bless the LORD, O my soul.

---

generation or two at most, we will be forgotten by all but Him. He therefore pities us, forgives us, and shows us His infinite kindness.

Furthermore, He often rewards us and renders us immortal. He does it by granting us progeny: *His righteousness reaches out to the children's children.*

After all is said and done, is that not what we all hope for?

יח לְשֹׁמְרֵי בְרִיתוֹ
וּלְזֹכְרֵי פִקֻּדָיו לַעֲשׂוֹתָם׃

יט יהוה בַּשָּׁמַיִם הֵכִין כִּסְאוֹ
וּמַלְכוּתוֹ בַּכֹּל מָשָׁלָה׃

כ בָּרְכוּ יהוה מַלְאָכָיו
גִּבֹּרֵי כֹחַ עֹשֵׂי דְבָרוֹ
לִשְׁמֹעַ בְּקוֹל דְּבָרוֹ׃

כא בָּרְכוּ יהוה כָּל־צְבָאָיו
מְשָׁרְתָיו עֹשֵׂי רְצוֹנוֹ׃

כב בָּרְכוּ יהוה ׀ כָּל־מַעֲשָׂיו
בְּכָל־מְקֹמוֹת מֶמְשַׁלְתּוֹ
בָּרְכִי נַפְשִׁי אֶת־יְהוָה׃

When the wind passes over it, it is gone, and its place knows it no more. We are fragile; our lives are more easily snuffed out than a candle. A wind can vanquish us; it can cause us to vanish. We are easily forgotten. We find that impossible to internalize. But God knows full well that in a short time, a

PSALM 104

Twenty-first day of the month

1. Bless the Lord, O my soul!
Lord, my God, You are very great,
You are clothed in glory and majesty.

2. He wraps Himself with light as with a garment;
He has spread out the heavens like a veil.

3. He has laid the girders of His chambers on the waters;
He makes the clouds His chariot,
and speeds along on the wings of the wind.

4. He makes the winds His messengers,
fiery flames His ministers.

5. He established the earth on its foundations,
so that it shall never be moved.

6. You covered it with the deep like a cloak;
the waters stood above the mountains.

7. But at Your rebuke they* fled,
at the sound of Your thunders they rushed away,

8. rising over the hills,
flowing down into the valleys,
to the place You appointed for them.

9. You set a boundary which they were not to pass;
never again shall they cover the earth.

* I.e., the waters.

מזמור קד *Psalm 104:* The term *Halleluya,* which Rabbi Cashdan consistently translates as *Praise the Lord*, is used very frequently in Jewish liturgy, and is familiar to worshippers of other faiths as well.

Our psalm, Psalm 104, is the first in which this term is used. Why was it never used earlier?

The Talmud (*Berakhot* 9b) answers: "King David waited to utter the phrase

מזמור קד

I was just a city boy. City boys think they know everything, but they don't. They know Man's world, but not the world Where the "grass grows" and "the trees are well watered." That's God's world. He showed His world to me. Now I'm not just a city boy. I am His world's boy. What a difference!

כא לחודש

א בָּרְכִ֥י נַפְשִׁ֗י אֶת־יְה֫וָ֥ה
יְהוָ֣ה אֱ֭לֹהַי גָּדַ֣לְתָּ מְּאֹ֑ד
ה֖וֹד וְהָדָ֣ר לָבָֽשְׁתָּ׃

ב עֹֽטֶה־א֭וֹר כַּשַּׂלְמָ֑ה
נוֹטֶ֥ה שָׁ֝מַ֗יִם כַּיְרִיעָֽה׃

ג הַֽמְקָרֶ֥ה בַמַּ֗יִם עֲֽלִיּ֫וֹתָ֥יו
הַשָּׂם־עָבִ֥ים רְכוּב֑וֹ
הַ֝מְהַלֵּ֗ךְ עַל־כַּנְפֵי־רֽוּחַ׃

ד עֹשֶׂ֣ה מַלְאָכָ֣יו רוּח֑וֹת
מְ֝שָׁרְתָ֗יו אֵ֣שׁ לֹהֵֽט׃

ה יָֽסַד־אֶ֭רֶץ עַל־מְכוֹנֶ֑יהָ
בַּל־תִּ֝מּ֗וֹט עוֹלָ֥ם וָעֶֽד׃

ו תְּ֭הוֹם כַּלְּב֣וּשׁ כִּסִּית֑וֹ
עַל־הָ֝רִ֗ים יַֽעַמְדוּ־מָֽיִם׃

ז מִן־גַּעֲרָתְךָ֣ יְנוּס֑וּן
מִן־ק֥וֹל רַ֝עַמְךָ֗ יֵחָפֵזֽוּן׃

ח יַעֲל֣וּ הָ֭רִים יֵרְד֣וּ בְקָע֑וֹת
אֶל־מְ֝ק֗וֹם זֶ֤ה ׀ יָסַ֬דְתָּ לָהֶֽם׃

ט גְּֽבוּל־שַׂ֭מְתָּ בַּל־יַעֲבֹר֑וּן
בַּל־יְ֝שׁוּב֗וּן לְכַסּ֥וֹת הָאָֽרֶץ׃

10. He makes springs break out in the valleys,
their waters flow between the hills,

11. supplying drink to all the wild beasts;
there the wild asses quench their thirst.

12. Nearby nest the birds of the air;
among the branches they sing their song.

13. He waters the mountains from His lofty chambers;
the earth is sated with the fruit of His* work.

14. He makes grass grow for the cattle,
and vegetation for man's needs,
that he may produce bread from the earth,

15. and wine to cheer the heart of man;
oil to make his face shine,
and bread to strengthen man's heart.

16. The trees of the LORD are well watered,
so, too, the cedars of Lebanon which He planted.

17. There the birds build their nests;
the stork has its home on the fir trees.

18. The high mountains are for the wild goats,
the crags are a shelter for the badgers.

19. He made the moon to mark the seasons;
the sun knows the time of its setting.

20. You bring on darkness and it is night;
then all the beasts of the forest are astir.

* Hebrew "Your."

Halleluya until he first witnessed the downfall of the wicked, as is written (in the last verse of our psalm), *May sinners disappear from the earth, and the wicked exist no more!... Halleluya! Praise the LORD!*

Rabbi Joseph Dov Soloveitchik, twentieth-century Talmudic sage and philosopher, is astounded by this passage. Is this the first time David alludes to the downfall of the wicked? Did we not already read in the very first psalm

י הַֽמְשַׁלֵּ֣חַ מַ֭עְיָנִים בַּנְּחָלִ֑ים
בֵּ֥ין הָ֝רִ֗ים יְהַלֵּכֽוּן׃

יא יַ֭שְׁקוּ כָּל־חַיְת֣וֹ שָׂדָ֑י
יִשְׁבְּר֖וּ פְרָאִ֣ים צְמָאָֽם׃

יב עֲ֭לֵיהֶם עֽוֹף־הַשָּׁמַ֣יִם יִשְׁכּ֑וֹן
מִבֵּ֥ין עֳ֝פָאיִ֗ם יִתְּנוּ־קֽוֹל׃

יג מַשְׁקֶ֣ה הָ֭רִים מֵעֲלִיּוֹתָ֑יו
מִפְּרִ֥י מַ֝עֲשֶׂ֗יךָ תִּשְׂבַּ֥ע הָאָֽרֶץ׃

יד מַצְמִ֤יחַ חָצִ֨יר ׀ לַבְּהֵמָ֗ה
וְ֭עֵשֶׂב לַעֲבֹדַ֣ת הָאָדָ֑ם
לְה֥וֹצִיא לֶ֝֗חֶם מִן־הָאָֽרֶץ׃

טו וְיַ֤יִן ׀ יְשַׂמַּ֬ח לְֽבַב־אֱנ֗וֹשׁ
לְהַצְהִ֣יל פָּנִ֣ים מִשָּׁ֑מֶן
וְ֝לֶ֗חֶם לְֽבַב־אֱנ֥וֹשׁ יִסְעָֽד׃

טז יִ֭שְׂבְּעוּ עֲצֵ֣י יְהוָ֑ה
אַרְזֵ֥י לְ֝בָנ֗וֹן אֲשֶׁ֣ר נָטָֽע׃

יז אֲשֶׁר־שָׁ֭ם צִפֳּרִ֣ים יְקַנֵּ֑נוּ
חֲ֝סִידָ֗ה בְּרוֹשִׁ֥ים בֵּיתָֽהּ׃

יח הָרִ֣ים הַ֭גְּבֹהִים לַיְּעֵלִ֑ים
סְ֝לָעִ֗ים מַחְסֶ֥ה לַשְׁפַנִּֽים׃

יט עָשָׂ֣ה יָ֭רֵחַ לְמוֹעֲדִ֑ים
שֶׁ֝֗מֶשׁ יָדַ֥ע מְבוֹאֽוֹ׃

כ תָּֽשֶׁת־חֹ֭שֶׁךְ וִ֣יהִי לָ֑יְלָה
בּֽוֹ־תִ֝רְמֹשׂ כָּל־חַיְתוֹ־יָֽעַר׃

21. The young lions roar for their prey,
seeking their food from God.

22. When the sun rises they stalk away,
and lie down in their dens.

23. Then man goes to his work,
and to his labor until evening.

24. How manifold are Your works, LORD!
You made them all with wisdom;
the earth is full of Your creations.

25. There is the sea, vast and wide,
teeming with countless creatures,
large and small alike.

26. There ships go to and fro,
Leviathan also, which You formed to sport with.

27. They all look expectantly to You,
to give them their food in due season.

28. When You give it to them, they gather it up;
when You open Your hand, they are well satisfied.

29. When You hide Your face, they are dismayed;
when You take away their breath, they perish,
and return to dust.

30. When You send back Your spirit, they are created anew,
and You give new life to the earth.

---

that *the way of the wicked is doomed*? Did the third psalm not declare that God *smashes the teeth of the wicked*?

Rav Soloveitchik encourages us to read a bit further along in that Talmudic passage. There we read the fascinating story of R. Meir, taunted so cruelly by a band of hooligans in his neighborhood that he was about to pray for them to die.

כא הַכְּפִירִים שֹׁאֲגִים לַטָּרֶף
וּלְבַקֵּשׁ מֵאֵל אׇכְלָם׃

כב תִּזְרַח הַשֶּׁמֶשׁ יֵאָסֵפוּן
וְאֶל־מְעוֹנֹתָם יִרְבָּצוּן׃

כג יֵצֵא אָדָם לְפׇעֳלוֹ
וְלַעֲבֹדָתוֹ עֲדֵי־עָרֶב׃

כד מָה־רַבּוּ מַעֲשֶׂיךָ ׀ יְהוָה
כֻּלָּם בְּחׇכְמָה עָשִׂיתָ
מָלְאָה הָאָרֶץ קִנְיָנֶךָ׃

כה זֶה ׀ הַיָּם גָּדוֹל וּרְחַב יָדָיִם
שָׁם־רֶמֶשׂ וְאֵין מִסְפָּר
חַיּוֹת קְטַנּוֹת עִם־גְּדֹלוֹת׃

כו שָׁם אֳנִיּוֹת יְהַלֵּכוּן
לִוְיָתָן זֶה־יָצַרְתָּ לְשַׂחֶק־בּוֹ׃

כז כֻּלָּם אֵלֶיךָ יְשַׂבֵּרוּן
לָתֵת אׇכְלָם בְּעִתּוֹ׃

כח תִּתֵּן לָהֶם יִלְקֹטוּן
תִּפְתַּח יָדְךָ יִשְׂבְּעוּן טוֹב׃

כט תַּסְתִּיר פָּנֶיךָ יִבָּהֵלוּן
תֹּסֵף רוּחָם יִגְוָעוּן
וְאֶל־עֲפָרָם יְשׁוּבוּן׃

ל תְּשַׁלַּח רוּחֲךָ יִבָּרֵאוּן
וּתְחַדֵּשׁ פְּנֵי אֲדָמָה׃

31. May the glory of the LORD endure forever;
may the LORD rejoice in His works!

32. When He looks at the earth, it trembles;
when He touches the mountains, they pour forth smoke.

33. As long as I live I will sing to the LORD;
I will chant praises to my God all my life.

34. May my meditation be pleasing to Him;
I will rejoice in the LORD.

35. May sinners disappear from the earth,
and the wicked exist no more!
Bless the LORD, O my soul.
Praise the LORD!*

* Hebrew "*Halleluya*." The Hebrew term is a musical direction given to the singer. It comes as a surprise to many to learn that the term "*Halleluya*," so frequent in the Jewish liturgy, is found only in the last fifty chapters of the book of Psalms.

The message of the perennial possibility of repentance is embedded in every verse of our psalm. God is everywhere: *He wraps Himself with light.... He makes the clouds His chariot.... He makes the winds His messengers.... He waters the mountains.... He makes grass grow.* If God is to be found in every nook and cranny of nature, surely He can be found within the heart of man.

"There is some good in every person," writes Rav Soloveitchik. "In the shambles of his life and underneath the mountains of his misdeeds, a candle yet burns!"

לא יְהִי כְבוֹד יְהוָה לְעוֹלָם
יִשְׂמַח יְהוָה בְּמַעֲשָׂיו׃

לב הַמַּבִּיט לָאָרֶץ וַתִּרְעָד
יִגַּע בֶּהָרִים וְיֶעֱשָׁנוּ׃

לג אָשִׁירָה לַיהוָה בְּחַיָּי
אֲזַמְּרָה לֵאלֹהַי בְּעוֹדִי׃

לד יֶעֱרַב עָלָיו שִׂיחִי
אָנֹכִי אֶשְׂמַח בַּיהוָה׃

לה יִתַּמּוּ חַטָּאִים ׀ מִן־הָאָרֶץ
וּרְשָׁעִים ׀ עוֹד אֵינָם
בָּרְכִי נַפְשִׁי אֶת־יְהוָה
הַלְלוּיָהּ׃

However, his wife Bruriah objected: "You must be resorting to the phrase *may sinners disappear from the earth*. But the word *ḥata'im* has two different meanings: *sinners* and *sins*. I prefer the second meaning. Read it my way: *May the* **sins** *disappear from the* earth. Pray that the sinners repent. Then *the wicked will exist no more!*"

At first, David refused to use the term *Halleluya* with regard to the defeat of the wicked. God does not rejoice in the punishment of even the cruelest of His creatures. Celebrating their downfall with *Halleluya* was out of the question.

In our psalm David reaches the conclusion that there is a corrective option for the worst of the wicked – repentance! He can now exclaim *Halleluya. May sin disappear… Praise the Lord!*

PSALM 105

1. Give thanks to the LORD! Call upon His name;
make known His deeds among the peoples.

2. Sing to Him; sing praises to Him;
speak of all His marvelous deeds.

3. Take pride in His holy name;
let the hearts that seek the LORD rejoice.

4. Seek the LORD and His strength;
*seek His presence at all times.

5. Remember the miracles that He performed,
His wonders, and the judgments that He pronounced,

6. O descendants of Abraham, His servant,
O sons of Jacob, His chosen ones.

7. He is the LORD, our God;
His judgments cover the whole earth.

8. He remembers His covenant forever,
the promise that He made to a thousand generations:

9. the covenant that He made with Abraham,
the promise on oath that He gave to Isaac.

10. He confirmed it as a decree to Jacob,
to Israel as an eternal covenant,

* "His strength" represents "the Ark of God"; cf. Ps. 78:61, 132:8.

מזמור קה *Psalm 105:* The previous psalm spoke of the wonders of God's creation, of nature and its everlasting beauty. Our psalm speaks of God's care for His people, of history and its ever-changing events.

Our psalm summarizes the history of the Jewish people, beginning with the covenant He made with Abraham. It culminates with a concise and cogent description of our slavery in Egypt, the Exodus, and the years in the wilderness, and finally our entry into the Promised Land. The last verse in

מזמור קה

History repeats itself. We must learn its many lessons. The story of our forefathers is our story. It began with God's promise to Abraham. Abraham was just the beginning. Joseph's trials added suspense to the story. Slavery ensued. Finally, the climax: Exodus and Redemption. But the story didn't end there. The story continues.

א הוֹדוּ לַיהוָה קִרְאוּ בִּשְׁמוֹ
הוֹדִיעוּ בָעַמִּים עֲלִילוֹתָיו:

ב שִׁירוּ־לוֹ זַמְּרוּ־לוֹ
שִׂיחוּ בְּכָל־נִפְלְאוֹתָיו:

ג הִתְהַלְלוּ בְּשֵׁם קָדְשׁוֹ
יִשְׂמַח לֵב | מְבַקְשֵׁי יְהוָה:

ד דִּרְשׁוּ יְהוָה וְעֻזּוֹ
בַּקְּשׁוּ פָנָיו תָּמִיד:

ה זִכְרוּ נִפְלְאוֹתָיו אֲשֶׁר־עָשָׂה
מֹפְתָיו וּמִשְׁפְּטֵי־פִיו:

ו זֶרַע אַבְרָהָם עַבְדּוֹ
בְּנֵי יַעֲקֹב בְּחִירָיו:

ז הוּא יְהוָה אֱלֹהֵינוּ
בְּכָל־הָאָרֶץ מִשְׁפָּטָיו:

ח זָכַר לְעוֹלָם בְּרִיתוֹ
דָּבָר צִוָּה לְאֶלֶף דּוֹר:

ט אֲשֶׁר כָּרַת אֶת־אַבְרָהָם
וּשְׁבוּעָתוֹ לְיִשְׂחָק:

י וַיַּעֲמִידֶהָ לְיַעֲקֹב לְחֹק
לְיִשְׂרָאֵל בְּרִית עוֹלָם:

11. saying, "To you I will give the land of Canaan
as your allotted heritage."

12. When they were but few in number,
very few, and strangers in the land,

13. wandering from country to country,
from one kingdom to another.

14. He allowed no one to oppress them;
He rebuked kings on their account:

15. "Touch not My anointed ones;
do not harm My prophets."

16. He called down a famine on the land,
and cut off all supply of bread.

17. But He had sent a man ahead of them,
Joseph, who was sold into slavery.

18. They pressed his feet into fetters,
his neck was put in irons;

19. until what he foretold came to pass,
and the word of the LORD proved him true.

20. The king sent and released him,
the ruler of peoples set him free.

21. He made him master of his house,
ruler of all his possessions,

22. with power to imprison princes at will,
and to instruct the elders in wisdom.

---

our psalm is all-important, for it clearly states the purpose of the entire long and arduous process: *that they might keep His statutes and observe His laws.*

Our sages tells us that this psalm was composed by David to be sung as he brought the Holy Ark from its place in captivity to the City of David, Jerusalem. This moment was one of great triumph for David, and it is no wonder that he attempted to connect the moment to his nation's past glory.

יא לֵאמֹ֗ר לְךָ֗ אֶתֵּ֥ן אֶת־אֶֽרֶץ־כְּנָ֑עַן
חֶ֝֗בֶל נַחֲלַתְכֶֽם׃

יב בִּֽהְיוֹתָ֗ם מְתֵ֣י מִסְפָּ֑ר
כִּ֝מְעַ֗ט וְגָרִ֥ים בָּֽהּ׃

יג וַֽיִּתְהַלְּכוּ֮ מִגּ֪וֹי אֶל־גּ֫וֹי
מִ֝מַּמְלָכָ֗ה אֶל־עַ֥ם אַחֵֽר׃

יד לֹא־הִנִּ֣יחַ אָדָ֣ם לְעָשְׁקָ֑ם
וַ֖יּוֹכַח עֲלֵיהֶ֣ם מְלָכִֽים׃

טו אַל־תִּגְּע֥וּ בִמְשִׁיחָ֑י
וְ֝לִנְבִיאַ֗י אַל־תָּרֵֽעוּ׃

טז וַיִּקְרָ֣א רָ֭עָב עַל־הָאָ֑רֶץ
כָּֽל־מַטֵּה־לֶ֥חֶם שָׁבָֽר׃

יז שָׁלַ֣ח לִפְנֵיהֶ֣ם אִ֑ישׁ
לְ֝עֶ֗בֶד נִמְכַּ֥ר יוֹסֵֽף׃

יח עִנּ֣וּ בַכֶּ֣בֶל רגליו רַגְל֑וֹ
בַּ֝רְזֶ֗ל בָּ֣אָה נַפְשֽׁוֹ׃

יט עַד־עֵ֥ת בֹּֽא־דְבָר֑וֹ
אִמְרַ֖ת יְהוָ֣ה צְרָפָֽתְהוּ׃

כ שָׁ֣לַח מֶ֭לֶךְ וַיַּתִּירֵ֑הוּ
מֹשֵׁ֥ל עַ֝מִּ֗ים וַֽיְפַתְּחֵֽהוּ׃

כא שָׂמ֣וֹ אָד֣וֹן לְבֵית֑וֹ
וּ֝מֹשֵׁ֗ל בְּכָל־קִנְיָנֽוֹ׃

כב לֶאְסֹ֣ר שָׂרָ֣יו בְּנַפְשׁ֑וֹ
וּזְקֵנָ֥יו יְחַכֵּֽם׃

23. Then Israel came down to Egypt,
Jacob came to live in the land of Ham.

24. There God made His people very fruitful,
more numerous than their foes.

25. He turned their hearts to hate His people,
to conspire against His servants.

26. He sent Moses His servant,
and Aaron whom He had chosen.

27. They performed among them His wonderful signs,
and His miracles in the land of Ham.

28. He sent darkness and all was dark,
and none disobeyed His word.*

29. He turned their waters into blood,
and caused their fish to die.

30. Their land swarmed with frogs,
even in the royal apartments.

31. He commanded and there came a mixture of harmful creatures,
and lice too, throughout their country.

32. He turned their rain into hail,
with lightning flashing throughout their land.

33. He struck down their vines and fig trees,
and shattered the trees of their territory.

34. He commanded and the locusts came,
and grasshoppers without number.

* I.e., the plagues carried out the tasks they were sent to do (Rashi).

There was no greater glory in its past than the exodus from Egypt. He celebrated his present achievement and his future destiny by remembering the past and its significance. In doing so he set the pattern for all future Jewish celebrations to follow. They all must be *zekher liyetziat Mitzrayim*. They must recall the exodus from Egypt.

כג וַיָּבֹא יִשְׂרָאֵל מִצְרָיִם
וְיַעֲקֹב גָּר בְּאֶרֶץ־חָם׃

כד וַיֶּפֶר אֶת־עַמּוֹ מְאֹד
וַיַּעֲצִמֵהוּ מִצָּרָיו׃

כה הָפַךְ לִבָּם לִשְׂנֹא עַמּוֹ
לְהִתְנַכֵּל בַּעֲבָדָיו׃

כו שָׁלַח מֹשֶׁה עַבְדּוֹ
אַהֲרֹן אֲשֶׁר בָּחַר־בּוֹ׃

כז שָׂמוּ־בָם דִּבְרֵי אֹתוֹתָיו
וּמֹפְתִים בְּאֶרֶץ חָם׃

כח שָׁלַח חֹשֶׁךְ וַיַּחְשִׁךְ
וְלֹא־מָרוּ אֶת־דבריו׃ דְּבָרוֹ

כט הָפַךְ אֶת־מֵימֵיהֶם לְדָם
וַיָּמֶת אֶת־דְּגָתָם׃

ל שָׁרַץ אַרְצָם צְפַרְדְּעִים
בְּחַדְרֵי מַלְכֵיהֶם׃

לא אָמַר וַיָּבֹא עָרֹב
כִּנִּים בְּכָל־גְּבוּלָם׃

לב נָתַן גִּשְׁמֵיהֶם בָּרָד
אֵשׁ לֶהָבוֹת בְּאַרְצָם׃

לג וַיַּךְ גַּפְנָם וּתְאֵנָתָם
וַיְשַׁבֵּר עֵץ גְּבוּלָם׃

לד אָמַר וַיָּבֹא אַרְבֶּה
וְיֶלֶק וְאֵין מִסְפָּר׃

35. They devoured every blade of grass in their land,
and consumed the produce of their soil.

36. Then He struck down all the first-born in the land,
the first fruits of their manhood.

37. He led out His people, laden with silver and gold,
and among their tribes not one stumbled.

38. The Egyptians were glad when they left,
for the dread of Israel had fallen on them.

39. He spread a cloud to screen them,
and fire to light up the night.

40. They asked [for food], and He sent them quails;
He satisfied them with bread from heaven.

41. He opened a rock and water gushed out;
it flowed like a river in the parched land.

42. Mindful of His sacred promise
that He made to His servant Abraham,

43. He brought out His people with joy,
His chosen ones with songs of triumph.

---

occasions not just for remembering past glory, but for appreciating God's ongoing place in our lives. We celebrate not just by singing, but by singing to Him. We *remember the miracles that He performed, His wonders, and the judgments that He pronounced*. And we acknowledge that the events we currently celebrate were also accompanied by His miracles and wonders, perhaps not quite as miraculous or as wondrous as were those of the past, but miracles and wonders nonetheless.

God is ever present in Jewish history; in days of yore, and in our own time and place. Our psalm befits David's successes. It also befits every success we experience in our own lives, down to this very day. *Sing to Him, sing praises to Him, and speak of all His marvelous deeds.*

לה וַיֹּאכַל כׇּל־עֵשֶׂב בְּאַרְצָם
וַיֹּאכַל פְּרִי אַדְמָתָם׃

לו וַיַּךְ כׇּל־בְּכוֹר בְּאַרְצָם
רֵאשִׁית לְכׇל־אוֹנָם׃

לז וַיּוֹצִיאֵם בְּכֶסֶף וְזָהָב
וְאֵין בִּשְׁבָטָיו כּוֹשֵׁל׃

לח שָׂמַח מִצְרַיִם בְּצֵאתָם
כִּי־נָפַל פַּחְדָּם עֲלֵיהֶם׃

לט פָּרַשׂ עָנָן לְמָסָךְ
וְאֵשׁ לְהָאִיר לָיְלָה׃

מ שָׁאַל וַיָּבֵא שְׂלָו
וְלֶחֶם שָׁמַיִם יַשְׂבִּיעֵם׃

מא פָּתַח צוּר וַיָּזוּבוּ מָיִם
הָלְכוּ בַּצִּיּוֹת נָהָר׃

מב כִּי־זָכַר אֶת־דְּבַר קׇדְשׁוֹ
אֶת־אַבְרָהָם עַבְדּוֹ׃

מג וַיּוֹצִא עַמּוֹ בְשָׂשׂוֹן
בְּרִנָּה אֶת־בְּחִירָיו׃

In every age, and in all circumstances, present and future must be linked to the past. This perspective is fundamental to the Jewish experience. A celebration of national achievement, which is not accompanied by the component of memory of the past, is not a fully Jewish celebration.

But recollection of history is in itself insufficient. It must be accompanied by the recognition of God's role in our history. Current celebrations are

44. He gave them the lands of nations;
they took possession of what other people had toiled for,

45. so that they might keep His statutes
and observe His laws.
Praise the Lord!

מד וַיִּתֵּ֣ן לָ֭הֶם אַרְצ֣וֹת גּוֹיִ֑ם
וַעֲמַ֖ל לְאֻמִּ֣ים יִירָֽשׁוּ׃

מה בַּעֲב֤וּר ׀ יִשְׁמְר֣וּ חֻ֭קָּיו
וְתוֹרֹתָ֥יו יִנְצֹ֗רוּ
הַֽלְלוּיָֽהּ׃

PSALM 106

Twenty-second day of the month

1. Praise the LORD!
Give thanks to the LORD for He is good;
His loving-kindness endures forever.

2. Who can put into words the mighty acts of the LORD?
Who can declare all the praise due to Him?

3. Happy are those who act with justice,
who do what is right at all times.

4. Remember me, LORD, when You favor Your people,
count me among those who enjoy Your saving power,

5. that I too may share the welfare of Your chosen ones,
rejoice in the happiness of Your own people,
and take pride in Your heritage.

6. We have sinned like our forefathers;
we have done wrong,
we have acted wickedly.

7. Our fathers in Egypt did not appreciate Your miracles;
they did not remember Your many acts of kindness,
but they rebelled at the sea, at the Sea of Reeds.

8. Nevertheless He saved them because of His name,
to make known His power.

9. He rebuked the Sea of Reeds and it dried up;
He led them through the deep as through a desert.

10. He saved them from the hand of the enemy,
and freed them from the grip of the foe.

מזמור קו *Psalm 106:* Our psalm is a continuation of the previous one, but with one sharp difference. In Psalm 105, we recount God's glory, the wondrous acts He performed for His people. In that psalm the people suffer, but they do not sin. They certainly do not rebel.

In our psalm, God's wondrous acts are also recounted. But the people do

מזמור קו

We sin. He forgives us. We take that for granted. After all, He is a forgiving God. We sin again, and again. He still forgives us. That's unbelievable! Who can declare all the praise due to Him?

א הַֽלְלוּיָ֨הּ ׀ ה֣וֹדוּ לַיהֹוָ֣ה כִּי־ט֑וֹב כב לחודש
כִּ֖י לְעוֹלָ֣ם חַסְדּֽוֹ׃

ב מִ֗י יְ֭מַלֵּל גְּבוּר֣וֹת יְהֹוָ֑ה
יַ֝שְׁמִ֗יעַ כׇּל־תְּהִלָּתֽוֹ׃

ג אַ֭שְׁרֵי שֹׁמְרֵ֣י מִשְׁפָּ֑ט
עֹשֵׂ֖ה צְדָקָ֣ה בְכׇל־עֵֽת׃

ד זׇכְרֵ֣נִי יְ֭הֹוָה בִּרְצ֣וֹן עַמֶּ֑ךָ
פׇּ֝קְדֵ֗נִי בִּישׁוּעָתֶֽךָ׃

ה לִרְא֤וֹת ׀ בְּט֬וֹבַת בְּחִירֶ֗יךָ
לִ֭שְׂמֹחַ בְּשִׂמְחַ֣ת גּוֹיֶ֑ךָ
לְ֝הִתְהַלֵּ֗ל עִם־נַחֲלָתֶֽךָ׃

ו חָטָ֥אנוּ עִם־אֲבוֹתֵ֑ינוּ
הֶ֝עֱוִ֗ינוּ הִרְשָֽׁעְנוּ׃

ז אֲבוֹתֵ֬ינוּ בְמִצְרַ֨יִם ׀ לֹא־הִשְׂכִּ֡ילוּ נִפְלְאוֹתֶ֗יךָ
לֹ֣א זָ֭כְרוּ אֶת־רֹ֣ב חֲסָדֶ֑יךָ
וַיַּמְר֖וּ עַל־יָ֣ם בְּיַם־סֽוּף׃

ח וַ֭יּוֹשִׁיעֵם לְמַ֣עַן שְׁמ֑וֹ
לְ֝הוֹדִ֗יעַ אֶת־גְּבוּרָתֽוֹ׃

ט וַיִּגְעַ֣ר בְּיַם־ס֭וּף וַֽיֶּחֱרָ֑ב
וַיּוֹלִיכֵ֥ם בַּ֝תְּהֹמ֗וֹת כַּמִּדְבָּֽר׃

י וַ֭יּוֹשִׁיעֵם מִיַּ֣ד שׂוֹנֵ֑א
וַ֝יִּגְאָלֵ֗ם מִיַּ֥ד אוֹיֵֽב׃

11. The waters covered their adversaries,
not one of them survived.

12. Then they believed His words,
and they sang His praises.

13. But they quickly forgot what He had done;
they would not await [the working out of] His plan.

14. They craved for food in the desert,
and challenged God in the barren waste.

15. He gave them what they desired,
but sent a wasting disease among them.

16. They grew envious of Moses in the camp,
of Aaron, too, the holy one of the Lord.

17. The earth opened up and swallowed Dathan,
and covered over the company of Abiram.

18. Fire blazed up among their company,
and flames devoured the wicked.

19. They made a calf at Horeb,
and bowed down to a molten figure.

20. They exchanged Him who was their glory
for the image of a grass-eating ox.

21. They forgot God, their deliverer,
who had done great things in Egypt,

22. wonders in the land of Ham,
and awesome deeds at the Sea of Reeds.

---

sin, and indeed rebel. *Our fathers in Egypt did not appreciate Your miracles… they rebelled at the sea.* Any yet, God not only forgives them, but He does not cease to do wonders for them. *Nevertheless… He saved them from the hand of the enemy.*

If the previous psalm is an assertion of God's abiding place in the course of our history, our psalm is a testament to His fidelity to the Jewish people, even when they do not deserve His assistance.

יא וַיְכַסּוּ־מַיִם צָרֵיהֶם
אֶחָד מֵהֶם לֹא נוֹתָר׃

יב וַיַּאֲמִינוּ בִדְבָרָיו
יָשִׁירוּ תְּהִלָּתוֹ׃

יג מִהֲרוּ שָׁכְחוּ מַעֲשָׂיו
לֹא־חִכּוּ לַעֲצָתוֹ׃

יד וַיִּתְאַוּוּ תַאֲוָה בַּמִּדְבָּר
וַיְנַסּוּ־אֵל בִּישִׁימוֹן׃

טו וַיִּתֵּן לָהֶם שֶׁאֱלָתָם
וַיְשַׁלַּח רָזוֹן בְּנַפְשָׁם׃

טז וַיְקַנְאוּ לְמֹשֶׁה בַּמַּחֲנֶה
לְאַהֲרֹן קְדוֹשׁ יְהוָה׃

יז תִּפְתַּח־אֶרֶץ וַתִּבְלַע דָּתָן
וַתְּכַס עַל־עֲדַת אֲבִירָם׃

יח וַתִּבְעַר־אֵשׁ בַּעֲדָתָם
לֶהָבָה תְּלַהֵט רְשָׁעִים׃

יט יַעֲשׂוּ־עֵגֶל בְּחֹרֵב
וַיִּשְׁתַּחֲווּ לְמַסֵּכָה׃

כ וַיָּמִירוּ אֶת־כְּבוֹדָם
בְּתַבְנִית שׁוֹר אֹכֵל עֵשֶׂב׃

כא שָׁכְחוּ אֵל מוֹשִׁיעָם
עֹשֶׂה גְדֹלוֹת בְּמִצְרָיִם׃

כב נִפְלָאוֹת בְּאֶרֶץ חָם
נוֹרָאוֹת עַל־יַם־סוּף׃

23. He would have destroyed them,
were it not for Moses, His chosen one,
who stood in the breach before Him,
to restrain His fury from destroying them.

24. Then they spurned the most desirable land;
they had no faith in His word.

25. They grumbled in their tents;
they would not heed the voice of the LORD.

26. So He raised His hand and swore
to let them fall in the wilderness,

27. to scatter* their children among the nations,
and to disperse them throughout the lands.

28. They attached themselves to Baal Peor,
and ate offerings made to lifeless gods.

29. They provoked Him with their practices,
and a plague broke out among them.

30. Then Phinehas stood up and executed judgment,
and the plague was checked.

31. This was credited to him as a merit,
for all generations, forever.

32. They angered the LORD also at the waters of Meribah,
and Moses fared ill on their account.

33. For they rebelled against His spirit,
and he** spoke rashly with his lips.

* Lit. "to make fall"; cf. Targum.

** I.e., Moses.

Our psalm is thus of great theological significance. It is a resounding rebuttal of the contention that we are no longer God's Chosen People, that we have been superseded by others, because of our sins.

Our psalm records a lengthy catalog of our misdeeds: *they quickly forgot…*

כג וַיֹּאמֶר לְֽהַשְׁמִ֫ידָ֥ם
לוּלֵ֡י מֹשֶׁ֣ה בְחִיר֗וֹ עָמַ֣ד בַּפֶּ֣רֶץ לְפָנָ֑יו
לְהָשִׁ֥יב חֲ֝מָת֗וֹ מֵֽהַשְׁחִֽית׃

כד וַֽיִּמְאֲס֗וּ בְּאֶ֣רֶץ חֶמְדָּ֑ה
לֹא־הֶ֝אֱמִ֗ינוּ לִדְבָרֽוֹ׃

כה וַיֵּרָגְנ֥וּ בְאָהֳלֵיהֶ֑ם
לֹ֥א שָׁ֝מְע֗וּ בְּק֣וֹל יְהוָֽה׃

כו וַיִּשָּׂ֣א יָד֣וֹ לָהֶ֑ם
לְהַפִּ֥יל א֝וֹתָ֗ם בַּמִּדְבָּֽר׃

כז וּלְהַפִּ֣יל זַ֭רְעָם בַּגּוֹיִ֑ם
וּ֝לְזָר֗וֹתָם בָּאֲרָצֽוֹת׃

כח וַ֭יִּצָּמְדוּ לְבַ֣עַל פְּע֑וֹר
וַ֝יֹּאכְל֗וּ זִבְחֵ֥י מֵתִֽים׃

כט וַ֭יַּכְעִיסוּ בְּמַֽעַלְלֵיהֶ֑ם
וַתִּפְרָץ־בָּ֝֗ם מַגֵּפָֽה׃

ל וַיַּעֲמֹ֣ד פִּ֭ינְחָס וַיְפַלֵּ֑ל
וַ֝תֵּעָצַ֗ר הַמַּגֵּפָֽה׃

לא וַתֵּחָ֣שֶׁב ל֭וֹ לִצְדָקָ֑ה
לְדֹ֥ר וָ֝דֹ֗ר עַד־עוֹלָֽם׃

לב וַ֭יַּקְצִיפוּ עַל־מֵ֣י מְרִיבָ֑ה
וַיֵּ֥רַע לְ֝מֹשֶׁ֗ה בַּעֲבוּרָֽם׃

לג כִּֽי־הִמְר֥וּ אֶת־רוּח֑וֹ
וַ֝יְבַטֵּ֗א בִּשְׂפָתָֽיו׃

34. They did not exterminate the peoples
as the LORD had commanded them,

35. but they mingled with the nations,
and learned their practices.

36. They served their idols
which became a snare to them.

37. They even sacrificed their own sons
and daughters to demons.

38. They shed innocent blood,
the blood of their sons and daughters
whom they sacrificed to the idols of Canaan;
and the land was polluted with blood.

39. They became defiled by their actions,
and were wanton in their behavior.

40. So the LORD's anger blazed against His people,
and He abhorred His heritage.

41. He handed them over to the nations;
their foes ruled over them.

42. Their enemies oppressed them;
they were crushed under their rule.

43. Time and again He rescued them;
but they were defiant in their schemes,
and were brought low by their guilt.

44. Yet He heeded their distress
when He heard their cry.

---

they challenged God... they grew envious of Moses... they made a calf at Horeb... they exchanged Him for the image of a grass-eating ox... they spurned the land... they had no faith... they grumbled... they provoked Him... they angered Him... they shed innocent blood.

Indeed, He held them to account for all of this evil. He did not let them off lightly. *He handed them over to the nations.*

לד לֹֽא־הִ֭שְׁמִידוּ אֶת־הָֽעַמִּ֑ים
אֲשֶׁ֤ר אָמַ֖ר יְהֹוָ֣ה לָהֶֽם׃

לה וַיִּתְעָרְב֥וּ בַגּוֹיִ֑ם
וַֽ֝יִּלְמְד֗וּ מַעֲשֵׂיהֶֽם׃

לו וַיַּעַבְד֥וּ אֶת־עֲצַבֵּיהֶ֑ם
וַיִּהְי֖וּ לָהֶ֣ם לְמוֹקֵֽשׁ׃

לז וַיִּזְבְּח֣וּ אֶת־בְּ֭נֵיהֶם וְאֶת־בְּֽנוֹתֵיהֶ֗ם לַשֵּׁדִֽים׃

לח וַיִּשְׁפְּכ֨וּ דָ֪ם נָקִ֡י
דַּֽם־בְּנֵיהֶ֣ם וּבְנֽוֹתֵיהֶ֗ם
אֲשֶׁ֣ר זִ֭בְּחוּ לַעֲצַבֵּ֣י כְנָ֑עַן
וַתֶּחֱנַ֥ף הָ֝אָ֗רֶץ בַּדָּמִֽים׃

לט וַיִּטְמְא֥וּ בְמַעֲשֵׂיהֶ֑ם
וַ֝יִּזְנ֗וּ בְּמַעַלְלֵיהֶֽם׃

מ וַיִּֽחַר־אַ֣ף יְהֹוָ֣ה בְּעַמּ֑וֹ
וַ֝יְתָעֵ֗ב אֶת־נַחֲלָתֽוֹ׃

מא וַיִּתְּנֵ֥ם בְּיַד־גּוֹיִ֑ם
וַיִּמְשְׁל֥וּ בָ֝הֶ֗ם שֹׂנְאֵיהֶֽם׃

מב וַיִּלְחָצ֥וּם אוֹיְבֵיהֶ֑ם
וַ֝יִּכָּנְע֗וּ תַּ֣חַת יָדָֽם׃

מג פְּעָמִ֥ים רַבּ֗וֹת יַצִּ֫ילֵ֥ם
וְ֭הֵמָּה יַמְר֣וּ בַעֲצָתָ֑ם
וַ֝יָּמֹ֗כּוּ בַּעֲוֺנָֽם׃

מד וַיַּ֭רְא בַּצַּ֣ר לָהֶ֑ם
בְּ֝שָׁמְע֗וֹ אֶת־רִנָּתָֽם׃

45. For their sake He remembered His covenant,
and in His great loving-kindness relented.

46. He roused compassion for them
in the heart of all their captors.

47. LORD our God, save us!
Gather us from among the nations,
that we may give thanks to Your holy name,
and glory in Your praise.

48. Blessed be the LORD, the God of Israel,
from eternity to eternity!
And let all the people say, "Amen!"
Praise the LORD!

The answer lies in our verse 44, which reads, in Rabbi Cashdan's translation, *Yet He heeded their distress when He heard their cry.* The Hebrew word which Rabbi Cashdan translates as "cry" is *rina,* which in most instances means "song," not "cry." The rabbis of the hasidic dynasty of Modzitz, who are known for the emphasis they place upon the use of joyous melodies in spiritual worship, insist that "*rina*" should be translated, even in our verse, as "song." God heeds us when we sing in spite of our distress, when we preserve our sense of joy in His worship even while we suffer. This, they insist, is why He has not abandoned us. He will not abandon a people who resist despair, and remain joyously faithful no matter their situation.

Our psalm teaches us that He has kept His covenant with us precisely because of the joyful quality of our commitment to Him, a mode of worship which He especially cherishes, one which is the very essence of the Jewish people – "*rina,*" song!

מה וַיִּזְכֹּ֣ר לָהֶ֣ם בְּרִית֑וֹ
וַ֝יִּנָּחֵ֗ם כְּרֹ֣ב חֲסָדָֽו׃

מו וַיִּתֵּ֣ן אוֹתָ֣ם לְרַחֲמִ֑ים
לִ֝פְנֵ֗י כָּל־שׁוֹבֵיהֶֽם׃

מז הוֹשִׁיעֵ֨נוּ ׀ יהוה אֱלֹהֵ֗ינוּ
וְקַבְּצֵ֗נוּ מִֽן־הַ֫גּוֹיִ֥ם
לְ֭הוֹדוֹת לְשֵׁ֣ם קׇדְשֶׁ֑ךָ
לְ֝הִשְׁתַּבֵּ֗חַ בִּתְהִלָּתֶֽךָ׃

מח בָּר֤וּךְ יהוה ׀ אֱלֹהֵ֪י יִשְׂרָאֵ֡ל
מִן־הָעוֹלָ֨ם ׀ וְעַ֬ד הָעוֹלָ֗ם
וְאָמַ֣ר כׇּל־הָעָ֣ם אָ֭מֵן הַֽלְלוּיָֽהּ׃

But He did not reject them totally. He did not permanently displace them from His favor. He certainly did not allow them to be superseded by another people. *He remembered His covenant, and in His great loving-kindness relented.*

The theological significance of our psalm as an irrefutable statement of the unique place of the Jewish people cannot be overestimated.

One may legitimately ask for God's reason for such great forbearance. Why does He continue to redeem His people in spite of their tendency to sin and sin again?

PSALM 107

1. "Give thanks to the LORD, for He is good; *Friday*
His loving-kindness endures forever!"

2. Let the redeemed of the LORD say this –
those whom He redeemed from the hand of the enemy,

3. and those whom He gathered out of the lands,
from east and west, from the north and from the sea.

4. Some lost their way in the wilderness, in the wasteland,
finding no path to a town to live in.

5. Hungry and thirsty,
their spirit began to fail.

6. Then they cried to the LORD in their trouble,
and He rescued them from their distress.

7. He led them by a straight way
to a city where they could settle.

8. Let them give thanks to the LORD for His goodness,
and for His wonderful deeds for men;

9. for He satisfied the thirsty soul,
and filled the hungry with all good things.

10. Some were living in darkness and in gloom,
fettered in misery and irons,

מזמור קז *Psalm 107:* Our psalm charts the ups and downs of life. It portrays conditions of flourishing success, which suddenly deteriorate into arid deserts. And it contrasts those conditions with pitiful ones, which are transformed instantly and beneficially.

It describes four nightmarish scenarios: the wayfarer lost in the wilderness, the prisoner, the person suffering from illness, and the sailor in the stormy sea.

Those scenarios are timeless. We too cross seas and deserts, albeit more frequently by airplane than by ship or caravan. Jailed prisoners are as numerous

מזמור קז

I spend my week wandering in the wilderness. The path to safety eludes me. I feel shackled, chained to the dungeon's walls. No exit. Nausea denies me every pleasure. I am tossed about by the waves of circumstance. Shabbat draws near, and the path slowly emerges from its shroud. With Shabbat comes freedom, healing, and a safe harbor. With Shabbat comes gratitude, and the ability to express it.

ליום שישי

א הֹדוּ לַיהוָה כִּי־טוֹב
כִּי לְעוֹלָם חַסְדּוֹ׃

ב יֹאמְרוּ גְּאוּלֵי יהוָה
אֲשֶׁר גְּאָלָם מִיַּד־צָר׃

ג וּמֵאֲרָצוֹת קִבְּצָם
מִמִּזְרָח וּמִמַּעֲרָב מִצָּפוֹן וּמִיָּם׃

ד תָּעוּ בַמִּדְבָּר בִּישִׁימוֹן דָּרֶךְ
עִיר מוֹשָׁב לֹא מָצָאוּ׃

ה רְעֵבִים גַּם־צְמֵאִים
נַפְשָׁם בָּהֶם תִּתְעַטָּף׃

ו וַיִּצְעֲקוּ אֶל־יהוה בַּצַּר לָהֶם
מִמְּצוּקוֹתֵיהֶם יַצִּילֵם׃

ז וַיַּדְרִיכֵם בְּדֶרֶךְ יְשָׁרָה
לָלֶכֶת אֶל־עִיר מוֹשָׁב׃

ח יוֹדוּ לַיהוָה חַסְדּוֹ
וְנִפְלְאוֹתָיו לִבְנֵי אָדָם׃

ט כִּי־הִשְׂבִּיעַ נֶפֶשׁ שֹׁקֵקָה
וְנֶפֶשׁ רְעֵבָה מִלֵּא־טוֹב׃

י יֹשְׁבֵי חֹשֶׁךְ וְצַלְמָוֶת
אֲסִירֵי עֳנִי וּבַרְזֶל׃

11. because they had rebelled against God's commands,
and spurned the counsel of the Most High.

12. So He humbled their hearts with hardship;
they stumbled, and there was no one to help.

13. Then they cried to the LORD in their trouble,
and He saved them from their distress.

14. He brought them out from the darkness and gloom,
and snapped their bonds asunder.

15. Let them give thanks to the LORD for His goodness,
and for His wonderful deeds for men;

16. for He broke down gates of bronze,
and cut through iron bars.

17. Some were fools, suffering because of their rebellious ways,
and because of their iniquities.

18. They loathed all food,
and were near death's door.

19. Then they cried to the LORD in their trouble,
and He saved them from their distress.

20. He sent His word and healed them,
and delivered them from the pit of death.

21. Let them give thanks to the LORD for His goodness,
and for His wonderful deeds for men.

22. Let them offer sacrifices of thanksgiving,
and tell of His deeds with songs of joy.

---

as ever. Despite the advances of modern medicine, debilitating illnesses are still with us.

However, nowadays few of us are troubled by travel. We traverse oceans or wastelands with ease. Most of us do not face the threat of prison. But sickness remains a universal source of anxiety.

Radak focuses on the differences between sickness and the other three

יא כִּֽי־הִ֭מְרוּ אִמְרֵי־אֵ֑ל
וַעֲצַ֖ת עֶלְי֣וֹן נָאָֽצוּ׃

יב וַיַּכְנַ֣ע בֶּעָמָ֣ל לִבָּ֑ם
כָּ֝שְׁל֗וּ וְאֵ֣ין עֹזֵֽר׃

יג וַיִּזְעֲק֣וּ אֶל־יְ֭הוָה בַּצַּ֣ר לָהֶ֑ם
מִ֝מְּצֻ֥קוֹתֵיהֶ֗ם יוֹשִׁיעֵֽם׃

יד י֭וֹצִיאֵם מֵחֹ֣שֶׁךְ וְצַלְמָ֑וֶת
וּמוֹסְר֖וֹתֵיהֶ֣ם יְנַתֵּֽק׃

טו יוֹד֣וּ לַיהוָ֣ה חַסְדּ֑וֹ
וְ֝נִפְלְאוֹתָ֗יו לִבְנֵ֥י אָדָֽם׃

טז כִּֽי־שִׁ֭בַּר דַּלְת֣וֹת נְחֹ֑שֶׁת
וּבְרִיחֵ֖י בַרְזֶ֣ל גִּדֵּֽעַ׃

יז אֱ֭וִלִים מִדֶּ֣רֶךְ פִּשְׁעָ֑ם
וּ֝מֵעֲוֺנֹתֵיהֶ֗ם יִתְעַנּֽוּ׃

יח כָּל־אֹ֭כֶל תְּתַעֵ֣ב נַפְשָׁ֑ם
וַ֝יַּגִּ֗יעוּ עַד־שַׁ֥עֲרֵי מָֽוֶת׃

יט וַיִּזְעֲק֣וּ אֶל־יְ֭הוָה בַּצַּ֣ר לָהֶ֑ם
מִ֝מְּצֻ֥קוֹתֵיהֶ֗ם יוֹשִׁיעֵֽם׃

כ יִשְׁלַ֣ח דְּ֭בָרוֹ וְיִרְפָּאֵ֑ם
וִֽ֝ימַלֵּ֗ט מִשְּׁחִיתוֹתָֽם׃

כא יוֹד֣וּ לַיהוָ֣ה חַסְדּ֑וֹ
וְ֝נִפְלְאוֹתָ֗יו לִבְנֵ֥י אָדָֽם׃

כב וְ֭יִזְבְּחוּ זִבְחֵ֣י תוֹדָ֑ה
וִיסַפְּר֖וּ מַעֲשָׂ֣יו בְּרִנָּֽה׃

23. Others went down to the sea in ships,
plying their trade on the mighty waters.

24. They saw the works of the LORD,
and His wonderful deeds in the deep.

25. By His word He raised a storm,
that lifted high the waves.

26. They mounted up to heaven,
they went down to the depths;
their hearts melted away in their plight.

27. They reeled and staggered like drunken men;
all their skill was of no avail.

28. Then they cried to the LORD in their trouble,
and He delivered them from their distress.

29. He stilled the storm to a whisper,
and the waves were hushed.

30. They were glad when all was calm,
and He guided them to their desired haven.

31. Let them give thanks to the LORD for His goodness,
and for His wonderful deeds for men.

---

disease. He could have taken measures to ensure his health or at least to minimize the severity of the illness. Hence, the sick person is singled out as a "fool." His failure to care for himself is itself a sin.

Radak also notes that, alone among the four sufferers, the sick person offers *sacrifices of thanksgiving*. This is a consequence of the long duration of his recovery. Unlike the prisoner who may be freed in moment, or the wayfarer who suddenly discovers the road home, the ill person recovers slowly, over a long period of time. His feelings are allowed to ripen and slowly mature.

He thus does not spontaneously burst into a song of thanksgiving. Rather,

כג יוֹרְדֵי הַיָּם בָּאֳנִיּוֹת
עֹשֵׂי מְלָאכָה בְּמַיִם רַבִּים׃ ׆

כד הֵמָּה רָאוּ מַעֲשֵׂי יהוה
וְנִפְלְאוֹתָיו בִּמְצוּלָה׃ ׆

כה וַיֹּאמֶר וַיַּעֲמֵד רוּחַ סְעָרָה
וַתְּרוֹמֵם גַּלָּיו׃ ׆

כו יַעֲלוּ שָׁמַיִם יֵרְדוּ תְהוֹמוֹת
נַפְשָׁם בְּרָעָה תִתְמוֹגָג׃ ׆

כז יָחוֹגּוּ וְיָנוּעוּ כַּשִּׁכּוֹר
וְכָל־חָכְמָתָם תִּתְבַּלָּע׃ ׆

כח וַיִּצְעֲקוּ אֶל־יהוה בַּצַּר לָהֶם
וּמִמְּצוּקֹתֵיהֶם יוֹצִיאֵם׃

כט יָקֵם סְעָרָה לִדְמָמָה
וַיֶּחֱשׁוּ גַּלֵּיהֶם׃

ל וַיִּשְׂמְחוּ כִי־יִשְׁתֹּקוּ
וַיַּנְחֵם אֶל־מְחוֹז חֶפְצָם׃

לא יוֹדוּ לַיהוה חַסְדּוֹ
וְנִפְלְאוֹתָיו לִבְנֵי אָדָם׃

---

circumstances described in the text. He notes that the sick person is referred to as a fool. *Some were fools, suffering because of their rebellious ways.*

Long before he was immobilized by his illness, the sick person was forewarned. Early warning signs existed at the disease's onset, but were ignored. He could have mitigated his illness had he acted earlier in the course of the

32. Let them exalt Him in the assembly of the people,
and praise Him in the council of the elders.

33. Sometimes God turns rivers into a wilderness,
springs of water into thirsty ground;

34. the fruitful land into a salt waste,
because of the wickedness of the people who live there.

35. Sometimes He turns the desert into pools of water,
the parched ground into flowing springs.

36. There He settles the hungry,
and they build themselves a city to live in.

37. They sow fields and plant vineyards
that yield a fruitful harvest.

38. He blesses them, and their numbers increase,
and does not let their herds decrease.

39. And when people grow few and are brought low,
through tyranny, affliction and sorrow,

40. He pours contempt on those tyrants,
and makes them wander in a trackless waste.

---

recited in the synagogue by all who have crossed the sea or the wilderness, have been freed from prison, or have recovered from illness.

Why in the synagogue? The answer lies in our verse 32: *Let them exalt Him in the assembly of the people, and praise Him in the council of the elders.*

Thanksgiving is not a private moment. It is a public acknowledgment of one's indebtedness to God. Furthermore, it is a religious act, not to be exhibited before just any public, but before a *council of elders.*

Our psalm, which is recited in many congregations on the eve of the Sabbath, helps one recognize the degree to which he must feel grateful not just for emerging from the urgent challenges which occasionally confront us, but for the strength to cope with the struggles of the six days of the week, the ordinary problems of living.

לב וִירוֹמְמוּהוּ בִּקְהַל־עָם
וּבְמוֹשַׁב זְקֵנִים יְהַלְלוּהוּ׃

לג יָשֵׂם נְהָרוֹת לְמִדְבָּר
וּמֹצָאֵי מַיִם לְצִמָּאוֹן׃

לד אֶרֶץ פְּרִי לִמְלֵחָה
מֵרָעַת יוֹשְׁבֵי בָהּ׃

לה יָשֵׂם מִדְבָּר לַאֲגַם־מַיִם
וְאֶרֶץ צִיָּה לְמֹצָאֵי מָיִם׃

לו וַיּוֹשֶׁב שָׁם רְעֵבִים
וַיְכוֹנְנוּ עִיר מוֹשָׁב׃

לז וַיִּזְרְעוּ שָׂדוֹת וַיִּטְּעוּ כְרָמִים
וַיַּעֲשׂוּ פְּרִי תְבוּאָה׃

לח וַיְבָרְכֵם וַיִּרְבּוּ מְאֹד
וּבְהֶמְתָּם לֹא יַמְעִיט׃

לט וַיִּמְעֲטוּ וַיָּשֹׁחוּ
מֵעֹצֶר רָעָה וְיָגוֹן׃ ׆

מ שֹׁפֵךְ בּוּז עַל־נְדִיבִים
וַיַּתְעֵם בְּתֹהוּ לֹא־דָרֶךְ׃

he considers his response carefully, paying attention to his nuanced feelings as they become modified over the months and years. He plans the details of his sacrifice, and personalizes them. He returns to a healthy life, ennobled by gratefulness.

The Talmud finds in our psalm the source for the obligation to offer sacrifices of thanksgiving. Nowadays, in lieu of a sacrifice, a special blessing is

41. The needy He lifts high out of trouble,
and increases their families like flocks of sheep.

42. The upright see it and rejoice,
while the mouth of wickedness is silenced.

43. Whoever is wise, let him heed these things,
and ponder on the LORD's loving-kindness.

מא וַיְשַׂגֵּב אֶבְיוֹן מֵעוֹנִי
וַיָּשֶׂם כַּצֹּאן מִשְׁפָּחוֹת׃

מב יִרְאוּ יְשָׁרִים וְיִשְׂמָחוּ
וְכָל־עַוְלָה קָפְצָה פִּיהָ׃

מג מִי־חָכָם וְיִשְׁמָר־אֵלֶּה
וְיִתְבּוֹנְנוּ חַסְדֵי יְהוָה׃

PSALM 108

Twenty-third day of the month

1. A song. A psalm of David.
2. *My heart is steadfast, God.
I will sing and chant praises;
indeed, it is my honor to do so.
3. Awake, O harp and lyre!
I will awaken the dawn.
4. I will praise You, LORD, among the nations;
I will sing praises to You among the peoples.
5. For Your loving-kindness is higher than the heavens;
Your truth reaches to the sky.
6. Be exalted, God, above the heavens;
let Your glory be over all the earth.
7. In order that those dear to You may be delivered,
save with Your right hand and answer me.
8. God declared in His sanctuary that I would triumph;
I would divide Shechem,
and measure out the Valley of Sukkoth.
9. Gilead would be mine, Manasseh mine;
Ephraim my chief stronghold, Judah my scepter.

* This psalm is composed of portions of two psalms in Book II. Verses 2–6 are a repeat of Psalm 57:8 –12, and verses 7–14 of Psalm 60:7–14, with some slight differences.

The careful reader of Psalms will have himself noticed what is indicated in the asterisked comment at the beginning of our translation. Our psalm is an almost exact repetition of two earlier psalms. Our initial verses repeat a section of Psalm 57, while the last verses appeared in Psalm 60. The few minor differences between the texts do not seem sufficiently significant to warrant such repetition.

Furthermore, both earlier psalms carry prescripts which clearly identify the circumstances under which they were written. Psalm 57 was written

מזמור קח

We cannot brazenly knock on God's door and expect Him to answer. We must first prepare ourselves. He won't take us seriously unless we take ourselves seriously. Therefore, many meditate introspectively before they knock. That helps a bit. I do what David did. He summoned his harp and lyre. His music empowered him to pray. My music can't compare to his, so I just hum a tune. That gives me the confidence to knock on God's door.

א שִׁיר מִזְמוֹר לְדָוִד׃ כג לחודש

ב נָכוֹן לִבִּי אֱלֹהִים
אָשִׁירָה וַאֲזַמְּרָה אַף־כְּבוֹדִי׃

ג עוּרָה הַנֵּבֶל וְכִנּוֹר
אָעִירָה שָּׁחַר׃

ד אוֹדְךָ בָעַמִּים ׀ יְהוָה
וַאֲזַמֶּרְךָ בַּלְאֻמִּים׃

ה כִּי־גָדוֹל מֵעַל־שָׁמַיִם חַסְדֶּךָ
וְעַד־שְׁחָקִים אֲמִתֶּךָ׃

ו רוּמָה עַל־שָׁמַיִם אֱלֹהִים
וְעַל כָּל־הָאָרֶץ כְּבוֹדֶךָ׃

ז לְמַעַן יֵחָלְצוּן יְדִידֶיךָ
הוֹשִׁיעָה יְמִינְךָ ועננו׃ וַעֲנֵנִי

ח אֱלֹהִים ׀ דִּבֶּר בְּקָדְשׁוֹ אֶעְלֹזָה
אֲחַלְּקָה שְׁכֶם וְעֵמֶק סֻכּוֹת אֲמַדֵּד׃

ט לִי גִלְעָד ׀ לִי מְנַשֶּׁה
וְאֶפְרַיִם מָעוֹז רֹאשִׁי
יְהוּדָה מְחֹקְקִי׃

קח *Psalm 108:* Our psalm teaches us an important lesson about the nature of language. Sometimes identical words can be used to describe very different circumstances.

10. Moab would be my wash-basin,
over Edom I would fling my shoe;
I would shout in triumph over Philistia.

11. But who will conduct me to the fortified city?
Who will lead me to Edom?

12. Have You not rejected us, God?
You no longer, God, go out with our armies.

13. Give us aid against the foe,
for worthless is the help of man.

14. With God's help we shall triumph;
it is He who will trample our foes.

---

together with the stick of Judah to form one stick." Our psalm thus speaks of that future time when *Shechem… the Valley of Sukkoth… Manasseh… Ephraim* will all accept the leadership of *Judah my scepter.*

Radak is fully aware that the listing of Moab and Edom and Philistia in verses 10 and 11 is anachronistic. These nations fell into oblivion long before the drama of Israel's final redemption. Radak dismisses this difficulty: "These are references to the geographic locales which were once occupied by these ancient nations." He finds ample precedent for this use of the names of ancient nations in the prophecies of Isaiah and Daniel.

Radak's thesis allows him to reread these verses with inspirational results. One example: the very first verse now becomes the occasion for the "David" who endured the exile and now leads his people out of it to assert that his *heart is steadfast,* meaning he never despaired of redemption, and that he *will sing and chant* despite the exile's painful frustrations.

The repetition of sections of previous psalms in our psalm is a challenging puzzle. Radak offers an approach to the puzzle which is inspirational and educational. We are inspired by the hopefulness which pervades Jewish history. And our education is advanced as we learn that the psalmist is able to describe radically different human circumstances in identical words and phrases.

י מוֹאָב ׀ סִיר רַחְצִי
עַל־אֱדוֹם אַשְׁלִיךְ נַעֲלִי
עֲלֵי־פְלֶשֶׁת אֶתְרוֹעָע׃

יא מִי יֹבִלֵנִי עִיר מִבְצָר
מִי נָחַנִי עַד־אֱדוֹם׃

יב הֲלֹא־אֱלֹהִים זְנַחְתָּנוּ
וְלֹא־תֵצֵא אֱלֹהִים בְּצִבְאֹתֵינוּ׃

יג הָבָה־לָּנוּ עֶזְרָת מִצָּר
וְשָׁוְא תְּשׁוּעַת אָדָם׃

יד בֵּאלֹהִים נַעֲשֶׂה־חָיִל
וְהוּא יָבוּס צָרֵינוּ׃

---

when David *fled from Saul into a cave.* Psalm 60 was written on the occasion of David's battle *against Aram-Nuharaim and Aram-Zobah.* Yet our psalm mentions neither of those historical contexts.

Radak therefore suggests that the previous psalms refer to David's own lived experiences, historical happenings. Our psalm, on the other hand, foretells events which have not yet occurred, prophetic visions.

Taking this approach further, Radak demonstrates just how the identical language can fit both the circumstances of David's ordeals and the promise of Israel's ultimate redemption. He begins by pointing out that Psalms 57 and 60 both contain very specific references to King David's life which would be entirely out of place in a psalm foretelling the future redemption. Thus, our psalm omits those references.

He argues that verses 8 and 9 take on a new meaning once they are understood as references to the prophetic vision of a unified Jewish people. He alludes to the prophecy of Ezekiel (37:19) which speaks of the eventual coming together of all the tribes of Israel under the leadership of the tribe of Judah: "*Behold I will take the stick of Joseph… and the tribes of Israel his companions…*

PSALM 109

1. For the Chief Musician. Of David. A psalm.
God, to whom I offer praise, do not be silent.

2. For wicked and deceitful men open their mouths against me;
they speak to me with lying tongues.

3. They surround me with words of hate;
they attack me without cause.

4. In return for my love they accuse me,
yet I pray [for them].

5. They repay me evil for good,
hatred for my love.

6. [They say:] "Appoint over him a wicked man [as his judge];
let the accuser stand at his right hand.

7. When he is tried, let him be found guilty;
may his plea incriminate him.

8. May his days be few;
may another take over his office!

9. May his children be fatherless,
and his wife a widow!

10. May his children be wandering beggars,
seeking [bread] far from their ruined homes!

מזמור קט *Psalm 109:* In our psalm David is confronted with a thoroughly treacherous enemy, one that our people, and many of us as individuals, have encountered all too frequently. This enemy maligns us viciously behind our backs, but to our face professes friendship. They *open their mouths **against** me,* but when *they speak **to** me* it is *with lying tongues.*

Such a foe is all the more intolerable because of the relationship we have previously had with him. We showed him love and friendship, but now he has reciprocated with hatred and enmity.

מזמור קט

Why do they hate me? I love them. I love Him. Do they hate me because I love Him? Can they not tolerate my love for Him? Is it Him they really hate? Or is it my love for them that they despise? These questions have no answer. They necessitated the invention of a new term: "anti-Semitism."

א לַמְנַצֵּ֗חַ לְדָוִ֥ד מִזְמ֑וֹר
אֱלֹהֵ֥י תְ֝הִלָּתִ֗י אַֽל־תֶּחֱרַֽשׁ׃

ב כִּ֤י פִ֪י רָשָׁ֡ע וּֽפִי־מִ֭רְמָה עָלַ֣י פָּתָ֑חוּ
דִּבְּר֥וּ אִ֝תִּ֗י לְשׁ֣וֹן שָֽׁקֶר׃

ג וְדִבְרֵ֣י שִׂנְאָ֣ה סְבָב֑וּנִי
וַיִּֽלָּחֲמ֥וּנִי חִנָּֽם׃

ד תַּֽחַת־אַהֲבָתִ֥י יִשְׂטְנ֗וּנִי
וַאֲנִ֥י תְפִלָּֽה׃

ה וַיָּ֤שִׂימוּ עָלַ֣י רָ֭עָה תַּ֣חַת טוֹבָ֑ה
וְ֝שִׂנְאָ֗ה תַּ֣חַת אַהֲבָתִֽי׃

ו הַפְקֵ֣ד עָלָ֣יו רָשָׁ֑ע
וְ֝שָׂטָ֗ן יַעֲמֹ֥ד עַל־יְמִינֽוֹ׃

ז בְּ֭הִשָּׁפְטוֹ יֵצֵ֣א רָשָׁ֑ע
וּ֝תְפִלָּת֗וֹ תִּהְיֶ֥ה לַחֲטָאָֽה׃

ח יִֽהְיוּ־יָמָ֥יו מְעַטִּ֑ים
פְּ֝קֻדָּת֗וֹ יִקַּ֥ח אַחֵֽר׃

ט יִֽהְיוּ־בָנָ֥יו יְתוֹמִ֑ים
וְ֝אִשְׁתּ֗וֹ אַלְמָנָֽה׃

י וְנ֤וֹעַ יָנ֣וּעוּ בָנָ֣יו וְשִׁאֵ֑לוּ
וְ֝דָרְשׁ֗וּ מֵֽחָרְבוֹתֵיהֶֽם׃

11. May a creditor seize everything he has,
and strangers plunder the fruits of his labor!

12. May no one show him any kindness
or take pity on his fatherless children!

13. May his posterity be cut off;
by the next generation may their names be blotted out!

14. May the iniquity of his fathers
be remembered before the Lord;
may the sin of his mother never be blotted out;

15. may they be continually before the Lord,
till He cuts off all memory of them from the earth!

16. For he never thought of doing a kind deed,
but persecuted the poor and the needy
and hounded to death the broken-hearted.

17. He loved to curse – may the curse light on him!
He would not bless – may blessing be far from him!

18. He clothed himself with cursing like a garment;
may it enter his body like water
and into his bones like oil!

19. May it wrap him round like the clothes that he wears,
like the belt that he puts on every day!"

20. May this* be the punishment of my accusers from the Lord,
and of those who speak evil against me.

21. But You, God my Lord,
deal with me as befits Your name,
Your loving-kindness benefits all – save me!

* I.e., the curses enumerated above.

It would therefore not be surprising that David would respond with great resentment, and angrily curse such a foe. Most traditional commentators indeed see verses 6 to 19 as such an angry response. They understand these

יא יְנַקֵּ֣שׁ נ֭וֹשֶׁה לְכׇל־אֲשֶׁר־ל֑וֹ
וְיָבֹ֖זּוּ זָרִ֣ים יְגִיעֽוֹ׃

יב אַל־יְהִי־ל֭וֹ מֹשֵׁ֣ךְ חָ֑סֶד
וְאַל־יְהִ֥י ח֝וֹנֵ֗ן לִיתוֹמָֽיו׃

יג יְהִֽי־אַחֲרִית֥וֹ לְהַכְרִ֑ית
בְּד֥וֹר אַ֝חֵ֗ר יִמַּ֥ח שְׁמָֽם׃

יד יִזָּכֵ֤ר ׀ עֲוֺ֣ן אֲ֭בֹתָיו אֶל־יְהֹוָ֑ה
וְחַטַּ֥את אִ֝מּ֗וֹ אַל־תִּמָּֽח׃

טו יִהְי֣וּ נֶגֶד־יְהֹוָ֣ה תָּמִ֑יד
וְיַכְרֵ֖ת מֵאֶ֣רֶץ זִכְרָֽם׃

טז יַ֗עַן אֲשֶׁ֤ר ׀ לֹ֥א זָכַר֮ עֲשׂ֢וֹת חָ֥סֶד
וַיִּרְדֹּ֡ף אִישׁ־עָנִ֣י וְ֭אֶבְיוֹן
וְנִכְאֵ֥ה לֵ֝בָ֗ב לְמוֹתֵֽת׃

יז וַיֶּאֱהַ֣ב קְ֭לָלָה וַתְּבוֹאֵ֑הוּ
וְֽלֹא־חָפֵ֥ץ בִּ֝בְרָכָ֗ה וַתִּרְחַ֥ק מִמֶּֽנּוּ׃

יח וַיִּלְבַּ֣שׁ קְ֭לָלָה כְּמַ֫דּ֥וֹ
וַתָּבֹ֣א כַמַּ֣יִם בְּקִרְבּ֑וֹ
וְ֝כַשֶּׁ֗מֶן בְּעַצְמוֹתָֽיו׃

יט תְּהִי־ל֭וֹ כְּבֶ֣גֶד יַעְטֶ֑ה
וּ֝לְמֵ֗זַח תָּמִ֥יד יַחְגְּרֶֽהָ׃

כ זֹ֤את ׀ פְּעֻלַּ֣ת שֹׂ֭טְנַי מֵאֵ֣ת יְהֹוָ֑ה
וְהַדֹּבְרִ֥ים רָ֝֗ע עַל־נַפְשִֽׁי׃

כא וְאַתָּ֤ה ׀ יֱהֹוִ֬ה אֲדֹנָ֗י
עֲשֵׂה־אִ֭תִּי לְמַ֣עַן שְׁמֶ֑ךָ
כִּי־ט֥וֹב חַ֝סְדְּךָ֗ הַצִּילֵֽנִי׃

22. For I am poor and needy,
and my heart is deeply wounded within me.

23. I fade away like a declining shadow;
I am shaken off like a locust.

24. My knees give way from fasting,
my body is lean for lack of fatness.

25. I have become an object of scorn to them;
when they see me they shake their heads.

26. Help me, LORD my God.
Save me, in accordance with Your loving-kindness,

27. that men may know that this is Your hand,
that You alone, LORD, have done it.

28. So let them curse,
but You will bless;
let them rise up, only to be put to shame,
while Your servant rejoices.

29. My accusers shall be clothed in disgrace,
wrapped in their shame as in a cloak.

David asks that these curses, if they must be fulfilled, be directed at those who uttered them and not at him, their intended victim.

This is then an expression of David's refinement and nobility. He has been cursed by his enemies, but he has not cursed them. *So let them curse, but You will bless.* They evoked the harshest of curses against him: *May his days be few... may his children be fatherless.* He merely asks that their curses be ignored and their designs against him frustrated. He asks only that they *be put to shame... clothed in disgrace.*

Victory over such a foe, all the while retaining one's moral decency, calls for a special public expression of thanks to God. *In the midst of the throng I will praise Him.*

כב כִּי־עָנִי וְאֶבְיוֹן אָנֹכִי
וְלִבִּי חָלַל בְּקִרְבִּי׃

כג כְּצֵל כִּנְטוֹתוֹ נֶהֱלָכְתִּי
נִנְעַרְתִּי כָּאַרְבֶּה׃

כד בִּרְכַּי כָּשְׁלוּ מִצּוֹם
וּבְשָׂרִי כָּחַשׁ מִשָּׁמֶן׃

כה וַאֲנִי ׀ הָיִיתִי חֶרְפָּה לָהֶם
יִרְאוּנִי יְנִיעוּן רֹאשָׁם׃

כו עָזְרֵנִי יְהוָה אֱלֹהָי
הוֹשִׁיעֵנִי כְחַסְדֶּךָ׃

כז וְיֵדְעוּ כִּי־יָדְךָ זֹּאת
אַתָּה יְהוָה עֲשִׂיתָהּ׃

כח יְקַלְלוּ־הֵמָּה וְאַתָּה תְבָרֵךְ
קָמוּ ׀ וַיֵּבֹשׁוּ וְעַבְדְּךָ יִשְׂמָח׃

כט יִלְבְּשׁוּ שׂוֹטְנַי כְּלִמָּה
וְיַעֲטוּ כַמְעִיל בָּשְׁתָּם׃

verses as a litany of curses directed by David against his foes. Such a reaction would be natural, but it would not be morally exemplary.

Rav Hirsch argues that these verses are not emanating from David. Quite the contrary, they are the curses which David's foes hurled at him. He is quoting them. He is saying to God: "Look at how treacherous they are! They are cursing me so viciously. Please God; do not be influenced by these curses."

Rabbi Cashdan has wisely followed Rav Hirsch in his translation, and in his punctuation, putting verses 6–19 into quotation marks. David is quoting his enemies, citing the words they have used against him. Then, in verse 20,

30. I will greatly extol the LORD with my voice;
in the midst of the throng I will praise Him,

31. because He stands at the right hand of the needy
to save his life from those who would condemn him.

ל אֽ֫וֹדֶ֥ה יהוָ֣ה מְאֹ֣ד בְּפִ֑י
וּבְת֭וֹךְ רַבִּ֣ים אֲהַֽלְלֶֽנּוּ׃

לא כִּֽי־יַ֭עֲמֹד לִימִ֣ין אֶבְי֑וֹן
לְ֝הוֹשִׁ֗יעַ מִשֹּׁפְטֵ֥י נַפְשֽׁוֹ׃

PSALM 110

1. A psalm of David.
The LORD said to my lord,*
"Remain at My right hand,
while I make your enemies your footstool."

2. The LORD will send your mighty scepter from Zion, saying,
"hold sway in the midst of your enemies."

3. Your people will offer themselves willingly in holy attire
on the day of battle.
You retain the freshness of your youth,
like the dew that falls from the womb of the dawn.

4. The LORD has sworn, and will not relent;
"You are a priest forever
after the manner of Melchizedek."**

5. The LORD is at your right hand!
On the day when His anger is aroused,
he*** will crush kings.

* I.e., God's chosen king.

** The king and priest to the Most High God; see Gen. 14:18.

*** God's chosen king.

Following this approach, the psalm is centered about the life story of Abraham, especially his venture to combat the four kings, as described in Genesis 14. And so our psalm begins with *the LORD*, God, offering reassurance to *my* lord, Abraham, that if he would but be patient and remain at His right hand, his enemies would be vanquished. Abraham is frequently addressed by other characters in the Genesis narrative, particularly in chapter 23, as "my lord." So, "the LORD" addresses "my lord."

The mighty scepter that God sends Abraham from Zion is none other than Melchizedek, the king of Salem, who visits Abraham soon after his return from the battle. Salem, Jerusalem, and Zion are one and the same in rabbinic commentary.

מזמור קי

The Midrash paints a bloody scene. Revenge against millennia of evil is not a pretty sight. God the Judge will wear His royal robe. It will be stained with the blood of every martyr ever. God the Avenger will shatter the heads of all their murderers. Rivers of their blood will flow. A bird will try to drink from one such river, but will lift his head in flight. He will be repelled by the river's raging waves. The rivers will not quench the poor bird's thirst.

א לְדָוִד מִזְמוֹר
נְאֻם יהוה ׀ לַאדֹנִי שֵׁב לִימִינִי
עַד־אָשִׁית אֹיְבֶיךָ הֲדֹם לְרַגְלֶיךָ׃

ב מַטֵּה עֻזְּךָ יִשְׁלַח יהוה מִצִּיּוֹן
רְדֵה בְּקֶרֶב אֹיְבֶיךָ׃

ג עַמְּךָ נְדָבֹת בְּיוֹם חֵילֶךָ
בְּהַדְרֵי־קֹדֶשׁ מֵרֶחֶם מִשְׁחָר
לְךָ טַל יַלְדֻתֶיךָ׃

ד נִשְׁבַּע יהוה ׀ וְלֹא יִנָּחֵם
אַתָּה־כֹהֵן לְעוֹלָם
עַל־דִּבְרָתִי מַלְכִּי־צֶדֶק׃

ה אֲדֹנָי עַל־יְמִינְךָ
מָחַץ בְּיוֹם־אַפּוֹ מְלָכִים׃

מזמור קי *Psalm 110:* The theme of our psalm is very difficult to decipher. It has thus become the subject of multitudinous interpretations by the sages of Talmud and Midrash, and by the classical Jewish commentators. Radak goes so far as to present a Christian interpretation of our psalm, which he persuasively refutes on both linguistic and theological grounds. This refutation was censored in most editions for centuries, and was inaccessible to the average student until recently.

Rashi offers two alternate interpretations to our psalm, the first of which is especially interesting. He relies upon the Midrash on Psalms for this interpretation, although a slightly different version of it can be found in the Talmud (*Nedarim* 32b).

6. He will execute judgment upon the nations,
he will pile up the corpses,
shattering heads far and wide.

7. He will drink from the stream by the wayside;
therefore he will hold his head high.

The brutal images, near the end of our psalm, of *crushed kings, shattered heads,* and *piled up corpses,* refer to the fates of two sets of enemies. Firstly, they refer to the fate of the four kings against whom Abraham did battle, who were *smitten and pursued* (Gen. 14:15).

Ultimately, those phrases refer to the fate of the Egypt which enslaved Abraham's descendants. Abraham was foretold in Genesis 15:14: *And also that nation which they shall serve will I judge.* Their judgment will be especially severe because of their hubris, believing of the River Nile that *my river is my own and I have made it for myself* (Ezek. 29:3).

Hence, the concluding verse in our psalm: *He will drink from the stream by the wayside; therefore he will hold his head high.* It is Egypt, whose confidence in its "Nile stream" would lead it to arrogantly and defiantly "hold his head high" eventuated in its final downfall.

This is Rashi's preferred approach to interpreting our psalm, and it leaves most readers astonished by the precision with which each word and phrase of our psalm fits the Abraham narrative.

ו יָדִין בַּגּוֹיִם מָלֵא גְוִיּוֹת
מָחַץ רֹאשׁ עַל־אֶרֶץ רַבָּה׃

ז מִנַּחַל בַּדֶּרֶךְ יִשְׁתֶּה
עַל־כֵּן יָרִים רֹאשׁ׃

God then assures Abraham that *your people will offer themselves willingly on the day of battle,* and indeed Abraham has no difficulty in *leading forth his trained servants* (Gen. 14:14) and in enlisting the allegiance of his friends, *the men who went with me, Aner, Eshkol, and Mamre.*

Abraham warrants God's assistance because of his lifelong devotion to God. Thus, *like the dew that falls from the womb,* Abraham was devout almost from birth, recognizing His creator at the age of three.

We know that Abraham feared that the blood he shed in warfare would lead to his punishment and loss of the various rewards which God had promised him. But in our verse 4 he is assured that *the Lord has sworn, and will not relent.* He is reminded of the eternal blessing and the tithe that Melchizedek bestowed upon him.

PSALM 111

1. Praise the LORD!*
I will praise the LORD with all my heart
in the company and the assembly of the upright.

2. Great are the works of the LORD,
sought by all who delight in them.

3. Glorious and majestic are His deeds;
His righteousness endures forever.

4. He has won renown for His marvelous deeds;
the LORD is gracious and compassionate.

5. He gives food to those who fear Him;
He keeps His covenant ever in mind.

6. He showed His people His powerful works,
by giving them the lands of other nations.

7. His handiwork is truth and justice;
all His precepts are trustworthy.

* An alphabetical psalm, of twenty-two lines, corresponding to the twenty-two letters of the alphabet.

---

every alphabetically arranged psalm, then these two psalms are especially exalted. They differ only in the exalted theme which they each treat. The theme of our psalm is God, His might and His providence. The theme of the next psalm is Man and his capacity for piety, righteousness, and generosity.

But the brevity of these two psalms should not be mistaken for simplicity. The conception of God which our psalm enunciates is complex and subtle. God is not merely "high and mighty." He cares. Yes, He is a transcendent Being, but He does "come down to earth." *Glorious and majestic are His deeds,* but those deeds are not limited to the wonders of the solar system or the marvels of nature. Rather, they encompass His righteousness, graciousness, and compassion.

The power of our psalm is its ability to convey, in just a few short phrases, so many of the aspects of the Divine which characterize the Jewish notion

מִזְמוֹר קיא

Help me begin my search for wisdom. This world is vast and wonderful. Can I ever understand it? It is the Creator's world. Can I ever understand Him? I stand in awe of Him and revere the world He created. I must preserve that awe and never lose that reverence. They are my first steps on the path to wisdom.

א הַלְלוּיָהּ ׀ אוֹדֶה יְהוָה בְּכׇל־לֵבָב
בְּסוֹד יְשָׁרִים וְעֵדָה׃

ב גְּדֹלִים מַעֲשֵׂי יְהוָה
דְּרוּשִׁים לְכׇל־חֶפְצֵיהֶם׃

ג הוֹד־וְהָדָר פׇּעֳלוֹ
וְצִדְקָתוֹ עֹמֶדֶת לָעַד׃

ד זֵכֶר עָשָׂה לְנִפְלְאֹתָיו
חַנּוּן וְרַחוּם יְהוָה׃

ה טֶרֶף נָתַן לִירֵאָיו
יִזְכֹּר לְעוֹלָם בְּרִיתוֹ׃

ו כֹּחַ מַעֲשָׂיו הִגִּיד לְעַמּוֹ
לָתֵת לָהֶם נַחֲלַת גּוֹיִם׃

ז מַעֲשֵׂי יָדָיו אֱמֶת וּמִשְׁפָּט
נֶאֱמָנִים כׇּל־פִּקּוּדָיו׃

מזמור קיא *Psalm 111:* Our psalm and the next one have so much in common that they are best viewed as mirror images of each other. They are equally brief, each containing only ten verses. They are equally clear, consisting of direct assertions which leave little room for interpretive commentary. They contain no allusions to other biblical narratives.

Furthermore, they both begin with *"Halleluya!" Praise the Lord.* Even more striking, they both follow the Hebrew alphabet, with every verse containing two letters of the alphabet, except for the final two verses which each contain three letters of the alphabet.

If Radak is correct in his insistence that there is something exalted about

8. They are valid forever and ever,
enacted in truth and equity.

9. He sent freedom to His people;
He ordained His covenant for all time;
holy and awe-inspiring is His name.

10. Fear of the LORD is the beginning of wisdom;
all who act accordingly show good judgment.
His praise endures forever.

---

for God. More than that, to the extent that God is inextricably involved in every aspect of human existence, no area of human knowledge, neither science nor history nor ethics, can commence without taking God into account.

The statement heard in some philosophical circles to the effect that "God is dead" can only refer to a one-dimensional deity. But the God portrayed in our psalm is part and parcel of every aspect of the natural world and of human existence. To say that such a God is dead is tantamount to saying that the world does not exist.

ח סְמוּכִים לָעַד לְעוֹלָם
עֲשׂוּיִם בֶּאֱמֶת וְיָשָׁר׃

ט פְּדוּת ׀ שָׁלַח לְעַמּוֹ
צִוָּה־לְעוֹלָם בְּרִיתוֹ
קָדוֹשׁ וְנוֹרָא שְׁמוֹ׃

י רֵאשִׁית חָכְמָה ׀ יִרְאַת יהוה
שֵׂכֶל טוֹב לְכָל־עֹשֵׂיהֶם
תְּהִלָּתוֹ עֹמֶדֶת לָעַד׃

---

of God. He is Creator, Judge, Lawgiver, and Redeemer. *He gives food… keeps His covenant…* and shows *His people His powerful works.*

The concluding verse of our psalm is frequently quoted in our liturgy and is familiar even to schoolchildren. But from the perspective of its description of God as being infinitely multifaceted this verse takes on a much more profound meaning. It is not just that *fear of the Lord is the beginning of wisdom* in that one must preface one's search for wisdom upon a firm basis of reverence

8. His heart is firm, he has no fears;
in the end he will see the downfall of his enemies.

9. He gives to the needy indiscriminately;
his righteousness endures forever;
his dignity* rises high in honor.

10. The wicked man shall see it and be infuriated,
he will gnash his teeth and slink away;
the desire of the wicked will come to nothing.

* Lit. "horn."

He is a balanced person, and it is this inner equilibrium that sustains his dignity and earns him the honor, and the envy, of others. No wonder there are those who are so envious of him that they *gnash their teeth* in fury. They cannot tolerate his company, because his proximity makes them feel inadequate and guilty. But the scorn and even the hostility of others do not affect him. He remains who he is, a "good man," with an inner sense of right and wrong that cannot be shaken by the whims and winds of circumstance.

ח סָמ֣וּךְ לִ֭בּוֹ לֹ֣א יִירָ֑א
עַ֖ד אֲשֶׁר־יִרְאֶ֣ה בְצָרָֽיו׃

ט פִּזַּ֤ר ׀ נָ֘תַ֤ן לָֽאֶבְיוֹנִ֗ים
צִ֭דְקָתוֹ עֹמֶ֣דֶת לָעַ֑ד
קַ֝רְנ֗וֹ תָּר֥וּם בְּכָבֽוֹד׃

י רָשָׁ֤ע יִרְאֶ֨ה ׀ וְכָעָ֗ס
שִׁנָּ֣יו יַחֲרֹ֣ק וְנָמָ֑ס
תַּאֲוַ֖ת רְשָׁעִ֣ים תֹּאבֵֽד׃

Even when he attains wealth, power, and prestige, his essential righteousness remains unchanged. *Wealth and riches are in his house, yet his righteousness endures forever.*

Nor do times of difficulty cause him to lose his essential goodness. *Even in darkness* he continues to maintain his own standards of behavior. Furthermore, he *shines a light* to illuminate the path of others.

He is thrifty, but not stingy; generous, but not extravagant. He gives charity to a wide variety of needy persons, careful not to discriminate among them in a manner that would make them feel degraded.

PSALM 113

Twenty-fourth day of the month

1. Praise the LORD!
Praise, O servants of the LORD,
praise the name of the LORD.

2. May the name of the LORD be blessed
now and forevermore.

3. From the rising of the sun to its setting
the name of the LORD is praised.

4. High above all nations is the LORD;
His glory is above the heavens.

5. Who is like the LORD our God,
enthroned so high,

6. yet deigns to look down
on heaven and on earth?

Rav Hirsch suggests that there is an aspect to mundane life which also calls for Hallel, if only a muted incomplete Hallel. He writes:

It is out of a profound recognition of the fact that the wonders of God's loving-kindness are not limited to unusual events that we recite Hallel on Rosh Ḥodesh. Even in the course of our ordinary routine we must be aware of God's benevolence. As the sages insist, "Just as Redemption is wondrous, so is our capacity to earn a livelihood wondrous; and just as earning our livelihood is a daily occurrence, so does Redemption occur daily."

Our psalm enunciates its theme with a startling contrast: the contrast of God as envisioned by all the nations of the world, *from the rising of the sun to its setting,* to God as we, the People of Israel, envision Him. Our psalm insists that all humans praise God in some fashion. The Book of Psalms does not fathom pure atheism.

But the God of the nations is *high... His glory is above the heavens.* He is mighty and fearsome, but He is distant. Whereas the People of Israel envision Him differently: *Who is like the LORD our God, enthroned so high, yet deigns to look down on heaven and on earth?*

מזמור קיג

It is hard to find a word strong enough to describe her suffering. She desperately wants a child, but cannot conceive. "Frustration" is inadequate. "Tragic" is stronger, but her tragedy is in a league of its own. Ask her, and she'll tell you that no pain can compare with hers. Should she conceive, she'll tell you, no joy will compare with hers. She is right. The height of happiness is the former "barren woman," now the happy mother. Halleluya! Praise the LORD*!*

כד לחודש

א הַֽלְלוּיָ֨הּ ׀
הַ֭לְלוּ עַבְדֵ֣י יְהוָ֑ה
הַ֝לְל֗וּ אֶת־שֵׁ֥ם יְהוָֽה׃

ב יְהִ֤י שֵׁ֣ם יְהוָ֣ה מְבֹרָ֑ךְ
מֵ֝עַתָּ֗ה וְעַד־עוֹלָֽם׃

ג מִמִּזְרַח־שֶׁ֥מֶשׁ עַד־מְבוֹא֑וֹ
מְ֝הֻלָּ֗ל שֵׁ֣ם יְהוָֽה׃

ד רָ֖ם עַל־כָּל־גּוֹיִ֥ם ׀ יְהוָ֑ה
עַ֖ל הַשָּׁמַ֣יִם כְּבוֹדֽוֹ׃

ה מִ֭י כַּיהוָ֣ה אֱלֹהֵ֑ינוּ
הַֽמַּגְבִּיהִ֥י לָשָֽׁבֶת׃

ו הַֽמַּשְׁפִּילִ֥י לִרְא֑וֹת
בַּשָּׁמַ֥יִם וּבָאָֽרֶץ׃

מזמור קיג *Psalm 113:* Our psalm begins the series of psalms which have been incorporated into our liturgy as the Hallel, the ultimate expression of joy and thanksgiving. Thus, it is recited on the three major festivals and on Ḥanukka, all occasions for celebration of God's powers of redemption.

But Hallel is also recited on the first day of each Hebrew month, on the occasion of the New Moon, Rosh Ḥodesh. What redemption do we celebrate on this occasion? Unlike the three major festivals and Ḥanukka, the New Moon celebrates neither agricultural bounty nor historical glory.

7. He lifts the poor from the dust,
raises the needy from the dunghill,

8. to seat him with princes,
with the princes of His people.

9. He settles the childless woman in her home
as a happy mother of children.
Praise the LORD!

---

least a natural part of God's earth. The *evyon*, on the other hand, is in the dunghill, symbolic of an unspeakably degraded place.

Hallel begins with this assertion, then. God is close even to the lowliest person. The poor, the needy, even the infertile woman. Not only is He close, but He cares. He cares enough to raise the poor and needy *to seat him... with the princes of His people.* He cares enough so that even the barren woman can hope to be *settled in her home as the happy mother of children.*

Indeed, *Halleluya! Praise the LORD!*

ז מְקִימִ֣י מֵעָפָ֣ר דָּ֑ל
מֵ֝אַשְׁפֹּ֗ת יָרִ֥ים אֶבְיֽוֹן׃

ח לְהוֹשִׁיבִ֥י עִם־נְדִיבִ֑ים
עִ֝֗ם נְדִיבֵ֥י עַמּֽוֹ׃

ט מֽוֹשִׁיבִ֨י ׀ עֲקֶ֬רֶת הַבַּ֗יִת
אֵֽם־הַבָּנִ֥ים שְׂמֵחָ֗ה
הַֽלְלוּיָֽהּ׃

What distinguishes the Jewish concept of God is not His exaltedness, but rather the inner appreciation of His closeness, of His proximity and accessibility to even the lowest of the low.

Our verse 7 speaks of God lifting up *the poor from the dust… and the needy from the dunghill.* The "poor" man, *dal* in Hebrew, is unfortunate, true. But he is not totally without resources. He is merely missing something that he once had. He is "deprived."

The "needy" person, the *evyon,* is abjectly helpless, impotent, and completely dependent upon others. Note that the *dal* is in the dust, which is at

PSALM 114

1. When Israel came out of Egypt,
the house of Jacob from an alien folk,

2. Judah became His sacred people,
Israel His sovereign nation.

3. The sea saw Him and fled,
the Jordan turned back on its course;

4. the mountains skipped like rams,
the hills like young sheep.

5. What alarmed you, O sea, that you fled?
Jordan, why did you turn back?

6. Mountains, why did you skip like rams?
You hills, like young sheep?

---

title as *SheLaH,* or even as the *SheLaH HaKadosh,* the holy SheLaH. He draws our attention to an aspect of our psalm's language which has gone unnoticed by other commentators.

Our psalm emphasizes the impact of the exodus on the various components of nature's landscape. They all react with fear and with trembling. But Rabbi Horowitz makes us aware that not only do they all react, but they each react differently from the others. The sea flees, the Jordan reverses course. The mountains and hills both skip, but the former skip like adult rams, energetically and skillfully, whereas the latter skip timidly and playfully.

Rabbi Horowitz uses this insight to make an important homiletic point. There are events in life which are so wondrous and so forceful that we cannot help but be moved by them. But we do not necessarily all react in the same way. We retain our individuality even in the face of the most powerful and most unusual of events. Mountains react one way, and hills another. Neither is correct, neither is wrong. Reactions can differ in quality but be equally strong in force.

Rabbi Horowitz' insightful interpretation not only allows for diversity in worship, but it encourages it. There are many legitimate ways of responding to the exodus. There are equally many ways to respond to God.

מזמור קיד

"Earthshaking" is a powerful word. It is a word that we misuse. When we are surprised we say we heard "earthshaking" news. But "earthshaking" means so much more than "surprising." "Earthshaking" means that objects which never moved before are now shaking. "Earthshaking" means that they are shaking with fear. "Earthshaking" means that the entire earth is shaking. "Earthshaking" means unprecedented. Our exodus from Egypt was an "earthshaking" event.

א בְּצֵאת יִשְׂרָאֵל מִמִּצְרָיִם
בֵּית יַעֲקֹב מֵעַם לֹעֵז׃

ב הָיְתָה יְהוּדָה לְקָדְשׁוֹ
יִשְׂרָאֵל מַמְשְׁלוֹתָיו׃

ג הַיָּם רָאָה וַיָּנֹס
הַיַּרְדֵּן יִסֹּב לְאָחוֹר׃

ד הֶהָרִים רָקְדוּ כְאֵילִים
גְּבָעוֹת כִּבְנֵי־צֹאן׃

ה מַה־לְּךָ הַיָּם כִּי תָנוּס
הַיַּרְדֵּן תִּסֹּב לְאָחוֹר׃

ו הֶהָרִים תִּרְקְדוּ כְאֵילִים
גְּבָעוֹת כִּבְנֵי־צֹאן׃

מזמור קיד *Psalm 114:* Our psalm is best read as a climactic exclamation. It calls upon the reader to exult in the exodus from Egypt, as did the freed Jewish people and as did the animal kingdom, and indeed the entire world. The exodus was not a political or historical event; it was a cosmic event, literally "earthshaking." When recited in the synagogue our psalm is typically set to music, for only thereby can the words approximate the cosmic grandeur of this event.

There exists a remarkably insightful late medieval work entitled *Shnei Luḥot HaBrit,* or "The Two Tablets of the Covenant." Its author, Rabbi Isaiah Horowitz, is known by the acronym formed by the first letters of the book's

7. It was the presence of the Master, the Creator of the earth;
it was the presence of the God of Jacob,

8. who turns the rock into a pool of water,
the flinty rock into a flowing fountain.

ז מִלִּפְנֵי אָדוֹן חוּלִי אָרֶץ
מִלִּפְנֵי אֱלוֹהַּ יַעֲקֹב׃

ח הַהֹפְכִי הַצּוּר אֲגַם־מָיִם
חַלָּמִישׁ לְמַעְיְנוֹ־מָיִם׃

PSALM 115

1. Not for us, Lord, not for us,
but for Your name give glory,
because of Your loving-kindness and Your truth.

2. Why should the nations say,
"Where is their God now?"

3. But our God is in heaven;
whatever He wills He does.

4. Their idols are silver and gold,
the work of men's hands.

5. They have mouths, but cannot speak;
they have eyes, but cannot see;

6. they have ears, but cannot hear;
they have a nose, but cannot smell.

7. With their hands they cannot feel;
with their feet they cannot walk;
they utter no sound with their throat.

We know to whom the psalmist refers when he speaks of *Israel* or *the house of Israel.* He is referring to the entire Jewish nation. Similarly, we have no problem understanding that the *house of Aaron* refers to the *kohanim*, the descendants of Aaron, a specific tribe of their own. But who precisely are *those who fear the Lord*? Are they some elite and saintly sect, distinct and aloof from the rest of us?

Rashi's comment regarding the identity of *those who fear the Lord* is so terse that we almost overlook his provocative suggestion. He states that *those who fear the Lord* are "the *geirim*," the strangers and newcomers in our midst, the converts. Rashi disabuses us of our assumption that *those who fear the Lord* are an exceptional group of saints, recognizable by their dress or demeanor. He insists that *those who fear the Lord* are not the elite and outwardly

מזמור קטו

Are we entitled to pray? Do we deserve His answer to our prayers? Let's be honest with ourselves. We deserve very little. At most, we are entitled to pity. We ask that He answer us for His own sake. He is better off having us alive and well. Then we can at least try to do His will. Dead, we can do nothing for Him. Maybe we deserve more than we think we do.

א לֹא לָנוּ יהוה לֹא לָנוּ
כִּי־לְשִׁמְךָ תֵּן כָּבוֹד
עַל־חַסְדְּךָ עַל־אֲמִתֶּךָ׃

ב לָמָּה יֹאמְרוּ הַגּוֹיִם
אַיֵּה־נָא אֱלֹהֵיהֶם׃

ג וֵאלֹהֵינוּ בַשָּׁמָיִם
כֹּל אֲשֶׁר־חָפֵץ עָשָׂה׃

ד עֲצַבֵּיהֶם כֶּסֶף וְזָהָב
מַעֲשֵׂה יְדֵי אָדָם׃

ה פֶּה־לָהֶם וְלֹא יְדַבֵּרוּ
עֵינַיִם לָהֶם וְלֹא יִרְאוּ׃

ו אָזְנַיִם לָהֶם וְלֹא יִשְׁמָעוּ
אַף לָהֶם וְלֹא יְרִיחוּן׃

ז יְדֵיהֶם ׀ וְלֹא יְמִישׁוּן
רַגְלֵיהֶם וְלֹא יְהַלֵּכוּ
לֹא־יֶהְגּוּ בִּגְרוֹנָם׃

מזמור קטו *Psalm 115:* Twice, our psalm makes reference to three groups of people: *Israel, the house of Aaron,* and those *who fear the Lord.* Beginning in verse 9, the psalmist invites each of the three to *trust in the Lord.* Then, in verse 12, he assures each of the three of God's blessing. But this time, when he refers to *those who fear the Lord,* he adds the phrase *small and great alike.*

8. May their makers become like them;
and so too, all who trust in them.

9. O Israel, trust in the LORD!
He is their help and their shield.

10. O house of Aaron, trust in the LORD!
He is their help and their shield.

11. You who fear the LORD, trust in the LORD!
He is their help and their shield.

12. The LORD remembers us;
He will give us His blessing.
He will bless the house of Israel;
He will bless the house of Aaron;

13. He will bless those who fear the LORD,
small and great alike.

14. May the LORD grant you increase,
you and your children.

15. May you be blessed by the LORD,
the maker of heaven and earth.

---

wishes us to avoid. Thus, he defines *those who fear the LORD* as "those wise men who sit in solitude in the house of God, studying and preoccupying themselves with their quest to know God." Like us, he first assumed that *those who fear the LORD* must be detached from society, and totally dedicated to spiritual endeavors.

But then Radak offers an alternative definition of *those who fear the LORD.* He says that "there are others who explain that the psalmist is referring to those in each and every nation who fear the LORD."

We are called upon by Rashi to consider that an otherwise neglected minority are the sincerely God-fearing persons. Radak encourages us to be mindful that such spiritually gifted folk are to be found even outside our own faith community. They too trust in God and are blessed by Him, *small and great alike.*

ח כְּמוֹהֶם יִהְיוּ עֹשֵׂיהֶם
כֹּל אֲשֶׁר־בֹּטֵחַ בָּהֶם׃

ט יִשְׂרָאֵל בְּטַח בַּיהוָה
עֶזְרָם וּמָגִנָּם הוּא׃

י בֵּית אַהֲרֹן בִּטְחוּ בַיהוָה
עֶזְרָם וּמָגִנָּם הוּא׃

יא יִרְאֵי יהוה בִּטְחוּ בַיהוָה
עֶזְרָם וּמָגִנָּם הוּא׃

יב יהוה זְכָרָנוּ יְבָרֵךְ
יְבָרֵךְ אֶת־בֵּית יִשְׂרָאֵל
יְבָרֵךְ אֶת־בֵּית אַהֲרֹן׃

יג יְבָרֵךְ יִרְאֵי יְהוָה
הַקְּטַנִּים עִם־הַגְּדֹלִים׃

יד יֹסֵף יהוה עֲלֵיכֶם
עֲלֵיכֶם וְעַל־בְּנֵיכֶם׃

טו בְּרוּכִים אַתֶּם לַיהוָה
עֹשֵׂה שָׁמַיִם וָאָרֶץ׃

---

pious, but rather people whom we tend to look upon with condescension, even rejecting them from our inner circles.

We did not ourselves consider that it is the convert among us who is being singled out by the psalmist. Rashi, knowing well the inclinations of his readership, calls our attention to the *geirim* and insists that we recognize them and their uniquely justified claim to the title *those who fear the Lord.*

How interesting it is that Radak seems to fall into the very trap that Rashi

16. The heavens belong to the LORD,
but the earth He has given to man.

17. It is not the dead who praise the LORD,
nor those who go down into silence.*

18. But we will bless the LORD,
now and forevermore.
Praise the LORD!

* I.e., the grave.

טז הַשָּׁמַיִם שָׁמַיִם לַיהוָה
וְהָאָרֶץ נָתַן לִבְנֵי־אָדָם׃

יז לֹא הַמֵּתִים יְהַלְלוּ־יָהּ
וְלֹא כָּל־יֹרְדֵי דוּמָה׃

יח וַאֲנַחְנוּ ׀ נְבָרֵךְ יָהּ
מֵעַתָּה וְעַד־עוֹלָם
הַלְלוּיָהּ׃

PSALM 116

1. I love the LORD,
for He hears my voice and my supplications;

2. for He inclines His ear to me
whenever I call.

3. When the pangs of death encircled me,
and the anguish of Sheol overtook me,
when I found nothing but distress and sorrow,

4. I invoked the name of the LORD:
"I beg You, LORD, deliver my soul."

5. Gracious indeed is the LORD, and just;
our God is full of compassion.

6. The LORD protects the simple-hearted;
I was brought low and He saved me.

7. Turn back, O my soul, to your rest,
for the LORD has treated you kindly.

He confesses that *I spoke rashly*: *"All men are liars."*

What brings a man to such a sorry state that he accuses all others of being liars?

Rashi modulates the severity of the connotation of the Hebrew original: *kol haadam kozev.* This is not an accusation against mankind. It simply means that all men disappoint; all men fail to live up to others' expectations of them.

Neither is this a paranoid statement. It is no more than a truism about humanity. None of us is perfect. We are all fallible. We let each other down.

Radak interprets the verse not as a condemnation of man, but rather as an affirmation of faith in God.

For Radak, David is the speaker here and he is saying, "*I kept my faith,* and when people attempted to dissuade me from my faith, pessimistically predicting that God would not keep His promises to me, *I called them all liars.*"

מזמור קטז

My life has been a turbulent one. But I have found peace. I have known failure and defeat. But now I am on the right track. I was suspicious and distrustful. But faithful friends now surround me. Thank you, God.

א אָהַבְתִּי כִּי־יִשְׁמַע ׀ יְהוָה
אֶת־קוֹלִי תַּחֲנוּנָי׃

ב כִּי־הִטָּה אָזְנוֹ לִי
וּבְיָמַי אֶקְרָא׃

ג אֲפָפוּנִי ׀ חֶבְלֵי־מָוֶת
וּמְצָרֵי שְׁאוֹל מְצָאוּנִי
צָרָה וְיָגוֹן אֶמְצָא׃

ד וּבְשֵׁם־יְהוָה אֶקְרָא
אָנָּה יְהוָה מַלְּטָה נַפְשִׁי׃

ה חַנּוּן יְהוָה וְצַדִּיק
וֵאלֹהֵינוּ מְרַחֵם׃

ו שֹׁמֵר פְּתָאיִם יְהוָה
דַּלּוֹתִי וְלִי יְהוֹשִׁיעַ׃

ז שׁוּבִי נַפְשִׁי לִמְנוּחָיְכִי
כִּי־יְהוָה גָּמַל עָלָיְכִי׃

מזמור קטז *Psalm 116:* Our psalm reads like the happy ending of a long and sad story.

The story teller loves God, and feels that God has heard his prayers. The LORD has treated him kindly, and he wishes to repay Him.

But once he was quite a tortured soul. Distress and sorrow were his lot. His eyes shed tears and his feet stumbled. He even knew the *pangs of death.*

8. For You have delivered my soul from death,
my eyes from tears,
my feet from stumbling.

9. I shall walk before the LORD
in the land of the living.

10. I kept my faith,
even when I complained, "I am sorely afflicted,"

11. even when I spoke rashly, "All men are liars."

12. How can I repay the LORD
for all His benefits to me?

13. I will raise the cup of salvation
and invoke the name of the LORD.

14. I will pay my vows to the LORD
in the presence of all His people.

15. Precious in the LORD's sight
is the death of His faithful ones.

16. Truly, LORD, I am Your servant;
I am Your servant, the son of Your maidservant;
O free me from my fetters.

As the eminent sociologist Ervin Goffman demonstrates in his book, *The Presentation of Self in Everyday Life,* each of us exposes but a façade to others in our interactions with them. Our genuine selves are seldom disclosed.

Rav Soloveitchik views each of us as a *homo absconditus,* a "hidden man," whom no one really knows.

Following this approach we can perhaps translate the phrase not as "all men are liars" but as "all men are imposters." Such a statement does not attribute malice to every member of the human race. Instead it recognizes that we can never really know each other. There is no real self. We each possess a multiplicity of roles, and play different roles in different circumstances.

It is frustrating that we can never really know one another. It is dreadful that we can never even know ourselves.

ח כִּי חִלַּצְתָּ נַפְשִׁי מִמָּוֶת
אֶת־עֵינִי מִן־דִּמְעָה
אֶת־רַגְלִי מִדֶּחִי׃

ט אֶתְהַלֵּךְ לִפְנֵי יְהֹוָה
בְּאַרְצוֹת הַחַיִּים׃

י הֶאֱמַנְתִּי כִּי אֲדַבֵּר
אֲנִי עָנִיתִי מְאֹד׃

יא אֲנִי אָמַרְתִּי בְחָפְזִי
כָּל־הָאָדָם כֹּזֵב׃

יב מָה־אָשִׁיב לַיהֹוָה
כָּל־תַּגְמוּלוֹהִי עָלָי׃

יג כּוֹס־יְשׁוּעוֹת אֶשָּׂא
וּבְשֵׁם יְהֹוָה אֶקְרָא׃

יד נְדָרַי לַיהֹוָה אֲשַׁלֵּם
נֶגְדָה־נָּא לְכָל־עַמּוֹ׃

טו יָקָר בְּעֵינֵי יְהֹוָה
הַמָּוְתָה לַחֲסִידָיו׃

טז אָנָּה יְהֹוָה כִּי־אֲנִי עַבְדֶּךָ
אֲנִי־עַבְדְּךָ בֶּן־אֲמָתֶךָ
פִּתַּחְתָּ לְמוֹסֵרָי׃

Rav Soloveitchik offers a decidedly modern reinterpretation of our verse. He insists that "liars" here does not describe an intentionally fraudulent person. In existential terms we are all "liars." None of us is quite the person he appears to be. We all put up a front, at least some of the time.

17. To You I will offer a sacrifice of thanksgiving,
and invoke the name of the LORD.

18. I will pay my vows to the LORD
in the presence of all His people,

19. in the courts of the LORD's house,
in the midst of you, O Jerusalem.
Praise the LORD!

מזמור קיח

I had no exit. I was rejected, scorned, and pitied. There was no one to trust. I surprised myself. I trusted God. He surprised me.

א הוֹדוּ לַיהוָה כִּי־טוֹב
כִּי לְעוֹלָם חַסְדּוֹ׃

ב יֹאמַר־נָא יִשְׂרָאֵל
כִּי לְעוֹלָם חַסְדּוֹ׃

ג יֹאמְרוּ־נָא בֵית־אַהֲרֹן
כִּי לְעוֹלָם חַסְדּוֹ׃

ד יֹאמְרוּ־נָא יִרְאֵי יְהוָה
כִּי לְעוֹלָם חַסְדּוֹ׃

ה מִן־הַמֵּצַר קָרָאתִי יָּהּ
עָנָנִי בַמֶּרְחָב יָהּ׃

ו יְהוָה לִי לֹא אִירָא
מַה־יַּעֲשֶׂה לִי אָדָם׃

ז יְהוָה לִי בְּעֹזְרָי
וַאֲנִי אֶרְאֶה בְשֹׂנְאָי׃

ח טוֹב לַחֲסוֹת בַּיהוָה
מִבְּטֹחַ בָּאָדָם׃

ט טוֹב לַחֲסוֹת בַּיהוָה
מִבְּטֹחַ בִּנְדִיבִים׃

מזמור קיח *Psalm 118:* Our psalm is the last of a series of six psalms which comprise the Hallel service, recited in the synagogue on the occasion of the major Jewish festivals.

Many of the verses of Hallel have been set to music, and are customarily

10. All nations surround me;
by the LORD's name I will cut them down.

11. They surround me, they surround me completely;
by the LORD's name I will cut them down.

12. They surround me like bees;
they shall be extinguished like a fire of thorns;
by the LORD's name I will cut them down.

13. I was hard pressed* so that I nearly fell;
but the LORD helped me.

14. The LORD is my strength and my song;
He has become my savior.

15. Joyous songs and shouts of deliverance resound
in the tents of the righteous:
"The LORD's right hand has triumphed!

16. The LORD's right hand is exalted!
The LORD's right hand has triumphed!"

17. I shall not die, but live,
and proclaim the deeds of the LORD.

18. The LORD chastised me severely,
but He did not hand me over to death.

* Lit. "You [i.e., each one of my adversaries] pressed me hard."

At first, the seeker assumes that there must be many gates.

"Surely," the seeker reasons, "there cannot be just one path to a righteous life. People are different. For those who follow a rational path there are philosophical gates. For those who are gregarious, there are social gates. For those who are curious about the world, scientific gates must exist. I must find my own individual path to righteousness."

י כָּל־גּוֹיִם סְבָבוּנִי
בְּשֵׁם יהוה כִּי אֲמִילַם׃

יא סַבּוּנִי גַם־סְבָבוּנִי
בְּשֵׁם יהוה כִּי אֲמִילַם׃

יב סַבּוּנִי כִדְבוֹרִים
דֹּעֲכוּ כְּאֵשׁ קוֹצִים
בְּשֵׁם יהוה כִּי אֲמִילַם׃

יג דַּחֹה דְחִיתַנִי לִנְפֹּל
וַיהוה עֲזָרָנִי׃

יד עָזִּי וְזִמְרָת יָהּ
וַיְהִי־לִי לִישׁוּעָה׃

טו קוֹל ׀ רִנָּה וִישׁוּעָה בְּאָהֳלֵי צַדִּיקִים
יְמִין יהוה עֹשָׂה חָיִל׃

טז יְמִין יהוה רוֹמֵמָה
יְמִין יהוה עֹשָׂה חָיִל׃

יז לֹא־אָמוּת כִּי־אֶחְיֶה
וַאֲסַפֵּר מַעֲשֵׂי יָהּ׃

יח יַסֹּר יִסְּרַנִּי יָּהּ
וְלַמָּוֶת לֹא נְתָנָנִי׃

---

plural *gates of righteousness,* and then shifts to the singular *the* LORD*'s gate*. How are we to understand this change?

One approach to this problem is to understand the two phrases as representing two stages in the search for *the gates of righteousness.*

19. Open for me the gates of righteousness
that I may enter them and praise the LORD.

20. This is the LORD's gate,
the righteous shall enter through it.

21. I will praise You, for You have answered me,
and have become my deliverer.

22. The stone which the builders rejected
has become the chief corner-stone.

23. This is the LORD's doing;
it is marvelous in our eyes.

24. This is the day the LORD has made,
let us rejoice and be happy on it.

25. We beg You, LORD, save us!
We beg You, LORD, send prosperity!

26. Blessed is he who comes in the name of the LORD;
we bless you from the house of the LORD.

27. The LORD is God;
He has caused His light to shine upon us.
With myrtle branches in hand,
form the festal procession
up to the horns of the altar.

---

seeks, there is only one gate. One can approach that gate through scientific achievements, through friendly behavior, through a principled system of ethics, or through prayer and contemplation.

But one's underlying motivation must be to do the will of God, to sanctify His name.

With that motivation, almost every path is legitimate. Without that motivation, the paths culminate in a dead end.

In the words of a later psalm, Psalm 127:

יט פִּתְחוּ־לִי שַׁעֲרֵי־צֶדֶק
אָבֹא־בָם אוֹדֶה יָהּ׃

כ זֶה־הַשַּׁעַר לַיהוָה
צַדִּיקִים יָבֹאוּ בוֹ׃

כא אוֹדְךָ כִּי עֲנִיתָנִי
וַתְּהִי־לִי לִישׁוּעָה׃

כב אֶבֶן מָאֲסוּ הַבּוֹנִים
הָיְתָה לְרֹאשׁ פִּנָּה׃

כג מֵאֵת יהוה הָיְתָה זֹּאת
הִיא נִפְלָאת בְּעֵינֵינוּ׃

כד זֶה־הַיּוֹם עָשָׂה יהוָה
נָגִילָה וְנִשְׂמְחָה בוֹ׃

כה אָנָּא יהוה הוֹשִׁיעָה נָּא
אָנָּא יהוה הַצְלִיחָה נָּא׃

כו בָּרוּךְ הַבָּא בְּשֵׁם יהוָה
בֵּרַכְנוּכֶם מִבֵּית יהוָה׃

כז אֵל ׀ יהוה וַיָּאֶר לָנוּ
אִסְרוּ־חַג בַּעֲבֹתִים
עַד־קַרְנוֹת הַמִּזְבֵּחַ׃

Thus, the seeker wishes to wander along many paths, aspiring to find the one that best suits him.

As the seeker matures, however, he gradually discovers that the many paths lead inexorably to but one gate. That gate is the spirituality gate, *the Lord's gate.*

Many diverse paths may lead to it, but if it is the *gate of righteousness* that one

28. You are my God and I will praise You;
You are my God, and I will exalt You.

29. Give thanks to the LORD, for He is good,
for His loving-kindness endures forever.

His gate can only be entered by those whose motives are righteous. That's the "bad news." The "good news" is that with the proper motive His gate is open to travelers of many differing paths.

כח אֵלִ֣י אַתָּ֣ה וְאוֹדֶ֑ךָּ
אֱ֝לֹהַ֗י אֲרוֹמְמֶֽךָּ׃

כט הוֹד֣וּ לַיהֹוָ֣ה כִּי־ט֑וֹב
כִּ֖י לְעוֹלָ֣ם חַסְדּֽוֹ׃

Unless the LORD builds the house; in vain do its builders labor.
In the words of our psalm:
This is the LORD's gate; the righteous shall enter through it.

PSALM 119 *

ALEF

1. Happy are they whose way is blameless, who follow the Torah of the LORD. *Twenty-fifth day of the month*

2. Happy are they who keep His decrees, who seek Him with all their heart;

3. who have done no wrong, but walk in His ways.

4. You have commanded that Your precepts must be diligently kept.

5. How I wish that my ways were steadfast in keeping Your statutes!

6. Then I would never be put to shame when I regard all Your commandments.

7. I will praise You with a sincere heart as I learn Your just laws.

8. I mean to observe Your statutes; do not utterly forsake me.

* An extended alphabetical psalm. For each letter of the Hebrew alphabet there is a stanza of eight verses which all begin with that letter; thus there are twenty-two stanzas.

His two most famous works are *Avnei Nezer*, a multi-volume collection of his responsa on a wide array of subjects, and *Eglei Tal*, a treatise on the laws of the Sabbath. In his preface to the latter work, he records a question which was asked of him.

"Is it permissible," the questioner asked, "for a Jew to enjoy studying the Torah? After all, Torah study is a mitzva, a divine commandment. As such, we should study it because it is commanded of us. If we take pleasure in our

מזמור קיט

Enjoy life! I do. But have you tasted worldly pleasures? I have.
Why then do you study Torah day and night? It gives me the greatest pleasure of all.

א

כה לחודש

א אַשְׁרֵי תְמִימֵי־דָרֶךְ
הַהֹלְכִים בְּתוֹרַת יְהוָה׃

ב אַשְׁרֵי נֹצְרֵי עֵדֹתָיו
בְּכָל־לֵב יִדְרְשׁוּהוּ׃

ג אַף לֹא־פָעֲלוּ עַוְלָה
בִּדְרָכָיו הָלָכוּ׃

ד אַתָּה צִוִּיתָה פִקֻּדֶיךָ
לִשְׁמֹר מְאֹד׃

ה אַחֲלַי יִכֹּנוּ דְרָכָי
לִשְׁמֹר חֻקֶּיךָ׃

ו אָז לֹא־אֵבוֹשׁ בְּהַבִּיטִי
אֶל־כָּל־מִצְוֹתֶיךָ׃

ז אוֹדְךָ בְּיֹשֶׁר לֵבָב בְּלָמְדִי
מִשְׁפְּטֵי צִדְקֶךָ׃

ח אֶת־חֻקֶּיךָ אֶשְׁמֹר
אַל־תַּעַזְבֵנִי עַד־מְאֹד׃

מזמור קיט *Psalm 119:* Rabbi Abraham of Sochaczew was a great hasidic Rebbe who lived into the early twentieth century. He was the son-in-law of the famous Rabbi Menachem Mendel of Kotzk. He was also an accomplished rabbinic scholar, whose halakhic decisions remain authoritative to this very day.

BEIT

9. How can a young man keep his way pure?
By holding to Your word.

10. I seek You with all my heart;
do not let me stray from Your commandments.

11. In my heart I treasure Your promise,
for fear that I might sin against You.

12. Blessed are You, LORD;
teach me Your statutes.

13. With my lips I repeat
all the laws You have stated.

14. I rejoice in following Your decrees,
as one rejoices over great wealth.

15. I meditate on Your precepts,
and regard Your paths.

16. I delight in Your statutes;
I will not forget Your word.

GIMMEL

17. Deal kindly with Your servant,
that I may live and keep Your word.

18. Unveil my eyes that I may behold
the wonders of Your Torah.

19. I am a passing stranger on earth;
do not hide Your commandments from me.

---

study, are we not studying for an ulterior motive, thereby diminishing the mitzva, and perhaps even rendering our study entirely invalid?"

The Rebbe was astonished by this question. His reaction was clear and

ב

ט בַּמֶּה יְזַכֶּה־נַּעַר אֶת־אָרְחוֹ
לִשְׁמֹר כִּדְבָרֶךָ׃

י בְּכָל־לִבִּי דְרַשְׁתִּיךָ
אַל־תַּשְׁגֵּנִי מִמִּצְוֺתֶיךָ׃

יא בְּלִבִּי צָפַנְתִּי אִמְרָתֶךָ
לְמַעַן לֹא אֶחֱטָא־לָךְ׃

יב בָּרוּךְ אַתָּה יְהוָה
לַמְּדֵנִי חֻקֶּיךָ׃

יג בִּשְׂפָתַי סִפַּרְתִּי
כֹּל מִשְׁפְּטֵי־פִיךָ׃

יד בְּדֶרֶךְ עֵדְוֺתֶיךָ שַׂשְׂתִּי
כְּעַל כָּל־הוֹן׃

טו בְּפִקֻּדֶיךָ אָשִׂיחָה
וְאַבִּיטָה אֹרְחֹתֶיךָ׃

טז בְּחֻקֹּתֶיךָ אֶשְׁתַּעֲשָׁע
לֹא אֶשְׁכַּח דְּבָרֶךָ׃

ג

יז גְּמֹל עַל־עַבְדְּךָ אֶחְיֶה
וְאֶשְׁמְרָה דְבָרֶךָ׃

יח גַּל־עֵינַי וְאַבִּיטָה
נִפְלָאוֹת מִתּוֹרָתֶךָ׃

יט גֵּר אָנֹכִי בָאָרֶץ
אַל־תַּסְתֵּר מִמֶּנִּי מִצְוֺתֶיךָ׃

20. My heart is breaking with longing
for Your laws at all times.

21. You rebuke the accursed proud
who stray from Your commandments.

22. Remove from me scorn and contempt,
for I keep Your decrees.

23. Though princes sit together and scheme against me,
Your servant studies Your statutes.

24. For Your decrees are my delight;
they are my counselors.

DALET

25. My soul clings to the dust;
revive me according to Your word.

26. I confessed my ways, and You answered me;
teach me Your statutes.

27. Make me understand the way of Your precepts,
and I will meditate on Your wonders.

28. My soul weeps with grief;
raise my spirits according to Your word.

29. Remove from me the way of falsehood;
favor me with Your Torah.

30. I have chosen the way of truth;
I have set Your judgments before me.

---

forceful. The enjoyment of Torah study is an essential component of the mitzva. God wants us to take pleasure in His Torah to the extent that our fulfillment of the mitzva is diminished if we fail to take pleasure in our study.

כ גָּרְסָה נַפְשִׁי לְתַאֲבָה
אֶל־מִשְׁפָּטֶיךָ בְכָל־עֵת׃

כא גָּעַרְתָּ זֵדִים אֲרוּרִים
הַשֹּׁגִים מִמִּצְוֺתֶיךָ׃

כב גַּל מֵעָלַי חֶרְפָּה וָבוּז
כִּי עֵדֹתֶיךָ נָצָרְתִּי׃

כג גַּם יָשְׁבוּ שָׂרִים בִּי נִדְבָּרוּ
עַבְדְּךָ יָשִׂיחַ בְּחֻקֶּיךָ׃

כד גַּם־עֵדֹתֶיךָ שַׁעֲשֻׁעָי
אַנְשֵׁי עֲצָתִי׃

ד

כה דָּבְקָה לֶעָפָר נַפְשִׁי
חַיֵּנִי כִּדְבָרֶךָ׃

כו דְּרָכַי סִפַּרְתִּי וַתַּעֲנֵנִי
לַמְּדֵנִי חֻקֶּיךָ׃

כז דֶּרֶךְ־פִּקּוּדֶיךָ הֲבִינֵנִי
וְאָשִׂיחָה בְּנִפְלְאוֹתֶיךָ׃

כח דָּלְפָה נַפְשִׁי מִתּוּגָה
קַיְּמֵנִי כִּדְבָרֶךָ׃

כט דֶּרֶךְ־שֶׁקֶר הָסֵר מִמֶּנִּי
וְתוֹרָתְךָ חָנֵּנִי׃

ל דֶּרֶךְ־אֱמוּנָה בָחָרְתִּי
מִשְׁפָּטֶיךָ שִׁוִּיתִי׃

31. I cling to Your decrees;
LORD, do not put me to shame.

32. I eagerly pursue the way of Your commandments,
for You free* my heart [from anxiety].

HEH

33. Teach me, LORD, the way of Your statutes,
and I will observe them meticulously.

34. Give me understanding that I may observe Your Torah,
and keep it with all my heart.

35. Guide me in the path of Your commandments,
for that is my sole delight.

36. Incline my heart toward Your decrees,
and not toward love of gain.

37. Turn my eyes away from worthless things;
grant me life to follow in Your way.

38. Fulfill for Your servant the promise
which [You made] to those who fear You.

39. Remove the reproach which I dread,
for Your judgments are good.

40. See, how I long for Your precepts!
By Your righteousness grant me life.

VAV

41. May Your loving-kindness come to me, LORD,
and Your deliverance, as You have promised.

* Lit. "broaden."

לא דָּבַ֥קְתִּי בְעֵדְוֺתֶ֑יךָ
יְ֝הֹוָ֗ה אַל־תְּבִישֵֽׁנִי׃

לב דֶּֽרֶךְ־מִצְוֺתֶ֥יךָ אָר֑וּץ
כִּ֖י תַרְחִ֣יב לִבִּֽי׃

ה

לג ה֤וֹרֵ֣נִי יְ֭הֹוָה דֶּ֣רֶךְ חֻקֶּ֑יךָ
וְאֶצְּרֶ֥נָּה עֵֽקֶב׃

לד הֲ֭בִינֵנִי וְאֶצְּרָ֥ה תֽוֹרָתֶ֗ךָ
וְאֶשְׁמְרֶ֥נָּה בְכָל־לֵֽב׃

לה הַ֭דְרִיכֵנִי בִּנְתִ֣יב מִצְוֺתֶ֑יךָ
כִּי־ב֥וֹ חָפָֽצְתִּי׃

לו הַט־לִ֭בִּי אֶל־עֵ֝דְוֺתֶ֗יךָ
וְאַ֣ל אֶל־בָּֽצַע׃

לז הַעֲבֵ֣ר עֵ֭ינַי מֵרְא֣וֹת שָׁ֑וְא
בִּדְרָכֶ֥ךָ חַיֵּֽנִי׃

לח הָקֵ֣ם לְ֭עַבְדְּךָ אִמְרָתֶ֑ךָ
אֲ֝שֶׁ֗ר לְיִרְאָתֶֽךָ׃

לט הַעֲבֵ֣ר חֶ֭רְפָּתִי אֲשֶׁ֣ר יָגֹ֑רְתִּי
כִּ֖י מִשְׁפָּטֶ֣יךָ טוֹבִֽים׃

מ הִ֭נֵּה תָּאַ֣בְתִּי לְפִקֻּדֶ֑יךָ
בְּצִדְקָתְךָ֥ חַיֵּֽנִי׃

ו

מא וִיבֹאֻ֣נִי חֲסָדֶ֣ךָ יְהֹוָ֑ה
תְּ֝שׁוּעָתְךָ֗ כְּאִמְרָתֶֽךָ׃

42. Then I shall have an answer for him who reviles me;
for I trust in Your word.

43. Do not utterly take away the true word from my mouth;
for I put my hope in Your just rulings.

44. I will always obey Your Torah,
forever and ever.

45. I will walk about in all freedom,
because I seek Your precepts.

46. I will speak of Your decrees before kings,
and shall not be ashamed.

47. I find delight in Your commandments,
because I love them.

48. I reach out my hands for Your commandments which I love,
and meditate on Your statutes.

ZAYIN

49. Remember the word [You spoke] to Your servant,
by which You have given me hope.

50. This is my comfort in my suffering:
that Your promise gives me life.

51. Though the arrogant bitterly mock me,
I do not swerve from Your Torah.

52. I remember Your judgments of old, Lord,
and am comforted by them.

The Rebbe supports his contention with a lengthy, learned essay, based on many rabbinic sources. He could easily have quoted our psalm to corroborate his view. Our psalm eloquently and graphically describes the pleasures of Torah study. It is a paean to the beauty of the Torah and to the delights to be discovered in its contemplation.

מב וְאֶעֱנֶה חֹרְפִי דָבָר
כִּי־בָטַחְתִּי בִּדְבָרֶךָ׃

מג וְאַל־תַּצֵּל מִפִּי דְבַר־אֱמֶת עַד־מְאֹד
כִּי לְמִשְׁפָּטֶךָ יִחָלְתִּי׃

מד וְאֶשְׁמְרָה תוֹרָתְךָ תָמִיד
לְעוֹלָם וָעֶד׃

מה וְאֶתְהַלְּכָה בָרְחָבָה
כִּי פִקֻּדֶיךָ דָרָשְׁתִּי׃

מו וַאֲדַבְּרָה בְעֵדֹתֶיךָ נֶגֶד מְלָכִים
וְלֹא אֵבוֹשׁ׃

מז וְאֶשְׁתַּעֲשַׁע בְּמִצְוֺתֶיךָ
אֲשֶׁר אָהָבְתִּי׃

מח וְאֶשָּׂא־כַפַּי אֶל־מִצְוֺתֶיךָ אֲשֶׁר אָהָבְתִּי
וְאָשִׂיחָה בְחֻקֶּיךָ׃

ז

מט זְכׇר־דָּבָר לְעַבְדֶּךָ
עַל אֲשֶׁר יִחַלְתָּנִי׃

נ זֹאת נֶחָמָתִי בְעׇנְיִי
כִּי אִמְרָתְךָ חִיָּתְנִי׃

נא זֵדִים הֱלִיצֻנִי עַד־מְאֹד
מִתּוֹרָתְךָ לֹא נָטִיתִי׃

נב זָכַרְתִּי מִשְׁפָּטֶיךָ מֵעוֹלָם ׀ יהוה
וָאֶתְנֶחָם׃

53. Burning indignation grips me
because of the wicked who forsake Your Torah.

54. Your statutes are the theme of my song
wherever I sojourn.

55. In the night I remember Your name, LORD,
and I dwell upon Your Torah.

56. This has been my merit,
that I always kept Your precepts.

ḤET

57. [You are] my portion, Lord;
so I promise to obey Your words.

58. I implore You with all my heart;
have pity on me according to Your promise.

59. I have considered my ways,
and have turned my steps to Your decrees.

60. I hasten, and never delay,
to keep Your commandments.

61. Bands of wicked men prey on me,
but I do not forget Your Torah.

62. At midnight I rise to praise You
for Your righteous judgments.

63. I am a friend to all who fear You,
to all who observe Your precepts.

I delight in Your statutes.... I yearn to *behold the wonders of Your Torah*.... *I find delight in Your commandments*.... *Your statutes are the theme of my song*.... *More precious to me is the Torah You proclaimed than thousands of gold and silver pieces*.... *How sweet to my palate are Your words, sweeter than honey to my mouth.*

נג זַלְעָפָה אֲחָזַתְנִי מֵרְשָׁעִים
עֹזְבֵי תּוֹרָתֶךָ׃

נד זְמִרוֹת הָיוּ־לִי חֻקֶּיךָ
בְּבֵית מְגוּרָי׃

נה זָכַרְתִּי בַלַּיְלָה שִׁמְךָ יְהוָה
וָאֶשְׁמְרָה תּוֹרָתֶךָ׃

נו זֹאת הָיְתָה־לִּי
כִּי פִקֻּדֶיךָ נָצָרְתִּי׃

ח

נז חֶלְקִי יְהוָה אָמַרְתִּי
לִשְׁמֹר דְּבָרֶיךָ׃

נח חִלִּיתִי פָנֶיךָ בְכָל־לֵב
חָנֵּנִי כְּאִמְרָתֶךָ׃

נט חִשַּׁבְתִּי דְרָכָי
וָאָשִׁיבָה רַגְלַי אֶל־עֵדֹתֶיךָ׃

ס חַשְׁתִּי וְלֹא הִתְמַהְמָהְתִּי
לִשְׁמֹר מִצְוֹתֶיךָ׃

סא חֶבְלֵי רְשָׁעִים עִוְּדֻנִי
תּוֹרָתְךָ לֹא שָׁכָחְתִּי׃

סב חֲצוֹת־לַיְלָה אָקוּם לְהוֹדוֹת לָךְ
עַל מִשְׁפְּטֵי צִדְקֶךָ׃

סג חָבֵר אָנִי לְכָל־אֲשֶׁר יְרֵאוּךָ
וּלְשֹׁמְרֵי פִּקּוּדֶיךָ׃

64. The earth is filled with Your loving-kindness, LORD;
teach me Your statutes.

TET

65. Do good to Your servant, Lord,
according to Your word.

66. Teach me good sense and knowledge,
because I believe in Your commandments.

67. Before I applied myself [to the Torah] I went astray,
but now I heed Your bidding.

68. You are good, and what You do is good;
teach me Your statutes.

69. Though proud men besmear me with lies,
I observe Your precepts with all my heart.

70. Their heart is gross like fat;
*but as for me, Your Torah is my delight.

71. It was good for me that I was afflicted,
so that I might learn Your statutes.

72. More precious to me is the Torah You proclaimed
than thousands of gold and silver pieces.

YOD

73. Your hands made me and formed me;
give me understanding that I may learn Your commandments.

74. Those who fear You will see me and rejoice,
for I put my hope in Your word.

* I.e., they are callous and unfeeling.

These are just some of the phrases which abound in our psalm, all testifying that it is acceptable, and indeed praiseworthy, to derive pleasure from the study of the Torah.

סד חַסְדְּךָ֣ יהוה מָלְאָ֣ה הָאָ֑רֶץ
חֻקֶּ֥יךָ לַמְּדֵֽנִי׃

ט

סה ט֗וֹב עָשִׂ֣יתָ עִֽם־עַבְדְּךָ֑
יְ֝הוָ֗ה כִּדְבָרֶֽךָ׃

סו ט֤וּב טַ֣עַם וָדַ֣עַת לַמְּדֵ֑נִי
כִּ֖י בְמִצְוֺתֶ֣יךָ הֶאֱמָֽנְתִּי׃

סז טֶ֣רֶם אֶ֭עֱנֶה אֲנִ֣י שֹׁגֵ֑ג
וְ֝עַתָּ֗ה אִמְרָתְךָ֥ שָׁמָֽרְתִּי׃

סח טוֹב־אַתָּ֥ה וּמֵטִ֗יב
לַמְּדֵ֥נִי חֻקֶּֽיךָ׃

סט טָֽפְל֬וּ עָלַ֣י שֶׁ֣קֶר זֵדִ֑ים
אֲ֝נִ֗י בְּכָל־לֵ֤ב ׀ אֱצֹּ֬ר פִּקּוּדֶֽיךָ׃

ע טָפַ֣שׁ כַּחֵ֣לֶב לִבָּ֑ם
אֲ֝נִ֗י תּוֹרָתְךָ֥ שִׁעֲשָֽׁעְתִּי׃

עא טוֹב־לִ֥י כִי־עֻנֵּ֑יתִי
לְ֝מַ֗עַן אֶלְמַ֥ד חֻקֶּֽיךָ׃

עב טֽוֹב־לִ֥י תֽוֹרַת־פִּ֑יךָ
מֵ֝אַלְפֵ֗י זָהָ֥ב וָכָֽסֶף׃

י

עג יָדֶ֣יךָ עָ֭שׂוּנִי וַיְכוֹנְנ֑וּנִי
הֲ֝בִינֵ֗נִי וְאֶלְמְדָ֥ה מִצְוֺתֶֽיךָ׃

עד יְ֭רֵאֶיךָ יִרְא֣וּנִי וְיִשְׂמָ֑חוּ
כִּ֖י לִדְבָרְךָ֣ יִחָֽלְתִּי׃

75. I know, LORD, that Your judgments are just,
and in faithfulness You have afflicted me.

76. O let Your loving-kindness comfort me,
in accordance with Your promise to Your servant.

77. May Your mercies come to me that I may live,
for Your Torah is my delight.

78. May the proud be ashamed, for they wrong me with lies;
but I will meditate on Your precepts.

79. May those who fear You turn to me,
those who know Your decrees.

80. May my heart be blameless toward Your statutes;
then I shall never be put to shame!

KAF

81. My soul yearns for Your deliverance;
I have put my hope in Your word.

82. My eyes fail awaiting Your promise;
I say, "When will You comfort me?"

83. Though I have become [shriveled]
like a wine-skin in the smoke,
I have not forgotten Your statutes.

84. How many are the days of Your servant?
When will You execute judgment on my persecutors?

85. The proud have dug pits for me,
in defiance of Your Torah.

Our psalm extols the virtues of finding delight in God's statutes. But it also contains quite a few passages which restrain our exuberance over such pleasures, and which caution us to remember that there are much more serious dimensions to Torah study.

עה יָדַעְתִּי יְהוָה כִּי־צֶדֶק מִשְׁפָּטֶיךָ
וֶאֱמוּנָה עִנִּיתָנִי׃

עו יְהִי־נָא חַסְדְּךָ לְנַחֲמֵנִי
כְּאִמְרָתְךָ לְעַבְדֶּךָ׃

עז יְבֹאוּנִי רַחֲמֶיךָ וְאֶחְיֶה
כִּי־תוֹרָתְךָ שַׁעֲשֻׁעָי׃

עח יֵבֹשׁוּ זֵדִים כִּי־שֶׁקֶר עִוְּתוּנִי
אֲנִי אָשִׂיחַ בְּפִקּוּדֶיךָ׃

עט יָשׁוּבוּ לִי יְרֵאֶיךָ
וידעו עֵדֹתֶיךָ׃ וִידְעֵי

פ יְהִי־לִבִּי תָמִים בְּחֻקֶּיךָ
לְמַעַן לֹא אֵבוֹשׁ׃

כ

פא כָּלְתָה לִתְשׁוּעָתְךָ נַפְשִׁי
לִדְבָרְךָ יִחָלְתִּי׃

פב כָּלוּ עֵינַי לְאִמְרָתֶךָ
לֵאמֹר מָתַי תְּנַחֲמֵנִי׃

פג כִּי־הָיִיתִי כְּנֹאד בְּקִיטוֹר
חֻקֶּיךָ לֹא שָׁכָחְתִּי׃

פד כַּמָּה יְמֵי־עַבְדֶּךָ
מָתַי תַּעֲשֶׂה בְרֹדְפַי מִשְׁפָּט׃

פה כָּרוּ־לִי זֵדִים שִׁיחוֹת
אֲשֶׁר לֹא כְתוֹרָתֶךָ׃

86. All Your commandments are true;
men persecute me without cause; help me!

87. They had almost swept me off the earth,
but I would not abandon Your precepts.

88. By Your kindness grant me life,
that I may keep the decree that You uttered.

LAMED

89. You, LORD, are eternal,
Your word stands firm in the heavens;

90. Your faithfulness endures for all generations;
You established the earth and it stands.

91. They stand today according to Your ordinances.
for all things are Your servants.

92. Had Your Torah not been my delight,
I should have perished in my affliction.

93. Never shall I forget Your precepts,
for by them You have given me life.

94. I am Yours; save me!
for I have sought Your precepts.

95. The wicked lie in wait to destroy me,
but I ponder Your decrees.

96. I have seen that everything, however perfect, has a limit,
but Your commandment is wide beyond measure.

One example is verse 24: *For Your decrees are my delight; they are my counselors.* Dayan Abramsky tells us that he knew many who studied Torah because they found it intellectually stimulating and emotionally fulfilling. But when these individuals needed guidance for some practical issue in their lives, they invariably turned to secular advisors. He wisely applied to them our verse, stressing that *Your decrees* are not merely a source of *delight*. They must also be your *counselors* in your everyday worldly affairs.

פו כָּל־מִצְוֺתֶיךָ אֱמוּנָה
שֶׁקֶר רְדָפוּנִי עָזְרֵנִי׃

פז כִּמְעַט כִּלּוּנִי בָאָרֶץ
וַאֲנִי לֹא־עָזַבְתִּי פִקֻּדֶיךָ׃

פח כְּחַסְדְּךָ חַיֵּנִי וְאֶשְׁמְרָה
עֵדוּת פִּיךָ׃

ל

פט לְעוֹלָם יְהוָה דְּבָרְךָ
נִצָּב בַּשָּׁמָיִם׃

צ לְדֹר וָדֹר אֱמוּנָתֶךָ
כּוֹנַנְתָּ אֶרֶץ וַתַּעֲמֹד׃

צא לְמִשְׁפָּטֶיךָ עָמְדוּ הַיּוֹם
כִּי הַכֹּל עֲבָדֶיךָ׃

צב לוּלֵי תוֹרָתְךָ שַׁעֲשֻׁעָי
אָז אָבַדְתִּי בְעָנְיִי׃

צג לְעוֹלָם לֹא־אֶשְׁכַּח פִּקּוּדֶיךָ
כִּי־בָם חִיִּיתָנִי׃

צד לְךָ־אֲנִי הוֹשִׁיעֵנִי
כִּי פִקּוּדֶיךָ דָרָשְׁתִּי׃

צה לִי קִוּוּ רְשָׁעִים לְאַבְּדֵנִי
עֵדֹתֶיךָ אֶתְבּוֹנָן׃

צו לְכָל־תִּכְלָה רָאִיתִי קֵץ
רְחָבָה מִצְוָתְךָ מְאֹד׃

MEM

97. O how I love Your Torah!
I meditate on it all day long.

Twenty-sixth day of the month

98. Your commandments
make me wiser than my enemies,
for they are ever with me.

99. I have gained more insight
than all my teachers,
for Your decrees are my study.

100. I have more understanding
than the aged,
for I keep Your precepts.

101. I restrain my feet from every evil path,
so that I may keep Your word.

102. I have not departed from Your ordinances,
for You Yourself have taught me.

103. How sweet to my palate are Your words,
sweeter than honey to my mouth!

104. I gain wisdom from Your precepts,
therefore I hate every false way.

NUN

105. Your word is a lamp to my feet
and a light for my path.

106. I have sworn –
and I will keep my oath –
to observe Your just regulations.

Our psalm glorifies the aesthetic value of Torah study. But it also pleads with us not to be so bedazzled by its delights that we lose sight of it practical value and down-to-earth utility.

כו לחודש

מ

צז מָֽה־אָהַ֥בְתִּי תוֹרָתֶ֑ךָ
כׇּל־הַ֝יּ֗וֹם הִ֣יא שִׂיחָתִֽי׃

צח מֵ֭אֹיְבַי תְּחַכְּמֵ֣נִי מִצְוֺתֶ֑ךָ
כִּ֖י לְעוֹלָ֣ם הִיא־לִֽי׃

צט מִכׇּל־מְלַמְּדַ֥י הִשְׂכַּ֑לְתִּי
כִּ֥י עֵ֝דְוֺתֶ֗יךָ שִׂ֣יחָה לִֽי׃

ק מִזְּקֵנִ֥ים אֶתְבּוֹנָ֑ן
כִּ֖י פִקּוּדֶ֣יךָ נָצָֽרְתִּי׃

קא מִכׇּל־אֹ֣רַח רָ֭ע כָּלִ֣אתִי רַגְלָ֑י
לְ֝מַ֗עַן אֶשְׁמֹ֥ר דְּבָרֶֽךָ׃

קב מִמִּשְׁפָּטֶ֥יךָ לֹא־סָ֑רְתִּי
כִּֽי־אַ֝תָּ֗ה הוֹרֵתָֽנִי׃

קג מַה־נִּמְלְצ֣וּ לְ֭חִכִּי אִמְרָתֶ֑ךָ
מִדְּבַ֥שׁ לְפִֽי׃

קד מִפִּקּוּדֶ֥יךָ אֶתְבּוֹנָ֑ן
עַל־כֵּ֝ן שָׂנֵ֤אתִי ׀ כׇּל־אֹ֬רַח שָֽׁקֶר׃

נ

קה נֵר־לְרַגְלִ֥י דְבָרֶ֑ךָ
וְ֝א֗וֹר לִנְתִיבָתִֽי׃

קו נִ֭שְׁבַּעְתִּי וָאֲקַיֵּ֑מָה
לִ֝שְׁמֹ֗ר מִשְׁפְּטֵ֥י צִדְקֶֽךָ׃

107. I am sorely afflicted;
LORD, preserve my life according to Your word.

108. Accept, LORD, the willing offerings of my mouth,
and teach me Your ordinances.

109. Though my life is in constant danger,*
yet I never forget Your Torah.

110. Evil men have set a trap for me,
yet I do not stray from Your precepts.

111. Your decrees are my everlasting heritage;
for they are the joy of my heart.

112. I have resolved to carry out Your statutes;
the reward is eternal.

SAMEKH

113. I hate skeptics,**
but I love Your Torah.

114. You are my shelter and my shield;
I await the fulfillment of Your word.

115. Away from me, you evildoers,
that I may keep the commandments of my God.

116. Support me as You have promised,
that I may live;
do not disappoint my hope.

117. Sustain me that I may be saved,
and I shall always occupy myself with Your statutes.

* Lit. "My life is continually in my hand."

** Or: "waverers"; i.e., those who are undecided and waver in their religious loyalties.

קז נַעֲנֵ֥יתִי עַד־מְאֹ֑ד
יְ֝הֹוָ֗ה חַיֵּ֥נִי כִדְבָרֶֽךָ׃

קח נִדְב֣וֹת פִּ֭י רְצֵה־נָ֣א יְהֹוָ֑ה
וּ֝מִשְׁפָּטֶ֗יךָ לַמְּדֵֽנִי׃

קט נַפְשִׁ֣י בְכַפִּ֣י תָמִ֑יד
וְ֝תוֹרָתְךָ֗ לֹ֣א שָׁכָֽחְתִּי׃

קי נָתְנ֬וּ רְשָׁעִ֣ים פַּ֣ח לִ֑י
וּ֝מִפִּקּוּדֶ֗יךָ לֹ֣א תָעִֽיתִי׃

קיא נָחַ֣לְתִּי עֵדְוֺתֶ֣יךָ לְעוֹלָ֑ם
כִּֽי־שְׂשׂ֖וֹן לִבִּ֣י הֵֽמָּה׃

קיב נָטִ֣יתִי לִ֭בִּי לַעֲשׂ֥וֹת חֻקֶּ֗יךָ
לְעוֹלָ֥ם עֵֽקֶב׃

ס

קיג סֵעֲפִ֥ים שָׂנֵ֑אתִי
וְֽתוֹרָתְךָ֥ אָהָֽבְתִּי׃

קיד סִתְרִ֣י וּמָגִנִּ֣י אָ֑תָּה
לִדְבָרְךָ֥ יִחָֽלְתִּי׃

קטו ס֣וּרוּ מִמֶּ֣נִּי מְרֵעִ֑ים
וְ֝אֶצְּרָ֗ה מִצְוֺ֥ת אֱלֹהָֽי׃

קטז סָמְכֵ֣נִי כְאִמְרָתְךָ֣ וְאֶחְיֶ֑ה
וְאַל־תְּ֝בִישֵׁ֗נִי מִשִּׂבְרִֽי׃

קיז סְעָדֵ֣נִי וְאִוָּשֵׁ֑עָה
וְאֶשְׁעָ֖ה בְחֻקֶּ֣יךָ תָמִֽיד׃

118. You reject all who stray from Your statutes;
for their scheming is in vain.

119. You discard as dross all the wicked of the earth;
therefore I love Your decrees.

120. My flesh creeps from dread of You;
I stand in awe of Your ordinances.

AYIN

121. I have done what is just and right;
do not abandon me to my oppressors.

122. Assure the well-being of Your servant;
do not let the proud oppress me.

123. My eyes languish for Your deliverance,
and for Your righteous promise.

124. Deal with Your servant according to Your true loving-kindness;
teach me Your statutes.

125. I am Your servant; give me insight,
that I may know Your decrees.

126. It is a time for the LORD to act;
for they have violated Your Torah.

127. Truly I love Your commandments
more than gold, even the finest gold.

128. Truly I consider all Your precepts right in all matters;*
I hate every false way.

* Or: "I order my life in all things in accordance with Your precepts."

קיח סָלִיתָ כׇּל־שׁוֹגִים מֵחֻקֶּיךָ
כִּי־שֶׁקֶר תַּרְמִיתָם׃

קיט סִגִים הִשְׁבַּתָּ כׇל־רִשְׁעֵי־אָרֶץ
לָכֵן אָהַבְתִּי עֵדֹתֶיךָ׃

קכ סָמַר מִפַּחְדְּךָ בְשָׂרִי
וּמִמִּשְׁפָּטֶיךָ יָרֵאתִי׃

ע

קכא עָשִׂיתִי מִשְׁפָּט וָצֶדֶק
בַּל־תַּנִּיחֵנִי לְעֹשְׁקָי׃

קכב עֲרֹב עַבְדְּךָ לְטוֹב
אַל־יַעַשְׁקֻנִי זֵדִים׃

קכג עֵינַי כָּלוּ לִישׁוּעָתֶךָ
וּלְאִמְרַת צִדְקֶךָ׃

קכד עֲשֵׂה עִם־עַבְדְּךָ כְחַסְדֶּךָ
וְחֻקֶּיךָ לַמְּדֵנִי׃

קכה עַבְדְּךָ־אָנִי הֲבִינֵנִי
וְאֵדְעָה עֵדֹתֶיךָ׃

קכו עֵת לַעֲשׂוֹת לַיהֹוָה
הֵפֵרוּ תּוֹרָתֶךָ׃

קכז עַל־כֵּן אָהַבְתִּי מִצְוֺתֶיךָ
מִזָּהָב וּמִפָּז׃

קכח עַל־כֵּן ׀ כׇּל־פִּקּוּדֵי כֹל יִשָּׁרְתִּי
כׇּל־אֹרַח שֶׁקֶר שָׂנֵאתִי׃

PEH

129. Your decrees are wonderful;
that is why I keep them.

130. Your opening words shed light;
they give understanding to the simple.

131. I open wide my mouth,
I pant,
longing for Your commandments.

132. Turn to me
and be gracious to me,
as You always do
to those who love Your name.

133. Direct my footsteps according to Your word;
let no iniquity dominate me.

134. Redeem me from the oppression of men,
that I may keep Your precepts.

135. Let Your face shine upon Your servant,
and teach me Your statutes.

136. My eyes stream with tears
because men do not obey Your Torah.

TZADI

137. You are righteous, LORD,
and Your judgments are just.

138. You have imposed Your decrees with fairness;
they are fully trustworthy.

139. My zeal devastates me
because my enemies ignore Your words.

פ

קכט פְּלָא֥וֹת עֵדְוֺתֶ֑יךָ
עַל־כֵּ֝֗ן נְצָרָ֥תַם נַפְשִֽׁי׃

קל פֵּ֣תַח־דְּבָרֶ֣יךָ יָאִ֑יר
מֵבִ֥ין פְּתָיִֽים׃

קלא פִּֽי־פָ֭עַרְתִּי וָאֶשְׁאָ֑פָה
כִּ֖י לְמִצְוֺתֶ֣יךָ יָאָֽבְתִּי׃

קלב פְּנֵה־אֵ֭לַי וְחָנֵּ֑נִי כְּ֝מִשְׁפָּ֗ט
לְאֹהֲבֵ֥י שְׁמֶֽךָ׃

קלג פְּ֭עָמַי הָכֵ֣ן בְּאִמְרָתֶ֑ךָ
וְאַל־תַּשְׁלֶט־בִּ֥י כָל־אָֽוֶן׃

קלד פְּ֭דֵנִי מֵעֹ֣שֶׁק אָדָ֑ם
וְ֝אֶשְׁמְרָ֗ה פִּקּוּדֶֽיךָ׃

קלה פָּ֭נֶיךָ הָאֵ֣ר בְּעַבְדֶּ֑ךָ
וְ֝לַמְּדֵ֗נִי אֶת־חֻקֶּֽיךָ׃

קלו פַּלְגֵי־מַ֭יִם יָרְד֣וּ עֵינָ֑י
עַ֝֗ל לֹא־שָׁמְר֥וּ תוֹרָתֶֽךָ׃

צ

קלז צַדִּ֣יק אַתָּ֣ה יְהֹוָ֑ה
וְ֝יָשָׁ֗ר מִשְׁפָּטֶֽיךָ׃

קלח צִ֭וִּיתָ צֶ֣דֶק עֵדֹתֶ֑יךָ
וֶֽאֱמוּנָ֥ה מְאֹֽד׃

קלט צִמְּתַ֥תְנִי קִנְאָתִ֑י
כִּֽי־שָׁכְח֖וּ דְבָרֶ֣יךָ צָרָֽי׃

140. Your word is well tested,
and Your servant cherishes it.

141. I may be of little account and despised,
but I do not forget Your precepts.

142. Your righteousness
is an everlasting righteousness;
Your Torah is truth.

143. Though distress
and anxiety have overtaken me,
Your commandments are still my delight.

144. Your decrees are ever just;
give me understanding that I may live.

KUF

145. I call with all my heart;
answer me, Lord,
that I may keep Your statutes.

146. I call out to You: save me,
that I may keep Your decrees.

147. I rise before dawn and cry for help;
I await the fulfillment of Your word.

148. My eyes stay open through the watches of the night,
to meditate on Your word.

149. Hear my voice in accordance
with Your constant loving-kindness;
grant me life, Lord, as is Your rule.

150. My malicious pursuers are coming closer,
they are far from Your Torah.

קמ צְרוּפָה אִמְרָתְךָ מְאֹד
וְעַבְדְּךָ אֲהֵבָהּ׃

קמא צָעִיר אָנֹכִי וְנִבְזֶה
פִּקֻּדֶיךָ לֹא שָׁכָחְתִּי׃

קמב צִדְקָתְךָ צֶדֶק לְעוֹלָם
וְתוֹרָתְךָ אֱמֶת׃

קמג צַר־וּמָצוֹק מְצָאוּנִי
מִצְוֺתֶיךָ שַׁעֲשֻׁעָי׃

קמד צֶדֶק עֵדְוֺתֶיךָ לְעוֹלָם
הֲבִינֵנִי וְאֶחְיֶה׃

ק

קמה קָרָאתִי בְכָל־לֵב עֲנֵנִי יהוה
חֻקֶּיךָ אֶצֹּרָה׃

קמו קְרָאתִיךָ הוֹשִׁיעֵנִי
וְאֶשְׁמְרָה עֵדֹתֶיךָ׃

קמז קִדַּמְתִּי בַנֶּשֶׁף וָאֲשַׁוֵּעָה
לדבריך יִחָלְתִּי׃ לִדְבָרְךָ

קמח קִדְּמוּ עֵינַי אַשְׁמֻרוֹת
לָשִׂיחַ בְּאִמְרָתֶךָ׃

קמט קוֹלִי שִׁמְעָה כְחַסְדֶּךָ
יהוה כְּמִשְׁפָּטֶךָ חַיֵּנִי׃

קנ קָרְבוּ רֹדְפֵי זִמָּה
מִתּוֹרָתְךָ רָחָקוּ׃

151. Yet You are near, Lord,
and all Your commandments are true.

152. I have long known from Your decrees
that You have established them forever.

REISH

153. See my affliction and deliver me,
for I have not forgotten Your Torah.

154. Defend my cause and redeem me;
grant me life according to Your promise.

155. Deliverance is far from the wicked,
for they do not seek Your statutes.

156. Great is Your compassion, Lord;
grant me life, as is Your rule.

157. Though my persecutors
and foes are many,
I have not swerved from Your decrees.

158. When I see faithless men,
I am disgusted,
because they do not keep Your word.

159. See how I love Your precepts;
grant me life, Lord,
according to Your loving-kindness.

160. The essence of Your word is truth;
all Your righteous laws are eternal.

SHIN

161. Princes persecute me without cause,
yet my heart fears only for Your word.

קנא קָרוֹב אַתָּה יְהוָה
וְכָל־מִצְוֺתֶיךָ אֱמֶת:

קנב קֶדֶם יָדַעְתִּי מֵעֵדֹתֶיךָ
כִּי לְעוֹלָם יְסַדְתָּם:

ר

קנג רְאֵה־עָנְיִי וְחַלְּצֵנִי
כִּי־תוֹרָתְךָ לֹא שָׁכָחְתִּי:

קנד רִיבָה רִיבִי וּגְאָלֵנִי
לְאִמְרָתְךָ חַיֵּנִי:

קנה רָחוֹק מֵרְשָׁעִים יְשׁוּעָה
כִּי־חֻקֶּיךָ לֹא דָרָשׁוּ:

קנו רַחֲמֶיךָ רַבִּים ׀ יְהוָה
כְּמִשְׁפָּטֶיךָ חַיֵּנִי:

קנז רַבִּים רֹדְפַי וְצָרָי
מֵעֵדְוֺתֶיךָ לֹא נָטִיתִי:

קנח רָאִיתִי בֹגְדִים וָאֶתְקוֹטָטָה
אֲשֶׁר אִמְרָתְךָ לֹא שָׁמָרוּ:

קנט רְאֵה כִּי־פִקּוּדֶיךָ אָהָבְתִּי
יְהוָה כְּחַסְדְּךָ חַיֵּנִי:

קס רֹאשׁ־דְּבָרְךָ אֱמֶת
וּלְעוֹלָם כָּל־מִשְׁפַּט צִדְקֶךָ:

ש

קסא שָׂרִים רְדָפוּנִי חִנָּם
וּמדבריך פָּחַד לִבִּי: וּמִדְּבָרְךָ

162. I rejoice over Your promise
like one who finds much spoil.

163. I hate falsehood,
I loathe it,
but I love Your Torah.

164. Seven times each day I praise You
for Your just rulings.

165. Great peace have they who love Your Torah;
there is no stumbling for them.

166. I wait for Your deliverance, LORD,
and I fulfill Your commandments.

167. My soul heeds Your decrees,
for I love them dearly.

168. I observe Your precepts
and Your decrees,
for all my ways are before You.

TAV

169. Let my cry come before You, LORD;
give me understanding
as You have promised.

170. Let my entreaty reach You;
save me according to Your promise.

171. My lips shall pour forth praise,
because You teach me Your statutes.

172. My tongue shall sing of Your promise,
for all Your commandments are righteous.

קסב שָׂשׂ אָנֹכִי עַל־אִמְרָתֶךָ
כְּמוֹצֵא שָׁלָל רָב׃

קסג שֶׁקֶר שָׂנֵאתִי וַאֲתַעֵבָה
תּוֹרָתְךָ אָהָבְתִּי׃

קסד שֶׁבַע בַּיּוֹם הִלַּלְתִּיךָ
עַל מִשְׁפְּטֵי צִדְקֶךָ׃

קסה שָׁלוֹם רָב לְאֹהֲבֵי תוֹרָתֶךָ
וְאֵין־לָמוֹ מִכְשׁוֹל׃

קסו שִׂבַּרְתִּי לִישׁוּעָתְךָ יְהוָה
וּמִצְוֺתֶיךָ עָשִׂיתִי׃

קסז שָׁמְרָה נַפְשִׁי עֵדֹתֶיךָ
וָאֹהֲבֵם מְאֹד׃

קסח שָׁמַרְתִּי פִקּוּדֶיךָ וְעֵדֹתֶיךָ
כִּי כָל־דְּרָכַי נֶגְדֶּךָ׃

ת

קסט תִּקְרַב רִנָּתִי לְפָנֶיךָ יְהוָה
כִּדְבָרְךָ הֲבִינֵנִי׃

קע תָּבוֹא תְּחִנָּתִי לְפָנֶיךָ
כְּאִמְרָתְךָ הַצִּילֵנִי׃

קעא תַּבַּעְנָה שְׂפָתַי תְּהִלָּה
כִּי תְלַמְּדֵנִי חֻקֶּיךָ׃

קעב תַּעַן לְשׁוֹנִי אִמְרָתֶךָ
כִּי כָל־מִצְוֺתֶיךָ צֶדֶק׃

173. May Your hand be ready to help me,
for I have chosen Your precepts.

174. I long for Your deliverance, LORD;
Your Torah is my delight.

175. Let me live to praise You;
may Your judgments help me.

176. I have strayed like a lost sheep;
come and seek Your servant,
for I have not forgotten Your commandments.

קעג תְּֽהִי־יָדְךָ֥ לְעָזְרֵ֑נִי
כִּ֖י פִקּוּדֶ֣יךָ בָחָֽרְתִּי׃

קעד תָּאַ֣בְתִּי לִישׁוּעָתְךָ֣ יְהֹוָ֑ה
וְ֝תוֹרָתְךָ֗ שַֽׁעֲשֻׁעָֽי׃

קעה תְּֽחִי־נַ֭פְשִׁי וּֽתְהַֽלְלֶ֑ךָּ
וּֽמִשְׁפָּטֶ֥ךָ יַעֲזְרֻֽנִי׃

קעו תָּעִ֗יתִי כְּשֶׂ֣ה אֹ֭בֵד בַּקֵּ֣שׁ עַבְדֶּ֑ךָ
כִּ֥י מִ֝צְוֺתֶ֗יךָ לֹ֣א שָׁכָֽחְתִּי׃

PSALM 120

1. A song of Ascents.
In my distress I called to the LORD
and He answered me.

Twenty-seventh day of the month

Shabbat

2. LORD, deliver my soul from lying lips,
from the deceitful tongue.

3. What can be done to you,
what can be added to you,
deceitful tongue?

4. You are like the sharp arrows of the warrior,
the burning coals of the broom tree!

5. Alas, that I must dwell in Meshech,
that I must live among the tents of Kedar.

---

of secretiveness and profound disappointment. It expresses the plight of the exile, helplessly struggling against those most treacherous of weapons – malicious words.

Those words are dangerous in two ways. First of all, their damage is not limited to the here and now. They travel great distances, and they endure well into the future. They are *like the sharp arrows of the warrior.*

Secondly they are impossible to detect. Outwardly, they seem harmless. They are deceptively benevolent. They are like *the burning coals of the broom tree,* whose flames burn deep within, but are invisible on the surface.

Fraud and deception take an even more frightening turn in the concluding verses, as Malbim reads them. These verses express the disillusionment of the exile as he learns to his horror that his friends are no better than his foes. Not enough that is he compelled to *dwell in Meshech* and *live among the tents of Kedar,* among alien persecutors. Even his compatriots cannot be trusted!

He has lived all his life with his fellow exiles. He was sure that since they shared his plight, they must also have shared his goals and desires. He is

מזמור קכ

This is my world: lies, malicious gossip, and slander. Everyone schemes and plots against me. I'm not paranoid. This is my real world. It is foolish to be honest, and futile to seek peace.

כו לחודש
ליום השבת

א שִׁיר הַמַּעֲלוֹת
אֶל־יְהוָה בַּצָּרָתָה לִּי
קָרָאתִי וַיַּעֲנֵנִי׃

ב יְהוָה הַצִּילָה נַפְשִׁי מִשְּׂפַת־שֶׁקֶר
מִלָּשׁוֹן רְמִיָּה׃

ג מַה־יִּתֵּן לְךָ וּמַה־יֹּסִיף לָךְ
לָשׁוֹן רְמִיָּה׃

ד חִצֵּי גִבּוֹר שְׁנוּנִים
עִם גַּחֲלֵי רְתָמִים׃

ה אוֹיָה־לִי כִּי־גַרְתִּי מֶשֶׁךְ
שָׁכַנְתִּי עִם־אָהֳלֵי קֵדָר׃

מזמור קכ *Psalm 120:* Our psalm is the first in a series of fifteen psalms, all labeled songs of ascent. It is commonly assumed that that they correspond to the fifteen steps which led from the Holy Temple's lower courtyard to its upper one, and that the Levites sang these songs as they ascended those steps, one by one.

But there are other opinions as to their significance, opinions which will guide us in our study of all fifteen songs of ascent.

Saadia Gaon, for example, believes that they are called songs of ascent because they are meant to be sung more and more loudly, or perhaps in an increasingly higher pitch, as the singer progresses from the first song to the last.

Radak sees these fifteen psalms as collectively giving voice to the hopeful ascent from the depths of the Exile to the heights of Redemption.

Following Saadia, we hear this psalm sung in a whisper, suggesting a mood

6. Too long have I lived
among men who hate peace.

7. I am for peace;
but whenever I speak of it,
they are for war.

This psalm anticipates some of the most shameful episodes in Jewish history. There have been too many occasions when Jews betrayed other Jews, sometimes even acting worse than the alien tormentors. This lamentable state of affairs is the sad note upon which our psalm abruptly ends.

ו רַבַּת שָֽׁכְנָה־לָּהּ נַפְשִׁי
עִם שׂוֹנֵא שָׁלוֹם׃

ז אֲנִי־שָׁלוֹם וְכִי אֲדַבֵּר
הֵמָּה לַמִּלְחָמָה׃

---

tragically disabused of that certainty as he discovers that *too long have I lived among men who hate peace.*

He knows how sincerely he speaks of peace, and how confident he is that he can at least find it among his brethren. How shocked he is to discover that *whenever I speak of it, they are for war.*

PSALM 121

1. A song to the Ascents.
I lift up my eyes to the mountains;
from where will my help come?

2. My help comes from the Lord,
maker of heaven and earth.

3. He will not let your foot slip;
He who guards you does not slumber.

4. Indeed, the guardian of Israel
neither slumbers nor sleeps!

5. The Lord is your guardian;
the Lord is your shade at your right hand.

6. The sun will not strike you by day,
nor the moon by night.

---

connects to the previous one: *I lift up my eyes to the mountains; from where will my help come?*

What does he seek in the mountains? What kind of help can he expect from them? The Midrash (*Bereshit Raba 68*), notes the similarity between the Hebrew words for mountains, *harim,* and the word for parents, *horim.* David hopes for enlightenment from those in his personal and historical past who educated him and shaped his personality – who made him who he is.

But neither the literal mountains nor his forebears have answers for him. His enemies are intransigently committed to war; and the solutions he seeks are not to be found even in the experiences of his ancestors.

He has hit bottom. He has no resort. Now he is prepared to turn to God.

In God he finds the sense of protection he so desires. In Him he finds a guardian who *neither slumbers nor sleeps,* a guardian who will protect him from all harm.

His confidence is renewed, and he can now find within himself the resources he requires to overcome his paralyzing frustration. He hears that *The Lord will guard your coming and going,* and that message assures him

מזמור קכא

I am without hope, utterly alone. I have no answers for my problems. I've looked everywhere for some ray of light. I can't afford to fail again. Who will help me?

א שִׁיר לַמַּעֲלוֹת
אֶשָּׂא עֵינַי אֶל־הֶהָרִים
מֵאַיִן יָבֹא עֶזְרִי׃

ב עֶזְרִי מֵעִם יְהוָה
עֹשֵׂה שָׁמַיִם וָאָרֶץ׃

ג אַל־יִתֵּן לַמּוֹט רַגְלֶךָ
אַל־יָנוּם שֹׁמְרֶךָ׃

ד הִנֵּה לֹא־יָנוּם וְלֹא יִישָׁן
שׁוֹמֵר יִשְׂרָאֵל׃

ה יְהוָה שֹׁמְרֶךָ
יְהוָה צִלְּךָ עַל־יַד יְמִינֶךָ׃

ו יוֹמָם הַשֶּׁמֶשׁ לֹא־יַכֶּכָּה
וְיָרֵחַ בַּלָּיְלָה׃

מזמור קכא *Psalm 121:* This is the second in the series of fifteen psalms that began with the previous one. Unlike all the others, which begin *A song of Ascents, Shir HaMaalot,* this one begins *A song* **to the** *Ascents, Shir LaMaalot.*

Why the change? What might it signify?

Dayan Abramsky suggests that whereas all the subsequent psalms in this series stand alone, our psalm is linked to the previous one. The Hebrew letter "*lamed*," "to the," hints at that link.

The previous psalm began with a desperate prayer: *deliver my soul from lying lips,* and ended with absolute frustration: *I am for peace; but whenever I speak of it, they are for war.*

David feels paralyzed, helpless. He longs for peace, but all he hears is the brandishing of swords. His reaction is described in our psalm, which

7. The LORD will guard you from all harm;
He will guard your life.

8. The LORD will guard your coming and going,
now and forevermore.

Nothing has changed in the "real" world described in the first psalm. In the second psalm everything has changed in David's spiritual condition. He has learned not to fear the challenges that once seemed insurmountable, and he has learned not to depend upon the "mountains" of his past.

He is prepared to do it by himself, with the awareness that his *help comes from the LORD, maker of heaven and earth.*

ז יְהוָה יִשְׁמׇרְךָ מִכׇּל־רָע
יִשְׁמֹר אֶת־נַפְשֶׁךָ׃

ח יְהוָה יִשְׁמׇר־צֵאתְךָ וּבוֹאֶךָ
מֵעַתָּה וְעַד־עוֹלָם׃

---

that he can cope with the "comings and goings" of the predicament he once considered impossible.

Our psalm and the immediately preceding one are thus a couplet. The first describes the crisis; the second the resolution of that crisis.

PSALM 122

1. A song of Ascents. Of David.
I rejoiced when people said to me,
"Let us go up to the house of the Lord."

2. Our feet now stand within your gates,
O Jerusalem:

3. Jerusalem, built up,
like a city compacted together.

4. There the tribes would go up,
the tribes of the Lord,
as was decreed for Israel,
to praise the name of the Lord.

5. There the thrones of judgment are set,
the thrones of the house of David.

6. Pray for the peace of Jerusalem:
"May those who love you live harmoniously;

---

times, that strife was internal, as factions within the city fought viciously with each other for causes petty and noble.

Frequently, Jerusalem found itself besieged by enemies. The major empires of history have laid claim to the city, and war was never a stranger to its citizens.

More than once, those citizens were exiled from Jerusalem for years, for decades, and for centuries.

Our psalm expresses the abundant joy of one of those exiles when he hears the long awaited words: *"Let us go up to the house of the Lord."* His joy becomes exultant when he not only hears the good tidings, but actually stands at Jerusalem's gates.

Our psalmist knows well the power of a rebuilt Jerusalem. It can do what no other force has ever accomplished. It can heal the discord which has historically plagued Jerusalem. *Jerusalem, built up, is like a city compacted together,* which our sages take to mean that it can transform all of Israel's factions into companions of each other.

מזמור קכב

When I really need a spiritual boost, I think of Jerusalem. I recall her glorious past. I imagine her eternal future. I envision her citizens together at last. I pray for her peace.

א שִׁיר הַמַּעֲלוֹת לְדָוִד
שָׂמַחְתִּי בְּאֹמְרִים לִי
בֵּית יְהוָה נֵלֵךְ׃

ב עֹמְדוֹת הָיוּ רַגְלֵינוּ
בִּשְׁעָרַיִךְ יְרוּשָׁלִָם׃

ג יְרוּשָׁלִַם הַבְּנוּיָה
כְּעִיר שֶׁחֻבְּרָה־לָּהּ יַחְדָּו׃

ד שֶׁשָּׁם עָלוּ שְׁבָטִים שִׁבְטֵי־יָהּ עֵדוּת לְיִשְׂרָאֵל
לְהֹדוֹת לְשֵׁם יְהוָה׃

ה כִּי שָׁמָּה ׀ יָשְׁבוּ כִסְאוֹת לְמִשְׁפָּט
כִּסְאוֹת לְבֵית דָּוִד׃

ו שַׁאֲלוּ שְׁלוֹם יְרוּשָׁלִָם
יִשְׁלָיוּ אֹהֲבָיִךְ׃

מזמור קכב *Psalm 122:* Jerusalem is comprised of many diverse components. It is the seat of justice, and it is the seat of royalty: *There the thrones of judgment are set, the thrones of the house of David.*

Pilgrims journey great distances to visit the city, and its residents give thanks for the privilege of living there. *There the tribes would go up… to praise the name of the Lord.*

Like any city, it has its divisions of rank, status, and wealth. Priests attend to the Temple services, scholars teach, craftsmen labor, and merchants sell their wares.

It is very much like a body with its many organs, all so different from each other.

Like no other city, it has been the scene of strife for many centuries. At

7. may there be peace within your ramparts,
harmony in your palaces."

8. For the sake of my brothers and my friends,
I will say, "Peace be within you."

9. For the sake of the house of the LORD our God,
I will pray for your well-being.

---

love you, those who love the city, must *live harmoniously*. When can peace be achieved at the *ramparts* which protect the city from enemies without? The answer is: only when there is *harmony in the palaces* within.

What a pertinent lesson for our time! The goal of peace with Israel's foes can be realized only to the extent that harmony exists in Israel's midst. *Shalva* is a prerequisite for *shalom.*

ז יְהִי־שָׁלוֹם בְּחֵילֵךְ
שַׁלְוָה בְּאַרְמְנוֹתָיִךְ:

ח לְמַעַן אַחַי וְרֵעָי
אֲדַבְּרָה־נָּא שָׁלוֹם בָּךְ:

ט לְמַעַן בֵּית־יְהוָה אֱלֹהֵינוּ
אֲבַקְשָׁה טוֹב לָךְ:

Verses 6 and 7 each contain two words which are essentially synonymous, *shalom* and *shalva*. We have translated them *peace* and *harmony,* basing our translation upon Malbim's suggestion that *shalom* refers to peace between the city and its external enemies, whereas *shalva* connotes peace within the city, harmony among its inhabitants.

Following Malbim's suggestion, we can paraphrase these verses to convey a vital lesson: If there is a wish to *pray for the peace of Jerusalem,* then *those who*

PSALM 123

1. A song of Ascents.
To You, enthroned in heaven, I lift up my eyes.

2. As the eyes of slaves look to their master's hand,
as the eyes of a maid to the hand of her mistress,
so our eyes look to the LORD our God,
awaiting His favor.

3. Favor us, LORD, favor us,
for we have had more than enough of contempt.

4. Too long have we suffered the scorn of the complacent,
the contempt of haughty oppressors.

The author of *Mishna Berura*, the final authority on such matters, does not agree that the *Amida* should be repeated in such a case. However, he does urge that one try one's best to follow the *Shulḥan Arukh*'s prescription.

He further counsels, "One should remain aware that it is in the power of no entity, neither an angel nor good fortune nor the stars in the heavens, to fulfill one's prayers. That can only be achieved by His will, may He be blessed."

The nineteenth-century German theologian Friedrich Schleiermacher described this attitude as *kreaturgefuhl*, a feeling of "creatureness." He was almost certainly unaware that Ramban, centuries earlier, in his commentary on Exodus 13, had already identified the words which define the essence of prayer. Those words, he wrote in his commentary on Exodus 13, are "we are Your creatures."

Ramban's source might very well be our psalm, which precisely expresses his idea, albeit in metaphoric terms: *As the eyes of slaves… so our eyes look to the LORD our God, awaiting His favor.*

מזמור קכג

I feel like the lowest of the low. I am mocked and teased at every turn. I don't know what's worse, the names they call me or their supercilious smiles. I have had enough.

א שִׁ֗יר הַֽמַּ֫עֲל֥וֹת
אֵ֭לֶיךָ נָשָׂ֣אתִי אֶת־עֵינַ֑י
הַ֝יֹּשְׁבִ֗י בַּשָּׁמָֽיִם׃

ב הִנֵּ֨ה כְעֵינֵ֪י עֲבָדִ֡ים אֶל־יַ֬ד אֲֽדוֹנֵיהֶ֗ם
כְּעֵינֵ֣י שִׁפְחָה֮ אֶל־יַ֪ד גְּבִ֫רְתָּ֥הּ
כֵּ֣ן עֵ֭ינֵינוּ אֶל־יהוה אֱלֹהֵ֑ינוּ עַ֝֗ד שֶׁיְּחָנֵּֽנוּ׃

ג חָנֵּ֣נוּ יהוה חָנֵּ֑נוּ
כִּֽי־רַ֝֗ב שָׂבַ֥עְנוּ בֽוּז׃

ד רַבַּת֮ שָֽׂבְעָה־לָּ֪ה נַ֫פְשֵׁ֥נוּ
הַלַּ֥עַג הַשַּׁאֲנַנִּ֑ים הַ֝בּ֗וּז לגאיונים׃ לִגְאֵ֥י יוֹנִֽים

מזמור קכג *Psalm 123:* These days none of us really knows what it feels like to be a slave.

The experience of being totally dependent upon another person, powerless but for his favor, is alien to us.

Yet, feeling like a slave is precisely the frame of mind which characterizes prayer. *As the eyes of slaves look to their master's hand... so our eyes look to the* L*ORD*.

In the section of his *Shulḥan Arukh* which deals with the laws of prayer, Rabbi Yosef Karo prescribes a subservient posture as a singular prerequisite for proper prayer. He writes, "One should pray in a pleading manner, like a beggar seeking alms at the door, meekly" (ch. 98:3).

Some later halakhic authorities even go so far as to rule that failure to recite the *Amida* prayer in a "pleading manner" invalidates that prayer, thereby requiring its repetition.

PSALM 124

1. A song of Ascents. Of David.
If the LORD had not been on our side –
Israel can truly say so –

2. if the LORD had not been on our side,
when man rose up against us,

3. then they would have swallowed us alive
in their fierce anger against us;

4. the waters would have swept us away,
the torrent would have surged over our heads,

5. the raging waters would have surged over us.

6. Blessed be the LORD, who did not leave us
a prey for their teeth.

---

an entire nation to *rise up against us*. We are all too familiar with the nefarious power of one madman, a Haman or a Hitler, to sway multitudes to enact his murderous schemes.

Our psalm celebrates God's rescue of His people from two distinct threats: the physical threat, *they would have swallowed us alive,* and the spiritual threat symbolized by *the raging waters*.

We survived bodily, and were not left as *a prey for their teeth.*

And we survived spiritually.

For a time, our innermost soul, so aptly symbolized by the frail and delicate bird, was indeed ensnared. It was seduced by the attractions of other cultures and alien beliefs. But eventually the bird became free of that trap. Our souls emerged intact.

We readily acknowledge that without God's assistance we could not have survived physically. We also readily admit that it was not only by dint of our own efforts that we avoided the many attempts to capture our souls.

That too required *seyata deshemaya,* heaven's helping hand. *Our help is the name of the LORD, maker of heaven and earth.*

מזמור קכד

That was a close call. I never thought I'd make it. The odds were against me. My friends and family gave up hope. But I am here to tell the tale. Thank God.

א שִׁיר הַמַּעֲלוֹת לְדָוִד
לוּלֵי יהוה שֶׁהָיָה לָנוּ
יֹאמַר־נָא יִשְׂרָאֵל:

ב לוּלֵי יהוה שֶׁהָיָה לָנוּ
בְּקוּם עָלֵינוּ אָדָם:

ג אֲזַי חַיִּים בְּלָעוּנוּ
בַּחֲרוֹת אַפָּם בָּנוּ:

ד אֲזַי הַמַּיִם שְׁטָפוּנוּ
נַחְלָה עָבַר עַל־נַפְשֵׁנוּ:

ה אֲזַי עָבַר עַל־נַפְשֵׁנוּ
הַמַּיִם הַזֵּידוֹנִים:

ו בָּרוּךְ יהוה
שֶׁלֹּא נְתָנָנוּ טֶרֶף לְשִׁנֵּיהֶם:

מזמור קכד *Psalm 124:* The relationship between God and Israel is a reciprocal one. We trust in Him, and He reciprocates with His divine providence. Note that it is another human being, *adam,* who is the implacable foe in our psalm. This is reminiscent of another biblical verse: *And David said to Gad, "I am in great distress. Let us fall into God's hand… but do not let me fall into the hand of man"* (II Sam. 24:14). David learned from his personal experience that no natural danger is as sinister as a human adversary.

Note too that it is one single human being who is the ultimate threat. *When man rose up against us,* and not *when men rose up against us.* The Jewish people have learned from their historical experience that it is frequently just one hateful man, possessed with diabolical charisma, who is capable of inciting

7. We have escaped like a bird from the fowler's snare;
the snare broke and we escaped.

8. Our help is the name of the LORD,
maker of heaven and earth.

ז נַ֭פְשֵׁנוּ כְּצִפּ֥וֹר נִמְלְטָה֮ מִפַּ֪ח י֫וֹקְשִׁ֥ים
הַפַּ֥ח נִשְׁבָּ֗ר וַאֲנַ֥חְנוּ נִמְלָֽטְנוּ׃

ח עֶ֭זְרֵנוּ בְּשֵׁ֣ם יְהוָ֑ה
עֹ֝שֵׂ֗ה שָׁמַ֥יִם וָאָֽרֶץ׃

PSALM 125

1. A song of Ascents.
Those who trust in the Lord are like Mount Zion,
which cannot be moved, but stands forever.

2. As mountains are around Jerusalem,
so the Lord is around His people, both now and forevermore.

3. Surely the rule* of wickedness shall not rest
in the land allotted to the righteous,
for then the righteous may set their hands to wrongdoing.

4. Do good, Lord, to those who do good,
and to them who are upright in their hearts.

5. But as for them who turn to crooked ways,
may the Lord lead them along the way of the evildoers.
Then there will be peace upon Israel!

*Lit. "scepter."

Our verse reads:

As mountains are around Jerusalem, so the Lord is around His people, both now and forevermore.

Radak intersperses these words with comments of his own, thus changing its meaning significantly:

> *Jerusalem,* in spite of *the mountains around her,* is not invincible. Nations have dominated her, and other nations have conquered the city, one from the other. Jerusalem will not be secure until God's people are within it. Then He will be a circle *around His people.* His name will be a stronger source of strength for them than the mighty mountains, and the enemy will never again dominate them, *now and forevermore.*

Implicit in Radak's interpretation is a word of caution to the Jewish people. *The Lord is around His people.* God's presence in Jerusalem is but one component of its security. The other component is that we behave as *His people,* that we live ethical and moral lives, in accordance with His will. Only then are we assured that He will surround us with an invulnerable circle, superior to the mightiest circle of mountains.

מזמור קכה

I've heard that nice guys finish last. But that doesn't tempt me to become a bad guy. I'll stick with the nice guys. Our time will come. We'll finish first.

א שִׁיר הַמַּעֲלוֹת
הַבֹּטְחִים בַּיהוָה
כְּהַר־צִיּוֹן לֹא־יִמּוֹט לְעוֹלָם יֵשֵׁב׃

ב יְרוּשָׁלִַם הָרִים סָבִיב לָהּ
וַיהוָה סָבִיב לְעַמּוֹ מֵעַתָּה וְעַד־עוֹלָם׃

ג כִּי לֹא יָנוּחַ שֵׁבֶט הָרֶשַׁע עַל גּוֹרַל הַצַּדִּיקִים
לְמַעַן לֹא־יִשְׁלְחוּ הַצַּדִּיקִים ׀ בְּעַוְלָתָה יְדֵיהֶם׃

ד הֵיטִיבָה יְהוָה לַטּוֹבִים
וְלִישָׁרִים בְּלִבּוֹתָם׃

ה וְהַמַּטִּים עֲקַלְקַלּוֹתָם
יוֹלִיכֵם יְהוָה אֶת־פֹּעֲלֵי הָאָוֶן
שָׁלוֹם עַל־יִשְׂרָאֵל׃

מזמור קכה *Psalm 125:* Is our psalm the ultimate expression of optimism and hope? Is the circle of mountains of verse 2 a metaphor for Jerusalem's invincibility?

Many commentators definitely think so. Rashi states: "Just as the mountains encircle Jerusalem, so does the Holy One blessed be He encircle His people."

A much more recent commentator, Dayan Abramsky, goes even further: "Just as the 'mountains surrounding Jerusalem' are plainly visible for all to see, so too 'the Lord surrounding His people' is apparent and obvious to anyone who hasn't deliberately clouded his eyes from seeing clearly" (*Ḥazon Yeḥezkel, Sukka* 3:4).

Radak, on the other hand, questions whether those mountains are in fact a symbol of perfect protection for the Holy City. After all, the armies of many nations have successfully scaled those mountains, capturing the city again and again in the course of its long history.

It is not the circle of mountains that protects Jerusalem, insists Radak. It is the Lord God who protects Jerusalem.

PSALM 126

1. A song of Ascents.
When the Lord brings back Zion's exiles,
we were like dreamers.*

2. Then our mouths will be filled with laughter,
and our tongues with songs of joy.
Then shall they say among the nations,
"The Lord has done great things for them."

3. Indeed, the Lord will have done great things for us;
we shall surely be glad.

4. Bring back our exiles, Lord,
like streams coming to the dry south.

5. They who sow in tears
will reap with songs of joy.

6. He who goes out weeping, carrying precious seed,
will come back with songs of joy, carrying his sheaves.

* Or: "We see it as in a dream." Ibn Ezra.

For Ibn Ezra, redemption itself is the dream. For Radak's father, the dream is the nightmare of our long exile.

Rav Kook, in his *Orot HaKodesh*, offers yet another interpretation. For him, the realm of the dream is the ideal realm. What we refer to as the "real world" is bereft of dreams, and as such is a diminished and contaminated world.

He points out that the best of humanity regularly dream. Prophets dream, poets dream, and, in our psalm, the returned captives of Zion dream.

Ordinary life "removes from the world the light of the dream." Paradoxically, the dream is the ultimate reality, the ground of true existence.

For Rav Kook, the message of our psalm is this: During our long and tragic exile our capacity to dream was lost. With the redemption, that capacity is restored.

The tears of exile become songs of joy because of the transformative powers of the dream.

מזמור קכו

It was all worth it. We suffered. We cried. But look at us now. We laugh and sing with joy.

א שִׁ֗יר הַֽמַּ֫עֲל֥וֹת
בְּשׁ֣וּב יְ֭הוָה אֶת־שִׁיבַ֣ת צִיּ֑וֹן
הָ֝יִ֗ינוּ כְּחֹלְמִֽים׃

ב אָ֤ז יִמָּ֪לֵ֡א שְׂח֡וֹק פִּינוּ֮ וּלְשׁוֹנֵ֪נוּ רִ֫נָּ֥ה
אָ֭ז יֹאמְר֣וּ בַגּוֹיִ֑ם
הִגְדִּ֥יל יְ֝הוָ֗ה לַעֲשׂ֥וֹת עִם־אֵֽלֶּה׃

ג הִגְדִּ֣יל יְ֭הוָה לַעֲשׂ֥וֹת עִמָּ֗נוּ
הָיִ֥ינוּ שְׂמֵחִֽים׃

ד שׁוּבָ֣ה יְ֭הוָה אֶת־שבותנו ‏ שְׁבִיתֵ֑נוּ
כַּאֲפִיקִ֥ים בַּנֶּֽגֶב׃

ה הַזֹּרְעִ֥ים בְּדִמְעָ֗ה
בְּרִנָּ֥ה יִקְצֹֽרוּ׃

ו הָ֘ל֤וֹךְ יֵלֵ֨ךְ ׀ וּבָכֹה֮ נֹשֵׂ֪א מֶֽשֶׁךְ־הַזָּ֫רַע
בֹּֽא־יָבֹ֥א בְרִנָּ֑ה נֹ֝שֵׂ֗א אֲלֻמֹּתָֽיו׃

מזמור קכו *Psalm 126:* The great cantor, Yossele Rosenblatt, recommended our psalm to be the national anthem of the State of Israel. He popularized a stirring melody for it, composed by Pinhas Minkowski, which expresses its theme dramatically, and one which is suitable as an anthem for a redeemed nation. To this very day, many sing the words of our psalm to his melody.

In its opening verse, our psalm presents a potent image: *we were like dreamers.*

Abraham ibn Ezra understands this image to mean that only in a dream could humans experience such a wondrous event as the Return to Zion.

In his commentary on our verse, Radak offers a very different interpretation. He quotes his father, as he frequently does: "The sufferings of our exile will be like a fleeting dream in our eyes, because of the great joy that we will experience when we return to our land."

PSALM 127

1. A song of Ascents. Of Solomon.
Unless the LORD builds the house,
in vain do its builders labor.
Unless the LORD guards the city,
in vain does the guard keep watch.

2. In vain do you rise early and stay up late,
toiling hard for the bread you eat;
He provides as much for His loved ones in their sleep.

3. Truly children are a gift from the LORD,
the fruit of the womb is His reward.

4. Like arrows in the hand of a warrior
are the children of one's youth.

5. Happy is the man who has his quiver full of them;
they shall not be put to shame
when they contend with the enemy at the gate.

---

insists Rav Hirsch, "is the most worrisome concern of all. With each child come more worries, and preoccupation with the problems of one's children and grandchildren endures for the entire course of one's life."

For the "friend" of God, however, children are not just drains on one's resources. They are divine gifts and blessed rewards. *Happy is the man who has his quiver full of them.*

Our psalm employs a most unusual metaphor for children. They are *like arrows in the hand of a warrior*. Like the arrow which must be aimed, so the child must have parental direction. Like the arrow which continues its flight long after it has left the archer's bow, so the child must embody his parents' teachings long after he has left their home.

Malbim finds yet another lesson for parents in our psalm. He notes in verse 3 that children are both a gift and a reward. Gifts are given out of love, in this case, God's love, for which the parents must live a life of prayer and devotion.

But rewards are earned by hard work, without which successful parenting is impossible.

מזמור קכז

I've worked long hours. I've built a house. I've been involved in my community. I've raised a family. I've known success. But it wasn't my doing. I had His help.

א שִׁיר הַמַּעֲלוֹת לִשְׁלֹמֹה
אִם־יהוה ׀ לֹא־יִבְנֶה בַיִת שָׁוְא עָמְלוּ בוֹנָיו בּוֹ
אִם־יהוה לֹא־יִשְׁמָר־עִיר שָׁוְא ׀ שָׁקַד שׁוֹמֵר׃

ב שָׁוְא לָכֶם ׀ מַשְׁכִּימֵי קוּם מְאַחֲרֵי־שֶׁבֶת
אֹכְלֵי לֶחֶם הָעֲצָבִים
כֵּן יִתֵּן לִידִידוֹ שֵׁנָא׃

ג הִנֵּה נַחֲלַת יהוה בָּנִים
שָׂכָר פְּרִי הַבָּטֶן׃

ד כְּחִצִּים בְּיַד־גִּבּוֹר
כֵּן בְּנֵי הַנְּעוּרִים׃

ה אַשְׁרֵי הַגֶּבֶר אֲשֶׁר מִלֵּא אֶת־אַשְׁפָּתוֹ מֵהֶם
לֹא־יֵבֹשׁוּ כִּי־יְדַבְּרוּ אֶת־אוֹיְבִים בַּשָּׁעַר׃

מזמור קכז *Psalm 127:* Our psalm and the next are "domestic" psalms. They both describe the delights of family life and contain good counsel for parents. Whereas the first teaches that personal efforts are futile when they are not blessed with divine providence, the second instructs us how and when to exercise our own efforts successfully.

The average person feels frustrated by life's disappointments. When things do not work out for him, he merely redoubles his efforts, trying ever harder to repetitively perform the same activities that were unsuccessful in the first place.

The man of faith knows disappointments too, but he sees them as the will of God. In the words of Rav Hirsch, "He knows that even if he was to expend all of his energies, neither sleeping nor resting, he will ultimately achieve nothing without God's help." Instead, the man of faith is confident that his Friend will *provide for His loved ones*.

Life provides many occasions for worry. "Concern about one's children,"

PSALM 128

1. A song of Ascents.
Happy are all who fear the Lord,
who walk in His ways!

2. You shall eat the labor of your hands,
you shall be happy and prosperous.

3. Your wife shall be like a fruitful vine within your house;
your children like olive shoots around your table.

4. And thus shall the man be blessed who fears the Lord.

5. May the Lord bless you from Zion;
may you see the prosperity of Jerusalem
all the days of your life;

6. and may you live to see your children's children!
Peace be on Israel!

He comments insightfully: "A life of luxury achieved effortlessly forces a person to seek out peculiar pleasures, whereas those who support themselves by means of their own toil find joy even in the simplest of life's moments."

And finally, writes Rav Hirsch inspirationally: "The God-fearing Jew does not see in himself and in his family the ultimate source of blessing, for he knows that he is only a branch, a small part, of a large circle whose center is Zion and Jerusalem."

The fortunate man finds his work life productive and his family life gratifying. However, he feels incomplete unless he finds a role to play in the larger community of Israel. He strives to *see the prosperity of Jerusalem*.

Even when surrounded by his *children's children* he exclaims:

Peace be on Israel!

מזמור קכח

I am truly blessed. I work hard, but productively. I love my wife.
I am proud of my children. If Jerusalem was at peace, all would be perfect.

א שִׁ֗יר הַֽמַּ֫עֲל֥וֹת
אַ֭שְׁרֵי כׇּל־יְרֵ֣א יְהוָ֑ה הַ֝הֹלֵ֗ךְ בִּדְרָכָֽיו׃

ב יְגִ֣יעַ כַּ֭פֶּיךָ כִּ֣י תֹאכֵ֑ל
אַ֝שְׁרֶ֗יךָ וְט֣וֹב לָֽךְ׃

ג אֶשְׁתְּךָ֤ ׀ כְּגֶ֥פֶן פֹּרִיָּ֮ה בְּיַרְכְּתֵ֪י בֵ֫יתֶ֥ךָ
בָּ֭נֶיךָ כִּשְׁתִלֵ֣י זֵיתִ֑ים סָ֝בִ֗יב לְשֻׁלְחָנֶֽךָ׃

ד הִנֵּ֣ה כִי־כֵ֭ן יְבֹ֥רַךְ גָּ֗בֶר יְרֵ֣א יְהוָֽה׃

ה יְבָרֶכְךָ֥ יְהוָ֗ה מִצִּ֫יּ֥וֹן
וּ֭רְאֵה בְּט֣וּב יְרוּשָׁלָ֑͏ִם כֹּ֝֗ל יְמֵ֣י חַיֶּֽיךָ׃

ו וּרְאֵֽה־בָנִ֥ים לְבָנֶ֑יךָ
שָׁ֝ל֗וֹם עַל־יִשְׂרָאֵֽל׃

מזמור קכח *Psalm 128:* Our psalm continues to paint the picture of the ideal home. Wife and children, and even grandchildren, are in the foreground of the picture. In the background we find the hardworking husband and father, who *eats the labor of his hands.*

Rav Hirsch comments incisively about the value of eating *the labor of your hands.* He writes that when one earns his livelihood through his own hard work he experiences "a sweetness of success which is absent from him whose material possessions and luxurious lifestyle comes to him without effort, not having to work hard to sustain his wife and children."

PSALM 129

1. A song of Ascents.
Since my youth men have often attacked me –
Israel can truly say so –

2. since my youth men have often attacked me,
but they never prevailed against me.

3. Plowmen have plowed across my back,
they made long their furrows.

4. But the Lord is just,
He has snapped the ropes of the wicked.

5. Let all who hate Zion
be ashamed and driven back.

6. Let them be like grass growing on the roof,
which withers before it can be pulled up;

---

their plowing. No ally intervenes on the victim's behalf. Aware that they are free to plow as they please, the persecutors escalate their atrocities. *They make long their furrows.*

Thankfully, the darkness is never total. Sadly, the light too is incomplete. *They never prevailed against me.* The enemy failed to achieve his genocidal goal, but in the process so many perished.

Our psalm does not conclude with the hope that resounds in the final words of the preceding psalm: *Peace be upon Israel.*

In our psalm the hope that is expressed is much more modest. May the haters of Zion *be ashamed and driven back. Let them be like grass growing on the roof, which withers before it can be pulled up.* May the enemy's plans be thwarted early on. May his objective *to destroy, to murder, to eradicate* not be fully achieved.

Our psalm is not a song of glorious victory. It is a desperate prayer that a remnant be spared, and a plea that the survivors rebuild what was destroyed.

מזמור קכט

They hate me because I am a Jew. They've hated us from the very beginning. They've tried to exterminate us. Had they had their way, none of us would be here now. Thank God, I survived, and so did you. But others didn't.

א שִׁ֗יר הַֽמַּ֫עֲל֥וֹת
רַ֭בַּת צְרָר֣וּנִי מִנְּעוּרָ֑י
יֹֽאמַר־נָ֝א יִשְׂרָאֵֽל׃

ב רַ֭בַּת צְרָר֣וּנִי מִנְּעוּרָ֑י
גַּ֝֗ם לֹא־יָ֥כְלוּ לִֽי׃

ג עַל־גַּ֭בִּי חָרְשׁ֣וּ חֹרְשִׁ֑ים
הֶ֝אֱרִ֗יכוּ למענותָֽם׃ לְמַעֲנִיתָֽם

ד יְהוָ֥ה צַדִּ֑יק
קִ֝צֵּ֗ץ עֲב֣וֹת רְשָׁעִֽים׃

ה יֵ֭בֹשׁוּ וְיִסֹּ֣גוּ אָח֑וֹר
כֹּ֝֗ל שֹׂנְאֵ֥י צִיּֽוֹן׃

ו יִ֭הְיוּ כַּחֲצִ֣יר גַּגּ֑וֹת
שֶׁקַּדְמַ֖ת שָׁלַ֣ף יָבֵֽשׁ׃

מזמור קכט *Psalm 129:* The term "anti-Semitism" is an invention of the nineteenth century. But the phenomenon it describes is an ancient one. The story of Israel's suffering at the hands of her despisers is a long and sordid story.

Our psalm, brief as it is, tells some of that story. The story begins when Israel began. *Since my youth men have often attacked me.*

The story alternates between darkness and light.

In the dark times we were often helpless victims, as defenseless against our tormentors as is the soil against the plow.

Plowmen have plowed across my back. To their surprise, no one protests

7. with which the reaper cannot fill his hand,
nor the binder of sheaves his lap,

8. so that passers-by will never exchange greetings with them:
"The LORD's blessing be upon you!"
"We bless you in the name of the LORD!"

ז שֶׁלֹּא מִלֵּא כַפּוֹ קוֹצֵר
וְחִצְנוֹ מְעַמֵּר:

ח וְלֹא אָמְרוּ ׀ הָעֹבְרִים
בִּרְכַּת־יְהוָה אֲלֵיכֶם
בֵּרַכְנוּ אֶתְכֶם בְּשֵׁם יְהוָה:

PSALM 130

1. A song of Ascents.
Out of the depths I call to You, Lord.

2. Lord, hear my voice;
let Your ears be attentive to my plea for mercy.

3. If You, Lord, should keep account of sins,
who could survive?

4. But with You there is forgiveness;
therefore You are feared.

5. I wait for the Lord;
my soul waits;
hopefully I wait for His word.

6. My soul waits for the Lord
more eagerly than watchmen for the morning;
yes, more than watchmen for the morning.

---

a forgiving God, knowing that He would not punish us but would readily forgive us.

There are two approaches which are helpful here.

One is that of Rashi, who points out that much of God's work is done through intermediaries: angels, in biblical terms; nature, in modern terms. But forgiveness is an act of God for which there are no intermediaries. Only God can forgive by undoing not only sin but the consequences of sin. Men thus discover that they cannot appeal to intermediaries to find forgiveness. Therefore, men come to fear God, knowing that only by confronting Him can they attain ultimate forgiveness.

Abraham Ibn Ezra, in his commentary on Psalms, offers us a profound insight which helps us understand this verse differently. He points out that if sinners were convinced that there was no forgiveness for their iniquities, they would persuade themselves that repentance is hopeless. Why reform one's ways if one was damned to punishment anyway? Precisely the fact that

מזמור קל

I am in deep trouble. I am down deep, and You are up so high. My depth will release me from the depths. Deep faith, deep sincerity, and deep humility will elevate me once again. I must descend in order to ascend. I must not pray from upon a chair. I must pray from here.

א שִׁיר הַמַּעֲלוֹת
מִמַּעֲמַקִּים קְרָאתִיךָ יהוה:

ב אֲדֹנָי שִׁמְעָה בְקוֹלִי
תִּהְיֶינָה אָזְנֶיךָ קַשֻּׁבוֹת לְקוֹל תַּחֲנוּנָי:

ג אִם־עֲוֺנוֹת תִּשְׁמָר־יָהּ
אֲדֹנָי מִי יַעֲמֹד:

ד כִּי־עִמְּךָ הַסְּלִיחָה
לְמַעַן תִּוָּרֵא:

ה קִוִּיתִי יהוה
קִוְּתָה נַפְשִׁי
וְלִדְבָרוֹ הוֹחָלְתִּי:

ו נַפְשִׁי לַאדֹנָי
מִשֹּׁמְרִים לַבֹּקֶר
שֹׁמְרִים לַבֹּקֶר:

מזמור קל *Psalm 130:* Our psalm is frequently recited in the synagogue at times when the community feels greatly threatened. It is brief, forthright, and easily understood. No wonder that many incorporate it into the liturgy for the Ten Days of Repentance, just before the "*Barekhu*" prayer which begins the series of blessings preceding the recitation of *Shema Yisrael.*

One verse, however, presents difficulty: *But with You there is forgiveness; therefore You are feared.* How does God's forgiveness lead to our fear of Him? Quite the contrary; one would think that we would be less fearful of

7. O Israel, put your hope in the LORD;
for with the LORD there is loving-kindness,
and with Him there is great power to redeem.

8. He Himself will redeem Israel from all their sins.

The messages of both Rashi and Ibn Ezra help us understand the special relevance of our psalm for the Ten Days of Repentance between Rosh HaShana and Yom Kippur. As we contemplate the special blessing of God's forgiveness, a favor which only He can bestow upon us, we are motivated to fear Him and change our ways.

ז יַחֵל יִשְׂרָאֵל אֶל־יְהֹוָה
כִּי־עִם־יְהֹוָה הַחֶסֶד
וְהַרְבֵּה עִמּוֹ פְדוּת:

ח וְהוּא יִפְדֶּה אֶת־יִשְׂרָאֵל
מִכֹּל עֲוֺנֹתָיו:

God does forgive removes that hopelessness from them. They realize that if, out of fear of God, they approach Him and beg His forgiveness, they can be hopeful of attaining it.

The fact that God forgives thus leads to fear of Him, and motivates repentance and personal change.

PSALM 131

1. A song of Ascents. Of David.
LORD, my heart is not proud,
nor are my eyes haughty;
I do not concern myself with matters,
too great or too wonderful for me.

2. But I have stilled and calmed my soul,
like a weaned child with its mother;
like a weaned child is my soul within me.

3. O Israel, put your hope in the LORD,
now and forevermore.

David offers advice based upon his own experience with persecution, wandering, and powerlessness.

What worked for me, he is saying, is keeping a low profile and realizing how helpless I was. Only then did God hear me. As we will read in Psalm 138, *The LORD is exalted, yet He cares for the lowly.*

This is his message: Don't concern yourself with matters that are over your head. Go slow, step by step. Realize your limitations. Think of yourself as a babe just weaned from your mother's breast. Depend upon God, realizing that without Him you are totally lost. Only with such extreme humility, in thought and in action, can you *put your hope in the LORD, now and forevermore.*

Rav Hirsch sees it differently. He believes that David is contrasting his own ability to be satisfied with little, to what he thinks that his people deserve. For Rav Hirsch, David is saying: "As far as I am concerned, my soul now asks for nothing more.... But as for Israel, they have an eternal claim to progress, growth, and prosperity. Let them *hope in the LORD, now and evermore.*"

We have here two different approaches, each with great validity. One sees David as giving advice to the people to follow his humble example. The other concurs with David's approach, but insists that David will only preach humility to himself, and perhaps to other individuals. But a nation, a collective, can never be humble. A nation must have proud goals and lofty objectives, and must insist on its right to achieve them.

מזמור קלא

I am a charitable person. Yet I refuse to help someone who can help himself. Send me someone who is truly helpless. I won't turn him away empty handed. It is the same way with God. If you want Him to answer your prayers, You had better convince Him that you're truly helpless. You are helpless, you know. You are as helpless as a just-weaned child.

א שִׁיר הַמַּעֲלוֹת לְדָוִד
יהוה ׀ לֹא־גָבַהּ לִבִּי וְלֹא־רָמוּ עֵינַי
וְלֹא־הִלַּכְתִּי ׀ בִּגְדֹלוֹת וּבְנִפְלָאוֹת מִמֶּנִּי׃

ב אִם־לֹא שִׁוִּיתִי ׀ וְדוֹמַמְתִּי נַפְשִׁי
כְּגָמֻל עֲלֵי אִמּוֹ
כַּגָּמֻל עָלַי נַפְשִׁי׃

ג יַחֵל יִשְׂרָאֵל אֶל־יהוה
מֵעַתָּה וְעַד־עוֹלָם׃

מזמור קלא *Psalm 131:* It has been said that arrogance is the worst of all sins. Our psalm makes that claim eloquently, and very succinctly.

David declares that he has fought every man's natural tendency toward prideful self-confidence. He has struggled to maintain an image of himself as an infant: totally helpless, and totally dependent upon his mother. He has done so inwardly, through introspection: *My heart is not proud*. And he has done so outwardly, in his behavior: *Nor are my eyes haughty.*

Some men proclaim their humility arrogantly. They boast that they are the humblest of men. Such paradoxical statements seem foolish, and hearing them we cannot suppress a dismissive chuckle. Is that what David is doing in our psalm? Is he boasting of his humility?

Radak insists otherwise. He maintains that David is giving advice to others. As Radak puts it, David is giving advice to the Jewish people, knowing prophetically that they are destined to spend centuries in exile.

How can you survive the trials and tribulations of many years of persecution and wandering? How especially can one maintain one's faith in the face of all the suffering which lies in store for those without a land of their own?

PSALM 132

1. A song of Ascents.
LORD, remember in David's favor
all the hardships he endured.

2. How he swore an oath to the LORD
and vowed to the Mighty One of Jacob:

3. "I will not enter my house,
nor will I mount the couch spread for me;

4. I will give no sleep to my eyes,
no slumber to my eyelids,

5. until I find a place for the LORD,
a dwelling for the Mighty One of Jacob."

6. We first heard of it* in Ephrata,
and then we learned it was to be in the wooded field.**

7. Let us enter His dwelling,
let us worship at His footstool.

* I.e., the Ark of God.

** David and his men discovered that the Ark and God's dwelling-place were to be located in Jerusalem; the places named in this verse are in the vicinity of Jerusalem: Ephrat (another name for Bethlehem) about six miles south of Jerusalem, and Jaar (probably Kiriath-Yearim) about eight miles north of Jerusalem. Cf. Tractate *Zevaḥim*, 54b.

---

son who will be a tranquil man… Solomon will be his name… he will build a house for My name." (1 Chr. 22:8–10)

David's reaction is epitomized in our psalm, and it serves as a model for all of us who reach a point in our lives when we realize that we will not live to see some of our greatest ambitions fulfilled.

David accepts his disappointment with a combination of resignation and

מזמור קלב

There's the external and there's the internal. God's Temple must have both. External does not mean pompous gilded glitter. It means exemplary behavior, priests robed in righteousness. Internal does not mean plans and schemes. It means music and melody, joyous and eternal. Righteousness and song – together, that's the Temple.

א שִׁיר הַמַּעֲלוֹת
זְכוֹר־יְהוָה לְדָוִד אֵת כָּל־עֻנּוֹתוֹ׃

ב אֲשֶׁר נִשְׁבַּע לַיהוָה
נָדַר לַאֲבִיר יַעֲקֹב׃

ג אִם־אָבֹא בְּאֹהֶל בֵּיתִי
אִם־אֶעֱלֶה עַל־עֶרֶשׂ יְצוּעָי׃

ד אִם־אֶתֵּן שְׁנַת לְעֵינָי
לְעַפְעַפַּי תְּנוּמָה׃

ה עַד־אֶמְצָא מָקוֹם לַיהוָה
מִשְׁכָּנוֹת לַאֲבִיר יַעֲקֹב׃

ו הִנֵּה־שְׁמַעֲנוּהָ בְאֶפְרָתָה
מְצָאנוּהָ בִּשְׂדֵי־יָעַר׃

ז נָבוֹאָה לְמִשְׁכְּנוֹתָיו
נִשְׁתַּחֲוֶה לַהֲדֹם רַגְלָיו׃

מזמור קלב *Psalm 132:* Our psalm masks a tragic story. Like Moses, David was denied his most fervent desire. He wished to build the Temple, which until his time had no permanent place. He was judged unfit to be the one to build the Temple, as he personally told his son and successor, Solomon:

> *My son, I wanted to build a house for the name of the Lord my God. But the word of the Lord came to me, saying, "You have shed much blood and fought great battles; you shall not build a house for My name… but you will have a*

8. Arise, LORD, and enter Your resting place,
You and the Ark [the symbol] of Your strength.

9. Your priests are robed in righteousness,
Your loyal ones sing for joy.

10. For the sake of Your servant David,
do not reject Your anointed one.

11. The LORD swore to David,
a sure oath that He will not revoke:
"One born of your own body
I will set upon your throne.

12. If your sons keep My covenant,
and My decrees that I teach them,
then their sons also, to the end of time,
shall sit upon your throne."

13. For the LORD has chosen Zion;
He desired her for His seat.

14. This is My resting-place forever;
here will I dwell, for such is My desire.

15. I will amply bless her provision,
I will satisfy her needy with bread.

---

and trials, but rather to the energy he expended and sleepless nights he devoted to devising plans to build the Temple. The hardships he endured are thus the frustrations he experienced working so effortfully to accomplish the monumental task that he was not destined to complete.

David remains with his hopes for the Temple, which he articulates so gently: God, help my son and his descendants build a Temple which will last, and a kingdom that shall know only peace. God, make sure that those who serve in Your Temple will be righteous men, men who can serve as models for Your people, and that my "sweet songs" of devotion are sung to You there.

God grants David's modest and selfless wish, albeit with one condition: *If your sons keep My covenant.*

ח קוּמָה יְהוָה לִמְנוּחָתֶךָ
אַתָּה וַאֲרוֹן עֻזֶּךָ׃

ט כֹּהֲנֶיךָ יִלְבְּשׁוּ־צֶדֶק
וַחֲסִידֶיךָ יְרַנֵּנוּ׃

י בַּעֲבוּר דָּוִד עַבְדֶּךָ
אַל־תָּשֵׁב פְּנֵי מְשִׁיחֶךָ׃

יא נִשְׁבַּע־יְהוָה ׀ לְדָוִד
אֱמֶת לֹא־יָשׁוּב מִמֶּנָּה
מִפְּרִי בִטְנְךָ אָשִׁית לְכִסֵּא־לָךְ׃

יב אִם־יִשְׁמְרוּ בָנֶיךָ ׀ בְּרִיתִי
וְעֵדֹתִי זוֹ אֲלַמְּדֵם
גַּם־בְּנֵיהֶם עֲדֵי־עַד
יֵשְׁבוּ לְכִסֵּא־לָךְ׃

יג כִּי־בָחַר יְהוָה בְּצִיּוֹן
אִוָּהּ לְמוֹשָׁב לוֹ׃

יד זֹאת־מְנוּחָתִי עֲדֵי־עַד
פֹּה אֵשֵׁב כִּי אִוִּתִיהָ׃

טו צֵידָהּ בָּרֵךְ אֲבָרֵךְ
אֶבְיוֹנֶיהָ אַשְׂבִּיעַ לָחֶם׃

---

hope. He resigns himself to God's decision and does not protest. But he expresses the hope that his fervent dedication to the Temple's construction not be forgotten, and that his suffering be rewarded by Solomon's success.

Hence, Radak insists that in the phrase *remember in David's favor all the hardships he endured,* those hardships refer, not to David lifelong struggles

16. I will clothe her priests with salvation,
and her loyal ones shall forever sing for joy.

17. There I will make David's majesty* flourish;
I will prepare a lamp for My anointed.

18. His enemies I will clothe with shame;
but on him his crown shall sparkle.

* Lit. "horn."

Her priests will be robed not only in righteousness, but in salvation, and her singers will not just sing, but sing forever. And the crown, your crown, will rest securely on the head of your successors. More than that – it will sparkle resplendently, and that sparkle will be your legacy.

טז וְכֹהֲנֶיהָ אַלְבִּישׁ יֶשַׁע
וַחֲסִידֶיהָ רַנֵּן יְרַנֵּנוּ׃

יז שָׁם אַצְמִיחַ קֶרֶן לְדָוִד
עָרַכְתִּי נֵר לִמְשִׁיחִי׃

יח אוֹיְבָיו אַלְבִּישׁ בֹּשֶׁת
וְעָלָיו יָצִיץ נִזְרוֹ׃

If that big "if" is kept, God promises David all he asked for, and more: your son and his sons will sit upon your throne *until the end of time… I will amply bless her provision, I will satisfy her needy.*

PSALM 133

1. A song of Ascents. Of David.
How good and pleasant it is
to dwell together as brothers in unity!

2. It is like precious oil poured on the head,
running down on to the beard,
like the oil on Aaron's beard,
which ran down on to the collar of his robes;

3. as the dew of Hermon,
and as the dew that falls on the hills of Zion.
There the Lord commands His blessing,
life forevermore.

---

and Zebulun. The former was scholarly, introspective, and devout. The latter was a sea-farer: active, energetic, and outgoing. They chose to establish a complementary relationship. Zebulun engaged in foreign trade and supported Issachar in his studies and devotions. This is, for Malbim, the ultimate blessing, for which the anointing oil serves as a metaphor. It is poured on the head, reaching first the intellect and spirit of Issachar, but from there it descends to more mundane and Zebulun-like *collar of his robes*. Zebulun's material support of his brother eventually allows him to derive benefit from the spiritual blessings which Issachar has garnered.

Rav Hirsch transcends both of these approaches in his interpretation of the *brothers* in our psalm. They are not one pair of archetypal brothers, such as Issachar and Zebulun. Nor are they one sub-group, be it Priests or Princes.

Rather, the *brothers* are the Jewish people as a whole: "How good and pleasant will it be when those separated by dispersion will dwell together once more in one land."

The vision of our psalm is of brothers living together in peace and harmony. Tragically, it is a vision that was only rarely achieved in our past. But it most certainly remains a vision for us to set as our objective, and to arduously strive to achieve.

מזמור קלג

All good things come from Zion. Torah and blessing come from Zion. Beauty and sustenance come from Zion. Greatness, redemption, and life itself come from Zion What's Zion's secret? Friendship comes from Zion.

א שִׁ֥יר הַֽמַּֽעֲל֗וֹת לְדָ֫וִ֥ד
הִנֵּ֣ה מַה־טּ֭וֹב וּמַה־נָּעִ֑ים
שֶׁ֖בֶת אַחִ֣ים גַּם־יָֽחַד׃

ב כַּשֶּׁ֤מֶן הַטּ֨וֹב ׀ עַל־הָרֹ֗אשׁ
יֹ֭רֵד עַל־הַזָּקָ֣ן
זְקַֽן־אַהֲרֹ֑ן שֶׁ֝יֹּרֵ֗ד עַל־פִּ֥י מִדּוֹתָֽיו׃

ג כְּטַל־חֶרְמ֗וֹן שֶׁיֹּרֵד֮ עַל־הַרְרֵ֪י צִ֫יּ֥וֹן
כִּ֤י שָׁ֨ם ׀ צִוָּ֣ה יְ֭הוָה אֶת־הַבְּרָכָ֑ה
חַ֝יִּ֗ים עַד־הָעוֹלָֽם׃

מזמור קלג *Psalm 133:* Our psalm extols the glory of friendship, of brothers who dwell together amicably. It does so by comparing the attributes of friendship to ointment and to dew.

In certain circumstances friendship is particularly difficult. Those circumstances are often the very occasions at which friendly cooperation is the most necessary. This insight is made explicit in the works of various traditional commentaries, who suggest a wide range of examples of the *brothers* in our psalm, and who exemplify the desirability, and the possibility, of genuine friendship.

Who might these *brothers* be? Some suggest that our psalm is picking up where the previous psalm left off, with God's promise to *clothe her priests with salvation* and to *make David's majesty flourish*. Our psalm begins by exclaiming *how good and pleasant it is* to see the priests cooperating in the performance of their onerous and complex Temple duties; *how good and pleasant it is* to see the members of David's royal family rise above their intense rivalries and dwell together as one.

Malbim offers another example of brothers working together harmoniously, each with very different skills and interests from the other, Issachar

PSALM 134

1. A song of Ascents.
Come, bless the LORD, all you servants of the LORD,
who stand in the house of the LORD by night.

2. Raise your hands in holy devotion
and bless the LORD.

3. The LORD, maker of heaven and earth,
will bless you from Zion!

---

aging us to pronounce formulaic words of blessing. Rather, it is demanding that we perform good deeds and act in a blessed manner, like true servants who are on duty not only by day, but each and every night. Like a parent who blesses his child by placing his hand upon the child's head, we are asked to act in a holy manner, symbolically placing our hand upon the source of blessing, and stimulating the effusion of divine bounty.

In Malbim's bold theology much power is given to us humans. The words may sound blasphemous to our ears, but we have control over God. Our actions determine His.

Our "blessings," which Malbim translates as our ethical and moral conduct, enable Him to bless us directly, from Zion. Although He is *maker of heaven and earth*, and controls the forces of nature, our actions allow Him to bypass the natural means at His disposal. We enable Him to bless us directly from a supernatural source, epitomized by Zion.

Malbim's theology is a provocative one, and many will consider it heretical. We can imagine Malbim arguing that David kept our psalm so teasingly brief because of the boldness of its message.

But one thing is certain. Malbim's interpretation challenges us and empowers us. It challenges us to bless God, and it empowers us with the realization that God's blessings from above depend entirely upon our blessed behavior here below.

מזמור קלד

I have known night. As a child, its dark shadows frightened me. Later, it became my symbol for the dark moments of history. Eventually, I learned that night is an opportunity. God is closest to us then. It is the best time to study Torah. It is the best time to pray. It is when He prays.

שִׁיר הַמַּעֲלוֹת א
הִנֵּה ׀ בָּרְכוּ אֶת־יהוה כָּל־עַבְדֵי יהוה
הָעֹמְדִים בְּבֵית־יהוה בַּלֵּילוֹת:

שְׂאוּ־יְדֵכֶם קֹדֶשׁ ב
וּבָרְכוּ אֶת־יהוה:

יְבָרֶכְךָ יהוה מִצִּיּוֹן ג
עֹשֵׂה שָׁמַיִם וָאָרֶץ:

מזמור קלד *Psalm 134:* Our psalm provides the opportunity to reflect upon the meaning of the word *berakha*, generally translated as "blessing." The word appears three times in our very brief psalm. Twice, we are enjoined to *bless the Lord*. Once, in the final verse, we learn that *the Lord will bless* us.

It is easy to understand what "the Lord will bless us" means. But what does it mean for us to bless Him? Does He require our human blessing? This dilemma has perplexed theologians through the ages.

Malbim begins his explication of our psalm by asserting "a wondrous aspect of the fundamentals of faith." He speaks of a heavenly fountain which waxes and wanes, expands and contracts, in correspondence to mankind's deeds. The blessings of mankind are its good deeds. Those good deeds allow that heavenly fountain to expand and pour down its bountiful waters beneficially. Should mankind act in an evil fashion, the waters of that fountain dry up and the source of divine bounty withers.

The word *berakha* supports this explanation, because the Hebrew word for a body of water, a fountain or a lake, is *berekha*, similar in spelling, if not in exact pronunciation, to the word *berakha*, or blessing.

For Malbim, when our psalm urges us to *bless the Lord*, it is not encour-

PSALM 135

Twenty-eighth day of the month

1. Praise the LORD!
Praise the name of the LORD.
Give praise, you servants of the LORD,

2. who stand in the house of the LORD,
in the courts of the house of our God.

3. Praise the LORD, for the LORD is good;
sing praises to His name, for it is pleasant.

4. For the LORD has chosen Jacob for Himself,
Israel as His treasured possession.

5. For I know that the LORD is great,
that our LORD is above all gods.

6. Whatever the LORD desires He does,
in heaven and on earth,
in the seas and in all the depths.

7. He brings up mists from the ends of the earth;
He makes lightnings for the rain;
He brings out the wind from His storehouses.

---

omnipotent, eternal, and unknowable. How can He be compared to idols, the mere *work of men's hands*?

Especially troublesome is our verse 5: *For I know that the LORD is great, that our LORD is above all gods.* All gods? What other gods are there?

An approach to this dilemma can be found in the writings of Rabbi Shneur Zalman of Liadi, fondly referred to by his followers as "*der Alter Rebbe*," "the old Rabbi."

In a collection of his teachings known as *Torah Or* the Alter Rebbe addresses this perplexing verse.

He distinguishes between two of the names by which we refer to God.

מזמור קלה

My God is special, incomparable. He controls nature. He protects His people. He protects me. I sing His praises. All His people join me in praising Him.

כח לחודש

א הַלְלוּיָהּ ׀ הַלְלוּ אֶת־שֵׁם יהוָה
הַלְלוּ עַבְדֵי יהוָה׃

ב שֶׁעֹמְדִים בְּבֵית יהוָה
בְּחַצְרוֹת בֵּית אֱלֹהֵינוּ׃

ג הַלְלוּיָהּ כִּי־טוֹב יהוָה
זַמְּרוּ לִשְׁמוֹ כִּי נָעִים׃

ד כִּי־יַעֲקֹב בָּחַר לוֹ יָהּ
יִשְׂרָאֵל לִסְגֻלָּתוֹ׃

ה כִּי אֲנִי יָדַעְתִּי כִּי־גָדוֹל יהוָה
וַאֲדֹנֵינוּ מִכָּל־אֱלֹהִים׃

ו כֹּל אֲשֶׁר־חָפֵץ יהוה עָשָׂה
בַּשָּׁמַיִם וּבָאָרֶץ
בַּיַּמִּים וְכָל־תְּהֹמוֹת׃

ז מַעֲלֶה נְשִׂאִים מִקְצֵה הָאָרֶץ
בְּרָקִים לַמָּטָר עָשָׂה
מוֹצֵא־רוּחַ מֵאוֹצְרוֹתָיו׃

מזמור קלה *Psalm 135:* Our psalm extols God in a dazzling variety of ways. *The LORD is good.... Whatever the LORD desires He does.... He struck down the first-born of Egypt... and slew mighty kings.*

Our psalm also compares God to other gods, and denigrates *the idols of the nations.* This comparison is very troublesome. The Almighty God is

8. He struck down the first-born of Egypt,
both of man and beast.

9. He sent signs and wonders into the midst of Egypt,
against Pharaoh and against all his servants.

10. He smote many nations
and slew mighty kings:

11. Sihon, king of the Amorites,
Og, king of Bashan,
and all the kingdoms of Canaan.

12. He gave their land as a heritage,
a heritage to His people Israel.

13. LORD, Your name endures forever;
Your renown, LORD, throughout all generations.

14. For the LORD will vindicate His people,
and have pity on His servants.

15. The idols of the nations are silver and gold,
the work of men's hands.

16. They have mouths, but cannot speak;
they have eyes, but cannot see;

This latter aspect shields us from being blinded by the Divine Light of the former aspect. This latter aspect of God is apprehensible through our contact with the world of nature. The former aspect is supernatural and thus not normally accessible to us.

Our psalm declares that *our LORD is above all gods*. That is, there are "gods" out there that are merely emanations of the true God. They are by no means deities themselves, but are manifestations of *our LORD*, the infinite *Ein Sof*. These "gods" impede our ability to draw close to the Divine Light.

In our psalm, however, the psalmist asserts that he has been able to see

ח שֶׁ֭הִכָּה בְּכוֹרֵ֣י מִצְרָ֑יִם
מֵ֝אָדָ֗ם עַד־בְּהֵמָֽה׃

ט שָׁלַ֤ח ׀ אוֹתֹ֣ת וּ֭מֹפְתִים בְּתוֹכֵ֣כִי מִצְרָ֑יִם
בְּ֝פַרְעֹ֗ה וּבְכָל־עֲבָדָֽיו׃

י שֶׁ֭הִכָּה גּוֹיִ֣ם רַבִּ֑ים
וְ֝הָרַ֗ג מְלָכִ֥ים עֲצוּמִֽים׃

יא לְסִיח֤וֹן ׀ מֶ֤לֶךְ הָֽאֱמֹרִ֗י
וּ֭לְעוֹג מֶ֣לֶךְ הַבָּשָׁ֑ן
וּ֝לְכֹ֗ל מַמְלְכ֥וֹת כְּנָֽעַן׃

יב וְנָתַ֣ן אַרְצָ֣ם נַחֲלָ֑ה
נַ֝חֲלָ֗ה לְיִשְׂרָאֵ֥ל עַמּֽוֹ׃

יג יהוה שִׁמְךָ֣ לְעוֹלָ֑ם
יהוה זִכְרְךָ֥ לְדֹר־וָדֹֽר׃

יד כִּֽי־יָדִ֣ין יהוה עַמּ֑וֹ
וְעַל־עֲ֝בָדָ֗יו יִתְנֶחָֽם׃

טו עֲצַבֵּ֣י הַ֭גּוֹיִם כֶּ֣סֶף וְזָהָ֑ב
מַ֝עֲשֵׂ֗ה יְדֵ֣י אָדָֽם׃

טז פֶּֽה־לָ֭הֶם וְלֹ֣א יְדַבֵּ֑רוּ
עֵינַ֥יִם לָ֝הֶ֗ם וְלֹ֣א יִרְאֽוּ׃

One, in our verse translated as *our* LORD, is pronounced *Adonai* and spelled *YHWH*. This name refers to God the Ultimate Creator, the infinite *Ein Sof*.

The other, here translated as "gods" with a lower case G, is spelled and pronounced *Elohim*. This name refers to the guise by which God makes Himself known to man.

17. they have ears, but cannot hear;
neither is there breath in their mouths.

18. Their makers become like them;
and so do all who trust in them.

19. House of Israel, bless the LORD!
House of Aaron, bless the LORD!

20. House of Levi, bless the LORD!
You who fear the LORD, bless the LORD!

21. Blessed from Zion be the LORD,
who dwells in Jerusalem!
Praise the LORD!

With such uplifting assurance, it is no wonder that our psalm concludes with the many diverse "houses" of Israel all singing in unison. *Blessed from Zion be the LORD, who dwells in Jerusalem!*

יז אׇזְנַיִם לָהֶם וְלֹא יַאֲזִינוּ
אַף אֵין־יֶשׁ־רוּחַ בְּפִיהֶם׃

יח כְּמוֹהֶם יִהְיוּ עֹשֵׂיהֶם
כֹּל אֲשֶׁר־בֹּטֵחַ בָּהֶם׃

יט בֵּית יִשְׂרָאֵל בָּרְכוּ אֶת־יְהֹוָה
בֵּית אַהֲרֹן בָּרְכוּ אֶת־יְהֹוָה׃

כ בֵּית הַלֵּוִי בָּרְכוּ אֶת־יְהֹוָה
יִרְאֵי יְהֹוָה בָּרְכוּ אֶת־יְהֹוָה׃

כא בָּרוּךְ יְהֹוָה ׀ מִצִּיּוֹן
שֹׁכֵן יְרוּשָׁלָ͏ִם
הַלְלוּיָהּ׃

---

past the impediments that the natural world sets before us. *I know that the Lord is great.* He "knows" God.

Our psalm assures us that it is possible, however mysteriously, to glimpse the *Ein Sof.* If only for rare and fleeting moments, the unknowable can be known.

PSALM 136

1. Give thanks to the LORD, for He is good;
His loving-kindness endures forever!

2. Give thanks to the God of gods,
His loving-kindness endures forever!

3. Give thanks to the LORD of LORDS,
His loving-kindness endures forever!

4. To Him who alone works great wonders,
His loving-kindness endures forever!

5. To Him who made the heavens with wisdom,
His loving-kindness endures forever!

6. To Him who spread out the earth above the waters,
His loving-kindness endures forever!

7. To Him who made the great lights;
His loving-kindness endures forever!

8. the sun to rule by day,
His loving-kindness endures forever!

---

and morality, mankind had no way of earning God's favor. Only God's loving-kindness then sustained the world.

Thus, our psalm conveys, again and again, the message that man receives God's benevolence even when he is undeserving. This is the meaning of the persistent refrain: God's *loving-kindness,* His unconditional loving relationship with mankind, *endures forever,* no matter the state of humanity's morality.

Our psalm is known as *Hallel HaGadol,* the "Great Hallel," or the "Great Praise." It deserves this appellation because it tells of God's mastery over every aspect of the universe, as well as His special role in the history of the People of Israel.

Especially poignant is the manner in which our psalm begins with God's grandest cosmic "accomplishments," but yet concludes with what initially seems quite modest: He *gives food to all flesh.* Further thought, however, leads

מזמור קלו

Danger surrounds us. We are in the dark, oblivious. We'll never know what could have gone wrong. Even the person for whom a miracle has occurred has no clue that he owes his life to a miracle. We don't even see what our vision equips us to see. We see only what we want to see. God alone sees the whole picture. He alone works great wonders!

א הוֹדוּ לַיהוָה כִּי־טוֹב
כִּי לְעוֹלָם חַסְדּוֹ׃

ב הוֹדוּ לֵאלֹהֵי הָאֱלֹהִים
כִּי לְעוֹלָם חַסְדּוֹ׃

ג הוֹדוּ לַאֲדֹנֵי הָאֲדֹנִים
כִּי לְעוֹלָם חַסְדּוֹ׃

ד לְעֹשֵׂה נִפְלָאוֹת גְּדֹלוֹת לְבַדּוֹ
כִּי לְעוֹלָם חַסְדּוֹ׃

ה לְעֹשֵׂה הַשָּׁמַיִם בִּתְבוּנָה
כִּי לְעוֹלָם חַסְדּוֹ׃

ו לְרֹקַע הָאָרֶץ עַל־הַמָּיִם
כִּי לְעוֹלָם חַסְדּוֹ׃

ז לְעֹשֵׂה אוֹרִים גְּדֹלִים
כִּי לְעוֹלָם חַסְדּוֹ׃

ח אֶת־הַשֶּׁמֶשׁ לְמֶמְשֶׁלֶת בַּיּוֹם
כִּי לְעוֹלָם חַסְדּוֹ׃

מזמור קלו *Psalm 136:* Our psalm contains twenty-six verses, each of which proclaims the eternity of God's loving-kindness.

The Talmud (*Pesaḥim* 118a) tells us that the twenty-six verses correspond to the twenty-six generations which preceded God's revelation upon Mount Sinai, at which time the Torah was given. Absent a God-given system of law

9. the moon and the stars to rule by night;
His loving-kindness endures forever!

10. To Him who struck Egypt through their first-born,
His loving-kindness endures forever!

11. and brought out Israel from their midst,
His loving-kindness endures forever!

12. with a strong hand and outstretched arm,
His loving-kindness endures forever!

13. To Him who split apart the Sea of Reeds,
His loving-kindness endures forever!

14. and made Israel pass through it,
His loving-kindness endures forever!

15. but Pharaoh and his army He drove into the Sea of Reeds;
His loving-kindness endures forever!

16. To Him who led His people through the wilderness;
His loving-kindness endures forever!

17. To Him who struck down great kings,
His loving-kindness endures forever!

18. and slew mighty kings,
His loving-kindness endures forever!

---

are much more likely to be moved to religious ecstasy by sunsets, starry skies, and the momentous wonders of nature. But the truly pious person sees God's gifts in the ordinary blessings which the rest of us take for granted.

The Talmud puts it succinctly and graphically: "Man's daily sustenance is as much of a miracle as the splitting of the Sea of Reeds." The Talmud derives this insight from the proximity in our psalm of the verse *To Him who split apart the Sea of Reeds* to the verse *To Him who gives food to all flesh* Both are wondrous acts of God, and for both the psalmist exclaims: *His loving-kindness endures forever!*

ט אֶת־הַיָּרֵחַ וְכוֹכָבִים לְמֶמְשְׁלוֹת בַּלָּיְלָה
כִּי לְעוֹלָם חַסְדּוֹ׃

י לְמַכֵּה מִצְרַיִם בִּבְכוֹרֵיהֶם
כִּי לְעוֹלָם חַסְדּוֹ׃

יא וַיּוֹצֵא יִשְׂרָאֵל מִתּוֹכָם
כִּי לְעוֹלָם חַסְדּוֹ׃

יב בְּיָד חֲזָקָה וּבִזְרוֹעַ נְטוּיָה
כִּי לְעוֹלָם חַסְדּוֹ׃

יג לְגֹזֵר יַם־סוּף לִגְזָרִים
כִּי לְעוֹלָם חַסְדּוֹ׃

יד וְהֶעֱבִיר יִשְׂרָאֵל בְּתוֹכוֹ
כִּי לְעוֹלָם חַסְדּוֹ׃

טו וְנִעֵר פַּרְעֹה וְחֵילוֹ בְיַם־סוּף
כִּי לְעוֹלָם חַסְדּוֹ׃

טז לְמוֹלִיךְ עַמּוֹ בַּמִּדְבָּר
כִּי לְעוֹלָם חַסְדּוֹ׃

יז לְמַכֵּה מְלָכִים גְּדֹלִים
כִּי לְעוֹלָם חַסְדּוֹ׃

יח וַיַּהֲרֹג מְלָכִים אַדִּירִים
כִּי לְעוֹלָם חַסְדּוֹ׃

---

to the conclusion that God's provision of *food to all flesh* is not at all trivial. Indeed, from the perspective of most of us, this is His greatest gift, although perhaps His least appreciated one. Few of us are religiously inspired when we open our cupboard in the morning and find our breakfast on the shelf. We

19. Sihon, king of the Amorites,
His loving-kindness endures forever!

20. and Og, king of Bashan,
His loving-kindness endures forever!

21. and gave their land as a heritage,
His loving-kindness endures forever!

22. a heritage to His servant Israel;
His loving-kindness endures forever!

23. To Him who remembered us in our low estate,
His loving-kindness endures forever!

24. and rescued us from our enemies,
His loving-kindness endures forever!

25. To Him who gives food to all flesh,
His loving-kindness endures forever!

26. Give thanks to the God of heaven,
His loving-kindness endures forever!

---

nent of the Passover Haggada. Rather than run the risk of our psalm losing its majestic message because of routine and frequent recitation, the sages wisely suggested that we stand when reciting it, and restricted its recital to special moments.

יט לְסִיחוֹן מֶלֶךְ הָאֱמֹרִי
כִּי לְעוֹלָם חַסְדּוֹ׃

כ וּלְעוֹג מֶלֶךְ הַבָּשָׁן
כִּי לְעוֹלָם חַסְדּוֹ׃

כא וְנָתַן אַרְצָם לְנַחֲלָה
כִּי לְעוֹלָם חַסְדּוֹ׃

כב נַחֲלָה לְיִשְׂרָאֵל עַבְדּוֹ
כִּי לְעוֹלָם חַסְדּוֹ׃

כג שֶׁבְּשִׁפְלֵנוּ זָכַר לָנוּ
כִּי לְעוֹלָם חַסְדּוֹ׃

כד וַיִּפְרְקֵנוּ מִצָּרֵינוּ
כִּי לְעוֹלָם חַסְדּוֹ׃

כה נֹתֵן לֶחֶם לְכָל־בָּשָׂר
כִּי לְעוֹלָם חַסְדּוֹ׃

כו הוֹדוּ לְאֵל הַשָּׁמָיִם
כִּי לְעוֹלָם חַסְדּוֹ׃

Our psalm has a special place in Jewish liturgy. It is instructive that it is not chosen to be recited each and every day. It is instead reserved for special occasions: Sabbath and Festival Morning Services, and as a central compo-

PSALM 137

1. By the rivers of Babylon we sat,
weeping loudly, as we remembered Zion.

2. On the willow trees there
we hung up our lyres.

3. For there our captors had asked us for songs,
our tormentors called for merriment:
"Sing for us one of the songs of Zion."

4. How can we sing the LORD's song
on foreign soil?

5. If I forget you, O Jerusalem,
may my right hand forget its skill;

6. may my tongue cling to my palate
if I do not remember you,
if I do not set Jerusalem
above my greatest joy.

---

him to cling even more tenaciously to his nation's religious values. He will not freely use his creative talents on behalf of an alien culture. He is bound by his sense of loyalty to Zion and all that Zion represents.

One Holocaust survivor relates a story in his memoirs that illustrates our psalm's theme. This survivor was a devoutly observant Jew, who refrained from eating non-kosher meat even in the concentration camp. One SS guard found out about his refusal, and was determined to force the stubborn Jew to violate his practice. However, he misidentified the "culprit," and instead began to whip another Jew, one who was far from religious observance, and who freely indulged in non-kosher meat long before the Holocaust. This Jew, although previously unconcerned with the kosher status of his food, refused to eat at the Nazi soldier's command. He apparently reasoned that submission to the Nazi's coercion would constitute a betrayal of his people's time-honored tradition. That was sufficient cause for him to stand up and resist the Nazi's sadistic beating, although it cost him his life.

מזמור קלז

I am homeless. Zion was my home. I am hopeless. Zion was my hope. Songs cannot be coaxed from a homeless harp; Hopeless hearts cannot be forced to sing. I will never forget my home. Remembrance is my only hope. Revenge is my bitter wish.

א עַל־נַהֲרוֹת ׀ בָּבֶל שָׁם יָשַׁבְנוּ גַּם־בָּכִינוּ
בְּזָכְרֵנוּ אֶת־צִיּוֹן׃

ב עַל־עֲרָבִים בְּתוֹכָהּ
תָּלִינוּ כִּנֹּרוֹתֵינוּ׃

ג כִּי שָׁם ׀ שְׁאֵלוּנוּ שׁוֹבֵינוּ
דִּבְרֵי־שִׁיר וְתוֹלָלֵינוּ שִׂמְחָה
שִׁירוּ לָנוּ מִשִּׁיר צִיּוֹן׃

ד אֵיךְ נָשִׁיר אֶת־שִׁיר־יְהוָה
עַל אַדְמַת נֵכָר׃

ה אִם־אֶשְׁכָּחֵךְ יְרוּשָׁלָםִ
תִּשְׁכַּח יְמִינִי׃

ו תִּדְבַּק לְשׁוֹנִי ׀ לְחִכִּי אִם־לֹא אֶזְכְּרֵכִי
אִם־לֹא אַעֲלֶה אֶת־יְרוּשָׁלַםִ עַל רֹאשׁ שִׂמְחָתִי׃

מזמור קלז *Psalm 137:* Our psalm is a prophetic one. The Talmud (*Gittin* 57b) states that it foretells the destruction of both the First and Second Temples. Thus, the first several verses speak of Babylon, whereas the final verses allude to Edom, traditionally identified as Rome, before reverting to the mention of Babylon near the end of the psalm.

For nearly two millennia of exile our psalm has served as the quintessential expression of the pain of the Jewish people. *How can we sing the Lord's song on foreign soil?*

Our psalm gives voice to the Jew whose spiritual commitment to Judaism remains intact despite his suffering. In fact, his physical tribulations cause

7. Remember, Lord, against the Edomites
the day when Jerusalem fell,
how they cried, "Lay it bare, lay it bare,
to its very foundations!"

8. O daughter of Babylon, doomed to devastation,
happy is he who repays you
for what you did to us!

9. Happy is he who seizes your babes
and dashes them against a rock!

In our psalm the secret of the Jewish people's ability to return to the Land of Israel, even after the many centuries of Diaspora, lies hidden. Their backs were stiffened by their suffering, not broken by it. The fires of hope were fueled by suffering, not extinguished by it. They remembered Jerusalem above their greatest joys, because all of their joys were dimmed by the loss of Jerusalem.

Thankfully, today our people's joys are no longer dimmed by that loss, but have begun to be enhanced by our return to Zion and Jerusalem.

זְכֹר יהוה ׀ לִבְנֵי אֱדוֹם אֵת יוֹם יְרוּשָׁלָםִ ז
הָאֹמְרִים עָרוּ ׀ עָרוּ עַד הַיְסוֹד בָּהּ:

בַּת־בָּבֶל הַשְּׁדוּדָה ח
אַשְׁרֵי שֶׁיְשַׁלֶּם־לָךְ
אֶת־גְּמוּלֵךְ שֶׁגָּמַלְתְּ לָנוּ:

אַשְׁרֵי ׀ שֶׁיֹּאחֵז ט
וְנִפֵּץ אֶת־עֹלָלַיִךְ אֶל־הַסָּלַע:

One rabbi, upon reading this story, commented: "This man couldn't draw close to God in his many years of light. It took the darkness to drive him into his Creator's arms."

That comment epitomizes the theme of our psalm. It was the very darkness of the Babylonian exile that empowered the captives to defy their captors. The captives may have lacked an appreciation of Zion when they were yet in Zion. But once they experienced the trauma of Zion's loss, they fervently dedicated themselves never to forget her.

PSALM 138

1. Of David.
I will praise You with all my heart;
in the presence of the mighty I will sing Your praises.

2. I will bow down toward Your Holy Temple,
and praise Your name for Your loving-kindness and faithfulness;
for You have magnified Your word
above all Your name.*

3. Whenever I called, You answered me;
You inspired me with courage and strength.

4. All the kings of the earth shall praise You, LORD,
when they have heard the words of Your mouth.

5. They shall sing of the LORD's ways;
for great is the glory of the LORD.

6. The LORD is exalted, yet He cares for the lowly;
from afar He takes note of the proud.

* God has fulfilled His promise far in excess of all expectation.

---

fear not *the presence of the mighty*, and they feel *inspired with courage and strength.*

If they are in touch with their spiritual selves they attribute their self-confidence to God. They have known great challenges, and they have called upon God for His help. They gratefully exclaim: *Whenever I called, You answered me.*

Such leaders are not blinded by their talents and resources. They know that they have been blessed, and they feel indebted to the Almighty God who has blessed them. They are humble, but are secure in their knowledge that it is their very humility which brings God close to them. *The LORD is exalted, yet He cares for the lowly.*

Such leaders excel in times of crisis. They are firmly convinced that *though I walk in the midst of trouble, You preserve my life.* That firm conviction is contagious, and encourages others to follow them devotedly.

מזמור קלח

Some of us are lowly, and know it. Others hold themselves high, and think they really are. They are convinced that the Highest is closest to them. They believe that He takes no notice of the low. But they are in for a surprise. The Almighty is different. He is high, but distant from those who hold themselves high. He is high, but He is closest to the low.

א לְדָוִ֨ד ׀
אוֹדְךָ֥ בְכָל־לִבִּ֑י
נֶ֖גֶד אֱלֹהִ֣ים אֲזַמְּרֶֽךָּ׃

ב אֶשְׁתַּחֲוֶ֨ה אֶל־הֵיכַ֪ל קָדְשְׁךָ֡
וְא֘וֹדֶ֤ה אֶת־שְׁמֶ֗ךָ עַל־חַסְדְּךָ֥ וְעַל־אֲמִתֶּ֑ךָ
כִּֽי־הִגְדַּ֥לְתָּ עַל־כָּל־שִׁ֝מְךָ֗ אִמְרָתֶֽךָ׃

ג בְּי֣וֹם קָ֭רָאתִי וַֽתַּעֲנֵ֑נִי
תַּרְהִבֵ֖נִי בְנַפְשִׁ֣י עֹֽז׃

ד יוֹד֣וּךָ יְ֭הוָה כָּל־מַלְכֵי־אָ֑רֶץ
כִּ֥י שָׁ֝מְע֗וּ אִמְרֵי־פִֽיךָ׃

ה וְ֭יָשִׁירוּ בְּדַרְכֵ֣י יְהוָ֑ה
כִּ֥י גָ֝ד֗וֹל כְּב֣וֹד יְהוָֽה׃

ו כִּי־רָ֣ם יְ֭הוָה וְשָׁפָ֣ל יִרְאֶ֑ה
וְ֝גָבֹ֗הַּ מִמֶּרְחָ֥ק יְיֵדָֽע׃

מזמור קלח *Psalm 138:* In our psalm David speaks of his confidence in God's promise to him. He models the effective leader who trusts himself and who has a clear and firm vision of his mission and purpose.

Of course, David's confidence is based upon prophetic insight, and few other leaders are granted that advantage. Nevertheless, even those leaders who are devoid of such supernatural guidance frequently possess a sure sense of their purpose in life, and of the nature of their vocation.

Such individuals trust themselves, and exude a sense of self-mastery. They

7. Though I walk in the midst of trouble,
You preserve my life;
against the raging of my enemies
You wield Your power;
and with Your right hand You save me.

8. The Lord will fulfill His purpose for me;
Your loving-kindness, Lord, endures forever.
Do not abandon the work of Your hands.

Our psalm is an expression of both thanksgiving and petitionary prayer. It is not a tale of woe and worry, and not a poem of praise and wonder. It is an exquisite statement of a person who knows of his blessings and acknowledges their source. But he also knows his limitations.

Our psalm is the prayer of a person who has experienced great success and who is thankful to God. He knows full well that he is still in need of divine assistance, and he fully trusts that God will not let him down.

If there is one psalm which should be required reading for all who are in positions of power and leadership, this is that psalm.

ז אִם־אֵלֵךְ ׀ בְּקֶרֶב צָרָה תְּחַיֵּנִי
עַל אַף אֹיְבַי תִּשְׁלַח יָדֶךָ וְתוֹשִׁיעֵנִי יְמִינֶךָ׃

ח יהוה יִגְמֹר בַּעֲדִי יהוה חַסְדְּךָ לְעוֹלָם
מַעֲשֵׂי יָדֶיךָ אַל־תֶּרֶף׃

Such a leader knows that he is not perfect. He is aware that even after he achieves success his entire mission is not yet completed. But he trusts that God will remain with him until he can see his task to completion. *The LORD will fulfill His purpose for me.* He knows that he must persist with his prayers to God. He cannot relent and rely upon his own skills. And so he pleads, *do not abandon the work of Your hands.*

PSALM 139

1. To the Chief Musician. Of David. A psalm.
LORD, You have examined me, and You know me.

2. You know when I sit down and when I rise up;
You discern my thoughts from afar.

3. You scrutinize* my walking and my resting;
You are familiar with all my ways.

4. Before ever a word is on my tongue,
You, LORD, know it all.

5. You have hemmed me in on all sides,
and laid Your hand upon me.

6. Such knowledge is too wonderful for me;
too high, I cannot reach it.

7. Where can I escape from Your spirit?
Where can I flee from Your presence?

8. If I ascend to heaven, You are there;
if I make my bed in Sheol, You are there.

9. If I take the wings of the dawn,
and dwell at the sea's furthest end,

* Lit. "You sift."

We decide to do various actions: sitting, standing, walking, resting. When we are healthy our bodies respond instantly. We are hardly conscious of the mental instructions which we give to our bodies. But *You discern my thoughts from afar.*

A thought occurs to us, and we attempt to articulate it. But somehow, we rarely express it exactly as we intended. There is a great gap between our thoughts and our speech. What we thought seemed brilliant to us, nuanced and persuasive. But the spoken words were heard as dull and trivially simple, and made hardly an impression upon our listeners. Others appear not to fully

מזמור קלט

I know myself well, but You know me better. You were there when I was conceived. I spent nine months in my mother's womb. I began as a microscopic speck. Each day I developed a bit more. After many days I was fully formed. Then, in an instant, I was born. I recall none of those many days, but I thank You for them all. I thank You for giving me me.

א לַמְנַצֵּחַ לְדָוִד מִזְמוֹר
יְהוָה חֲקַרְתַּנִי וַתֵּדָע׃

ב אַתָּה יָדַעְתָּ שִׁבְתִּי וְקוּמִי
בַּנְתָּה לְרֵעִי מֵרָחוֹק׃

ג אָרְחִי וְרִבְעִי זֵרִיתָ
וְכׇל־דְּרָכַי הִסְכַּנְתָּה׃

ד כִּי אֵין מִלָּה בִּלְשׁוֹנִי
הֵן יְהוָה יָדַעְתָּ כֻלָּהּ׃

ה אָחוֹר וָקֶדֶם צַרְתָּנִי
וַתָּשֶׁת עָלַי כַּפֶּכָה׃

ו פלאיה דַעַת מִמֶּנִּי
פְּלִיאָה
נִשְׂגְּבָה לֹא־אוּכַל לָהּ׃

ז אָנָה אֵלֵךְ מֵרוּחֶךָ
וְאָנָה מִפָּנֶיךָ אֶבְרָח׃

ח אִם־אֶסַּק שָׁמַיִם שָׁם אָתָּה
וְאַצִּיעָה שְּׁאוֹל הִנֶּךָּ׃

ט אֶשָּׂא כַנְפֵי־שָׁחַר
אֶשְׁכְּנָה בְּאַחֲרִית יָם׃

מזמור קלט *Psalm 139:* Our psalm is complicated, because the human being is so complicated. Science has helped us know so much about ourselves, yet we still know next to nothing. We do not know ourselves.

10. even there Your hand will be guiding me,
Your right hand will be holding me fast.

11. Then I realized, even in the darkness He sees me;
even in the night there is light all around me.

12. For darkness is not dark to You;
night is as light as day;
darkness and light are the same.

13. It was You who created my inward parts;*
You knit me together in my mother's womb.

14. I praise You because I am fearfully and wondrously made;
wonderful are Your works; I know that full well.

15. My frame was not hidden from You,
when I was made in the secret place,
woven together in the lowest depths of the earth.

16. Your eyes saw my shapeless mass;
all the days ordained [for me] were recorded in Your book,
before one of them ever came into being.

17. How precious to me are Your thoughts, God!
How vast their number!

* Lit. "my kidneys."

---

try to hide from Him, to avoid His probing questions. We do not want to be known, and attempt to conceal our real selves from others. In a certain sense, we are all imposters. But we cannot deceive God, and He forces us to confront our real selves. We cannot escape that self-confrontation, hard as we might try. *Where can I flee from Your presence ... even in the darkness He sees me.*

The faithful are forced to be honest with themselves. One who believes in God cannot continually live a lie. The believer is aware the He knows his secrets, so that he cannot suppress them forever. God's profound and precise knowledge of who we are compels us, sooner or later, to live a life of greater authenticity.

י גַּם־שָׁם יָדְךָ תַנְחֵנִי
וְתֹאחֲזֵנִי יְמִינֶךָ׃

יא וָאֹמַר אַךְ־חֹשֶׁךְ יְשׁוּפֵנִי
וְלַיְלָה אוֹר בַּעֲדֵנִי׃

יב גַּם־חֹשֶׁךְ לֹא־יַחְשִׁיךְ מִמֶּךָ
וְלַיְלָה כַּיּוֹם יָאִיר
כַּחֲשֵׁיכָה כָּאוֹרָה׃

יג כִּי־אַתָּה קָנִיתָ כִלְיֹתָי
תְּסֻכֵּנִי בְּבֶטֶן אִמִּי׃

יד אוֹדְךָ עַל כִּי נוֹרָאוֹת נִפְלֵיתִי
נִפְלָאִים מַעֲשֶׂיךָ
וְנַפְשִׁי יֹדַעַת מְאֹד׃

טו לֹא־נִכְחַד עָצְמִי מִמֶּךָּ
אֲשֶׁר־עֻשֵּׂיתִי בַסֵּתֶר
רֻקַּמְתִּי בְּתַחְתִּיּוֹת אָרֶץ׃

טז גָּלְמִי ׀ רָאוּ עֵינֶיךָ
וְעַל־סִפְרְךָ כֻּלָּם יִכָּתֵבוּ
יָמִים יֻצָּרוּ וְלֹא אֶחָד בָּהֶם׃ וְלוֹ

יז וְלִי מַה־יָּקְרוּ רֵעֶיךָ אֵל
מֶה עָצְמוּ רָאשֵׁיהֶם׃

---

comprehend what we are trying to say. But that is not so with God. *Before ever a word is on my tongue, You, Lord, know it all.*

We are ashamed and frightened of God because He knows us so well. We

18. Were I to count them, they would outnumber the grains of sand.
Were I to finish the count, I must be like You [eternal].

19. If only, God, You would slay the wicked!
Away from me, you bloodthirsty men!

20. They speak of You with wicked intent;
Your adversaries swear by You falsely.

21. Do I not hate those who hate You, LORD,
and loathe those who rise up against You?

22. I have nothing but utter hatred for them;
I count them my enemies.

23. Examine me, God, and know my mind;
test me, and know my inmost thoughts.

24. See if there be any grievous way in me;
and lead me in the way everlasting.

We are frustrated because He does not punish the wicked, at least not in a manner which is apparent to us. Instead, He persistently trains His gaze on me, expecting me to dig deeper into my own psyche, and to expunge whatever is wicked or perverse within it. He wants me to declare unto Him: *Examine me... test me, and know my inmost thoughts.*

Only after a sincere and thorough course of introspection does He promise to *lead me in the way everlasting*

יח אֶסְפְּרֵם מֵחוֹל יִרְבּוּן
הֱקִיצֹתִי וְעוֹדִי עִמָּךְ׃

יט אִם־תִּקְטֹל אֱלוֹהַּ ׀ רָשָׁע
וְאַנְשֵׁי דָמִים סוּרוּ מֶנִּי׃

כ אֲשֶׁר יֹמְרוּךָ לִמְזִמָּה
נָשֻׂא לַשָּׁוְא עָרֶיךָ׃

כא הֲלוֹא־מְשַׂנְאֶיךָ יְהוָה ׀ אֶשְׂנָא
וּבִתְקוֹמְמֶיךָ אֶתְקוֹטָט׃

כב תַּכְלִית שִׂנְאָה שְׂנֵאתִים
לְאוֹיְבִים הָיוּ לִי׃

כג חָקְרֵנִי אֵל וְדַע לְבָבִי
בְּחָנֵנִי וְדַע שַׂרְעַפָּי׃

כד וּרְאֵה אִם־דֶּרֶךְ־עֹצֶב בִּי
וּנְחֵנִי בְּדֶרֶךְ עוֹלָם׃

Convinced of His infinite wisdom, we wonder why He allows the wicked to flourish. In His wisdom He has brought to light the wickedness which has been buried within me. Why can He not do the same with the truly wicked? *If only, God, You would slay the wicked.*

PSALM 140

1. For the Chief Musician. A psalm of David. *Twenty-ninth day of the month*

2. Rescue me, LORD, from the evil man;
protect me from the violent man,

3. who devise evil in their hearts,
and stir up wars day after day.

4. They sharpen their tongues like a serpent's;
spider's poison is under their lips. *Selah*

5. Guard me, LORD, from the hands of the wicked man;
protect me from the violent man,
who plan to trip up my feet.

6. Arrogant men have hidden a trap for me;
they have spread a net with its cords along my path;
they have set snares for me. *Selah*

7. I say to the LORD, "You are my God."
Hear, LORD, my cry for mercy.

But the enemy in this psalm can also be interpreted as the enemy within us, the psychic passions which undermine our determination to act ethically and morally. There are forces within us, call them the devil or the evil urge or whatever name you choose, which sabotage our spiritual ideals. The enemy in our psalm can be understood as an exquisitely apt metaphor for these nefarious forces.

The Jewish tradition views man as being subject to a profound duality, an inner schism. On the one hand, he is capable of approaching the sublime. "*You made him little less than divine, and crowned him with glory and honor*" (Ps. 8:6). On the other hand, man can sink to the very depths of depravity.

Thus, our psalm can be read as the struggle of one who has glimpsed his sublime potential, but who feels attacked by the internal seductive pressures that impede that potential. As he fights these voices of temptation he envisions them as serpents, and their weapons as a spider's poison. He enlists God's assistance in suppressing these powerful inner foes, and exclaims

מזמור קמ

I am not as afraid of a good fight as I am of facing a sneak. It is the schemer whom I really fear. He is deceitful, and I cannot trust his peace-loving gestures. He is plotting and planning to do me in. But he pretends that we are friends. He is treacherous. How can I protect myself from such an enemy? That's where God comes in. He'll signal me: "Beware." Then I'll know how to defend myself.

א לַמְנַצֵּחַ מִזְמוֹר לְדָוִד׃ כט לחודש

ב חַלְּצֵנִי יְהוָה מֵאָדָם רָע
מֵאִישׁ חֲמָסִים תִּנְצְרֵנִי׃

ג אֲשֶׁר חָשְׁבוּ רָעוֹת בְּלֵב
כָּל־יוֹם יָגוּרוּ מִלְחָמוֹת׃

ד שָׁנְנוּ לְשׁוֹנָם כְּמוֹ־נָחָשׁ
חֲמַת עַכְשׁוּב
תַּחַת שְׂפָתֵימוֹ סֶלָה׃

ה שָׁמְרֵנִי יְהוָה ׀ מִידֵי רָשָׁע
מֵאִישׁ חֲמָסִים תִּנְצְרֵנִי
אֲשֶׁר חָשְׁבוּ לִדְחוֹת פְּעָמָי׃

ו טָמְנוּ־גֵאִים ׀ פַּח לִי וַחֲבָלִים
פָּרְשׂוּ רֶשֶׁת לְיַד־מַעְגָּל
מֹקְשִׁים שָׁתוּ־לִי סֶלָה׃

ז אָמַרְתִּי לַיהוָה אֵלִי אָתָּה
הַאֲזִינָה יְהוָה קוֹל תַּחֲנוּנָי׃

מזמור קמ *Psalm 140:* This is the last of the psalms to begin "For the Chief Musician. A psalm of David." It is the last opportunity to read David's personal experiences with his many enemies into the text, and many commentaries have done just that. Radak, for example, identifies David's enemy in this psalm as Doeg, the treacherous informer, who maligned David to Saul, thus condemning him to the trials of flight and hiding.

8. O God, Lord, the strength of my salvation,
shield my head in the day of battle.

9. Lord, do not grant the desires of the wicked;
do not let their plans succeed,
lest they exalt themselves. *Selah*

10. As for the leaders of those who beset me –
let the mischief of their lips overwhelm them.

11. Let burning coals drop down upon them,
let them be cast into the fire,
into miry pits, never to rise again.

12. Let the slanderer have no place in the land;
let disaster hound the violent man to destruction.

13. I know that the Lord will maintain the cause of the poor,
the rights of the needy.

14. Surely the righteous will praise Your name;
the upright shall live in Your presence.

---

into miry pits, never to rise again. He knows that temporary defeat will not suffice against such sly enemies, for they can rise again. Only if they are totally vanquished can he feel secure of a life of spiritual rectitude.

Every self-conscious person of faith has known this tortuous inner journey, and has traversed its peaks and its valleys. But he has also known the sense of confidence that accompanies one who travels this road. He has come to *know that the Lord will maintain the cause of the poor.*

He is confident that no matter the tenacity of his inner foes, the final result will be that *the upright shall live in Your presence.*

ח יֱהֹוִה אֲדֹנָי עֹז יְשׁוּעָתִי
סַכּוֹתָה לְרֹאשִׁי בְּיוֹם נָשֶׁק׃

ט אַל־תִּתֵּן יְהוָה מַאֲוַיֵּי רָשָׁע
זְמָמוֹ אַל־תָּפֵק יָרוּמוּ סֶלָה׃

י רֹאשׁ מְסִבָּי
עֲמַל שְׂפָתֵימוֹ יכסומו׃ יְכַסֵּמוֹ

יא ימיטו עֲלֵיהֶם גֶּחָלִים יִמּוֹטוּ
בָּאֵשׁ יַפִּלֵם
בְּמַהֲמֹרוֹת בַּל־יָקוּמוּ׃

יב אִישׁ לָשׁוֹן בַּל־יִכּוֹן בָּאָרֶץ
אִישׁ־חָמָס רָע יְצוּדֶנּוּ לְמַדְחֵפֹת׃

יג יָדַעְתָּ כִּי־יַעֲשֶׂה יְהוָה דִּין עָנִי
מִשְׁפַּט אֶבְיֹנִים׃

יד אַךְ צַדִּיקִים יוֹדוּ לִשְׁמֶךָ
יֵשְׁבוּ יְשָׁרִים אֶת־פָּנֶיךָ׃

Rescue me… guard me… hear my cry for mercy. The battle is no easy one, and he turns to the Almighty to help him prevail.

He feels surrounded, overwhelmed, by a multitude of temptations. He imagines them to be a band of wicked men with a leader who guides them. Hence, he prays: *as for the leaders of those who beset me… let them be cast…*

PSALM 141

1. A psalm of David.
I call to You, LORD; come quickly to me.
Hear my voice when I call to You.

2. May my prayer be like an incense offering set before You,
the lifting up of my hands as the evening offering.

3. LORD, set a guard over my mouth;
keep watch at the door of my lips.

4. Do not let my heart turn to an evil thing,
or take part in wicked deeds
with men who are evildoers;
let me not eat of their delicacies.

5. Were a righteous man to strike me, it would be an act of kindness.
Were he to reprove me, it would be like choice oil,
my head would not refuse it.
But while I live my prayer is ever against their wickedness.

6. When their rulers slip down by the rock,
then the people will listen to my words for they are pleasant.

---

the sacrifices, in terms of its purity and fragrance. It alone, and not the animal or vegetable sacrifices, was offered daily upon the inner golden altar. On the holiest day of the year, the incense penetrated the innermost sanctum of the Temple; the closest one can get to God.

Our psalm suggests that for a prayer to be as propitious as the incense offering, the person who prays must attain the level of inner purity which is described, albeit with frustrating brevity, in our psalm.

The English word "prayer" refers to the words which are uttered. But the word can also refer to the one who prays. Just as one who plays is a "player," so too one who prays is a "prayer." What are the prerequisites for the "prayer" if God is to pay heed to his words *to come quickly to me*?

The "prayer" must be ready to confront himself, his motives and his deeds, critically and candidly. He must be open to a painful "no holds

מזמור קמא

Before I pray I must pray. I must pray that I find the words to express my thoughts. I must pray that my thoughts be pure. I must pray lovingly, and not hatefully. I must avoid bitterness and cynicism. I must not surrender to despair. Before I begin praying I must pray. When I conclude my prayers, I am not yet finished. I know well: The constant prayer of the soul.

א מִזְמוֹר לְדָוִד
יְהוָה קְרָאתִיךָ חוּשָׁה לִּי
הַאֲזִינָה קוֹלִי בְּקׇרְאִי־לָךְ׃

ב תִּכּוֹן תְּפִלָּתִי קְטֹרֶת לְפָנֶיךָ
מַשְׂאַת כַּפַּי מִנְחַת־עָרֶב׃

ג שִׁיתָה יְהוָה שׇׁמְרָה לְפִי
נִצְּרָה עַל־דַּל שְׂפָתָי׃

ד אַל־תַּט־לִבִּי ׀ לְדָבָר ׀ רָע
לְהִתְעוֹלֵל עֲלִלוֹת ׀ בְּרֶשַׁע
אֶת־אִישִׁים פֹּעֲלֵי־אָוֶן
וּבַל־אֶלְחַם בְּמַנְעַמֵּיהֶם׃

ה יֶהֶלְמֵנִי צַדִּיק ׀ חֶסֶד
וְיוֹכִיחֵנִי שֶׁמֶן רֹאשׁ
אַל־יָנִי רֹאשִׁי
כִּי־עוֹד וּתְפִלָּתִי בְּרָעוֹתֵיהֶם׃

ו נִשְׁמְטוּ בִידֵי־סֶלַע שֹׁפְטֵיהֶם
וְשָׁמְעוּ אֲמָרַי כִּי נָעֵמוּ׃

מזמור קמא *Psalm 141:* In our psalm, the psalmist asks God not just that his prayer be answered, but that it be the equivalent of the most sublime ritual offering. *May my prayer be like an incense offering… as the evening offering.*

This incense offering in the ancient Holy Temple was the epitome of all

7. As when one harrows and breaks up the ground,
so were our bones strewn at the mouth of Sheol.*

8. But to You, God, my LORD, my eyes are turned;
in You I take refuge; let not my life ebb away.

9. Keep me from the trap which they have set for me,
and from the snares of evildoers.

10. Let the wicked, one and all, fall into their own nets,
while I pass on my way.

* By the hands of those cruel rulers.

Our psalm gives voice to just such an attitude: *Were a righteous man to strike me;* that is, "strike" me verbally with words which force me to confront myself, I will not be insulted. Quite the contrary, I will consider it *an act of kindness.* Words of reproof do not daunt me, but are to me like *choice oil.*

It is no wonder that the Hebrew word for the one who prays is *mitpalel*, in the reflexive mode, indicating that one must look inward before reaching upward in prayer. Looking inward honestly and being able to hear the constructive criticism of others without defensiveness is a rare attribute indeed. But it is a necessary attribute for the exalted level of prayer described in our psalm.

כְּמ֣וֹ פֹלֵ֣חַ וּבֹקֵ֣עַ בָּאָ֑רֶץ ז
נִפְזְר֥וּ עֲ֝צָמֵ֗ינוּ לְפִ֣י שְׁאֽוֹל׃

כִּ֤י אֵלֶ֨יךָ ׀ יֱהֹוִ֣ה אֲדֹנָ֣י עֵינָ֑י ח
בְּכָ֥ה חָ֝סִ֗יתִי אַל־תְּעַ֥ר נַפְשִֽׁי׃

שָׁמְרֵ֗נִי מִ֣ידֵי פַ֭ח יָ֣קְשׁוּ לִ֑י ט
וּ֝מֹקְשׁ֗וֹת פֹּ֣עֲלֵי אָֽוֶן׃

יִפְּל֣וּ בְמַכְמֹרָ֣יו רְשָׁעִ֑ים י
יַ֥חַד אָ֝נֹכִ֗י עַֽד־אֶעֱבֽוֹר׃

---

barred" criticism which few of us can tolerate. We all have our rationalizations and self-justifications, which diminish our faults in our eyes. The "prayer" cannot do so. He must unflinchingly "face the music" of harsh feedback. He must eschew excuses and apologies, and be ready to say, as King David said, *"Against You have I sinned, and done what is evil in Your sight"* (Ps. 51:6).

The person who is eager to hear criticism, and ready to correct his wrongdoings, is the person who can be a "prayer."

PSALM 142

1. A *maskil* of David,
when he was in the cave.* A prayer.

2. With all my voice I shout to the LORD;
with all my voice I entreat the LORD.

3. I pour out my speech before Him;
I declare my troubles before Him

4. when my spirit grows faint within me.
You know the course I take;
yet in the path where I walk
men have hidden a snare for me.

5. Look to the right and see,
there is no one who takes notice of me.
I have no means of escape;
no one cares for me.

* Cf. 1 Sam. 24:3–4.

---

organize the structure of prayer so that the petitioner would first give vent to his own feelings of distress, and only afterward acknowledge his faith in the presence of God. They base their opinion upon an earlier verse in Psalms, Psalm 102:1, which reads "*A prayer of a poor man who is overwhelmed, and pours out his speech before the LORD.*" In that verse, the poor man first rushes to tell God of his woes, and only later, almost as an afterthought, directs his attention to God Himself.

The other opinion recorded in the Talmud is based instead on our verse, in which the proper acknowledgment of God is the troubled person's priority. First, he *pours out his speech*, addressing God with words of praise. He suppresses his emotions, and postpones the expression of his urgent needs until after he praises God.

מזמור קמב

I am overwhelmed by my troubles. They are too much for me to bear. I turn to You, for only You can help me. But as I turn to You I am overwhelmed by You. You are the Almighty, Creator of the Universe. I must first acknowledge that. So I begin, "Blessed are You, our God and the God of our fathers." Only then can I enumerate my many woes. First, I pour out my speech before Him. Then, I tell Him of my distress.

א מַשְׂכִּיל לְדָוִד
בִּהְיוֹתוֹ בַמְּעָרָה תְפִלָּה׃

ב קוֹלִי אֶל־יְהוָה אֶזְעָק
קוֹלִי אֶל־יְהוָה אֶתְחַנָּן׃

ג אֶשְׁפֹּךְ לְפָנָיו שִׂיחִי
צָרָתִי לְפָנָיו אַגִּיד׃

ד בְּהִתְעַטֵּף עָלַי ׀ רוּחִי
וְאַתָּה יָדַעְתָּ נְתִיבָתִי
בְּאֹרַח־זוּ אֲהַלֵּךְ
טָמְנוּ פַח לִי׃

ה הַבֵּיט יָמִין ׀ וּרְאֵה
וְאֵין־לִי מַכִּיר
אָבַד מָנוֹס מִמֶּנִּי
אֵין דּוֹרֵשׁ לְנַפְשִׁי׃

מזמור קמב *Psalm 142:* Our psalm is a favorite of those who feel overwhelmingly distressed. Its brevity belies its poignancy and power. It contains many lessons for the person who feels so desperately trapped, so hopeless, that his only resort is to God Himself.

One lesson that is derived from our psalm is discussed in the Talmud (*Avoda Zara* 7b). There, a debate is recorded between those who would

6. I cry to You, Lord;
I say, "You are my refuge;
You are my portion in the land of the living."

7. Listen to my cry,
for I am brought very low;
rescue me from those who pursue me,
for they are too strong for me.

8. Set me free from prison,
that I may praise Your name.
Then the righteous will gather around me,
because of Your kind dealings with me.

---

the Lord that Saul not fall into my hands!" David desperately wishes to be rescued; he just as much wishes to avoid harming his enemies.

There are then two distinct, but supremely important, lessons in our psalm. One is not to lose sight of God's infinite majesty, even in the face of one's own personal distress. The other is to desist from praying that vengeance be wreaked upon one's tormentors.

As is true of many psalms, our psalm sets a very high spiritual standard for us. Like all such high standards, they are ideals for us to be inspired by and to strive for, even if we cannot fulfill them perfectly.

ו זָעַקְתִּי אֵלֶיךָ יְהוָה
אָמַרְתִּי אַתָּה מַחְסִי
חֶלְקִי בְּאֶרֶץ הַחַיִּים׃

ז הַקְשִׁיבָה ׀ אֶל־רִנָּתִי
כִּי־דַלּוֹתִי מְאֹד
הַצִּילֵנִי מֵרֹדְפַי
כִּי אָמְצוּ מִמֶּנִּי׃

ח הוֹצִיאָה מִמַּסְגֵּר ׀ נַפְשִׁי
לְהוֹדוֹת אֶת־שְׁמֶךָ
בִּי יַכְתִּרוּ צַדִּיקִים
כִּי תִגְמֹל עָלָי׃

The sequence of prayer adopted by our psalm is the one that is preserved in Jewish liturgy. In the words of the Talmud, "a person should always set forth the praise of God and only afterward beseech Him for his needs."

Rav Hirsch draws our attention to another aspect of this prayer. The psalmist, in this case King David himself, is beset by enemies who wish to annihilate him. Yet he never utters a harsh word about them, even refraining from praying for their defeat. He urges God to listen to him, to rescue him, but never even hints that God should punish them, his hostile foes.

Hence the Midrash explains the repetitiveness of verse 2: "*With all my voice I shout to the Lord* that I not fall into Saul's hands. *With all my voice I entreat*

PSALM 143

1. A psalm of David.
LORD, hear my prayer,
listen to my plea;
in Your faithfulness and righteousness answer me.

2. Do not enter into judgment with Your servant,
for no man living is righteous before You.

3. For an enemy pursues me;
he crushes my life to the ground;
he makes me dwell in darkness like those long dead.

4. So my spirit is faint within me,
my heart within me is appalled.

5. I remember the days of long ago;
I meditate on all Your doings;
I reflect on the work of Your hands.

6. I spread out my hands to You;
my soul longs for You like a thirsty land. *Selah*

---

his prayers are answered? And how is he to cope with the surprising set of circumstances in which he is likely to find himself after he is released from his dire straits?

Verse 8 begins: *Let me hear of Your loving-kindness in the morning.* Many commentators, chief among them both Rashi and Radak, understand "morning" to be a symbol of salvation, of the resolution of the psalmist's troubles. The question then presents itself: If the "morning" has arrived, if the redemption has occurred, why does the psalmist need to plead that he be allowed to *hear of Your loving-kindness*? Can he not see it for himself?

The answer is based upon a simple fact about us humans. We often do not see what is before our very eyes. It is quite possible that morning has dawned, but that we haven't noticed. The redemption is here, but we do not realize it. We still believe that we are mired in our woes, and are blind to the fact that things have turned around, and that morning is here. And so the psalmist

מזמור קמג

Sometimes I am so sure of myself that I say to God, shafteini. Judge me. That's when I am convinced that my cause is just. After all, compared to my enemies I am a tzaddik. At other times, I realize that it foolhardy of me to ask to be judged. That's when I'm honest with myself – I am no tzaddik. Truth to tell, no one is a tzaddik. We all have our faults. Thankfully, He overlooks them.

א מִזְמוֹר לְדָוִד
יְהוָה ׀ שְׁמַע תְּפִלָּתִי
הַאֲזִינָה אֶל־תַּחֲנוּנַי
בֶּאֱמֻנָתְךָ עֲנֵנִי בְּצִדְקָתֶךָ׃

ב וְאַל־תָּבוֹא בְמִשְׁפָּט אֶת־עַבְדֶּךָ
כִּי לֹא־יִצְדַּק לְפָנֶיךָ כָל־חָי׃

ג כִּי רָדַף אוֹיֵב ׀ נַפְשִׁי
דִּכָּא לָאָרֶץ חַיָּתִי
הוֹשִׁיבַנִי בְמַחֲשַׁכִּים כְּמֵתֵי עוֹלָם׃

ד וַתִּתְעַטֵּף עָלַי רוּחִי
בְּתוֹכִי יִשְׁתּוֹמֵם לִבִּי׃

ה זָכַרְתִּי יָמִים ׀ מִקֶּדֶם
הָגִיתִי בְכָל־פָּעֳלֶךָ
בְּמַעֲשֵׂה יָדֶיךָ אֲשׂוֹחֵחַ׃

ו פֵּרַשְׂתִּי יָדַי אֵלֶיךָ
נַפְשִׁי ׀ כְּאֶרֶץ־עֲיֵפָה לְךָ סֶלָה׃

מזמור קמג *Psalm 143:* Our psalm, like so very many others, eloquently expresses the passion of prayer, and cogently portrays the inspiring confidence demonstrated by the person who prays. But our psalm goes further, and allows us to glimpse at the aftermath of prayer. It hints at the answers to the following two questions: How does the person who prays know when

7. Speedily answer me, LORD, for my spirit fails.
Do not hide Your face from me,
or I shall be like those who go down into the pit.

8. Let me hear of Your loving-kindness in the morning,
for I put my trust in You.
Show me the way I should take,
for to You I lift up my soul.

9. Rescue me, LORD, from my enemies,
for to You I [reveal my plight, which I]
have kept covered [from others].

10. Teach me to do Your will,
for You are my God;
let Your good spirit
lead me on level ground.

11. For Your name's sake, LORD, preserve my life;
in Your righteousness free me from distress.

12. Because of Your loving-kindness
You will make an end of my enemies;
and destroy all who oppress me,
for I am Your servant.

---

be totally different from anything he imagined. What does he do now? How does he cope with this surprisingly new environment, with the challenges of a "new world"?

And so, he prays again: *Show me the way I should take… teach me to do Your will… let Your good spirit lead me on level ground.* Even after one's problems are resolved, one does not just "live happily ever after." The redeemed world is not without its own pitfalls and dangers, physical and spiritual. New roads open up as soon as prayers are answered, and they require God's teaching and guidance.

Our psalm recognizes full well that one needs to remain connected to God even after his prayers are answered. At that point, he may no longer need Him to deliver him from enemies and illness, but he does need Him to show him the way forward, so that he makes the most of the new set of circumstances with which he has been blessed.

ז מַהֵר עֲנֵנִי ׀ יהוה כָּלְתָה רוּחִי
אַל־תַּסְתֵּר פָּנֶיךָ מִמֶּנִּי
וְנִמְשַׁלְתִּי עִם־יֹרְדֵי בוֹר׃

ח הַשְׁמִיעֵנִי בַבֹּקֶר ׀ חַסְדֶּךָ
כִּי־בְךָ בָטָחְתִּי
הוֹדִיעֵנִי דֶּרֶךְ־זוּ אֵלֵךְ
כִּי־אֵלֶיךָ נָשָׂאתִי נַפְשִׁי׃

ט הַצִּילֵנִי מֵאֹיְבַי ׀ יהוה
אֵלֶיךָ כִסִּתִי׃

י לַמְּדֵנִי ׀ לַעֲשׂוֹת רְצוֹנֶךָ
כִּי־אַתָּה אֱלוֹהָי
רוּחֲךָ טוֹבָה
תַּנְחֵנִי בְּאֶרֶץ מִישׁוֹר׃

יא לְמַעַן־שִׁמְךָ יהוה תְּחַיֵּנִי
בְּצִדְקָתְךָ ׀ תּוֹצִיא מִצָּרָה נַפְשִׁי׃

יב וּבְחַסְדְּךָ תַּצְמִית אֹיְבָי
וְהַאֲבַדְתָּ כָּל־צֹרְרֵי נַפְשִׁי
כִּי אֲנִי עַבְדֶּךָ׃

---

prays, "*Let me hear of Your loving-kindness in the morning!* Help me be aware that the worst is over, that the tide has turned, and that although my redemption may be in its earliest and most tentative stages, it has finally begun. My prayers have already been answered."

But once awareness sets in, and the desperate person realizes that he is no longer engulfed by pain and woe, a new problem arises. The new set of circumstances is likely to be unexpected and confounding to the person who prayed. He prayed that his troubles be resolved, but he did not at all specify the nature of the redeemed world for which he yearned. It is likely to

PSALM 144

1. Of David.
Blessed be the LORD, my rock,
who trains my hands for war,
my fingers for battle.

2. He is my benefactor, my fortress,
my stronghold, and my deliverer;
He is my shield, in whom I take refuge,
who subdues peoples under me.

3. LORD, what is man that You care for him,
mortal man that You think of him?

4. Man is like a breath,
his days are like a passing shadow.

5. LORD, bend Your heavens and come down;
touch the mountains and they will pour forth smoke.

6. Flash Your lightnings and scatter them;*
shoot Your arrows and rout them.

* I.e., "the proud foes of God's people."

> the following: "*When our cattle are heavily laden, when there is no breaching of our walls, no going into captivity, no cries of distress in our streets – happy are the people who have it so; happy are the people whose God is the LORD*" (*Berakhot* 17a)

These are, of course, the concluding verses of our psalm.

Our psalm plays a role in the daily liturgy, at the conclusion of the Sabbath, and as an expression of farewell to the study hall. What is distinctive about these spiritual moments, and what connection does our psalm have to them?

Rav Soloveitchik notes the tension in Jewish life between the spiritual world of the synagogue and study hall and the mundane world of the city,

מזמור קמד

I fight many battles in my life. Dare I ask Him to help me?
He is wondrous, but I wonder: Does He care? I silently sing to Him.
Does He hear my song? I am happy. How do I thank Him?

א לְדָוִ֨ד ׀ בָּ֘ר֤וּךְ יְהוָ֨ה ׀ צוּרִ֗י
הַֽמְלַמֵּ֣ד יָדַ֣י לַקְרָ֑ב
אֶ֝צְבְּעוֹתַ֗י לַמִּלְחָמָֽה׃

ב חַסְדִּ֥י וּמְצוּדָתִי֮ מִשְׂגַּבִּ֪י וּֽמְפַלְטִ֫י לִ֥י
מָ֭גִנִּי וּב֣וֹ חָסִ֑יתִי
הָרוֹדֵ֖ד עַמִּ֣י תַחְתָּֽי׃

ג יְהוָ֗ה מָֽה־אָ֭דָם וַתֵּדָעֵ֑הוּ
בֶּן־אֱ֝נ֗וֹשׁ וַתְּחַשְּׁבֵֽהוּ׃

ד אָ֭דָם לַהֶ֣בֶל דָּמָ֑ה
יָ֝מָ֗יו כְּצֵ֣ל עוֹבֵֽר׃

ה יְ֭הוָה הַט־שָׁמֶ֣יךָ וְתֵרֵ֑ד
גַּ֖ע בֶּהָרִ֣ים וְיֶעֱשָֽׁנוּ׃

ו בְּר֣וֹק בָּ֭רָק וּתְפִיצֵ֑ם
שְׁלַ֥ח חִ֝צֶּ֗יךָ וּתְהֻמֵּֽם׃

מזמור קמד *Psalm 144:* The final verse of our psalm is familiar to the synagogue Jew. It serves, along with the fifth verse of Psalm 84, as a prelude to *Ashrei*, the thrice-daily recitation of Psalm 145.

In many synagogues, our psalm is sung to an uplifting melody at the conclusion of the Sabbath, just before the evening service.

Our psalm was also used in a fascinating ancient practice, recorded in the Talmud:

> When the sages took leave of the study hall of Rav Ḥisda, and some say it was the study hall of Rav Shmuel bar Naḥmani, they would say to him

7. Reach out Your hand from on high;
rescue me and deliver me from mighty waters,
from the hands of foreigners,

8. whose mouths speak lies,
and whose right hand is raised in perjury.

9. To You, God, I will sing a new song;
on a ten-stringed harp I will chant praises to You,

10. who gave victory to kings,
who rescued His servant David from the deadly sword.

11. Rescue me and deliver me
from the hands of foreigners,
whose mouths speak lies,
and whose right hand is raised in perjury.

12. When our sons are like saplings,
carefully trained from their youth,
and our daughters like sculptured corner columns,
fit to adorn a palace;

13. when our storehouses are filled to overflowing,
affording every kind of provision;
when our flocks increase by thousands,
even by myriads, in our fields;

---

dwell in the "house of the LORD," as he regretfully returns to the challenging world outside. *Happy are the people who have it so.*

Rav Soloveitchik encourages us to contemplate King David's travails in this regard. He was the "sweet singer of Israel," the sensitive musician who had a harp suspended above his bed. He was a prophet, a poet, a scholar. But his moments of seclusion in the houses of prayer and study were precious and rare. He was consumed by the urgent needs of his people, which often required waging war and unavoidable bloodshed. How delighted he must have been whenever he found the tranquility necessary for his preferred pursuits.

ז שְׁלַח יָדֶיךָ מִמָּרוֹם
פְּצֵנִי וְהַצִּילֵנִי מִמַּיִם רַבִּים
מִיַּד בְּנֵי נֵכָר׃

ח אֲשֶׁר פִּיהֶם דִּבֶּר־שָׁוְא
וִימִינָם יְמִין שָׁקֶר׃

ט אֱלֹהִים שִׁיר חָדָשׁ אָשִׁירָה לָּךְ
בְּנֵבֶל עָשׂוֹר אֲזַמְּרָה־לָּךְ׃

י הַנּוֹתֵן תְּשׁוּעָה לַמְּלָכִים
הַפּוֹצֶה אֶת־דָּוִד עַבְדּוֹ מֵחֶרֶב רָעָה׃

יא פְּצֵנִי וְהַצִּילֵנִי מִיַּד בְּנֵי־נֵכָר
אֲשֶׁר פִּיהֶם דִּבֶּר־שָׁוְא
וִימִינָם יְמִין שָׁקֶר׃

יב אֲשֶׁר בָּנֵינוּ ׀ כִּנְטִעִים
מְגֻדָּלִים בִּנְעוּרֵיהֶם
בְּנוֹתֵינוּ כְזָוִיֹּת
מְחֻטָּבוֹת תַּבְנִית הֵיכָל׃

יג מְזָוֵינוּ מְלֵאִים מְפִיקִים מִזַּן אֶל זַן
צֹאונֵנוּ מַאֲלִיפוֹת
מְרֻבָּבוֹת בְּחוּצוֹתֵינוּ׃

---

farm, marketplace, and battlefield. The Jew cherishes the moments he can spend in the former world, and accepts reluctantly the necessity of returning to the latter.

Our psalm is the quintessential expression of this tension. Its concluding verses express the gratitude the Jew feels when he has the good fortune to

14. when our cattle are heavily laden;*
when there is no breaching [of our walls],
no going into captivity,
no cries of distress in our streets –

15. happy are the people who have it so;
happy are the people whose God is the LORD.

* Others: "heavy with young."

---

had to return home to the worries of daily life, earning a livelihood, living among gentiles. They left the study hall to engage in the battles of life. How apt was the verse: *Blessed be the LORD… who trains my hands for war, my fingers for battle… rescue me and deliver me from mighty waters, from the hands of foreigners, whose mouths speak lies.*

When they did return home, and were successful in their struggles, they could best articulate their feelings with the words of our psalm: *To You, God, I will sing a new song… I will chant praises to You, who gave victory to kings, who rescued His servant David from the deadly sword.*

יד אַלּוּפֵינוּ מְסֻבָּלִים
אֵין פֶּרֶץ וְאֵין יוֹצֵאת
וְאֵין צְוָחָה בִּרְחֹבֹתֵינוּ׃

טו אַשְׁרֵי הָעָם שֶׁכָּכָה לּוֹ
אַשְׁרֵי הָעָם שֶׁיהוָה אֱלֹהָיו׃

Our Talmudic anecdote now assumes a broader significance. Here was a group of sages who had come to Babylon to study under Rav Ḥisda's tutelage from the far-flung corners of the Diaspora. They came from the Holy Land, from Yemen, Spain, and even Germany. At the end of the study season they

PSALM 145

1. *A song of praise by David.
I will extol You, my God and King,
and bless Your name forever and ever.

Thirtieth day of the month

2. Every day will I bless You,
and praise Your name forever and ever.

3. Great is the LORD and most worthy of praise;
His goodness no one can fathom.

4. One generation shall laud Your works to another;
they will declare Your mighty deeds.

5. On the splendor of Your glorious majesty,
and on Your marvelous deeds, I will meditate.

6. And men shall talk of Your awe-inspiring power,
and I will tell of Your greatness.

7. They shall recite the record of Your abundant goodness,
and sing joyously of Your righteousness.

8. Gracious and compassionate is the LORD,
slow to anger and abounding in kindness.

* An alphabetical psalm; the "*nun*" verse is missing.

---

song." They serve as a kind of introduction to the more essential subsequent components of the daily prayer service.

Not only is our psalm the first of this series of six, it is also of distinctive significance. The Talmud assures the person who recites our psalm three times a day that he will have a share in the World to Come (*Berakhot* 4b). Indeed, our psalm appears three times in the daily prayer service, and may therefore be the single psalm with which observant Jews are most familiar.

Why is our psalm so distinctive? For one thing, each verse begins with a different letter in alphabetical sequence. The first verse begins with *alef*, the second with *beit*, and so on.

מזמור קמה

When He is so close that I can speak to Him directly, I call Him "You." Every day I will bless You. When You overwhelm me with Your splendor and might, I call You "Him." His mercy is upon all His works. I praise Him and sing Your praises to all who hear me. They join me and sing His praise, Your praise.

ל לחודש

א תְּהִלָּה לְדָוִד
אֲרוֹמִמְךָ אֱלוֹהַי הַמֶּלֶךְ
וַאֲבָרְכָה שִׁמְךָ לְעוֹלָם וָעֶד:

ב בְּכָל־יוֹם אֲבָרְכֶךָּ
וַאֲהַלְלָה שִׁמְךָ לְעוֹלָם וָעֶד:

ג גָּדוֹל יהוה וּמְהֻלָּל מְאֹד
וְלִגְדֻלָּתוֹ אֵין חֵקֶר:

ד דּוֹר לְדוֹר יְשַׁבַּח מַעֲשֶׂיךָ
וּגְבוּרֹתֶיךָ יַגִּידוּ:

ה הֲדַר כְּבוֹד הוֹדֶךָ
וְדִבְרֵי נִפְלְאֹתֶיךָ אָשִׂיחָה:

ו וֶעֱזוּז נוֹרְאֹתֶיךָ יֹאמֵרוּ
וגדלותיך אֲסַפְּרֶנָּה: וּגְדוּלָּתְךָ

ז זֵכֶר רַב־טוּבְךָ יַבִּיעוּ
וְצִדְקָתְךָ יְרַנֵּנוּ:

ח חַנּוּן וְרַחוּם יהוה
אֶרֶךְ אַפַּיִם וּגְדָל־חָסֶד:

מזמור קמה *Psalm 145:* Our psalm and the five that follow it are psalms of praise to God. They are so exuberant and so eloquent that they were selected by our sages to comprise the series known as *Pesukei DeZimra*, the "verses of

9. The LORD is good to all,
and His mercy is upon all His works.

10. All Your works shall praise You, LORD,
and Your devout ones shall bless You.

11. They shall talk of the glory of Your kingdom,
and speak of Your might,

12. to make known to the sons of men His mighty acts,
and the glorious splendor of His kingship.

13. Your kingdom is an everlasting kingdom,
and Your dominion endures throughout all generations.

14. The LORD supports all who fall,
and raises all who are bowed down.

15. The eyes of all look hopefully to You,
and You give them their food at the proper time.

16. You open Your hand,
and satisfy the desire of every living thing.

17. The LORD is righteous in all His ways,
and kind in all that He does.

18. The LORD is near to all who call Him,
to all who call Him with sincerity.

---

hand, and satisfy the desire of every living thing. The concept that God provides for our well-being and is the ultimate source of our livelihood is a fundamental element of our system of belief. So important is this verse that we are cautioned to recite it with conscious intention. Many authorities even insist that if one fails to recite the verse with adequate attentiveness, he must repeat the entire verse.

Our psalm is remarkable in yet another way. It contains no petitionary prayer. The exclusive focus of every verse is the praise of God. We ask Him for nothing.

ט טוֹב־יְהוָה לַכֹּל
וְרַחֲמָיו עַל־כָּל־מַעֲשָׂיו׃

י יוֹדוּךָ יְהוָה כָּל־מַעֲשֶׂיךָ
וַחֲסִידֶיךָ יְבָרְכוּכָה׃

יא כְּבוֹד מַלְכוּתְךָ יֹאמֵרוּ
וּגְבוּרָתְךָ יְדַבֵּרוּ׃

יב לְהוֹדִיעַ ׀ לִבְנֵי הָאָדָם גְּבוּרֹתָיו
וּכְבוֹד הֲדַר מַלְכוּתוֹ׃

יג מַלְכוּתְךָ מַלְכוּת כָּל־עֹלָמִים
וּמֶמְשַׁלְתְּךָ בְּכָל־דּוֹר וָדֹר׃

יד סוֹמֵךְ יְהוָה לְכָל־הַנֹּפְלִים
וְזוֹקֵף לְכָל־הַכְּפוּפִים׃

טו עֵינֵי־כֹל אֵלֶיךָ יְשַׂבֵּרוּ
וְאַתָּה נוֹתֵן־לָהֶם אֶת־אָכְלָם בְּעִתּוֹ׃

טז פּוֹתֵחַ אֶת־יָדֶךָ
וּמַשְׂבִּיעַ לְכָל־חַי רָצוֹן׃

יז צַדִּיק יְהוָה בְּכָל־דְּרָכָיו
וְחָסִיד בְּכָל־מַעֲשָׂיו׃

יח קָרוֹב יְהוָה לְכָל־קֹרְאָיו
לְכֹל אֲשֶׁר יִקְרָאֻהוּ בֶאֱמֶת׃

Only the letter *nun* is missing. The Talmud explains that the letter *nun* brings to mind the Hebrew word for "fallen" or "defeated," *nafal.* The very notion of "defeat" is unsuitable for inclusion in a psalm of exultation.

Also contributing to our psalm's distinctiveness is verse 16: *You open Your*

19. He fulfills the will of those who fear Him;
He hears their cry for help and saves them.

20. The Lord watches over all who love Him,
but all the wicked He will destroy.

21. My mouth shall declare the praise of the Lord,
and all people shall bless His holy name
forever and ever.

---

ourselves without His providence, while the exclusion of a verse beginning with *nun* is the result of our wish to praise God for His role in our triumphs and accomplishments, and not to associate Him with our defeats and failures.

Finally, our psalm declares that it is the praise of God which is primary, and that beseeching Him for His favors, while legitimate, is not the essence of prayer.

יט רְצוֹן־יְרֵאָיו יַעֲשֶׂה
וְאֶת־שַׁוְעָתָם יִשְׁמַע וְיוֹשִׁיעֵם׃

כ שׁוֹמֵר יהוה אֶת־כָּל־אֹהֲבָיו
וְאֵת כָּל־הָרְשָׁעִים יַשְׁמִיד׃

כא תְּהִלַּת יהוה יְדַבֶּר פִּי
וִיבָרֵךְ כָּל־בָּשָׂר שֵׁם קָדְשׁוֹ לְעוֹלָם וָעֶד׃

Thus, our psalm's distinctiveness reflects several essential components of our religious faith.

The alphabetic arrangement symbolizes our desire to employ every literary means at our disposal in praise of God.

The inclusion of the verse *You open Your hand* asserts that we cannot sustain

PSALM 146

1. Praise the LORD!
Praise the LORD, O my soul.

2. I will praise the LORD as long as I live;
I will sing praises to my God as long as I exist.

3. Put no trust in princes,
or in mortal man who has no power to save.

4. His spirit departs, he returns to the dust;
on that day his plans come to nothing.

5. Happy is he whose help is the God of Jacob,
whose hope is in the LORD his God,

6. maker of heaven and earth,
the sea and all that is in them.
It is He who keeps faith forever.

7. He secures justice for the oppressed,
He gives food to the hungry.
The LORD sets captives free,

Our psalm maintains that we know Him best with our soul. *Praise the LORD, O my soul.* Why is our soul the part of us that is in the best position to praise God? The answer lies in the fact that, as the Talmud points out, the soul of man has much in common with the nature of God.

"Just as the Holy One blessed be He fills the world, so the soul fills the body; just as the Holy One blessed be He sees, but is not seen, so the soul sees but is not seen" (*Berakhot* 10a).

The essence of the soul is spiritual wisdom, and its most outstanding, and frustrating, attribute is its invisibility. But the very fact that the soul is invisible is what qualifies it to apprehend the invisible God.

God cannot be seen in the world. But He can be discerned by the soul of man. Eyes of flesh cannot perceive Him, but that which is itself invisible can envision Him who is invisible.

מזמור קמו

Will God redeem us? Yes, but He will use His emissaries to do so. Sure, we are not to put our trust in mortal men. But they are the ones God will send to help us. I don't pray that my doctor should heal me. I pray that God give my doctor the skills to do so. I can't be sure that my soldier will shoot straight. But I can pray to God that he won't miss. That He won't miss.

א הַלְלוּיָהּ
הַלְלִי נַפְשִׁי אֶת־יְהוָה:

ב אֲהַלְלָה יְהוָה בְּחַיָּי
אֲזַמְּרָה לֵאלֹהַי בְּעוֹדִי:

ג אַל־תִּבְטְחוּ בִנְדִיבִים
בְּבֶן־אָדָם ׀ שֶׁאֵין לוֹ תְשׁוּעָה:

ד תֵּצֵא רוּחוֹ יָשֻׁב לְאַדְמָתוֹ
בַּיּוֹם הַהוּא אָבְדוּ עֶשְׁתֹּנֹתָיו:

ה אַשְׁרֵי שֶׁאֵל יַעֲקֹב בְּעֶזְרוֹ
שִׂבְרוֹ עַל־יְהוָה אֱלֹהָיו:

ו עֹשֶׂה ׀ שָׁמַיִם וָאָרֶץ
אֶת־הַיָּם וְאֶת־כָּל־אֲשֶׁר־בָּם
הַשֹּׁמֵר אֱמֶת לְעוֹלָם:

ז עֹשֶׂה מִשְׁפָּט ׀ לַעֲשׁוּקִים
נֹתֵן לֶחֶם לָרְעֵבִים
יְהוָה מַתִּיר אֲסוּרִים:

מזמור קמו *Psalm 146:* We know God in many ways. We know Him emotionally, intellectually, and even physically. We feel Him and experience Him in sadness and in sorrow. We conceptualize Him philosophically and learn from Him by studying His Torah. We sense His life-giving force when we are strong, and its absence when we are ill.

8. the LORD opens the eyes of the blind,
the LORD raises those who are bowed down,
the LORD loves the righteous.

9. The LORD watches over the stranger;
He gives courage to the fatherless and the widow,
but subverts the course of the wicked.

10. The LORD shall reign forever,
your God, O Zion, for all generations.
Praise the LORD!

---

ignore God. It mistakenly is under the impression that its physicality is incompatible with spirituality. It is prepared to expend its healthy energies on its passions.

The soul protests against the body. It says to it, "No! It is precisely when you feel the life-forces within you that you can draw close to God."

The soul also understands that even when the body is racked with pain and illness, even when it is in throes of death, it can still connect with God. The soul of a man can sing upon his very deathbed. As long as there is life there is hope.

How apt are the opening verses of our psalm given this perspective: *Halleluya! Praise the LORD, O my soul. I will praise the LORD as long as I live; I will sing praises to my God as long as I exist.*

ח יְהוָ֨ה ׀ פֹּ֘קֵ֤חַ עִוְרִ֗ים
יְֽהוָה֮ זֹקֵ֪ף כְּפוּפִ֥ים
יְ֝הוָ֗ה אֹהֵ֥ב צַדִּיקִֽים׃

ט יְהוָ֤ה ׀ שֹׁ֘מֵ֤ר אֶת־גֵּרִ֗ים
יָת֣וֹם וְאַלְמָנָ֣ה יְעוֹדֵ֑ד
וְדֶ֖רֶךְ רְשָׁעִ֣ים יְעַוֵּֽת׃

י יִמְלֹ֤ךְ יְהוָ֨ה ׀ לְעוֹלָ֗ם
אֱלֹהַ֣יִךְ צִ֭יּוֹן לְדֹ֥ר וָדֹ֗ר
הַֽלְלוּיָֽהּ׃

What the Talmud, in the above passage, does not say about the soul is that its language is music and song. The soul communicates neither in words and sentences nor in concepts, but rather in tones and melodies and moods.

Our psalm initiates the final series of psalms, each of which begins and ends with the exclamation *Halleluya*. *Hallel* is generally translated as "praise," but that term is inadequate. It does indeed mean to praise, but it carries the additional connotations of "joy" and of "song." The soul sings; it does not merely speak.

Above all, the soul knows the body even better than the body knows itself. The soul knows that the body can sing *as long as I live*. The body erroneously believes that when it *lives*, that is, when it is full of vigor and vitality, it can

PSALM 147

1. Praise the Lord!
How good it is to sing praises to our God!
How pleasant and fitting to praise Him!

2. The Lord rebuilds Jerusalem;
He gathers in the scattered people of Israel.

3. He heals the broken-hearted
and binds up their wounds.

4. He counts the number of the stars
and calls each by name.

5. Great is our Lord and mighty in power;
His wisdom is infinite.

6. The Lord gives courage to the lowly;
He brings the wicked down to the ground.

7. Sing to the Lord a song of thanksgiving;
sing praises to our God on the harp.

---

number of the stars and calls each by name. What does it mean that He *calls each by name*?

In response to this question, Rav Kook (Commentary on the Siddur, *Olat Re'iya,* p. 227) points out that a name indicates the ultimate purpose of an object. Although the complex totality of the world has its divinely determined ultimate purpose, so too does every composite part of the world, however tiny and seemingly insignificant, have its particular purpose. God's benevolence does not merely extend to the stars as a totality, but to every single individual star. Hence, while *He counts the number of the stars,* ordaining for "stars" a role in His universe, He does not overlook the individual star, for which He has a preordained particular role, a name.

We can extend this concept to humanity. Humanity as a totality has a purpose in God's creation. One dominant view in our tradition is that the human race is the central purpose of God's creation. But each individual person also

מזמור קמז

At times like this, His cosmic greatness does not do it for me. Sure, He is the Master of the Universe. What about little old me? It helps me to hear that He is rebuilding Jerusalem. It helps more to hear that He blesses her with peace. It helps most of all to know that He heals the broken-hearted, and that He gives courage to the needy. I am broken-hearted, and so is Jerusalem. I need courage, and so does she.

א הַ֥לְלוּיָ֨הּ ׀
כִּי־ט֭וֹב זַמְּרָ֣ה אֱלֹהֵ֑ינוּ
כִּֽי־נָ֝עִ֗ים נָאוָ֥ה תְהִלָּֽה׃

ב בּוֹנֵ֣ה יְרוּשָׁלַ֣ם יְהוָ֑ה
נִדְחֵ֖י יִשְׂרָאֵ֣ל יְכַנֵּֽס׃

ג הָ֭רוֹפֵא לִשְׁב֣וּרֵי לֵ֑ב
וּ֝מְחַבֵּ֗שׁ לְעַצְּבוֹתָֽם׃

ד מוֹנֶ֣ה מִ֭סְפָּר לַכּוֹכָבִ֑ים
לְ֝כֻלָּ֗ם שֵׁמ֥וֹת יִקְרָֽא׃

ה גָּד֣וֹל אֲדוֹנֵ֣ינוּ וְרַב־כֹּ֑חַ
לִ֝תְבוּנָת֗וֹ אֵ֣ין מִסְפָּֽר׃

ו מְעוֹדֵ֣ד עֲנָוִ֣ים יְהוָ֑ה
מַשְׁפִּ֖יל רְשָׁעִ֣ים עֲדֵי־אָֽרֶץ׃

ז עֱנ֣וּ לַיהוָ֣ה בְּתוֹדָ֑ה
זַמְּר֖וּ לֵאלֹהֵ֣ינוּ בְכִנּֽוֹר׃

מזמור קמז *Psalm 147:* Our psalm teaches us a great deal about God. It describes His dominion over the world of nature, it tells of His special concern for Jerusalem and the people of Israel, and it assures us that He watches over the lowly and the broken-hearted.

Careful and learned readers of our psalm have uncovered treasured teachings in its every phrase. One such phrase appears in verse 4: *He counts the*

8. He covers the heavens with clouds,
provides rain for the earth,
and makes grass grow on the hills.

9. He gives food to the cattle,
and to the young ravens when they cry.

10. He does not delight in the strength of a horse;
He takes no pleasure in the fleetness* of a man.

11. The LORD is pleased with those who fear Him,
with those who wait for His loving-kindness.

12. Sing to the LORD, O Jerusalem,
praise your God, O Zion.

13. For He has strengthened the bars of your gates;
He has blessed Your children within you.

14. He brings peace within your frontiers,
and satisfies you with the finest wheat.

15. He sends forth His command to the earth;
His word runs swiftly.

16. He spreads snow like fleece,
and scatters frost like ashes.

* Lit. "thighs."

---

the stars. God counts us as He does the stars. We are His people. But He also gives each of us names. We are each persons in our own right, with a special part to play in His cosmic drama.

This is an important lesson in the life of all groups: families, classrooms, or places of work. Every group has certain common goals, and often the individual must suppress his needs in order to achieve the overarching goals of the group. But a good parent, or teacher, or manager, must never lose sight

ח הַֽמְכַסֶּה שָׁמַיִם ׀ בְּעָבִים
הַמֵּכִין לָאָרֶץ מָטָר
הַמַּצְמִיחַ הָרִים חָצִיר׃

ט נוֹתֵן לִבְהֵמָה לַחְמָהּ
לִבְנֵי עֹרֵב אֲשֶׁר יִקְרָאוּ׃

י לֹא בִגְבוּרַת הַסּוּס יֶחְפָּץ
לֹא־בְשׁוֹקֵי הָאִישׁ יִרְצֶה׃

יא רוֹצֶה יְהוָה אֶת־יְרֵאָיו
אֶת־הַמְיַחֲלִים לְחַסְדּוֹ׃

יב שַׁבְּחִי יְרוּשָׁלַםִ אֶת־יְהוָה
הַלְלִי אֱלֹהַיִךְ צִיּוֹן׃

יג כִּי־חִזַּק בְּרִיחֵי שְׁעָרָיִךְ
בֵּרַךְ בָּנַיִךְ בְּקִרְבֵּךְ׃

יד הַשָּׂם־גְּבוּלֵךְ שָׁלוֹם
חֵלֶב חִטִּים יַשְׂבִּיעֵךְ׃

טו הַשֹּׁלֵחַ אִמְרָתוֹ אָרֶץ
עַד־מְהֵרָה יָרוּץ דְּבָרוֹ׃

טז הַנֹּתֵן שֶׁלֶג כַּצָּמֶר
כְּפוֹר כָּאֵפֶר יְפַזֵּר׃

---

has a special purpose. As the Talmud has it (*Sanhedrin* 37a), "a person should always say 'the world was created for me!'"

So it is for the Jewish people. We are a nation, a totality. As such we have a role to play in God's world. We are to be a "light unto the nations." But each one of us has his or her unique role to play as well. In that sense we are like

17. He hurls down His icy hail like crumbs;
who can stand His cold blast?

18. He issues His command and melts them;
He stirs up His wind, and the waters flow.

19. He declared His words to Jacob,
His statutes and laws to Israel.

20. He has not done so for any other nation;
of such laws they have no knowledge.
Praise the Lord!

The good parent, teacher, or manager does not just "count the number" of his stars. Rather, he knows their names, and calls each of them by name.

He counts the number of stars and calls each by name.

יז מַשְׁלִ֣יךְ קַֽרְח֣וֹ כְפִתִּ֑ים
לִפְנֵ֥י קָ֝רָת֗וֹ מִ֣י יַעֲמֹֽד׃

יח יִשְׁלַ֣ח דְּבָר֣וֹ וְיַמְסֵ֑ם
יַשֵּׁ֥ב ר֝וּח֗וֹ יִזְּלוּ־מָֽיִם׃

יט מַגִּ֣יד דְּבָרָ֣ו לְיַעֲקֹ֑ב
חֻקָּ֥יו וּ֝מִשְׁפָּטָ֗יו לְיִשְׂרָאֵֽל׃

כ לֹ֘א עָ֤שָׂה כֵ֨ן ׀ לְכָל־גּ֗וֹי
וּמִשְׁפָּטִ֥ים בַּל־יְ֝דָע֗וּם
הַֽלְלוּיָֽהּ׃

---

of the uniqueness of the individuals in his or her charge. Each individual has a role to play, a unique role. Ignoring the individual inevitably impedes the progress of the group toward its larger goal.

PSALM 148

1. Praise the Lord!
Praise the Lord, from the heavens;
praise Him in the heights.

2. Praise Him, all His angels;
praise Him, all His hosts.

3. Praise Him, sun and moon;
praise Him, all you shining stars.

4. Praise Him, you highest heavens,
and you waters that are above the heavens.

5. Let them praise the name of the Lord,
for He commanded and they were created.

6. He established them forever and ever,
by a decree that shall never pass away.

7. Praise the Lord, from the earth,
you sea monsters and ocean depths;

---

and moon and stars. This world is unchanging. It has not changed over the millennia, and it never will. The heavens constantly obey the will of God, and as such they model the ideal relationship with Him – absolute loyalty.

Our psalm contrasts this world with the world of the earth. There order, stability, and predictability are absent. The elements, *fire and hail, snow and mist,* may indeed *obey His command,* but they appear dynamic, fluid, unpredictable. The creatures of the *ocean depths... all cattle, creeping things, and winged birds* conjure up images of tumultuous motion, even chaos, in spite of the inscrutable laws of instinct to which they are subject. The behavior of human beings, however great and mighty, stands in sharp contrast to the orderliness which pervades the heavens.

The world of heaven is thus a paradigm for immutability, constancy, and even eternity. The world of earth is a paradigm for flux and change and upheaval.

Our psalm has a vision, and in this vision the world of earth will fuse and

מזמור קמח

I often wonder how the world will end. Will it end with a bang? Or will it end with a whimper, as some say? We're all in for a surprise. Nature's wonders will not end at all. He established them forever and ever. Persecution will end, and war, and intolerance. Class distinctions will end. Genders and generations will end their rivalry. That's how this world will end. A new world will begin.

א הַֽלְלוּיָהּ ׀
הַֽלְלוּ אֶת־יְהוָה מִן־הַשָּׁמַיִם
הַֽלְלוּהוּ בַּמְּרוֹמִֽים׃

ב הַֽלְלוּהוּ כָל־מַלְאָכָיו
הַֽלְלוּהוּ כָּל־צְבָאָֽו׃

ג הַֽלְלוּהוּ שֶׁמֶשׁ וְיָרֵחַ
הַֽלְלוּהוּ כָּל־כּוֹכְבֵי אֽוֹר׃

ד הַֽלְלוּהוּ שְׁמֵי הַשָּׁמָיִם
וְהַמַּיִם אֲשֶׁר ׀ מֵעַל הַשָּׁמָֽיִם׃

ה יְֽהַלְלוּ אֶת־שֵׁם יְהוָה
כִּי הוּא צִוָּה וְנִבְרָֽאוּ׃

ו וַיַּעֲמִידֵם לָעַד לְעוֹלָם
חָק־נָתַן וְלֹא יַעֲבֽוֹר׃

ז הַֽלְלוּ אֶת־יְהוָה מִן־הָאָרֶץ
תַּנִּינִים וְכָל־תְּהֹמֽוֹת׃

מזמור קמח *Psalm 148:* As the Book of Psalms draws to a close we no longer read of the fears, hopes, and prayers of individual persons. Instead, the themes become much grander in scope – universal, cosmic. Our psalm epitomizes this trend. It is clearly divided into two halves, one which describes the world of heaven and the other the world of the earth.

Our psalm first describes the world of heaven, of angels and hosts, sun

8. fire and hail, snow and mist,
storm winds that obey His command;

9. you mountains and all hills,
fruit trees and all cedars;

10. wild animals and all cattle,
creeping things and winged birds;

11. you kings of the earth and all nations,
you princes and all judges on earth,

12. young men, too, and maidens,
old men and young together.

13. Let them praise the name of the LORD,
for His name alone is exalted;
His majesty is above the earth and the heavens.

14. He has exalted the renown* of His people,
for the glory of all His faithful ones,
the children of Israel, the people close to Him.
Praise the LORD!

* Lit. "horn."

It is noteworthy that our psalm, according to Rav Hirsch, concludes with a subtle allusion to the coming together of human history's most prominent antagonists, the Jewish people and the nations of the world. Rav Hirsch insists that the *faithful ones* whose glory is mentioned in the last verse are the faithful ones of the other nations of the world, who will also share in that ultimate moment when *He has exalted the renown of His people.* This theme becomes even more pronounced as we proceed to the next psalm, which is arguably the culmination of the entire Book of Psalms.

ח אֵשׁ וּבָרָד שֶׁלֶג וְקִיטוֹר
רוּחַ סְעָרָה עֹשָׂה דְבָרוֹ׃

ט הֶהָרִים וְכָל־גְּבָעוֹת
עֵץ פְּרִי וְכָל־אֲרָזִים׃

י הַחַיָּה וְכָל־בְּהֵמָה
רֶמֶשׂ וְצִפּוֹר כָּנָף׃

יא מַלְכֵי־אֶרֶץ וְכָל־לְאֻמִּים
שָׂרִים וְכָל־שֹׁפְטֵי אָרֶץ׃

יב בַּחוּרִים וְגַם־בְּתוּלוֹת
זְקֵנִים עִם־נְעָרִים׃

יג יְהַלְלוּ ׀ אֶת־שֵׁם יהוה
כִּי־נִשְׂגָּב שְׁמוֹ לְבַדּוֹ
הוֹדוֹ עַל־אֶרֶץ וְשָׁמָיִם׃

יד וַיָּרֶם קֶרֶן ׀ לְעַמּוֹ
תְּהִלָּה לְכָל־חֲסִידָיו
לִבְנֵי יִשְׂרָאֵל עַם קְרֹבוֹ
הַלְלוּיָהּ׃

---

merge, however slowly, with the world of heaven. The discord which prevails in the world of earth will diminish, and all the antagonistic forces which populate the world of earth will somehow come into harmony with each other. The lower world too will come to obey God's primeval will, becoming more unified and more stable in the process.

This is of course consistent with the vision of all the Hebrew prophets, and our psalm is but a precursor of that vision.

PSALM 149

1. Praise the LORD!
Sing to the LORD a new song,
His praise in the assembly of the faithful.

2. Let Israel rejoice in their Maker;
let the people of Zion exult in their King.

3. Let them praise His name with dancing;
and sing praises to Him with timbrel and harp.

4. For the LORD delights in His people;
He crowns the humble with victory.

5. Let the faithful exult in glory;
let them sing for joy upon their couches.

6. Let the high praises of God be in their throats,
and a two-edged sword in their hand;

7. to wreak vengeance on the nations,
punishment upon the peoples;

---

nation, Israel, and to His faithful, "*ḥasidav*," traditional commentaries, Radak especially, do not distinguish between Israel and "the faithful." In fact, Radak insists that "the assembly of the faithful" in verse 1 refers to Israel, and repeats his insistence in verse 9: "*The glory of all His faithful* refers to Israel."

Rav Hirsch takes a radically different approach. He understands the era referred to in our psalm as a time all men of faith will join together, Jew and non-Jew. "Even those of the rest of humanity who now draw close to God in devotion and love will bond together in praise of Him."

For Rav Hirsch the end of days is not just a time of spiritual triumph for the people of Israel. It is a universal human phenomenon. Yes it will be a time when God judges the nations, and even *wreaks vengeance on the nations*. But he insists that there will be those among the nations who will escape that harsh judgment. They will be those exceptional individuals who were not part of Israel but who devoted themselves loyally to God in their own way.

מזמור קמט

As our body ages so does our spirit. The spirit we fashioned when we were young remains with us. But the spirit of a twenty year old can't quench the thirst of a middle-aged man. It became tired and stale. Old men need renewed souls. The soul becomes new when it sings a new song. We can indulge our nostalgia and sing old songs. But our souls urge us to compose new songs. New times demand new songs. New songs create new times.

א הַֽלְלוּיָ֨הּ ׀
שִׁ֣ירוּ לַ֭יהוה שִׁ֣יר חָדָ֑שׁ
תְּ֝הִלָּת֗וֹ בִּקְהַ֥ל חֲסִידִֽים׃

ב יִשְׂמַ֣ח יִשְׂרָאֵ֣ל בְּעֹשָׂ֑יו
בְּנֵֽי־צִ֝יּ֗וֹן יָגִ֥ילוּ בְמַלְכָּֽם׃

ג יְהַלְל֣וּ שְׁמ֣וֹ בְמָח֑וֹל
בְּתֹ֥ף וְ֝כִנּ֗וֹר יְזַמְּרוּ־לֽוֹ׃

ד כִּֽי־רוֹצֶ֣ה יְהֹוָ֣ה בְּעַמּ֑וֹ
יְפָאֵ֥ר עֲ֝נָוִ֗ים בִּישׁוּעָֽה׃

ה יַעְלְז֣וּ חֲסִידִ֣ים בְּכָב֑וֹד
יְ֝רַנְּנ֗וּ עַל־מִשְׁכְּבוֹתָֽם׃

ו רוֹמְמ֣וֹת אֵ֭ל בִּגְרוֹנָ֑ם
וְחֶ֖רֶב פִּֽיפִיּ֣וֹת בְּיָדָֽם׃

ז לַעֲשׂ֣וֹת נְ֭קָמָה בַּגּוֹיִ֑ם
תּ֝וֹכֵח֗וֹת בַּלְאֻמִּֽים׃

מזמור קמט *Psalm 149:* Our psalm is the culmination of the Book of Psalms. It describes the climax of history, the triumph of Israel and the judgment of the nations. The next psalm is more than the culmination. It is the epilogue, and refers to a time beyond the bounds of history.

Our psalm heralds the era near the end of days when Israel will rejoice in God and God will rejoice in Israel. Although the text refers both to His

8. to bind their kings in chains,
and their nobles in fetters of iron;

9. carrying out the judgment decreed against them.
This is the glory of all His faithful.
Praise the Lord!

Furthermore, the final verse 9 suggests according to Rav Hirsch that the very judgment of the nations will bring glory to these rare individuals, whose religious behavior contrasts with those others upon whom God will wreak vengeance. So that *carrying out the judgment decreed against them,* the non-Jews who are found wanting, are *the glory of all His faithful*, meaning those of His faithful who are not part of Israel.

Rav Hirsch emphasizes this point so close to the end of his magnificent commentary because he wishes us to realize that there are indeed "*ḥasidei umot haolam*," heroically pious people outside the Jewish fold. He wants to leave us with the awareness that they too will rejoice in their Maker at this wonderful climactic moment, and that they too will *sing a new song*.

ח לֶאְסֹ֣ר מַלְכֵיהֶ֣ם בְּזִקִּ֑ים
וְ֝נִכְבְּדֵיהֶ֗ם בְּכַבְלֵ֥י בַרְזֶֽל׃

ט לַעֲשׂ֤וֹת בָּהֶ֨ם ׀ מִשְׁפָּ֬ט כָּת֗וּב
הָדָ֣ר ה֭וּא לְכָל־חֲסִידָ֗יו
הַֽלְלוּ־יָֽהּ׃

Rav Hirsch divides our psalm into its component parts: verses 2–4 do indeed speak only of Israel, for the joy of that wondrous time will mainly be theirs. And verses 7–9 do indeed speak of those among the nations who will receive their ultimate punishments: *their kings in chains and their nobles in fetters*. But he sees in verses 5 and 6 reference to all those outside of the Jewish people who were faithful in their own way to God throughout history and who dedicated themselves to Him in humility and love. These verses even extend to those who have come close to God only of late, at the moment of history's final episode. All of these devotees of God, new and old, will exult along with Israel.

PSALM 150

1. Praise the LORD!
Praise God in His sanctuary,
praise Him in His mighty heavens.

2. Praise Him for His acts of power.
praise Him according to His exceeding greatness.

3. Praise Him with blasts of the shofar,
praise Him with lyre and harp.

4. Praise Him with timbrel and dance,
praise Him with strings and pipe.

5. Praise Him with resounding cymbals,
praise Him with clanging cymbals.

6. Let every breathing soul praise the LORD! Praise the LORD!

---

kol haneshama, every breathing organism, contains God's sprit, and is given the capacity to praise Him.

He is praised *in His sanctuary,* for the aspect of divinity that inspires faith, devotion, and moral behavior. He is praised *in His mighty heavens,* for the dominion He exercises over the awesome forces of nature.

He is praised *for His acts of power,* for *midat hadin,* the demands He makes of us and the discipline with which He holds us accountable. He is praised for *His exceeding greatness, midat haraḥamim,* His boundless mercy and the gift of His forgiveness.

He is praised with the entire gamut of music's repertoire, with every conceivable nuance of humanity's emotional life: the reverence evoked by *the shofar;* the contemplative mood stimulated by the *lyre and harp;* the joyful abandon which *timbrel and dance* call forth; the longing and sorrow which are stirred up by the mournful sounds of *strings and pipe;* the long-repressed thunderous joy which the *resounding cymbals* release; and the deafening glee to which the *clanging cymbals* give voice.

Every living and breathing soul has a stake in this wondrous experience. No emotion is invalid here, every conceivable expression of devotion and faith has its place. Contrition, reflection, celebration, happiness, fear and trembling – all are legitimate in this enclave of pure spirituality.

Every breathing soul, praise the LORD!

מזמור קנ

Can you imagine how King David felt when he finally finished his book? Remember how you felt when you finished a long and arduous task? He felt, as you did, that he was on top of the world. "Over the moon," as they say. Ancient Perek Shira, "Chapter of Song," tells us the rest of the story. David turned to the Holy One, blessed be He. "Has any other living creature ever praised You with such songs?" Proud David then met a frog, a single lowly frog. The frog said, "David, don't gloat. I've composed many more songs than you have. What's more, I attach three thousand fables to every song I compose." Did David get the frog's message? Do you?

א הַֽלְלוּיָ֨הּ ׀
הַֽלְלוּ־אֵ֥ל בְּקָדְשׁ֑וֹ
הַ֝לְל֗וּהוּ בִּרְקִ֥יעַ עֻזּֽוֹ׃

ב הַֽלְל֥וּהוּ בִגְבוּרֹתָ֑יו
הַ֝לְל֗וּהוּ כְּרֹ֣ב גֻּדְלֽוֹ׃

ג הַֽ֭לְלוּהוּ בְּתֵ֣קַע שׁוֹפָ֑ר
הַ֝לְל֗וּהוּ בְּנֵ֣בֶל וְכִנּֽוֹר׃

ד הַֽ֭לְלוּהוּ בְתֹ֣ף וּמָח֑וֹל
הַ֝לְל֗וּהוּ בְּמִנִּ֥ים וְעֻגָֽב׃

ה הַֽלְל֥וּהוּ בְצִלְצְלֵי־שָׁ֑מַע
הַ֝לְל֗וּהוּ בְּֽצִלְצְלֵ֥י תְרוּעָֽה׃

ו כֹּ֣ל הַ֭נְּשָׁמָה תְּהַלֵּ֥ל יָ֗הּ הַֽלְלוּיָֽהּ׃

מזמור קנ *Psalm 150:* Our psalm is not the culmination of the Book of Psalms. The book already culminated in the vision of the previous psalm, the vision of a world where the righteous exult in God, and the wicked are finally brought to justice.

Our psalm transcends that vision. It is an epilogue to history. It is not limited to a time or to a place. It describes a mood, a mode of being. No persons are mentioned, no warring nations, no woes and no worries. Body has no place in our psalm, just soul. Praise, music, and song pervade our psalm. They are all that exist.

Our psalm contains no less than thirteen calls to praise God. To whom are those calls addressed? Who is invited to praise Him? Every living creature,

PRAYER AFTER READING PSALMS

After reading Psalms it is customary to say the following:

מִי O that the deliverance of Israel might come from Zion! Ps. 14
When the LORD restores the fortunes of His people, Jacob will rejoice;
Israel will be glad.
The deliverance of the righteous comes from the LORD; Ps. 37
He is their stronghold in times of trouble.
The LORD helps them and delivers them; He delivers them from the
wicked and saves them, because they seek refuge in Him.

On weekdays say:

יְהִי רָצוֹן May it be Your will, LORD our God, God of our ancestors, that by the merit of the first / second / third / fourth / fifth book of Psalms that we have read before You, corresponding to the Book of Genesis / Exodus / Leviticus / Numbers / Deuteronomy – by the merit of its songs, by the merit of its verses and its words, by the merit of Your holy and pure names found therein – You shall grant us atonement for all our sins, and forgive us all the transgressions by which we have sinned, we have done wrong, we have rebelled before You. And bring us back in perfect repentance before You, and guide us in the service of You, and open our hearts in the study of Your Torah, and send a complete recovery to all the afflicted of Your people [and among them the patient (*name*) son/daughter of (*mother's name*)], and announce the freedom Is. 61 of captives, and the liberation of prisoners. Save all the travelers among Your people Israel, and all those journeying by sea, from any distress or harm; and bring them to their desired destinations in life and in peace. And remember all those deprived of sons and daughters, bringing them healthy children who will serve You and hold You in awe. And protect the pregnant women among Your people Israel, that none of them miscarry. And as for those who are now in labor – in Your great compassion save them from all evil; and give of Your own plenty to the nursing mothers, that their breasts may never lack milk. And never let the plague or demons, spirits or liliths, injuries or illness exert power on any of the children of Your people; raise them by Your Torah, to study Torah for its own sake, and save them from the evil eye, and from pestilence, plague and adversary and the evil instinct. Nullify all harsh and evil decrees, for us and for all Your people Israel, wherever they may be. And incline the heart of the government to favor us, decree good decrees regarding us, and send blessing and success to all that we do. Prepare our sustenance,

תפילה לאחר אמירת תהלים

After reading Psalms it is customary to say the following:

מִי יִתֵּן מִצִּיּוֹן יְשׁוּעַת יִשְׂרָאֵל תהלים יד
בְּשׁוּב יהוה שְׁבוּת עַמּוֹ, יָגֵל יַעֲקֹב, יִשְׂמַח יִשְׂרָאֵל:
וּתְשׁוּעַת צַדִּיקִים מֵיהוה, מָעוּזָּם בְּעֵת צָרָה: תהלים לז
וַיַּעְזְרֵם יהוה וַיְפַלְּטֵם, יְפַלְּטֵם מֵרְשָׁעִים וְיוֹשִׁיעֵם, כִּי־חָסוּ בוֹ:

On weekdays say:

יְהִי רָצוֹן מִלְּפָנֶיךָ יהוה אֱלֹהֵינוּ וֵאלֹהֵי אֲבוֹתֵינוּ, בִּזְכוּת סֵפֶר רִאשׁוֹן / שֵׁנִי / שְׁלִישִׁי / רְבִיעִי / חֲמִישִׁי שֶׁבַּתְּהִלִּים שֶׁקָּרָאנוּ לְפָנֶיךָ שֶׁהוּא כְּנֶגֶד סֵפֶר בְּרֵאשִׁית / שְׁמוֹת / וַיִּקְרָא / בְּמִדְבַּר / דְּבָרִים בִּזְכוּת מִזְמוֹרָיו וּבִזְכוּת פְּסוּקָיו וּבִזְכוּת תֵּבוֹתָיו וּבִזְכוּת שְׁמוֹתֶיךָ הַקְּדוֹשִׁים וְהַטְּהוֹרִים הַיּוֹצְאִים מִמֶּנּוּ, שֶׁתְּכַפֵּר לָנוּ עַל כָּל חַטֹּאתֵינוּ, וְתִסְלַח לָנוּ עַל כָּל פְּשָׁעֵינוּ שֶׁחָטָאנוּ וְשֶׁעָוִינוּ וְשֶׁפָּשַׁעְנוּ לְפָנֶיךָ, וְהַחֲזִירֵנוּ בִּתְשׁוּבָה שְׁלֵמָה לְפָנֶיךָ, וְהַדְרִיכֵנוּ לַעֲבוֹדָתֶךָ, וְתִפְתַּח לִבֵּנוּ בְּתַלְמוּד תּוֹרָתֶךָ, וְתִשְׁלַח רְפוּאָה שְׁלֵמָה לְחוֹלֵי עַמֶּךָ (לַחוֹלֶה/לַחוֹלָה פלוני/ת בֶּן/בַּת פלונית), וְתִקְרָא לִשְׁבוּיִם דְּרוֹר, וְלַאֲסוּרִים פְּקַח־קוֹחַ: וּלְכָל הוֹלְכֵי דְרָכִים וְעוֹבְרֵי יַמִּים וּנְהָרוֹת מֵעַמְּךָ יִשְׂרָאֵל תַּצִּילֵם מִכָּל צַעַר וָנֶזֶק, וְתַגִּיעֵם לִמְחוֹז חֶפְצָם לְחַיִּים וּלְשָׁלוֹם. וְתִפְקֹד לְכָל חֲשׂוּכֵי בָנִים בְּזֶרַע שֶׁל קַיָּמָא לַעֲבוֹדָתֶךָ וּלְיִרְאָתֶךָ, וְעֻבָּרוֹת שֶׁל עַמְּךָ בֵּית יִשְׂרָאֵל תַּצִּילֵן שֶׁלֹּא תַפֵּלְנָה וְלָדוֹתֵיהֶן, וְהַיּוֹשְׁבוֹת עַל הַמַּשְׁבֵּר בְּרַחֲמֶיךָ הָרַבִּים תַּצִּילֵן מִכָּל רָע, וְאֶל הַמֵּינִיקוֹת תַּשְׁפִּיעַ שֶׁלֹּא יֶחְסַר חָלָב מִדְּדֵיהֶן. וְאַל יִמְשֹׁל אַסְכָּרָה וְשֵׁדִין וְרוּחִין וְלִילִין וְכָל פְּגָעִים וּמַרְעִין בִּישִׁין בְּכָל יַלְדֵי עַמְּךָ בֵּית יִשְׂרָאֵל, וּתְגַדְּלֵם לְתוֹרָתֶךָ לִלְמֹד תּוֹרָה לִשְׁמָהּ, וְתַצִּילֵם מֵעַיִן הָרָע וּמִדֶּבֶר וּמִמַּגֵּפָה וּמִשָּׂטָן וּמִיֵּצֶר הָרָע. וּתְבַטֵּל מֵעָלֵינוּ וּמִכָּל עַמְּךָ בֵּית יִשְׂרָאֵל בְּכָל מָקוֹם שֶׁהֵם כָּל גְּזֵרוֹת קָשׁוֹת וְרָעוֹת. וְתַטֶּה לֵב הַמַּלְכוּת עָלֵינוּ לְטוֹבָה, וְתִגְזֹר עָלֵינוּ גְּזֵרוֹת טוֹבוֹת, וְתִשְׁלַח בְּרָכָה וְהַצְלָחָה בְּכָל מַעֲשֵׂה יָדֵינוּ. וְהָכֵן פַּרְנָסָתֵנוּ מִיָּדְךָ הָרְחָבָה וְהַמְּלֵאָה, וְלֹא יִצְטָרְכוּ עַמְּךָ

(ישעיה סא)

coming from Your own broad, full hand, and let Your people Israel never be dependent on the charity of one another or of any other people; grant every single person what he needs, and every single body what it lacks, and hurry and make haste to redeem us, and build the house of our sanctuary, our glory. All this by the merit of Your thirteen attributes of compassion, as they
are written in Your Torah – "The Lord, the Lord, compassionate and gra- *Ex. 34*
cious God, slow to anger, abounding in loving-kindness and truth, extending loving-kindness to a thousand generations, forgiving iniquity, rebellion and sin, and absolving [the guilty who repent]" – for never do they come empty-
handed away from Your presence. Help us, God our Deliverer, for the glory of *Ps. 79*
Your name; rescue us and forgive our sins for the sake of Your name. Blessed *Ps. 89*
be the Lord forever. Amen and Amen.

On Shabbat and Festivals say:

May it be Your will, Lord our God, God of our ancestors, that by the merit of the first / second / third / fourth / fifth book of Psalms that we have read before You, corresponding to the Book of Genesis / Exodus / Leviticus / Numbers / Deuteronomy – by the merit of its songs, by the merit of its verses and its words, by the merit of Your holy and pure names found therein – that these psalms we have spoken may be considered as if it were David, king of Israel himself who had spoken them (may his merit protect us) – and may he stand up for us, to join the Bride of His youth with the Beloved, in friendship and in brotherhood and love – and from that place may plenty be drawn down to us, to soul and spirit and higher soul. And just as we sing songs in this world, so may we have the merit to sing before You, Lord our God, God of our ancestors, song and praise in the world to come. And through our speak-
ing these Psalms, may the Rose of Sharon be awakened to sing with a lovely *Is. 35*
voice, rejoicing and song, for the glory of Lebanon is given to her. Glory and splendor in the house of our God, speedily in our days: Amen, Selah!

בֵּית יִשְׂרָאֵל זֶה לָזֶה וְלֹא לְעַם אַחֵר, וְתֵן לְכָל אִישׁ וָאִישׁ דֵּי פַּרְנָסָתוֹ וּלְכָל גְּוִיָּה וּגְוִיָּה דֵּי מַחְסוֹרָהּ וּתְמַהֵר וְתָחִישׁ לְגָאֳלֵנוּ, וְתִבְנֶה בֵּית מִקְדָּשֵׁנוּ וְתִפְאַרְתֵּנוּ. וּבִזְכוּת שְׁלֹשׁ עֶשְׂרֵה מִדּוֹתֶיךָ שֶׁל רַחֲמִים הַכְּתוּבוֹת בְּתוֹרָתֶךָ,
שמות לד כְּמוֹ שֶׁנֶּאֱמַר: יהוה, יהוה, אֵל רַחוּם וְחַנּוּן, אֶרֶךְ אַפַּיִם וְרַב־חֶסֶד וֶאֱמֶת: נֹצֵר חֶסֶד לָאֲלָפִים, נֹשֵׂא עָוֹן וָפֶשַׁע וְחַטָּאָה, וְנַקֵּה: שֶׁאֵינָן חוֹזְרוֹת רֵיקָם
תהלים עט מִלְּפָנֶיךָ. עָזְרֵנוּ אֱלֹהֵי יִשְׁעֵנוּ עַל־דְּבַר כְּבוֹד־שְׁמֶךָ, וְהַצִּילֵנוּ וְכַפֵּר עַל־
תהלים פט חַטֹּאתֵינוּ לְמַעַן שְׁמֶךָ: בָּרוּךְ יהוה לְעוֹלָם אָמֵן וְאָמֵן:

On שבת *and* יום טוב *say:*

יְהִי רָצוֹן מִלְּפָנֶיךָ יהוה אֱלֹהֵינוּ וֵאלֹהֵי אֲבוֹתֵינוּ, בִּזְכוּת סֵפֶר רִאשׁוֹן / שֵׁנִי / שְׁלִישִׁי / רְבִיעִי / חֲמִישִׁי שֶׁבַּתְּהִלִּים שֶׁקָּרָאנוּ לְפָנֶיךָ שֶׁהוּא כְּנֶגֶד סֵפֶר בְּרֵאשִׁית / שְׁמוֹת / וַיִּקְרָא / בְּמִדְבַּר / דְּבָרִים בִּזְכוּת מִזְמוֹרָיו וּבִזְכוּת פְּסוּקָיו וּבִזְכוּת תֵּבוֹתָיו וּבִזְכוּת שְׁמוֹתֶיךָ הַקְּדוֹשִׁים וְהַטְּהוֹרִים הַיּוֹצְאִים מִמֶּנּוּ שֶׁתְּהֵא נֶחְשֶׁבֶת לָנוּ אֲמִירַת מִזְמוֹרֵי תְהִלִּים אֵלּוּ כְּאִלּוּ אֲמָרָם דָּוִד מֶלֶךְ יִשְׂרָאֵל בְּעַצְמוֹ, זְכוּתוֹ תָּגֵן עָלֵינוּ, וְיַעֲמָד לָנוּ לְחַבֵּר אֵשֶׁת נְעוּרִים עִם דּוֹדָהּ בְּאַהֲבָה וְאַחֲוָה וְרֵעוּת, וּמִשָּׁם יִמָּשֵׁךְ לָנוּ שֶׁפַע לְנֶפֶשׁ רוּחַ וּנְשָׁמָה. וּכְשֵׁם שֶׁאֲנַחְנוּ אוֹמְרִים שִׁירִים בָּעוֹלָם הַזֶּה, כָּךְ נִזְכֶּה לוֹמַר לְפָנֶיךָ יהוה אֱלֹהֵינוּ וֵאלֹהֵי אֲבוֹתֵינוּ, שִׁיר וּשְׁבָחָה לָעוֹלָם הַבָּא. וְעַל יְדֵי אֲמִירַת
ישעיה לה תְּהִלִּים תִּתְעוֹרֵר חֲבַצֶּלֶת הַשָּׁרוֹן לָשִׁיר בְּקוֹל נָעִים גִּילַת וְרַנֵּן, כְּבוֹד הַלְּבָנוֹן נִתַּן־לָהּ: הוֹד וְהָדָר בְּבֵית אֱלֹהֵינוּ בִּמְהֵרָה בְיָמֵינוּ, אָמֵן סֶלָה.

תפילות נוספות

ADDITIONAL PRAYERS

THE TRAVELER'S PRAYER

If one intends to return home on the same day, add the words in parentheses:

יְהִי רָצוֹן May it be Your will,
Lord our God and God of our fathers,
to lead us to peace, direct our steps to peace,
guide us to peace, and bring us to our desired destination in life,
joy and peace
(and bring us back to our home in peace).
Rescue us from any enemy or ambush on the way,
and from all afflictions that trouble the world.
Send blessing to the work of our hands,
and let us find grace, kindness and compassion
from You and from all who see us.
Hear our pleas,
for You are a God who hears prayer and pleas.
Blessed are You, Lord, who listens to prayer.

May the Lord guard your going out and your return, *Ps. 121*
from now and for all time.

Repeat three times:

וַיַּעֲקֹב And Jacob went on his way *Gen. 32*
and angels of God met him.
When he saw them, Jacob said, "This is God's camp"
and he named the place Maḥanaim [two camps].

Repeat three times:

יְבָרֶכְךָ May the Lord bless you and protect you. *Num. 6*
May the Lord make His face shine on you and be gracious to you.
May the Lord turn His face toward you and grant you peace.

שִׁיר לַמַּעֲלוֹת A song of ascents. I lift my eyes up to the hills; from where will *Ps. 121*
my help come? My help comes from the Lord, Maker of heaven and earth. He will not let your foot stumble; He who guards you does not slumber. See: the Guardian of Israel neither slumbers nor sleeps. The Lord is your Guardian; the Lord is your Shade at your right hand. The sun will not strike you by day, nor the moon by night. The Lord will guard you from all harm; He will guard your life. The Lord will guard your going and coming, now and for evermore.

תפילת הדרך

If one intends to return home on the same day, add the words in parentheses:

יְהִי רָצוֹן מִלְּפָנֶיךָ, יהוה אֱלֹהֵינוּ וֵאלֹהֵי אֲבוֹתֵינוּ
שֶׁתּוֹלִיכֵנוּ לְשָׁלוֹם, וְתַצְעִידֵנוּ לְשָׁלוֹם, וְתַדְרִיכֵנוּ לְשָׁלוֹם
וְתַגִּיעֵנוּ לִמְחוֹז חֶפְצֵנוּ לְחַיִּים וּלְשִׂמְחָה וּלְשָׁלוֹם
(וְתַחֲזִירֵנוּ לְבֵיתֵנוּ לְשָׁלוֹם)
וְתַצִּילֵנוּ מִכַּף כָּל אוֹיֵב וְאוֹרֵב בַּדֶּרֶךְ
וּמִכָּל מִינֵי פֻּרְעָנִיּוֹת הַמִּתְרַגְּשׁוֹת לָבוֹא לָעוֹלָם
וְתִשְׁלַח בְּרָכָה בְּמַעֲשֵׂה יָדֵינוּ
וְתִתְּנֵנוּ לְחֵן וּלְחֶסֶד וּלְרַחֲמִים בְּעֵינֶיךָ וּבְעֵינֵי כָל רוֹאֵינוּ
וְתִשְׁמַע קוֹל תַּחֲנוּנֵינוּ
כִּי אֵל שׁוֹמֵעַ תְּפִלָּה וְתַחֲנוּן אָתָּה.
בָּרוּךְ אַתָּה יהוה, שׁוֹמֵעַ תְּפִלָּה.

יהוה יִשְׁמָר־צֵאתְךָ וּבוֹאֶךָ, מֵעַתָּה וְעַד־עוֹלָם: תהלים קכא

Repeat three times:

וְיַעֲקֹב הָלַךְ לְדַרְכּוֹ, וַיִּפְגְּעוּ־בוֹ מַלְאֲכֵי אֱלֹהִים: בראשית לב
וַיֹּאמֶר יַעֲקֹב כַּאֲשֶׁר רָאָם, מַחֲנֵה אֱלֹהִים זֶה
וַיִּקְרָא שֵׁם־הַמָּקוֹם הַהוּא מַחֲנָיִם:

Repeat three times:

יְבָרֶכְךָ יהוה וְיִשְׁמְרֶךָ: במדבר ו
יָאֵר יהוה פָּנָיו אֵלֶיךָ וִיחֻנֶּךָּ:
יִשָּׂא יהוה פָּנָיו אֵלֶיךָ וְיָשֵׂם לְךָ שָׁלוֹם:

שִׁיר לַמַּעֲלוֹת, אֶשָּׂא עֵינַי אֶל־הֶהָרִים, מֵאַיִן יָבֹא עֶזְרִי: עֶזְרִי מֵעִם יהוה, תהלים קכא
עֹשֵׂה שָׁמַיִם וָאָרֶץ: אַל־יִתֵּן לַמּוֹט רַגְלֶךָ, אַל־יָנוּם שֹׁמְרֶךָ: הִנֵּה לֹא־יָנוּם
וְלֹא יִישָׁן, שׁוֹמֵר יִשְׂרָאֵל: יהוה שֹׁמְרֶךָ, יהוה צִלְּךָ עַל־יַד יְמִינֶךָ: יוֹמָם
הַשֶּׁמֶשׁ לֹא־יַכֶּכָּה, וְיָרֵחַ בַּלָּיְלָה: יהוה יִשְׁמָרְךָ מִכָּל־רָע, יִשְׁמֹר אֶת־נַפְשֶׁךָ:
יהוה יִשְׁמָר־צֵאתְךָ וּבוֹאֶךָ, מֵעַתָּה וְעַד־עוֹלָם:

SHEMA BEFORE SLEEP AT NIGHT

הֲרֵינִי I hereby forgive anyone who has angered or provoked me or sinned against me, physically or financially or by failing to give me due respect, or in any other matter relating to me, involuntarily or willingly, inadvertently or deliberately, whether in word or deed: let no one incur punishment because of me.

בָּרוּךְ Blessed are You, LORD our God, King of the Universe, who makes the bonds of sleep fall on my eyes, and slumber on my eyelids. May it be Your will, LORD my God and God of my fathers, that You make me lie down in peace and arise in peace. Let not my imagination, bad dreams or troubling thoughts disturb me. May my bed be flawless before You. Enlighten my eyes lest I sleep the sleep of death, for it is You who illuminates the pupil of the eye. Blessed are You, LORD, who gives light to the whole world in His glory.

When saying all three paragraphs of Shema, say:

God, faithful King!

The following verse should be said aloud, while covering the eyes with the right hand:

Listen, Israel: the LORD is our God, *Deut. 6*
the LORD is One.

Quietly: Blessed be the name of His glorious kingdom for ever and all time.

וְאָהַבְתָּ Love the LORD your God with all your heart, with all your *Deut. 6*
soul, and with all your might. These words which I command you today shall be on your heart. Teach them repeatedly to your children, speaking of them when you sit at home and when you travel on the way, when you lie down and when you rise. Bind them as a sign on your hand, and they shall be an emblem between your eyes. Write them on the doorposts of your house and gates.

וִיהִי May the pleasantness of the LORD our God be upon us. Establish for us *Ps. 90*
the work of our hands, O establish the work of our hands.

יֹשֵׁב He who lives in the shelter of the Most High dwells in the shadow of the *Ps. 91*
Almighty. I say of God, my Refuge and Stronghold, my LORD in whom I trust, that He will save you from the fowler's snare and the deadly pestilence. With His pinions He will cover you, and beneath His wings you will find shelter; His faithfulness is an encircling shield. You need not fear terror by night, nor

קריאת שמע על המיטה

הֲרֵינִי מוֹחֵל לְכָל מִי שֶׁהִכְעִיס וְהִקְנִיט אוֹתִי אוֹ שֶׁחָטָא כְּנֶגְדִּי, בֵּין בְּגוּפִי בֵּין בְּמָמוֹנִי בֵּין בִּכְבוֹדִי בֵּין בְּכָל אֲשֶׁר לִי, בֵּין בְּאֹנֶס בֵּין בְּרָצוֹן, בֵּין בְּשׁוֹגֵג בֵּין בְּמֵזִיד, בֵּין בְּדִבּוּר בֵּין בְּמַעֲשֶׂה, וְלֹא יֵעָנֵשׁ שׁוּם אָדָם בְּסִבָּתִי.

בָּרוּךְ אַתָּה יהוה אֱלֹהֵינוּ מֶלֶךְ הָעוֹלָם, הַמַּפִּיל חֶבְלֵי שֵׁנָה עַל עֵינַי וּתְנוּמָה עַל עַפְעַפָּי. וִיהִי רָצוֹן מִלְּפָנֶיךָ, יהוה אֱלֹהַי וֵאלֹהֵי אֲבוֹתַי, שֶׁתַּשְׁכִּיבֵנִי לְשָׁלוֹם וְתַעֲמִידֵנִי לְשָׁלוֹם, וְאַל יְבַהֲלוּנִי רַעְיוֹנַי וַחֲלוֹמוֹת רָעִים וְהִרְהוּרִים רָעִים, וּתְהֵא מִטָּתִי שְׁלֵמָה לְפָנֶיךָ, וְהָאֵר עֵינַי פֶּן אִישַׁן הַמָּוֶת, כִּי אַתָּה הַמֵּאִיר לְאִישׁוֹן בַּת עָיִן. בָּרוּךְ אַתָּה יהוה, הַמֵּאִיר לָעוֹלָם כֻּלּוֹ בִּכְבוֹדוֹ.

When saying all three paragraphs of שמע*, say:*

אֵל מֶלֶךְ נֶאֱמָן

The following verse should be said aloud, while covering the eyes with the right hand:

שְׁמַע יִשְׂרָאֵל, יהוה אֱלֹהֵינוּ, יהוה ׀ אֶחָד׃ דברים ו

Quietly בָּרוּךְ שֵׁם כְּבוֹד מַלְכוּתוֹ לְעוֹלָם וָעֶד.

וְאָהַבְתָּ אֵת יהוה אֱלֹהֶיךָ, בְּכָל־לְבָבְךָ וּבְכָל־נַפְשְׁךָ וּבְכָל־ דברים ו
מְאֹדֶךָ׃ וְהָיוּ הַדְּבָרִים הָאֵלֶּה, אֲשֶׁר אָנֹכִי מְצַוְּךָ הַיּוֹם, עַל־לְבָבֶךָ׃
וְשִׁנַּנְתָּם לְבָנֶיךָ וְדִבַּרְתָּ בָּם, בְּשִׁבְתְּךָ בְּבֵיתֶךָ וּבְלֶכְתְּךָ בַדֶּרֶךְ,
וּבְשָׁכְבְּךָ וּבְקוּמֶךָ׃ וּקְשַׁרְתָּם לְאוֹת עַל־יָדֶךָ וְהָיוּ לְטֹטָפֹת בֵּין
עֵינֶיךָ׃ וּכְתַבְתָּם עַל־מְזֻזוֹת בֵּיתֶךָ וּבִשְׁעָרֶיךָ׃

וִיהִי נֹעַם אֲדֹנָי אֱלֹהֵינוּ עָלֵינוּ וּמַעֲשֵׂה יָדֵינוּ כּוֹנְנָה עָלֵינוּ וּמַעֲשֵׂה יָדֵינוּ תהלים צ
כּוֹנְנֵהוּ׃

יֹשֵׁב בְּסֵתֶר עֶלְיוֹן, בְּצֵל שַׁדַּי יִתְלוֹנָן׃ אֹמַר לַיהוה מַחְסִי וּמְצוּדָתִי, אֱלֹהַי תהלים צא
אֶבְטַח־בּוֹ׃ כִּי הוּא יַצִּילְךָ מִפַּח יָקוּשׁ, מִדֶּבֶר הַוּוֹת׃ בְּאֶבְרָתוֹ יָסֶךְ לָךְ,
וְתַחַת־כְּנָפָיו תֶּחְסֶה, צִנָּה וְסֹחֵרָה אֲמִתּוֹ׃ לֹא־תִירָא מִפַּחַד לָיְלָה, מֵחֵץ

the arrow that flies by day; not the pestilence that stalks in darkness, nor the plague that ravages at noon. A thousand may fall at your side, ten thousand at your right hand, but it will not come near you. You will only look with your eyes and see the punishment of the wicked. Because you said, "The Lord is my Refuge," taking the Most High as your shelter, no harm will befall you, no plague come near your tent, for He will command His angels about you, to guard you in all your ways. They will lift you in their hands, lest your foot stumble on a stone. You will tread on lions and vipers; you will trample on young lions and snakes. [God says:] "Because he loves Me, I will rescue him; I will protect him, because he acknowledges My name. When he calls on Me, I will answer him; I will be with him in distress, I will deliver him and bring him honor. With long life I will satisfy him and show him My salvation.
With long life I will satisfy him and show him My salvation.

יהוה Lord, how numerous are my enemies, how many rise against me. Many *Ps. 3*
say of me: "There is no help for him in God," Selah. But You, Lord, are a shield around me. You are my glory; You raise my head high. I cry aloud to the Lord, and He answers me from His holy mountain, Selah. I lie down to sleep and I wake again, for the Lord supports me. I will not fear the myriad forces ranged against me on all sides. Arise, Lord, save me, O my God; strike all my enemies across the cheek; break the teeth of the wicked. From the Lord comes deliverance; may Your blessing rest upon Your people, Selah.

הַשְׁכִּיבֵנוּ Help us lie down, O Lord our God, in peace, and rise up, O our King, to life. Spread over us Your canopy of peace. Direct us with Your good counsel, and save us for the sake of Your name. Shield us and remove from us every enemy, plague, sword, famine and sorrow. Remove the adversary from before and behind us. Shelter us in the shadow of Your wings, for You, God, are our Guardian and Deliverer; You, God, are a gracious and compassionate King. Guard our going out and our coming in, for life and peace, from now and for ever.

בָּרוּךְ Blessed is the Lord by day, blessed is the Lord by night. Blessed is the Lord when we lie down; blessed is the Lord when we rise. For in Your
hand are the souls of the living and the dead, [as it is written:] "In His hand *Job 12*
is every living soul, and the breath of all mankind." Into Your hand I entrust *Ps. 31*
my spirit: You redeemed me, Lord, God of truth. Our God in heaven, bring unity to Your name, establish Your kingdom constantly and reign over us for ever and all time.

יָעוּף יוֹמָם: מִדֶּבֶר בָּאֹפֶל יַהֲלֹךְ, מִקֶּטֶב יָשׁוּד צָהֳרָיִם: יִפֹּל מִצִּדְּךָ אֶלֶף, וּרְבָבָה מִימִינֶךָ, אֵלֶיךָ לֹא יִגָּשׁ: רַק בְּעֵינֶיךָ תַבִּיט, וְשִׁלֻּמַת רְשָׁעִים תִּרְאֶה: כִּי־אַתָּה יהוה מַחְסִי, עֶלְיוֹן שַׂמְתָּ מְעוֹנֶךָ: לֹא־תְאֻנֶּה אֵלֶיךָ רָעָה, וְנֶגַע לֹא־יִקְרַב בְּאָהֳלֶךָ: כִּי מַלְאָכָיו יְצַוֶּה־לָּךְ, לִשְׁמָרְךָ בְּכָל־דְּרָכֶיךָ: עַל־כַּפַּיִם יִשָּׂאוּנְךָ, פֶּן־תִּגֹּף בָּאֶבֶן רַגְלֶךָ: עַל־שַׁחַל וָפֶתֶן תִּדְרֹךְ, תִּרְמֹס כְּפִיר וְתַנִּין: כִּי בִי חָשַׁק וַאֲפַלְּטֵהוּ, אֲשַׂגְּבֵהוּ כִּי־יָדַע שְׁמִי: יִקְרָאֵנִי וְאֶעֱנֵהוּ, עִמּוֹ־אָנֹכִי בְצָרָה, אֲחַלְּצֵהוּ וַאֲכַבְּדֵהוּ: אֹרֶךְ יָמִים אַשְׂבִּיעֵהוּ, וְאַרְאֵהוּ בִּישׁוּעָתִי: אֹרֶךְ יָמִים אַשְׂבִּיעֵהוּ, וְאַרְאֵהוּ בִּישׁוּעָתִי:

תהלים ג יהוה מָה־רַבּוּ צָרָי, רַבִּים קָמִים עָלָי: רַבִּים אֹמְרִים לְנַפְשִׁי, אֵין יְשׁוּעָתָה לּוֹ בֵאלֹהִים, סֶלָה: וְאַתָּה יהוה מָגֵן בַּעֲדִי, כְּבוֹדִי וּמֵרִים רֹאשִׁי: קוֹלִי אֶל־יהוה אֶקְרָא, וַיַּעֲנֵנִי מֵהַר קָדְשׁוֹ, סֶלָה: אֲנִי שָׁכַבְתִּי וָאִישָׁנָה, הֱקִיצוֹתִי כִּי יהוה יִסְמְכֵנִי: לֹא־אִירָא מֵרִבְבוֹת עָם, אֲשֶׁר סָבִיב שָׁתוּ עָלָי: קוּמָה יהוה, הוֹשִׁיעֵנִי אֱלֹהַי, כִּי־הִכִּיתָ אֶת־כָּל־אֹיְבַי לֶחִי, שִׁנֵּי רְשָׁעִים שִׁבַּרְתָּ: לַיהוה הַיְשׁוּעָה, עַל־עַמְּךָ בִרְכָתֶךָ סֶּלָה:

הַשְׁכִּיבֵנוּ, יהוה אֱלֹהֵינוּ, לְשָׁלוֹם. וְהַעֲמִידֵנוּ, מַלְכֵּנוּ, לְחַיִּים. וּפְרֹשׂ עָלֵינוּ סֻכַּת שְׁלוֹמֶךָ, וְתַקְּנֵנוּ בְּעֵצָה טוֹבָה מִלְּפָנֶיךָ, וְהוֹשִׁיעֵנוּ לְמַעַן שְׁמֶךָ. וְהָגֵן בַּעֲדֵנוּ, וְהָסֵר מֵעָלֵינוּ אוֹיֵב, דֶּבֶר וְחֶרֶב וְרָעָב וְיָגוֹן. וְהָסֵר שָׂטָן מִלְּפָנֵינוּ וּמֵאַחֲרֵינוּ, וּבְצֵל כְּנָפֶיךָ תַּסְתִּירֵנוּ, כִּי אֵל שׁוֹמְרֵנוּ וּמַצִּילֵנוּ אָתָּה, כִּי אֵל מֶלֶךְ חַנּוּן וְרַחוּם אָתָּה. וּשְׁמֹר צֵאתֵנוּ וּבוֹאֵנוּ לְחַיִּים וּלְשָׁלוֹם מֵעַתָּה וְעַד עוֹלָם.

בָּרוּךְ יהוה בַּיּוֹם, בָּרוּךְ יהוה בַּלָּיְלָה, בָּרוּךְ יהוה בְּשָׁכְבֵנוּ, בָּרוּךְ יהוה
איוב יב בְּקוּמֵנוּ. כִּי בְיָדְךָ נַפְשׁוֹת הַחַיִּים וְהַמֵּתִים. אֲשֶׁר בְּיָדוֹ נֶפֶשׁ כָּל־חָי,
תהלים לא וְרוּחַ כָּל־בְּשַׂר־אִישׁ: בְּיָדְךָ אַפְקִיד רוּחִי, פָּדִיתָה אוֹתִי יהוה אֵל אֱמֶת:
אֱלֹהֵינוּ שֶׁבַּשָּׁמַיִם, יַחֵד שִׁמְךָ וְקַיֵּם מַלְכוּתְךָ תָּמִיד, וּמְלֹךְ עָלֵינוּ לְעוֹלָם וָעֶד.

יִרְאוּ May our eyes see, our hearts rejoice, and our souls be glad in Your true salvation, when Zion is told, "Your God reigns." The LORD is King, the LORD was King, and the LORD will be King for ever and all time. For sovereignty is Yours, and to all eternity You will reign in glory, for we have no king but You.

הַמַּלְאָךְ May the angel who rescued me from all harm, bless these boys. May they be called by my name and the names of my fathers Abraham and Isaac, and may they increase greatly on the earth. *Gen. 48*

וַיֹּאמֶר He said, "If you listen carefully to the voice of the LORD your God and do what is right in His eyes, if you pay attention to His commandments and keep all His statutes, I will not bring on you any of the diseases I brought on the Egyptians, for I am the LORD who heals you." The LORD said to the accuser, "The LORD shall rebuke you, accuser. The LORD who has chosen Jerusalem shall rebuke you! Is not this man a burning stick snatched from the fire?" Look! It is Solomon's bed, escorted by sixty warriors, the noblest of Israel, all of them wearing the sword, experienced in battle, each with his sword at his side, prepared for the terror of the nights. *Ex. 15* *Zech. 3* *Song. 3*

Say three times:

יְבָרֶכְךָ May the LORD bless you and protect you. *Num. 6*
May the LORD make His face shine on you and be gracious to you.
May the LORD turn His face toward you and grant you peace.

Say three times:

הִנֵּה See – the Guardian of Israel neither slumbers nor sleeps. *Ps. 121*

Say three times:

לִישׁוּעָתְךָ For Your salvation I hope, LORD. *Gen. 49*
I hope, LORD, for Your salvation.
LORD, for Your salvation I hope.

Say three times:

בְּשֵׁם In the name of the LORD, God of Israel:
may Michael be at my right hand,
Gabriel, at my left;
in front of me, Uriel,
behind me, Raphael;
and above my head the Presence of God.

יִרְאוּ עֵינֵינוּ וְיִשְׂמַח לִבֵּנוּ, וְתָגֵל נַפְשֵׁנוּ בִּישׁוּעָתְךָ בֶּאֱמֶת, בֶּאֱמֹר לְצִיּוֹן מָלַךְ אֱלֹהָיִךְ. יהוה מֶלֶךְ, יהוה מָלָךְ, יהוה יִמְלֹךְ לְעוֹלָם וָעֶד. כִּי הַמַּלְכוּת שֶׁלְּךָ הִיא, וּלְעוֹלְמֵי עַד תִּמְלֹךְ בְּכָבוֹד, כִּי אֵין לָנוּ מֶלֶךְ אֶלָּא אָתָּה.

בראשית מח הַמַּלְאָךְ הַגֹּאֵל אֹתִי מִכָּל־רָע יְבָרֵךְ אֶת־הַנְּעָרִים, וְיִקָּרֵא בָהֶם שְׁמִי וְשֵׁם אֲבֹתַי אַבְרָהָם וְיִצְחָק, וְיִדְגּוּ לָרֹב בְּקֶרֶב הָאָרֶץ:

שמות טו וַיֹּאמֶר אִם־שָׁמוֹעַ תִּשְׁמַע לְקוֹל יהוה אֱלֹהֶיךָ, וְהַיָּשָׁר בְּעֵינָיו תַּעֲשֶׂה,
וְהַאֲזַנְתָּ לְמִצְוֹתָיו וְשָׁמַרְתָּ כָּל־חֻקָּיו, כָּל־הַמַּחֲלָה אֲשֶׁר־שַׂמְתִּי בְמִצְרַיִם
זכריה ג לֹא־אָשִׂים עָלֶיךָ, כִּי אֲנִי יהוה רֹפְאֶךָ: וַיֹּאמֶר יהוה אֶל־הַשָּׂטָן, יִגְעַר
יהוה בְּךָ הַשָּׂטָן, וְיִגְעַר יהוה בְּךָ הַבֹּחֵר בִּירוּשָׁלָיִם, הֲלוֹא זֶה אוּד מֻצָּל
מֵאֵשׁ: הִנֵּה מִטָּתוֹ שֶׁלִּשְׁלֹמֹה, שִׁשִּׁים גִּבֹּרִים סָבִיב לָהּ, מִגִּבֹּרֵי יִשְׂרָאֵל:
שיר השירים ג כֻּלָּם אֲחֻזֵי חֶרֶב, מְלֻמְּדֵי מִלְחָמָה, אִישׁ חַרְבּוֹ עַל־יְרֵכוֹ מִפַּחַד בַּלֵּילוֹת:

Say three times:

במדבר ו יְבָרֶכְךָ יהוה וְיִשְׁמְרֶךָ:
יָאֵר יהוה פָּנָיו אֵלֶיךָ וִיחֻנֶּךָּ:
יִשָּׂא יהוה פָּנָיו אֵלֶיךָ וְיָשֵׂם לְךָ שָׁלוֹם:

Say three times:

תהלים קכא הִנֵּה לֹא־יָנוּם וְלֹא יִישָׁן שׁוֹמֵר יִשְׂרָאֵל:

Say three times:

בראשית מט לִישׁוּעָתְךָ קִוִּיתִי יהוה:
קִוִּיתִי יהוה לִישׁוּעָתְךָ
יהוה לִישׁוּעָתְךָ קִוִּיתִי

Say three times:

בְּשֵׁם יהוה אֱלֹהֵי יִשְׂרָאֵל
מִימִינִי מִיכָאֵל, וּמִשְּׂמֹאלִי גַּבְרִיאֵל
וּמִלְּפָנַי אוּרִיאֵל, וּמֵאֲחוֹרַי רְפָאֵל
וְעַל רֹאשִׁי שְׁכִינַת אֵל.

שִׁיר הַמַּעֲלוֹת A song of ascents. *Ps. 128*
Happy are all who fear the Lord, who walk in His ways.
When you eat the fruit of your labor, happy and fortunate are you.
Your wife shall be like a fruitful vine within your house;
your sons like olive saplings around your table.
So shall the man who fears the Lord be blessed.
May the Lord bless you from Zion;
may you see the good of Jerusalem all the days of your life;
and may you live to see your children's children. Peace be on Israel!

Say three times:

רִגְזוּ Tremble, and do not sin. *Ps. 4*
Search your heart as you lie on your bed, and be silent. Selah.

אֲדוֹן עוֹלָם Lord of the Universe,
who reigned before the birth of any thing;
when by His will all things were made,
then was His name proclaimed King.
And when all things shall cease to be,
He alone will reign in awe.
He was, He is, and He shall be glorious for evermore.
He is One, there is none else, alone, unique, beyond compare;
Without beginning, without end, His might, His rule are everywhere.
He is my God; my Redeemer lives.
He is the Rock on whom I rely –
my banner and my safe retreat, my cup, my portion when I cry.
Into His hand my soul I place, when I awake and when I sleep.
The Lord is with me, I shall not fear;
body and soul from harm will He keep.

שִׁיר הַמַּעֲלוֹת, אַשְׁרֵי כָּל־יְרֵא יהוה, הַהֹלֵךְ בִּדְרָכָיו: תהלים קכח
יְגִיעַ כַּפֶּיךָ כִּי תֹאכֵל, אַשְׁרֶיךָ וְטוֹב לָךְ:
אֶשְׁתְּךָ כְּגֶפֶן פֹּרִיָּה בְּיַרְכְּתֵי בֵיתֶךָ
בָּנֶיךָ כִּשְׁתִלֵי זֵיתִים, סָבִיב לְשֻׁלְחָנֶךָ:
הִנֵּה כִי־כֵן יְבֹרַךְ גָּבֶר יְרֵא יהוה:
יְבָרֶכְךָ יהוה מִצִּיּוֹן, וּרְאֵה בְּטוּב יְרוּשָׁלָםִ, כֹּל יְמֵי חַיֶּיךָ:
וּרְאֵה־בָנִים לְבָנֶיךָ, שָׁלוֹם עַל־יִשְׂרָאֵל:

Say three times:

רִגְזוּ וְאַל־תֶּחֱטָאוּ תהלים ד
אִמְרוּ בִלְבַבְכֶם עַל־מִשְׁכַּבְכֶם, וְדֹמּוּ סֶלָה:

אֲדוֹן עוֹלָם אֲשֶׁר מָלַךְ בְּטֶרֶם כָּל־יְצִיר נִבְרָא.
לְעֵת נַעֲשָׂה בְחֶפְצוֹ כֹּל אֲזַי מֶלֶךְ שְׁמוֹ נִקְרָא.
וְאַחֲרֵי כִּכְלוֹת הַכֹּל לְבַדּוֹ יִמְלֹךְ נוֹרָא.
וְהוּא הָיָה וְהוּא הֹוֶה וְהוּא יִהְיֶה בְּתִפְאָרָה.
וְהוּא אֶחָד וְאֵין שֵׁנִי לְהַמְשִׁיל לוֹ לְהַחְבִּירָה.
בְּלִי רֵאשִׁית בְּלִי תַכְלִית וְלוֹ הָעֹז וְהַמִּשְׂרָה.
וְהוּא אֵלִי וְחַי גּוֹאֲלִי וְצוּר חֶבְלִי בְּעֵת צָרָה.
וְהוּא נִסִּי וּמָנוֹס לִי מְנָת כּוֹסִי בְּיוֹם אֶקְרָא.
בְּיָדוֹ אַפְקִיד רוּחִי בְּעֵת אִישַׁן וְאָעִירָה.
וְעִם רוּחִי גְּוִיָּתִי יהוה לִי וְלֹא אִירָא.

PRAYER FOR RECOVERY FROM ILLNESS

מִזְמוֹר לְדָוִד A psalm of David. The LORD is my Shepherd, I shall not want. He makes me lie down in green pastures. He leads me beside the still waters. He refreshes my soul. He guides me in the paths of righteousness for His name's sake. Though I walk through the valley of the shadow of death, I will fear no evil, for You are with me; Your rod and Your staff, they comfort me. You set a table before me in the presence of my enemies; You anoint my head with oil; my cup is filled to overflowing. May goodness and kindness follow me all the days of my life, and may I live in the house of the LORD for evermore. *Ps. 23*

לְדָוִד Of David. Bless the LORD, my soul; with all my being I bless His holy name. Bless the LORD, my soul, and forget none of His benefits. He forgives all your sins. He heals all your ills. He redeems your life from the pit. He crowns you with love and compassion. He satisfies your soul with good things, so that your youth is renewed like the eagle's. The LORD is righteous in all He does; He brings justice to all the oppressed. He made known His ways to Moses, His deeds to the people of Israel. The LORD is compassionate and gracious, slow to anger, abounding in love. He will not always accuse or nurse His anger for ever. He has not treated us as our sins deserve, or repaid us according to our misdeeds. For as high as the heavens are above the earth, so great is His love for those who fear Him. As far as the east is from the west, so far has He removed our transgressions from us. As a father has compassion on his children, so the LORD has compassion on those who fear Him. For He knows how we are formed; He remembers that we are dust. As for man, his days are like grass; like a flower of the field he flourishes. For a wind passes over it and it is gone, and its place knows it no more. But the kindness of the LORD is for all eternity to those who fear Him; His righteousness is with their children's children – with those who keep His covenant, and remember to obey His precepts. The LORD has established His throne in heaven, and His kingdom rules over all. Bless the LORD, you His angels, mighty in power, who do His bidding, who obey His word. Bless the LORD, all you His host, the ministers who do His will. Bless the LORD, all His works, everywhere in His dominion. Bless the LORD, my soul. *Ps. 103*

לַמְנַצֵּחַ For the conductor of music. A psalm of David. O LORD, You have examined me and You know me. You know when I sit and when I rise; You understand my thoughts from afar. You encompass my going out and lying down. You are familiar with all my ways. Before a word is on my tongue, You, LORD, know it all. You keep close guard behind and before me. You have laid *Ps. 139*

תפילה לחולה

מִזְמוֹר לְדָוִד, יהוה רֹעִי לֹא אֶחְסָר: בִּנְאוֹת דֶּשֶׁא יַרְבִּיצֵנִי, עַל־מֵי מְנֻחוֹת תהלים כג
יְנַהֲלֵנִי: נַפְשִׁי יְשׁוֹבֵב, יַנְחֵנִי בְמַעְגְּלֵי־צֶדֶק לְמַעַן שְׁמוֹ: גַּם כִּי־אֵלֵךְ בְּגֵיא צַלְמָוֶת לֹא־אִירָא רָע, כִּי־אַתָּה עִמָּדִי, שִׁבְטְךָ וּמִשְׁעַנְתֶּךָ הֵמָּה יְנַחֲמֻנִי: תַּעֲרֹךְ לְפָנַי שֻׁלְחָן נֶגֶד צֹרְרָי, דִּשַּׁנְתָּ בַשֶּׁמֶן רֹאשִׁי, כּוֹסִי רְוָיָה: אַךְ טוֹב וָחֶסֶד יִרְדְּפוּנִי כָּל־יְמֵי חַיָּי, וְשַׁבְתִּי בְּבֵית־יהוה לְאֹרֶךְ יָמִים:

לְדָוִד, בָּרְכִי נַפְשִׁי אֶת־יהוה, וְכָל־קְרָבַי אֶת־שֵׁם קָדְשׁוֹ: בָּרְכִי נַפְשִׁי תהלים קג
אֶת־יהוה, וְאַל־תִּשְׁכְּחִי כָּל־גְּמוּלָיו: הַסֹּלֵחַ לְכָל־עֲוֺנֵכִי, הָרֹפֵא לְכָל־תַּחֲלוּאָיְכִי: הַגּוֹאֵל מִשַּׁחַת חַיָּיְכִי, הַמְעַטְּרֵכִי חֶסֶד וְרַחֲמִים: הַמַּשְׂבִּיעַ בַּטּוֹב עֶדְיֵךְ, תִּתְחַדֵּשׁ כַּנֶּשֶׁר נְעוּרָיְכִי: עֹשֵׂה צְדָקוֹת יהוה, וּמִשְׁפָּטִים לְכָל־עֲשׁוּקִים: יוֹדִיעַ דְּרָכָיו לְמֹשֶׁה, לִבְנֵי יִשְׂרָאֵל עֲלִילוֹתָיו: רַחוּם וְחַנּוּן יהוה, אֶרֶךְ אַפַּיִם וְרַב־חָסֶד: לֹא־לָנֶצַח יָרִיב, וְלֹא לְעוֹלָם יִטּוֹר: לֹא כַחֲטָאֵינוּ עָשָׂה לָנוּ, וְלֹא כַעֲוֺנֹתֵינוּ גָּמַל עָלֵינוּ: כִּי כִגְבֹהַּ שָׁמַיִם עַל־הָאָרֶץ, גָּבַר חַסְדּוֹ עַל־יְרֵאָיו: כִּרְחֹק מִזְרָח מִמַּעֲרָב, הִרְחִיק מִמֶּנּוּ אֶת־פְּשָׁעֵינוּ: כְּרַחֵם אָב עַל־בָּנִים, רִחַם יהוה עַל־יְרֵאָיו: כִּי־הוּא יָדַע יִצְרֵנוּ, זָכוּר כִּי־עָפָר אֲנָחְנוּ: אֱנוֹשׁ כֶּחָצִיר יָמָיו, כְּצִיץ הַשָּׂדֶה כֵּן יָצִיץ: כִּי רוּחַ עָבְרָה־בּוֹ וְאֵינֶנּוּ, וְלֹא־יַכִּירֶנּוּ עוֹד מְקוֹמוֹ: וְחֶסֶד יהוה מֵעוֹלָם וְעַד־עוֹלָם עַל־יְרֵאָיו, וְצִדְקָתוֹ לִבְנֵי בָנִים: לְשֹׁמְרֵי בְרִיתוֹ, וּלְזֹכְרֵי פִקֻּדָיו לַעֲשׂוֹתָם: יהוה בַּשָּׁמַיִם הֵכִין כִּסְאוֹ, וּמַלְכוּתוֹ בַּכֹּל מָשָׁלָה: בָּרְכוּ יהוה מַלְאָכָיו, גִּבֹּרֵי כֹחַ עֹשֵׂי דְבָרוֹ, לִשְׁמֹעַ בְּקוֹל דְּבָרוֹ: בָּרְכוּ יהוה כָּל־צְבָאָיו, מְשָׁרְתָיו עֹשֵׂי רְצוֹנוֹ: בָּרְכוּ יהוה כָּל־מַעֲשָׂיו, בְּכָל־מְקֹמוֹת מֶמְשַׁלְתּוֹ, בָּרְכִי נַפְשִׁי אֶת־יהוה:

לַמְנַצֵּחַ לְדָוִד מִזְמוֹר, יהוה חֲקַרְתַּנִי וַתֵּדָע: אַתָּה יָדַעְתָּ שִׁבְתִּי וְקוּמִי, תהלים קלט
בַּנְתָּה לְרֵעִי מֵרָחוֹק: אָרְחִי וְרִבְעִי זֵרִיתָ, וְכָל־דְּרָכַי הִסְכַּנְתָּה: כִּי אֵין מִלָּה בִּלְשׁוֹנִי, הֵן יהוה יָדַעְתָּ כֻלָּהּ: אָחוֹר וָקֶדֶם צַרְתָּנִי, וַתָּשֶׁת עָלַי

Your hand upon me. Knowledge so wonderful is beyond me; so high, it is above my reach. Where can I escape from Your spirit? Where can I flee from Your presence? If I climb to heaven, You are there; if I make my bed in the underworld, You are there. If I rise on the wings of the dawn, if I settle on the far side of the sea, even there Your hand will guide me, Your right hand will hold me fast. Were I to say, "Surely the darkness will hide me, and light become night around me," to You the darkness would not be dark; night is light as day; to You dark and light are one. For You created my innermost being; You knitted me together in my mother's womb. I praise You because I am awesomely, wondrously made; wonderful are Your works; I know that full well. My frame was not hidden from You when I was formed in the secret place, woven in the depths of the earth. Your eyes saw my unformed body. All the days ordained for me were written in Your book before one of them came to be. How precious to me are Your thoughts, God, how vast in number they are. Were I to count them, they would outnumber the grains of the sand. I awake and I am still with You. God, if only You would slay the wicked – away from me, you bloodthirsty men. They speak of You with evil intent; Your adversaries misuse Your name. Do I not hate those who hate You, Lord, and loathe those who rise up against You? I have nothing but hatred for them; I count them my enemies. Search me, God, and know my heart; test me and know my innermost thoughts. See if there is grief in the way I follow, and lead me in the everlasting way.

תְּפִלָּה לְעָנִי A prayer of one who is afflicted, when he is faint, and pours out his anguish before the Lord. Lord, hear my prayer and let my cry come before You. Do not hide Your face from me in my day of distress. Turn Your ear toward me; answer me swiftly on the day I call. *Ps. 102*

אָנָּא Please, Lord, Healer of all flesh, have pity on me, and support me on my sick bed, in Your great love, for I am weak. Send relief and healing to me and to the others of Your children who are sick. Heal my pain and renew my youth as the eagle's. Grant wisdom to the physician that he may cure my illness, so that my healing may spring up swiftly. Hear my prayer, prolong my life, and let me complete my years in happiness, so that I may be able to serve You and keep Your precepts with a perfect heart. Grant me the understanding to know that this bitter trial has come upon me for my welfare. Let me not reject Your discipline or spurn Your rebuke.

אֱלוֹהַּ סְלִיחוֹת God of forgiveness, gracious and compassionate, slow to anger, abounding in love, I acknowledge before You with a broken and contrite heart that I have sinned and done evil in Your sight. I hereby repent of my evil and

כַּפֶּֽכָה: פְּלִיאָה דַעַת מִמֶּנִּי, נִשְׂגְּבָה לֹא־אוּכַל לָהּ: אָנָה אֵלֵךְ מֵרוּחֶךָ, וְאָנָה מִפָּנֶיךָ אֶבְרָח: אִם־אֶסַּק שָׁמַיִם שָׁם אָתָּה, וְאַצִּיעָה שְּׁאוֹל הִנֶּךָּ: אֶשָּׂא כַנְפֵי־שָׁחַר, אֶשְׁכְּנָה בְּאַחֲרִית יָם: גַּם־שָׁם יָדְךָ תַנְחֵנִי, וְתֹאחֲזֵנִי יְמִינֶךָ: וָאֹמַר אַךְ־חֹשֶׁךְ יְשׁוּפֵנִי, וְלַיְלָה אוֹר בַּעֲדֵנִי: גַּם־חֹשֶׁךְ לֹא־יַחְשִׁיךְ מִמֶּךָ, וְלַיְלָה כַּיּוֹם יָאִיר, כַּחֲשֵׁיכָה כָּאוֹרָה: כִּי־אַתָּה קָנִיתָ כִלְיֹתָי, תְּסֻכֵּנִי בְּבֶטֶן אִמִּי: אוֹדְךָ עַל כִּי נוֹרָאוֹת נִפְלֵיתִי, נִפְלָאִים מַעֲשֶׂיךָ, וְנַפְשִׁי יֹדַעַת מְאֹד: לֹא־נִכְחַד עָצְמִי מִמֶּךָּ, אֲשֶׁר־עֻשֵּׂיתִי בַסֵּתֶר, רֻקַּמְתִּי בְּתַחְתִּיּוֹת אָרֶץ: גָּלְמִי רָאוּ עֵינֶיךָ, וְעַל־סִפְרְךָ כֻּלָּם יִכָּתֵבוּ, יָמִים יֻצָּרוּ, וְלֹא אֶחָד בָּהֶם: וְלִי מַה־יָּקְרוּ רֵעֶיךָ אֵל, מֶה עָצְמוּ רָאשֵׁיהֶם: אֶסְפְּרֵם מֵחוֹל יִרְבּוּן, הֱקִיצֹתִי וְעוֹדִי עִמָּךְ: אִם־תִּקְטֹל אֱלוֹהַּ רָשָׁע, וְאַנְשֵׁי דָמִים סוּרוּ מֶנִּי: אֲשֶׁר יֹמְרוּךָ לִמְזִמָּה, נָשֻׂא לַשָּׁוְא עָרֶיךָ: הֲלוֹא־מְשַׂנְאֶיךָ יהוה אֶשְׂנָא, וּבִתְקוֹמְמֶיךָ אֶתְקוֹטָט: תַּכְלִית שִׂנְאָה שְׂנֵאתִים, לְאוֹיְבִים הָיוּ לִי: חָקְרֵנִי אֵל וְדַע לְבָבִי, בְּחָנֵנִי וְדַע שַׂרְעַפָּי: וּרְאֵה אִם־דֶּרֶךְ־עֹצֶב בִּי, וּנְחֵנִי בְּדֶרֶךְ עוֹלָם:

תְּפִלָּה לְעָנִי כִי־יַעֲטֹף, וְלִפְנֵי יהוה יִשְׁפֹּךְ שִׂיחוֹ: יהוה שִׁמְעָה תְפִלָּתִי, תהלים קב
וְשַׁוְעָתִי אֵלֶיךָ תָבוֹא: אַל־תַּסְתֵּר פָּנֶיךָ מִמֶּנִּי בְּיוֹם צַר לִי, הַטֵּה־אֵלַי אָזְנֶךָ, בְּיוֹם אֶקְרָא מַהֵר עֲנֵנִי:

אָנָּא יהוה רוֹפֵא כָל בָּשָׂר, רַחֵם עָלַי, וּסְעָדֵנִי בְּחַסְדְּךָ הַגָּדוֹל עַל עֶרֶשׂ דְּוָי, כִּי אֻמְלַל אָנִי. שְׁלַח לִי תְּרוּפָה וּתְעָלָה, בְּתוֹךְ שְׁאָר חוֹלֵי יִשְׂרָאֵל. רְפָא אֶת מַכְאוֹבִי, וְחַדֵּשׁ כַּנֶּשֶׁר נְעוּרָי. תֵּן בִּינָה לָרוֹפֵא, וְיִגְהֶה מִמֶּנִּי מְזוֹרִי, וַאֲרוּכָתִי מְהֵרָה תִצְמָח. שְׁמַע תְּפִלָּתִי, וְהוֹסֵף יָמִים עַל יָמַי, וַאֲכַלֶּה שְׁנוֹתַי בַּנְּעִימִים, לְמַעַן אוּכַל לַעֲבֹד אוֹתְךָ, וְלִשְׁמֹר פִּקּוּדֶיךָ בְּלֵב שָׁלֵם. הֲבִינֵנִי וְאֵדְעָה, כִּי לְשָׁלוֹמִי מַר לִי מָר. וְאַל אֶמְאַס אֶת מוּסָרְךָ, וּבְתוֹכַחְתְּךָ אַל אָקוּץ.

אֱלוֹהַּ סְלִיחוֹת, חַנּוּן וְרַחוּם אֶרֶךְ אַפַּיִם וְרַב חֶסֶד, מוֹדֶה אֲנִי לְפָנֶיךָ בְּלֵב נִשְׁבָּר וְנִדְכֶּה כִּי חָטָאתִי, וְהָרַע בְּעֵינֶיךָ עָשִׂיתִי. הִנֵּה נִחַמְתִּי עַל

turn to You in complete repentance. Help me, God of my salvation, that I may not turn to folly again, but instead walk before You in truth and integrity. Gladden Your servant's heart, for to You, Lord, I lift up my soul. Heal me, *Ps. 86*
Lord, and I will be healed, save me and I will be saved, for You are my glory. *Jer. 17*
Amen and Amen!

THANKSGIVING PRAYER AFTER RECOVERY FROM ILLNESS

Say Psalms 23 and 103 on pages 108 and 514. Then continue with:

אָנָּא O great, mighty and awesome God: By Your great love I come before You to offer thanks for all the good You have bestowed on me. In my distress I called to You and You answered me; from my sick bed I cried to You, and You heard my voice and my pleas. You chastened me severely, Lord, but You did not hand me over to death. In Your love and compassion You lifted my soul from the grave. For Your anger is for a moment, Your favor for a lifetime.
At night there may be weeping, but in the morning there is joy. The living, *Is. 38*
only the living, praise You as I do this day. My soul which You have redeemed shall tell of Your wonders to the children of men. Blessed are You, the faithful Healer of all flesh.

אֵל רַחוּם O God, compassionate and gracious, who grants favors to the undeserving: I am not worthy of all the kindness You have shown to me until now. Purify, please, my heart that I may be worthy to walk before You in the way of the upright. Extend Your help to Your servant. Grant me the strength and resolution to overcome my weakness, and bless me with physical health. Keep sorrow and grief far from me; protect me from all harm, and guide me with Your counsel. May the sun of righteousness shine for me, bringing healing in
its wings. May the words of my mouth and the meditation of my heart find *Ps. 19*
favor before You, O Lord, my Rock and my Redeemer. Amen.

רָעָתִי, וְאָשׁוּב בִּתְשׁוּבָה שְׁלֵמָה לְפָנֶיךָ. עָזְרֵנִי אֱלֹהֵי יִשְׁעִי, וְלֹא אָשׁוּב
תהלים פו לְכִסְלָה, וְאֶתְהַלֵּךְ לְפָנֶיךָ בֶּאֱמֶת וּבְתָמִים. שַׂמֵּחַ נֶפֶשׁ עַבְדֶּךָ, כִּי־אֵלֶיךָ
ירמיה יז אֲדֹנָי, נַפְשִׁי אֶשָּׂא: רְפָאֵנִי יהוה וְאֵרָפֵא, הוֹשִׁיעֵנִי וְאִוָּשֵׁעָה, כִּי תְהִלָּתִי
אָתָּה: אָמֵן וְאָמֵן.

תפילה לעומד מחליו

Say תהלים כג *and* קג *on pages 109 and 515. Then continue with:*

אָנָּא הָאֵל הַגָּדוֹל הַגִּבּוֹר וְהַנּוֹרָא, בְּרֹב חַסְדְּךָ אָבוֹא לְפָנֶיךָ לְהוֹדוֹת
לְךָ עַל כָּל הַטּוֹבוֹת אֲשֶׁר גְּמַלְתָּ עָלַי. מִן הַמֵּצַר קְרָאתִיךָ וַתַּעֲנֵנִי, מֵעֶרֶשׂ
דְּוַי שִׁוַּעְתִּי אֵלֶיךָ, וַתִּשְׁמַע אֶת קוֹלִי תַּחֲנוּנַי. יַסֹּר יִסְּרַנִּי יָהּ, וְלַמָּוֶת לֹא
נְתָנָנִי. בְּאַהֲבָתְךָ וּבְחֶמְלָתְךָ הֶעֱלִיתָ מִן שְׁאוֹל נַפְשִׁי. כִּי רֶגַע בְּאַפּוֹ,
ישעיה לח חַיִּים בִּרְצוֹנוֹ, בָּעֶרֶב יָלִין בֶּכִי וְלַבֹּקֶר רִנָּה. חַי חַי הוּא יוֹדֶךָ, כָּמוֹנִי
הַיּוֹם: וְנַפְשִׁי אֲשֶׁר פָּדִיתָ, תְּסַפֵּר נִפְלְאוֹתֶיךָ לִבְנֵי אָדָם. בָּרוּךְ אַתָּה,
רוֹפֵא נֶאֱמָן לְכָל בָּשָׂר.

אֵל רַחוּם וְחַנּוּן, הַגּוֹמֵל לְחַיָּבִים טוֹבוֹת, קָטֹנְתִּי מִכֹּל הַחֲסָדִים אֲשֶׁר
עָשִׂיתָ עִמָּדִי עַד הֵנָּה. אָנָּא טַהֵר לְבָבִי, וְזַכֵּנִי לָלֶכֶת בְּדֶרֶךְ יְשָׁרִים לְפָנֶיךָ,
וּמְשֹׁךְ עֶזְרְךָ לְעַבְדֶּךָ. חַזְּקֵנִי וְאַמְּצֵנִי מֵרִפְיוֹן, וּבְחִלּוּץ עֲצָמוֹת תְּבָרְכֵנִי.
הַרְחֵק מֵעָלַי כָּל צָרָה וְתוּגָה, שָׁמְרֵנִי מִכָּל רָע, וּבַעֲצָתְךָ תַנְחֵנִי. וְזָרְחָה לִי
תהלים יט שֶׁמֶשׁ צְדָקָה, וּמַרְפֵּא בִּכְנָפֶיהָ. יִהְיוּ לְרָצוֹן אִמְרֵי־פִי וְהֶגְיוֹן לִבִּי לְפָנֶיךָ,
יהוה צוּרִי וְגֹאֲלִי: אָמֵן.

PRAYERS AT THE CEMETERY

*On visiting a cemetery for the first time in thirty days,
it is customary to say the following:*

בָּרוּךְ Blessed are You, LORD our God, King of the universe,
who justly formed you,
and justly nourished and sustained you,
and justly brought death to you,
and justly knows you, one by one,
and is one day justly to bring you back and revive you;
blessed are You, LORD,
who revives the dead.

אַתָּה You are eternally mighty, LORD.
You give life to the dead and have great power to save.
He sustains the living with loving-kindness,
and with great compassion revives the dead.
He supports the fallen, heals the sick, sets captives free,
and keeps His faith with those who sleep in the dust.
Who is like You, Master of might,
and to whom can You be compared,
O King who brings death and gives life,
and makes salvation grow?
Faithful are You to revive the dead.

When visiting a cemetery, especially for a memorial service or on the anniversary of a death, it is customary to say the following seven psalms by the graveside. These are followed by the verses of Psalm 119 (which is arranged alphabetically in groups of eight verses for each letter) that spell out the deceased person's name (page 801), and then the groups of verses that spell out the word נשמה *("soul") (page 815).*

33 Sing joyfully to the LORD, you righteous; it is fitting for the upright to praise Him.
Praise the LORD with the harp; sing to Him with the ten-stringed lute.
Sing to Him a new song; play skillfully amid shouts of joy.
For the word of the LORD is right; His every deed is trustworthy.
He loves righteousness and justice; the earth is full of the goodness of the LORD.
By the word of the LORD the heavens were made, and all their host by the breath of His mouth.
He gathers the waters of the sea as in a heap; He puts the deep in storehouses.

תפילות לבית הקברות

On visiting a cemetery for the first time in thirty days,
it is customary to say the following:

בָּרוּךְ אַתָּה יהוה, אֱלֹהֵינוּ מֶלֶךְ הָעוֹלָם
אֲשֶׁר יָצַר אֶתְכֶם בַּדִּין
וְזָן וְכִלְכֵּל אֶתְכֶם בַּדִּין
וְהֵמִית אֶתְכֶם בַּדִּין
וְיוֹדֵעַ מִסְפַּר כֻּלְּכֶם בַּדִּין
וְעָתִיד לְהַחֲזִיר וּלְהַחֲיוֹתְכֶם בַּדִּין.
בָּרוּךְ אַתָּה יהוה, מְחַיֵּה הַמֵּתִים.

אַתָּה גִּבּוֹר לְעוֹלָם, אֲדֹנָי
מְחַיֵּה מֵתִים אַתָּה, רַב לְהוֹשִׁיעַ
מְכַלְכֵּל חַיִּים בְּחֶסֶד, מְחַיֵּה מֵתִים בְּרַחֲמִים רַבִּים
סוֹמֵךְ נוֹפְלִים, וְרוֹפֵא חוֹלִים, וּמַתִּיר אֲסוּרִים
וּמְקַיֵּם אֱמוּנָתוֹ לִישֵׁנֵי עָפָר.
מִי כָמוֹךָ, בַּעַל גְּבוּרוֹת וּמִי דּוֹמֶה לָּךְ
מֶלֶךְ, מֵמִית וּמְחַיֶּה וּמַצְמִיחַ יְשׁוּעָה.
וְנֶאֱמָן אַתָּה לְהַחֲיוֹת מֵתִים.

When visiting a cemetery, especially for a memorial service or on the anniversary of a death, it is customary to say the following seven תהלים *by the graveside. These are followed by the verses of* מזמור קיט *(which is arranged alphabetically in groups of eight verses for each letter) that spell out the deceased person's name* (page 801)*, and then the groups of verses that spell out the word* נשמה *("soul")* (page 815)*.*

לג רַנְּנוּ צַדִּיקִים בַּיהוָה לַיְשָׁרִים נָאוָה תְהִלָּה׃
הוֹדוּ לַיהוָה בְּכִנּוֹר בְּנֵבֶל עָשׂוֹר זַמְּרוּ־לוֹ׃
שִׁירוּ־לוֹ שִׁיר חָדָשׁ הֵיטִיבוּ נַגֵּן בִּתְרוּעָה׃
כִּי־יָשָׁר דְּבַר־יְהוָה וְכָל־מַעֲשֵׂהוּ בֶּאֱמוּנָה׃
אֹהֵב צְדָקָה וּמִשְׁפָּט חֶסֶד יְהוָה מָלְאָה הָאָרֶץ׃
בִּדְבַר יְהוָה שָׁמַיִם נַעֲשׂוּ וּבְרוּחַ פִּיו כָּל־צְבָאָם׃
כֹּנֵס כַּנֵּד מֵי הַיָּם נֹתֵן בְּאֹצָרוֹת תְּהוֹמוֹת׃

Let all the earth fear the LORD; let all the inhabitants of the world stand in awe of Him.
For He spoke, and it was; He commanded, and there it stood.
The LORD frustrates the plans of nations; He thwarts the designs of peoples.
But the LORD's own plan stands forever, the designs of His heart endure for all generations.
Happy is the nation whose God is the LORD; the people He has chosen for His own heritage.
The LORD looks down from heaven, He sees all mankind.
From His dwelling-place He surveys all the inhabitants of the earth.
It is He who fashions the hearts of them all, He notes all their doings.
No king is saved by the size of his army; no warrior is delivered by his great strength.
The horse is a vain hope for deliverance; despite its great strength, it provides no escape.
But the eye of the LORD is on those who fear Him, who wait for His loving care, to deliver them from death, and to keep them alive in famine.
Our soul waits for the LORD; He is our help and our shield.
In Him our hearts rejoice, for we trust in His holy name.
Let Your loving care, LORD, rest upon us, as we put our hope in You.

16 A *mikhtam* of David. Guard me, God, for I seek refuge in You.
I say to the LORD, "You are my Master." You are not bound to promote my welfare;
but [You do so] on account of the holy ones who were in the land, and the noble men, in whom was all my delight.
Many shall be the sorrows of those who woo another god. Never will I offer libations of blood to such gods; never will I take their names upon my lips.
The LORD alone is my portion, my share, my cup of destiny; You hold my lot secure.
A measured portion has fallen for me in delightful places; excellent indeed is my heritage.
I will bless the LORD who gives me counsel; at night my thoughts instruct me.
I set the LORD before me always; with Him at my right hand I shall not falter.
Therefore my heart is glad, my soul rejoices, my whole body is secure and at rest.
For You will not abandon my soul to the grave, nor suffer Your faithful servant to see the pit.
You will make known to me the path of life; in Your presence is fullness of joy, at Your right hand bliss forevermore.

יִירְאוּ מֵיהוה כָּל־הָאָרֶץ מִמֶּנּוּ יָגוּרוּ כָּל־יֹשְׁבֵי תֵבֵל:
כִּי הוּא אָמַר וַיֶּהִי הוּא־צִוָּה וַיַּעֲמֹד:
יהוה הֵפִיר עֲצַת־גּוֹיִם הֵנִיא מַחְשְׁבוֹת עַמִּים:
עֲצַת יהוה לְעוֹלָם תַּעֲמֹד מַחְשְׁבוֹת לִבּוֹ לְדֹר וָדֹר:
אַשְׁרֵי הַגּוֹי אֲשֶׁר־יהוה אֱלֹהָיו הָעָם ׀ בָּחַר לְנַחֲלָה לוֹ:
מִשָּׁמַיִם הִבִּיט יהוה רָאָה אֶת־כָּל־בְּנֵי הָאָדָם:
מִמְּכוֹן־שִׁבְתּוֹ הִשְׁגִּיחַ אֶל כָּל־יֹשְׁבֵי הָאָרֶץ:
הַיֹּצֵר יַחַד לִבָּם הַמֵּבִין אֶל־כָּל־מַעֲשֵׂיהֶם:
אֵין־הַמֶּלֶךְ נוֹשָׁע בְּרָב־חָיִל גִּבּוֹר לֹא־יִנָּצֵל בְּרָב־כֹּחַ:
שֶׁקֶר הַסּוּס לִתְשׁוּעָה וּבְרֹב חֵילוֹ לֹא יְמַלֵּט:
הִנֵּה עֵין יהוה אֶל־יְרֵאָיו לַמְיַחֲלִים לְחַסְדּוֹ:
לְהַצִּיל מִמָּוֶת נַפְשָׁם וּלְחַיּוֹתָם בָּרָעָב:
נַפְשֵׁנוּ חִכְּתָה לַיהוה עֶזְרֵנוּ וּמָגִנֵּנוּ הוּא:
כִּי־בוֹ יִשְׂמַח לִבֵּנוּ כִּי בְשֵׁם קָדְשׁוֹ בָטָחְנוּ:
יְהִי־חַסְדְּךָ יהוה עָלֵינוּ כַּאֲשֶׁר יִחַלְנוּ לָךְ:

טז מִכְתָּם לְדָוִד שָׁמְרֵנִי אֵל כִּי־חָסִיתִי בָךְ:
אָמַרְתְּ לַיהוה אֲדֹנָי אָתָּה טוֹבָתִי בַּל־עָלֶיךָ:
לִקְדוֹשִׁים אֲשֶׁר־בָּאָרֶץ הֵמָּה וְאַדִּירֵי כָּל־חֶפְצִי־בָם:
יִרְבּוּ עַצְּבוֹתָם אַחֵר מָהָרוּ
בַּל־אַסִּיךְ נִסְכֵּיהֶם מִדָּם וּבַל־אֶשָּׂא אֶת־שְׁמוֹתָם עַל־שְׂפָתָי:
יהוה מְנָת־חֶלְקִי וְכוֹסִי אַתָּה תּוֹמִיךְ גּוֹרָלִי:
חֲבָלִים נָפְלוּ־לִי בַּנְּעִמִים אַף־נַחֲלָת שָׁפְרָה עָלָי:
אֲבָרֵךְ אֶת־יהוה אֲשֶׁר יְעָצָנִי אַף־לֵילוֹת יִסְּרוּנִי כִלְיוֹתָי:
שִׁוִּיתִי יהוה לְנֶגְדִּי תָמִיד כִּי מִימִינִי בַּל־אֶמּוֹט:
לָכֵן ׀ שָׂמַח לִבִּי וַיָּגֶל כְּבוֹדִי אַף־בְּשָׂרִי יִשְׁכֹּן לָבֶטַח:
כִּי ׀ לֹא־תַעֲזֹב נַפְשִׁי לִשְׁאוֹל לֹא־תִתֵּן חֲסִידְךָ לִרְאוֹת שָׁחַת:
תּוֹדִיעֵנִי אֹרַח חַיִּים שֹׂבַע שְׂמָחוֹת אֶת־פָּנֶיךָ נְעִמוֹת בִּימִינְךָ נֶצַח:

17 A prayer of David. Hear, LORD, my righteous cause, listen to my cry. Give ear to my prayers from lips without deceit.
Let my judgment come forth from You; let Your eyes discern what is right.
Were You to test my heart, and watch me all night long. Were You to try me [as in a furnace], You would not find me innocent. I wish that my mouth had not transgressed.
With regard to man's activities – being mindful of the command of Your lips, I have protected others from the ways of the lawless.
My steps have held firmly to Your paths, my feet have never faltered.
I call on You, for You will answer me, God. Turn Your ear to me; listen to my words.
Favor me with Your compassion, You who rescues those who seek refuge from Your opponents with Your right hand.
Guard me like the apple of Your eye; hide me in the shadow of Your wings from the wicked who do me violence, from my deadly enemies who encircle me.
Their fat has enclosed their hearts, their mouths speak nothing but arrogance.
[They track] our steps; now they surround us; they set their eyes to throw us to the ground.
They are like a lion hungry for prey, like a young lion crouching in ambush.
Arise, LORD, confront them, bring them down; save my life from the wicked who act as Your sword.
I prefer to die at Your hand, LORD, among those who die of old age; whose portion is life, and whose bellies You will fill with Your hidden treasures.
May their sons have plenty, and have something to leave for their offspring.
Then I, in righteousness, will behold Your face; when I awake, I shall be content with the vision of You.

72 Of Solomon. God, endow the king with Your justice, the royal son with Your righteousness,
that he may judge Your people with righteousness, and Your poor with equity.
May the mountains bring forth prosperity for the people, the hills too, because of [his] justice.
May he defend the poor among the people; may he save the children of the needy, and crush the oppressor.
Then all will revere You as long as the sun endures, and as long as the moon lasts, throughout the ages.

יז תְּפִלָּה לְדָוִד
שִׁמְעָה יְהֹוָה ׀ צֶדֶק הַקְשִׁיבָה רִנָּתִי הַאֲזִינָה תְפִלָּתִי
בְּלֹא שִׂפְתֵי מִרְמָה:
מִלְּפָנֶיךָ מִשְׁפָּטִי יֵצֵא עֵינֶיךָ תֶּחֱזֶינָה מֵישָׁרִים:
בָּחַנְתָּ לִבִּי ׀ פָּקַדְתָּ לַּיְלָה צְרַפְתַּנִי בַל־תִּמְצָא
זַמֹּתִי בַּל־יַעֲבָר־פִּי:
לִפְעֻלּוֹת אָדָם בִּדְבַר שְׂפָתֶיךָ אֲנִי שָׁמַרְתִּי אָרְחוֹת פָּרִיץ:
תָּמֹךְ אֲשֻׁרַי בְּמַעְגְּלוֹתֶיךָ בַּל־נָמוֹטּוּ פְעָמָי:
אֲנִי־קְרָאתִיךָ כִי־תַעֲנֵנִי אֵל הַט־אָזְנְךָ לִי שְׁמַע אִמְרָתִי:
הַפְלֵה חֲסָדֶיךָ מוֹשִׁיעַ חוֹסִים מִמִּתְקוֹמְמִים בִּימִינֶךָ:
שָׁמְרֵנִי כְּאִישׁוֹן בַּת־עָיִן בְּצֵל כְּנָפֶיךָ תַּסְתִּירֵנִי:
מִפְּנֵי רְשָׁעִים זוּ שַׁדּוּנִי אֹיְבַי בְּנֶפֶשׁ יַקִּיפוּ עָלָי:
חֶלְבָּמוֹ סָּגְרוּ פִּימוֹ דִּבְּרוּ בְגֵאוּת:
אַשֻּׁרֵינוּ עַתָּה סְבָבוּנוּ עֵינֵיהֶם יָשִׁיתוּ לִנְטוֹת בָּאָרֶץ:
דִּמְיֹנוֹ כְּאַרְיֵה יִכְסוֹף לִטְרוֹף וְכִכְפִיר יֹשֵׁב בְּמִסְתָּרִים:
קוּמָה יְהֹוָה קַדְּמָה פָנָיו הַכְרִיעֵהוּ
פַּלְּטָה נַפְשִׁי מֵרָשָׁע חַרְבֶּךָ:
מִמְתִים יָדְךָ ׀ יְהֹוָה מִמְתִים מֵחֶלֶד חֶלְקָם בַּחַיִּים
וּצְפוּנְךָ תְּמַלֵּא בִטְנָם יִשְׂבְּעוּ בָנִים
וְהִנִּיחוּ יִתְרָם לְעוֹלְלֵיהֶם:
אֲנִי בְּצֶדֶק אֶחֱזֶה פָנֶיךָ אֶשְׂבְּעָה בְהָקִיץ תְּמוּנָתֶךָ:

עב לִשְׁלֹמֹה ׀
אֱלֹהִים מִשְׁפָּטֶיךָ לְמֶלֶךְ תֵּן וְצִדְקָתְךָ לְבֶן־מֶלֶךְ:
יָדִין עַמְּךָ בְצֶדֶק וַעֲנִיֶּיךָ בְמִשְׁפָּט:
יִשְׂאוּ הָרִים שָׁלוֹם לָעָם וּגְבָעוֹת בִּצְדָקָה:
יִשְׁפֹּט ׀ עֲנִיֵּי־עָם יוֹשִׁיעַ לִבְנֵי אֶבְיוֹן וִידַכֵּא עוֹשֵׁק:
יִירָאוּךָ עִם־שָׁמֶשׁ וְלִפְנֵי יָרֵחַ דּוֹר דּוֹרִים:

May he come down like rain falling on a mown field, like showers watering the earth!
In his days may the righteous flourish, and peace abound till the moon be no more.
May he rule from sea to sea, from the River to the ends of the earth.
Desert dwellers shall kneel before him; his enemies shall lick the dust.
The kings of Tarshish and of the isles shall pay him tribute, the kings of Sheba and Seba shall offer gifts;
all kings shall bow to him, all nations shall serve him.
For he saves the needy who call for help, and the poor who have no protector.
He has pity on the poor and the needy, and saves the lives of the helpless.
He redeems their lives from oppression and violence, for their blood is precious in his eyes.
Long may he live with them, sharing the gold he received from Sheba,
so that they will pray for him constantly, and bless him each day.
May there be an abundance of corn in the land, even on the mountain tops;
may its crops rustle like Lebanon; and men shall thrive in the cities like grass in the fields!
May his name endure forever; as long as the sun lasts may his name continue;
men shall wish to be blessed as he was; all nations shall call him happy!
Blessed be the Lord, the God of Israel, who alone does wondrous things!
Blessed be His glorious name forever;
let the whole earth be filled with His glory! Amen and Amen!
Here end the prayers of David, son of Jesse.

91 You who dwell in the shelter of the Most High, and abide in the shadow of the Almighty,
I say [to you], on behalf of the Lord, who is my refuge, my stronghold, my God in whom I trust,
that He will deliver you from the fowler's snare, from the destructive plague.
He will cover you with His pinions; under His wings you will find safety.
His faithfulness is your shield and buckler.
You will not fear the terrors of the night, or the arrow that flies by day;

יֵרֵד כְּמָטָר עַל־גֵּז כִּרְבִיבִים זַרְזִיף אָרֶץ׃
יִפְרַח־בְּיָמָיו צַדִּיק וְרֹב שָׁלוֹם עַד־בְּלִי יָרֵחַ׃
וְיֵרְדְּ מִיָּם עַד־יָם וּמִנָּהָר עַד־אַפְסֵי־אָרֶץ׃
לְפָנָיו יִכְרְעוּ צִיִּים וְאֹיְבָיו עָפָר יְלַחֵכוּ׃
מַלְכֵי תַרְשִׁישׁ וְאִיִּים מִנְחָה יָשִׁיבוּ
מַלְכֵי שְׁבָא וּסְבָא אֶשְׁכָּר יַקְרִיבוּ׃
וְיִשְׁתַּחֲווּ־לוֹ כָל־מְלָכִים כָּל־גּוֹיִם יַעַבְדוּהוּ׃
כִּי־יַצִּיל אֶבְיוֹן מְשַׁוֵּעַ וְעָנִי וְאֵין־עֹזֵר לוֹ׃
יָחֹס עַל־דַּל וְאֶבְיוֹן וְנַפְשׁוֹת אֶבְיוֹנִים יוֹשִׁיעַ׃
מִתּוֹךְ וּמֵחָמָס יִגְאַל נַפְשָׁם וְיֵיקַר דָּמָם בְּעֵינָיו׃
וִיחִי וְיִתֶּן־לוֹ מִזְּהַב שְׁבָא
וְיִתְפַּלֵּל בַּעֲדוֹ תָמִיד כָּל־הַיּוֹם יְבָרֲכֶנְהוּ׃
יְהִי פִסַּת־בַּר ׀ בָּאָרֶץ בְּרֹאשׁ הָרִים
יִרְעַשׁ כַּלְּבָנוֹן פִּרְיוֹ וְיָצִיצוּ מֵעִיר כְּעֵשֶׂב הָאָרֶץ׃
יְהִי שְׁמוֹ ׀ לְעוֹלָם לִפְנֵי־שֶׁמֶשׁ יִנּוֹן שְׁמוֹ
וְיִתְבָּרְכוּ בוֹ כָּל־גּוֹיִם יְאַשְּׁרֻהוּ׃
בָּרוּךְ ׀ יהוה אֱלֹהִים אֱלֹהֵי יִשְׂרָאֵל
עֹשֵׂה נִפְלָאוֹת לְבַדּוֹ׃
וּבָרוּךְ ׀ שֵׁם כְּבוֹדוֹ לְעוֹלָם
וְיִמָּלֵא כְבוֹדוֹ אֶת־כָּל־הָאָרֶץ אָמֵן ׀ וְאָמֵן׃
כָּלּוּ תְפִלּוֹת דָּוִד בֶּן־יִשָׁי׃

צא יֹשֵׁב בְּסֵתֶר עֶלְיוֹן בְּצֵל שַׁדַּי יִתְלוֹנָן׃
אֹמַר לַיהוה מַחְסִי וּמְצוּדָתִי אֱלֹהַי אֶבְטַח־בּוֹ׃
כִּי הוּא יַצִּילְךָ מִפַּח יָקוּשׁ מִדֶּבֶר הַוּוֹת׃
בְּאֶבְרָתוֹ ׀ יָסֶךְ לָךְ וְתַחַת־כְּנָפָיו תֶּחְסֶה
צִנָּה וְסֹחֵרָה אֲמִתּוֹ׃
לֹא־תִירָא מִפַּחַד לָיְלָה מֵחֵץ יָעוּף יוֹמָם׃

the plague that stalks in the darkness, or the pestilence that ravages at noon.
A thousand may fall at your side, ten thousand at your right hand; but you it will not reach.
You have but to look around and see the punishment of the wicked.
Because you [have said:] "The LORD is my refuge"; because you have made the Most High your dwelling,
no evil shall befall you, no plague shall come near your dwelling.
For He will charge His angels concerning you, to guard you wherever you go.
They will carry you in their hands, lest you strike your foot against a stone.
You will tread on lion and viper. You will trample on young lion and snake.
"Because he desires Me, [says the LORD,] I will deliver him. I will set him on high, for he knows My name.
Let him call to Me, so that I might answer him that I will be with him in time of trouble and so that I might rescue him and honor him.
With length of days I will satisfy him; I will show him My salvation."

104 Bless the LORD, O my soul! LORD, my God, You are very great, You are clothed in glory and majesty.
He wraps Himself with light as with a garment; He has spread out the heavens like a veil.
He has laid the girders of His chambers on the waters;
He makes the clouds His chariot, and speeds along on the wings of the wind.
He makes the winds His messengers, fiery flames His ministers.
He established the earth on its foundations, so that it shall never be moved.
You covered it with the deep like a cloak; the waters stood above the mountains.
But at Your rebuke they fled, at the sound of Your thunders they rushed away, rising over the hills, flowing down into the valleys, to the place You appointed for them.
You set a boundary which they were not to pass; never again shall they cover the earth.
He makes springs break out in the valleys, their waters flow between the hills, supplying drink to all the wild beasts; there the wild asses quench their thirst.
Nearby nest the birds of the air; among the branches they sing their song.
He waters the mountains from His lofty chambers;
the earth is sated with the fruit of His work.

מִדֶּבֶר בָּאֹפֶל יַהֲלֹךְ מִקֶּטֶב יָשׁוּד צׇהֳרָיִם:
יִפֹּל מִצִּדְּךָ אֶלֶף וּרְבָבָה מִימִינֶךָ אֵלֶיךָ לֹא יִגָּשׁ:
רַק בְּעֵינֶיךָ תַבִּיט וְשִׁלֻּמַת רְשָׁעִים תִּרְאֶה:
כִּי־אַתָּה יְהוָה מַחְסִי עֶלְיוֹן שַׂמְתָּ מְעוֹנֶךָ:
לֹא־תְאֻנֶּה אֵלֶיךָ רָעָה וְנֶגַע לֹא־יִקְרַב בְּאׇהֳלֶךָ:
כִּי מַלְאָכָיו יְצַוֶּה־לָּךְ לִשְׁמׇרְךָ בְּכׇל־דְּרָכֶיךָ:
עַל־כַּפַּיִם יִשָּׂאוּנְךָ פֶּן־תִּגֹּף בָּאֶבֶן רַגְלֶךָ:
עַל־שַׁחַל וָפֶתֶן תִּדְרֹךְ תִּרְמֹס כְּפִיר וְתַנִּין:
כִּי בִי חָשַׁק וַאֲפַלְּטֵהוּ אֲשַׂגְּבֵהוּ כִּי־יָדַע שְׁמִי:
יִקְרָאֵנִי וְאֶעֱנֵהוּ עִמּוֹ־אָנֹכִי בְצָרָה אֲחַלְּצֵהוּ וַאֲכַבְּדֵהוּ:
אֹרֶךְ יָמִים אַשְׂבִּיעֵהוּ וְאַרְאֵהוּ בִּישׁוּעָתִי:

קד בָּרְכִי נַפְשִׁי אֶת־יְהוָה יְהוָה אֱלֹהַי גָּדַלְתָּ מְּאֹד
הוֹד וְהָדָר לָבָשְׁתָּ:
עֹטֶה־אוֹר כַּשַּׂלְמָה נוֹטֶה שָׁמַיִם כַּיְרִיעָה:
הַמְקָרֶה בַמַּיִם עֲלִיּוֹתָיו
הַשָּׂם־עָבִים רְכוּבוֹ הַמְהַלֵּךְ עַל־כַּנְפֵי־רוּחַ:
עֹשֶׂה מַלְאָכָיו רוּחוֹת מְשָׁרְתָיו אֵשׁ לֹהֵט:
יָסַד־אֶרֶץ עַל־מְכוֹנֶיהָ בַּל־תִּמּוֹט עוֹלָם וָעֶד:
תְּהוֹם כַּלְּבוּשׁ כִּסִּיתוֹ עַל־הָרִים יַעַמְדוּ־מָיִם:
מִן־גַּעֲרָתְךָ יְנוּסוּן מִן־קוֹל רַעַמְךָ יֵחָפֵזוּן:
יַעֲלוּ הָרִים יֵרְדוּ בְקָעוֹת אֶל־מְקוֹם זֶה יָסַדְתָּ לָהֶם:
גְּבוּל־שַׂמְתָּ בַּל־יַעֲבֹרוּן בַּל־יְשׁוּבוּן לְכַסּוֹת הָאָרֶץ:
הַמְשַׁלֵּחַ מַעְיָנִים בַּנְּחָלִים בֵּין הָרִים יְהַלֵּכוּן:
יַשְׁקוּ כׇּל־חַיְתוֹ שָׂדָי יִשְׁבְּרוּ פְרָאִים צְמָאָם:
עֲלֵיהֶם עוֹף־הַשָּׁמַיִם יִשְׁכּוֹן מִבֵּין עֳפָאיִם יִתְּנוּ־קוֹל:
מַשְׁקֶה הָרִים מֵעֲלִיּוֹתָיו
מִפְּרִי מַעֲשֶׂיךָ תִּשְׂבַּע הָאָרֶץ:

He makes grass grow for the cattle, and vegetation for man's needs,
that he may produce bread from the earth,
and wine to cheer the heart of man; oil to make his face shine,
and bread to strengthen man's heart.
The trees of the LORD are well watered, so, too, the cedars of Lebanon which He planted.
There the birds build their nests; the stork has its home on the fir trees.
The high mountains are for the wild goats, the crags are a shelter for the badgers.
He made the moon to mark the seasons; the sun knows the time of its setting.
You bring on darkness and it is night; then all the beasts of the forest are astir.
The young lions roar for their prey, seeking their food from God.
When the sun rises they stalk away, and lie down in their dens.
Then man goes to his work, and to his labor until evening.
How manifold are Your works, LORD! You made them all with wisdom; the earth is full of Your creations.
There is the sea, vast and wide,
teeming with countless creatures, large and small alike.
There ships go to and fro, Leviathan also, which You formed to sport with.
They all look expectantly to You, to give them their food in due season.
When You give it to them, they gather it up; when You open Your hand, they are well satisfied.
When You hide Your face, they are dismayed; when You take away their breath, they perish, and return to dust.
When You send back Your spirit, they are created anew, and You give new life to the earth.
May the glory of the LORD endure forever; may the LORD rejoice in His works!
When He looks at the earth, it trembles; when He touches the mountains, they pour forth smoke.
As long as I live I will sing to the LORD; I will chant praises to my God all my life.
May my meditation be pleasing to Him; I will rejoice in the LORD.
May sinners disappear from the earth, and the wicked exist no more!
Bless the LORD, O my soul. Praise the LORD!

מַצְמִיחַ חָצִיר ׀ לַבְּהֵמָה וְעֵשֶׂב לַעֲבֹדַת הָאָדָם
לְהוֹצִיא לֶחֶם מִן־הָאָרֶץ׃
וְיַיִן ׀ יְשַׂמַּח לְבַב־אֱנוֹשׁ לְהַצְהִיל פָּנִים מִשָּׁמֶן
וְלֶחֶם לְבַב־אֱנוֹשׁ יִסְעָד׃
יִשְׂבְּעוּ עֲצֵי יְהוָה אַרְזֵי לְבָנוֹן אֲשֶׁר נָטָע׃
אֲשֶׁר־שָׁם צִפֳּרִים יְקַנֵּנוּ חֲסִידָה בְּרוֹשִׁים בֵּיתָהּ׃
הָרִים הַגְּבֹהִים לַיְּעֵלִים סְלָעִים מַחְסֶה לַשְׁפַנִּים׃
עָשָׂה יָרֵחַ לְמוֹעֲדִים שֶׁמֶשׁ יָדַע מְבוֹאוֹ׃
תָּשֶׁת־חֹשֶׁךְ וִיהִי לָיְלָה בּוֹ־תִרְמֹשׂ כָּל־חַיְתוֹ־יָעַר׃
הַכְּפִירִים שֹׁאֲגִים לַטָּרֶף וּלְבַקֵּשׁ מֵאֵל אָכְלָם׃
תִּזְרַח הַשֶּׁמֶשׁ יֵאָסֵפוּן וְאֶל־מְעוֹנֹתָם יִרְבָּצוּן׃
יֵצֵא אָדָם לְפָעֳלוֹ וְלַעֲבֹדָתוֹ עֲדֵי־עָרֶב׃
מָה־רַבּוּ מַעֲשֶׂיךָ ׀ יְהוָה כֻּלָּם בְּחָכְמָה עָשִׂיתָ
מָלְאָה הָאָרֶץ קִנְיָנֶךָ׃
זֶה ׀ הַיָּם גָּדוֹל וּרְחַב יָדָיִם
שָׁם־רֶמֶשׂ וְאֵין מִסְפָּר חַיּוֹת קְטַנּוֹת עִם־גְּדֹלוֹת׃
שָׁם אֳנִיּוֹת יְהַלֵּכוּן לִוְיָתָן זֶה־יָצַרְתָּ לְשַׂחֶק־בּוֹ׃
כֻּלָּם אֵלֶיךָ יְשַׂבֵּרוּן לָתֵת אָכְלָם בְּעִתּוֹ׃
תִּתֵּן לָהֶם יִלְקֹטוּן תִּפְתַּח יָדְךָ יִשְׂבְּעוּן טוֹב׃
תַּסְתִּיר פָּנֶיךָ יִבָּהֵלוּן תֹּסֵף רוּחָם יִגְוָעוּן
וְאֶל־עֲפָרָם יְשׁוּבוּן׃
תְּשַׁלַּח רוּחֲךָ יִבָּרֵאוּן וּתְחַדֵּשׁ פְּנֵי אֲדָמָה׃
יְהִי כְבוֹד יְהוָה לְעוֹלָם יִשְׂמַח יְהוָה בְּמַעֲשָׂיו׃
הַמַּבִּיט לָאָרֶץ וַתִּרְעָד יִגַּע בֶּהָרִים וְיֶעֱשָׁנוּ׃
אָשִׁירָה לַיהוָה בְּחַיָּי אֲזַמְּרָה לֵאלֹהַי בְּעוֹדִי׃
יֶעֱרַב עָלָיו שִׂיחִי אָנֹכִי אֶשְׂמַח בַּיהוָה׃
יִתַּמּוּ חַטָּאִים ׀ מִן־הָאָרֶץ וּרְשָׁעִים ׀ עוֹד אֵינָם
בָּרְכִי נַפְשִׁי אֶת־יְהוָה הַלְלוּיָהּ׃

130 A song of Ascents. Out of the depths I call to You, LORD.
LORD, hear my voice; let Your ears be attentive to my plea for mercy.
If You, LORD, should keep account of sins, who could survive?
But with You there is forgiveness; therefore You are feared.
I wait for the LORD; my soul waits; hopefully I wait for His word.
My soul waits for the LORD more eagerly than watchmen for the morning; yes, more than watchmen for the morning.
O Israel, put your hope in the LORD; for with the LORD there is loving-kindness, and with Him there is great power to redeem.
He Himself will redeem Israel from all their sins.

After reciting the initial seven psalms above, it is customary to spell out the name of the deceased by reciting the verses of Psalm 119 that correspond to the letters of the name.

ALEF

119 Happy are they whose way is blameless, who follow the Torah of the LORD.
Happy are they who keep His decrees, who seek Him with all their heart; who have done no wrong, but walk in His ways.
You have commanded that Your precepts must be diligently kept.
How I wish that my ways were steadfast in keeping Your statutes!
Then I would never be put to shame when I regard all Your commandments.
I will praise You with a sincere heart as I learn Your just laws.
I mean to observe Your statutes; do not utterly forsake me.

BEIT

How can a young man keep his way pure? By holding to Your word.
I seek You with all my heart; do not let me stray from Your commandments.
In my heart I treasure Your promise, for fear that I might sin against You.
Blessed are You, LORD; teach me Your statutes.
With my lips I repeat all the laws You have stated.
I rejoice in following Your decrees, as one rejoices over great wealth.
I meditate on Your precepts, and regard Your paths.
I delight in Your statutes; I will not forget Your word.

קל שִׁיר הַמַּעֲלוֹת מִמַּעֲמַקִּים קְרָאתִיךָ יְהוָה:
אֲדֹנָי שִׁמְעָה בְקוֹלִי תִּהְיֶינָה אָזְנֶיךָ קַשֻּׁבוֹת לְקוֹל תַּחֲנוּנָי:
אִם־עֲוֺנוֹת תִּשְׁמָר־יָהּ אֲדֹנָי מִי יַעֲמֹד:
כִּי־עִמְּךָ הַסְּלִיחָה לְמַעַן תִּוָּרֵא:
קִוִּיתִי יהוה קִוְּתָה נַפְשִׁי וְלִדְבָרוֹ הוֹחָלְתִּי:
נַפְשִׁי לַאדֹנָי מִשֹּׁמְרִים לַבֹּקֶר שֹׁמְרִים לַבֹּקֶר:
יַחֵל יִשְׂרָאֵל אֶל־יְהוָה כִּי־עִם־יְהוָה הַחֶסֶד וְהַרְבֵּה עִמּוֹ פְדוּת:
וְהוּא יִפְדֶּה אֶת־יִשְׂרָאֵל מִכֹּל עֲוֺנֹתָיו:

After reciting the initial seven psalms above, it is customary to spell out the name of the deceased by reciting the verses of מזמור קיט *that correspond to the letters of the name.*

א

קיט אַשְׁרֵי תְמִימֵי־דָרֶךְ הַהֹלְכִים בְּתוֹרַת יְהוָה:
אַשְׁרֵי נֹצְרֵי עֵדֹתָיו בְּכָל־לֵב יִדְרְשׁוּהוּ:
אַף לֹא־פָעֲלוּ עַוְלָה בִּדְרָכָיו הָלָכוּ:
אַתָּה צִוִּיתָה פִקֻּדֶיךָ לִשְׁמֹר מְאֹד:
אַחֲלַי יִכֹּנוּ דְרָכָי לִשְׁמֹר חֻקֶּיךָ:
אָז לֹא־אֵבוֹשׁ בְּהַבִּיטִי אֶל־כָּל־מִצְוֺתֶיךָ:
אוֹדְךָ בְּיֹשֶׁר לֵבָב בְּלָמְדִי מִשְׁפְּטֵי צִדְקֶךָ:
אֶת־חֻקֶּיךָ אֶשְׁמֹר אַל־תַּעַזְבֵנִי עַד־מְאֹד:

ב

בַּמֶּה יְזַכֶּה־נַּעַר אֶת־אָרְחוֹ לִשְׁמֹר כִּדְבָרֶךָ:
בְּכָל־לִבִּי דְרַשְׁתִּיךָ אַל־תַּשְׁגֵּנִי מִמִּצְוֺתֶיךָ:
בְּלִבִּי צָפַנְתִּי אִמְרָתֶךָ לְמַעַן לֹא אֶחֱטָא־לָךְ:
בָּרוּךְ אַתָּה יְהוָה לַמְּדֵנִי חֻקֶּיךָ:
בִּשְׂפָתַי סִפַּרְתִּי כֹּל מִשְׁפְּטֵי־פִיךָ:
בְּדֶרֶךְ עֵדְוֺתֶיךָ שַׂשְׂתִּי כְּעַל כָּל־הוֹן:
בְּפִקֻּדֶיךָ אָשִׂיחָה וְאַבִּיטָה אֹרְחֹתֶיךָ:
בְּחֻקֹּתֶיךָ אֶשְׁתַּעֲשָׁע לֹא אֶשְׁכַּח דְּבָרֶךָ:

GIMMEL

Deal kindly with Your servant, that I may live and keep Your word.
Unveil my eyes that I may behold the wonders of Your Torah.
I am a passing stranger on earth; do not hide Your commandments from me.
My heart is breaking with longing for Your laws at all times.
You rebuke the accursed proud who stray from Your commandments.
Remove from me scorn and contempt, for I keep Your decrees.
Though princes sit together and scheme against me, Your servant studies Your statutes.
For Your decrees are my delight; they are my counselors.

DALET

My soul clings to the dust; revive me according to Your word.
I confessed my ways, and You answered me; teach me Your statutes.
Make me understand the way of Your precepts, and I will meditate on Your wonders.
My soul weeps with grief; raise my spirits according to Your word.
Remove from me the way of falsehood; favor me with Your Torah.
I have chosen the way of truth; I have set Your judgments before me.
I cling to Your decrees; LORD, do not put me to shame.
I eagerly pursue the way of Your commandments, for You free my heart [from anxiety].

HEH

Teach me, LORD, the way of Your statutes, and I will observe them meticulously.
Give me understanding that I may observe Your Torah, and keep it with all my heart.
Guide me in the path of Your commandments, for that is my sole delight.
Incline my heart toward Your decrees, and not toward love of gain.
Turn my eyes away from worthless things; grant me life to follow in Your way.
Fulfill for Your servant the promise which [You made] to those who fear You.
Remove the reproach which I dread, for Your judgments are good.
See, how I long for Your precepts! By Your righteousness grant me life.

ג

גְּמֹל עַל־עַבְדְּךָ אֶחְיֶה וְאֶשְׁמְרָה דְבָרֶךָ׃
גַּל־עֵינַי וְאַבִּיטָה נִפְלָאוֹת מִתּוֹרָתֶךָ׃
גֵּר אָנֹכִי בָאָרֶץ אַל־תַּסְתֵּר מִמֶּנִּי מִצְוֺתֶיךָ׃
גָּרְסָה נַפְשִׁי לְתַאֲבָה אֶל־מִשְׁפָּטֶיךָ בְכָל־עֵת׃
גָּעַרְתָּ זֵדִים אֲרוּרִים הַשֹּׁגִים מִמִּצְוֺתֶיךָ׃
גַּל מֵעָלַי חֶרְפָּה וָבוּז כִּי עֵדֹתֶיךָ נָצָרְתִּי׃
גַּם יָשְׁבוּ שָׂרִים בִּי נִדְבָּרוּ עַבְדְּךָ יָשִׂיחַ בְּחֻקֶּיךָ׃
גַּם־עֵדֹתֶיךָ שַׁעֲשֻׁעָי אַנְשֵׁי עֲצָתִי׃

ד

דָּבְקָה לֶעָפָר נַפְשִׁי חַיֵּנִי כִּדְבָרֶךָ׃
דְּרָכַי סִפַּרְתִּי וַתַּעֲנֵנִי לַמְּדֵנִי חֻקֶּיךָ׃
דֶּרֶךְ־פִּקּוּדֶיךָ הֲבִינֵנִי וְאָשִׂיחָה בְּנִפְלְאוֹתֶיךָ׃
דָּלְפָה נַפְשִׁי מִתּוּגָה קַיְּמֵנִי כִּדְבָרֶךָ׃
דֶּרֶךְ־שֶׁקֶר הָסֵר מִמֶּנִּי וְתוֹרָתְךָ חָנֵּנִי׃
דֶּרֶךְ־אֱמוּנָה בָחָרְתִּי מִשְׁפָּטֶיךָ שִׁוִּיתִי׃
דָּבַקְתִּי בְעֵדְוֺתֶיךָ יהוה אַל־תְּבִישֵׁנִי׃
דֶּרֶךְ־מִצְוֺתֶיךָ אָרוּץ כִּי תַרְחִיב לִבִּי׃

ה

הוֹרֵנִי יהוה דֶּרֶךְ חֻקֶּיךָ וְאֶצְּרֶנָּה עֵקֶב׃
הֲבִינֵנִי וְאֶצְּרָה תוֹרָתֶךָ וְאֶשְׁמְרֶנָּה בְכָל־לֵב׃
הַדְרִיכֵנִי בִּנְתִיב מִצְוֺתֶיךָ כִּי־בוֹ חָפָצְתִּי׃
הַט־לִבִּי אֶל־עֵדְוֺתֶיךָ וְאַל אֶל־בָּצַע׃
הַעֲבֵר עֵינַי מֵרְאוֹת שָׁוְא בִּדְרָכֶךָ חַיֵּנִי׃
הָקֵם לְעַבְדְּךָ אִמְרָתֶךָ אֲשֶׁר לְיִרְאָתֶךָ׃
הַעֲבֵר חֶרְפָּתִי אֲשֶׁר יָגֹרְתִּי כִּי מִשְׁפָּטֶיךָ טוֹבִים׃
הִנֵּה תָּאַבְתִּי לְפִקֻּדֶיךָ בְּצִדְקָתְךָ חַיֵּנִי׃

VAV

May Your loving-kindness come to me, LORD, and Your deliverance, as You have promised.
Then I shall have an answer for him who reviles me; for I trust in Your word.
Do not utterly take away the true word from my mouth; for I put my hope in Your just rulings.
I will always obey Your Torah, forever and ever.
I will walk about in all freedom, because I seek Your precepts.
I will speak of Your decrees before kings, and shall not be ashamed.
I find delight in Your commandments, because I love them.
I reach out my hands for Your commandments which I love, and meditate on Your statutes.

ZAYIN

Remember the word [You spoke] to Your servant, by which You have given me hope.
This is my comfort in my suffering: that Your promise gives me life.
Though the arrogant bitterly mock me, I do not swerve from Your Torah.
I remember Your judgments of old, LORD, and am comforted by them.
Burning indignation grips me because of the wicked who forsake Your Torah.
Your statutes are the theme of my song wherever I sojourn.
In the night I remember Your name, LORD, and I dwell upon Your Torah.
This has been my merit, that I always kept Your precepts.

ḤET

[You are] my portion, LORD; so I promise to obey Your words.
I implore You with all my heart; have pity on me according to Your promise.
I have considered my ways, and have turned my steps to Your decrees.
I hasten, and never delay, to keep Your commandments.
Bands of wicked men prey on me, but I do not forget Your Torah.
At midnight I rise to praise You for Your righteous judgments.
I am a friend to all who fear You, to all who observe Your precepts.
The earth is filled with Your loving-kindness, LORD; teach me Your statutes.

ו

וִיבֹאֻנִי חֲסָדֶךָ יְהֹוָה תְּשׁוּעָתְךָ כְּאִמְרָתֶךָ׃
וְאֶעֱנֶה חֹרְפִי דָבָר כִּי־בָטַחְתִּי בִּדְבָרֶךָ׃
וְאַל־תַּצֵּל מִפִּי דְבַר־אֱמֶת עַד־מְאֹד כִּי לְמִשְׁפָּטֶךָ יִחָלְתִּי׃
וְאֶשְׁמְרָה תוֹרָתְךָ תָמִיד לְעוֹלָם וָעֶד׃
וְאֶתְהַלְּכָה בָרְחָבָה כִּי פִקֻּדֶיךָ דָרָשְׁתִּי׃
וַאֲדַבְּרָה בְעֵדֹתֶיךָ נֶגֶד מְלָכִים וְלֹא אֵבוֹשׁ׃
וְאֶשְׁתַּעֲשַׁע בְּמִצְוֺתֶיךָ אֲשֶׁר אָהָבְתִּי׃
וְאֶשָּׂא־כַפַּי אֶל־מִצְוֺתֶיךָ אֲשֶׁר אָהָבְתִּי וְאָשִׂיחָה בְחֻקֶּיךָ׃

ז

זְכֹר־דָּבָר לְעַבְדֶּךָ עַל אֲשֶׁר יִחַלְתָּנִי׃
זֹאת נֶחָמָתִי בְעָנְיִי כִּי אִמְרָתְךָ חִיָּתְנִי׃
זֵדִים הֱלִיצֻנִי עַד־מְאֹד מִתּוֹרָתְךָ לֹא נָטִיתִי׃
זָכַרְתִּי מִשְׁפָּטֶיךָ מֵעוֹלָם ׀ יְהֹוָה וָאֶתְנֶחָם׃
זַלְעָפָה אֲחָזַתְנִי מֵרְשָׁעִים עֹזְבֵי תּוֹרָתֶךָ׃
זְמִרוֹת הָיוּ־לִי חֻקֶּיךָ בְּבֵית מְגוּרָי׃
זָכַרְתִּי בַלַּיְלָה שִׁמְךָ יְהֹוָה וָאֶשְׁמְרָה תּוֹרָתֶךָ׃
זֹאת הָיְתָה־לִּי כִּי פִקֻּדֶיךָ נָצָרְתִּי׃

ח

חֶלְקִי יְהֹוָה אָמַרְתִּי לִשְׁמֹר דְּבָרֶיךָ׃
חִלִּיתִי פָנֶיךָ בְכָל־לֵב חָנֵּנִי כְּאִמְרָתֶךָ׃
חִשַּׁבְתִּי דְרָכָי וָאָשִׁיבָה רַגְלַי אֶל־עֵדֹתֶיךָ׃
חַשְׁתִּי וְלֹא הִתְמַהְמָהְתִּי לִשְׁמֹר מִצְוֺתֶיךָ׃
חֶבְלֵי רְשָׁעִים עִוְּדֻנִי תּוֹרָתְךָ לֹא שָׁכָחְתִּי׃
חֲצוֹת־לַיְלָה אָקוּם לְהוֹדוֹת לָךְ עַל מִשְׁפְּטֵי צִדְקֶךָ׃
חָבֵר אָנִי לְכָל־אֲשֶׁר יְרֵאוּךָ וּלְשֹׁמְרֵי פִּקּוּדֶיךָ׃
חַסְדְּךָ יְהֹוָה מָלְאָה הָאָרֶץ חֻקֶּיךָ לַמְּדֵנִי׃

TET

Do good to Your servant, LORD, according to Your word.
Teach me good sense and knowledge, because I believe in Your commandments.
Before I applied myself [to the Torah] I went astray, but now I heed Your bidding.
You are good, and what You do is good; teach me Your statutes.
Though proud men besmear me with lies, I observe Your precepts with all my heart.
Their heart is gross like fat; but as for me, Your Torah is my delight.
It was good for me that I was afflicted, so that I might learn Your statutes.
More precious to me is the Torah You proclaimed than thousands of gold and silver pieces.

YOD

Your hands made me and formed me; give me understanding that I may learn Your commandments.
Those who fear You will see me and rejoice, for I put my hope in Your word.
I know, LORD, that Your judgments are just, and in faithfulness You have afflicted me.
O let Your loving-kindness comfort me, in accordance with Your promise to Your servant.
May Your mercies come to me that I may live, for Your Torah is my delight.
May the proud be ashamed, for they wrong me with lies; but I will meditate on Your precepts.
May those who fear You turn to me, those who know Your decrees.
May my heart be blameless toward Your statutes; then I shall never be put to shame!

KAF

My soul yearns for Your deliverance; I have put my hope in Your word.
My eyes fail awaiting Your promise; I say, "When will You comfort me?"
Though I have become [shriveled] like a wine-skin in the smoke, I have not forgotten Your statutes.
How many are the days of Your servant? When will You execute judgment on my persecutors?
The proud have dug pits for me, in defiance of Your Torah.
All Your commandments are true; men persecute me without cause; help me!
They had almost swept me off the earth, but I would not abandon Your precepts.
By Your kindness grant me life, that I may keep the decree that You uttered.

ט

ט֭וֹב עָשִׂ֣יתָ עִֽם־עַבְדְּךָ֑ יְ֝הוה כִּדְבָרֶֽךָ׃
ט֤וּב טַ֣עַם וָדַ֣עַת לַמְּדֵ֑נִי כִּ֖י בְמִצְוֺתֶ֣יךָ הֶאֱמָֽנְתִּי׃
טֶ֣רֶם אֶ֭עֱנֶה אֲנִ֣י שֹׁגֵ֑ג וְ֝עַתָּ֗ה אִמְרָתְךָ֥ שָׁמָֽרְתִּי׃
טוֹב־אַתָּ֥ה וּמֵטִ֗יב לַמְּדֵ֥נִי חֻקֶּֽיךָ׃
טָֽפְל֘וּ עָלַ֣י שֶׁ֣קֶר זֵדִ֑ים אֲ֝נִ֗י בְּכׇל־לֵ֤ב ׀ אֶצֹּ֬ר פִּקּוּדֶֽיךָ׃
טָפַ֣שׁ כַּחֵ֣לֶב לִבָּ֑ם אֲ֝נִ֗י תּוֹרָתְךָ֥ שִׁעֲשָֽׁעְתִּי׃
טוֹב־לִ֥י כִֽי־עֻנֵּ֑יתִי לְ֝מַ֗עַן אֶלְמַ֥ד חֻקֶּֽיךָ׃
טוֹב־לִ֥י תֽוֹרַת־פִּ֑יךָ מֵ֝אַלְפֵ֗י זָהָ֥ב וָכָֽסֶף׃

י

יָדֶ֣יךָ עָ֭שׂוּנִי וַיְכוֹנְנ֑וּנִי הֲ֝בִינֵ֗נִי וְאֶלְמְדָ֥ה מִצְוֺתֶֽיךָ׃
יְ֭רֵאֶיךָ יִרְא֣וּנִי וְיִשְׂמָ֑חוּ כִּ֖י לִדְבָרְךָ֣ יִחָֽלְתִּי׃
יָדַ֣עְתִּי יְ֭הוה כִּי־צֶ֣דֶק מִשְׁפָּטֶ֑יךָ וֶ֝אֱמ֗וּנָה עִנִּיתָֽנִי׃
יְהִי־נָ֣א חַסְדְּךָ֣ לְנַחֲמֵ֑נִי כְּאִמְרָתְךָ֥ לְעַבְדֶּֽךָ׃
יְבֹא֣וּנִי רַחֲמֶ֣יךָ וְאֶֽחְיֶ֑ה כִּֽי־ת֝וֹרָתְךָ֗ שַׁעֲשֻׁעָֽי׃
יֵבֹ֣שׁוּ זֵ֭דִים כִּי־שֶׁ֣קֶר עִוְּת֑וּנִי אֲ֝נִ֗י אָשִׂ֥יחַ בְּפִקּוּדֶֽיךָ׃
יָשׁ֣וּבוּ לִ֣י יְרֵאֶ֑יךָ וְ֝יֹדְעֵ֗י עֵדֹתֶֽיךָ׃
יְהִֽי־לִבִּ֣י תָמִ֣ים בְּחֻקֶּ֑יךָ לְ֝מַ֗עַן לֹ֣א אֵבֽוֹשׁ׃

כ

כָּלְתָ֣ה לִתְשׁוּעָתְךָ֣ נַפְשִׁ֑י לִדְבָרְךָ֥ יִחָֽלְתִּי׃
כָּל֣וּ עֵ֭ינַי לְאִמְרָתֶ֑ךָ לֵ֝אמֹ֗ר מָתַ֥י תְּנַחֲמֵֽנִי׃
כִּֽי־הָ֭יִיתִי כְּנֹ֣אד בְּקִיט֑וֹר חֻ֝קֶּ֗יךָ לֹ֣א שָׁכָֽחְתִּי׃
כַּמָּ֥ה יְמֵֽי־עַבְדֶּ֑ךָ מָתַ֘י תַּעֲשֶׂ֖ה בְרֹדְפַ֣י מִשְׁפָּֽט׃
כָּֽרוּ־לִ֣י זֵדִ֣ים שִׁיח֑וֹת אֲ֝שֶׁ֗ר לֹ֣א כְתוֹרָתֶֽךָ׃
כׇּל־מִצְוֺתֶ֥יךָ אֱמוּנָ֑ה שֶׁ֖קֶר רְדָפ֣וּנִי עׇזְרֵֽנִי׃
כִּ֭מְעַט כִּלּ֣וּנִי בָאָ֑רֶץ וַ֝אֲנִ֗י לֹא־עָזַ֥בְתִּי פִקֻּדֶֽיךָ׃
כְּחַסְדְּךָ֥ חַיֵּ֑נִי וְ֝אֶשְׁמְרָ֗ה עֵד֥וּת פִּֽיךָ׃

LAMED

You, Lord, are eternal, Your word stands firm in the heavens;
Your faithfulness endures for all generations; You established the earth and it stands.
They stand today according to Your ordinances. for all things are Your servants.
Had Your Torah not been my delight, I should have perished in my affliction.
Never shall I forget Your precepts, for by them You have given me life.
I am Yours; save me! for I have sought Your precepts.
The wicked lie in wait to destroy me, but I ponder Your decrees.
I have seen that everything, however perfect, has a limit, but Your commandment is wide beyond measure.

MEM

O how I love Your Torah! I meditate on it all day long.
Your commandments make me wiser than my enemies, for they are ever with me.
I have gained more insight than all my teachers, for Your decrees are my study.
I have more understanding than the aged, for I keep Your precepts.
I restrain my feet from every evil path, so that I may keep Your word.
I have not departed from Your ordinances, for You Yourself have taught me.
How sweet to my palate are Your words, sweeter than honey to my mouth!
I gain wisdom from Your precepts, therefore I hate every false way.

NUN

Your word is a lamp to my feet and a light for my path.
I have sworn – and I will keep my oath – to observe Your just regulations.
I am sorely afflicted; Lord, preserve my life according to Your word.
Accept, Lord, the willing offerings of my mouth, and teach me Your ordinances.
Though my life is in constant danger, yet I never forget Your Torah.
Evil men have set a trap for me, yet I do not stray from Your precepts.
Your decrees are my everlasting heritage; for they are the joy of my heart.
I have resolved to carry out Your statutes; the reward is eternal.

ל

לְעוֹלָם יְהוָה דְּבָרְךָ נִצָּב בַּשָּׁמָיִם:
לְדֹר וָדֹר אֱמוּנָתֶךָ כּוֹנַנְתָּ אֶרֶץ וַתַּעֲמֹד:
לְמִשְׁפָּטֶיךָ עָמְדוּ הַיּוֹם כִּי הַכֹּל עֲבָדֶיךָ:
לוּלֵי תוֹרָתְךָ שַׁעֲשֻׁעָי אָז אָבַדְתִּי בְעָנְיִי:
לְעוֹלָם לֹא־אֶשְׁכַּח פִּקּוּדֶיךָ כִּי־בָם חִיִּיתָנִי:
לְךָ־אֲנִי הוֹשִׁיעֵנִי כִּי פִקּוּדֶיךָ דָרָשְׁתִּי:
לִי קִוּוּ רְשָׁעִים לְאַבְּדֵנִי עֵדֹתֶיךָ אֶתְבּוֹנָן:
לְכָל־תִּכְלָה רָאִיתִי קֵץ רְחָבָה מִצְוָתְךָ מְאֹד:

מ

מָה־אָהַבְתִּי תוֹרָתֶךָ כָּל־הַיּוֹם הִיא שִׂיחָתִי:
מֵאֹיְבַי תְּחַכְּמֵנִי מִצְוֺתֶךָ כִּי לְעוֹלָם הִיא־לִי:
מִכָּל־מְלַמְּדַי הִשְׂכַּלְתִּי כִּי עֵדְוֺתֶיךָ שִׂיחָה לִי:
מִזְּקֵנִים אֶתְבּוֹנָן כִּי פִקּוּדֶיךָ נָצָרְתִּי:
מִכָּל־אֹרַח רָע כָּלִאתִי רַגְלָי לְמַעַן אֶשְׁמֹר דְּבָרֶךָ:
מִמִּשְׁפָּטֶיךָ לֹא־סָרְתִּי כִּי־אַתָּה הוֹרֵתָנִי:
מַה־נִּמְלְצוּ לְחִכִּי אִמְרָתֶךָ מִדְּבַשׁ לְפִי:
מִפִּקּוּדֶיךָ אֶתְבּוֹנָן עַל־כֵּן שָׂנֵאתִי ׀ כָּל־אֹרַח שָׁקֶר:

נ

נֵר־לְרַגְלִי דְבָרֶךָ וְאוֹר לִנְתִיבָתִי:
נִשְׁבַּעְתִּי וָאֲקַיֵּמָה לִשְׁמֹר מִשְׁפְּטֵי צִדְקֶךָ:
נַעֲנֵיתִי עַד־מְאֹד יְהוָה חַיֵּנִי כִדְבָרֶךָ:
נִדְבוֹת פִּי רְצֵה־נָא יְהוָה וּמִשְׁפָּטֶיךָ לַמְּדֵנִי:
נַפְשִׁי בְכַפִּי תָמִיד וְתוֹרָתְךָ לֹא שָׁכָחְתִּי:
נָתְנוּ רְשָׁעִים פַּח לִי וּמִפִּקּוּדֶיךָ לֹא תָעִיתִי:
נָחַלְתִּי עֵדְוֺתֶיךָ לְעוֹלָם כִּי־שְׂשׂוֹן לִבִּי הֵמָּה:
נָטִיתִי לִבִּי לַעֲשׂוֹת חֻקֶּיךָ לְעוֹלָם עֵקֶב:

SAMEKH

I hate skeptics, but I love Your Torah.
You are my shelter and my shield; I await the fulfillment of Your word.
Away from me, you evildoers, that I may keep the commandments of my God.
Support me as You have promised, that I may live; do not disappoint my hope.
Sustain me that I may be saved, and I shall always occupy myself with Your statutes.
You reject all who stray from Your statutes; for their scheming is in vain.
You discard as dross all the wicked of the earth; therefore I love Your decrees.
My flesh creeps from dread of You; I stand in awe of Your ordinances.

AYIN

I have done what is just and right; do not abandon me to my oppressors.
Assure the well-being of Your servant; do not let the proud oppress me.
My eyes languish for Your deliverance, and for Your righteous promise.
Deal with Your servant according to Your true loving-kindness; teach me Your statutes.
I am Your servant; give me insight, that I may know Your decrees.
It is a time for the LORD to act; for they have violated Your Torah.
Truly I love Your commandments more than gold, even the finest gold.
Truly I consider all Your precepts right in all matters; I hate every false way.

PEH

Your decrees are wonderful; that is why I keep them.
Your opening words shed light; they give understanding to the simple.
I open wide my mouth, I pant, longing for Your commandments.
Turn to me and be gracious to me, as You always do to those who love Your name.
Direct my footsteps according to Your word; let no iniquity dominate me.
Redeem me from the oppression of men, that I may keep Your precepts.
Let Your face shine upon Your servant, and teach me Your statutes.
My eyes stream with tears because men do not obey Your Torah.

ס

סֵעֲפִים שָׂנֵאתִי וְתוֹרָתְךָ אָהָבְתִּי׃
סִתְרִי וּמָגִנִּי אָתָּה לִדְבָרְךָ יִחָלְתִּי׃
סוּרוּ מִמֶּנִּי מְרֵעִים וְאֶצְּרָה מִצְוֺת אֱלֹהָי׃
סָמְכֵנִי כְאִמְרָתְךָ וְאֶחְיֶה וְאַל־תְּבִישֵׁנִי מִשִּׂבְרִי׃
סְעָדֵנִי וְאִוָּשֵׁעָה וְאֶשְׁעָה בְחֻקֶּיךָ תָמִיד׃
סָלִיתָ כָּל־שׁוֹגִים מֵחֻקֶּיךָ כִּי־שֶׁקֶר תַּרְמִיתָם׃
סִגִים הִשְׁבַּתָּ כָל־רִשְׁעֵי־אָרֶץ לָכֵן אָהַבְתִּי עֵדֹתֶיךָ׃
סָמַר מִפַּחְדְּךָ בְשָׂרִי וּמִמִּשְׁפָּטֶיךָ יָרֵאתִי׃

ע

עָשִׂיתִי מִשְׁפָּט וָצֶדֶק בַּל־תַּנִּיחֵנִי לְעֹשְׁקָי׃
עֲרֹב עַבְדְּךָ לְטוֹב אַל־יַעַשְׁקֻנִי זֵדִים׃
עֵינַי כָּלוּ לִישׁוּעָתֶךָ וּלְאִמְרַת צִדְקֶךָ׃
עֲשֵׂה עִם־עַבְדְּךָ כְחַסְדֶּךָ וְחֻקֶּיךָ לַמְּדֵנִי׃
עַבְדְּךָ־אָנִי הֲבִינֵנִי וְאֵדְעָה עֵדֹתֶיךָ׃
עֵת לַעֲשׂוֹת לַיהוָה הֵפֵרוּ תּוֹרָתֶךָ׃
עַל־כֵּן אָהַבְתִּי מִצְוֺתֶיךָ מִזָּהָב וּמִפָּז׃
עַל־כֵּן ׀ כָּל־פִּקּוּדֵי כֹל יִשָּׁרְתִּי כָּל־אֹרַח שֶׁקֶר שָׂנֵאתִי׃

פ

פְּלָאוֹת עֵדְוֺתֶיךָ עַל־כֵּן נְצָרָתַם נַפְשִׁי׃
פֵּתַח־דְּבָרֶיךָ יָאִיר מֵבִין פְּתָיִים׃
פִּי־פָעַרְתִּי וָאֶשְׁאָפָה כִּי לְמִצְוֺתֶיךָ יָאָבְתִּי׃
פְּנֵה־אֵלַי וְחָנֵּנִי כְּמִשְׁפָּט לְאֹהֲבֵי שְׁמֶךָ׃
פְּעָמַי הָכֵן בְּאִמְרָתֶךָ וְאַל־תַּשְׁלֶט־בִּי כָל־אָוֶן׃
פְּדֵנִי מֵעֹשֶׁק אָדָם וְאֶשְׁמְרָה פִּקּוּדֶיךָ׃
פָּנֶיךָ הָאֵר בְּעַבְדֶּךָ וְלַמְּדֵנִי אֶת־חֻקֶּיךָ׃
פַּלְגֵי־מַיִם יָרְדוּ עֵינָי עַל לֹא־שָׁמְרוּ תוֹרָתֶךָ׃

TZADI

You are righteous, Lord, and Your judgments are just.
You have imposed Your decrees with fairness; they are fully trustworthy.
My zeal devastates me because my enemies ignore Your words.
Your word is well tested, and Your servant cherishes it.
I may be of little account and despised, but I do not forget Your precepts.
Your righteousness is an everlasting righteousness; Your Torah is truth.
Though distress and anxiety have overtaken me, Your commandments are still my delight.
Your decrees are ever just; give me understanding that I may live.

KUF

I call with all my heart; answer me, Lord, that I may keep Your statutes.
I call out to You: save me, that I may keep Your decrees.
I rise before dawn and cry for help; I await the fulfillment of Your word.
My eyes stay open through the watches of the night, to meditate on Your word.
Hear my voice in accordance with Your constant loving-kindness; grant me life, Lord, as is Your rule.
My malicious pursuers are coming closer, they are far from Your Torah.
Yet You are near, Lord, and all Your commandments are true.
I have long known from Your decrees that You have established them forever.

REISH

See my affliction and deliver me, for I have not forgotten Your Torah.
Defend my cause and redeem me; grant me life according to Your promise.
Deliverance is far from the wicked, for they do not seek Your statutes.
Great is Your compassion, Lord; grant me life, as is Your rule.
Though my persecutors and foes are many, I have not swerved from Your decrees.
When I see faithless men, I am disgusted, because they do not keep Your word.
See how I love Your precepts; grant me life, Lord, according to Your loving-kindness.
The essence of Your word is truth; all Your righteous laws are eternal.

צ

צַדִּיק אַתָּה יהוה וְיָשָׁר מִשְׁפָּטֶיךָ:
צִוִּיתָ צֶדֶק עֵדֹתֶיךָ וֶאֱמוּנָה מְאֹד:
צִמְּתַתְנִי קִנְאָתִי כִּי־שָׁכְחוּ דְבָרֶיךָ צָרָי:
צְרוּפָה אִמְרָתְךָ מְאֹד וְעַבְדְּךָ אֲהֵבָהּ:
צָעִיר אָנֹכִי וְנִבְזֶה פִּקֻּדֶיךָ לֹא שָׁכָחְתִּי:
צִדְקָתְךָ צֶדֶק לְעוֹלָם וְתוֹרָתְךָ אֱמֶת:
צַר־וּמָצוֹק מְצָאוּנִי מִצְוֹתֶיךָ שַׁעֲשֻׁעָי:
צֶדֶק עֵדְוֺתֶיךָ לְעוֹלָם הֲבִינֵנִי וְאֶחְיֶה:

ק

קָרָאתִי בְכָל־לֵב עֲנֵנִי יהוה חֻקֶּיךָ אֶצֹּרָה:
קְרָאתִיךָ הוֹשִׁיעֵנִי וְאֶשְׁמְרָה עֵדֹתֶיךָ:
קִדַּמְתִּי בַנֶּשֶׁף וָאֲשַׁוֵּעָה לִדְבָרְךָ יִחָלְתִּי:
קִדְּמוּ עֵינַי אַשְׁמֻרוֹת לָשִׂיחַ בְּאִמְרָתֶךָ:
קוֹלִי שִׁמְעָה כְחַסְדֶּךָ יהוה כְּמִשְׁפָּטֶךָ חַיֵּנִי:
קָרְבוּ רֹדְפֵי זִמָּה מִתּוֹרָתְךָ רָחָקוּ:
קָרוֹב אַתָּה יהוה וְכָל־מִצְוֹתֶיךָ אֱמֶת:
קֶדֶם יָדַעְתִּי מֵעֵדֹתֶיךָ כִּי לְעוֹלָם יְסַדְתָּם:

ר

רְאֵה־עָנְיִי וְחַלְּצֵנִי כִּי־תוֹרָתְךָ לֹא שָׁכָחְתִּי:
רִיבָה רִיבִי וּגְאָלֵנִי לְאִמְרָתְךָ חַיֵּנִי:
רָחוֹק מֵרְשָׁעִים יְשׁוּעָה כִּי־חֻקֶּיךָ לֹא דָרָשׁוּ:
רַחֲמֶיךָ רַבִּים ׀ יהוה כְּמִשְׁפָּטֶיךָ חַיֵּנִי:
רַבִּים רֹדְפַי וְצָרָי מֵעֵדְוֺתֶיךָ לֹא נָטִיתִי:
רָאִיתִי בֹגְדִים וָאֶתְקוֹטָטָה אֲשֶׁר אִמְרָתְךָ לֹא שָׁמָרוּ:
רְאֵה כִּי־פִקּוּדֶיךָ אָהָבְתִּי יהוה כְּחַסְדְּךָ חַיֵּנִי:
רֹאשׁ־דְּבָרְךָ אֱמֶת וּלְעוֹלָם כָּל־מִשְׁפַּט צִדְקֶךָ:

SHIN

Princes persecute me without cause, yet my heart fears only for Your word.
I rejoice over Your promise like one who finds much spoil.
I hate falsehood, I loathe it, but I love Your Torah.
Seven times each day I praise You for Your just rulings.
Great peace have they who love Your Torah; there is no stumbling for them.
I wait for Your deliverance, LORD, and I fulfill Your commandments.
My soul heeds Your decrees, for I love them dearly.
I observe Your precepts and Your decrees, for all my ways are before You.

TAV

Let my cry come before You, LORD; give me understanding as You have promised.
Let my entreaty reach You; save me according to Your promise.
My lips shall pour forth praise, because You teach me Your statutes.
My tongue shall sing of Your promise, for all Your commandments are righteous.
May Your hand be ready to help me, for I have chosen Your precepts.
I long for Your deliverance, LORD; Your Torah is my delight.
Let me live to praise You; may Your judgments help me.
I have strayed like a lost sheep; come and seek Your servant, for I have not forgotten Your commandments.

The following are the verses of Psalm 119 that spell out the word נשמה ("soul").

NUN

Your word is a lamp to my feet and a light for my path.
I have sworn – and I will keep my oath – to observe Your just regulations.
I am sorely afflicted; LORD, preserve my life according to Your word.
Accept, LORD, the willing offerings of my mouth, and teach me Your ordinances.
Though my life is in constant danger, yet I never forget Your Torah.
Evil men have set a trap for me, yet I do not stray from Your precepts.
Your decrees are my everlasting heritage; for they are the joy of my heart.
I have resolved to carry out Your statutes, the reward is eternal.

ש

שָׂרִים רְדָפוּנִי חִנָּם וּמִדְּבָרְךָ פָּחַד לִבִּי׃
שָׂשׂ אָנֹכִי עַל־אִמְרָתֶךָ כְּמוֹצֵא שָׁלָל רָב׃
שֶׁקֶר שָׂנֵאתִי וָאֲתַעֵבָה תּוֹרָתְךָ אָהָבְתִּי׃
שֶׁבַע בַּיּוֹם הִלַּלְתִּיךָ עַל מִשְׁפְּטֵי צִדְקֶךָ׃
שָׁלוֹם רָב לְאֹהֲבֵי תוֹרָתֶךָ וְאֵין־לָמוֹ מִכְשׁוֹל׃
שִׂבַּרְתִּי לִישׁוּעָתְךָ יְהוָה וּמִצְוֺתֶיךָ עָשִׂיתִי׃
שָׁמְרָה נַפְשִׁי עֵדֹתֶיךָ וָאֹהֲבֵם מְאֹד׃
שָׁמַרְתִּי פִקּוּדֶיךָ וְעֵדֹתֶיךָ כִּי כָל־דְּרָכַי נֶגְדֶּךָ׃

ת

תִּקְרַב רִנָּתִי לְפָנֶיךָ יְהוָה כִּדְבָרְךָ הֲבִינֵנִי׃
תָּבוֹא תְּחִנָּתִי לְפָנֶיךָ כְּאִמְרָתְךָ הַצִּילֵנִי׃
תַּבַּעְנָה שְׂפָתַי תְּהִלָּה כִּי תְלַמְּדֵנִי חֻקֶּיךָ׃
תַּעַן לְשׁוֹנִי אִמְרָתֶךָ כִּי כָל־מִצְוֺתֶיךָ צֶּדֶק׃
תְּהִי־יָדְךָ לְעָזְרֵנִי כִּי פִקּוּדֶיךָ בָחָרְתִּי׃
תָּאַבְתִּי לִישׁוּעָתְךָ יְהוָה וְתוֹרָתְךָ שַׁעֲשֻׁעָי׃
תְּחִי־נַפְשִׁי וּתְהַלְלֶךָּ וּמִשְׁפָּטֶךָ יַעְזְרֻנִי׃
תָּעִיתִי כְּשֶׂה אֹבֵד בַּקֵּשׁ עַבְדֶּךָ כִּי מִצְוֺתֶיךָ לֹא שָׁכָחְתִּי׃

The following are the verses of מזמור קיט *that spell out the word* נשמה *("soul").*

נ

נֵר־לְרַגְלִי דְבָרֶךָ וְאוֹר לִנְתִיבָתִי׃
נִשְׁבַּעְתִּי וָאֲקַיֵּמָה לִשְׁמֹר מִשְׁפְּטֵי צִדְקֶךָ׃
נַעֲנֵיתִי עַד־מְאֹד יְהוָה חַיֵּנִי כִדְבָרֶךָ׃
נִדְבוֹת פִּי רְצֵה־נָא יְהוָה וּמִשְׁפָּטֶיךָ לַמְּדֵנִי׃
נַפְשִׁי בְכַפִּי תָמִיד וְתוֹרָתְךָ לֹא שָׁכָחְתִּי׃
נָתְנוּ רְשָׁעִים פַּח לִי וּמִפִּקּוּדֶיךָ לֹא תָעִיתִי׃
נָחַלְתִּי עֵדְוֺתֶיךָ לְעוֹלָם כִּי־שְׂשׂוֹן לִבִּי הֵמָּה׃
נָטִיתִי לִבִּי לַעֲשׂוֹת חֻקֶּיךָ לְעוֹלָם עֵקֶב׃

SHIN

Princes persecute me without cause, yet my heart fears only for Your word.
I rejoice over Your promise like one who finds much spoil.
I hate falsehood, I loathe it, but I love Your Torah.
Seven times each day I praise You for Your just rulings.
Great peace have they who love Your Torah; there is no stumbling for them.
I wait for Your deliverance, LORD, and I fulfill Your commandments.
My soul heeds Your decrees, for I love them dearly.
I observe Your precepts and Your decrees, for all my ways are before You.

MEM

O how I love Your Torah! I meditate on it all day long.
Your commandments make me wiser than my enemies, for they are ever with me.
I have gained more insight than all my teachers, for Your decrees are my study.
I have more understanding than the aged, for I keep Your precepts.
I restrain my feet from every evil path, so that I may keep Your word.
I have not departed from Your ordinances, for You Yourself have taught me.
How sweet to my palate are Your words, sweeter than honey to my mouth!
I gain wisdom from Your precepts, therefore I hate every false way.

HEH

Teach me, LORD, the way of Your statutes, and I will observe them meticulously.
Give me understanding that I may observe Your Torah, and keep it with all my heart.
Guide me in the path of Your commandments, for that is my sole delight.
Incline my heart toward Your decrees, and not toward love of gain.
Turn my eyes away from worthless things; grant me life to follow in Your way.
Fulfill for Your servant the promise which [You made] to those who fear You.
Remove the reproach which I dread, for Your judgments are good.
See, how I long for Your precepts! By Your righteousness grant me life.

ש

שָׂרִים רְדָפוּנִי חִנָּם וּמִדְּבָרְךָ פָּחַד לִבִּי׃
שָׂשׂ אָנֹכִי עַל־אִמְרָתֶךָ כְּמוֹצֵא שָׁלָל רָב׃
שֶׁקֶר שָׂנֵאתִי וָאֲתַעֵבָה תּוֹרָתְךָ אָהָבְתִּי׃
שֶׁבַע בַּיּוֹם הִלַּלְתִּיךָ עַל מִשְׁפְּטֵי צִדְקֶךָ׃
שָׁלוֹם רָב לְאֹהֲבֵי תוֹרָתֶךָ וְאֵין־לָמוֹ מִכְשׁוֹל׃
שִׂבַּרְתִּי לִישׁוּעָתְךָ יהוה וּמִצְוֺתֶיךָ עָשִׂיתִי׃
שָׁמְרָה נַפְשִׁי עֵדֹתֶיךָ וָאֹהֲבֵם מְאֹד׃
שָׁמַרְתִּי פִקּוּדֶיךָ וְעֵדֹתֶיךָ כִּי כָל־דְּרָכַי נֶגְדֶּךָ׃

מ

מָה־אָהַבְתִּי תוֹרָתֶךָ כָּל־הַיּוֹם הִיא שִׂיחָתִי׃
מֵאֹיְבַי תְּחַכְּמֵנִי מִצְוֺתֶךָ כִּי לְעוֹלָם הִיא־לִי׃
מִכָּל־מְלַמְּדַי הִשְׂכַּלְתִּי כִּי עֵדְוֺתֶיךָ שִׂיחָה לִי׃
מִזְּקֵנִים אֶתְבּוֹנָן כִּי פִקּוּדֶיךָ נָצָרְתִּי׃
מִכָּל־אֹרַח רָע כָּלִאתִי רַגְלָי לְמַעַן אֶשְׁמֹר דְּבָרֶךָ׃
מִמִּשְׁפָּטֶיךָ לֹא־סָרְתִּי כִּי־אַתָּה הוֹרֵתָנִי׃
מַה־נִּמְלְצוּ לְחִכִּי אִמְרָתֶךָ מִדְּבַשׁ לְפִי׃
מִפִּקּוּדֶיךָ אֶתְבּוֹנָן עַל־כֵּן שָׂנֵאתִי ׀ כָּל־אֹרַח שָׁקֶר׃

ה

הוֹרֵנִי יהוה דֶּרֶךְ חֻקֶּיךָ וְאֶצְּרֶנָּה עֵקֶב׃
הֲבִינֵנִי וְאֶצְּרָה תוֹרָתֶךָ וְאֶשְׁמְרֶנָּה בְכָל־לֵב׃
הַדְרִיכֵנִי בִּנְתִיב מִצְוֺתֶיךָ כִּי־בוֹ חָפָצְתִּי׃
הַט־לִבִּי אֶל־עֵדְוֺתֶיךָ וְאַל אֶל־בָּצַע׃
הַעֲבֵר עֵינַי מֵרְאוֹת שָׁוְא בִּדְרָכֶךָ חַיֵּנִי׃
הָקֵם לְעַבְדְּךָ אִמְרָתֶךָ אֲשֶׁר לְיִרְאָתֶךָ׃
הַעֲבֵר חֶרְפָּתִי אֲשֶׁר יָגֹרְתִּי כִּי מִשְׁפָּטֶיךָ טוֹבִים׃
הִנֵּה תָּאַבְתִּי לְפִקֻּדֶיךָ בְּצִדְקָתְךָ חַיֵּנִי׃

MEMORIAL PRAYER

אָנָּא O Lord and King, full of compassion, God of the spirits of all flesh, in whose hand are the souls of the living and the dead, receive, we pray You, in Your great love the soul of

For a man, say:

(*name* son of *father's name*) who has been gathered to his people.
Have mercy on him, pardon all his transgressions, for there is no one Eccl. 7
so righteous on earth as to have done only good and never sinned. Remember the righteousness that he did, and let his reward be with him, his recompense before him. O shelter his soul in the shadow of Your wings. Make known to him the path of life. In Your presence is fullness of joy, at Your right hand bliss for evermore. Bestow upon him the great goodness that is stored up for the righteous.

For a woman, say:

(*name* daughter of *father's name*) who has been gathered to her people.
Have mercy on her, pardon all her transgressions, for there is no one Eccl. 7
so righteous on earth as to have done only good and never sinned. Remember the righteousness that she did, and let her reward be with her, her recompense before her. O shelter her soul in the shadow of Your wings. Make known to her the path of life. In Your presence is fullness of joy, at Your right hand bliss for evermore. Bestow upon her the great goodness that is stored up for the righteous.

For a boy, say:

(*name* son of *father's name*) who has been gathered to his people. Remember the righteousness that he did, and let his reward be with him, his recompense before him. O shelter his soul in the shadow of Your wings. Make known to him the path of life. In Your presence is fullness of joy, at Your right hand bliss for evermore. Bestow upon him the great goodness that is stored up for the righteous.

For a girl, say:

(*name* daughter of *father's name*) who has been gathered to her people. Remember the righteousness that she did, and let her reward be with her, her recompense before her. O shelter her soul in the shadow of Your wings. Make known to her the path of life. In Your presence is fullness of joy, at Your right hand bliss for evermore. Bestow upon her the great goodness that is stored up for the righteous.

אזכרה

אָנָּא יהוה מֶלֶךְ מָלֵא רַחֲמִים, אֱלֹהֵי הָרוּחוֹת לְכָל בָּשָׂר, אֲשֶׁר בְּיָדְךָ נַפְשׁוֹת הַחַיִּים וְהַמֵּתִים, אָנָּא קַבֵּל בְּחַסְדְּךָ הַגָּדוֹל אֶת נִשְׁמַת

For a man, say:

(פלוני בֶּן פלוני) אֲשֶׁר נֶאֱסַף אֶל עַמָּיו. חוּס וַחֲמֹל עָלָיו, סְלַח וּמְחַל לְכָל פְּשָׁעָיו. כִּי אָדָם אֵין צַדִּיק בָּאָרֶץ, אֲשֶׁר יַעֲשֶׂה־טּוֹב וְלֹא קהלת ז
יֶחֱטָא: זְכֹר לוֹ צִדְקָתוֹ אֲשֶׁר עָשָׂה, וִיהִי שְׂכָרוֹ אִתּוֹ, וּפְעֻלָּתוֹ לְפָנָיו. אָנָּא הַסְתֵּר אֶת נִשְׁמָתוֹ בְּצֵל כְּנָפֶיךָ, הוֹדִיעֵהוּ אֹרַח חַיִּים, שֹׂבַע שְׂמָחוֹת אֶת פָּנֶיךָ, נְעִימוֹת בִּימִינְךָ נֶצַח, וְתַשְׁפִּיעַ לוֹ מֵרֹב טוּב הַצָּפוּן לַצַּדִּיקִים.

For a woman, say:

(פלונית בַּת פלוני) אֲשֶׁר נֶאֶסְפָה אֶל עַמֶּיהָ. חוּס וַחֲמֹל עָלֶיהָ, סְלַח וּמְחַל לְכָל פְּשָׁעֶיהָ. כִּי אָדָם אֵין צַדִּיק בָּאָרֶץ, אֲשֶׁר יַעֲשֶׂה־טּוֹב וְלֹא קהלת ז
יֶחֱטָא: זְכֹר לָהּ צִדְקָתָהּ אֲשֶׁר עָשְׂתָה, וִיהִי שְׂכָרָהּ אִתָּהּ, וּפְעֻלָּתָהּ לְפָנֶיהָ. אָנָּא הַסְתֵּר אֶת נִשְׁמָתָהּ בְּצֵל כְּנָפֶיךָ, הוֹדִיעֶהָ אֹרַח חַיִּים, שֹׂבַע שְׂמָחוֹת אֶת פָּנֶיךָ, נְעִימוֹת בִּימִינְךָ נֶצַח, וְתַשְׁפִּיעַ לָהּ מֵרֹב טוּב הַצָּפוּן לַצַּדִּיקִים.

For a boy, say:

(פלוני בֶּן פלוני) אֲשֶׁר נֶאֱסַף אֶל עַמָּיו. זְכֹר לוֹ צִדְקָתוֹ אֲשֶׁר עָשָׂה, וִיהִי שְׂכָרוֹ אִתּוֹ, וּפְעֻלָּתוֹ לְפָנָיו. אָנָּא הַסְתֵּר אֶת נִשְׁמָתוֹ בְּצֵל כְּנָפֶיךָ, הוֹדִיעֵהוּ אֹרַח חַיִּים, שֹׂבַע שְׂמָחוֹת אֶת פָּנֶיךָ, נְעִימוֹת בִּימִינְךָ נֶצַח, וְתַשְׁפִּיעַ לוֹ מֵרֹב טוּב הַצָּפוּן לַצַּדִּיקִים.

For a girl, say:

(פלונית בַּת פלוני) אֲשֶׁר נֶאֶסְפָה אֶל עַמֶּיהָ. זְכוֹר לָהּ צִדְקָתָהּ אֲשֶׁר עָשְׂתָה, וִיהִי שְׂכָרָהּ אִתָּהּ, וּפְעֻלָּתָהּ לְפָנֶיהָ. אָנָּא הַסְתֵּר אֶת נִשְׁמָתָהּ בְּצֵל כְּנָפֶיךָ, הוֹדִיעֶהָ אֹרַח חַיִּים, שֹׂבַע שְׂמָחוֹת אֶת פָּנֶיךָ, נְעִימוֹת בִּימִינְךָ נֶצַח, וְתַשְׁפִּיעַ לָהּ מֵרֹב טוּב הַצָּפוּן לַצַּדִּיקִים.

As it is written, "How great is Your goodness which You have stored up for those who revere You, which You bestow on those that trust in You before the children of men." *Ps. 31*

אָנָּא May the Lord who heals the brokenhearted and binds up their wounds, grant consolation to the mourners.

For a young boy, add:

May the death of this boy
mark the end of all anguish and sorrow for his parents.

For a young girl, add:

May the death of this girl
mark the end of all anguish and sorrow for her parents.

If the mourners have children, add the words in parentheses:

חַזְּקֵם Strengthen and support them in the day of their sadness and grief; and remember them (and their children) for a long and good life. Put into their hearts love and reverence for You, so that they may serve You with a perfect heart; and let their end be peace. Amen.

כְּאִישׁ As a mother comforts her son, *Is. 66*
so will I comfort you;
and in Jerusalem you shall find comfort.
Your sun shall no more set, *Is. 60*
your moon shall no more withdraw itself,
for the Lord shall be your everlasting light,
and your days of mourning shall be ended.
He will destroy death for ever; *Is. 25*
and the Lord God will wipe away the tears from all faces,
and remove the reproach of His people from the whole earth;
for the Lord has spoken it.

כְּמוֹ שֶׁכָּתוּב: מָה רַב טוּבְךָ אֲשֶׁר־צָפַנְתָּ לִּירֵאֶיךָ, פָּעַלְתָּ לַחוֹסִים בָּךְ נֶגֶד בְּנֵי אָדָם: תהלים לא

אָנָּא יהוה, הָרוֹפֵא לִשְׁבוּרֵי לֵב וּמְחַבֵּשׁ לְעַצְּבוֹתָם, שַׁלֵּם נִחוּמִים לָאֲבֵלִים.

For a young boy, add:

וּתְהִי פְּטִירַת הַיֶּלֶד הַזֶּה קֵץ לְכָל צָרָה וְצוּקָה לְאָבִיו וּלְאִמּוֹ.

For a young girl, add:

וּתְהִי פְּטִירַת הַיַּלְדָּה הַזֹּאת קֵץ לְכָל צָרָה וְצוּקָה לְאָבִיהָ וּלְאִמָּהּ.

If the mourners have children, add the words in parentheses:

חַזְּקֵם וְאַמְּצֵם בְּיוֹם אֶבְלָם וִיגוֹנָם, וְזָכְרֵם (וּזְכֹר אֶת בְּנֵי בֵיתָם) לְחַיִּים טוֹבִים וַאֲרֻכִּים. תֵּן בְּלִבָּם יִרְאָתְךָ וְאַהֲבָתְךָ לְעָבְדְּךָ בְּלֵבָב שָׁלֵם, וּתְהִי אַחֲרִיתָם שָׁלוֹם, אָמֵן.

כְּאִישׁ אֲשֶׁר אִמּוֹ תְּנַחֲמֶנּוּ ישעיה סו
כֵּן אָנֹכִי אֲנַחֶמְכֶם
וּבִירוּשָׁלַיִם תְּנֻחָמוּ:
לֹא־יָבוֹא עוֹד שִׁמְשֵׁךְ, וִירֵחֵךְ לֹא יֵאָסֵף ישעיה ס
כִּי יהוה יִהְיֶה־לָּךְ לְאוֹר עוֹלָם
וְשָׁלְמוּ יְמֵי אֶבְלֵךְ:
בִּלַּע הַמָּוֶת לָנֶצַח ישעיה כה
וּמָחָה אֲדֹנָי יֱהֹוִה דִּמְעָה מֵעַל כָּל־פָּנִים
וְחֶרְפַּת עַמּוֹ יָסִיר מֵעַל כָּל־הָאָרֶץ
כִּי יהוה דִּבֵּר:

MOURNER'S KADDISH

The following prayer, said by mourners, requires the presence of a minyan. A transliteration can be found on page 831.

Mourner: יִתְגַּדַּל Magnified and sanctified
may His great name be,
in the world He created by His will.
May He establish His kingdom
in your lifetime and in your days,
and in the lifetime of all the house of Israel,
swiftly and soon –
and say: Amen.

All: May His great name be blessed for ever and all time.

Mourner: Blessed and praised,
glorified and exalted,
raised and honored,
uplifted and lauded
be the name of the Holy One,
blessed be He,
beyond any blessing,
song, praise and consolation
uttered in the world –
and say: Amen.

May there be great peace from heaven,
and life for us and all Israel –
and say: Amen.

Bow, take three steps back, as if taking leave of the Divine Presence, then bow, first left, then right, then center, while saying:

May He who makes peace in His high places,
make peace for us and all Israel –
and say: Amen.

קדיש יתום

The following prayer, said by mourners, requires the presence of a מנין*.*
A transliteration can be found on page 831.

אבל: יִתְגַּדַּל וְיִתְקַדַּשׁ שְׁמֵהּ רַבָּא (קהל: אָמֵן)
בְּעָלְמָא דִּי בְרָא כִרְעוּתֵהּ
וְיַמְלִיךְ מַלְכוּתֵהּ
בְּחַיֵּיכוֹן וּבְיוֹמֵיכוֹן וּבְחַיֵּי דְכָל בֵּית יִשְׂרָאֵל
בַּעֲגָלָא וּבִזְמַן קָרִיב, וְאִמְרוּ אָמֵן. (קהל: אָמֵן)

קהל ואבל: יְהֵא שְׁמֵהּ רַבָּא מְבָרַךְ לְעָלַם וּלְעָלְמֵי עָלְמַיָּא.

אבל: יִתְבָּרַךְ וְיִשְׁתַּבַּח וְיִתְפָּאַר
וְיִתְרוֹמַם וְיִתְנַשֵּׂא וְיִתְהַדָּר וְיִתְעַלֶּה וְיִתְהַלָּל
שְׁמֵהּ דְּקֻדְשָׁא בְּרִיךְ הוּא (קהל: בְּרִיךְ הוּא)
לְעֵלָּא מִן כָּל בִּרְכָתָא
/בעשרת ימי תשובה: לְעֵלָּא לְעֵלָּא מִכָּל בִּרְכָתָא/
וְשִׁירָתָא, תֻּשְׁבְּחָתָא וְנֶחֱמָתָא
דַּאֲמִירָן בְּעָלְמָא, וְאִמְרוּ אָמֵן. (קהל: אָמֵן)

יְהֵא שְׁלָמָא רַבָּא מִן שְׁמַיָּא
וְחַיִּים, עָלֵינוּ וְעַל כָּל יִשְׂרָאֵל, וְאִמְרוּ אָמֵן. (קהל: אָמֵן)

Bow, take three steps back, as if taking leave of the Divine Presence, then bow, first left, then right, then center, while saying:

עֹשֶׂה שָׁלוֹם/בעשרת ימי תשובה: הַשָּׁלוֹם/ בִּמְרוֹמָיו
הוּא יַעֲשֶׂה שָׁלוֹם עָלֵינוּ וְעַל כָּל יִשְׂרָאֵל
וְאִמְרוּ אָמֵן. (קהל: אָמֵן)

GOD, FULL OF MERCY

For a male close relative:

אֵל מָלֵא רַחֲמִים God, full of mercy, who dwells on high, grant fitting rest on the wings of the Divine Presence, in the heights of the holy and the pure who shine like the radiance of heaven, to the soul of (*name* son of *father's name*) who has gone to his eternal home, and to this I pledge (without formal vow) to give charity in his memory, may his resting place be in the Garden of Eden. Therefore, Master of compassion, shelter him in the shadow of Your wings forever and bind his soul in the bond of everlasting life. The LORD is his heritage; may he rest in peace, and let us say: Amen.

For a female close relative:

אֵל מָלֵא רַחֲמִים God, full of mercy, who dwells on high, grant fitting rest on the wings of the Divine Presence, in the heights of the holy and the pure who shine like the radiance of heaven, to the soul of (*name* daughter of *father's name*) who has gone to her eternal home, and to this I pledge (without formal vow) to give charity in her memory, may her resting place be in the Garden of Eden. Therefore, Master of compassion, shelter her in the shadow of Your wings forever and bind her soul in the bond of everlasting life. The LORD is her heritage; may she rest in peace, and let us say: Amen.

For the Israeli soldiers:

אֵל מָלֵא רַחֲמִים God, full of mercy, who dwells on high, grant fitting rest on the wings of the Divine Presence, in the heights of the holy, the pure and the brave, who shine like the radiance of heaven, to the souls of the holy ones who fought in any of Israel's battles, in clandestine operations and in Israel's Defense Forces, who fell in battle and sacrificed their lives for the consecration of God's name, for the people and the land, and for this we pray for the ascent of their souls. Therefore, Master of compassion, shelter them in the shadow of Your wings forever, and bind their souls in the bond of everlasting life. The LORD is their heritage; may the Garden of Eden be their resting place, may they rest in peace, may their

אל מלא רחמים

For a male close relative:

אֵל מָלֵא רַחֲמִים, שׁוֹכֵן בַּמְּרוֹמִים, הַמְצֵא מְנוּחָה נְכוֹנָה עַל כַּנְפֵי הַשְּׁכִינָה, בְּמַעֲלוֹת קְדוֹשִׁים וּטְהוֹרִים, כְּזֹהַר הָרָקִיעַ מַזְהִירִים, לְנִשְׁמַת (פלוני בֶּן פלוני) שֶׁהָלַךְ לְעוֹלָמוֹ, בַּעֲבוּר שֶׁבְּלִי נֶדֶר אֶתֵּן צְדָקָה בְּעַד הַזְכָּרַת נִשְׁמָתוֹ, בְּגַן עֵדֶן תְּהֵא מְנוּחָתוֹ. לָכֵן, בַּעַל הָרַחֲמִים יַסְתִּירֵהוּ בְּסֵתֶר כְּנָפָיו לְעוֹלָמִים, וְיִצְרֹר בִּצְרוֹר הַחַיִּים אֶת נִשְׁמָתוֹ, יהוה הוּא נַחֲלָתוֹ, וְיָנוּחַ בְּשָׁלוֹם עַל מִשְׁכָּבוֹ, וְנֹאמַר אָמֵן.

For a female close relative:

אֵל מָלֵא רַחֲמִים, שׁוֹכֵן בַּמְּרוֹמִים, הַמְצֵא מְנוּחָה נְכוֹנָה עַל כַּנְפֵי הַשְּׁכִינָה, בְּמַעֲלוֹת קְדוֹשִׁים וּטְהוֹרִים, כְּזֹהַר הָרָקִיעַ מַזְהִירִים, לְנִשְׁמַת (פלונית בַּת פלוני) שֶׁהָלְכָה לְעוֹלָמָהּ, בַּעֲבוּר שֶׁבְּלִי נֶדֶר אֶתֵּן צְדָקָה בְּעַד הַזְכָּרַת נִשְׁמָתָהּ, בְּגַן עֵדֶן תְּהֵא מְנוּחָתָהּ. לָכֵן, בַּעַל הָרַחֲמִים יַסְתִּירֶהָ בְּסֵתֶר כְּנָפָיו לְעוֹלָמִים, וְיִצְרֹר בִּצְרוֹר הַחַיִּים אֶת נִשְׁמָתָהּ, יהוה הוּא נַחֲלָתָהּ, וְתָנוּחַ בְּשָׁלוֹם עַל מִשְׁכָּבָהּ, וְנֹאמַר אָמֵן.

For the Israeli soldiers:

אֵל מָלֵא רַחֲמִים, שׁוֹכֵן בַּמְּרוֹמִים, הַמְצֵא מְנוּחָה נְכוֹנָה עַל כַּנְפֵי הַשְּׁכִינָה, בְּמַעֲלוֹת קְדוֹשִׁים טְהוֹרִים וְגִבּוֹרִים, כְּזֹהַר הָרָקִיעַ מַזְהִירִים, לְנִשְׁמוֹת הַקְּדוֹשִׁים שֶׁנִּלְחֲמוּ בְּכָל מַעַרְכוֹת יִשְׂרָאֵל, בַּמַּחְתֶּרֶת וּבִצְבָא הַהֲגָנָה לְיִשְׂרָאֵל, וְשֶׁנָּפְלוּ בְּמִלְחַמְתָּם וּמָסְרוּ נַפְשָׁם עַל קְדֻשַּׁת הַשֵּׁם, הָעָם וְהָאָרֶץ, בַּעֲבוּר שֶׁאָנוּ מִתְפַּלְּלִים לְעִלּוּי נִשְׁמוֹתֵיהֶם. לָכֵן, בַּעַל הָרַחֲמִים יַסְתִּירֵם בְּסֵתֶר כְּנָפָיו לְעוֹלָמִים, וְיִצְרֹר בִּצְרוֹר הַחַיִּים אֶת נִשְׁמוֹתֵיהֶם, יהוה הוּא נַחֲלָתָם,

merit stand for all Israel, and may they receive their reward at the End of Days, and let us say: Amen.

For the Holocaust victims:

אֵל מָלֵא רַחֲמִים God, full of mercy, Justice of widows and Father of orphans, please do not be silent and hold Your peace for the blood of Israel that was shed like water. Grant fitting rest on the wings of the Divine Presence, in the heights of the holy and the pure who shine and radiate light like the radiance of heaven, to the souls of the millions of Jews, men, women and children, who were murdered, slaughtered, burned, strangled, and buried alive, in the lands touched by the German enemy and its followers. They were all holy and pure; among them were great scholars and righteous individuals, cedars of Lebanon and noble masters of Torah, may the Garden of Eden be their resting place. Therefore, Master of compassion, shelter them in the shadow of Your wings forever, and bind their souls in the bond of everlasting life. The Lord is their heritage; may they rest in peace, and let us say: Amen.

בְּגַן עֵדֶן תְּהֵא מְנוּחָתָם, וְיָנוּחוּ בְשָׁלוֹם עַל מִשְׁכְּבוֹתֵיהֶם וְתַעֲמֹד לְכָל יִשְׂרָאֵל זְכוּתָם, וְיַעַמְדוּ לְגוֹרָלָם לְקֵץ הַיָּמִין, וְנֹאמַר אָמֵן.

For the Holocaust victims:

אֵל מָלֵא רַחֲמִים, דַּיַּן אַלְמָנוֹת וַאֲבִי יְתוֹמִים, אַל נָא תֶחֱשֶׁה וְתִתְאַפַּק לְדַם יִשְׂרָאֵל שֶׁנִּשְׁפַּךְ כַּמָּיִם. הַמְצֵא מְנוּחָה נְכוֹנָה עַל כַּנְפֵי הַשְּׁכִינָה, בְּמַעֲלוֹת קְדוֹשִׁים וּטְהוֹרִים, כְּזֹהַר הָרָקִיעַ מְאִירִים וּמַזְהִירִים, לְנִשְׁמוֹתֵיהֶם שֶׁל רִבְבוֹת אַלְפֵי יִשְׂרָאֵל, אֲנָשִׁים וְנָשִׁים, יְלָדִים וִילָדוֹת, שֶׁנֶּהֶרְגוּ וְנִשְׁחֲטוּ וְנִשְׂרְפוּ וְנֶחְנְקוּ וְנִקְבְּרוּ חַיִּים, בַּאֲרָצוֹת אֲשֶׁר נָגְעָה בָהֶן יַד הַצּוֹרֵר הַגֶּרְמָנִי וּגְרוּרָיו. כֻּלָּם קְדוֹשִׁים וּטְהוֹרִים, וּבָהֶם גְּאוֹנִים וְצַדִּיקִים, אַרְזֵי הַלְּבָנוֹן אַדִּירֵי הַתּוֹרָה. בְּגַן עֵדֶן תְּהֵא מְנוּחָתָם. לָכֵן, בַּעַל הָרַחֲמִים יַסְתִּירֵם בְּסֵתֶר כְּנָפָיו לְעוֹלָמִים, וְיִצְרֹר בִּצְרוֹר הַחַיִּים אֶת נִשְׁמָתָם, יהוה הוּא נַחֲלָתָם, וְיָנוּחוּ בְשָׁלוֹם עַל מִשְׁכָּבָם, וְנֹאמַר אָמֵן.

WEEKLY DIVISION OF PSALMS

Day of the Week	*Psalms*	*Psalms*
Sunday	א-כט	1–29
Monday	ל-נ	30–50
Tuesday	נא-עב	51–72
Wednesday	עג-פט	73–89
Thursday	צ-קו	90–106
Friday	קז-קיט	107–119
Shabbat	קכ-קנ	120–150

MONTHLY DIVISION OF PSALMS

Day of the Month	*Psalms*	*Psalms*
1	א-ט	1–9
2	י-יז	10–17
3	יח-כב	18–22
4	כג-כח	23–28
5	כט-לד	29–34
6	לה-לח	35–38
7	לט-מג	39–43
8	מד-מח	44–48
9	מט-נד	49–54
10	נה-נט	55–59
11	ס-סה	60–65
12	סו-סח	66–68
13	סט-עא	69–71
14	עב-עו	72–76
15	עז-עח	77–78

Day of the Month	*Psalms*	*Psalms*
16	עט-פב	79–82
17	פג-פז	83–87
18	פח-פט	88–89
19	צ-צו	90–96
20	צז-קג	97–103
21	קד-קה	104–105
22	קו-קז	106–107
23	קח-קיב	108–112
24	קיג-קיח	113–118
25	קיט:א-צו	119:1–96
26	קיט:צז-קעו	119:97–176
27	קכ-קלד	120–134
28	קלה-קלט	135–139
29	קמ-קמד	140–144
30	קמה-קנ	145–150

PSALMS FOR SPECIAL OCCASIONS

The following psalms may be said on special occasions:

On the day of one's wedding	Ps. 19 on page 89
On the birth of a child	Ps. 20 on page 93 and Ps. 139 on page 713
For someone who is ill	Ps. 23, page 109; Ps. 121, page 651; Ps. 130, page 677; and Ps. 139 on page 713
For safety in Israel	Ps. 20 on page 93; Ps. 120 on page 647; Ps. 121 on page 651 and Ps. 125 on page 665
On recovery from illness	Ps. 6 on page 23; Ps. 30 on page 141 and Ps. 103 on page 515
Thanksgiving	Ps. 95 on page 483; Ps. 116 on page 597
For guidance	Ps. 139 on page 713
For success	Ps. 121 on page 651
For repentance	Ps. 90 on page 461
For help in difficult times	Ps. 20 on page 93; Ps. 130 on page 677
When traveling	Ps. 91 on page 467
In thanksgiving for being saved	Ps. 124 on page 661

MOURNER'S KADDISH (Transliterated)

Mourner: Yitgadal ve-yitkadash shemeh raba. (*Cong:* Amen)
Be-alema di vera khir'uteh, ve-yamlikh malkhuteh,
be-ḥayyeikhon, uv-yomeikhon,
uv-ḥayyei de-khol beit Yisrael,
ba-agala uvi-zman kariv,
ve-imru Amen. (*Cong:* Amen)

All: Yeheh shemeh raba mevarakh le'alam ul-alemei alemaya.

Mourner: Yitbarakh ve-yishtabaḥ ve-yitpa'ar ve-yitromam ve-yitnaseh
ve-yit-hadar ve-yit'aleh ve-yit-hallal
shemeh dekudsha, berikh hu. (*Cong:* Berikh hu)
Le-ela min kol birkhata
/ *Between Rosh HaShana & Yom Kippur:* Le-ela le-ela mi-kol birkhata/
ve-shirata, tushbeḥata ve-neḥemata, da-amiran be-alema,
ve-imru, Amen. (*Cong:* Amen)

Yeheh shelama raba min shemaya
ve-ḥayyim aleinu ve-al kol Yisrael,
ve-imru Amen. (*Cong:* Amen)

Bow, take three steps back, as if taking leave of the Divine Presence, then bow, first left, then right, then center, while saying:

Oseh shalom/*Between Rosh HaShana & Yom Kippur:* ha-shalom/
bim-romav,
hu ya'aseh shalom aleinu, ve-al kol Yisrael,
ve-imru Amen. (*Cong:* Amen)

קורן ירושלים